Readings in
Physical Anthropology
and Archaeology

Readings in Physical Anthropology and Archaeology

edited by
David E. Hunter
Yale University

Phillip Whitten

HARPER & ROW, PUBLISHERS

New York   Hagerstown   San Francisco   London

Production Supervisor: Stefania J. Taflinska
Printer and Binder: The Murray Printing Company

**READINGS IN PHYSICAL ANTHROPOLOGY
AND ARCHAEOLOGY**

Copyright © 1978 by David E. Hunter and Phillip Whitten

Library of Congress Cataloging in Publication Data
Main entry under title:

Readings in physical anthropology and archaeology.

   1. Physical anthropology—Addresses, essays,
lectures. 2. Archaeology—Addresses, essays,
lectures. I. Hunter, David E. II. Whitten,
Phillip.
GN60.R35   573   78–18511
ISBN 0–06–043023–0

ACKNOWLEDGMENTS

I. AN INTRODUCTION. Photo by Robert F. Sisson, © National Geographic Society.

  1. STONES AND BONES: THE EMERGENCE OF PHYSICAL ANTHROPOLOGY AND ARCHAEOLOGY by David E. Hunter is printed by permission from the author. Drawing by Josefina Robirosa, Buenos Aires, Argentina.

II. ON THE CONCEPT OF EVOLUTION

  2. THE IDEA OF MAN'S ANTIQUITY by Glyn E. Daniel is reprinted with permission. Copyright © 1959 by Scientific American, Inc. All rights reserved. Artwork is courtesy New York Public Library.

  3. A CHAT WITH CHARLES DARWIN by Michael Hoskin is from *The Mind of the Scientist* by Michael Hoskin (Taplinger Publishing Company, 1972). Copyright © 1971 by Michael Hoskin. Reprinted by permission. Photos are courtesy of Radio Times Hulton Picture Library, B.B.C.

  4. DARWIN'S DILEMMA by Stephen Jay Gould is reprinted, with permission, from *Natural History* Magazine, June–July, 1974. Copyright © The American Museum of Natural History, 1974. Photo is by The Bettmann Archive.

  5. PHYSICAL EVOLUTION AND TECHNOLOGICAL EVOLUTION IN MAN: A PARALLELISM by François Bordes is reprinted from the June 1971 issue of *World Archaeology* by permission from the author.

III. ARCHAEOLOGY: AN OVERVIEW

  6. HOW WE LEARN ABOUT THE PREHISTORIC PAST by Robert J. Braidwood is from *Prehistoric Men,* 8th Edition by Robert J. Braidwood. Copyright © 1975, 1967, 1964 by Scott, Foresman and Company. Reprinted by permission.

  7. TOOLS FOR ARCHEOLOGY: AIDS TO STUDYING THE PAST by Allen L. Hammond is reprinted by permission, copyright 1971 by the American Association for the Advancement of Science.

  8. ARCHAEOLOGICAL RESEACH STRATEGIES by Robert McC. Adams is reprinted by permission, copyright 1968 by the American Association for the Advancement of Science.

  9. PILGRIMS ELUDE A PILGRIM HUNTER by Francis E. Wylie is reprinted by permission. Copyright 1971 Smithsonian Institution, from *Smithsonian* Magazine, October 1971. Photo by Norman Synder.

10. THE ARCHAEOLOGIST IN DEEP WATER by Willard Bascom is reprinted from the May 1972 issue of *UNESCO Courier.* Photographs are reproduced from the *UNESCO Courier,* photo IFP, Paris.

11. A STONE AGE ORCHESTRA by Sergei N. Bibikov is reprinted from the June 1975 issue of *UNESCO Courier.* Photos are by S. N. Bibikov, APN, Moscow.

12. LOOKING INTO THE STONE AGE by Valeri Simakov is reprinted with permission from *Soviet Life* Magazine, March 1976. Photographs are reprinted courtesy of *Soviet Life* Magazine.

13. ANCIENT ACHES AND PAINS by Calvin Wells is reprinted from the Autumn 1968 issue of *Horizon.* Copyright © 1968 American Heritage Publishing Co., Inc. Reprinted by permission. Photographs are from the Bildarchiv Foto Marburg, Germany, and the British Museum.

IV. RECOVERING THE PAST

14. STONE AGE BURIALS AT CUEVA MORÍN by L. G. Freeman and J. González Echegaray is printed by permission from the authors. Photos by L. G. Freeman and the Smithsonian Institution.

15. THE ENIGMA OF THE THRACIANS by Magdalina Stancheva is reprinted from the February 1973 issue of *UNESCO Courier.* Photographs are courtesy of the Bulgarian Committee for Friendship and Cultural Relations with Foreign Countries, Sofia, Bulgaria.

16. EASTER ISLAND by William Mulloy is reprinted, with permission, from *Natural History* Magazine, December 1967. Copyright © The American Museum of Natural History, 1967. The photograph is courtesy of George Holton.

17. THE DROWNED CITY OF PORT ROYAL by Robert F. Marx is reprinted from the May

We dedicate this book to Frederick S. Hulse whose lectures are extended moments of discovery—both for his students and himself.

CONTENTS

PREFACE

The marketplace for academic books is crammed, and new ones seem to appear with astonishing swiftness. As the editors of one such new arrival, we feel an obligation to explain what we think this work has to contribute in the domain of published materials on physical anthropology and archaeology.

Students have a nickname for courses in physical anthropology and archaeology: stones and bones. And like the stones and bones that are excavated and examined in our laboratories, much of what is written about these academic disciplines is dry—interesting only to committed college majors and their mentors. But what of the liberal arts student who is exposed to physical anthropology and archaeology for the first time? What of the person who has not yet developed a knowledge of the specialized vocabulary and a familiarity with the frequently terse and undramatic writing style found in so many professional works? Shall we not address ourselves to the needs of such persons?

That, precisely, is what we attempt to accomplish here. This book is composed of articles that we have carefully culled from a wide range of sources. Our concern was to find engagingly written and graphically well-illustrated articles that would be accessible to students with no prior knowledge of either discipline. However, we also maintained high standards of academic substance. The resulting reader is unique, we think. It is a fresh, lively, well-illustrated, and interest-sustaining work that presents both the traditional concerns of archaeology and physical anthropology, and the current hot debates as well.

We have produced this work because we believe that the perspectives of physical anthropology and archaeology are important, that they must be widely disseminated and understood if we are to make wise choices as we plan for the future of the human species. It is our hope that this reader will contribute to the spread of academically responsible yet inviting and accessible facts and theories that will provoke thought about human origins, accomplishments, and future possibilities.

This book is really the work of all the authors whose writings we have printed and reprinted here. We appreciate their permission to do so and the cooperation they have afforded us. We also would like to thank our student research assistants—Wendy Davis (Swarthmore) and David Riemer (Brown)—who helped us in the enormous task of scanning the professional and semi-professional literature, and the following persons who reviewed and critiqued various drafts of this book: Dean T. Arnold (Wheaton College), Nathan R. McClintic (East Los Angeles Community College), Ted A. Rathbun (University of South Carolina), and Catherine E. Read-Martin (California State University, Los Angeles); their comments were enormously helpful to us.

D.E.H.
P.W.

Readings in
Physical Anthropology
and Archaeology

I. An Introduction

Painstaking digging by anthropologists Louis and Mary Leakey in East Africa has pushed back the horizons of prehistory hundreds of thousands of years. The Leakeys work under an umbrella in the boiling sun of Olduvai Gorge, Tanzania.

No discipline is free of its history, just as no person is free of his or her childhood. The events of our childhood stay with us, molding our behavior, shaping our views. And the history of a discipline remains a part of it, even as new waters are charted, new territories conquered.

We think that you will understand and appreciate archaeology and physical anthropology much more if you have some idea of the history of their evolution as vital intellectual disciplines. Toward this end we begin this reader with Hunter's "Stones and Bones: The Emergence of Physical Anthropology and Archaeology," written especially for this work.

Stones and Bones: The Emergence of Physical Anthropology and Archaeology

David E. Hunter

The disciplines of physical anthropology and archaeology first emerged in the nineteenth century. But their roots are far deeper. In fact we can trace their origins back to thinkers in the classical civilizations of the Mediterranean and the Middle East—the cradle of our modern civilization.

Both physical anthropology and archaeology are built on the most profound intellectual breakthrough of the nineteenth century, the theory of evolution. Thus in order to understand and appreciate the emergence of these two disciplines it is necessary to learn something about the history of the concept of evolution itself.

History of the Concept of Evolution

As far as we know, all societies have beliefs about their own origins and often about the origins of the entire human species as well. The ancient Greeks had a number of origin myths, including the tale of Prometheus, who created people out of earth and water. The philosopher Thales (640?–546 B.C.) broke away from mythological stories and claimed that everything in the world had its ultimate origin in one substance—water. This perspective, if not the specific belief itself, was important because it explained the origins of the world in terms of natural rather than mythological events.

Writing in the following century, the Greek philosopher Empedocles (495?–435? B.C.) even suggested the idea of natural selection, which would become the cornerstone of Darwin's theory of evolution some 2300 years later. Empedocles believed that the various body parts originally existed in isolation from one another and combined randomly, often forming grotesque combinations such as the Minotaur, a mythological creature with a human body and the head of a bull. However, only combinations of body parts that functioned well enough to nourish and reproduce themselves ultimately survived; the human species was an outcome of this selective process.

But the speculations of the classical philosophers did not lead to concrete or systematic investigations into human origins. And the advent of Christianity, with its view of the universe as a static representation of God's creative drive, stifled the motivation for such research: Medieval scholars thought that their major task was to detect and formally to describe the natural laws governing the universe, thus providing people with a glimpse of the Creator's awesome ingenuity and perfection; any search for origins—which would imply development and hence change—was not compatible with this world view, because if the universe were an expression of God it must, perforce, be perfect. To believe that it had changed significantly meant that it had either been created imperfectly and then had become perfect or that it had been created perfectly and then become imperfect. Either way this led to the idea that God had directly or indirectly created an imperfect universe and thus, by extension, must himself be imperfect—a theological impossibility. Thus theories about human origins were confined to an acceptance of the Biblical story of Adam and Eve.

During the Renaissance and even beyond, a literal interpretation of the Bible continued to inhibit the investigation of human origins for hundreds of years. As late as the first part of the nineteenth century, most scholars accepted the calculations of Archbishop James Ussher and John Lightfoot (vice chancellor of the University of Cambridge), who, in the early 1600s, had deduced from a careful study of *Genesis* that the earth had been created at 9 o'clock in the morning on October 23, 4004 B.C. (Daniel 1963:24–25).[1]

However, the Christian doctrine that Creation had been a single event became more and more troublesome in the course of the sixteenth century. With Vasco Nuñez de Balboa's discovery in 1513 that America was not an

---

[1] Other dates for the moment of human creation that were given broad currency at the time were 3700 B.C.E., computed by rabbinical scholars, and Pope Clement's calculation of 5199 B.C.

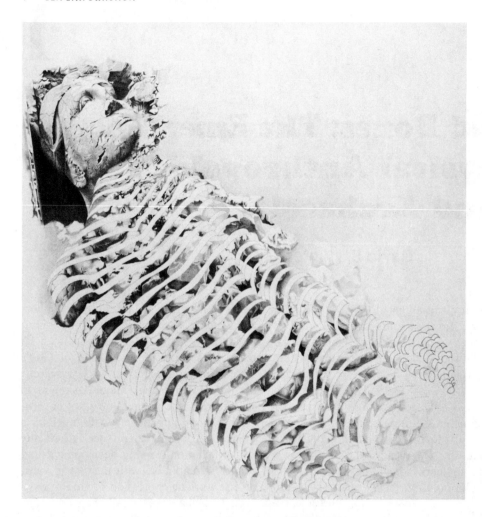

extension of Asia but, rather, a separate continent, the origin of the "Indians" became a source of heated argument. This debate rapidly expanded into controversy about the degree of relatedness—and inherent levels of ability—of all the diverse peoples around the world.

To the *polygenists* the differences between human groups were so vast that they could not accept even a common origin for all people. Rebelling against a narrow acceptance of *Genesis,* they insisted that scientific inquiry must prevail over the Bible (a courageous position at the time). They argued that God must have created human beings a number of times in different places and that all people were not, then, descendants of Adam and Eve. Their numbers included many of the period's leading skeptics and intellectuals, such as Voltaire and David Hume. It is hardly surprising that these thinkers, attaching as they did such great significance to human physical variation, should have been racial determinists and indeed racists, ascribing to their own "stock" superior mental abilities. Voltaire, for instance, discussing the state of civilization among Africans, argued:

> If their understanding is not of a different nature from ours, it is at least greatly inferior. They are not capable of any great application or association of ideas, and seemed [sic] formed neither for the advantages nor the abuses of philosophy (quoted in Harris 1968:87).

Monogenists defended the Scriptures' assertion of a single origin for all humans. Isolated groups, such as the "Indians," were accounted for by the claim that they had come from Atlantis (a mythical continent that was believed to have stretched from Spain to Africa before sinking beneath the waters of the Atlantic Ocean) or that they were the descendants of one of the lost tribes of Israel. Monogenists accounted for "racial" differences in terms of populations adapting to the problems posed by different environments—an idea that would become central to Darwin's principle of natural selection. But they also tended to believe, along with the French biologist Jean Baptiste de Lamarck (1744–1829), that physical characteristics acquired by an individual in the course of his or her lifelong development could be passed on biologically from one generation to the next (an idea rejected by Darwin and the mainstream of subsequent evolutionary thought).

Because monogenists tended to defend the validity of the Biblical version of human origins, they also accepted the very recent dates that Biblical scholars had established for human creation. Thus although they, like the polygenists, divided the human species into "races," they deduced that these "races" must be of very recent origin and that, although people exhibited differences in response to environmental pressures, these differences were of minimal importance with regard to basic human abilities. For instance, Johann Friedrich Blumenbach (1752–1840), a German physician who developed an interest in comparative human anatomy, published a study in 1775 in which he identified five "races": Caucasian, Mongolian, Ethiopian (including all sub-Saharan blacks), Malayan, and American. For this effort he is frequently called the "father" of physical anthropology. However, Blumenbach was far from convinced that these categories were anything more than artificial constructions of convenience in the service of science: "When the matter is thoroughly considered, you see that all [human groups] do so run into one another, and that one variety of mankind does so sensibly pass into the other, that you cannot mark out the limits between them" (cited in Montagu 1964:41). And he adds, with a tone of wryly modern wisdom: "Very arbitrary indeed both in number and definition have been the varieties of mankind accepted by eminent men" (ibid.).

It was Georges Buffon (1707–1788), a fellow monogenist, who first introduced the term *race* into the zoological literature in 1749. He also argued that environment determines the qualities of different human groups, that such differences are superficial and changeable, and that in no manner do they disprove the fundamental unity by eminent men" (ibid.).

The debate between monogenists and polygenists raged on through the nineteenth century and continues to this day. Although most human biologists since Darwin have aligned themselves in the monogenist camp, the writings of Carleton S. Coon, a contemporary anthropologist, are firmly polygenist. He argues in *The Origin of Races* (1963)—a highly controversial work—that the human species evolved five different times into the five "races" that he believes consitute the population of the world today.

Let us return, however, to our account of the emergence of the theory of evolution. By the late eighteenth and early nineteenth centuries, discoveries (especially in biology and geology) were gradually forcing scholars to reassess their acceptance of a date for the creation of the earth derived from scriptural study. More and more geological strata in the earth's crust were coming to light, and it became clear that the thickness of some strata, and the nature of the mineral contents of many, demanded a very long developmental process. In order to account for this process, these scientists faced the need to push back the date of Creation, as we will see shortly. In addition, the fossilized record of extinct life forms accumulated, obliging scientists to produce plausible explanations for the existence and subsequent disappearance of such creatures as the woolly mammoth and the saber-toothed tiger.

In 1833 Sir Charles Lyell (1797–1875) published the third and last volume of his *Principles of Geology,* a work that tremendously influenced Darwin. Lyell attacked such schools of thought as *diluvialism,* whose followers claimed that Noah's flood accounted for what was known of the earth's geological structure and history, and *catastrophism,* whose adherents proposed that localized catastrophes (of which the Biblical flood was merely the most recent) accounted for all the layers and cracks in the earth's crust. He argued that the processes shaping the earth are the same today as they always were—uniform and continous in character—a position that has come to be called *uniformitarianism.* However, Lyell was unable to free himself entirely from a doctrinaire Christian framework. Although he could envision gradual transformations in the inanimate world of geology, when he discussed living creatures he continued to believe in the divine creation of each (unchanging) species; and he accounted for the extinction of species in terms of small, localized natural catastrophes.

Some biologists did comprehend the implications of comparative anatomy and the fossil record. For instance, Lamarck advanced his "developmental hypothesis," in which he arranged all known animals into a sequence based on their increasing organic complexity. He clearly implied that human beings were the highest product of a process of organic transformation and had been created through the same processes that had created all other species. However, Lamarck's imagination was also bound by theological constraints, and he did not carry his research through to its logical conclusion. Rather than limiting himself to natural forces as the shapers of organic transformation, Lamarck assumed an underlying, divinely ordered patterning.

Before scholars could fully appreciate the antiquity of the earth and the processes that gave rise to all species—including the human species—they had to free themselves from the constraints of nineteenth-century Christian theology. A revolution of perspective was necessary, a change of viewpoint so convincing that it would overcome people's emotional and intellectual commitment to Christian dogma. The logic of the new position would have to be simple and straightforward, and rest on a unified, universally applicable principle.

As we shall see shortly, students of human *society* had been grappling with these issues for almost a century. Herbert Spencer (1820–1903) developed the theory of evolution as applied to societies and based it (in the now immortal phrase) on "survival of the fittest." His writings and those of Thomas Malthus (1766–1834), the political economist who pessimistically forecast a "struggle for survival" among humankind for dwindling resources, profoundly influenced two naturalists working independently on the problem of the origins of species: Both Alfred Russel Wallace (1823–1913) and Charles Robert Darwin (1809–1882) arrived at the solution at the same time. They hit on the single, unifying (and natural) principle that would account both for the origin and the extinction of species—*natural selection.* In 1858 they presented joint papers on this topic, and the next year Darwin published *On the Origin of Species,* a book that captured scholars' imaginations and became the first influential work that popularized the concept of evolution as applied to the world of living organisms.

What is natural selection? It can be put simply and straightforwardly: *Natural selection is the process through which certain environmentally adaptive features are perpetuated at the expense of less adaptive features.*

Two very important points must be stressed with regard to natural selection. *First, it is features—not individuals—that are favored. Second, no features are inherently "superior";* natural selection is entirely dependent on the environment. Change the environment, and the favored adaptive features change as well.

Evolutionism in Social Thought

As we have already mentioned, in medieval times Europeans were exposed, through the reports of adventurous travelers, to the existence of many "strange" peoples living in "exotic" places on distant shores. Knowledge of these peoples was expanded considerably during the Renaissance and Enlightenment periods as the lure of riches to be made through trade and conquest generated massive world exploration and colonization underwritten by European rulers—and of course, the Church, ever ready to extend its influence through missionary activities. As information (and a great deal of misinformation) about foreign people accumulated, European scholars increasingly attempted to study them through the systematic comparison of what they learned of their societies with what they believed were the important characteristics of their own society in Western Europe.

Inevitably these researches "proved" that European society was superior to all others, which were ranked at various levels of "advance" below Europe. Thus by the late eighteenth century and throughout the nineteenth century the *comparative method* of social science resulted in the elaboration of theories of social and intellectual progress that developed into full-blown evolutionary theories, frequently referred to as *classical* or *unilineal evolutionism.* The Marquis de Condorcet (1743–1794), for instance, identified ten stages of social evolution marked by the successive acquisition of technological and scientific knowledge: From the limited knowledge needed for hunting and gathering, humanity passes through the development of pastoralism, agriculture, writing, and the differentiation of the sciences, then through a temporary period of darkness and the decline of knowledge in the Middle Ages leading to the invention of the printing press in 1453, the skeptical rationalism of René Descartes' philosophy, then to the founding of the French Republic of Condorcet's day, and eventually, through the application of scientific knowledge, to a world of peace and equality among the nations and the sexes. His *Outline of the Intellectual Progress of Mankind* (orig. 1795) is viewed by many as the outstanding work of social science produced in eighteenth-century Europe, even though its ethnocentric bias is blatant (Harris 1968:35).

Auguste Comte (1798–1857), who is sometimes called one of the "fathers" of social science, followed Condorcet's approach to social evolution. For him, too, the progress of the human intellect moved social evolution forward. However, he identified only three stages of evolution, characterized respectively by "theological" thought, in which people perceive the universe as animated by a will much like their own (evolving from animism through polytheism to monotheism); "metaphysical" thought, in which abstract laws of nature are discovered; and finally "positive" thought, represented by the scientific method (of which his own writings were the embodiment in the social sciences). By the way, it is interesting to note that Comte also believed that each person passes through these three stages in the course of his or her individual development.

The writings of Herbert Spencer on social evolution were preeminent during much of the middle and late nineteenth century. As mentioned earlier, it was he who first introduced the term *evolution* into the scientific literature. And in his classic *First Principles,* published in 1862,[2] he provides a definition of the term that has not significantly been improved upon to this day. *Evolution,* Spencer points out, *is not merely change.* It is "change from an indefinite, incoherent homogeneity to a definite, coherent heterogeneity; through continuous differentiations and integrations" (cited in Carneiro 1973:89). In other words, to Spencer *evolution is the progress of life forms and social forms from the simple to the complex.*

Spencer's work is often neglected by contemporary anthropologists,[3] who tend to trace their historical roots to two other major nineteenth-century evolutionists, Sir Edward Burnett Tylor (1832–1917) and Lewis Henry Morgan (1818–1881). Morgan's work in many ways is derived from that of Spencer. Like Spencer, he viewed social evolution as the result of societies adapting to the stresses of their environments. In his classic study, *Ancient Society* (1877), Morgan identified seven stages of social evolution:

| I. Lower Status of Savagery | Marked by simple food gathering |
| II. Middle Status of Savagery | Marked by knowledge of fishing and the invention of fire |

---

[2] The word *evolution* does not even appear in Darwin's *On the Origin of Species* until the 1872 edition!

[3] This is at least partially because Spencer's writings have been associated with the so-called social Darwinists, who justify the exploitative characteristics of class-based society by appealing superficially to the notion of "survival of the fittest." As Irven Devore has pointed out, social Darwinism should more accurately be called "social anti-Darwinism."

III. Upper Status of Savagery	Marked by the invention of the bow and arrow
IV. Lower Status of Barbarism	Marked by the invention of pottery
V. Middle Status of Barbarism	Marked by the domestication of plants and animals, irrigation, and stone and brick architecture
VI. Upper Status of Barbarism	Marked by the invention of iron working
VII. Civilization	Marked by the invention of the phonetic alphabet

Sir Edward Tylor lacked the concern with social systems of Spencer and Morgan. He was more concerned with *culture* than with society, defining culture all-inclusively as "that complex whole which includes knowledge, belief, art, morals, law, custom, and any other capabilities and habits acquired by man as a member of society" (1958:1; orig. 1871). Tylor attempted to demonstrate that culture had evolved from simple to complex and that it is possible to reconstruct the simple beginnings of culture by the study of its "survivals" in contemporary "primitive" cultures.

In spite of the fact that their individual evolutionary schemes differed from one another in important ways, these classical evolutionists shared one overriding conviction: Society had evolved from simple to complex through identifiable stages. Although it could not be claimed that every single society had passed through each of the stages they described, nevertheless they believed they had found sequences of developmental stages through which a "preponderant number" of societies had passed (Carneiro 1973:91), and that these sequences represented progress. At the turn of the century this position came under furious assault by Franz Boas and his students and vanished from the American intellectual scene. It reemerged in the 1940s, and has become one of the major conceptual tools that prehistorians and archaeologists use to reconstruct the human past.

The Emergence of Specialized Disciplines

Until the middle of the eighteenth century there was no separate discipline that one might call social science. To the extent that society was studied, it was done within the all-purpose framework of history. But by around 1750 the study of society had become sufficiently specialized to deserve the label "social science"—a separate discipline having split off from historical studies and embarked upon its own development. For about 100 years the study of human nature and society evolved along the lines we have already described, embodying loosely all the different approaches to the building of a science of humankind.

A century later Darwinian evolutionism arrived.

As has already been observed, the impact of Darwinism on human thought was profound and its effects on social science were no less dramatic. The two outstanding changes in the study of human nature and society that resulted were the application of evolutionary theory to virtually all aspects of the study of humankind and the split of such studies into increasingly specialized, separate disciplines.

The Sociology–Anthropology Split

Perhaps the major splitting of the social sciences in the mid-nineteenth century was the emergence of the separate disciplines of sociology and anthropology, which to this day have maintained their distinct and individual identities. Sociologists tended to follow the positivist approach of Auguste Comte described earlier, and shared with Comte a preoccupying interest in European society. Anthropologists, on the other hand, remained interested in a far broader range of data: archaeological finds, the study of "races" and the distribution of diverse human physical traits, human evolution, the comparative study of cultures and cultural evolution—all more or less unified by evolutionary theory. And whereas sociologists focused on European society, anthropologists, in their worldwide search for data, tended to concentrate on the "primitive" or preindustrial societies (Voget 1975:114–116).

Major Splits Within Anthropology

Even within the newly emerging discipline of anthropology internal specializations developed. Four major subfields established themselves, each focusing on particular kinds of data and developing its own theories, methods, and techniques (as well as even more specialized internal subdivisions).

Cultural anthropology focuses on *ethnography,* the intensive description of individual societies, usually of the small, isolated, relatively homogeneous kind, and *ethnology,* the systematic comparison and analysis of ethnographic materials, usually with the specification of evolutionary stages of development of such things as legal systems, political systems, economic systems, technology, kinship systems, and religions in mind.

Linguistics emerged as the systematic study of language. *Structural linguistics* is the study of the internal structures of the world's languages; *historical linguistics* is the study of the evolutionary tree of language, reconstructing extinct "proto" forms by systematically comparing surviving language branches.

Archaeology is the retrieval and study of human organic and cultural remains left in the earth. *Prehistoric archaeology* is the use of archaeology to reconstruct prehistoric times; *classical archaeology* is the use of archaeology to reconstruct the classical civilizations; *historical archaeology* is the investigation of all literate civilizations; and *salvage archaeology* is the attempt to preserve archaeological remains from destruction by the large-scale proj-

ects of industrial society such as dam building, foundation excavation, and highway construction.

Physical anthropology is the study of human biology.
It has two primary subjects: *paleontology,* the study of
fossil ancestors, and *neontology,* the comparative study
of living primates (including the study of differences in
human physical traits).

The Emergence of Physical Anthropology

We mentioned earlier that the origins of physical
anthropology as a distinct discipline generally are traced
to the eighteenth-century scientist Johann Blumenbach.
He was among the first scholars to collect skulls in a
systematic manner and is credited with pioneering in their
careful measurement (craniometry). These researches
led him to develop his system of "racial" classification, the
prototype of many subsequent efforts.

One of Blumenbach's central ideas was that the
"races" developed as biological responses to environmental stresses. This notion was elaborated upon in the nineteenth century by numerous scholars such as Anders
Retzius (1796–1860), who in 1842 devised a formula
for computing long-headedness and narrow-headedness:

$$\frac{\text{head breadth}}{\text{head length}} \times 100 = \text{cephalic index}$$

A low cephalic index indicates a narrow head; a high
index a broad head. Fourteen years later Retzius published a survey of cranial indices based on the measurement of skulls from private collections, in which he distinguished a vast number of "races" determined by virtue
of their cephalic indexes.

Others followed the lead of Blumenbach and
Retzius, and a wide number of techniques were developed
through which the human body could be systematically
measured. Such measuring is called *anthropometry* and
remains to the present day an important aspect of physical anthropology. Anthropometry contributes to our
understanding of fossil remains by providing scholars
with precise methods for studying them. It also provides
concrete data on variations in body shape among human
populations, replacing what previously had been rather
impressionistic descriptions. Thus body measuring became
one of the major tools for determining "racial" classifications; however, by the end of the century it was being
attacked by scholars who pointed out that anthropometric
traits of all ranges could be found represented among
individuals of all the so-called "races."

We have already discussed at length the impact of
Darwinism on the human sciences. After the publication
of Darwin's *On the Origin of Species* in 1859, natural
selection became the core concept of physical anthropology and evolution its primary concern. Thomas
Huxley (1825–1895), a naturalist who enthusiastically
took up Darwin's theories, added great impetus to the
study of human evolution by showing that the human
species was not qualitatively distinct from other primates

but, rather, only the most complex in an evolutionary
continuum from the most primitive lower primates
through monkeys, the great apes, and finally humankind.

The study of the fossil evidence for human evolution
was slow in developing. By 1822 reports had come from
Germany about findings of the fossilized remains of many
extinct animals in limestone caves. These reports impelled
William Buckland (1784–1856), Reader of Geology
at Oxford University, to investigate the limestone Paviland
Cave on the Welsh coast. There Buckland found the same
kinds of extinct animals as had been reported in Germany—as well as flint tools and a human skeleton. This
skeleton came to be called the Red Lady of Paviland because it had become stained with red ochre.[4] As a Christian minister and a confirmed diluvialist, Buckland was
hardpressed to explain this human presence among extinct creatures. He resorted to the contorted conclusion
that the animal remains had probably been swept into the
cave by flooding and that the human skeleton had been
buried there long after Noah's flood by local inhabitants
(Leakey and Goodall 1969:11–12).

Similar mental gymnastics kept scholars from ac-
knowledging what, in fact, their eyes were seeing: ancient
human remains among extinct animals, attesting to a
vastly longer human existence than Christian doctrine
permitted. Only after the Darwinian revolution could
people permit themselves to make accurate interpretations of these fossil materials. In 1860, for example,
Edouard Lartet (1801–1873), while investigating a cave
near the village of Aurignac in southern France, found
human remains associated with the charred bones of such
extinct animals as the woolly mammoth, the woolly rhinoceros, the cave bear, and the bison. The evidence he
reported finally convinced many people, including the
prominent geologist Charles Lyell, of the antiquity of
humankind. It is hardly coincidental that these events
happened the year *after* the publication of Darwin's *On
the Origin of Species.*

Eight years later, in 1868, Louis Lartet followed
his father's lead and excavated an ancient rock shelter
that had been exposed in the course of the construction
of a railway in the Dordogne region of France. He found
five human skeletons, including three adult males, one
adult female, and one unborn baby. These people were
associated with the same kinds of extinct animals and
cultural artifacts as those found by his father at Aurignac.
They came to be viewed as representatives of the so-called
Cro-magnon population (fully modern humans) that produced the impressive Aurignacian Upper Paleolithic culture.

In 1857 fragments of a human skeleton were found
in a limestone cave near Düsseldorf in Germany. The
skull cap, however, displayed what at the time seemed to
be shockingly apelike features. It was extraordinarily

---

[4] Subsequently it was determined that the skeleton was that of a
male.

thick, had massive ridges over the eyes, and had little in the way of a forehead. This specimen, which came to be called Neanderthal man, raised for scholars the possibility of finding fossil populations of primitive people who were ancestral to the Cro-magnon types and, thus, to modern human beings. In 1889 Eugène Dubois (1858–1940) traveled to Southeast Asia with the deliberate intention of finding such fossilized evidence of human evolution. There, during 1891–1892, in a site on the bank of the Solo River on the island of Java, he found some molars, a skull cap, and a femur (thighbone) of so primitive a nature that he thought them at first to be the remains of an ancient chimpanzee. By 1892 he revised this assessment and decided that he had, indeed, found an evolutionary ancestor of the human species, a creature he eventually called *Pithecanthropus erectus* (erect Ape-man). Naturally, as with all such finds, a great debate about its evolutionary status ensued; but today we agree with Dubois that his Solo River find is indeed a human ancestor, one of many that have been found and are now grouped together under the term *Homo erectus.*

As we have seen, physical anthropology emerged during the nineteenth century. Although the beginnings of serious and systematic work on human biology can be found in the eighteenth and early nineteenth centuries, it was not until the theory of evolution asserted itself in the middle of the last century that the conceptual tools to integrate and inform such research became available. Evolution continues to be a central and unifying theme in the current practice of physical anthropology.

The Emergence of Archaeology

Like physical anthropology, archaeology gradually emerged as a separate discipline in the course of the nineteenth century. It split off from the generalized study of ancient history as scholars—mostly geologists, initially—began to focus on finding material remains of ancient precivilized populations in Europe.

Actually, it was a geological debate that helped lay the groundwork for the emergence of archaeology. As mentioned earlier, the prevailing view among geologists until well into the nineteenth century was that the series of strata that composed the earth's crust were the result of Noah's flood (diluvialism) or a series of catastrophes of which the flood was the most recent (catastrophism). One of the first geologists to dispute these notions was William Smith (1769–1839). Dubbed "Strata" Smith by his detractors, he assembled a detailed table of all the known strata and their fossil contents and argued a uniformitarian position: that the eternally ongoing processes of erosion, weathering, accumulation, and tectonic movement accounted for their large number. He was supported by James Hutton (1726–1797) in his influential work *Theory of the Earth,* published in 1795.

Combat was joined by the greatly respected William Buckland (the discoverer of the "Red Lady of Paviland"), who in 1823 published his work *Reliquiae Dilu-*

vianae, or Observations on the Organic Remains contained in Caves, Fissures and Diluvial Gravel, and on Other Geological Phenomena attesting to the Action of an Universal Deluge, in which he vigorously attacked the uniformitarian views that so directly contradicted Church dogma (Daniel 1959). Only the appearance of Sir Charles Lyell's *Principles of Geology* (1830–1833) managed finally to turn the tide of scholarly sentiment in favor of the uniformitarian view of the earth's history.

Because of the nature of their work, it was for the most part amateur and professional geologists who most frequently encountered fossilized human remains—generally embedded in strata in the floors of limestone caverns. In the roughly six decades beginning in the 1790s, an impressive array of evidence with regard to human antiquity was found in a number of such caves in Europe and England; but the finds were dismissed or their importance unrecognized. As early as 1797, for example, John Frere (1740–1807) found chipped flint tools twelve feet deep in his excavation at Hoxne (northeast of London). These stone tools were closely associated with the remains of extinct animal species. To Frere these finds suggested a very ancient human existence, even older than the commonly accepted 6000-year antiquity of Creation. Nobody listened. Forty years later, in 1838, Boucher de Perthes (1788–1868), a customs collector at Abbeville in the northwest of France, disclosed news of some flint "axes" he had found in gravel pit caves on the banks of the Somme River. The world laughed at his assertion that these tools were manufactured by "antediluvial man," even though they had been found in the immediate vicinity of the bones of extinct cold-adapted animals. In 1846 he published *Antiquités Celtiques et Antediluviennes,* in which he formally argued his thesis—and was attacked as a heretic by the Church.

We have already discussed William Buckland's inability in 1822 to comprehend the significance of his own find, the so-called Red Lady of Paviland. The powerful grip of Christian theology on scholars' minds blinded the intellectual establishment of the period, keeping them from seeing and appreciating the overwhelming pattern that these and numerous other finds presented. As we have emphasized repeatedly, it was the emergence of Darwinism in 1859 that freed people's vision and enabled them to face and reinterpret these materials correctly. The evolutionary perspective, then, was of critical importance for the emergence of archaeology. Without it there was no way to interpret accurately the significance of the ancient remains that were being turned up with increasing frequency.

The excavation of rock shelters revealing human cultural remains of great antiquity was only one of several kinds of archaeological research being undertaken in the nineteenth century. The excavation and description of large prehistoric monuments and burial mounds, begun in the wake of emergent nationalism in the seventeenth and eighteenth centuries, continued. So did the retrieval and preservation of materials accidentally brought to light by road, dam, and building excavations as the industrial revolution changed the face of the earth. By the early 1800s vast quantities of stone and metal implements had been recovered and had found their way into both private and public collections. As the volume of such artifacts mounted, museum curators were faced with the problem of how to organize and display them meaningfully.

In 1836 Christian Jurgensen Thomsen (1788–1865), curator of the Danish National Museum, published a guide to its collections in which he classified all artifacts in terms of the material from which they were made. He argued that the three classes he thus identified represented stages in cultural evolution: a *Stone Age* followed by a *Bronze Age* and then an *Iron Age*. The idea was not new—it had been proposed by Lucretius in ancient Rome—but it was new for its time. However, the *Three Age System* fit well with the contemporary writings of early nineteenth-century social evolutionists and was of such usefulness that it quickly spread to other countries.

The Three Age System was clearly evolutionary (and hence radical) in nature. It contained a geological perspective in that it proposed clearly defined sequences of cultural stages modeled after geological strata. It was of tremendous value in providing a conceptual framework through which archaeologists could begin systematically to study the artifacts they retrieved from the earth, and also in that it tended to support those scholars arguing for a greatly expanded vision of human antiquity.

Combined with Darwinian evolutionism, the Three Age System became an even more powerful conceptual tool. In 1865 Sir John Lubbock (1834–1913) published his tremendously influential book *Prehistoric Times,* in which he vastly extended the Stone Age and divided it in two. He thus proposed that human prehistory be viewed in terms of the following stages: the *Paleolithic* (Old Stone Age, marked by flint tools); the *Neolithic* (New Stone Age, marked by the appearance of pottery); the *Bronze Age;* and the *Iron Age.* Although this system has continued to be refined, it still forms the basis of our understanding of world prehistory, and we continue to make use of its terminology.

At about the time Lubbock was formulating his broad outline of the stages of cultural evolution, Edouard Lartet (whom we discussed earlier) and his English colleague Henry Christy were exploring the now famous rock shelters in the Dordogne region of France. In one cave, called La Madeleine, Christy and Lartet found not only an abundance of spectacular cave art and small engravings of extinct species such as the woolly mammoth, but also a magnificent collection of tools—including intricately carved implements of antler bone and ivory. These became the "type complex" for the identification of the Magdalenian culture, easily the most advanced and spectacular culture of Upper Paleolithic times.

Using the art work they found in the ten or so caves they explored in this region, Lartet and Christy developed a system to classify the materials they uncovered. Their approach was based on the fact that renderings of different species of animals predominated during different periods. The succession of stages they worked out for the Dordogne region was the following: (1) the Age of the Bison; (2) the Age of the Woolly Mammoth and Rhinoceros; (3) the Age of the Reindeer; and (4) the Age of the Cave Bear.

Gabriel de Mortillet (1821–1898) took the work of Lartet and Christy a step further by developing a chronology of the same region based on the tool industries found at *type sites* (sites used to represent the characteristic features of a culture). The series he ultimately settled on in the 1870s had six stages: Thenaisian, Chellean, Mousterian, Solutrean, Magdalenian, and Robenhausian. Although these materials have been reinterpreted a great deal since that time, prehistoric archaeologists still use Mortillet's approach to naming archaeological cultures and even most of the names he proposed.

The archaeologist of the late nineteenth century who most attracted public attention, however, was probably Heinrich Schliemann (1822–1890). After intensive study of the Homerian epics, Schliemann set out to find the ancient city of Troy. He accomplished this in 1871 at a place called Hissarlik, near the western tip of Anatolia (modern Turkey). He was a romantic figure, and his quest to find the sites of Homeric legend excited public fancy and brought forth private funds to support both his own and other archaeological research. Unfortunately he was not a very skilled excavator: While digging up the highly stratified site at Hissarlik he focused his attentions on what turned out to be the wrong layer—and virtually destroyed the real Troy in the process.

Developments in the New World

As the frontiers of knowledge about human origins expanded in Europe with the emergence of increasingly specialized subdisciplines, a parallel development was taking place in the Americas. Wild speculation about the origins of Native Americans gave way to increasingly systematic research by scholars and learned amateurs. In 1784, for example, Thomas Jefferson (1743–1826) excavated an Indian burial mound in Virginia. Although his digging techniques were crude, he set about his task in a very modern manner. Rather than setting out simply to collect *artifacts,* Jefferson cut into the mound to collect *information.* His cross-section of the mound revealed ancient burial practices similar to those of known historic groups, and refuted the popularly held notion that the mound builders had buried their dead in an upright position.

By the 1840s John Lloyd Stephens and Frederick Catherwood had established new standards for care in the recording of details in their magnificent reports about, and drawings of, the ruins of the Mayan civilization in the Yucatan peninsula, published in works such as Stephens'

Incidents of Travel in Central America: Chiapas and Yucatan (1842).

The mounds of the southeastern United States attracted a number of excavators, most notably E. G. Squier and E. H. Davis, who described their research in an important monograph published in 1848. By the middle of the century sufficient work had been done to justify a long synthesis of American archaeology by Samuel Haven published in 1856.

Archaeology in the New World was always very tightly connected to cultural anthropology—much more so than in Europe. This stemmed from the fact that whereas Europeans engaged in archaeological research as an extension of their researches backward from known historical times to their distant prehistoric past, Americans were investigating "foreign" societies—whether they were digging in their own backyards or engaging in ethnographic research with their displaced (and decimated) Native American neighbors. To this day this difference persists: In Europe archaeology is usually thought of as a humanity (an adjunct to history), while in the United States archaeology is practiced as a subdiscipline of anthropology and viewed as a social science.

On With the Show

Since the turn of the century anthropology has developed into an increasingly complex and segmented discipline. Less and less are theories and trends tied to particular scholars, and few giants inhabit the fields of physical anthropology and archaeology today. Thus we shall end here our historical account of the specific contributions of individuals to the origins and development of these disciplines. You will encounter twentieth-century anthropologists speaking to you directly through the articles we have collected in this anthology. We hope you enjoy reading what they have to say—and that you will think about what it all means. The central question, after all, is terribly important: What, really, are human beings?

And it remains true today—as it has been historically—that the answers to that question tell us as much about the nature of the times as about the subject. Here, then, are contemporary scholars' approaches to the subject; there is a lot here for you to learn about your species (*Homo sapiens*), its origins and evolution, its organic and cultural history. There is also much that you can learn about yourself and your own society today.

References

Carneiro, Robert. 1973. "The Four Faces of Evolution," in John J. Honigmann (ed.), *Handbook of Social and Cultural Anthropology*, Chicago: Rand McNally (pp. 89–110).

Condorcet, Marquis de. 1822 (orig. 1795). *Esquisse d'un Tableau Historique des Progres de l'Esprit Humain*, Paris: Masson.

Coon, Carleton S. 1963. *The Origin of Races*, New York: Alfred A. Knopf.

Daniel, Glyn. 1959. "The Idea of Man's Antiquity," *Scientific American*, November.

Daniel, Glyn. 1963. *The Idea of Prehistory*, Cleveland and New York: World

Harris, Marvin. 1968. *The Rise of Anthropological Theory: A History of Culture*, New York: Thomas Y. Crowell.

Haven, Samuel. 1856. *Archaeology of the United States*, Washington, D.C.: The Smithsonian Institution.

Leakey, L. S. B., and Vanne Morris Goodall. 1969. *Unveiling Man's Origins*, Cambridge, Mass.: Schenkman.

Lyell, Charles. 1850 (orig. 1830–1833). *Principles of Geology* (8th ed.), London: J. Murray.

Montagu, Ashley. 1964. *Man's Most Dangerous Myth: The Fallacy of Race* (4th ed., rev.), New York: Meridian Books.

Morgan, Lewis Henry. 1877. *Ancient Society*, New York: World.

Spencer, Herbert. 1862. *First Principles*, London: Williams and Norgate.

Squier, E. G., and E. H. Davis. 1848. *Ancient Monuments in the Mississippi Valley*, Washington, D.C.: The Smithsonian Institution.

Stephens, J. L. 1842. *Incidents of Travel in Central America: Chiapas and Yucatan*, New York: Harper & Row.

Tylor, Sir Edward Burnett. 1958 (orig. 1871). *The Origins of Culture Pt. I of Primitive Culture*, New York: Harper Torchbooks.

Voget, Fred W. 1975. *A History of Ethnology*, New York: Holt, Rinehart and Winston.

II. On the Concept of Evolution

As you learned in the article that opened this reader ("Stones and Bones"), the formal statement of the theory of evolution in the mid-nineteenth century was one of the great watersheds of human intellectual history. Certainly evolutionary theory is the foundation on which the disciplines of physical anthropology and archaeology both rest, and indeed most discussions of "human nature" that flood the popular market are phrased in evolutionary terms. It is unfortunate, therefore, that evolutionary theory is at best imperfectly understood by most laypersons—and not a few social scientists as well. Therefore we have included this section in our reader and placed it at the very beginning. It is intended to illuminate evolutionary theory, and especially to correct some popular misconceptions.

We open this section with Daniel's "The Idea of Man's Antiquity" because it provides a fine account of the historical setting in which the concept of evolution finally was formulated. Daniel demonstrates convincingly that the concept of evolution freed people's vision, allowing them to appreciate and interpret what their minds previously had failed to comprehend. Hoskin's imaginative "A Chat with Charles Darwin" follows. It is useful because it shows how ideas develop slowly and in roundabout ways—even in the "intellectual giants" that our civilization so prizes. Gould's article "Darwin's Dilemma" tackles one of the most lingering misunderstandings of evolutionary theory: the confounding of *evolution* with *progress.* Not only has this led to intellectual confusion (still present in not a few scientific discussions of the matter), but it has had damaging social consequences as well: Social Darwinism—a social philosophy that attempted to justify the ascendant position of society's elite groups in evolutionary terms—hung vacantly on the point of this fallacy but attracted a great number of politically powerful adherents. Social Darwinism is, in fact, inherently anti-Darwinian.

We close this section with Bordes' "Physical Evolution and Technological Evolution in Man: A Parallelism." It is a scholarly attempt to explore the nature of the undoubted relationship between changes in the nature of the evolving human brain, technological developments, and the emergence of human consciousness. You should keep in mind, however, that this article is primarily speculative in nature.

Having digested the materials in this section, you will be ready to tackle the more specialized sections that follow.

2

THE IDEA OF MAN'S ANTIQUITY

GLYN E. DANIEL

Digging near the Bavarian city of Bayreuth in 1771, Johann Friedrich Esper found human bones at the same level as the remains of extinct animals. He was more startled than elated by his find, because it confronted him with a disturbing anachronism in the then-accepted timetable of the world's history. In the preceding century Archbishop Ussher had worked out this chronology from the complicated genealogies of *Genesis;* he concluded that the world and man had been created in 4004 B.C. Six millennia took in everything, and man was only a trifle younger than time itself. In this view of human history there was no inkling that sources other than written ones existed. The antiquaries of the time were concerned with describing monuments and cataloguing portable relics; they had no idea that history lay in the soil, much less any notion of how to wrest it from its grave. Samuel Johnson spoke for the pre-archaeological scholar when he declared: "All that is really known of the ancient state of Britain is contained in a few pages. . . . We can know no more than what old writers have told us."

Except for a few pagan myths, the old writers did not suggest that there were men before Man. Geology in Esper's and Johnson's time was little more than an elaboration of the Biblical story of Creation and the Flood. In accordance with that tradition it was easy, and not without logic, to explain fossils and river gravels in terms of the Flood, or sometimes of several floods. This was catastrophist or diluvialist geology. There was, to be sure, some talk of animals antedating 4004 B.C., but their fossils were believed to be the remains of creatures discarded by the Creator before his culminating creation: the world of Genesis. But with the creation of Adam, according to the doctrine, further creation ceased. Opposed to this account were the antediluvians—the near-heretics who held that man may have lived before Adam. This was the danger apprehended by Esper, and it caused him to ask: "Did [the bones] belong to a Druid or to an Antediluvian or to a mortal man of more recent time? I dare not presume without sufficient reason these members to be of the same age as the other animal petrifactions. They must have got there by chance."

The "sufficient reason" Esper asked

Courtesy New York Library; previously published in *Scientific American,* November, 1959.

FLINT TOOL FROM HOXNE IN SUFFOLK is typical of the discoveries that caused speculation about man's antiquity. This hand-axe, dated according to the stratum in which it was found and the workmanship it displays, belongs to the Lower Paleolithic of about half a million years ago. The illustration appeared in 1800 in *Archeologia,* a publication of the Society of Antiquaries of London.

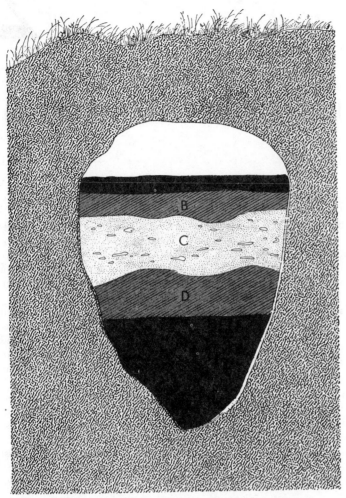 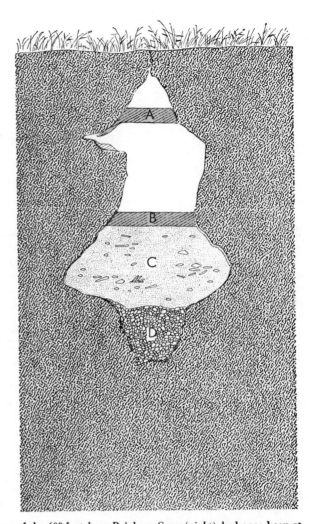

DEVON CAVES IN ENGLAND figured prominently in establishing the antiquity of man. Kent's Cavern (*left*) was the earlier find. Under surface layer (A) lay a stalagmite stratum (B) which sealed the cave earth (C) containing human artifacts amid the remains of extinct animals. Layers D and E are stalagmite and breccia. The floor of the 600-foot long Brixham Cave (*right*) had once been at A, but when excavated in 1858 the stalagmite at B was the cave floor. In the six feet of cave earth (C) were remains similar to those found in Kent's Cavern. Level D is gravel bed. Both the caves measure more than 20 feet from roof to gravel-bed bottom.

for was soon to be forthcoming. James Hutton, in his *Theory of the Earth*, published in 1785, offered the first persuasive alternative to cataclysmic geology. He suggested that the stratification of rocks was due not to floods and other supernatural calamities but to processes still going on in seas and rivers and lakes. He wrote: "No processes are to be employed that are not natural to the globe, no action to be admitted except those of which we know the principle." Hutton's reasoning was carried forward by William Smith—"Strata" Smith as he was called—who assigned relative ages to rocks according to their fossil contents, and who argued for an orderly, noncatastrophic deposition of strata over a long period of time—much longer than 6,000 years.

But the climate of opinion was still catastrophist. In 1797, just 26 years after Esper's discovery, John Frere, a gentleman of Suffolk, sent to the Secretary of the Society of Antiquaries of London some hand-axes and other implements of flint found at Hoxne, near Diss. In his accompanying letter he wrote: "If [these] weapons of war, fabricated and used by a people who had not the use of metals . . . are not particularly objects of curiosity in themselves, they must, I think, be considered in that light from the situation in which they are found, [which] may tempt us to refer them to a very remote period indeed; even beyond that of the present world."

They were indeed to be referred "to a very remote period": modern archaeologists would place them in the Lower Paleolithic of perhaps half a million years ago. But at the time no one took Frere's speculations seriously.

William Buckland, Reader in Geology at Oxford and later Dean of Westminster, perhaps typified catastrophist thinking. In 1823 he published his great book *Reliquiae Diluvianae, or Observations on the Organic Remains contained in Caves, Fissures and Diluvial Gravel, and on Other Geological Phenomena attesting the Action of an Universal Deluge.* Buckland himself had found evidence of the antiquity of man, but he refused to believe it. He had excavated Goat's Hole Cave near Paviland in South Wales and amid Upper Paleolithic implements had found the skeleton of a young man. (He believed it to be that of a young woman, and it is still referred to as the Red Lady of Paviland.) But he insisted that the skeleton was "clearly not coeval with the antediluvian bones of the extinct species" of animals. He made similar discoveries in the caves of the Mendip Hills of southwestern England but again refused to believe they were antediluvian. He argued instead that the caves had "been used either as a place of sepulture in early times or resorted to for refuge by the wretches that perished in it, when the country was suffering under one of our numerous military operations. . . . The state of the bones affords indication of very high antiquity but there is no reason for not considering them post-Diluvian."

When a Roman Catholic priest, Father MacEnery, discovered some flint implements at Kent's Cavern near Torquay in Devon, he wrote of them to Buckland. Buckland reacted characteristically. The flints had been found amid the stratified remains of rhinoceros and other animals under the unbroken, stalagmite-sealed floor of the cave. Buckland avoided the implications of this sealed evidence and offered another in-

genious and tortured explanation that preserved catastrophist doctrine. He told MacEnery that ancient Britons must have camped in the cave; they had probably scooped out ovens in the stalagmite and in that way the flint implements had got below. Thus, according to Buckland, the association of the flints with the skeletal remains of extinct animals was only apparent. It was all very reasonable, except that, as MacEnery noted, there were no such ovens in the way as important as Darwin's *Origin of Species*. Lyell took the many fragmentary observations and insights of the fluvialists and organized them into a coherent system. He stated the principle of uniformitarianism: the central geological idea that strata could only be interpreted correctly by assuming that the agencies that formed them had operated at a uniform rate and in a uniform way, just as they work in the present. Lyell's great book was a staggering blow to catastrophist geology. But though the discoveries of Esper and Frere were thus rationalized, and the work of Hutton and Smith endorsed, this was not yet suf-

ficient to swing general opinion behind belief in the true antiquity of man. More evidence was needed to shatter the old view and establish the new one; it soon came from Devon and northern France.

Boucher de Perthes was a customs official at Abbeville in the north of France. He had become interested in archaeology when he encountered neolithic artifacts and bones—"Celtic" remains as they were called—brought up by the dredging of the Somme Canal. His interest grew as more remains of "diluvial" man and animals were found in the quarries of nearby Manchecourt and Moulin-Quignon. By 1838, some five or six years after Lyell's *Principles* had appeared, de Perthes set forth his views in a five-volume work entitled *De la création: essai sur l'origine et la progression des êtres*. At about the same time he was exhibiting *haches diluviennes*, roughly chipped hand-axes, before the Société Imperiale d'Emulation de la Somme in Abbeville and at the Institut de Paris.

He was received with the same coldness suffered by his fellows in England, and like them he was regarded as a crank. "At the very mention of the words 'axe' and 'diluvium,'" he once remarked, "I observe a smile on the face of those to whom I speak. It is the workmen who help me, not the geologists." But de Perthes worked on and accumulated more evidence. The association he observed of human artifacts and extinct animals in the Somme gravels was compelling and no longer to be explained by the diluvial theory. In 1847 he published the first part of a three-volume work entitled *Antiquités celtiques et antédiluviennes*. The very title of the work indicates the effect his researches had on his thinking: the *haches diluviennes* were now *haches antédiluviennes*.

In England, meanwhile, the new archaeology had found other champions. William Pengelly, a schoolmaster, reworked MacEnery's cavern in Kent and, cave. But Buckland was insistent, and out of deference to his views MacEnery did not publish his evidence.

At about this time, however, the National Museum in Copenhagen had been opened to the public with its antiquities arranged in three ages: Stone, Bronze and Iron. This classification was the work of Christian Jurgenson Thomsen, director of the Museum, and he set forth its underlying idea in a treatise that served as a guidebook to the display. His three-age system has been described very

SKULL OF NEANDERTHAL WOMAN was found in Forbes Quarry at Gibraltar in 1848. First believed to be a new species, Neanderthal was later seen to be a human variant. Missing portions of skull are outlined in this drawing from Hugo Obermaier's *Fossil Man in Spain*.
Courtesy New York Public Library; previously published in *Scientific American*, December, 1959.

properly as "the cornerstone of modern archaeology"; it helped to secure recognition for the view that the human species had come through a long prehistory. (The word "prehistory" did not appear in print until 1851, when Daniel Wilson used it in *The Archaeology and Prehistoric Annals of Scotland*.)

The 1830's were eventful for the emerging new science of archaeology. In 1833 Sir Charles Lyell published his *Principles of Geology*, a powerful contribution to the cause of the fluvialists, as the supporters of Hutton and Smith were called. This book was in its viewing the evidence there in terms of Lyell's uniformitarianism, saw it as proof of man's antiquity. But he realized that objections could be raised because the cavern had been disturbed by other workers. He found an entirely new site in an undisturbed cave across the bay in Devon above Brixham Harbour—Windmill Hill Cave. To supervise his excavations here he enlisted a committee of distinguished geologists in London. Pengelly, carrying out the actual digging, worked from July, 1858, to the next summer. It was a successful year. On the floor of the cave "lay a sheet of stalagmite from three to eight inches thick having within it and on it relics of lion, hyena, bear, mammoth, rhinoceros and reindeer." Below the floor Pengelly found flint tools.

The Brixham discoveries were compelling. Sir Charles Lyell said of them: "The facts recently brought to light during the systematic investigation of the Brixham Cave must, I think, have prepared you to admit that scepticism in regard to the cave evidence in favour of the antiquity of man had previously been pushed to an extreme."

The revolution was nearing a crisis: within the immediately foreseeable future man's history was to reach back beyond Archbishop Ussher's 6,000 years. The catastrophist theory was once and for all to be discarded and with it the Biblical notion that the world and man represented unalterable acts of special creation.

In 1858, while Pengelly was digging in the Brixham cave, the Scottish geologist Hugh Falconer visited Boucher de Perthes at Abbeville. De Perthes' evidence of man's antiquity immediately convinced Falconer. When he returned

to London, he persuaded the geologist Joseph Prestwich and the antiquary John Evans to go and see the finds of Abbeville for themselves. As Evans was leaving for France, he wrote of the widely separated events that were revising men's beliefs: "Think of their finding flint axes and arrowheads at Abbeville in conjunction with the bones of elephants and rhinoceroses 40 feet below the surface in a bed of drift. In this bone cave in Devon now being excavated . . . they say they have found flint arrowheads among the bones and the same is reported of a cave in Sicily. I can hardly believe it. It will make my ancient Britons quite modern if man is carried back in England to the days when elephants, rhinoceroses, hippopotomuses and tigers were also inhabitants of the country."

Evans then records what happened when they got to France. De Perthes showed them his collection of flint axes and implements "found among the beds of gravel, . . . the remains of a race of men who existed at the time when the deluge or whatever was the origin of these gravel beds took place. One of the most remarkable features of the case is that nearly all . . . of the animals whose bones are found in the same beds as the axes are extinct. There is the mammoth, the rhinoceros, the urus, . . . etc." Then they arrive at the actual gravel pits: "Sure enough, the edge of an axe was visible in an entirely undisturbed bed of gravel and eleven feet from the surface. We had a photographer with us to take a view of it so as to corroborate our testimony."

The evidence at Abbeville convinced Evans and Prestwich as it had convinced Falconer, and this, with Pengelly's work at Windmill Hill Cave, brought the whole matter to a head. When they got back to London, Prestwich read a paper to the Royal Society in which he said: "It was not until I had myself witnessed the conditions under which these flint implements had been found at Brixham that I became fully impressed with the validity of the doubts thrown upon the previously prevailing opinions with respect to such remains in caves." That famous meeting of the Royal Society was on May 26, 1859, and of it John Evans wrote: "There were a good many geological nobs there: Sir Charles Lyell, Murchison, Huxley, Morris, Dr. Perry, Faraday, Wheatstone, Babbage, etc. . . . Our assertions as to the finding of the weapons seemed to be believed."

A week later Evans read a paper on

the same subject to the Society of Antiquaries of London. In his account of this meeting he remarked: "I think I was generally believed in."

In August Sir Charles Lyell himself went to see the evidence of the Abbeville pits. He too was convinced, and a month later, in his presidential address to Section C of the British Association for the Advancement of Science, with Prince Albert presiding, he said: "I am fully prepared to corroborate the conclusions recently laid before the Royal Society by Mr. Prestwich." The battle was over; the great antiquity of man was an established fact. Victorian thought had to adjust itself not only to organic evolution but also to the antiquity of man; 4004 B.C. was forgotten.

It is perhaps strange that Charles Darwin himself was not at first impressed by the findings of de Perthes. Later in life he confessed: "I am ashamed to think that I concluded the whole was rubbish. Yet [de Perthes] has done for man something like what Agassiz did for glaciers." Perhaps Darwin held back because he did not want to involve his theory of evolution, at least at the outset, in anything so controversial as the ancestry of man. In the first edition of the *Origin of Species* he refused to discuss the relationship of evolution to man, and made only one cryptic statement on the general thesis of his book: "Light will be thrown on the origin of man and his history." In later editions this sentence was modified to: "Much light will be thrown. . . ."

But Darwin threw no light, not at any rate until 1871, when he published his views on the relation between man and general evolutionary theory in his *Descent of Man*. But this was eight years after T. H. Huxley's *Evidence as to Man's Place in Nature* had been published, and a dozen years after the climactic events of 1859. Thus whatever contribution Darwin made to the discovery of the antiquity of man, it was indirect and unwitting. It consisted entirely in the new way of thinking that he exemplified: uniformitarianism and evolution. The doctrine of evolution had man evolving from a prehuman ancestor; obviously there must somewhere be evidence of his passage from savagery through barbarism to civilization. The roughly chipped tools from Devon and the Somme now were more than credible, they were essential. People now had to accept the discoveries of de Perthes and Pengelly, where only a generation or two before, when the immutability of the species and catastrophist diluvialism were the dominant ideas, such discoveries had been scorned or ignored. Thus though Darwinism did not create prehistoric archaeology, it did give a great impetus to its acceptance and study; it helped set the stage for the acceptance of the idea of man's antiquity.

But even after the idea seemed well established, many students of the mid-century discoveries had misgivings about them. There was one particularly troublesome point: Men had left their axes but no trace of their physical selves, no bones. "Find us human remains in the diluvium," some of de Perthes' countrymen said to him, "and we will believe you." For de Perthes it was a sad challenge; this was 1863 and he was an old man of 75. Unable to dig for himself, he offered a 200-franc reward to the first quarryman to find human remains. With four months' wages as the prize, the quarrymen could not leave it to honest luck. Soon after the offer was made, they "found" human remains; first a human tooth; five days later a human jaw.

Boucher de Perthes was vindicated,

and his French colleagues were at last satisfied. But the drama had not played out. Some British archaeologists had long suspected that de Perthes' gravel pits were being salted, and they proved that the jaw and several hand-axes had been inserted into the gravel faces by some of his workmen. It was a cruel blow.

Fortunately the case did not hang by so meager a thread. There was genuine skeletal evidence of man's antiquity. Two years before the 1859 pronouncements about the antiquity of man, the long bones and skullcap of a manlike being had been discovered in a limestone cave in the ravine of Neanderthal near the Rhenish city of Düsseldorf. Hermann Schaaffhausen, who first described these remains, noted the large size, low forehead and enormous brow-ridges of the skullcap. He believed that the Neanderthal skeleton belonged to "a barbarous and savage race," and he regarded it "as the most ancient memorial of the early inhabitants of Europe."

There was still more evidence. A female cranium had been found nine years before that, in 1848, during blasting operations in the Forbes Quarry at

Gibraltar. The significance of the relic was not realized at the time, but at this juncture, in 1859, George Busk read a paper on it before a meeting of the British Association. The ebullient Falconer, who had persuaded Evans and Prestwich to visit de Perthes six years before, again apprehended the importance of a crucial find. He perceived that here was a new species of man; he proposed to name it *Homo calpicus*, after Calpe, the ancient name for Gibraltar. He wrote his suggestion to Busk, referring somewhat redundantly to his "Grand, Priscan, Pithecoid, Agrioblematous, Platycnemic, wild *Homo calpicus* of Gibraltar." It was only later realized that this "grand, primitive, manlike, wild-eyed, flat-headed, wild Calpic man of Gibraltar" was not one of a new species but a member of that curious human variant, Neanderthal man.

And so by 1859 all the evidence for proper recognition of the antiquity of man was available: artifacts from the Somme and south Devon and fossils from Neanderthal and Gibraltar. The century since then has been given to building on that premise, to filling in its outlines with new evidence of man's physical and cultural evolution.

3

A Chat with Charles Darwin

The author of *The Origin of Species* was recently portrayed on British television.
His appearance was the brainchild of an imaginative science historian who re-created
an interview with the long-since departed champion of evolution

by Michael Hoskin

In his early manhood Darwin was capable of considerable feats of endurance in South American expeditions, but for many years now he has had to nurse his health. He is probably suffering from an obscure disease contracted in South America, one that leads to a feeling of lassitude and loss of drive. But the disease is not understood, and he is widely suspected of mere hypochondria. As a result he lives in the shelter of his large and devoted family, rarely venturing into the outside world and avoiding social contacts. He is fortunate in having been provided for by his father, so that he has never had to struggle to earn his own daily bread; instead he has enjoyed indefinite leisure in which to pursue his elaborate researches.

As a person he is simple to the point of naïveté. His wife said: "He is the most open transparent man I ever saw, and every word expresses his real thoughts." He has a sense of fun, and is exceedingly thoughtful and generous. He tends to avoid controversy and prefers others to fight his battles for him, but he has high principles and an ability to see many sides to a question.

Hoskin: Mr. Darwin, it's an extraordinary fact that most of the ideas that went into your theory of evolution are to be found in the writings of your own grandfather. How much did his work influence you?
Darwin: I read my grandfather's book *Zoonomia* when I was young, and I admired it greatly. But when I read it a second time after an interval of ten or fifteen years, I was disappointed in it—the proportion of speculation was so large in comparison with the facts he gave. In the same way a fellow undergraduate told me of my grandfather's French contemporary Lamarck, and his views on evolution; but as far as I can judge this had no effect on me.
Hoskin: But the idea of evolution was in the air?
Darwin: Well it had certainly been discussed, but I never came across a serious naturalist who believed

that species do change. But I think it is true that a great many well-observed facts were stored in the minds of naturalists, ready to take their proper places as soon as a theory was explained to account for them.
Hoskin: What was it like, having a famous grandfather?
Darwin: Oh, he died before I was born. It was my father who dominated the family. He was the largest man I ever saw, twenty-four stone of him. But his mind was not scientific. He didn't try to express his knowledge under general laws.
Hoskin: And your mother?
Darwin: She died when I was eight, and I can hardly remember anything about her. It was a year after that that I went to Dr. Butler's great school at Shrewsbury, where I stayed until I was sixteen. But the school as a means of education to me was simply a blank—the studies were strictly classical.
Hoskin: Latin and Greek? From what you say it sounds as though you didn't come top of the class.
Darwin: When I left the school all my masters thought me a very ordinary boy, rather below average. And my father once said to me, "You care for nothing but shooting, dogs, and rat-catching—you will be a disgrace to yourself and all your family."
Hoskin: You had no scientific interests at school?
Darwin: I collected minerals and insects—*dead* insects, as my sister told me it was wrong to kill insects just to make a collection. And towards the end of my school life I helped my brother in his chemical experiments—he had a laboratory with proper apparatus in the toolhouse in the garden. This was the best part of my education, though Dr. Butler didn't approve at all, and it showed me, practically, the meaning of experimental science.
Hoskin: What did your father make of all this?
Darwin: Well, I was doing no good at school, so when I was sixteen he sent me to Edinburgh University to study medicine. But I felt sure that he would leave me enough money to live on, and so I didn't make any

Drawing Ridiculing Darwin from "London Sketch Book."

great effort to learn medicine.

Hoskin: Did you find Edinburgh an improvement on Shrewsbury?

Darwin: No, the instruction was entirely by lectures, and these were intolerably dull. Dr. Duncan's lectures on drugs at eight o'clock on a winter's morning are something fearful to remember. Anyhow, human anatomy disgusted me.

Hoskin: Not a promising start to a medical career!

Darwin: No. And so when my father saw that I didn't like the thought of being a physician, he proposed that I should become a clergyman. This meant I must take a degree at one of the English universities.

Hoskin: Then your years at Edinburgh were a complete waste of time?

Darwin: No, I made friends with several young men fond of the natural sciences. I used to go with one of them to collect animals in the tidal pools, and I dissected them as well as I could. And during my second year I attended Professor Robert Jameson's lectures

on geology and zoology; but they were incredibly boring. The sole effect they produced on me was the determination never, as long as I lived, to read a book on geology or in any way to study the subject.

Hoskin: How did you react to your father's proposal that you become a clergyman?

Darwin: I asked for some time to consider. But as I did not then doubt the strict and literal truth of every word in the Bible, I soon persuaded myself that our creed must be fully accepted. So I went to Cambridge, early in 1828.

Hoskin: I hope you had better luck with the teaching there!

Darwin: No, I'm afraid my three years in Cambridge were wasted as completely as my time at Edinburgh and at school—as far as the academical studies were concerned.

Hoskin: You studied what, classics . . . ?

Darwin: . . . and mathematics, and William Paley's books, which we all *had* to study. The logic of Paley's reasoning appealed to me.

Hoskin: Paley gives the old argument for the existence of God, doesn't he? From the evidence of design in nature.

Darwin: Yes, Paley says that if we find a watch on the ground and pick it up and examine it, we soon convince ourselves that the watch had a maker who designed it for telling the time—even though we never actually saw him at work. In the same way, he argues, if we examine an eye we find it is wonderfully designed for seeing, and so must have a designer, who is God.

This argument—which then completely convinced me—was the basis for the then accepted belief that all species had remained fixed and immutable since their creation.

Hoskin: Did you go to any of the courses, in view of your experiences in Edinburgh?

Darwin: Not many, but I did attend John Henslow's lectures on botany. Henslow used to take his pupils on field excursions, and lectured on the rarer plants or animals which were seen. These excursions were delightful.

Hoskin: And very forward looking for their day.

Darwin: Yes. But nothing I did at Cambridge gave me so much pleasure as collecting beetles. It was the mere passion for collecting. I remember one day I tore off some old bark from a tree and saw two rare beetles there. I seized one in each hand—but then I saw a third and new kind, which I couldn't bear to lose. So I popped the one that I held in my right hand into my mouth! Alas, it ejected some intensely acrid fluid, which burned my tongue, so that I was forced to spit the beetle out—and I lost it and the third one as well.

Hoskin: But at least you held on to one of them!

Darwin: Yes! But at Cambridge what influenced my career more than anything else was my friendship with Professor Henslow. I took long walks with him most days, and some of the dons called me "the man who walks with Henslow." It was he who persuaded me to study geology in my last two terms in Cambridge, and it was he who asked Professor Sedgwick to let me accompany him on his geological investigations in North Wales.

Sedgwick's very first conversation with me made a big impression on my mind. I told him of a tropical shell that a laborer claimed he had found in an old gravel pit near Shrewsbury. But Sedgwick said at once that it must have been thrown away by someone into the pit—and he added that if it had really been embedded there it would be the greatest misfortune to geology.

Hoskin: Because it would disprove the current theories.

Darwin: Yes. But I was utterly astonished at Sedgwick not being delighted at so wonderful a fact as a tropical shell being found near the surface in the middle of England. Nothing before had ever made me realize that science consists in grouping facts so that general laws or conclusions may be drawn from them.

Hoskin: And one could go on to say that a fact only becomes a *scientific* fact when it is relevant to some theory—when it tells for or against some hypothesis. And one exception may be devastating.

Darwin: Yes. How odd it is that anyone should not see that all observation must be for or against some view if it is to be of any use.

Well, on returning home from Wales I found a letter from Henslow telling me that Captain Fitzroy of H.M.S. *Beagle* was willing to give up part of his own cabin to any young man who would volunteer to go with him as naturalist on a voyage round the world. Fitzroy wanted someone to gather evidence to help defend the strict and literal truth of every statement in the Bible.

Hoskin: But were you free to go? Weren't you studying for the Church?

Darwin: Yes, and my father thought that to go on this wild scheme would be disreputable to my character as a clergyman. You know, the voyage of the *Beagle* was by far the most important event in my life and determined my whole career. Yet it depended on my uncle offering to drive me thirty miles to Shrewsbury to talk with my father.

Hoskin: And your father gave his consent.

Darwin: In the kindest manner.

Hoskin: How long did the voyage last?

Darwin: Five years, most of which were spent along the shores of South America. I have always felt that I owe to the voyage the first real training or education of my mind. My powers of observation were improved—but far more important was the investigation of the geology of all the places we visited, because in geology you have to reason.

Hoskin: How do you mean?

Darwin: Well, when you first examine a new district the chaos of rocks seems hopeless. But if you record the layers and the nature of the rocks and fossils at many points, reasoning it out and predicting what you will find elsewhere, you discover that the general structure then becomes more or less intelligible.

Hoskin: You mean that you began to form hypotheses on the evidence that you first came across, and then you tested these hypotheses against the later evidence?

Darwin: Yes. And I studied the first volume of Lyell's *Principles of Geology,* which Henslow had given me, though he warned me on no account to accept Lyell's views.

Hoskin: He wanted you to use the book merely as a compendium of facts.

Darwin: Yes.

Hoskin: I suppose he didn't like Lyell's views because Lyell insisted that the Earth as we know it has been formed over millions of years, and simply by the forces we see at work today. No divine interventions, no great upheavals, only *continuous* processes—ones that science can investigate.

Darwin: Exactly. For example, Lyell claimed that long lines of inland cliffs have been formed and great valleys excavated by the agencies which we *still* see at work. But many geologists found this a great difficulty, because the mind cannot grasp the full meaning of even a million years.

In the same way the main cause of our unwillingness to admit that one species has given birth to other and distinct species is that we are always slow in admitting great changes of which we do not see the steps. The mind cannot add up the full effects of many slight variations accumulated during an almost infinite number of generations.

Now on the *Beagle* I studied Lyell's book *carefully.* And the very first district I examined showed me

Portrait of Thomas Huxley—scientist.

clearly the wonderful superiority of his method of treating geology.

Hoskin: And soon you were convinced that Lyell was right that the time-scale of the Earth is to be measured in millions of years.

Darwin: Yes.

Hoskin: But what led you to believe that species had changed? After all, Lyell himself was opposed to this, wasn't he?

Darwin: Yes, and he maintained this position for thirty years, but gave it up on reading my work—something which I think is without parallel in the records of science.

Hoskin: Yes, most scientists would rather die than alter their minds on a fundamental question! But what led you to believe that species change?

Darwin: Well, during the voyage of the *Beagle* I was deeply impressed by a number of things: by discovering in one place great fossil animals covered with armor like that on the existing armadillos; by the way in which closely allied animals replace one another as you proceed southwards over the continent of South America; and by the South American character of most of the animals of the Galápagos Islands; and more particularly by the way in which they differ slightly on each island of the group.

Hoskin: Could we take these in turn. First you found great animal fossils that looked like existing animals *except* that they were far bigger in size. And you wondered why they had died and others so similar were still living.

Then, in addition to these examples of similar animals separated in time, you found many examples of similar animals separated in *space*—as you traveled south the species changed *gradually* from place to place. And you wondered why this should be so. And the most striking example of this you found in some islands hundreds of miles out in the Pacific Ocean. There the animals were *nearly* the same on each island, but not *quite*.

Darwin: Yes. Unfortunately until my investigation was nearly complete it never occurred to me that on islands only a few miles apart and with the same physical conditions the animals would be dissimilar. Yet in the thirteen species of groundfinches you can trace a nearly perfect series of steps from a beak that is extraordinarily thick to one that's so fine you could compare it to a warbler. And if you show the Spaniards a tortoise from one of the islands they can tell you at once which island it has come from, simply from the form of its body, the shape of its scale, and its general size. It was clear that facts like these could only be explained on the supposition that species gradually become modified.

The subject haunted me. And so a few months after my return to England, I opened my first notebook for facts relating to the origin of species, and I never ceased working on this for the next twenty years.

Hoskin: But what about the question of what *causes* species to change?

Darwin: And the question of why organisms of every kind are so beautifully adapted to their habits of life—

a woodpecker to climb trees, or a seed to be scattered by hooks or plumes. Until these could be explained it seemed to me almost useless to try to prove by indirect evidence that species have been modified. And they couldn't be explained by the will of the organisms, or the action of the surrounding conditions, as some writers have tried to do—such as my grandfather and his French contemporary Lamarck.

Hoskin: Because, for example, conditions on each of those islands you visited were exactly the same, while at the same time the species of finches and tortoises were *different*. So somehow the barrier of a mile or two of water must have been enough to allow each species to develop its own characteristics.

Darwin: Yes.

Hoskin: So what did you do?

Darwin: Well, about fifteen months after I had opened my first notebook, I happened to read for amusement Thomas Malthus's *Essay on Population* and . . .

Hoskin: Excuse me. Malthus maintained, didn't he, that at each generation a population—human, animal, or plant—tends to multiply. For example if, on the average, two human parents have four children, then the population will double with each generation, *provided* the children survive. And after eight more generations you would have more than a thousand to take the place of the first parents.

Darwin: Yes, and he pointed out that in fact the food supplies increase much more slowly.

Hoskin: So that there is a constant check on the population.

Darwin: Yes. Now from my long-continued observations of the habits of animals and plants I was well able to appreciate the struggle for existence which everywhere goes on. And it struck me at once that under these circumstances *favorable* variations, however small, would tend to be preserved, and unfavorable ones destroyed. The result of this would be the formation of new species.

I called this process "natural selection" and the result is the survival of the fittest.

Hoskin: Could we see if I've got this clear? Let's suppose we have a lot of giraffes. Then some will of course be taller than others. But there is not enough food for them all, so the shorter giraffes go hungry and die, while the taller ones can reach higher in the trees for food and so manage to survive and have young ones.

But these young will tend to be tall like their parents—taller, that is, than the average giraffe *used* to be. In this way the average height will increase—and so the later giraffes will be different from their ancestors—in time perhaps so different that we would call it a *new species*.

Darwin: That would be one simple example, yes.

Hoskin: So now you had an idea of what *causes* species to change.

Darwin: Yes.

Hoskin: And this was a grand idea of yours, affecting every living species.

Darwin: Yes. So I was anxious to avoid prejudice. And it wasn't until 1842 that I first allowed myself the satisfacton of writing a very brief abstract of my theory in pencil. Two years later I enlarged it to 230 pages.

Hoskin: You were married by this time?

Darwin: Yes, I was married in 1839. My dear wife has been my greatest blessing; without her my life would have been miserable—because of my ill health.

Hoskin: Did you suffer from ill health during the *Beagle* voyage?

Darwin: No—then I could ride a horse for ten hours at a time, and I thought nothing of sleeping rough for weeks on end. But since my return I have lost much of my time through illness. This is why my wife and I have lived such a retired life. You see, I found that after meeting friends my health always suffered from the excitement, which brought on violent shivering and vomiting attacks. I get exhausted now by seeing and talking with anyone for even an hour—except my wife and children.

Hoskin: Yes, I must be careful not to tire you.

Darwin: Well, I have nothing to report during the rest of my life, except the publication of my various books.

Hoskin: You had time to write many books because you never had to go out and earn your living?

Darwin: Fortunately no—my father always provided for me. And so my chief enjoyment, and my sole employment throughout life, has been scientific work.

Hoskin: The world has left you to get on with it in peace.

Darwin: Yes, and the excitement of it makes me forget my daily discomfort.

Hoskin: We got as far as the longer sketch of your theory.

Darwin: Yes, that was in 1844. Twelve years later Lyell advised me to write out my views pretty fully, and I began to do so on a much larger scale than was afterwards published in my *Origin of Species.*

But my plans were all upset in 1858 when Mr. Alfred Russel Wallace, who was then in the Malay Archipelago, sent me an essay that contained exactly the same theory as mine.

Hoskin: What a dreadful thing to happen to you, and after twenty years' work on the theory! What did you do?

Darwin: With many misgivings, and on the advice of friends, I had Mr. Wallace's essay published jointly with some pieces of mine. But they didn't excite much attention—which shows how necessary it is that any new view should be explained at length.

Hoskin: But I expect the shock of Wallace's essay galvanized you into action.

Darwin: Yes! After thirteen months and ten days of hard labor, my *Origin of Species* was published in November, 1859.

Hoskin: Mr. Darwin, one of the most important implications of your theory is that man has animals for his ancestors.

Darwin: That is true.

Hoskin: Did you make this plain in your book?

Darwin: At the time when I first became convinced that species change I could not avoid believing that man must come under the same law. And so I collected notes on the subject—for my own satisfaction,

not for a long time with any intention of publishing. But in order that no honorable man should accuse me of concealing my views, I added in my book on *The Origin of Species* that "light will be thrown on the origin of man and his history."

Hoskin: What? You mean to say, only *one* sentence in the whole book?

Darwin: Yes—but of course when I found that many naturalists fully accepted my doctrine of the evolution of species, I worked up my notes into a special treatise on the origin of man. It was published in 1871 as *The Descent of Man.*

Hoskin: And that was no less than twelve years after *The Origin of Species.* And meanwhile friends like Thomas Henry Huxley were fighting your battles for you.

Darwin: That is true. I used to call Huxley "my general agent," and others called him my "bulldog."

After the *Origin* was published awful fights raged in the newspapers and drawing rooms. There was one pitched battle at a meeting in Oxford—I'm glad I wasn't there; I should have been overwhelmed, with my health in the state it was. But Huxley answered the Bishop of Oxford capitally—whereas I would as soon have died as tried to answer the bishop in such an assembly.

Hoskin: What did the bishop say?

Darwin: It seems he assured his listeners that there was nothing in the idea of evolution; and he asked Huxley whether he claimed descent from a monkey through his grandfather or his grandmother.

Hoskin: What did Huxley say to that?

Darwin: He said he would prefer to have a miserable ape for a grandfather, rather than a man who employed his great talents to introduce ridicule into a grave scientific discussion.

Hoskin: But was the bishop a scientist?

Darwin: No, but he was a spokesman for scientists.

Hoskin: There was no question of a fight with the scientists on one side and the bishop on the other?

Darwin: By no means. But it is true that the old argument for the existence of a personal God—the argument from design in nature, which used to seem so conclusive to me (you know, Paley's argument), fails now that the law of natural selection has been discovered.

Hoskin: You mean that giraffes have long necks, not because God decided to make them that way, but because long necks have helped their ancestors to survive periods of famine.

Darwin: Yes. There seems to be no more *design* in the variability of living things and in the action of natural selection than in the ways the wind blows.

Hoskin: But you are not saying that because one argument for the existence of God proves unsatisfactory, therefore God does not exist?

Darwin: No. But I cannot pretend to throw the least light on such abstruse problems. It is not in our power to solve the mystery of the beginning of all things; and I for one must be content to admit I do not know. I am agnostic.

Hoskin: Mr. Darwin, this caution seems to me to be

characteristic of your scientific work also. You took twenty years to publish your theory of evolution, and twelve more to make clear its implications for man. And yet your caution hasn't prevented you from bringing about a revolution in thought. How is this?

Darwin: It is hard to understand. My power to follow a purely abstract train of thought is very limited. And my memory is hazy—and I've no great quickness of wit, which is so remarkable in some clever men, like Huxley. But I don't think it's true to say, like some of my critics, "Oh, he's a good observer but he's no power of reasoning." After all, *The Origin of Species* is one long argument from beginning to end. And I notice things that easily escape attention, and observe them carefully. And I've always had the strongest desire to understand or explain whatever I observed—to group all facts under some general laws—though I've tried always to give up any hypothesis as soon as the facts are clearly against it.

But it's truly surprising that with such moderate abilities I should have influenced the beliefs of scientific men on some important points.

Hoskin: Mr. Darwin, I hope we have not tired you too much.

4

by Stephen Jay Gould

Darwin's Dilemma

*The father of evolution anticipated, but
failed to prevent, the misunderstanding that
has haunted his theory for a century*

Several readers have requested an explanation for the somewhat cryptic title of my column—"This View of Life." It is taken from the last sentence of Charles Darwin's *Origin of Species*:

> There is grandeur in this view of life, with its several powers, having been originally breathed by the Creator into a few forms or into one; and that, whilst this planet has gone cycling on according to the fixed law of gravity, from so simple a beginning endless forms most beautiful and most wonderful have been, and are being evolved.

This view of life, then, is the evolutionary perspective, the framework, for all my contributions to this column. As a personal statement, it also honors my heroes among past and present evolutionists—Charles Darwin, who coined the phrase, and George Gaylord Simpson, who used it as the title for a collection of essays.

The exegesis of evolution as a concept has occupied the lifetimes of a thousand scientists. Here, I shall present something almost laughably narrow in comparison—an exegesis of the word itself. I shall trace how "this view of life" came to be called *evolution*. The tale is complex and fascinating as a purely antiquarian exercise in etymological detection. But more is at stake, for a past usage of this word has contributed to the most common, current misunderstanding between laymen and scientists. their great works. Why not? And

how did their story of organic change acquire its present name?

Darwin, who spoke of "descent

To begin with a paradox: Darwin, Lamarck, and Haeckel—the greatest nineteenth-century evolutionists of England, France, and Germany, respectively—did not use evolution in the original editions of with modification," shunned evolution as a description of his theory for two reasons. In Darwin's day,

evolution already described a theory of embryology that could not be reconciled with his views of organic development.

In 1744, the German biologist Albrecht von Haller had coined the term *evolution* to describe the notion that embryos grew from preformed homunculi enclosed in the egg or sperm (and that, fantastic as it may seem today, all future generations had been created in the

THE BETTMANN ARCHIVE

In an 1871 cartoon, a gorilla complains, "That man . . . says he is one of my Descendants." The founder of the Society for the Prevention of Cruelty to Animals, Henry Bergh, adds: "Mr. Darwin, how could you insult him so?"

ovaries of Eve or testes of Adam, enclosed like Russian dolls, one within the next—a homunculus in each of Eve's ova, a tinier homunculus in each ovum of the homunculus, and so on). Haller chose his term carefully, for the Latin *evolvere* means "to unroll"; indeed, the tiny homunculus unfolded from its originally cramped quarters and simply increased in size during its embryonic development.

Yet Haller's embryological evolution seemed to preclude Darwin's descent with modification. If the entire history of the human race was prepackaged into Eve's ovaries, how could natural selection (or any other force) alter the preordained course of our sojourn on earth?

Our mystery seems only to deepen. How could Haller's term be transformed into a nearly opposite meaning? This became possible only because Haller's theory was in its death throes by 1859; with its demise, the term that Haller had used became available for other purposes.

Evolution, in Darwin's day, had become a common English word with a meaning quite different from Haller's technical sense. The *Oxford English Dictionary* traces it to a 1647 poem of H. More: "Evolution of outward forms spread in the world's vast spright [spirit]." But this was "unrolling" in a sense very different from Haller's. It implied "the appearance in orderly succession of a long train of events," and more important, it embodied a *concept of progressive development*—an orderly unfolding from simple to complex. The *O.E.D.* continues, "The process of developing from a rudimentary to a mature or complete state." Thus evolution, in the vernacular, was firmly tied to a concept of progress.

Darwin did use evolve in this vernacular sense—in fact it is the very last word of his book. He chose it for this passage because he wanted to contrast the flux of organic development with the fixity of such physical laws as gravitation. But it was a word he used very rarely indeed, for Darwin explicitly rejected the common equation of what we now call evolution with any notion of progress.

In a famous epigram, Darwin reminded himself never to say "higher" or "lower" in describing the structure of organisms—for if an amoeba is as well adapted to its environment as we are to ours, who is to say that we are higher creatures? Thus Darwin shunned evolution as a description for his descent with modification, both because its technical meaning contrasted with his position and because he was uncomfortable with the notion of inevitable progress inherent in its vernacular meaning.

The propaganda of the indefatigable Herbert Spencer, Victorian pundit of nearly everything, brought evolution into the English language as a synonym for descent with modification. Evolution, to Spencer, was the overarching law of all development. And, to a smug Victorian, what principle other than progress could rule the developmental processes of the universe? Thus, Spencer defined the universal law in his *First Principles* of 1862: "Evolution is an integration of matter and concomitant dissipation of motion; during which the matter passes from an indefinite, incoherent homogeneity to a definite coherent heterogeneity."

Two other aspects of Spencer's work contributed to the establishment of evolution in its present meaning: First, in writing his very popular *Principles of Biology* (1864–1867), Spencer constantly used "evolution" as a description of organic change. Second, he did not view progress as an intrinsic capacity of matter, but as a result of "cooperation" between internal and external (environmental) forces. This view fit nicely with most nineteenth-century concepts of organic evolution, for Victorian scientists easily equated organic change with organic progress. Thus evolution was available when many scientists felt a need for a term more succinct than Darwin's descent with modification. And since most evolutionists saw organic change as a process directed toward increasing complexity (that is, to us), their appropriation of Spencer's general term did no violence to his definition.

Ironically, Darwin, with his aversion to saying "higher" or "lower,"

stood almost alone in insisting that organic change led only to increasing adaptation between organisms and their own environment and not to an abstract ideal of progress defined by structural complexity. Had we heeded Darwin's warning, we would have been spared much of the confusion and misunderstanding that exists between scientists and laymen today. Scientists long ago abandoned the concept of necessary links between evolution and progress as the worst kind of anthropocentric bias. Yet most laymen still equate evolution with progress and define human evolution not simply as change, but as increasing intelligence, increasing height, or some other measure of assumed improvement.

In what may well be the most widespread antievolutionary document of modern times, the Jehovah's Witnesses' pamphlet "Did Man Get Here by Evolution or by Creation" proclaims: "Evolution, in very simple terms, means that life progressed from one-celled organisms to its highest state, the human being, by means of a series of biological changes taking place over millions of years. . . . Mere change within a basic type of living thing is not to be regarded as evolution."

This fallacious equation of organic evolution with a man-centered concept of progress continues to have unfortunate consequences. Historically, it engendered the abuses of Social Darwinism (which Darwin himself held in such suspicion). This discredited theory ranked human groups and cultures according to assumed level of evolutionary attainment, with (not surprisingly) "advanced" white Europeans at the top and "primitive" people dwelling in their conquered colonies at the bottom.

Today, it remains a primary component of our global arrogance, our belief in dominion over, rather than fellowship with, more than a million other species that inhabit our planet. The moving finger has written, of course, and nothing can be done; yet I am rather sorry that scientists contributed to a fundamental misunderstanding by selecting a vernacular word meaning progress as a name for "this view of life."

5

Physical evolution and technological evolution in man: a parallelism

François Bordes

This is a controversial paper, which is more a call for comments and criticism than an attempt to solve the question. We would be grateful to the physical anthropologists to voice their views, and to archaeologists, too. It is, in a way, the product of reflections made while chipping flint or analysing and classifying implements, for more than thirty-five years.

Man's technology changed a lot during the last two and a half million years, from pebble tool to spaceship and nuclear power. It seems to me, however, that changes were not always of the same nature all through this time. Man began with a small enough brain, at the australopithecine stage, and did not get his present brain organization till the first modern men appeared, that is probably towards the end of the Mousterian. However, the division between Mousterian Man (Neanderthal) and Upper Palaeolithic man (Modern man) is not so clear cut as was thought of old, especially since the latest discoveries: modern-looking man in the Mousterian of Jebel Kafzeh (Vandermeersch, 1969); non-Neanderthal men, maybe 60,000 years ago, in the Omo valley (Leakey *et al.* 1969); and a skull with perhaps a modern type frontal at La Chaise (Charente), maybe 100,000 years ago (Debenath and Piveteau, 1969). Nevertheless, real modern man dates back at most to the Mousterian, as we had hypothetized in 1959.

During the very long time between the first tools, and the Upper Palaeolithic, man's technology has undergone change, but so did his brain. It should not be preposterous then to imagine that there is some kind of relationship, more or less direct, between the changes in the brain and the progress of technology with all the subsequent changes that this progress brings to man's life. The relationship is probably not a simple one, but let us see if we can establish some points.

When the first tool was used depends on the definition one gives to the word 'tool'. It is known today that even a chimpanzee may be capable of a certain amount of abstract thinking, since some of them at least are able to take a branch and *transform* it by taking off the ramifications before licking it and putting it into a hole in a termite nest to catch termites (Pfeiffer 1969:278). This supposes that the ape foresees, in the branch with all its leaves, the twig it will use as a tool. For in a way it is a tool, and a fabricated one, not just a chance tool, as a stone picked up to break a nut.

One of the first steps of man may have been to observe that some naturally broken stones had a sharp edge, with which it was possible to cut the skin of dead animals to get at the meat. Not all the stones will do, only the ones with a sharp edge. But these stones are not present everywhere, when needed. Some day, a genius among the australopithecines may have noticed that stone struck against stone gives a break, and that often this break has a sharp edge. Also, flakes obtained in such a way have sharp edges too, and can be used. Maybe the invention was made many times, and lost when the inventor died, the others of the group being not intelligent enough, or clever enough, to be able to imitate him.

Theoretically, by the way, such an invention, the pebble tool, could have been made earlier, since one can make a chopper by using only the 'power grip'. Nothing, except its brain, prevents a chimpanzee from making such crude stone tools. But maybe it just has not the right connections in its brain. This may be comparable (let us hear what the psychologists will say) to the fact that young children, who know perfectly well all the characters of the alphabet, cannot grasp the arrangement of these letters into words. They know A, B, C and up to Z, but cannot see that C+A+B is 'cab'. Then, one day, they grasp it, and progress is very swift afterwards.

So, the first degree of abstraction in the evolution of

man's thinking may have been the comprehension that, inside the rock, there *is* a cutting edge, waiting to be released by some blows with another stone. This was done at australopithecine level.

For a very long time, there are only variations of this invention. Pebble tools may become bifacially worked, but it seems that some of them were made that way very early. At the bottom of layer II, in Olduvai, where man is represented by forms that some authors, like Clark Howell, interpreted as small pithecanthropines, we are still at that pebble-tool level. By progressive evolution, one can get to the proto-handaxe, which is nothing more than a pointed chopping-tool.

The true handaxe appears soon after, under the crude 'Abbevillian' type, where the shape seems to be very variable, and we have to wait till the Lower Acheulean, which may be the level of true pithecanthropines with bigger and better brains, to begin to find shapes that really repeat themselves, as a group. Or maybe the true handaxes were already the contribution of the pithecanthropines and the regularly shaped ones the contribution of a yet unknown type of humanity. Anyway, this may be the second level of abstraction, the idea that inside the rock there is not only a cutting edge, but also *a shape,* and that this shape can be obtained at will. This is facilitated by another invention, the observation that hard flint can be worked with soft bones, or even wood. This permits one to flake at a different angle, to get flatter tools and sharper edges. These edges can also be made less sinuous, straighter, without blunting them as is often the result of trying to produce a straight edge with a stone hammer.

Once the idea that a given shape can be obtained at will had been accepted, it probably became clear enough that certain of these shapes were better for such and such work. Thence came the first specialization of tools, and improvement in the efficiency of work. In other branches of mankind, where handaxes do not seem to have been used much, if at all, the shape was imposed on the flake tools (as was also done in the Acheulean).

With the Middle Acheulean, we come to the Swanscombe–Steinheim man level. No matter if these remains belong to the end of the Great Interglacial, or are later, as I think they may be. Those individuals we have found are certainly not the first representatives of this type of mankind. There, at a level well above the pithecanthropines, comes the next step towards abstraction, the invention of the Levallois flaking technique. Not only is there a cutting edge in the stone; not only can one shape at will this cutting edge; but one can predetermine its shape before striking it out of the flint. Let us have a look at this technique, which is more complicated than it seems at first sight. Levallois *débitage* does not consist of preparing the striking platform by small facets, even if it is often the case, but of predetermining the shape of the flake by shaping the core. First the general shape is given to the nodule, then the cortex is peeled off, so to speak, from

the upper part, then the striking platform is prepared, if preparation is needed. All of that presupposes a mastery of different flaking techniques: flat flaking for peeling off the top, steep flaking to prepare the sides and the platform. Then comes the most delicate part, striking off the flake. The angle has to be just right; if not, the flake will hinge out, and be too short, or hinge in, and take with it the end of the core.

There are several variants of this technique, depending upon whether one wants a flake, a point or a blade, the preparation of the core being different each time, although the basic idea stays the same.

It is interesting to note that this Levallois technique was probably discovered several times at different places, and maybe in a different way. In Africa, the true Levallois technique seems to have been preceded by the Victoria-West technique, which, as far as I know, is unknown in Europe, or at least very rare. In Africa, the Victoria-West technique was developed for obtaining laterally struck flakes, ready to be transformed into flake cleavers. It seems that it is only later that this technique became truly Levallois. In Europe, the Levallois technique seems to appear in the lower part of the Middle Acheulean, and may have been a result of observation of accidents in the fabrication of handaxes, when a flake, taken too 'deep', removes most of the face of the handaxe, and so has more or less the same shape.

This idea that one can get flakes which have a given shape was clearly a very promising one, since the Upper Palaeolithic type of blade is nothing more than an elaboration of the Levallois blade technique, as also are the very long blades of the Chalcolithic (Grand Pressigny type).

The next crucial step was taken by modern type man in the Upper Palaeolithic period. The idea, this time, was not only you could obtain a given shape, in the case of tool making either by retouch or by Levallois technique, but that you could also *represent* one. This is not a direct continuation of the previous process, since what was represented was not a tool, but animals; the representation, however, seems to denote now an ability to *separate* the shape from the object shaped. Drawing of lines on bone or stone may be a very old occupation, as witnessed by the 'engraved bone' we found in the Acheulean of Pech de l'Azé (Bordes 1969), but reproduction of a real shape, taken from the outside world and transferred in two dimensions to a flat surface is something totally different. Representation in three dimensions is perhaps less abstract, and we have very good examples of this as early as the Aurignacian I at Vogelherd (Germany) during a period when drawings are still very crude in the Aurignacian I of other sites.

This figurative art had probably been preceded, for a very long time, by the use of colour for lines or spots, as we can infer from the numerous fragments of mineral colourants found in Mousterian contexts, or even earlier.

Other abstract concepts, and other technical innovations, are more difficult to date. The punch technique in tool manufacture, for instance, derives from the idea that shock can be transmitted, and that you can, using an intermediate tool, apply the force exactly where you want to, since it will be transmitted along the length of the punch down to the tip, and you can place this tip exactly where you like. We do not know when this observation was made and understood. Perhaps it was during Mousterian times, but, if so, was it made by Neanderthalers or modern type men? It is by no means as easy as some think to tell if a blade has been punch-struck or directly struck. When there are many blades, it becomes possible, but at any time people probably went on making some blades and most flakes by the old direct percussion technique, which does not work so badly when one is clever with one's hands.

After the transmission of force came the multiplication of force, that is, the principle of the lever. Maybe levers were already used pretty early, if Clark Howell's hypothesis about Torralba is right. These were first or second order levers, easy to discover by chance. We would, however, put this discovery rather at the level of Swanscombe man than of the pithecanthropines, another reason for believing in a Riss, and not Mindel, age for Torralba. For the third type of lever, which is used in the spear-throwers, there is less evidence. We do not know exactly when it was discovered, but certainly by Upper Palaeolithic times. The oldest spear-throwers we know of are, if I remember rightly, Solutrean, but wooden ones could have been in use for a long time before they began to be made in more durable materials.

It is not at all proven that there was no evolution at all, as far as mental power is concerned, since the beginning of the Upper Palaeolithic. But we will probably never know whether Aurignacian man, for instance, was able or not to master mathematics beyond a basic level. It seems difficult to believe that these people did not have a rudimentary idea of numbers, but how accurate was their reckoning, and how far did it go?

Funeral practices seems to begin with Neanderthal man, as far as we know. Some would see in them an abstract concept of a life after death, but one wonders if it is not the other other way round, and if the abstract concept which is difficult to grasp is not the one of death itself.

Multiple tools, that is the manufacture on the same piece of flint of two scrapers, for instance, seem old enough, and go back at least to the Acheulean. Composite tools, that is the making on the same piece of stone of two different tools, is mainly a modern man idea, even if there are some forerunners: scraper-denticulates, for instance. We even know of two burin-end scrapers in the Mousterian, but they remain quite exceptional.

So it seems that there may be a relationship between the size or complexity of the brain and the complexity of the techniques used by prehistoric man. But this relationship seems limited to the period of physical evolution. Even if, as we said, there is no proof that there has been any change in the human brain since the emergence of true modern man, there is no proof the other way, either. Maybe the Aurignacians were already mentally equipped to handle nuclear physics. Maybe the capacity for abstraction was already as good as it is today. The cause of technical progress, which then began to accelerate, must have changed. The augmented capacity for abstraction can have had, as a result, a more elaborate language, giving a better way of transmitting knowledge, in a more subtle and precise manner. Also, as we have noticed elsewhere (Bordes 1968), there is a difference between intelligence and creativity. Even today, people who really contribute to progress are rare. There could be a relationship between the size of the populations, and the number of creative minds. Upper Palaeolithic people seem to have been more numerous than the Mousterians, even if the population seems to have fluctuated. With the coming of agriculture, population was augmented. Indeed it began to increase even before then, following perhaps the invention of better ways of preserving food, and so too did the rate of progress.

So we would see the evolution of technology as having depended on two factors of a different nature. First, development of the brain and of its complexity, until 'modern man level' was attained. Then there was a change in the mechanism: there was augmentation of the population (and so of the chances of creative minds being born and their ideas accepted) and an application of the new brain power to better communication and storage of knowledge. This capacity of storing and communicating knowledge was later augmented by the invention of writing; then, closer to us, by the invention of printing. Maybe punched cards and computers represent the present step in this direction.

References

Bordes, F. 1968. *The Old Stone Age.* London. *Laboratoire de Géologie quaternaise et Préhistoire Associé au C.N.R.S.*
Bordes, F. 1969. Os percé moustérien et os gravé acheuléen du Pech de l'Azé II. *Quaternaria.* Rome.
Debenath, A. and Piveteau, J. 1969. Unpublished communication at the symposium on the origin of modern man (UNESCO–INQUA). September 1969.
Leakey, R. E. F., Butzer, K. and Day, M. H. 1969. Early *Homo sapiens* remains from the Omo River region of southwest Ethiopia. *Nature.*
Pfeiffer, J. 1969. *The Emergence of Man.* Harper & Row, New York.
Vandermeersch, B. 1969. Les nouveaux squelettes moustériens découverts à Qafzeh (Israel) et leur signification. *Comptes rendus de l'Académie des Sciences.* 268. Paris.

III. Archaeology: An Overview

This is a "nuts and bolts" section. It is intended to teach you about the major methods and techniques that archaeologists and prehistorians employ to retrieve and interpret the remains of the past. The first selection is taken from an introductory book by Braidwood and explains just what its title suggests—namely, "How We Learn About the Prehistoric Past." It is especially useful in its discussion of stratigraphy, a central concern of archaeological research. Hammond's "Tools for Archeology: Aids to Studying the Past" focuses on some of the more spectacular technology at archaeologists' disposal. This article perhaps overstates the case a bit in its enthusiasm—many of the techniques discussed are still being developed and are not used in the course of everyday archaeology.

Adams' "Archaeological Research Strategies" is a discussion of conceptual developments in the field. He begins by characterizing early archaeology as concerned primarily with exploration and the confirmation of stratigraphic sequences, the verification of written records (including the Bible), and the search for origins. Adams then chronicles trends and developments within the discipline, including the split that emerged between "New World" archaeologists, who view archaeology as a social science, and "Old World" archaeologists, who think of it as part of the humanities. Finally, Adams sees the emergence of what some people call the "new archaeology" (which we deal with in Section X) with the elaboration of an "ecological" approach. It is useful to see how the perspective of a discipline can change, and to appreciate how this affects what practitioners of the discipline undertake to do.

Wylie's article on James Deetz ("Pilgrims Elude a Pilgrim Hunter") conveys the more personal side of academic work. Deetz is a committed teacher who involves his students in both his personal and his professional life. He sees archaeology as a crucial component of human undertaking. "We can't have social change," he says, "until we understand what we are, and we can't understand that until we understand where we came from." This article is especially interesting because it displays an archaeologist at work—and the processes through which he arrives at research strategies and tactics.

Very few of you might ever have thought of a sunken ship as a "neatly packaged collection of artifacts representing the culture of its time." "The Archaeologist in Deep Water," obviously does. And he is going to great lengths to develop the technology necessary to recover some of the thousands of ships that have settled on the ocean floor in the course of some 4000 years of shipping. In a different key, Bibikov narrates the discovery of "A Stone Age Orchestra" consisting of mammoth bones found in a 20,000-year-old Ukrainian settlement. Even more interesting than the fact that these finds represent the earliest documented remains of prehistoric musical activity is Bibikov's description of the way in which the significance of the remains came to be understood.

The study of what Simakov calls "traceology" helps archaeologists concerned with "Looking into the Stone Age." He describes how microscopic traces of wear on Stone Age tools allow archaeologists to reconstruct their use and estimate the productive capacities of Stone Age peoples.

Wells, on the other hand, is interested in what the skeletal remains and art work left behind by prehistoric people can tell us about "Ancient Aches and Pains." He makes the important point that "disease never comes haphazardly" and that it is a reflection of the circumstances in which people live. Prehistoric diets, habits of clothing, and ecological stresses can be inferred from evidence with regard to prevalent illnesses.

Armed with an understanding of the major methods and techniques that archaeologists employ, you will be, we hope, adequately prepared to venture ahead into the body of this book.

6

How we learn about the prehistoric past

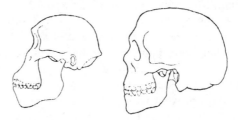

Prehistory means the time before written history began. Actually, more than 99 percent of the human story is prehistory. Human beings are certainly well over a million years old, but they did not begin to write history (or anything) until about 5000 years ago.

The people who lived in prehistoric times left us no history books, but they did unintentionally leave a record of their presence and their way of life. This record is studied and interpreted by different kinds of scientists.

Scientists Who Find Out About the Prehistoric Past

The scientists who study the bones and teeth and any other parts they find of the bodies of prehistoric people are called *physical anthropologists*. Physical anthropologists are trained, much like doctors, to know all about the human body. They study living people, too; they know more about the biological facts of human "races" than anybody else. If the police find a badly decayed body in a trunk, they ask a physical anthropologist to tell them what the person originally looked like. The physical anthropologists who specialize in prehistory work with fossils, so they are sometimes called *human paleontologists*.

Archeologists

There is a kind of scientist who studies the things that prehistoric people made and did. Such a scientist is called an *archeologist*. It is the archeologist's business to look for the stone and metal tools, the pottery, the graves, and the caves or huts of the people who lived before written history began.

But there is more to archeology than just looking for things. In Professor V. Gordon Childe's words, archeology "furnishes a sort of history of human activity, provided always that the actions have produced concrete results and left recognizable material traces."

You will see that there are at least three points in what Childe says:

1. The archeologist has to find the traces of things left behind by ancient people, and
2. Only a few objects may be found, for most of these were probably too soft or too breakable to last through the years. However,
3. The archeologist must use whatever he can find to tell a story—to make a "sort of history"—from the objects and living places and graves that have escaped destruction.

What I mean is this: Let us say you are walking through a dump yard, and you find a rusty old spark plug. If you want to think about what the spark plug means, you quickly remember that it is a part of an automobile motor. This tells you something about the person who threw the spark plug on the dump. He either had an automobile, or he knew or lived near someone who did. He couldn't have lived so very long ago, you'll remember, because spark plugs and automobiles are less than a century old.

When you think about the old spark plug in this way, you have just been making the beginnings of what we call an archeological *interpretation;* you have been making the spark plug tell a story. It is the same way with the man-made things we archeologists find and put in museums. Usually, only a few of these objects are pretty to look at; but each of them has some sort of story to tell. Making the interpretation of his finds is the most important part of the archeologist's job. It is the way he gets at the "sort of history of human activity" which is expected of archeology.

Some Other Scientists

There are many other scientists who help the archeologist and the physical anthropologist find out about prehistoric people. The geologists help us tell the age of the rocks or caves or gravel beds in which human bones or man-made objects are found. There are other scientists with names which all begin with "paleo" (the Greek word for "old"). The *paleontologists* study fossil animals. There are also *paleobotanists* and *paleoclimatologists,* who study ancient plants and climates. These scientists help us know the kinds of animals and plants that were living in prehistoric times and so could be used for food by ancient people; what the weather was like; and whether there were glaciers. Also, when I tell you that prehistoric men and women did not appear until long after the great dinosaurs had disappeared, I go on the say-so of the paleontologists. They know that fossils of humans and of dinosaurs are not found in the same geological period. The dinosaur fossils come in early periods, the fossils of people much later.

Since World War II even the atomic scientists have been helping the archeologists. By testing the amount of radioactivity left in charcoal, wood, or other vegetable matter obtained from archeological sites, it has been possible to assess the approximate age of the sites. Shell has been used also, and even the hair of Egyptian mummies. The dates of geological and climatic events have also been discovered. Some of this work has been done from drillings taken from the bottom of the sea.

It has also proved possible to assess the time when certain volcanic rocks were formed. If a bed of such rocks was formed later than (and hence sealed in) an archeological or human fossil site, then we may say that the site must be at least earlier than the "date" of the covering rock bed. Unfortunately, we do not always find such volcanic beds where we'd like to find them—nicely sealing in our own sites. The method depends on measuring the amount of argon in the rock, the result of potassium-argon transformation. Measurements of less than about 100,000 years ago are difficult to make so the method deals mainly with traces of early people.

Such dating by radioactivity has considerably changed the dates which the archeologists used to give. If you find that some of the dates I give here are more recent (or more ancient) than the dates you see in other books on prehistory, it is because I am using one of the new dating systems.

How the Scientists Find Out

So far, this chapter has been mainly about the people who find out about prehistoric people. We also need a word about *how* they find out.

All our finds came by accident until about a hundred years ago. People digging wells, or digging in caves for fertilizer, often turned up ancient swords or pots or stone arrowheads. People also found some odd pieces of stone that didn't look like natural forms, but they also didn't look like any known tool. As a result, the people who found them gave them queer names, such as "thunderbolts." The people thought the strange stones came to earth as bolts of lightning. We know now that these strange stones were prehistoric stone tools.

Many important finds still come to us by accident. In 1935, a British dentist, A. T. Marston, found the first of two fragments of a very important fossil human skull in a gravel pit at Swanscombe, on the River Thames, England. He had to wait nine months, until the face of the gravel pit had been dug eight yards farther back, before the second fragment appeared. They fitted! Then, twenty years later, still another piece appeared. In 1928, workmen who were blasting out rock for the breakwater in the port of Haifa began to notice flint tools. Thus the story of cave-dwellers on Mount Carmel, in Palestine, began to be known.

Planned archeological digging is only about a century old. Even before this, however, a few realized the significance of objects they dug from the ground; one of these early archeologists was our own Thomas Jefferson. An early digger of mounds was a German grocer's clerk, Heinrich Schliemann. Schliemann made a fortune as a merchant, first in Europe and then in the California gold rush of 1849. He became an American citizen. Then he retired and had both money and time to test an old idea of his. He believed that the heroes of ancient Troy and Mycenae were once real Trojans and Greeks. He proved it by going to Turkey and Greece and digging up the mounds that contained the remains of both cities.

Schliemann had the great good fortune to find rich and spectacular treasures, and he also had the common sense to keep notes and make descriptions of what he found. He proved beyond doubt that many ancient city mounds can be *stratified*. This means that there may be the remains of many towns in a mound, one above another, like layers in a cake. (The only trouble with that analogy—as I can tell you from well-learned experience—is that the layers in the mounds aren't always horizontal, while the cake layers usually are!)

You might like to have an idea of how mounds come to be in

layers. The original settlers may have chosen the spot because it had a good spring and there were good fertile lands nearby, or perhaps because it was close to some road or river or harbor. These settlers probably built their town of stone and—in many parts of the world—of *sun-dried mud-brick*. Finally, something would have happened to the town—a flood, or a burning, or a raid by enemies—and the walls of the houses would have fallen in or the sun-dried bricks would have melted down as mud in the rain. Nothing would have remained but the mud and debris of a low mound of *one* layer.

The second settlers would have wanted the spot for the same reasons the first settlers did—good water, land, and roads. Also, the

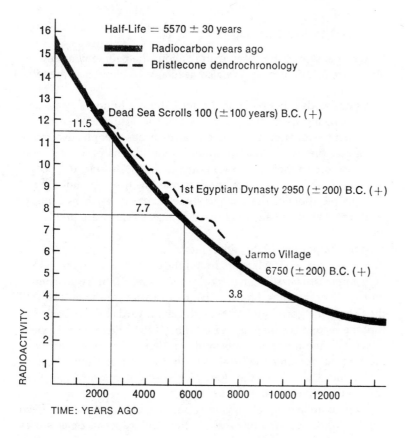

Radiocarbon Chart—The rate of disappearance of radioactivity as time passes*

*It is very important that the limitations of the radioactive carbon age determination system be kept in mind. (1) As the statistics involved in the system are used, there are two chances out of three that the "date" of a sample falls within the span of the plus-minus tolerance expressed in the full determination. For example, 6750 ± 200 B.C. means there are only two chances in three that the real "date" fell between 6950 and 6550 B.C. (2) The "best now obtainable" value of the half life of C14 is 5730 ± 40 yrs. Nevertheless, so many determinations have already been issued in the "old" or Libby value that there is agreement among the laboratories that the 5570 ± 30 yr. value shall be retained. Some archeologists have ignored this agreement, and quote their "dates" in 5730 ± 40 yr. half-life terms. This naturally causes confusion. (3) There is increasing evidence that the natural production of radioactive carbon in the earth's atmosphere (by cosmic rays) has not been constant, as was first assumed. This means that a determination is really given in terms of *radiocarbon years ago*, and that these are *not* necessarily equivalent to true calendar years ago. The black dashed line in the chart above indicates that dendrochronological ages (indicated by tree rings of bristlecone pine) are actually older than ages in radiocarbon years, as we go back in time. We assume that the dendrochronological years are equivalent to true calendar years. Thus, beyond about 2000 years ago, radiocarbon determinations (and radiocarbon years) are short or later than calendar (dendrochronological) years. Unfortunately, the dendrochronology only goes back about 7000 years, so that we cannot recalibrate our radiocarbon age determinations earlier than that. Corrections for the possible contamination of samples *in situ* remains a problem. Hence any single radioactive age determination is not really a "date" in a true time sense. A group of consistent determinations from several sites for a given type of archeological material is more impressive.

second settlers would have found a nice low mound to build their houses on, a protection from floods. But again, something would finally have happened to the second town, and the walls of *its* houses would have come tumbling down. This would make the *second* layer. And so on.

In Syria I once had the good fortune to dig on a large mound that had no less than fifteen layers. Also, most of the layers were thick, and there were signs of rebuilding and repairs within each layer. The mound was more than a hundred feet high. In each layer, the building material used had been a soft, unbaked mud-brick, and most of the debris consisted of fallen or rain-melted mud from these mud-bricks.

This idea of *stratification* was already a familiar one to the geologists by Schliemann's time. They could show that their lowest layer of rock was oldest or earliest, and that the overlying layers became more recent as one moved upward. Schliemann's digging proved the same thing at Troy. His first (lowest and earliest) city had at least nine layers above it; he thought that the second layer contained the remains of Homer's Troy. We now know that Homeric Troy was layer VIIa from the bottom; also, we count eleven layers or sublayers in total.

Schliemann's work marks the beginnings of modern archeology in southwestern Asia. Scholars soon set out to dig on ancient sites from Egypt to Central America.

Archeological Information

As time went on, the study of archeological materials—found either by accident or by digging on purpose—began to show certain things. Archeologists began to get ideas as to the kinds of objects that belonged together. If you compared a mail-order catalogue of 1890 with one of today, you would see a lot of differences. If you really studied the two catalogues hard, you would also begin to see that certain objects "go together." Horseshoes and metal buggy tires and pieces of harness would begin to fit into a picture with certain kinds of coal stoves and furniture and china dishes and kerosene lamps. Our friend the spark plug, and radios, and electric refrigerators, and light bulbs would fit into a picture with different kinds of furniture and dishes and tools. You aren't old enough to remember the kind of hats that women wore in 1890, but you've probably seen pictures of them, and you know very well they couldn't be worn today.

This is one of the ways that archeologists begin the study of their materials. The various tools and weapons and jewelry, the pottery, the kinds of houses, and even the ways of burying the dead tend to fit into a picture. Some archeologists call all of the things that go together to make such a picture an *assemblage.* The assemblage of the first layer of Schliemann's Troy was even more different from that of the seventh layer than our 1890 mail-order catalogue is from the one of today.

The archeologists who came after Schliemann began to notice other things and to compare them with occurrences in modern times. The idea that people will buy better mousetraps goes back into very ancient times. Today, if we make good automobiles or radios, we can sell some of them in Siam or even in Timbuktu. This means that some present-day types of American automobiles and radios form part of present-day "assemblages" in both Siam and Timbuktu. The total present-day "assemblage" of Siam (especially the rural parts) is quite different from that of Timbuktu or that of America, but they have at least some automobiles and some radios in common.

Now these automobiles and radios will eventually wear out. Let us suppose we could go to some remote part of Siam or to Timbuktu in a dream. We don't know what the date is in our dream, but we see all sorts of strange things and ways of living in both places. Nobody tells us what the date is. But suddenly we see a 1960 Ford; so we know that in our dream it has to be at least the year 1960, and only as many years after that as we could reasonably expect a Ford to keep in running order. The Ford would probably break down in twenty years' time, so the Siamese or Timbuktu "assemblage" we're seeing in our dream has to date at about A.D. 1960–1980.

Archeologists not only "date" their ancient materials in this way; they also see over what distances and between which peoples trading was done. It turns out that there was a good deal of trading in ancient times, probably all on a barter and exchange basis.

Everything Begins to Fit Together

Now we need to pull all these ideas together and see the complicated structure the archeologists can build with their materials.

Even the earliest archeologists soon found that there was a very long range of prehistoric time which would yield only very simple things. For this very long early part of prehistory, there was little to be found but the flint tools which wandering, hunting, and gathering people made, and the bones of the wild animals they ate. Toward the end of prehistoric time there was an increasing tendency toward settling down—even more so with the coming of agriculture—and all sorts of new things began to be made. Archeologists soon got a general notion of what ought to appear with what. Thus, it would upset a French prehistorian digging at the bottom of a very early cave if he found a fine bronze sword, just as much as it would upset him if he found a beer bottle. The people of his very early cave layer simply could not have made bronze swords, which came later, just as did beer bottles. Some accidental disturbance of the layers of his cave must have happened.

With any luck, archeologists do their digging in a layered, stratified site. They find the remains of everything that would last through time, in several different layers. They know that the assemblage in the bottom layer was laid down earlier than the assemblage in the next layer above, and so on up to the topmost layer, which is the latest. They look at the results of other "digs" and find that some other archeologist 200 miles away has found ax-heads in his lowest layer exactly like the ax-heads of their fifth layer. This means that their fifth layer must have been lived in at about the same time as was the first layer in the site 200 miles away. It also may mean that the people who lived in the two layers knew and traded with each other. Or it could mean that they didn't necessarily know each other, but simply that both traded with a third group at about the same time.

You can see that the more we dig and find, the more clearly the main facts begin to stand out. We begin to be more sure of which peoples lived at the same time, which earlier and which later. We begin to know who traded with whom, and which peoples seemed to live off by themselves. We begin to find enough skeletons in burials so that the physical anthropologists can tell us what the people looked like. We get animal bones, and a paleontologist may tell us they are all bones of wild animals; or he may tell us that some or most of the bones are those of domesticated animals, for instance, sheep or cattle, and therefore the people must have kept herds.

So far, so good, as these kinds of evidence come to hand. In the jargon, we've been establishing the "time-space systematics" of the general region of our concern. As archeologists, we cannot ignore this step; we must know where we are, so to speak, and how various parts of our evidence are interrelated in both time and space. Once we have this time-space systematics level of study reasonably blocked out, however, we can then turn to the how and why questions, the so-called processual studies. Here we become concerned with such things as the subtle hints our evidence gives of man-nature relationships, of how these change with time and with possibly changing environments and developing technologies, types of settlements, and population changes. More important than anything else—as our structure grows more complicated and our materials increase—is the fact that "a sort of history of human activity" does begin to appear.

We must do all this without one word of written history to aid us. Everything we are concerned with goes back to the time *before* people learned to write. That is the prehistorian's job—to find out what happened before written history began.

7

Tools for Archeology: Aids to Studying the Past

Allen L. Hammond

The archeological dig or excavation is still the primary method for exploring man's prehistoric past. Increasingly, however, archeologists have been borrowing techniques from physics, chemistry, and space technology to help recover artifacts and information from early civilizations. Prospecting techniques, such as aerial photography and magnetometer surveys, aid in locating potential sites and in selecting where to dig. Excavation technology itself has been improved by the development of flotation techniques and the application of power machinery for earth moving and screening. More accurate age determinations of artifacts are now possible because of improvements in radiocarbon methods and the development of new techniques such as thermoluminescence. Many of the new tools are still being developed, many are not universally applicable, and there are some archeologists who dismiss "gadgetry" as subsidiary to the main concerns in the field. But taken all together, physical instrumentation seems likely to have a major impact on the practice of archeology and the precision of its analysis of the past.

Many of the new instruments and improvements in analytic techniques are being developed at the Museum Applied Science Center for Archeology (MASCA) of the University Museum in Philadelphia, and at the Research Laboratory for Archeology (RLA) in Oxford, England—the two largest centers for this work. But archeologists and applied scientists in many fields, and at many different universities, have also been active in improving archeological tools. The familiarity with phys-

ics and chemistry required to use these new tools properly is indicative of the greater degree of technical sophistication that is increasingly common among archeologists today.

Prospecting

Aerial photography has been used to help locate archeological formations for many years. Often, geometrical shapes that are visible only from the air are marked by variations in the growth of a crop—wheat, for example —indicating the presence of an ancient wall or ditch. In other types of terrain, photographs can indicate patterns in plant cover, rock types, and terracing, which an observer on the ground would miss. But finding traces of archeological formations with standard photography is often a hit or miss affair. Crop marks, for example, are usually visible only for short periods of the growing season, or during a drought; different crops and soils have different peak times. Recently, archeologists have been attempting to improve remote sensing techniques, by using multispectral methods, in the hope of finding better contrasts with infrared film, and by recording the natural, as opposed to the cultural, landscape. In this latter technique, archeologists use photographs to help identify former springs, shorelines of ancient lakes, and other preferred areas for habitation or hunting which may be potential excavation sites.

Experiments with black-and-white, color, and infrared films have shown that each has certain advantages and that simultaneous recording with two or more often gives the best results

(1). Archeologists at MASCA, headed by Froelich Rainey, have been experimenting with special cameras that are capable of recording, in spectral bands, from the near ultraviolet to the medium infrared by means of nine lenses and three films. George Gumerman of Prescott College in Arizona has used a combination of infrared and black-and-white film to map the types of soil and groundcover in a Mexican valley; the photographs were used to determine how several known archeological sites fitted into the various microenvironments of the valley. Infrared scanning equipment, although too expensive for normal archeological applications, has been used to discover buried cultural features—in one instance, prehistoric garden plots in Arizona—by recording patterns in the far infrared spectrum, where film is no longer practical.

It is usually impossible to excavate all of a site, but preliminary surveys with resistivity or magnetic intensity measurements can sometimes locate buried structures or artifacts before excavation. Resistivity instruments, which measure the electrical conductivity of surface soils, can usually locate features only in the upper 2 meters of soil. Proton magnetometers, developed for archeological use by scientists at RLA, can sense features somewhat deeper and have been used to locate buried kilns and firepits. The graphs of magnetic contours prepared with the instrument show anomalies when the contrast between the magnetic susceptibility or the remanent magnetism of the buried objects and the surrounding clay is large enough.

More recently, rubidium and cesium magnetometers that are more sensitive and that can detect anomalies 6 or 7 meters into the ground have been developed by Varian Associates and used by Elizabeth Ralph of MASCA to help find the ancient Greek city of Sybaris in southern Italy. The exact location of the city had not been known, because the plain on which it was built had been covered by up to 6 meters of silt. The properties of the area—slightly magnetic, extremely uniform soil—exemplify the conditions under which magnetometer surveys seem to be most useful (2). Where there is a high level of background magnetic noise, magnetometers do not provide much useful information.

Two sensors are often used in magnetometer surveys, one as a fixed reference, so that diurnal and other temporal variations in the magnetic field are canceled out; any buried anomaly shows up as a difference in the readings. The maps of the magnetic field strength, prepared from magnetometer surveys, may show linear shapes that can be interpreted as walls or other large structures. In Greece, for example, the entire street plan of the ancient town of Elis was mapped out in this manner.

Underwater exploration for archeological remains has until recently been limited to the small area that a man with scuba equipment could cover. Two-man submarines that have been constructed especially for archeological exploration extend the range somewhat. George Bass of the University Museum in Philadelphia has been applying side-scanning sonar techniques that make possible the exploration of much larger underwater areas.

Because of practical limitations on the size of the screens that can be used to sift dirt at an archeological site, as much as 20 to 50 percent of the small artifacts are missed in most digs. These include such things as fossilized remains of plants, small animal bones, and other food items. A novel flotation method of recovering these remains in quantity has been developed by Stewart Struever of Northwestern University. In the first stage, running water and a fine mesh screen are used to process large quantities of soil, separating out leaves, roots, nut shells, animal vertebra, and similar items. Then,

in a chemical flotation stage, the plant remains are separated from bones and pottery chips with a solution of zinc chloride in which the lighter remains float. The system, although crude (Struever built the first model out of old wash tubs), allows the processing of large quantities of soil in a short period of time and works well enough to recover thousands of samples that would otherwise be lost.

Analysis of recovered material is increasingly being done in the field as part of the excavation procedure. Kent Schneider at the University of Georgia, for example, has assembled a flotation system basically similar to that described above, a carbon-14 dating laboratory, and other instruments and fitted them in a mobile van that can be driven into the field.

Age Determination

One of the recurring needs in archeological research is accurate determination of the age of artifactual material. The most widely used radiochemical method of dating, the carbon-14 method, is based on the radioactive decay of the trace amounts of the ^{14}C isotope present in all organic substances. The accuracy of the method depends on the assumption that the amount of ^{14}C in atmospheric CO_2 has been constant in the past, but this assumption has been shown to be incorrect; discrepancies between ^{14}C dates and those based on archeological evidence for the ages of the Egyptian dynasties, and more recently, the comparison of the ages of wood samples dated both by reference to a tree-ring chronology and by the ^{14}C method have confirmed that there are large systematic errors in the older ^{14}C dates.

Tree-ring dating for the earlier periods is based on the slow rate of growth and the extremely long lifetime of the bristlecone pine trees that are found in parts of the southwestern United States; specimens as old as 4900 years have been found, making them the oldest of living trees. The growth of these trees varies perceptibly with climatic changes, so that characteristic patterns often occur in the tree rings, especially in trees subjected to extremes of drought and temperature. When the tree rings are counted microscopically and the annual growth patterns are analyzed with

a computer, it is possible to link up the record preserved in dead trees with that of still living trees. In this way Wesley Ferguson, of the University of Arizona at Tuscon, has been able to build up a chronology that extends back some 8200 years.

Only the outer growth ring of a mature tree is actively growing and taking in ^{14}C from the atmosphere; within a small margin of error, therefore, the ^{14}C content of a given piece of wood should be that which was present at the time its growth rings were formed. If the ^{14}C content of the atmosphere had been constant throughout the past, the ^{14}C and tree ring ages should agree. But comparison of these dates has shown that the ^{14}C dates are consistently more recent than the true age for periods earlier than 800 B.C. According to a table of correction factors established by Ralph and Henry Michael of MASCA, the discrepancy increases steadily with the age of the sample, reaching 750 years for the period between 4000 and 4500 B.C. (3). Thus the accuracy and reliability of the ^{14}C method has been improved.

The cause of the past fluctuations in the ^{14}C content of the biosphere is not known. One explanation is based on the assumption that climatic changes are responsible. The melting of glaciers after the last ice age may have altered the equilibrium balance between the oceans and the atmosphere sufficiently to temporarily increase the amount of ^{14}C in the air. If this explanation is correct, then the discrepancy between tree ring ages and ^{14}C dates should decrease for periods earlier than about 7000 B.C.—a possibility that can be tested if the tree ring chronology can be extended back to that time. A more probable explanation, according to many geophysicists, is that changes in the earth's magnetic field has altered the intensity of the cosmic rays reaching the earth's atmosphere and thus the ^{14}C concentration—^{14}C is produced in the atmosphere by irradiation of nitrogen with neutrons from cosmic rays.

Carbon-14 techniques are also being improved by more elaborate chemical refinement of samples before they are dated. Bones, for example, are often unreliable items for ^{14}C dating because they may have exchanged calcium carbonate with groundwater, thus contaminating the sample with carbon of more recent origin. But William Berger of the University of California at Los Angeles has developed a method of dating the organic collagen fraction within bones, after first purifying the material chemically.

Despite its usefulness to archeology, ^{14}C dating is limited to organic materials and a few inorganic carbon compounds. Other artifacts, such as pottery and bricks, are often dated by their association with ^{14}C dated material, although this is often unsatisfactory. But the thermoluminescence method of dating, which is still being developed, will allow the age of those artifacts that are made from fired clays to be directly determined as well. Crystal imperfections in the clay can trap electrons that have been raised to high-

er energy levels by bombardment during the radioactive decay of the trace amounts of uranium, thorium, and potassium that are found in most clays. When the clay is fired, these trapped electrons are released, giving off their energy in the form of light. The amount of light given off is proportional to the amount of radioactive material in the sample, the susceptibility of the material to radiation damage, and the length of time since the clay was last fired; by determining all except the last in the laboratory, the age of manufacture of a piece of pottery or a tile can be determined.

In applying the method, small pieces of an artifact are ground up, their radioactive content is measured, and then the sample is heated rapidly by a

furnace equipped with a photomultiplier tube to measure the emitted light. The procedure is repeated, after the material has been irradiated with a known dosage of x-rays, to determine the susceptibility. By dating samples of known age, Mark Han of MASCA has been able to calibrate the method and then to show that it gives reasonable accuracy for ages back to about 1000 B.C. The improvement of the method, he believes, will eventually allow acceptable accuracy for older artifacts as well.

References

1. G. Gumerman and T. Lyons, *Science* **172**, 126 (1971).
2. E. Ralph, F. Morrison, D. O'Brien, *Geoexploration* **6**, 109 (1967).
3. H. N. Michael and E. Ralph, *Nobel Symp.* **12**, 109 (1970).

8

ARCHAEOLOGICAL RESEARCH STRATEGIES

Robert McC. Adams

Archaeology, in the minds of most laymen, probably has two aspects. One involves explorations in exotic lands— sun and sand, the menace of wild tribesmen, the lure of treasures from the East. The other involves the painstaking excavation, restoration, and display of individual antiquities that are thought to be the primary focus of study—a kind of philately of art styles or material objects abstracted from their cultural surroundings and handsomely illustrated on quarto volume plates or placed in museum cases.

At first glance, neither of these images of archaeology has much to do with prevailing concepts of scientific research as they are usually formulated with especial reference to the natural sciences. Instead, both seem to stress a subjective quality of scholarship—beginning with the inexplicable act of discovery beneath the sand and then proceeding almost mystically from physical description to intuitive reconstruction of forgotten historical events. Any attempt to wrest meaning from broken, unrecognizable artifacts seems, after all, to partake more of imagination than of plausibility. In fact, this is almost the direct antithesis of laboratory-generated procedures involving the inductive fashioning of explanatory hypotheses and then rigorous empirical testing.

Now that science is in the ascendancy, and the expansion of research frontiers into interstellar space and subatomic structure are proclaimed virtually as national goals, archaeology nonetheless thrives as never before. Paperback books, popular articles, and news media communicate even quite specialized or rather doubtful findings of archaeological research to an ever larger public;

the number of recognized practitioners of the subject climbs at every professional meeting; and the scale and diversity of archaeological undertakings mounts steadily. In a recent article the director of the University Museum in Philadelphia (one of the outstanding institutions in the field) speaks of "the archeology explosion." Why is this? Is the growth of the field a mere epiphenomenon of the powerful forward surge of research in the natural sciences? Is it a consequence of international attempts to solve balance of payments problems by attracting growing numbers of tourists to newly opened archaeological monuments and museums? Worse still, is it possible that man's increasing interest in the unearthing of his past is an outgrowth of increasing uncertainties over his future —that archaeology has prospered because it panders to a prevailing mood of escapism?

To some degree, all of these possibilities may be true. But the deeper truth is that the scientific dimensions of archaeology have grown most rapidly. Although the process is disorderly and controversial at many points, profound changes can be discerned not only in immediate research strategies but also in underlying structures of thought. This is less an explosion than a revolution in the sense that is a broad shift from one paradigm to another not unlike the shifts which Thomas S. Kuhn has metaphorically outlined for the history of physics. In any case, the major current changes offer parallels with many disciplines in the natural sciences. In choosing to discuss them, I am perhaps throwing another slender bridge across the void between the hard and soft sciences, or even between the sciences and the humanities. We all deplore this void; I attempt to span it because frequently we may overestimate its breadth and importance.

A brief description of the earlier stages in the maturation of archaeology as a discipline may help to clarify the issues in dispute at the present turning point. As the field emerged, one concern was the confirmation of its basic stratigraphic assumptions. Exploration in its own right was equally important, at least until the maps of empty continents began to fill with archaeological discoveries. Some geographical voids still remain, but the once commanding appeal of exploration has cumulatively been reduced to a secondary level. The last lost civilization was brought to light in the Indus Valley during the 1920's. It can reasonably be said that no unsuspected discovery of like magnitude awaits the spade of any future digger.

In addition to purely exploratory and methodological concerns, several other themes dominated early work. Viewed retrospectively, the most repugnant was an often highly competitive interest on the part of the major museums in excavating or otherwise acquiring beautiful objects with a minimum of supervision or record keeping. Such activities are now prevented by law in most countries—the United States is not one of them—but the two generations or so that have elapsed since the end of that era of pillaging have not erased its memory in much of the underdeveloped world.

Another major concern was the verification and amplification of written records that play a central role in our cultural heritage. Schliemann's work at Troy falls into this category; so also does the heavy concentration on biblical sites in Palestine. This objective persists, although tempered by increasing cautiousness in interpretation and much reduced in relative importance. So also, more regrettably, does a preoccupation with seeking origins. The quest for origins has contributed very little of scholarly importance, but continues to be encouraged by the distorted values that the news media attach to what is first.

This heterogeneous assortment of initial objectives reflects the diversity in modes of thought among those who, in the latter part of the 19th century, called themselves archaeologists. Recent work in the history of ideas is making us increasingly aware of the degree to which the intellectual paternity we proclaim for ourselves today often has more in common with the origin myths of primitive peoples recorded by anthropologists than with the actual roots which nourished our contemporary academic disciplines. Nevertheless, two partially distinct paths of development may be traced well into the past. The first to take shape involved the rediscovery of the classical world as a complex, viable, and aesthetically pleasing civilization that yet was culturally distinct, pagan, and temporally remote. This brought together almost from the beginning the private collector, the historian of art, and the philologist. The acquisition of monuments through excavations stimulated the formation of an objective, external view of entities like style and culture.

The other intellectual taproot of archaeology led largely through the terrain of the natural sciences. It probably began in the 18th century, with the uniformitarian assertions that the earth's surface should be regarded as a system of matter in motion over immensely long time periods. Later this was linked with speculations on natural selection and evolution in the biological world, and ultimately with Darwin's classic synthesis. Of course, the separation we draw retrospectively between these two sources of ideas may be somewhat artificial. Only as scholarship became a specialized, university-based activity, in the later 19th century, did the outward form of archaeological reports in both categories cease to be that of a description of travels that could appeal to a wide audience.

With the shift in focus of activity from private travelers and collectors, to public museums, and finally to university departments, began the bifurcation of the field that continues today. At least in the United States, all of prehistory and all of the aboriginal New World fell within the province of anthropology, a discipline in the generalizing, comparative tradition of the social sciences. Each of the literate civilizations of the Old World, in distinction, became the province of a more specialized, humanistic tradition of study in which archaeological interests generally have been secondary to those of documentary historians and philologists. Even though a few individuals manage to keep an uneasy foot in each camp, the division is nonetheless deep and genuine. This makes the task of speaking of the field as a whole considerably more difficult. Since most of the visible ferment has at least originated in the domain of the anthropologists, one is justified in placing major emphasis there.

The next broad stage in the growth of archaeology involved a virtual preoccupation with systematics. The guiding assumption was that styles uniformly followed a curve of normal distribution, changing gradually in both time and space, so that a plotting of the distribution of formal similarities in time and space would provide a reliable index of cultural and historical relationships. Consciously conducted, empirical tests of this assumption have been conspicuous by their absence; it supplied the seemingly self-evident paradigm of normal science by which alone a pattern of order and significance could be imposed on increasing masses of descriptive data. The main objectives of new research became the extension and progressive refinement of chronological charts showing the succession and distribution of clusters of formal similarities in artifacts that were called "cultures." Except in the hands of a few vigorous theorists of the time like V. Gordon Childe, interpretation was generally confined to descriptions of changing architectural and artifact inventories at individual sites, and to assessments of trade, migration, and culture contact that could be deduced from formal similarities linking different sites.

With due allowance for obvious regional variability, this was roughly the state of affairs at the time of the long hiatus that the second world war induced in fieldwork. In spite of the small number of institutions actively involved, there had been some impressive accomplishments. Leaving aside substantive discoveries, a number of classic monographs had been published by meticulous excavators, or soon would be finished on the basis of materials already in hand. Imposing standards of excavation technique and descriptive analysis had been erected, in other words, against which archaeological undertakings everywhere were increasingly subject to critical comparison. A systematic framework of temporal and spatial distributions had been at least roughed out for most areas and in some had been highly refined. Without such a framework, the more analytic, causally oriented approaches of more recent decades never could have been initiated. Nevertheless, we can best describe and evaluate present trends in the field not as they have built continuously upon this underlying body of methods and assumptions but as they have radically enlarged it and even departed from it.

Of the greatest importance has been the elaboration of an emphasis on an ecological approach. Descriptive statements on climate and environment already were included in some traditional site reports, but now the questions asked and the methods followed bear little resemblance to this prototype. What is seen as crucially important for study is no longer some uniform, predetermined set of obvious environmental features but the points of articulation between the subsistence activities of a particular human group and the wider natural and social setting within which it operated. The focus of concern, then, is the shifting, complex set of adaptive responses which must characterize any community, ancient or modern, and which in turn can help to explain the changes it undergoes through time. Average annual rainfall, for example, is an obvious and once frequently cited statistic which now is seldom regarded as important. What counts more is the reliability of its onset and periodicity during the growing season, the frequency with which it fails to meet the minimum needs of cultivation, or the destructive intensity of the storms in which it falls. Factors like these are critical in explaining changing subsistence productivities and hence also many related sociocultural changing features including patterns of settlement. As often as not, a perceptive assessment of the setting of an archaeological site along such lines goes far beyond even the best contemporary data gathered for other purposes, and requires the gathering of additional data as a part of the archaeological project itself.

Rainfall is only one among a very large number of features which might be used as an example. The trend has been toward reliance on greater and greater numbers of converging lines of evidence for both ancient and modern environments—soils, bones, pollen, geomorphology—in order to discover unsuspected cultural variables, to reduce ambiguities in interpretation, and to deal with the interlocking effects of the widest possible range of adaptive relationships. This in turn requires other reorienta-

tions, principally in the training of students and in the increased funding of projects. In some of the most important and productive undertakings of recent years, such as those concerned with the locally differentiated processes by which plants and animals were independently domesticated in the Old and New worlds soon after the end of the Pleistocene, the greater part of the effort and expense has been directed at the analysis of ecological variables rather than at all of the traditional classes of archaeological findings taken together.

The immense broadening of effort that an ecological approach requires has altered the social milieu of the research itself. The organizational model increasingly being followed is not dissimilar in some ways to that of the physical sciences. Groups of collaborators form, whether on one faculty or several, and institutionalize their relations in a variety of ways. Unlike the very large research groups currently active in physics, however, such groups in archaeology still remain characteristically fluid in internal structure and egalitarian in outlook; a serious deficiency is that these groups do not have long-term support from technicians. The groups are not tied to particular laboratories or to expensive equipment like particle accelerators, but they are constrained by equally effective geographical limits. Long experience in an area is almost a necessity in fashioning a valid ecological approach, and in the case of work overseas one must add to this the need for linguistic competence and for a wide knowledge of administrative procedures and political realities within a host country. Moreover, these groups also generally tend to work within the bounds of a particular focal problem, probably in large part because of close operating relationships with natural scientists whose contributions are most appropriate for those problems. Natural scientists, in fact, form a major component of such groups. However, since the core problems remain those of understanding changes in human culture, the responsibilities for direction, coordination, synthesis, and fund raising generally remain with the archaeologist.

The increasing emphasis on an ecological approach also is related to a growing dissatisfaction with narration or description for its own sake. This has brought in its wake a correspondingly heightened interest in seeking causal explanations of a deterministic character, and such explanations usually have stressed ecological factors. At the extreme, it has been suggested that environmental differences are virtually the only explanation of cultural differences, aside from periodic quantum jumps in the availability of nonhuman energy resulting from the growth of technology. More persuasive, although less sweeping, is the position taken on this question by a coherent, highly innovative group of "new" or "process-oriented" archaeologists, one of whose number recently formulated it as follows.

> . . . [T]he process school would like to move crucial decisions . . . farther from the individual by arguing

that systems, once set in motion, are self-regulating to the point where they do not even necessarily allow rejection or acceptance of new traits by a culture. Once a system has moved in a certain direction, it automatically sets up the limited range of possible moves it can make at the next critical turning point. This view is not original with the process-school archeologists—it is borrowed from Ludwig von Bertalanffy's framework for the developing embryo, where systems trigger behavior at critical junctures and, once they have done so, cannot return to their original pattern. The process school argues that there are systems so basic in nature that they can be seen operating in virtually every field—prehistory not excepted. Culture is about as powerless to divert these systems as the individual is to change his culture [Binford, 1968a: 14].

There are several points worthy of notice here. For one, this is by no means to be equated with the naive assertions of geographical determinism that were in wide circulation a generation or two ago. Cultural and environmental features are seen as closely interacting, rather than the former being either the helpless pawn of the latter or else free to improvise within well-defined limits imposed by the environment. At the same time, the stimulus and model are quite explicitly of biological rather than historical origin. It is fair to say that all schools of historical thought today, including the Marxists, have moved well away from rigorously deterministic modes of interpretation which tend to limit and distort all but the grossest, most self-evident kinds of social and cultural change. By taking its lead from ontogenetic analogies rather than from the broad trend of historical studies of human groups, this school of archaeologists lays itself open to the serious charge of reductionism.

That the dominant regularities of cultural behavior should be imposed by sustaining or unstabilizing ecological interactions is surely only a hypothesis. The extent of validity of that hypothesis is a matter for empirical determination rather than prejudgment, and hardly can be determined convincingly so long as attention is confined to systems that fit biological patterns alone. There is, to be sure, a heuristic defense for pursuing this strategy, at least where documentary evidence is not available.

> Obviously, individuals *do* make decisions but evidence of these individual decisions cannot be recovered by archeologists. Accordingly it is more useful for the archeologist to study and understand the system, whose behavior is detectable over and over again. Obviously, this approach is too deterministic for some purposes, but for others it is of great theoretical value [Flannery, 1967: 119].

Included in the program of this small but growing group of process-oriented archaeologists are a number of other features which serve to differentiate their approach from the traditional one. To begin with, they place heavy emphasis on formal procedures for critically testing deductively drawn hypotheses against independent sets of data. Hence very little tolerance is shown for intuitive in-

terpretations or analogies, on the grounds that judgments about the correctness of the latter must depend to a large extent on a subjective sense of internal consistency and fit that cannot be replicated.

In addition, their attitude toward the limits of interpretation attainable from archaeological findings is characteristically an expansive, optimistic one. The traditional starting point for archaeology has been that differing degrees of preservation and later disturbance usually limit the evidence directly recoverable from the ground to only a fragment of that laid down originally. Moreover, even before they were diminished by the effects of time, archaeological data were only the material vestiges of much more complex behavioral patterns of which no direct trace survives. But rather than limiting their concerns to questions of subsistence, technology, and economy that can be most directly and unambiguously answered from the archaeological record, the process-oriented archaeologists observe that social organization and even ideology must have influenced and been influenced by these other realms of organized behavior at innumerable points. On this basis, a leading spokesman states flatly that "data relevant to most, if not all, the components of past socio-cultural systems *are* preserved in the archaeological record. Our task, then, is to devise means for extracting this information from our data." Clearly, this group has moved away from sifting and synthesizing what is known of an extinct way of life as a whole through its archaeological vestiges, and has centered its interests instead on the formulation of more sharply focused, but also more adequately testable, hypotheses.

I do not mean to imply that process-oriented archaeology will or should replace the traditional reliance on induction. Its protagonists have called attention to defects in prevailing strategies of study, and have fashioned an approach within which ecology becomes not merely a fashionable slogan but an organizing concept. Nevertheless, relatively few propositions have been advanced and fully documented by members of the process school as to systemic interrelationships involving material, ecological, and sociological components. The bane of subjective interpretations and categories still affects much of the primary data on which they depend, albeit somewhat disguised by increasingly sophisticated quantitative manipulations. Although of great methodological interest, most such propositions to date remain merely plausible; validation, or even the evaluation of probability, has proved again to be a difficult goal to pursue through the complexities that surround man and his works.

Moreover, it seems hard to deny that the central creative activity in archaeology, like in all scholarship, lies in induction, in outstripping the narrow base of available facts to suggest new and essentially speculative unities. Formal analytical procedures are surely a useful adjunct to qualities of reflective judgment in assessing the consistency, utility, and fit to these hypothetical unities or explanations, but they are hardly likely to become a full-scale substitute. Both will surely remain, their complementarity enhancing archaeology's claims to work within the framework of a genuinely scientific methodology when the current agitation subsides. What the ferment does indicate, however, is that issues at the core of any philosophy of science now have become critical for a discipline many would unhesitatingly assign to the humanities.

Another major trend of thought in archaeology involves the increasing tendency to study cultural change as evolutionary change, recognizing the unique properties that culture imparts to the human record but nonetheless employing biological models for certain of its most significant or widely recurrent features. Most emphatically, this does not imply a return to crude popular notions of cultural Darwinism, such as the direct competition of inherently unequal and antagonistic groups for survival. I refer instead to some of the underlying conceptions of contemporary evolutionary biology: variable populations, rather than individuals or types, as the units upon which alone the action of selective pressures can be understood; the delicate, many-vectored mechanisms of the process of natural selection itself; adaptive radiations, through which populations rapidly evolve to fill new ecological niches; and, finally, the conceptualization of the results of evolution as a progression of irregular but irreversible transformations.

How are these conceptions reflected in current archaeological research? Partly in the increasing attention being given to ecology that has already been mentioned. But equally important, greater emphasis is being given to the critical processes of transformation that have led from one general level of organizational complexity in human society to another. Unlike the earlier use of stages as little more than typological constructs, the problem of the basic structural features of these successive quantum levels, and of the detailed sequence of steps by which they emerged in parallel instances, now are becoming uppermost. Transitional processes rather than static conditions are the focus of an unprecedented, if still loosely coordinated, attack by a considerable number of individuals at different institutions here and abroad, providing clusterings of greatly heightened activity within what previously had been a diffuse scattering of projects and problems. Among such developmental processes are, for example, the independent origins of agriculture, urban centers, and primary technological complexes like metallurgy or, more generally, pyrotechnics. And in the same way that key processes of change have been identified, key regions of change are receiving correspondingly increased attention. Central Mexico apparently was such a region within the much broader area where aboriginal civilization once flourished in Middle America, and the intensified surveys and excavations there in recent years are a good illustration of the point.

Having alluded to variable populations as the cru-cial unit of evolutionary analysis, I must return to this theme to describe an important additional trend in thought. Variability is always present in the inventory of artifacts that the archaeologist recovers, but from former acceptance of curves of normal distribution in space and time as a priori assumptions, archaeologists have moved to empirical studies of geographic variability and tempos of change. Processes of innovation, stylistic drift, and diffusion all are brought under scrutiny wherever circumstances permit adequate control over differences in time. Similarly, patterns of spatial variation that do not approximate the normal ones now are being regarded as significant clues to the kinship and other social groups of which the makers of the artifacts were members. A variety of new models and methods are required in the search for correspondences of this type, most of them originally developed by locational geographers; among them are linear regression and multivariant-factor analyses in order to detect nonrandom clusterings of variables dependent upon one another. From a holistic conception of extinct cultures as bodies of shared norms, changing only in response to the slow movement of stylistic variables except where subjected involuntarily to external influences, we have come to expect sharp accelerations and retardations of change and wide differences in the range of variability. By relating such differences to their cultural and natural setting, a new and powerful tool has been fashioned not merely for documenting the fact of change more accurately and interestingly than heretofore, but also for supplying convincing explanations of it.

And what of advances stemming from the physical sciences? It may have struck some as odd that I have yet to mention the dating and detection devices whose impact on archaeology is perhaps the most widely publicized aspect of my subject. The delay to the end is deliberate, for while their contribution is certainly very great it does not alter the whole structure of thought to the same degree as the other new features with which I have dealt.

Radiocarbon dating is the best and most important example. In one sense, as a recent overview states, it has "revolutionized archaeological ideas concerning the chronology of human events during the last 40,000 years." The worldwide synchronism of late glacial and postglacial climatic phases, the timing of agricultural origins and dispersals, the succession of cultural periods in many areas where long stratigraphic sequences do not exist to provide them securely, and the correlation of the Maya and Christian calendars are among the many important issues to which radiocarbon determinations have contributed decisively. One can argue also that the use of radiocarbon led indirectly to a considerable improvement in prevailing standards of fieldwork, requiring greater sophistication in sampling, in the detection of disturbances and contaminants, and in the evaluation of context if the resultant dates were to withstand critical comparison with others. Moreover, the slowly advancing precision of the system, both with regard to individual determinations and more especially to the cumulative series of them, has opened up the prospect of more carefully controlled studies of change in the future than any heretofore possible.

Errors and misinterpretations on the part of archaeologists have not been uncommon, but the principal deterrents to the realization of this potential are inherent in the radiocarbon process itself. The expression of standard deviations from the mean determination at times has been taken to imply absolute limits within which the age of the specimen must fall, and at other times has been ignored altogether by archaeologists. But even in the absence of these two linked forms of confusion the existence of a still fairly large plus or minus range for each dated specimen limits any fine-grained analysis of change. There has been considerable progress in recognizing sources of contamination, but this also implies that the reliability of determinations is to some degree dependent on when, how, and by whom they were made. Most important, the recognition of a number of factors which have exercised an irregularly distorting influence on the production of the carbon-14 isotope in the upper atmosphere for a time threatened to increase our interpretive uncertainties almost beyond tolerable limits. Recent empirical determinations based on bristlecone pine tree-ring sequences of known age are helping to correct these very considerable sources of error from the late sixth millennium B.C. onward, but determinations of greater age still remain disturbingly uncertain. None of this is intended to minimize the major contribution that radiocarbon dating has made. In the aggregate, it has supplied a system of absolute chronology that was essentially lacking previously. But numerous examples could be cited indicating that it remains unwise to rely very heavily on individual dates or even groups of dates. And unless ways can be found to obtain a further increase in optimum accuracy by an order of magnitude, studies of the dynamics of change based on the archaeological record will continue to be noteworthy more for their promise than for their performance.

In some ways, the availability of a whole series of supplements and alternatives to radiocarbon provides the greatest hopes for archaeology. Even within the age range for which radiocarbon is now the preeminent method, determinations based on the thermoluminescence of pottery offer certain potential advantages. Principal among these is that pottery is itself a human artifact, while occasionally there has been a considerable interval between the lifespan of some organic material dated by radiocarbon and its employment as an artifact. Thus far, however, the margin of error in the thermoluminescent method is still much larger than with the radiocarbon method. Of greater current importance are measurements of the thickness of a hydration layer that forms continuously on chipped artifacts of obsidian. Since the rate of hydration varies with temperature, the method at first

sight is not very promising for absolute chronology. However, it can very sharply distinguish components of different relative age within a particular site or area where the temperature is essentially a constant, and its low cost permits multiple determinations. Finally, for sites too old to be subjected to radiocarbon analysis, thorium-uranium, protactinium-uranium, and potassium-argon dating also are in use. The remote geochronological horizons to which they are applicable make them of particular importance for advances in the understanding of the biological evolution of the human species.

Space permits only the briefest mention of the promising beginnings made with a variety of detecting and locating systems. Magnetometers of rapidly increasing sensitivity have been shown to be effective in mapping ruined settlements beneath as much as 5 meters of overburden. Grids of soil resistivity measurements have been employed for the same purpose at shallower depths. Aerial photography is becoming an increasingly commonplace adjunct of both surveys and excavations, and there is considerable experimentation with the use of high resolution, multiband and photogrammetric techniques. Underwater archaeology, only the romantic province of the untrained skin diver a few years ago, is now an elaborately equipped, highly specialized field of its own. Without any doubt at all, the use of these and similar approaches will become a regular, even dominant, feature of archaeology in the decades immediately ahead. But again, their present importance is more in the realm of promise than of published performance. And the changes in the basic tenets of archaeological thought that I have emphasized are largely anterior to and independent of them.

Some of my colleagues will object that the emphasis I have given to these new trends of thought also is more of a hope or a promise than a balanced estimate of accomplishments to date. Probably they are at least partly correct. My personal bias has always been to look less at what the world is—or was at a given time—than at what it is—or was then in the process of—becoming. I would insist that the new paradigm I have tried to describe is taking hold, particularly among the younger members of the profession. On balance, however, there is little doubt that most of the work in the field is still descriptively, rather than causally, oriented.

In relatively few studies is the central problem of explaining change directly considered in terms of either the relevant data sought or the conceptual apparatus used. In spite of the widespread acceptance in theory of regional-ecological models that should depend on rigorous statistical sampling, the predominant focus of research for most investigators remains the arbitrarily chosen slice of a particular ancient site that is excavated. Specialists in the natural environment are still too often employed as technicians "expected to provide ready answers to poorly formulated questions," rather than engaged in a genuinely collaborative study. Problems and objectives too often are formulated only as armchair generalizations, rather than as sharply focused hypotheses to which definitive answers must be sought in regional or local sequences. Meanwhile, separated by a wide gulf from the former, the conduct of much research at the local level remains practically innocent of relevance to any theoretical problem whatever.

Holistic presuppositions about societies in general also have not been sufficiently clarified and tested. As a result, there may well be an excessive emphasis in archaeological interpretation on stability rather than instability as the salient human condition. To phrase this differently, an oddly antiquated, almost Victorian emphasis continues on institutions and behavior that performed integrative functions—art styles, rituals, elites—at the expense of conflict, marginality, and dissonance as sources of creativity and change. Possibly for the same reason, most reconstructions of archaeological sequences still consist of a succession of qualitatively distinct, smoothly functioning phases or stages rather than of the continuous interplay of forces marked at intervals by new transformational forms. Finally, most of us remain excessively timid, reluctant to tackle the grand problems of comparison, generalization, and synthesis, even though the certainty of being found in frequent error if we did so ought to be heavily outweighed by the opportunity to deepen, sharpen, and ultimately justify our inquiries. But, before I allow these criticisms of the present state of archaeology to seem overwhelming, perhaps I should ask whether at least some of them do not have analogs in the natural sciences as well.

9

By Francis E. Wylie

Pilgrims elude a Pilgrim-hunter

James Deetz, one of archaeology's new breed, seeks artifacts and laws of behavior in colonial trash heaps and cemeteries

"Maybe there never were any Pilgrims. Maybe the *Mayflower* story is just a legend."

Dr. James Deetz was expressing in his wry way the frustration of months of digging during the hot Massachusetts summer without finding any traces of the first settlers. In fact, Deetz has recovered thousands of artifacts from the rich trash heaps of the last three centuries, but nothing that can be positively identified with the 50 years before.

Last July Deetz and a group of student volunteers were at a site in the center of Plymouth, just behind a shoe store which occupies a house built in the early 18th century. The site probably marked the northern side of the Pilgrims' first village. Deetz thought there was just a chance the diggers would uncover evidence of the log stockade built around the village. Post holes, perhaps. A volunteer dug the soil from around the rotted stumps of three cedar posts.

"Could this be it?"

"If it is, we still have to find some proof," said Deetz, following the archaeologist's rule to be skeptical about anything he turns up. "Cedar lasts a long time, but these could have been the posts for a lady's clothesline 50 years ago."

The question was answered in a few days. In further digging the bottom of the posts was reached, and beneath one of them was a fragment of Mocha pottery.

"At the very earliest, 1790," Deetz said. "We can't tell how old the posts are, but we can be sure the Pilgrims didn't put them there."

A few days later the diggers gave up and shoveled back the dirt they had so carefully sifted. They had found Indian arrowheads, possibly contemporary with the Pilgrims. They were able to piece together much of a fragile Whieldon ware teapot, which could be dated to 1760, and they glued together 36 pieces of a handsome English agateware bowl of the same date (see p. 39). Shattered chamber pots were harvested in abundance, particularly creamware ones of about 1800. In fact, the excavation produced a remarkable cross section of New England culture, from clay pipes and pewter spoons to modern alarm clock remnants. But no Pilgrim artifacts.

Deetz (left), Geoff Moran (right) and a youthful
band of volunteers dug last summer for the
home of Governor Winslow—and they found a barn.

Nonetheless, the cross section is important to Deetz, one of the leaders of a new breed of investigators who are as much anthropologists as archaeologists. While archaeologists have always sought to make inferences from what they find, their work in the past has tended to be merely descriptive. Deetz and other practitioners of what is sometimes called the New Archaeology would like, through rigorous scientific method, to develop unifying theory and basic laws explaining the behavior of Man in all ages.

A pioneer of this approach, Deetz did not start out as an archaeologist. He wanted to be a doctor until, at Harvard university, he failed chemistry and switched to anthropology. After his sophomore year, he went to South Dakota for a summer of salvage archaeology, digging Indian sites which were about to be covered by dammed-up water.

It was during a subsequent trip to South Dakota that Deetz made a remarkable find: While digging, he saw something brown and shiny gleaming in the dirt. "Hey, what's this?" he yelled, and colleagues gathered around him. He carefully brushed away the soil and unearthed his own polished shoe. He again returned

51

to that state for his doctoral thesis work. By rigorous computer analysis of potshards from an Arikara Indian site, he demonstrated three distinct cultural phases between 1700 and 1780. He showed how, under the impact of trade in guns and horses and of the white man's smallpox, a stable society quickly altered to one of great mobility and small units.

He became a professor at the University of California at Santa Barbara, but summer fieldwork brought him back to New England. He recalls that he set out in 1965 in a Ford station wagon with his wife, eight children, one babysitter and 140 reptiles and amphibians. A consignment of 16 cats—two mothers and their litters—had been flown ahead, as well as cages containing additional lizards, including a three-foot iguana.

All went well in the station wagon until, after a 900-mile day, they discovered that a king snake had escaped and eaten 30 lizards. "He looked like a Christmas stocking," says Deetz.

In contrast to the unstratified and exuberant chaos of Deetz's mobile household, his precise archaeological method was sharpened in the summers of 1965 and 1966. Without digging so much as a spoonful of dirt, Deetz and a Harvard student, Edwin Dethlefsen, studied the carvings in over 20,000 tombstones in southern New England cemeteries. They traced the evolution of a grim death's head motif into a relatively cheerful cherub, correlating the change with the transition from stern Calvinistic doctrine to a theology in which the Resurrection played a more conspicuous part. His "archaeological" inferences could in turn be confirmed by written records of the time, serving to prove the validity of the archaeological method. His most exciting moment was "sitting in a Concord cemetery and suddenly realizing that all those gravestones made sense."

By 1967, Deetz had decided he was a New Englander, not a Californian. He resigned from Santa Barbara, driven also by the failure of the protest movement there. He had been on a faculty-student committee which organized the first protest march on the state capitol after the firing of Clark Kerr. A television network collected a group of bearded, wild-looking kids and made pictures of them pouring out of the dormitories. They appeared on national television as well as the 5,000 soberly dressed and legitimate protestors marching on Sacramento. "I decided to give it up," says Deetz, "because one, it doesn't do any good, and two, no matter how hard you try they're going to mess you up."

In answer to activists, who say his archaeology is an escape from the important things in the world, Deetz replies: "That's a lot of nonsense. We can't have social change until we understand what we are, and we can't understand that until we understand where we come from. More than any other generation, the kids today are interested in history, and what we are doing is to help them understand the past."

Deetz became professor of anthropology at Brown University and assistant director of the Plimoth Plantation at Plymouth, Massachusetts. A re-creation of the original Pilgrim village, Plimoth Plantation was organized principally by a serious amateur archaeologist and successful businessman, Henry Hornblower II. In addition to the village, the organization built the ocean-going *Mayflower II* and has sponsored archaeological research into the colonial past. Authenticity was a key word in the venture, and Deetz was looked to as a scholar who could help provide it.

Pottery and barns but no turkey bones

At 41, Jim Deetz is exuberant and animated. His blond curly hair is shaggy, and he wears snug, belled trousers on his lean hips, like the young people with whom he works. Wherever he goes, he is surrounded by admiring youngsters who dig for days on end without pay and without college credit, in a common acceptance with Deetz of modest scholarly goals.

"No one really knows what the Pilgrims were like," he says. "There are valuable written records, to be sure, and some of the furniture and weapons have survived. But in more than three centuries a lot of legend and folklore have accumulated, and no one knows how much of it is true.

"Through digging in the ground where they lived we believe we can learn a great deal more—not only about the Pilgrims but about the evolution of American society and culture since then."

Thus far, some 100,000 pieces of colonial pottery and other artifacts have been uncovered, but no momentous conclusions have yet been reached. There is evidence that while the Pilgrims were all equal to begin with, Plymouth society was distinctly stratified by 1700. And Deetz observes that in spite of the Thanksgiving tradition no turkey bones have been found.

A year ago Plimoth Plantation and the National Park Service sponsored a major Deetz excavation at the site of a tavern on Great Island in Wellfleet Harbor on Cape Cod, where whalers apparently made their headquarters between 1690 and 1740.

In midsummer this year another Deetz crew started digging in Marshfield, a dozen miles north of Plymouth, for debris left by Edward Winslow, a *Mayflower* passenger who settled there about 1635 and later served as governor of the colony, as did his son Josiah.

In 1941, Henry Hornblower conducted an excavation on the Winslow lands and found the foundation of a house built in about 1650. Two years ago two amateurs did some digging in the same general area. They wouldn't reveal where, which is the sort of thing that makes an archaeologist climb a wall, but Deetz saw some of their finds and, he says, "They were getting some real jazzy stuff."

So he decided to make a try at the Hornblower site. The dig's director was Geoffrey Moran, a history teacher at Bradford Junior College. The crew varied from day to day, but there were some regulars, including Barbara Haines, a rosy-cheeked blond from Pembroke College, who has been attracted to archaeology ever since she took a course under Deetz at Brown. (There were about 500 in the class—quite large for Brown but proof of his popularity. "I would always sit in one of the front rows because I didn't want to miss anything," Barbara remembers. "He has a habit of making comments aside, almost to himself, in a low voice—like 'I guess I'd better try that sentence again. I confused everyone.' The next year I went back to visit the class and he said, 'Hey, what are you doing here?' He remembered me as a person.")

The early days of digging for the Winslow house were not very rewarding. There were small mounds of crumbled brick—"soft as peanut butter," as Deetz put it, and obviously very old. There were some small pieces of a black glazed ware commonly used in 17th-century England but rarely found in America. As the string-marked squares were extended and the excavation deepened, prospects became more promising.

Some 18 inches below the surface dark bands of earth began to show against the yellow sand and clay. They looked as though they marked the foundations of buildings. Stones large enough to serve as foundations are not native to this shore area of Marshfield and would have had to be carted from elsewhere. Since such stones would have a value, they could have been dug from the original trenches and used for the foundations of new structures. Topsoil would wash into the trenches, accounting for the dark bands.

The diggers followed one band for 80 feet, where it turned a precise right angle—clearly the corner of a building. If three other corners could be found the complete dimensions would be established. But 80 feet! "We believe the Pilgrims may have had houses 30 or 40 feet long, built in three bays about ten feet square," explained Deetz. "There is evidence of such houses, although previously Pilgrim homes were supposed to be much smaller. A building 80 feet long would have to be a barn. And we believe there were such barns—funny looking buildings, long and low."

The excavation was extended in other directions, and after a few days Deetz came back for an inspection. Moran handed him an odd assortment of objects taken from a new hole—some rusted wire nails, a corroded brass cotter pin and a curious little glass tube about an inch long, containing a clear fluid.

"What in the hell is that?" exclaimed Deetz. They finally determined that it was the bubble chamber from a carpenter's level, the wooden frame of which had rotted away. Wire nails, cotter pin and such an artifact certainly didn't belong to the Pilgrims, even though they were found at a depth in the soil indicating the right age.

Further digging failed to reveal the other corners of the building or anything else of special value, and in another week the site was abandoned. But there were other projects to undertake; the exuberant Deetz was not discouraged. He and his band would continue their search elsewhere for remains of the Pilgrims. And meanwhile, he continues to perfect his analytical methods and to seek broad anthropological conclusions from those artifacts they do dig up.

Digging, of course, is only the beginning of the job. Every shard and scrap from an excavation is carefully numbered, showing the exact position of discovery. Bags of material are taken back to the Plimouth Plantation laboratory for careful study. Students work for hours and days trying to fit together jagged pieces of pottery, often gluing together recognizable and even beautiful reconstructions of the original ware. The bore of every clay pipestem fragment, of which there are bushels, is measured. (Between 1590 and 1800 the bore became 1/64 of an inch smaller every 30 years and pipestems serve as reliable indicators of the age of associated artifacts.)

However productive of theory his research may prove to be, it is very productive of artifacts and students. Plimouth Plantation now has one of the largest collections of 17th-century artifacts, surpassed, perhaps, only by that at Jamestown, Virginia. And the students who have worked with Deetz now number in the hundreds. On Friday nights they are likely to gather at his house to celebrate the end of a week's work. The house is a big gray Victorian summer place a half-mile from Plimouth Plantation.

Some of the college students who spend the day in gray Pilgrim garb, as inhabitants of Plimouth Plantation, show up in the quaint costumes of the 1971 youth culture. A record player blares with Bluegrass music, the staple in the Deetz household. When it stops, Deetz yells, "Where's the music? It's too damned quiet here." Traffic to the kitchen increases, where a makeshift bar offers everything from milk to Scotch. Tomorrow is Saturday and artifacts can wait.

10

The archaeologist in deep water

by
Willard Bascom

ALL kinds of ships from the earliest crude vessel to the most modern supertankers have had a disconcerting way of getting into trouble on the high seas and suddenly sinking. They sink for many reasons, often with all hands, far from shore.

The hulks may have landed in shallow water—which we will define as less than 200 metres—or perhaps they came to rest on the continental shelf, or even in the abyss. Each sunken ship is a neatly packaged collection of artifacts representing the culture of its time. Since these marine disasters have been going on steadily for 4,000 years, the accumulated record of the history of civilization is now spread for our choice on the floor of the sea.

Archaeological techniques for the examination of old ships in water less than 30 metres deep are well developed. But ship hulls in such shallow graves have been largely destroyed by wave action, sand abrasion, chemical

WILLARD BASCOM *began his career as a mining engineer, but switched to oceanography in 1945 as a research engineer at the University of California, Berkeley, and later at the Scripps Institution of Oceanography, La Jolla, California. After joining the U.S. National Academy of Sciences in 1954, he organized and directed the first phase of the Mohole Project to drill in deep water through the earth's crust (see "Unesco Courier", Oct. 1963). He has written many scientific and technical studies and is the author or editor of "A Hole in the Bottom of the Sea", "Waves and Beaches" and "Great Sea Poetry", for the general reader.*

changes, marine borers and divers. The destruction has usually been so complete we have come to think of shallow water wrecks as mounds of amphoras, piles of ballast stones, and scattered cannon. Only beneath the mud or sand does one find wood in the form of bottom ribs and planking. Often the associated artifacts have been scattered around over half a kilometre and buried deep in the sand by great waves over hundreds of years.

These shallow wrecks have encouraged us by providing much information; they also urge us on by raising questions about the parts that are missing and holding out hope that we can find better preserved examples.

There may be many ancient wooden ships in reasonably good condition lying on the deep-sea floor of the Mediterranean.

The weather in the Mediterranean is known for sudden violent change, and the old ships could not respond rapidly nor sail into wind very well. In the Aegean, the early mariners feared the "meltem", a northerly afternoon gale, known in the Adriatic as the "bora", which brings winds of 60 mph and more. It would be very easy for a ship to be blown offshore and sunk in a sudden squall.

The ancient ships were generally small (less than 40 metres long) and made of wooden planks held edge to edge. If the planks came apart, the weight of cargo and ballast would take a ship down in a few minutes. Many

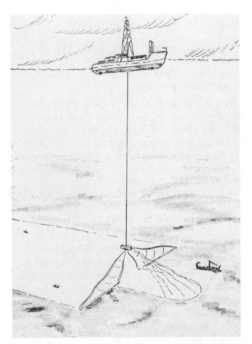

Impression of a specially designed archaeological research vessel, the "Alcoa Seaprobe," designed by Dr. W. Bascom, making a sonar search of the sea bed. An instrument pod, lowered through the ship's central well, contains forward and side-scanning sonars that can sweep a pathway 400 to 800 metres wide. Projections, such as rocks or the wreck of a ship, reflect sound waves better and produce a darker spot on the record. The sea bed pattern, below, was recorded by side-scanning sonar apparatus during a survey voyage by another research vessel.

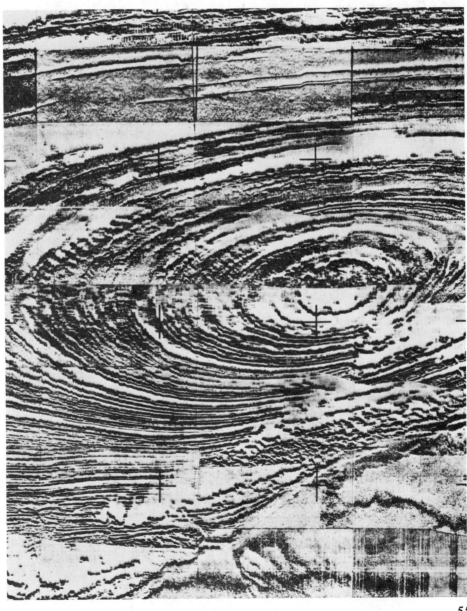

vessels were not completely decked and in heavy weather they could take water over the sides and quickly founder or capsize.

Pirates were the scourge of shipping for many centuries: they doubtless sank many of the vessels they caught. Fire was also a frequent cause of loss —coals would fall from a galley stove as the ship pitched, or a carelessly held torch would start a blaze. Warships, subject to all these hazards, also had a chance of being rammed in battle or scuttled after capture.

What happened to the ships that sank in water deeper than 200 metres? They must have settled rapidly to the bottom (the velocity depending on the weight) where they landed upright (because of the drag of the masts and rigging) on a sea floor made of mud, ooze or fine sand. Probably the impact would not be very damaging to a hull. Once on the bottom the hull is protected from most of the things that would destroy it in shallow water.

In water over 200 metres deep, wave action at the bottom is virtually nil. In most places the current is of low velocity, not capable of rearranging the bottom materials. It is dark at those depths, and photosynthesis, required to sustain plant growth, is not possible. The temperature is near-freezing so that chemical reactions proceed very slowly. And of course man, until now, has not been able to reach these depths and disturb the site. Deep water is a perfect place for old ship storage—almost.

The largest unknown in this consideration of whether old wooden wrecks survive in deep water is the question of whether marine borers consume them. The evidence is not clear and the answer is—perhaps.

If, for example, the ship was badly infected with shipworm when it sank, these creatures may have survived the increased pressure and finished their work. But teredos (shipworms) do not ordinarily live at depths as great as 200 metres. The most likely destruction will have been caused by a borer clam, xylophaga, which attacks wood down to 2,000 metres. Since samples of very old wood have been found on the deep sea bottom, these creatures are not universal and we are left with hope. Or perhaps there are other, unknown, biological attackers.

Variations in the survival of wood are probably caused by differences in salinity, oxygen, nutrients, metallic ions, currents, or just accident. In the reducing environment that exists in some marine depressions and in the Black Sea, one would expect wood on the sea bottom to survive very well.

IF the ship survives the borers, will it soon be covered with sediment? In deep water the sea dust usually accumulates very slowly. The mid-ocean sedimentation rate is as little as one or two millimetres per thousand years; in the central basins of the Mediterranean it is about 10 cm. per thousand years. In intermediate depths (200 to 2,000 m), except near large river discharges, an average might be 20 cm. per thousand years. Thus, in such depths, the general outline of even a very old ship will not be greatly changed by that blanket of sediment.

The net effect of the above arguments is that there is good reason to believe that somewhere on the deep sea floor wooden ships are well preserved for very long periods of time. Certainly they are in better condition than those found in shallow water.

Wrecks in shallow water have generally been found accidently by sponge divers, fishing boats, or sports divers. But to locate vessels sunk in deep water, other leads are needed. In the Mediterranean, useful information can be gleaned from statistics based on knowledge of the ancient ports and cities, the location of trade routes, the nature of the old ships and their cargoes.

It is believed that there were over 300 active ports in the Mediterranean by the 4th century B.C., and that during the first millenium B.C. some 150,000 ships were built. Other calculations suggest that as many as 15,000 of these vessels foundered—many in deep water.

If the total length of the trade routes in the eastern Mediterranean were 6,000 nautical miles (1 nautical mile equals 1.9 kilometres) and the average width 10 nautical miles, there is a reasonable chance of one sunken ship in every four square nautical miles along these routes.

By selecting specific areas where ships were known to get into trouble, it is possible to improve the chances considerably. There are numerous high-probability sites in the straits between islands, between islands and mainland, and at major "jumping off points", where ships left the security of nearby land and set out into open waters.

Such sites exist between the Peloponnese and Crete, east of Crete to Rhodes and Turkey, between Italy and Yugoslavia, between Tunis and Sicily, around Malta, near Gibraltar, and along the coasts of Lebanon, Israel and Cyprus.

Somewhat more is known about the

losses of military ships in the same period, and there are more fixed points to guide estimates. There are literally hundreds of historical references to sea battles in which astonishing numbers of ships were involved.

For example, at the battle of Cape Ecnomus, Sicily, in 255 B.C., 250 Roman ships faced 200 Carthaginian vessels. Only 16 ships were lost in the battle, but in a storm off Camarina, on the southern Sicilian coast, shortly afterward, 250 of the remaining ships were wrecked. When Anthony and Cleopatra met Augustus at Actium in 37 B.C., about 100 ships of the 900 engaged were lost.

Ships that sank much later than the ancient ones may be even more interesting. For example, in 1571 the Battle of Lepanto was fought between a fleet of 300 ships from Venice, Spain and the Papal States and a 273-ship Turkish fleet, not far from Actium, just over 1,600 years after the fleet of Anthony and Augustus fought there. Another 100-odd ships went down, this time with a very different array of artifacts.

So the obvious first place to look is in the Mediterranean along trade routes that have been travelled for thousands of years. Although that sea has a maximum depth of over 4,500 metres, the major part of these ancient pathways traversed waters less than half that depth, within easy reach of the system about to be described.

It is nearly ten years since I reached this conclusion and devised a method for systematic searching, inspection and the recovery of heavy objects. The system was awarded a U.S. Patent in 1965 and with few changes has been developed into a beautiful new ship completed in late 1971: the *Alcoa Seaprobe*. Now the technology is in existence.

THE *Alcoa Seaprobe* looks much like a deep ocean drilling ship —and indeed it is capable of drilling— but instead it uses its semi-rigid pipe to lower a pod containing sensors into the depths. These sensors include two sonars, television cameras and photographic equipment. When these are moved along a short distance above the bottom they transmit information about a wide swath of bottom up a cable to instrument watchers in the control room above.

It is not necessary to send men down; the pod at the tip of the pipe extends their vision into the depths. From the surface they can inspect objects on the bottom, dusting away sediment with propellers. Items of interest can be photographed and perhaps recovered with scoops and grasping devices.

The *Alcoa Seaprobe* is 75 metres long, 17 metres wide, and draws 4 metres. It is propelled by two vertical-axis manoeuvering propellers which can exert thrust to move the ship in any direction, including skewed and sidewise. The ship is all-electric with its power plant forward and quarters for 50 men aft. It is built of an aluminium alloy to demonstrate the excellent marine properties of that material.

The ship is steered by a console on the bridge which manually or automatically controls the propellers in such a way as to hold the ship in position above a point on the bottom in deep water. This capability, called "dynamic positioning", was invented by the author and associates in 1959, and is the key to doing precise work on the bottom in water too deep for anchoring.

In the centre of the ship is a rectangular opening to the sea 4 metres by 12 metres, called a "well". Directly above it is an aluminium derrick that can lift up to 400,000 kg (200 metric tons working load).

The derrick and pipe-handling system is capable of lowering or recovering drill pipe at an average rate of about 0.25 metres per second to a depth of 6,000 metres (although only 2,000 metres of pipe will normally be aboard). The pipe is ordinary oil drilling pipe 11.5 cm. in diameter, handled in "doubles", 20 metres long.

Pipe has the advantage that the pod and the tongs at its tip can be oriented and that sea water can be pumped down the inside at high pressure to operate hydraulic devices at the bottom. In order to ensure that the lower tip of the pipe remains close beneath the ship, the lower end of it is weighted with 20 tons of very thick-walled pipe.

The power-information cable between ship and pod is secured to the outside of the pipe with special clips and stored on a huge reel on deck. More pipe can be added or removed quickly as the depth changes and the cable length is readily adjusted.

As with any searching system, precise navigation is required so that there is a clear record of where the ship has been at every moment. Then any object found can be refound.

The ship's position can be determined closely enough by one of the electronic navigation systems. But careful searching out of sight of land requires local references such as taut-moored buoys supporting radar transponders (combined transmitter and receiver) or bottom-mounted sonar transponders. A systematic search is then conducted relative to these fixed points and the ship's position is plotted at short intervals of time as it moves back and forth along parallel pathways.

Once the navigation markers are installed we are ready to search. The pod is lowered to a position 20 to 50 metres above the bottom and the ship moves slowly forward at less than one metre per second. The sonars send out high frequency (177.5kh) pings of sound, one looking at the bottom directly ahead, the other scanning each side to a distance of at least 200 metres (twice that in some circumstances).

The side-looking sonar sends and receives sound pulses in such a fashion that objects that rise above the bottom, like a ship or a pile of ballast stones, reflect the sound and produce a dark spot on the record. Since the sea floor immediately beyond is in the sonic shadow and does not reflect sound, that part of the record remains white.

Thus each ping produces a line on the record and as the pod moves forward a sound picture of the bottom develops. The approximate size of bottom objects can be determined.

Because the side-looking sonar beam must strike the bottom at a small angle in order to be effective, it does not see objects on the bottom directly beneath the pod. Therefore the forward-looking sonar, which works in a similar fashion, is used to get information about the centre of the pathway.

When a ship-like object is detected with the sonar, it is necessary to verify it with television and to determine its approximate age and value. For this

the pod is lowered into television range (about 10 metres above the bottom) at the position plotted for the wreck. The sea dust can be blown away with water jets and the hulk inspected and photographed. The amount of work to be done will be determined by its value relative to other wrecks which could be studied.

If there are artifacts to be recovered an appropriate tool or device will be attached beneath the television. It may be a net, a grasping mechanism, or a large pair of tongs. Major pieces of a ship, heavy cannon, anchors, stone columns, etc., can be recovered as well as small items. Probably it will be possible to make reasonably good maps of the wreck from the photos and observations.

IT also may be possible to raise entire small wrecks in one or more lifts. Large wooden ship structures thus recovered would immediately be placed in fresh water in a prepared barge so as to prevent their deterioration while they are being studied and exhibited.

With the search method described here it should be possible to examine 30 square kilometres of bottom per day. The examination of wrecks and other objects will take the bulk of the time but it should be very rewarding.

So it seems that a great treasure house of information about the ancient world—the bottom of the Mediterranean—is almost within our grasp. In the New World, examination of 300 year-old wrecks will begin this year. Hopefully we will learn how well wood survives, how to identify and study old wrecks, and how to salvage major items.

If that is successful the next step will be to organize similar exploration work in the Mediterranean.

11

A STONE AGE ORCHESTRA

The earliest musical instruments were made from the bones of mammoths

by Sergei N. Bibikov

SERGEI N. BIBIKOV, *historian and corresponding member of the U.S.S.R. Academy of Sciences, is a researcher at the Archaeological Institute of the Academy of Sciences of the Ukraine.*

ARCHAEOLOGICAL excavations carried out at the site of a Palaeolithic settlement (some 20,000 years old) in the village of Mezin, near Chernigov in the Ukraine, between 1954 and 1962, brought to light the remains of a house built of the bones of a mammoth.

Inside the house, Ukrainian archaeologists I.G. Pidoplichko and I.G. Shovkoplyas found some large mammoth bones decorated with a cut-out geometrical design and coloured red. They were in a place apart and appeared to form a set, although their purpose was not immediately clear.

The finds included a shoulder blade, a thigh bone, two jaw bones, a fragment of pelvis and a portion of a mammoth's skull. Two ivory rattles, a mallet fashioned from a reindeer's antler and a large number of sea shells were also discovered on the floor of the house, together with a "rattling" bracelet with a simple but highly artistic design and consisting of five pieces of mammoth-tusk ivory with carved open-work decoration.

Near to the bones were found four heaps of pure yellow and red mineral ochre and also eight bone perforators. The floor of the dwelling bore the traces of three fireplaces and four pairs of bone struts for supporting the wigwam-type poles which had formerly held up the roof.

Detailed analysis of the finds has revealed that the history of this Palaeolithic construction falls neatly into two periods. At first it was used as a winter dwelling, but in the course of time it became unsafe—the whole three-ton edifice was in danger of collapse—and was abandoned by its inhabitants.

As the settlement grew, the villagers needed a public building, so they took over the old house, re-furbishing it, shoring it up from the inside, cleaning out the rubbish and using it as a building for festive occasions and rites.

It was then that the decorated mammoth bones and other objects of a non-utilitarian nature were brought into the building. It should be pointed out that some of the minority peoples in the north of Russia were still using abandoned houses for similar ceremonial purposes until fairly recent times.

Examination of the mammoth bones eventually made it possible, in 1974, to establish that they all formed part of a set of percussion instruments. The reindeer-horn mallet and the rattle fulfilled similar functions, while the

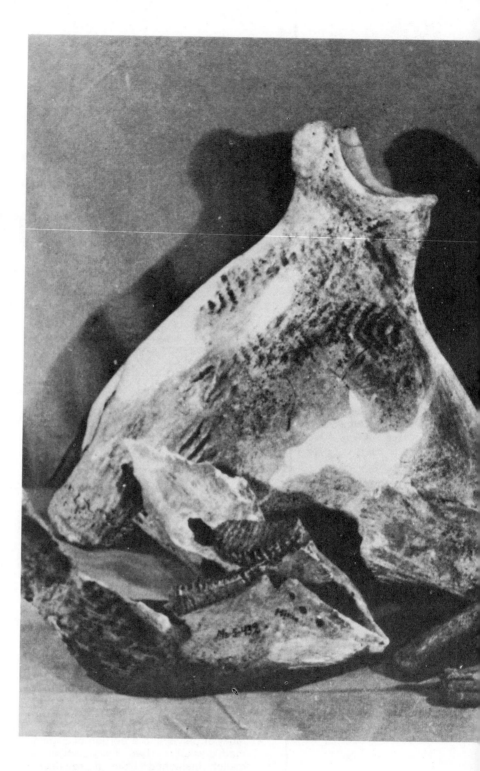

bracelet undoubtedly has some connexion with dancing, corresponding roughly in function to a pair of castanets. The red dye and the bone perforators were part of the "props"

The purpose of the objects found at Mezin was established by a team of archaeologists, palaeontologists, forensic scientists and medical experts. The way in which the surface of the bones is worn in places, the way the outer part of the bone tissue is compacted and has flaked away from the

inner, spongy part, the way in which the deformation of parts of the bone is strictly localized, and in which certain points on the surface have been polished, as well as a number of other clues, left the investigators in no doubt that these were in fact percussion instruments.

The discovery of such instruments dating from nearly 20,000 years ago is of the greatest significance, and is the first such discovery to have been made. Previously, only bone flutes,

In this collection of bones are instruments from one of the world's oldest orchestras, dating back some 20,000 years. Made from the bones of mammoths, these percussion instruments were unearthed at a Palaeolithic site near the village of Mezin, Ukraine. The largest include a shoulder-blade (left), a leg-bone (below), and a hip-bone (right).

Photo S.N. Bibikov © APN, Moscow

which incidentally have still not been scientifically investigated, had been discovered from Palaeolithic times in the U.S.S.R., and in Central and Western Europe.

The "castanet" bracelet is the first such instrument ever to have been found, and the only Palaeolithic object to have been discovered in the U.S.S.R. which confirms that the art of dancing was known in Central and Eastern Europe in Cro-Magnon times. Although music is generally recog-

nized to be one of the supreme manifestations of culture, its early history has not yet been very thoroughly explored, as Professors Maurice Freedman and Bruno Nettl made clear in a "Unesco Courier" article ("Music of the Centuries", June 1973). Music has generally been regarded as dating back to the civilizations of the ancient Orient and to Antiquity.

As a result of the discovery of these Palaeolithic instruments, this dating has now been pushed back by at least

Photos © APN. Moscow

Prehistoric pan-pipes

While most of the musical instruments unearthed at the Palaeolithic site at Mezin (Ukraine) were percussion instruments, flutes like this one (top) have been discovered in Moldavia (U.S.S.R.), France, U.K., Czechoslovakia, and elsewhere. Fashioned from a stag's antler, this flute found in Moldavia may be between 12 and 15,000 years old. The antler was hollowed out and six holes (four on one side, two on the other) pierced to modulate the sound. Later, in Neolithic times (some 5,000 years ago) greater numbers of more sophisticated musical instruments were made, like these bone Pan-pipes (above) reconstructed from fragments. In form and conception they are remarkably similar to Pan-pipes still used in various parts of the world today (Latin America, Rumania, Greece, etc.).

Cro-Magnon castanets

Formed of flattened rings of mammoth-tusk ivory with carved decoration, this "castanet bracelet" discovered at Mezin, in the Ukraine, is the first Palaeolithic instrument of its kind ever found. The rings make a harmonious sound when rattled together, and it is thought that the bracelet may have been used to accompany dances, thus suggesting that dancing was already practised in Cro-Magnon times some 20,000 years ago.

Photo S.N Bibikov © APN, Moscow

15,000 years, and rhythmic music is seen to have been already in existence in Cro-Magnon times. It thus appears that Cro-Magnon man had already mastered the elements of musical rhythm, tone and phrasing and was aware of the emotional impact of music. Music is thus probably as old as working skills and crafts and as old as society itself.

Dancing, which can also express the whole complexity of human experience —from imitations of the gestures of workers and craftsmen to the expression of the most subtle emotions—has also existed for as long as music. One of the earliest forms of the combined musical and choreographic performance—whether of ritual significance or simply dancing for pleasure —was done to the accompaniment of percussion instruments and also possibly to a sung accompaniment.

The structure of music and dancing is frequently compared with that of language. This emphasizes the correlation between words and sounds, between speech and music as a vehi-

cle for the expression of thought and ideas.

With the help of ethnography and other specialized fields of study, using the methods of cultural history and comparative analysis and even experimental methods, it should be possible to find out the basic facts about the musical culture of Palaeolithic times. This will give us a deeper insight into the mentality of *homo sapiens*, how he perceived the world, his emotional make-up, his behaviour and other aspects of his mental activity.

In order to get a rough idea of the sounds produced by the bone instruments, rather than relying only on the ethnographic evidence, an experiment was carried out at the Institute of Forensic Science, in Kiev (Ukraine). A musician carefully tapped out a rhythm on different parts of the shoulder-blade instrument. Sounds of various timbres—hard, resonant and musically expressive—were obtained. This experiment was a first step in the direction of investigating the range of sounds of Palaeolithic untuned percussion instruments.

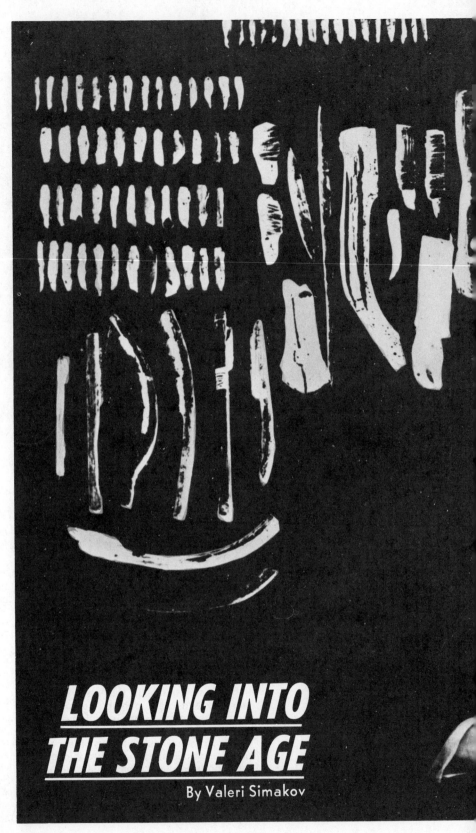

12

Among last year's State Prize winners in the fields of science and engineering was archeologist Sergei Semyonov, who received the award for his books on the history of primitive technology. Semyonov is widely known abroad. French scholar François Bordes has said that Semyonov's books will be permanent source works for the archeologist. The American archeologist N. Hoar believes that Semyonov has done the most important work in archeology of the last 50 years. The French magazine *Anthropologie* called the Soviet professor a "revolutionary in science." The National Library of London asked to register his book among the outstanding books of the world.

This is how primitive man drove piles when he built houses on lakes and rivers.

LOOKING INTO THE STONE AGE

By Valeri Simakov

THE RECENT AWARD of the State Prize to Sergei Semyonov stirred up considerable lay interest in the activities of the laboratory he heads. But archeologists, paleontologists and ethnographers have long appreciated the discoveries of their Leningrad colleague. Among scholars the world over Semyonov's monographs *Prehistoric Technology: An Experimental Study of the Oldest Tools and Artifacts from Traces of Manufacture and Wear* (1970) and *The Development of Technology in*

the Stone Age have become continuing best sellers. They are responsible for a veritable revolution in archeology.

Primitive tools and work techniques are the subjects of study of Semyonov and his staff. They are, in effect, investigating the dawn of human civilization.

To appreciate the importance of Semyonov's work, consider the rapidly growing role of archeology in studies of the history of society. It is consistent with the dynamism of present-day progress. Up to the time of the Revolution, that is, about 60 years ago, only 12 Paleolithic camps had been found in our country. Today there are almost a thousand. In collections throughout the world are millions of stone tools, from very large ones to microliths.

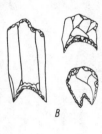

The books of archeologist Sergei Semyonov on the tools and work techniques of primitive man are scholarly best sellers the world over. His use of precise data has disposed of many long-held theories.

In studying stone tools, the first task, to properly name the find and thus determine its function, is not at all a simple one. Is it an axe, an adz or a knife? What was it used for?

Science must be precise. It must use exact methods. Semyonov has suggested and used such a method for archeology, which he calls traceology; his main instrument is the stereoscopic microscope. On the surface of the flint tools he dug up, he found rubbed spots, scratches, knobs, and the like—traces of labor. It took Semyonov 20 years to decipher these traces. His task

Researchers in Semyonov's laboratory learned to make and use the stone, wood and bone tools that the caveman employed. To make a boat, they studied the remains of ancient craft in museums and the drawings and findings of ethnographers.

Imitating our ancestors. Anatoli Filippov and Vyacheslav Shchelinsky are carving this stylized wooden head with stone tools.

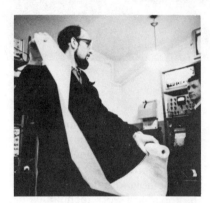

Yuri Markov and Vladimir Molebnikov use the most sensitive modern techniques to determine the age of ancient artifacts.

was no easier than the problems of Jean Champollion, who unraveled the mystery of ancient Egyptian hieroglyphics. And now, using Semyonov's method, we can accurately determine the function of a primitive tool, say what material it processed (wood, leather or stone), at what angle and with how much pressure, in short,

compile a full "process chart." We come out with a better way of ascertaining the economic activities of primitive society.

It was only after this rather practical, more than spectacular, part of the job was over that it was possible to confirm the findings by means of field experiments. Duplicating cavemen's work experience, Leningrad archeologists learned to make and use various stone, wooden and bone tools—exact replicas of primitive tools. They felled trees, made clothes, plowed and harvested as the Stone Age people did.

The experiments disposed of legends, something that could not have been done earlier because exact data were lacking. For instance, a student of the life of Kamchatka people had written that they had made their boats (and bowls) from wood with such difficulty that it took them three months to build a boat. On an expedition to the Angara River two research workers with no special experience worked for

eight hours a day, spelling each other (we do not know the work patterns of Neanderthal men); they made a pine-tree boat in 10 days.

So productivity in a caveman's workshop has turned out to be surprisingly high. Another ethnographer claimed that it took more than a primitive man's lifetime to grind a stone axe. But in a strictly controlled experiment, the job took from 2.5 to 25 hours, depending on the hardness of the material.

It took 50 seconds to light a fire by friction using the Stone Age method.

Semyonov thoroughly traced the evolution of the technology of manual labor in the Stone Age. He studied the way new methods of work set to functioning ever stronger groups of muscles (the rise in work capacity), how new speeds were reached and how the accuracy of work was increased.

He summed up the results of his studies of the past several years in a major contribution *The*

Theory being tested by practice: working with a wood plow made with the tools our ancestors made.

Origin of Agriculture, in which he continued the studies of Nikolai Vavilov, the eminent Soviet botanist and geneticist.

Our ancestors were keen-witted. Today we can see more clearly how and why they could settle great areas as far back as the Stone Age. Without exaggerating the technological progress of that period, we can pay our considerably greater respect to the tools and work techniques of primitive peoples.

13

Ancient Aches and Pains

The ills of ancient man, traced in his bones and art, tell us
how he lived and died and link his world to ours

By CALVIN WELLS

Disease never comes haphazardly. It always reflects the circumstances of our lives. Dental decay, cancer of the lung, tennis elbow, coronary thrombosis, beriberi, and innumerable other ailments are very precise indicators of the things we use, eat, do, or lack. This holds true for creatures other than modern man. Fossil sea urchins millions of years old bear the tooth marks of animals that took a snap at them. Dinosaurs developed arthritis from chronic stress and strain, and primeval trilobites fell victim to bacterial infection. The bones of ancient men often preserve a record of injury or affliction that reveals how these people lived, what they ate and wore, what weapons they used, and even what kind of society they lived in. The study of ancient disease and injury is called palaeopathology, and it has much to say about life in antiquity and in more recent times as well.

Not all the evidence is in bones. Ancient ailments have often been faithfully recorded in works of art. Sometimes the skeletal evidence supplements the artistic. For example, no one really knows whether American Indians were

afflicted with tuberculosis before 1492 or whether the Europeans imported the disease. Tuberculosis of the vertebrae, or Pott's disease, produces hunchbacks, and many hunchbacked spines have been found in the New World. The one at left below belonged to a Seneca Indian of around the thirteenth century A.D. Pott's disease probably caused the deformation, though other infections could conceivably have had the same result. But the fact that figurines of hunchbacks, all quite similar, are frequently found among American Indians is evidence that the deformity was widespread, and it is probable that tuberculosis was responsible. The hunchbacked figurine shown on this page is from San Domingo. It was used to pound grain.

From the nameless hordes of ancient cadavers a famous man is sometimes lifted from his sepulcher to be examined by the palaeopathologist. Tamerlane is such a case. This Mongol conqueror, whose name means simply "Timur the Lame," died in 1405. When the Gur Amir Mausoleum in Samarkand was opened in 1941, the remains were identified as Tamerlane's by the

An Egyptian dwarf and his family

extensive tubercular destruction of the right thigh and shin bones and by the bony union that had immobilized his knee joint and his right arm. The historical record was thus confirmed, but the old tradition that he was an albino was refuted. The parts of his beard that had survived were a graying chestnut color.

Apart from solving such minor historical puzzles as this, the chief interest of the palaeopathologist is in what he can learn about ancient society. The bronze figure of the dwarf below is

from Benin in West Africa. One of several beautiful and serious studies of dwarfism from Benin, it shows an achondroplastic dwarf, the kind seen in circuses and in the canvases of Velásquez. This sympathetic portrayal is a clear indication of a kindly attitude toward dwarfs, in a society where deformed children were usually regarded as bewitched. In ancient Egypt dwarfs seem to have been regarded with the same mixture of respect and affection. They also were allowed to take their place in society, as this limestone statue of 2500 B.C. makes clear. It shows a dwarf called Seneb with his wife and children, who are all of normal size.

The evidence of disease

Facial palsy caused by stroke has been deliberately and vividly portrayed, particularly in the arts of Africa and Peru, and there is no doubt that this ailment is an old one. Anthropomorphic vases are common in the arts of ancient Peru, and the asymmetrical features of the Mochica vase below surely reflect a deliberate attempt to re-create the lopsided expression of a sufferer from cranial hemorrhage or some other paralyzing lesion. The wooden dance mask at right, from Liberia, is a most accurate picture of what happens to a face that is paralyzed on one side.

A disease that has always been rare, yet was occasionally portrayed in the ancient world, is acromegaly. It is a pituitary abnormality that produces a thickened, bulbous nose, coarse lips, prominent brow ridges, and great elongation of the jaw. The hands and feet of the sufferer sometimes enlarge, and his personality may undergo changes. The pharaoh Akhenaten undoubtedly had some such pituitary malfunction. The portrait opposite, which dates from about 1365 B.C., clearly emphasizes the exceptional length of his lower jaw.

Later rulers of Egypt were also afflicted with acromegaly. The Ptolemies were Macedonian Greeks who ruled Egypt from the conquest of Alexander in 323 B.C. until the death of Cleopatra in 30 B.C. From their portrait coins, as well as from the historical record, we can see that for three hundred years this intensely inbred family repeatedly produced persons with this disorder. Ptolemy I Soter, the first of the line, had prominent brow ridges, an enlarged nose and lips, and a heavy, jutting jaw, all realistically reproduced on the coin opposite.

The nicknames of later rulers hint at abnormalities. A grandson of Ptolemy VI Philometer became Antiochus VIII of Syria. Does his nickname, Grypus, "hooknose," mean that he, too, was a victim of acromegaly? His brother was called Physkon, "the sausage," which was perhaps a reference to the obesity caused by endocrine malfunction.

Another glandular disorder that shows up in art is goiter, an enlargement of the thyroid gland. Some forms of it are closely linked to environmental factors, especially the chemistry of the available drinking water, and Pliny the Elder was only one of several classical writers to observe that certain localities had a high incidence of the disease. Greece and Asia Minor were two of these, and the coins of many of the major cities—Corinth, Seleucia, Athens—occasionally show a ruler with a swollen neck. In Africa the disease also appears. The carving opposite, from the Babwende tribe of the lower Congo, is an accurate representation of goiter. The Mochica pottery jug, from the Chicama valley in Peru, takes the form of a very dumpy little boy. It may also represent some form of thyroid or pituitary malfunction.

What flesh is heir to...

What people wore, or didn't wear, is often detectable from their skeletons. The early Saxons apparently wore some sort of tightly laced buskin, for evidence of inflammation is frequently found on their shinbones. Misshapen toe bones are one of the commoner skeletal defects of our own day—usually traceable to the vanity of squeezing a size seven foot into a size five shoe. Such defects are occasionally found in Saxon foot bones, so we can assume that they, too, must have worn tight boots at times. By contrast, foot defects rarely occur among the dynastic Egyptians, presumably because they habitually went barefoot. The Mochica

Indian shown on the vase above also went barefoot, but with less happy results. Parasites have invaded the soles of his feet, causing severe infection.

Another form of infection that was, and is, common in Africa and South America is trachoma, which causes blindness. The wooden mask at the top of the page, from Nigeria, is used in a mime. It shows a blind man trying to find his mouth with a stick. A carving like this leaves no doubt about the emotional impact of such an abnormality on the people who observe it. The Mochica vase below it has also been given an expressive blind face.

The queen of the land of Punt, above right, is surely suffering from something, but palaeopathologists have not been able to agree on a diagnosis. This relief, found in the temple of Queen Hatshepsut at Deir el-Bahri, depicts the reigning queen of a country that Hatshepsut visited about 1500 B.C. A reasonable guess is that the lady had congenital dislocation of the hips, a condition that causes protruding buttocks.

The disease depicted on the opposite page is readily diagnosed. This Egyptian stela of the New Kingdom portrays a temple official named Ruma. The shriveling of his right leg was probably caused by poliomyelitis. His disability did not prevent him from rising to high estate, and he performs his priestly duties with serenity.

Disease is mankind's unwelcome companion. Surprisingly enough, in this great age of science and medical innovation, man is still heir to all the fleshly ills portrayed in these ancient works of art and—to some extent—to most of the diseases of his ancestors.

Amulets or case studies?

Artists of ancient Mexico seem almost to have been obsessed with illness. The figurines on this page, from the collection of Dr. Kurt Stavenhagen in Mexico City, are pre-Columbian grave of-

Mochica vase from Peru

ferings that describe medically interesting cases. The man clutching his neck is suffering from tuberculosis of the spine. The figure of a pregnant woman is one of many that show various stages of pregnancy and birth. A mother's concern for her sick child is movingly portrayed in clay. The Indians must have undergone the ravages of malnutrition: one of the two victims shown here is starving to death. In addition there were less tractable diseases. The skin lesions sustained by the unfortunate at far right are thought to illustrate the final phase of syphilis or cancer. The visored bed or stretcher may show a method of strapping down a violent patient. Were these figurines supposed to ward off disease? Probably not. From the accuracy of their detail they could have been used by doctors for teaching, diagnosis, and treatment. Similar diagnostic figures have long been used by Chinese physicians when treating modest women.

IV. Recovering the Past

In this section you are invited to observe archaeologists at work. We begin with the article by Freeman and Echegaray discussing "Stone Age Burials at Cueva Morín" in Spain. It is a remarkable tale of international and interdisciplinary cooperation involving the excavation and preservation of two ritually mutilated and buried Upper Paleolithic figures whose remains had vanished long ago but had left behind exact replicas of themselves in the form of "soil shadows." By way of contrast, Stancheva's article "The Enigma of the Thracians" shows how a wide range of historical and archaeological information can be brought to bear in attempting to reconstruct the lifeways of historically known, though marginal, peoples.

Mulloy is faced with an even more difficult problem in "Easter Island." He is attempting to reconstruct the cultural and social history of a people very nearly obliterated by European slave raiders in the nineteenth century. However, not all the troubles on this island were caused by outsiders. It appears that the native population's great success at plant cultivation led to drastic population increases that induced a period of chronic internecine warfare by the seventeenth century. Those of you who have read Thor Heyerdahl's somewhat sensational *Aku-Aku* will find a more plausible treatment of Easter Island's history here.

We end this section with Marx' account of an impressive reclamation project in the domain of historical anthropology. "The Drowned City of Port Royal" was for the four decades before June 7, 1692 the dominant port and trading center in the Caribbean. On that day it was hit by three terrible earth tremors and then smashed by a tidal wave—and 90 percent of the city vanished beneath the sea. Using innovative underwater reclamation techniques and historical records, researchers are able to identify possessions of specific individuals and locate shops and other buildings that now rest in silt at the bottom of the sea.

This section is intended to give you some idea of the impressively broad range of problems that archaeologists tackle, and also to indicate some of the very difficult conditions under which they work.

14

Stone Age Burials at Cueva Morín

L. G. Freeman and J. González Echegaray

Most prehistorians spend the majority of their research time excavating and analyzing the debris produced by daily activities in the past in an attempt to discover just what those activities were. Prehistorians whose study is the Paleolithic period seldom encounter human remains; the age and condition of the sediments containing Old Stone Age occupations have frequently resulted in the destruction of most of the organic remains they once held, and apparently many Paleolithic societies disposed of their dead in special ways or in special places that are as yet undiscovered. If human remains of the Paleolithic period are not at all abundant, deliberate human burials (involving the intentional disposal of a corpse or its parts in a specially prepared area of a site—as in a grave or under a stone cairn) are so very rare that only a handful of prehistorians have ever had the opportunity to excavate one in an entire lifetime of research. We are among the fortunate few.

The burial complex we discovered at Cueva Morín, in the province of Santander in northern Spain, yielded a great wealth of scientific information. What is more, its extraordinary state of preservation—calling for rather unorthodox techniques of excavation and analysis and unusual conservation procedures—involved us with the Smithsonian Institution in a unique program of interdisciplinary cooperation on an international scale. That program has been far more successful than we ever imagined it could be. The story of the Morín burials illustrates nicely several dimensions of modern research in prehistory, and has an added degree of interest provided by the

unique nature of the finds and the operations that were employed to study and preserve them.

The discovery of the burial complex in the Morín cave was a happy and completely unexpected by-product of a research project designed to recover other kinds of evidence about the prehistoric past. Our choice of a site for investigation and our research objectives were a result of several years of previous planning. We selected Cueva Morín from a long list of previously discovered sites in northern Spain. Like so many other caves in the area, Morín was first recognized as a prehistoric human occupation site during the early part of the century; in fact extensive archaeological excavations were undertaken there by Father J. Carballo and Count de la Vega del Sella from 1917 to 1920, and the results of their studies were published in two detailed reports. Those monographs revealed Morín to be one of the most important Paleolithic localities in Spain. First of all, it contained substantial Middle Paleolithic (Mousterian) occupation levels (probably dating from more than 40,000 years ago); next, the site had a complex stratigraphic sequence bracketing several stages of Upper Paleolithic industrial development (Aurignacian, Perigordian, Solutrean, Magdalenian, and Azilian levels were recognized); and last, the earliest Upper Paleolithic horizon seemed to the earlier excavators to have many characteristics held over from the earlier Mousterian industrial stages. It was thought to be a level of transition between the Mousterian and Aurignacian complexes. A test trench revealed that the work conducted at Morín during the early part of the century had left a major part of the occupation levels undisturbed. Reexcavation of this important site began in 1966, but that year Freeman could only participate very briefly in the work, which was directed by the Santander Provincial Museum. In 1968 and 1969, financed

L. G. Freeman is an associate professor of anthropology at the University of Chicago. J. González Echegaray is vice director of the Provincial Museum of Prehistory and Archaeology, Santander, Spain.

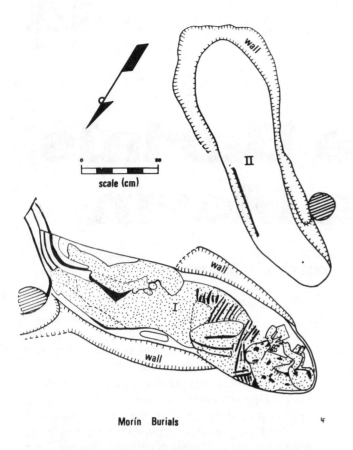

scale (cm)

Morín   Burials

Schematic illustration of the Morín I and II graves and their contents. No body was found in Morín II. Morín I held the three dimensional cast of a cadaver. The small ungulate deposited atop the head of Morín I, the animal ribs over the foot of the trench, and the offering pits near the foot of each grave are indicated.

by grants from the National Science Foundation, the Ford Foundation, and the Patronato de las Cuevas Prehistóricas de la Provincia de Santander, excavations at Morín were undertaken under our joint direction.

The selection of the site and the choice of problems for investigation dictated the location of our excavations within the cave. We hoped to verify and refine the published Upper Paleolithic stratigraphy, so Echegaray's part of our field crew concentrated on an area where those strata were preserved and accessible—in the witness section left by our predecessors along the cave's southwest wall. We hoped to find large horizontal expanses of Mousterian occupation debris—tools and trash covered up by sediments in the very places where they were abandoned by the cave occupants—so Freeman and his group worked mostly in the central and eastern parts of the cave, where our predecessors had removed most of the Upper Paleolithic strata. The possibility of discovering Paleolithic burials played no part in our plans—it never seriously entered our minds.

As it happens, we recovered the information needed for the problems we had set out to solve, and a great deal

more. Not one but several Mousterian levels were discovered, and in one the cave inhabitants had built a partition of limestone blocks dividing the cave into two main areas where different activities were undertaken. The same level provided a completely unexpected collection of tools made of bone instead of stone. With the worked bone are some pieces with deliberate linear engravings that seem to be among the earliest "art" in the world (apparently nonrepresentational, by the way). These bits of evidence add immensely to our appreciation of the intellectual capabilities of Neanderthal man.

We also recovered the facts needed to scotch the idea of a Moustero-Aurignacoid level at Morín completely. The curious transitional horizon noted by earlier workers was simply a result of bad excavation, mixing distinct Mousterian and Aurignacian levels. More important, we found the first *in situ* Chatelperronian level known from Iberia. In fact the site yielded an astonishingly complete sequence of Chatelperronian and very early Aurignacian industrial development: The sequence is not represented elsewhere in Spain and is as complete as any in France for the period it covers. Any one of these finds, taken alone, would have made us feel that our research time at Morín had been more than adequately rewarded. As it happens, among our "accidental" finds was a very spectacular discovery that caused considerable stir in the press in the summer of 1969—the burial complex that has been conserved at the Smithsonian.

We had just begun work in the "Mousterian sector" of the cave when the first of the related discoveries was made. Cutting cleanly into the tan Mousterian sediment was a large rectangular depression filled with dark organic earth. In places the fill was layered horizontally into almost paper-thin compacted lenses that yielded hundreds

The partly destroyed mounds atop the Morín I (left) and Morín II (right) graves.

The Morín I burial seen from the south. Scale in cm.

of fragments of worked stone. Inside the pit and against one wall there was a fireplace. All the characteristics of this structure suggest that what we found was the dugout substructure of a substantial dwelling or shelter within the cave. The stone tools from the dwelling pertain to a very early stage of the Aurignacian complex, which we have called Archaic Aurignacian because it is not quite like the earliest classical Aurignacian in France. Further excavations revealed a line of post holes extending from the southeast corner of the dwelling toward the cave's interior. Eventually a total of four post-holes were revealed in this alignment, which seems to have formed part of a screening wall separating the structure and the living area in this level from a mortuary precinct. The Aurignacian builder even left the marks of his digging implement—a simple pointed tool like the "digging sticks" still in use by some of the world's peoples today—in the cave earth.

Toward the end of the 1969 field season, our crew began to clear what we thought would prove to be two more post holes near the alignment found in 1968. To our great surprise, these turned out to be elongated trenches, both of which had been capped by low earthen mounds. From the size and shape of the trenches, it was immediately suspected that they might prove to be human graves. The excavation of Paleolithic burials is such a delicate process that we felt it was more responsibility than we could reasonably ask our assistants to share, so the two of us proceeded alone with work on the trenches from that point on. Each of us concentrated on the excavation of one grave. It took several days to clear away the mounds and record their contents. Echegaray, working with the smaller of the two graves, finished this preliminary work first and began immediately on the trench fill. The slow and painstaking task of excavation of the smaller trench did not reward us with the discovery of human remains. It contained only dark organic earth and patches of black buttery sediment. The bottom of the pit was striped with the marks of a digging stick like those discovered the pre-

vious year. Even though this evidence was extremely important, we both felt somewhat disappointed.

Then, while he was clearing the fill from the larger grave, Freeman's knife met an obstruction in the trench. Soon this was found to be one of a series of parallel ridges of dense earth. At first they looked so much like the ridges between the digging stick marks recovered earlier that we thought they must be more of the same. As excavation progressed, however, the ridges turned into a complex pattern quite unlike digging-stick marks. Flecks of recognizable, severely decayed bone began to appear in some of the ridges. The pattern looked suspiciously like the upper part of a human body—a flexed arm and a chest with flesh sunken into grooves between the ribs. In fact that is what it proved to be. We had found human remains, but not in the form we had expected. Instead of the skeleton we were prepared to find, a three-dimensional "soil shadow" or pseudomorph of the dead man lay revealed. As the flesh decayed, the hollow it left filled in with fine compact sediment, forming an earthen cast of the body that showed the shape of muscles and flesh "in the round."

Once the upper surface of the figure had been completely cleared, one could see that the dead man had been placed in the grave on his left side. His body was extended but the legs were slightly bent, and the left leg lay forward of the right one. The left arm was flexed tightly upward, bringing the hand up in front of the neck. The head was concealed from view by another interesting pseudomorph, which proved to be the cast of a small hoofed animal placed whole into the grave atop the human burial in a curled-up position, front legs tucked between the hind

The mold of a small hoofed mammal, forelegs tucked between its hindlegs, was found atop the head of Morín I.

legs, the way sheep are still trussed for market. From the small size of the creature, it could be a fawn or perhaps a young chamois or ibex. If it was a full-grown animal, it was most probably a roe deer. Perhaps this offering was placed in the grave to ensure an adequate supply of game or food for the hunter's spirit. The animal offering has maintained its original form considerably better than the hunter, whose body was squashed out of shape by the weight of the earth atop him.

The dead man's feet were covered by a pseudo-morph made up of several parallel ridges. We think this may have been a slab of ribs from a large game animal (an aurochs, or a horse, perhaps) included as another offering. We had a vague sense that the legs were too short for the body, but since the lower legs and feet were concealed by the grave offering the feeling remained insubstantial as we worked in the cave. Outside the trench in front of the lower legs of the dead man, we found a small pit filled with bits of burned bone and fragments of red coloring material (ochre). The pit communicated with the grave by means of a narrow channel. During excavation of the mound we found numerous patches and flecks of powdered red ochre in the earth. The remnants of the mound atop the smaller trench had also been flecked with ochre, and exactly such a pit as that just described was linked to one end of that trench too. These parallels strongly suggest that the small trench (Morín II) was in fact a grave like the larger one (Morín I), found empty because the body (probably that of a juvenile) decayed completely before a pseudomorph was formed. The mound atop Morín I provided one other interesting discovery—after the mound was completed, the cave occupants built a small fire in a saucer-shaped depression atop it. Perhaps this fire was another part of the elaborate burial ritual the Morín Aurignacians practiced.

Once it was certain that we had discovered human burials at Cueva Morín, we notified the police and the scientific authorities, as was our obligation. Our announcement brought crowds of reporters and visitors in addition to the necessary officials. We had to take elaborate precautions to see to it that the public could satisfy its curiosity without damaging the burials or the site, or hurting themselves in any way, and of course this meant some curtailment of our operations. However, among the visitors were several interested anthropologists, and without the intervention of one of them there would be no more to the story.

The Morín I pseudomorph is made of fragile sediment: It is not hard enough to be durable. We had not considered the possibility that it could be permanently preserved. With the means at our disposal that would have been out of the question. We intended to excavate the find completely, taking extensive samples and recording the appearance of the burial at each step by means of drawings, photographs, and motion pictures. To get to the under surface of the burial, we intended gradually to peel away the upper surface. When finished, we would have excavated and documented the burial more carefully than any previously recovered Paleolithic interment, but the process would have involved the total destruction of the find.

One of our visitors, Professor Sol Tax of the Smithsonian's Center for the Study of Man, saw the burial and put matters in an entirely different light. To him the find seemed far too important to destroy. After all, the facilities needed to preserve the burial were available somewhere in the world, and if we could bring those facilities together with the burial our problems would be solved. At first we were very skeptical about that possibility. Preservation of the burial inside the cave was absolutely out of the question. Even if we could have moved the burial to a large city like Madrid or Barcelona, the technicians, materials, and conditions necessary for its preservation would have to be found and brought to the specimen or created on the spot. Even if we found the right people and the right material for the job, we could think of no one with experience in consolidating such a large specimen. The engineer of the Santander Provincial Deputation, the late García Lorenzo, visited the site and assured us that the burial probably *could* be removed from the cave *en bloc*. The block of earth we would have to deal with would weigh nearly two tons, but there were facilities at hand that were adequate to attempt such a move if conservation elsewhere were only feasible.

Fortunately Tax had gone on to an international congress, where he discussed the find with Smithsonian physical anthropologists Lawrence Angel and T. Dale Stewart. Together they came to the conclusion that perhaps the only institution in the Western world with adequate space, facilities, and material, and a staff of experts fully familiar with the problems of conserving a find as large and delicate as our burial, was the Smithsonian it-

The underside of the grave was excavated in a specially controlled climate at the Smithsonian Institution. The football-shaped cast at the lower left is the head of Morín I, and the legs of Morín III are shown at the top of the grave, just right of center. Parallel stripes on the left side of Morín I show that the weight of the tomb forced the flesh into furrows left by a digging stick.

self. They then placed the question of using the facilities of the Smithsonian for the attempt before S. Dillon Ripley, secretary of that institution. The secretary gave them the go-ahead, generously offering to arrange for air transportation of the burial from Santander to Washington and back, and to undertake the conservation of the find as an act of international scientific collaboration. It would then fall to the Patronato de las Cuevas Prehistóricas to move the burial from the cave to the airport in Santander. Officials of the Patronato accepted the secretary's offer with enthusiasm, and we began preparations to remove the burial from the site.

The delicacy of the specimen required elaborate precautions. First the exposed surface of the burial was covered with a thick layer of quarry sand and a sheet of plaster of paris. This served to protect the surface during subsequent operations. Then a deep trench was dug all around the grave, isolating it in a solid block separated from the surrounding sediment. A technical crew from a boat-building concern owned by Angel Bedía then encased the block in a closefitting plastic and fiberglass box. The Bolado Brothers metalworking enterprise provided us with a thin steel plate and a pair of heavy mechanical jacks; we laid the steel sheet flat and gradually forced it to slice through the block. The plate was then firmly united to the fiberglass box, serving as its bottom. Supporting members were welded to the plate, and a pair of steel side rails, like runners, completed the transformation of the encased burial into a sort of sled. This sled, placed on rollers, was winched along a miniature "railway" leading up an earthen ramp to the cave mouth. Then the sled was lowered from the cave to a platform halfway down the hillside so that a crane could transfer it to a truck. It was then taken to the Velarde Museum, close to the airport, for storage until air transport could be arranged. The process, as we have just described it, sounds simple—actually, of course, the delicate task of moving an unimaginably bulky specimen like the Morín burial was terribly laborious and complicated. It was some time before we could really bring ourselves to believe that the move had at last been accomplished—and without mishap.

In the meantime Secretary Ripley had contacted former U.S. Air Force Secretary Seamans about flying the find to Washington. Thanks to his good offices and those of Deputy Undersecretary Hilbert, a C-130 transport belonging to the 36th Tactical Air Squadron was diverted to Santander to bring the burial to Andrews Air Force Base. The squadron commander, Lt. Col. Gordon Mulvey, took personal charge of the flight. Owing to the care he and members of the plane's crew exercised, the burial arrived in Washington in perfect shape, despite unexpected rough weather in the crossing.

When the case arrived at the Smithsonian, it had to be subjected to a long conditioning before we could open it. The climate in Washington in spring is drier than that in the cave in Santander, and if we had simply cut the

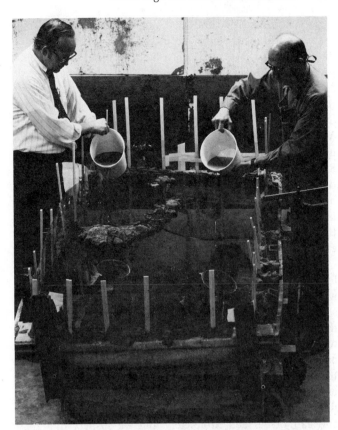

Smithsonian specialists embed the underside of the grave in transparent plastic. (Smithsonian photograph)

package open immediately the burial might have crumbled to bits. At the Smithsonian it was first stored in a sealed room whose climate was constantly controlled in order to keep the humidity above 90 percent. The case was kept in the climate-controlled room for about two months before it was opened, and all the remaining stages of excavation were performed under the same controlled conditions. The box was opened in our presence (Echegaray flew to the U.S. from Spain especially to help in this operation), and after it had been cleaned the burial was shown to a group of prehistoric archeologists at a conference on the Morín work sponsored by the Wenner-Gren Foundation.

The problem of preserving the burial fell to the lot of John Widener of the Smithsonian's Office of Exhibits Programs. His first operation was to stabilize the upper surface of the burial. Then silicon rubber was poured over the pseudomorph to form a mold from which plastic replicas could be made. The rubber also served to cushion the burial later. A new protective case was built over the rubber mold, and the burial was turned upside down. After the steel plate had been cut away from the plastic case it was lifted free, and the job of excavating the underside of the burial began. Since Freeman could work at this task only when his other duties at the University of Chicago would permit, this operation proceeded sporadically for over a year. During this phase of work we were astonished to find that the grave contained the pseudomorph of the hips and thighs of a third burial antedating Morín I. Morín III must have been buried for some time when Morín I was interred, and the small grave excavated by Echegaray, Morín II, actually cut through this earlier burial, destroying it from the midsection up. Since the hips and legs of Morín III were lower than the Morín I burial, Freeman found them before he found the underside of the pseudomorph we had recognized in Spain. At first he thought they might be part of the body of Morín I, and since they crossed the grave at an angle, he was concerned that our earlier reconstruction might have been in error. However, the body of Morín I eventually appeared above the enigmatic legs, and the true explanation for their position became clear.

On the underside of the Morín I burial, color differences between the body and the earth filling the grave were quite striking. As predicted, the left arm was flexed sharply up before the chest like the right. The outline of the shoulder, back, and chest was clearly visible, but where the head should have been there was nothing. The cast of the severed head was identified below the rest of the body, well in front of the hands. There was still enough decayed bone present in the cast so that it fluoresced brightly under ultraviolet light. The lower legs still cannot be seen completely, but we suspect that they too must have been mutilated, since the grave is short enough so that it would not hold them otherwise. The feet of the Morín III cast had been cut off above the ankle, and the legs were charred. We think that this was done deliberately to both burials. All the evidence suggests that the Morín burials were mutilated after death: We think we may even have found the stone knife used in the decapitation of Morín I in the grave next to his neck. Similar postmortem mutilation of the dead is practiced among some living societies to prevent the spirit of the deceased from returning to haunt the community. The Morín I burial would make a formidable ghost—Smithsonian anthropologists have estimated his stature at well over six feet.

Once the underside of the burial had been studied and samples taken for analysis, the serious work of conservation started. Widener tested several techniques before finally deciding to attempt complete embedment of the specimen in a transparent block of plastic. First another rubber mold of the lower surface was poured and removed from the find. Then Widener built a retaining dam around the specimen and began pouring the clear liquid over its surface in thin layers. The great danger at this point was that the reaction of the plastic as it hardens generates some heat; if it was poured in too large quantities, the "exotherm" produced could crack the block and damage the burial, and at the very least this would have rendered the specimen useless for exhibition. Since each layer took some time to harden, the process of pouring the embedment on one side of the burial, turning the burial back over to its normal position, and embedding

The preserved burial on display at the National Museum of Natural History. Suspended above the original are plastic replicas of its upper and lower surfaces. The embedded burial is mounted on a stand telling the story of the find in Spanish and English. (Smithsonian photograph)

the upper side required more months of painstaking labor. Finally the burial was completely embedded. As far as we are aware, the Morín burial is the world's largest plastic embedment; its successful production is a remarkable testimonial to the ability of Widener and his staff of specialists. The huge plastic block was the focal point of a special Smithsonian exhibit.

In 1972, after the Smithsonian display, the Aurignacian hunter was returned to Santander, where the Patronato prepared a final resting place for it in a special museum building adjacent to the famous painted cave of Altamira. A replica is on permanent exhibit at the Spanish National Archeological Museum in Madrid.

The specimens are not intended solely as exhibits; interesting though they may be to the public, their real importance is as scientific documents. Their preservation ensures that the story they can tell will be accessible to future generations of students and professional historians. We hope that they will serve to remind our generation of the many different kinds of evidence about the past that can be recovered by proper excavation, given good conditions of preservation. Perhaps one day in the future, when even better techniques of excavation and analysis have been developed, a scientist much better prepared than ourselves will open the plastic block to obtain much more information from the pseudomorph it contains than we could.

And we sincerely hope that as long as the burial and the replicas endure they will serve to remind us all of the advantages of scientific collaboration on an international scale. Without the cooperation of governments, institutions, and scientists from many nations, those precious documents would not exist.

Further Reading

Our excavations at Cueva Morín are the subject of two lengthy monographs in Spanish:

J. González, Echegaray, et al.

> 1971 *Cueva Morín: excavaciones 1966–1968* Patronato de las Cuevas Prehistóricas de la Provincia de Santander
> 1973 *Cueva Morín: excavaciones 1969* Patronato de las Cuevas Prehistóricas de la Provincia de Santander

We published a preliminary note about the burials in English as well:

Freeman, L. G., and J. González Echegaray

> 1970 "Aurignacian Structural Features and Burials at Cueva Morín (Santander, Spain)," *Nature* 226:722–726

15

THE ENIGMA OF THE THRACIANS

Tomb discoveries on the plains of Bulgaria shed new light on a civilization of hunters and goldsmiths dating back 3,000 years

Right, a hunting scene decorating part of a link from a Thracian silver-gilt belt of the 4th century B.C. The chase figures prominently in the decorative art of the Thracians, who were great horsemen and hunters. Unearthed near Letnitsa (central Bulgaria) the complete belt link is inset with pearls forming three panels. In this one the archer's conical cap and fringed tunic and the attitude of the horseman urging his mount to jump recall similar figures discovered in Persia. The Thracian craftsman who made the belt during the 4th century B. C. may have drawn inspiration from Achaemenid art of the same period. Left, a silver knee-piece embellished with a human face (350-300 B.C.) found in a Bulgarian burial mound at Vratza. When pursuing dangerous game such as wolves and bears, Thracian hunters wore protective armour including knee-pieces of this type.

Photos © Sofia Press, Bulgaria

by *Magdalina Stancheva*

THE Thracians and their culture pose one of the most fascinating enigmas in the early history of Europe. Today their ancient territories lie within the frontiers of Bulgaria, Greece and Turkey-in-Europe; and though the Thracians bequeathed their cultural heritage to Europe, they were bound to Asia by strong and abiding links.

Mention of the Thracians may bring to mind the name of Spartacus, who led a great slave uprising against ancient Rome, or passages from Homer's *Iliad*. It may also conjure up an image of gold treasures or of a region in south-eastern Europe.

As early as the 13th century B.C. the Thracians crossed the narrow strip of water separating them from Asia Minor and indisputable traces of their presence have been found in the earliest archaeological layers at the

MAGDALINA STANCHEVA *is one of the leading archaeologists and philologists of Bulgaria. Head of the Archaeological Department of the Historical Museum in Sofia for the past twenty years, she has carried out investigations at all the major archaeological sites in her country. For her pioneer work on Serdica (the ancient name for Sofia) she was recently awarded the Sofia Prize.*

site of Troy. In this way they occupied areas of contact between the two continents and remained open to influences from both East and West.

Answers to some of the mysteries surrounding the Thracians are today being found in the burial and settlement mounds that dot the Bulgarian landscape. Archaeologists excavating the many cultural layers of the settlement mounds have uncovered strata dating back to the Neolithic and Bronze Ages and found apparent evidence of links with Thracian and pre-Thracian tribes. Much painstaking work remains to be done, however, before it is possible to determine the date from which the inhabitants of these settlements can be considered with certainty as Thracians.

Altogether, over 15,000 mounds have been charted and listed by Bulgarian archaeologists and are now protected by law as important cultural relics. What do they hide? Some may be princely tombs rich with priceless vessels and jewellery; others may be soldiers' graves, containing merely an urn full of ashes and a bent iron spear. There is work enough for generations of archaeologists.

But it is not always the biggest mound that conceals the most valuable treasure. Two years ago, during the construction of a canal near Sofia, the scoop of a mechanical shovel bit deep into a slight rise in the ground

and brought up in its load of earth a clay urn, a copper cauldron and a huge gold bowl. With its exquisite shape and ornamental flutes and spirals, the gold bowl, dating back to just over one thousand years B.C., was clearly the work of a skilled goldsmith.

Prior to this discovery the only known gold vessels from this period of Thracian history were those found near the village of Vulchitrun, in northern Bulgaria, and known as "The Vulchitrun Treasure". More than 14 kilogrammes of gold had gone into the making of these vessels of various shapes and sizes, which it seems were intended for ritual use, possibly in connexion with sun-worship.

From about 500 B.C. the Thracian principalities flourished, and many of the Thracian tribes united to form the powerful kingdom of Odrysae. They traded with Greece and with the Greek colonies established along the shores of the Aegean and the Black Sea. Greek influence made itself felt among the ruling classes. But it was a two-way traffic and Thracian culture in turn left its imprint on the arts and crafts and even the cultural life of the Greeks.

One example of this was the spread of the cult of the god Dionysius which was rooted in Thracian religion. Another is the tragic story of the legendary Thracian poet and musician, Orpheus, which became a familiar theme in Greek and Roman poetry.

In those prosperous times, Seuthopolis, the capital of the kingdom of Odrysae, named after its ruler Seuthes, was built on the model of the Greek towns in the valley of the river Tundja. Here, where the king's palace was built, archaeologists found an inscription in Greek giving the name of the town, among the ruins that had lain undisturbed for centuries beneath the soil of the Valley of the Roses.

Two other magnificent examples of Thracian art were also discovered in the Valley of the Roses: the Panagyurishté treasure and the Kazanluk tomb, burial place of a Thracian chieftain.

The Kazanluk tomb is a small building with a narrow passage and a round chamber covered with a cone-shaped dome (see "Unesco Courier", June 1968). The walls are covered with some of the most perfect paintings in Europe, the finest to come down to us from the fourth century B.C.

In the centre is depicted the classical scene of a funeral feast with the chieftain and his wife seated at a well-laden table. The wife has placed her hand in that of the Thracian prince, her head is bent, her exquisite face expresses grief at the parting. Around them are servants bringing gifts, and leading

This three-headed serpent, left, is one of the fabulous beasts that decorate silver-gilt plaques, dating back to the 4th century B.C., found at the village of Letnitsa, northern Bulgaria. Other plaques bear scenes of everyday life. Measuring between 4 and 8 cm., each plaque has a ring on the back of which it was attached to the straps of a horse's harness.

the dead chieftain's favourite horses. The atmosphere of solemnity is softened by these touches of intimacy. Up above, in the dome, four-in-hand chariots are being raced.

The paintings reveal the hand of a highly trained and skilful artist, possibly a Greek, but the spirit and the content of the scenes depict Thracian customs and the life of a princely Thracian home.

The set of gold wine vessels, or rhyta, found near Panagyurishté is another example of the penetration of

Greek art. The rhyta are made in a variety of forms: the heads of women or animals, amphoras with mythological scenes, the forequarters of a goat. The flat cup (Phiale) is ornamented with concentric circles of small negro heads in relief (see photo page 19).

This exquisite work was made in the city of Lampsakos on the coast of Asia Minor.

Many other masterpieces have been unearthed in recent years and named from the places where they were found: the Loukovit, Letnitsa, Vratsa and Stara Zagora treasures. Gold or silver, they were almost all made by Thracian goldsmiths.

Many of the objects found in tombs were made to ornament the trappings of horses, for Thracian funeral customs included the burial of the dead man's horse in the same mound. A Thracian warrior's proudest possessions were his horse and the arms he bore, and their decorations were true works of art.

Figures of animals usually formed part of the decoration. Skilful stylization transformed their strained and contorted bodies into intricate entwined ornaments—extraordinary combinations of four-footed animals, birds and reptiles.

This art, which was possibly alien and incomprehensible to the Greeks, was the product of centuries of development, during which its forms attained a remarkable degree of stylization, without, however, losing their initial traits. Some researchers have recently looked for the sources of this art in pre-Achaemenid Iran, where new finds from Luristan show interesting similarities with those of Bulgaria.

Man, the warrior and mounted hunter, is the main subject of the decorative plaques found near the village of Letnitsa. In contrast to the animal forms, the human figures appear rather stiff and clumsy. The engraver shows little concern for proportion, but carefully records details of the chain-mail and weapons, and notably the face, which is large and expressive. Human and horses' heads, unconnected with the rest of the composition, are boldly placed in the spaces around the figures.

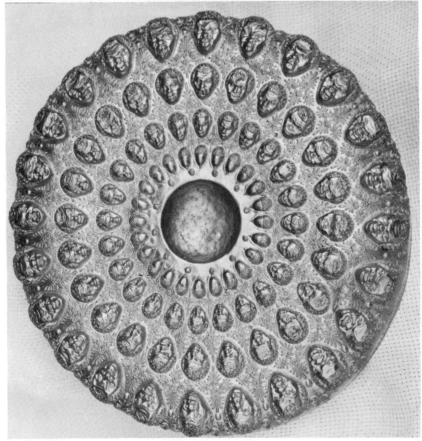

One of the finest items in the treasure trove discovered at Panagyurishté, 70 km. south-east of Sofia, is this 4th-3rd century B.C. gold libation bowl. Detail shows the outside of the bowl richly decorated with three concentric circles of negro heads and a circle of acorns. These motifs are repeated on the inside of the bowl. Photo below shows complete bowl (measuring 3.5 cm. high by 25 cm. across) which was fashioned by craftsmen of Lampsakos, one of the Greek colonies that flourished on the coast of the Sea of Marmara.

THE variety and abundance of finds in the tombs is linked with the Thracian attitude towards death. The Greek historian, Herodotus, (5th century B.C.) described the Thracian custom of lamenting over a new-born baby, but of bidding farewell to the dead with feasting and merrymaking.

This attitude to life and death must have expressed the hardships of everyday life, which led the Thracians to the ritual rejection of life and to the concept of death as a deliverance.

Having become a deeply-rooted tradition, this attitude accounts for the extraordinary magnificence of the funerals of the rich. No less than five richly adorned chariots together with the horses required by the ritual were found buried near the tomb of their master in a mound not far from the town of Stara Zagora.

In the early years of our era the hand of Roman rule was laid heavily on this martial and freedom-loving people. The prolonged resistance to Roman conquest was marked by acts of desperate courage, which we learn about from Roman authors. Far from his native land (today in south-western Bulgaria) Spartacus the Thracian became the leader of the greatest rebellion of slaves in history.

But in time many Thracians joined the Roman army and administration, while the nobles preserved their privileges and their estates, as inscriptions on the Thracian villa-castle near Stara Zagora and burial finds of the Roman period affirm.

Yet the spirit of Thracian culture survived, and although luxurious temples to the gods of the Graeco-Roman Pantheon were built, shrines of Heros, the Horseman, the beloved and most honoured Thracian deity, are still found scattered over the Thracian lands.

Like his worshippers, Heros was a hunter and warrior. He is associated with the powers of life as well as the underworld and he was the god of both fertility and death. Bendis, the forest huntress, who is identified with Artemis-Diana, the huntress, is Heros' feminine incarnation.

In the following centuries the Thracians had to endure the invasions of the Goths, the Visigoths and the Huns. They withdrew many times to the hills and again returned to the ravaged

A lovely example of Thracian art, this 16 cm. high, stylized stag of the 7th century B.C. was found at Sevlievo (Bulgaria). The points of the antlers are carved in the form of birds' heads.

plains, into which, in the sixth century, the Slavs gradually penetrated and settled. They were the last wave of the Great Migration of the Peoples. The surviving Thracians merged into the new ethnic community formed here by the Slavs and the Proto-Bulgarians.

Today, after 1,300 years, a distant echo of the Thracian past is still heard in Bulgarian folklore, in those special features which distinguish it from the folklore of the other Slav peoples, and which are rooted in the ancient history of present-day Bulgaria.

16

Easter Island

*Stark monuments and ruins that dot
the landscape tell of a complex culture, which once
flourished on this isolated Pacific island*

by William Mulloy

On Easter Sunday, 1722, a Dutch explorer, Jacob Roggeveen, landed on a remote volcanic island some 2,200 miles west of the South American coast. There, on the easternmost island of Polynesia, which he named Easter Island, the Dutchman found an advanced society suffering from violent internal conflict, its people living to a considerable extent among the ruins of their former spectacular achievements. Monumental stone statues had been pushed from their pedestals and lay broken, while the island inhabitants hid from one another in caves. Roggeveen was no doubt impressed by the huge sculptures and the other signs of an advanced civilization, but, like other European explorers who later visited Easter Island, he did not feel that the place had much economic potential and consequently assigned it no significance in his log.

So Easter Island, now well known for its gigantic, brooding statues, and for the mystery surrounding the origin and growth of its complex culture, was largely ignored for almost one hundred years. Then, in 1805 the schooner *Nancy*, out of New London, Connecticut, carried away twenty-two islanders for use as slaves, and the Western world realized that the island had economic possibilities that appealed to its value system. With time, the slave raids increased, and between 1859 and 1862, Peruvian raiders carried off about one thousand people to work at guano mining off the coast of Peru. As a result of a protest lodged by the Bishop of Tahiti, the few survivors of this crime were returned to Easter Island. But the returning islanders had contracted smallpox, and the introduction of this disease to the island all but annihilated the remaining inhabitants. Thus, the once high Easter Island culture, already torn by internal warfare, was dealt a death

blow by the slave raids. In 1877, a visiting Frenchman reported that only 111 islanders remained.

While the population of Easter Island has now increased to about a thousand individuals, the cultural collapse took with it most of the clues for answering a question of considerable importance to anthropology: How, on this remote ocean-bound island, had such an advanced society developed in the first place?

An elementary principle of culture growth, documented by countless examples, states that culture is largely a product of idea swapping. Complex civilizations have developed where large populations had outside contacts, and where advantage could be taken of ideas invented elsewhere. It is no accident that the first civilizations developed in southwestern Asia where Africa, Asia, and Europe meet. Conversely, the ultimate simplicity of human life is seen at the ends of the earth among such people as the Alacaluf and the Yahgan of Tierra del Fuego, the Bushmen of the Kalahari Desert, and the Tasmanians. These small groups live where foreign contacts have been rare and the flow of ideas sharply restricted.

Easter Island is one of the more isolated localities of the world. Surrounded by the sea, it is outside the range, so far as we know, of systematic two-way Polynesian voyages. It was probably discovered several

times by lost wanderers who could not return to their original homes. Although most of the culture, including the language, seems to be Polynesian, a few traits strongly suggest that American Indians may have made landings and settled on the island. But more important than their origin is the accomplishment of these fearless seamen after they arrived, for it stands as a real contradiction of the "idea swapping" philosophy of cultural development. Throughout their history these people could have received only minimal foreign stimulation beyond ideas brought with them. And with a population that could never have exceeded three or four thousand people, one would expect the most simple ways of life. Yet we find such hallmarks of cultural complexity as written texts not known to be related to any foreign script, a political structure capable of planning and co-ordinating public works, an organized priesthood, and a sophisticated interest in such celestial phenomena as the equinoxes and the solstices. In addition the islanders developed a remarkable religious building compulsion, which resulted in about a thousand statues, some of which weigh hundreds of tons, in addition to numerous other religious structures. All this on so small and remote an island understandably evokes genuine astonishment.

87

Seven statues, each weighing about sixteen tons, gaze from the restored altar of Ahu Akivi.

A reliable radiocarbon date of A.D. 857, ± 200 years, indicates that a human population had already arrived on the island during the ninth century. Since this date was obtained from a large statue-bearing altar unlikely to have been built among the first activities of new arrivals, it is probable that initial discovery occurred much earlier. The first immigrants certainly devoted many years exclusively to such basic problems as the development of food and shelter sources. Their economy was based on fishing and the cultivation of such crops as sweet potatoes, yams, bananas, sugar cane, taro, gourds, and the paper mulberry so useful for making tapa cloth. It is not known which of these were brought by the first

migrants, but all were in use at the time of first European contact. The chicken and the *kioe*, or Polynesian rat, were also present and used for food. The relative ease with which food crops can now be grown best explains the rapid development of what was to become by far the most spectacular religious building compulsion in all of Polynesia. This required an economy that permitted a good deal of leisure.

The scattered distribution of the religious structures indicates that the people were widely dispersed along the coasts and adjacent interior areas. Local traditions relate that the population was divided into semi-independent kin groups of some sort. Each group seems to have had one or more religious structures, usually large open-air altars. These were variants of the well-known Polyne-

sian marae, locally called *ahu*. Although they varied greatly, the typical form was a narrow dry masonry platform, at times as much as 650 feet long and 16 feet high, which sometimes had an elevated central section and lateral wings. This platform usually had a sloping paved ramp built against one side. An artificially flattened plaza, where religious ceremonies were held, frequently faced the ramp. Beyond this was a row of long, narrow houses shaped like overturned canoes, where, according to tradition, members of the priesthood lived. These had thatched roofs and foundations of large, precisely cut and fitted basalt blocks, which supported the superstructure. Entrances were lateral and opened on a crescent-shaped area paved with large, rounded beach boulders, which formed a kind of porch. Some *ahu* platforms were of relatively crude uncut masonry, while others had gigantic blocks precisely cut and fitted in a technique strongly reminiscent of Inca masonry. Most *ahu* lay near shores with plazas on the inland side. Farther inland were domestic establishments and cultivated lands.

We do not know whether or not the earliest of the *ahu* had statues on their platforms, but at some point in their history statues began to be placed on them, singly or in rows, facing toward the plazas and thus usually away from the sea. Through time they increased in size and stylization until a highly uniform type developed. The classic statue reveals a human figure from the hips upward, with a protruding abdomen, arms held stiffly at the sides, and hands unnaturally turned toward each other. Heads are elongated, with pursed lips and prominent, usually slightly concave noses. Earlobes are extended and often carved to represent inserted earspools. Sometimes, large cylindrical headpieces, or topknots, made of separate stones were added. Some, perhaps all, statues were painted in several colors. Tradition relates that statues represented ancestors and had supernatural power.

Within this general conception, *ahu* ruins vary greatly in size and individual characteristics. Many have been rebuilt several times; innovations have been added; usually size and height have increased. Perhaps competition among kin groups produced the impressive structures. It is likely that size and ostentation of features increased with the numbers of the groups that owned them.

Although some statues were of stone obtained in a variety of locations, it would seem that early in the statue-building period a single source became dominant. This was the tuff from the interior and exterior south slope of the volcanic cone of Rano Raraku in the southeastern part of the island. Here intensive quarrying was done, with statues being completely carved while still attached to the rock. When detached they were lowered down the side of the volcano on their backs. Some were initially slid into prepared holes near the base

of the talus and erected in these. Here more than seventy still remain, of which the tallest is 37 feet high. Nearby are about thirty others lying mostly prone. These may have been tipped forward out of their holes in preparation for movement to *ahu* in other locations. Many others, presumably in the process of transportation, lie along roads in various parts of the island. Remains of extensive quarrying operations are also found above the talus slope, where at least two hundred statues can be seen in every stage of preparation.

Everywhere in the quarry are the discarded basalt chisels or picks that were used in carving. Some might have been laid down on the day quarrying ceased. The number of statues in various stages of completion suggests that many crews worked at the same time. It is not known whether each *ahu*-owning community sent its own representatives or whether the carving was in the hands of specialists, but in any event, a large proportion of the island's small population must have engaged in one or another aspect of the statue-building labor, judging from the amount of work that can now be found.

The largest statue known to have been moved to an *ahu* is almost 32 feet long and weighs about 90 tons—a formidable transportation problem, even in 1967. On some sort of sledge and with enough men such a statue might have been pulled by brute force. More ingenious methods were probably used, but we do not have unequivocal evidence as to what they were. Islanders have a simpler explanation—the statues walked to the *ahu* with the aid of magic.

The problem of erecting the statues on the *ahu* also required engineering skill. It is highly probable that statues were levered up in stages while a platform of stones and earth was gradually built under them. This platform was elevated toward the head until the statue could be tipped into place. In 1955, a statue about 16 feet high, weighing close to 27 tons, was re-erected in this way by Pedro Atan, an Easter Islander. Atan said he had been told of the method by his grand-

father and the latter's brother-in-law. In 1960, seven somewhat smaller statues were similarly re-erected as part of the restoration of *Ahu Akivi*.

The previously mentioned cylindrical topknots were carved from red scoria, which contrasted sharply with the gray tuff of the statues themselves. The scoria was obtained from a quarry at the volcanic cone of Punapau near the west coast. The quarry is much smaller than the one at Rano Raraku, which suggests that the idea of the headpieces was conceived rather late in the statue-building period. Like the statues, the topknots were carved in place and rolled to their *ahu* locations. Some of these weighed over 10 tons, and raising them in such a manner that they would remain in position and not topple the statue required a combination of delicate manipulation and brute force. Probably they were placed at the statue heads while the latter were still horizontal, and raised on an extension of the same earth and stone platform.

At the southwestern corner of the island lies the village of Orongo, which occupies a spectacular location on the narrow-crested western lip of the crater of Rano Kau. To the west is a steep cliff descending more than 800 feet to the sea where lie the three islets called Motu Nui, Motu Iti, and Motu Kaokao. On the east an almost equally steep slope descends some 650 feet to the almost mile-wide crater lake of Rano Kau, which is covered by a varicolored mat of totora reeds solid enough to walk on—a hauntingly beautiful setting.

Formerly, Orongo was occupied during part of each September by representatives of the various kin groups. A ceremony was held that involved, among other things, a contest in which the participants descended the cliff and swam to the islet of Motu Nui about a mile offshore. The first to bring back an egg of the *manutara*, or Sooty Tern, was declared winner. His sponsor became *tangata manu*, or bird man, and occupied a position of special ceremonial importance during the following year.

Orongo is the site of about 47

houses, which are constructed differently from those found elsewhere on the island. The typical form is a narrow ellipse with walls made principally of thin stone slabs. Large roof slabs are carefully corbeled and interlocked to join at the center. Most houses are built into slopes so that one side is below ground level.

South of the village an extensive area of basalt outcroppings is beautifully decorated with large, excellently executed petroglyphs done in high relief. Many figures of the *tangata manu* (man wearing a bird mask) commemorate the egg race winner's sponsor, and others depict a local god called *Makemake*. The one small *ahu* at Orongo has a kind of sundial which marks the position of the rising sun at the equinoxes and summer and winter solstices. Ceremonies were held here as late as 1866 or 1867, and we have more complete information about these events than of those associated with the *ahu*.

Although *ahu*, statues, quarries, and the village of Orongo are among the better-known ruins, there are many other monuments and examples of architectural excellence, artistic accomplishment, and engineering skill. These range from elevated tombs and crematoriums to circular, clustered enclosures in which paper mulberry was grown; from the hundreds of conical towers that marked the boundaries of land owned by adjoining groups to the masonry-lined caves that were used as residences and refuges from hostile kin groups. Scattered throughout the island are the remains of thatched dwellings and masonry chicken coops erected during prehistoric times. The house of the common man was simpler than that of the priest and was usually located inland, adjoining agricultural areas.

Taken as a whole these and many other structural remains tell of an industrious population with a prosperous economy capable of producing significant amounts of leisure, which could be devoted to time-consuming religious endeavors. This architectural and artistic activity reached its zenith about 1680, at a time shortly before the first historic contacts, when the available land supported an optimum population and the economy had developed its greatest productivity. These factors contributed to maximum organization and made it possible for Easter Islanders to produce a remarkable quantity of religious statuary and architecture.

But an effective equilibrium between population and resources rarely lasts long in any culture, and this one was no exception. Perhaps in the fate of the inhabitants of Easter Island we see a preview in microcosm of what may ultimately be the fate of the whole of mankind. The land and resources of the island were sharply finite, and here the line between optimum population and overpopulation was a thin one indeed. It seems likely that this balance began to deteriorate shortly before the first European contacts, because of overpopulation that resulted in competition for agricultural land and fishing rights. Although ritual cannibalism may have been present earlier, it appears to have become a more practical matter once population pressure became intense. The groups carving statues at Rano Raraku were probably no longer safe and work at the quarries ceased. The extensive unfinished work and the tools lying at hand give the impression that labor there halted suddenly. Perhaps all the workers fled to the protection of their kinsmen on a single day, thus terminating a stoneworking tradition that had taken centuries to develop.

One of the characteristic goals of the ensuing warfare was the overthrowing of statues of enemy groups and destruction of their *ahu*. Possibly the ten or so kin groups, driven by hunger and desperation, attacked each other's monuments to destroy their enemies' source of supernatural power. Excavations were dug under the statue pedestals, and as the figures crashed down, the red scoria topknots rolled many yards inland. Sometimes, basalt slabs were carefully set on edge in front of the statues so that when they fell they were sure to break across the neck, and could not be erected again. The islanders still tell with intense emotion of defeated people hiding in caves who were hunted down and eaten by the victors. Once the older leaders and the priests lost their power, and their lives, all vestiges of order and security vanished. Many people sought the protection of the *matatoa*, the strongest of the island's warriors. Predatory bands appeared. This warfare may have lasted for more than one hundred and fifty years (from about 1680 to 1860), with some groups able to maintain their religious structures and organization intact much longer than others. It continued until well after European contact, for as late as 1838 a visitor reported nine statues still standing on two *ahu* on the west coast. There are no reports of statues standing on *ahu* after this time. The only ones to be seen today are the previously mentioned eight, which have been re-erected in modern times.

Warfare brought a serious cultural decline. While evidence suggests that the dead were once cremated, after warfare began, many stone-lined tombs were built among the fallen statues and in the ramps and platforms of the destroyed *ahu*. Other cadavers were simply laid out on the ramps and among fallen statues and covered with stones. As a result, many destroyed *ahu* were almost entirely covered with stones so that few vestiges of their formerly impressive masonry and architectural characteristics remain visible. Some took on the appearance of long, sloping piles of stone. New *ahu* were built of easily piled small stones in new locations, apparently to provide additional burial places.

Upon this chaotic scene was superimposed the attention of the New World slavers and whalers, who harassed the Easter Islanders for an additional two-thirds of a century and who wrote the final page in the history of the culture's destruction. It was during this period that vast amounts of knowledge concerning the history and culture of Easter Island were forever lost—information that would have made clear the meaning of much that is enigmatic in the island's maze of ruins. The few people left could maintain little of the complex culture of earlier times.

Most of it was soon forgotten. All of the priests who could read the script engraved on thousands of wooden tablets died as a result of the slave raids. When systematic attempts were made to find local people who could read the tablets, the stunning discovery was made that none were left. The unique Easter Island written language was lost, and despite nearly a century of effort by several highly trained linguists, the few surviving wooden tablets remain undeciphered.

Thus, when Lay Brother Eugéne Eyraud of the Congregation des Sacres Cóeurs de Picipus arrived in 1864 he found a remnant population, which had lost its priesthood and most of the concepts that formed its older religion. He noted little or no religious practice of any kind among them. Although he experienced difficulties with the islanders, who stole his supplies and treated him badly, he persisted with missionary zeal and established the first permanent European settlement in 1866. Within the next few years the islanders were converted to the Catholic faith and remain Catholic to this day.

Soon afterward, outside influences began their slow intrusion, but the island was again "forgotten" by the Western world until the Norwegian archeologist Thor Heyerdahl refocused world attention on it with his popular book *Aku Aku*. Subsequently, it has become evident that Easter Island is a remarkable monument to human capacity—a unique example of what can be accomplished by a tiny group of people forced to build their lives with a minimum of outside stimulation.

Increasing attention has been devoted to the preservation of monuments and to further investigation of the island's anthropological significance. Islanders are proud of their heritage, and are apparently happy to see the influx of tourists resulting from recent interest in the island as an outstanding example of achievement in isolation.

Ten years ago, an average of only two ships per year visited this Pacific outpost. Today, the first of several planned hotels is already under construction. An airstrip was recently completed and a regular schedule of tourist flights is in operation. It seems that the islanders' long isolation is at an end and that in the twentieth century they are to become a part of the world community. It is to be devoutly hoped that they will find minimal cause for regret.

17

The drowned city of Port Royal

by Robert F. Marx

SHIPWRECKS are not the only source of data for the marine archaeologist working in the Caribbean. Ringed almost completely by an earthquake belt, it has provided another type of underwater site: the submerged town.

Two of the three recorded—Jamestown, off the Island of Nevis, and Orangetown, off the Island of St. Eustatius—sank as the result of the same earthquake on April 30, 1680. The couple of hundred buildings of Jamestown, the main sugar port, lie in from 3 to 10 metres of water, covered now by about one metre of sand. Of the 150 buildings in Orangetown, a smugglers' base located on a bluff overlooking the sea, about a third toppled into the sea, in depths of from 7 to 20 m.

Neither town came anywhere close in size and importance to Port Royal, in Jamaica, the third earthquake victim. In four decades, thanks to privateering and the contraband trade with the Spanish colonies, it had become the most important trading

ROBERT F. MARX, *specialist in maritime history and marine archaeology, particularly of the Spanish colonial period in the Caribbean, directed the mapping and excavation of the sunken city of Port Royal, Jamaica (1965-68). He has discovered and explored a number of Mayan archaeological sites and "cenotes" (sacred wells) as well as many wrecks in the Caribbean and off the coasts of Spain. This article is a condensation of the chapter, "The Submerged Ruins of Port Royal, Jamaica", from Unesco's new book "Underwater Archaeology".*

centre in the Caribbean and possibly in the whole New World.

Shortly before noon on June 7, 1692, there were three strong earth tremors, quickly followed by a tidal wave. Within minutes, nine-tenths of the city's 2,000 buildings, many two and three storeys high, had either sunk or slid into the sea, and over 2,000 persons perished. No accurate estimate is available of the material losses.

Apart from the number and variety of sites, the Caribbean has two other advantages for marine archaeology. First, an enormous wealth of sources is available, mainly in Spanish archives, to aid in locating and identifying sites and furnish information about the artifacts recovered. Secondly, the working conditions are extremely favourable. The clarity of the water in most areas facilitates location, and photography *in situ* or as an aid in mapping.

Most sites are in shallow waters. These can be rough on an exposed reef, but there are no strong tides or, in most places, even currents, and no danger to divers of nitrogen narcosis or the "bends". Uniformly warm temperatures and fine weather permit work to continue throughout the year—even in the hurricane season, weeks of complete calm are common.

Port Royal offers the most extensive and important underwater site in the western hemisphere. Salvage operations began there on the very day it sank beneath the sea in 1692, and continued for many years.

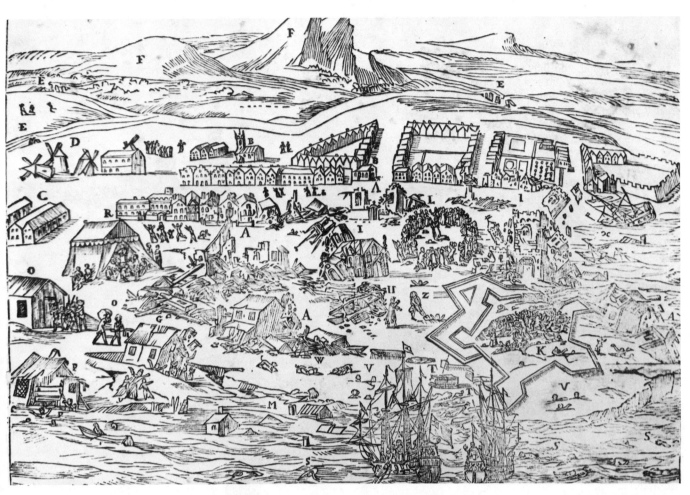

Above, contemporary drawing of the 1692 earthquake that brought disaster to the great Caribbean trading centre and pirate lair of Port Royal, Jamaica. Within minutes of the first tremor, 2,000 men, women and children had died and nine-tenths of the city's 2,000 buildings had disappeared into the sea. Major underwater excavations at Port Royal began in 1966. More artifacts have now been recovered than from all the wreck sites explored in the Caribbean during the past two decades. Below left, diver brings up a bucket of items recovered from the drowned city, while an air-lift spouts sand and water. Debris brought up by the air-lift is retained by a huge sieve in the centre of the barge. Below, two drawings, dated 1622, of salvage operations in Caribbean waters. Left, Spaniards attempting to recover a small vessel; right, primitive scoop used by early salvage engineers.

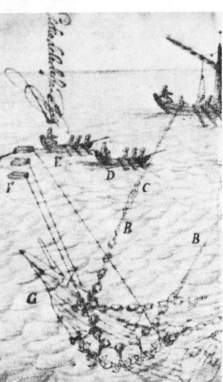

In January 1966, the Jamaican government began a long-term, proper excavation of the site which is expected to continue for many years. It was my good fortune to be selected to direct the project, and I spent the first four months of 1966 making a thorough survey.

This indicated that the site measured some 140,000 square metres in depths of from 1 to 20 m. of water with 75 per cent in less than 10 m.

The composition of the bottom sediment varies greatly. On average, below the silt there is a 1 to 1.8 metre deposit of hard packed mud and dead coral fragments; below this deposit, the sediment is about 70 per cent black sand and 30 per cent coarse gravel.

A variety of excavation tools were tested: two types of "prop-wash", several types of water and air jets, hydrolifts and air-lifts. Our final selection was a 10 cm. diameter air-lift, with a screen to prevent any artifacts larger than a small coin from going up the tube. We found that all the other excavation tools, and even larger-diameter air-lift tubes, could damage artifacts.

The sediment is pumped to a barge where it passes through a fine-mesh screen and small objects (beads, musket balls, pins, etc.) are recovered. Larger artifacts are recovered on the bottom and sent up in buckets.

A minimum of three divers are required on the bottom: one to hold the air-lift tube, one to send or carry artifacts to the surface, and one to send up bricks and other debris which are too large to pass through the screen on the air-lift tube.

Visibility rarely exceeds 30 to 60 cm before the day's excavation starts. Once pumping begins, it is reduced to a few centimetres (around the mouth of the air-lift tube) or zero. This makes the work more difficult, as everything must be done by touch.

The sophisticated horizontal and vertical control method used by land archaeologists and by George Bass on some of the Mediterranean sites (see article page 8) was ruled out by the lack of visibility and by the nature of the sediment in which cave-ins are the rule rather than the exception. Although most of the artifacts are recovered from the first 3 m. of sediment, we excavate to 5 m. and occasionally find artifacts in the lower sediment.

Marx surfacing holding an onion bottle and cannon ball with the airlift in operation in background.

Horizontal control is maintained by marking with four buoys the square to be excavated and each day recording the position of the top of the air-lift tube whenever important objects are recovered and brought up. Vertical control is maintained by establishing the depth of water, and noting the depth that the air-lift tube is down each time that artifacts are brought up for tagging.

Excavation began on the site on May 1, 1966 and has since gone on continuously, six days a week. We have systematically excavated a rectangular hole 133 by 50 m. to an average depth of 5 m. Only three intact brick buildings have so far been uncovered, but hundreds of fragments of brick walls and thousands of brickbats have been located.

On the basis of old maps and property records, we estimate that the area excavated contained from thirty to forty buildings. By checking owners' initials on pewter and silver artifacts with the old property records, we have been able to identify many of the sites. Most were private homes, but we also found two taverns, a carpenter's shop, a cobbler's shop, a pewterer's (or silversmith's) shop, the fish and meat markets, and two turtle crawls. In this same area we located two shipwrecks dating from the 1692 earthquake and another dating from a hurricane in 1722.

Excluding treasure, more artifacts have now been recovered than from all the wreck sites worked in the Caribbean over the past two decades. Over 20,000 iron objects have been recovered—most still await a suitable method of preservation. Other finds include 2,000 glass bottles, 6,500 clay smoking pipes, and over 500 pewter or silverware items.

Two large hoards of Spanish silver coins were found: the first in a wooden chest bearing a brass keyhole plate with the coat-of-arms of Philip IV of Spain, the other under a fallen wall believed to be part of a pewterer's or silversmith's shop.

Yet, after almost two years of operations, we have not excavated even five per cent of the site, and many years of work remain. It is to be hoped that Port Royal will eventually be used as a training centre for students of marine archaeology.

Unfortunately, there is both very little official interest and little financial support; at the moment, only the Mexican and Jamaican Governments are sponsoring projects.

In the Caribbean, as elsewhere, marine archaeology is still in its infancy as a discipline. The techniques are still experimental and there are few really expert archaeologists. Yet, compared with the Mediterranean, and considering the opportunities it offers, the Caribbean has attracted less than its share of archaeological effort.

V. The Fossil Record

Where, how, and when did human beings evolve? The question of human origins has vexed people since ancient times. Since the concept of evolution finally won acceptance in the mid-nineteenth century, archaeologists and paleontologists (biologists who study fossilized skeletal remains) have been studying this question systematically. Although a good many issues have yet to be resolved, the overall pattern of hominid evolution (evolution of the human line) is now quite well understood. In this section and the following one the fossil evidence of human evolution is examined. Here we will be concerned with the larger picture; in Section VI we will focus on specific problems of interpretation.

Pilbeam's article "Human Origins" is a very useful introduction to the entire topic. He quickly indicates what Darwinian evolution is all about, then sets about the task of clarifying terms; and it is essential that you follow his differentiation between hominids (humans and their ancestors) and pongids (apes and their ancestors). Next Pilbeam enumerates the most significant characteristics of human beings and traces their emergence in the course of human evolution. When this article was written in 1968, it appeared that one branch of *Australopithecus* was a direct ancestor of humans. As you will see in the next section, this is now a doubtful proposition; but that in no way diminishes the importance of Pilbeam's discussion of the Australopithecines, since such an ancestor certainly is to be found at that general stage of development. Finally, Pilbeam lays the groundwork for appreciating the importance of primate studies for the ongoing investigation of human nature, a topic we cover in Section VII.

Howells' "*Homo sapiens:* 20 Million Years in the Making" covers some of the same ground that Pilbeam did, but with a somewhat narrower focus and more up-to-date information. He is concerned with describing the fossil sequence of human evolution and does so admirably, slanting his discussion toward the question of the kinds of adaptations that are represented at each evolutionary stage. Two problems should be noted in this paper. The first is with regard to the size of the brains of the first tool producers, which Howells calls australopiths. It is true that gracile australopiths' brains were roughly the size of modern chimpanzees'. But they may well not have been the first stone tool makers; rather, the larger-skulled finds that Richard Leakey classifies as *Homo* (species indeterminate) may well have produced the earliest stone tools, as you will note in Leakey's article in the following section. Secondly, Howells assumes that it was in fact australopiths who evolved into *Homo erectus.* This, too, is disputed by Leakey and others. Otherwise this presentation of the fossil sequence and the cultural remains left behind by our ancestors is both comprehensive and accurate.

Solecki's article arguing that "Neanderthal Is Not an Epithet but a Worthy Ancestor" bridges Sections V and VI. It is both a detailed discussion of the Neanderthal phase of hominid evolution and a masterpiece of interpretive reconstruction. Using sophisticated archaeological techniques and a lively imaginative eye, Solecki conjures up for us a vision of the moving humanness of our ancestors.

18

HUMAN ORIGINS*

D. R. PILBEAM *University Demonstrator in Physical Anthropology, Duckworth Laboratory, Faculty of Archaeology and Anthropology, University of Cambridge*

Introduction

PERHAPS THE MOST FAMOUS British Association meeting ever was held at Oxford just over 100 years ago, in 1860. The meeting followed the publication in the preceding year of Charles Darwin's *The Origin of Species*. This book not only divided biological opinion on the one hand from popular and religious opinion on the other, but also divided biologists themselves. The debate at Oxford between Huxley, Hooker, and other Darwinian protagonists and Samuel Wilberforce, the Bishop of Oxford, is well known.

During the debate, Wilberforce facetiously asked Huxley whether he was descended from an ape on his grandfather's or grandmother's side. Huxley is said to have replied:

'If I am asked whether I would choose to be descended from the poor animal of low intelligence and stooping gait, who grins and chatters as we pass, or from a man, endowed with great ability and a splendid position, who should use these gifts to discredit and crush humble seekers after truth, I hesitate what answer to make.'

Although Darwin's book covered general evolutionary theory, it seems to have been the human implications which caused most anxiety. It bothered not only biologists and bishops but others too, for in 1860 the wife of a canon of Worcester Cathedral is reputed to have said to her husband, 'Descended from the apes! My dear, we will hope that it is not true. But if it is, let us pray that it may not become generally known.' How could man, the fallen angel, have such brutish ancestors!

In 1871, Darwin wrote another book, *The Descent of Man*, this time devoted specifically to human

* Text of Evening Discourse delivered on September 4, 1967, at the Leeds Meeting of the British Association.

evolution. In his characteristically cautious manner, he pointed out that man's ancestors, although not identical to, nor even closely resembling, the living apes, might nevertheless, when discovered, be described as 'apes'. He continued:

'We are naturally led to enquire, where was the birthplace of man . . .? In each great region of the world the living mammals are closely related to the extinct species of the same region. It is therefore probable that Africa was formerly inhabited by extinct apes closely allied to the gorilla and chimpanzee; and as these two species are now man's nearest allies, it is somewhat more probable that our early progenitors lived on the African continent than elsewhere.'[6]

So, almost 100 years ago, Charles Darwin had concluded first, that man's earliest ancestors were closely related to the apes, and second, that these early human ancestors most probably originated in Africa.

I want to tell you here about some of the exciting discoveries which have been made in the past few decades, discoveries which are beginning to throw light on those Darwinian speculations of a century or more ago. However, before talking about human origins, I think that I should try to explain some of the words that I shall be using.

Terminology

Zoologists divide the mammals into a number of basic groups known as 'orders'. The order to which man belongs, together with his closest relatives, the apes, monkeys, and prosimians, and their ancestors, is called Primates. Orders are further subdivided. The living great apes—chimpanzees, gorillas and orang-utans — are grouped into a 'family' known as the Pongidae. Their extinct ancestors are also included in this family, and it therefore has a time dimension. Living and extinct men are classified in another family, the Hominidae. We can describe the contents of these families by the more convenient colloquial terms 'pongids' and 'hominids'; these are broadly equivalent to the words 'apes' and 'men', although they are used—we hope—in more precise ways.

As Darwin noted, the Hominidae and Pongidae are more closely related to each other than either is to any other primate family. The exact time at which the early primates first split into human and ape stocks has been debated for more than 100 years. Estimates have fluctuated, some authorities favouring an ancient split, others a very recent one. Although we still do not know the exact time of the bifurcation, we do know that it had occurred in all probability at least 20 million years ago; but more of that later.

I have discussed the terms 'pongid' and 'hominid'. One other remains to be discussed. Few, I think, will have any doubts about the meaning of the word 'human'; human is what we are, and we are members of the species *Homo sapiens*. But when did we become human? If we accept the fact that evolution has occurred, and that evolution applies as much to us as to any other species, then clearly, somewhere in our past, there are ancestors that differ from us in their anatomy and behaviour. There will be no sharp jumps in this evolutionary record, and as we discover more and more fossils, as we fill in the gaps, our record of human evolution will become ever more continuous. With continuity, of course, definitions and boundary lines become harder to draw, and so it is with 'human'. However, it is generally agreed that the term 'human' should be applied to the first hominids to be recognizable as members of the genus *Homo*.

The hominid fossil record is most complete during the last two million years or so. Before that it is exceedingly sparse. This two-million year period falls within the epoch called by geologists the Pleistocene (Fig. 1). The Pleistocene is now known to have begun about two million years ago. (Only recently, one million years has been regarded as a liberal estimate.) Before the Pleistocene we have the Pliocene, which began 11 or 12 million years ago, and before that the Miocene, beginning more than 25 million years ago. However, it is to the Pleistocene hominids that we turn first.

The genus Homo

Men physically indistinguishable from ourselves first appeared about 40,000 years ago. Before that our ancestors did not look exactly like us. Although there is a danger in labouring this point, if we accept the fact that evolution has occurred in the human line, it is surely not too illogical to expect that at some stage our ancestors will *not* resemble us. I am emphasizing this because a few anthro-

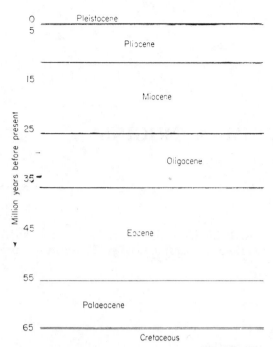

Fig. 1. Geological epochs of the Tertiary and Quaternary periods, following the Cretaceous period. The earliest primates appeared in the Cretaceous, the first monkeys and apes in the Oligocene, and the first hominids in the Miocene. Men of the genus *Homo* are not known before the Pleistocene.

pologists seem to forget this point when constructing human evolutionary trees.

One of the distinctive characteristics of living *Homo sapiens* is the ability to walk and run bipedally—that is, on two legs. Bipedal running and walking probably evolved quite early on in hominid evolution, perhaps as an aid to more efficient hunting. Certainly, by the time of Neandertal man, hominid hunting had become very efficient.

Modern man is also characterized by his enormous brain. The average skull volume,[2] the normal estimate of brain size, for both sexes of all races of *Homo sapiens* is 1320 cm³. This is three times as great as the average volume for apes. The average for gorillas is around 500 cm³, and for chimpanzees around 400 cm³. Only very rarely does one find capacities above 700 cm³ in gorillas or above 500 cm³ in chimpanzees. Most normal human beings have capacities between 900 and 1800 cm³. Of course there are microcephalics with smaller volumes, but these are almost always mentally subnormal. At least 900 cm³ of brain would seem to be an absolute minimum for the type of intelligence found in *Homo sapiens*; this is well outside the ape range.

This relatively enormous brain of ours has clearly been very important to us. If we want to find just one character which distinguishes us from all other animals it is surely the magnitude and quality of our intelligence. (I do not wish to get involved here in a discussion of the meaning of 'intelligence'. However it is defined, we certainly are more intelligent than any other animal.) It is our great brain size which enables human social behaviour to be so complex. Anthropologists term this specifically human complexity 'culture'. Broadly, culture includes those parts of human behaviour which are transmitted by learning from one generation to another. These include the legal, political, and religious institutions of societies, the technological traditions of tool-making, as well as many other features. Some other mammals have complex social behaviour depending on individual learning, but human learned behaviour is infinitely richer. Humans communicate by means of vocal language while other animals do not; human language is a wonderfully efficient way of conveying information, information not only about the here and now, but about yesterday and tomorrow, and over-there-out-of-sight.

For much of our existence, we have been stone-age hunters. At a conservative estimate, this phase of our history lasted for a quarter of a million years. Little more than 10,000 years ago, some groups of men discovered a new way of living. They took to domesticating plants and animals, and turned from hunting to farming, from a shifting to a settled existence. This change is called by archaeologists, the *Neolithic*, following the Palaeolithic, or stone age.

Populations which are settled and which can rely on regular supplies of vegetable and animal food can increase greatly in size, and they can support far more non-productive, specialized politicians, priests, soldiers, inventors, artists, and craftsmen than before. The Neolithic heralded a great burst in human social evolution, changes which are still going on. From the first farmers to the hydrogen bomb took just 10,000 years, and this 'progress' was due not to organic evolution, not to a change in brain structure, but to new social inventions, to cultural evolution; two very different types of evolution. There is little reason to doubt that our brains are structured in a way essentially similar to those of our ancestors 10,000 years, or even 50,000 years ago. It is as though once the brain had reached a certain evolutionary threshold, no more physical changes followed.

Stone-age *Homo sapiens* was a superb big-game hunter, making up for his comparative lack of size, strength, and speed with his intelligence, planning, and co-operation. His stone, wood and bone tool kits were of great complexity; he buried his dead, and has left behind carvings and paintings of great beauty. This much we know from the archaeological record. Doubtless his social, political and religious institutions were as well-developed as his technology. We are dealing then with men very similar to ourselves, or at least to the non-literate peoples of the world today.

The best known fossil hominids are those caricatures of cave-men, the Neandertals.[3] It is rather improbable that the Neandertalers from Western Europe were ancestral to any modern men. However, the ancestors of modern man were obviously alive at that time, living probably in Eastern Europe, Western Asia, and elsewhere; it is unlikely that they would have looked very different from the Western European Neandertals, but for convenience we shall use the term 'Neandertaloids' to describe those which were living at this time (50,000 and more years ago) in Eastern Europe, Asia and Africa, retaining 'Neandertal' for Western European men.

It can be inferred from their skeletons that these Neandertaloids were bipeds as efficient as ourselves. Although their jaws, teeth and faces were larger than ours and their skulls shaped differently, their brains were as large as those of modern man. They too buried their dead, and apparently believed in an after-life. They understood the uses of fire. Their tools were varied and well-made, though not as beautifully made as those of later man.

Although they differ a little from us anatomically, most anthropologists would now classify the Neandertaloids as *Homo sapiens* too, in this way conveying the opinion that the similarities between modern men and the Neandertaloids are more important than the difference. Viewed in the perspective of 20 million years or more of hominid evolution, these earliest *Homo sapiens* are close to us not only in time but also in anatomy and in what we can infer of their behaviour.

Before about 150,000 years ago the picture is more indistinct, and there are many gaps in the hominid fossil record. It becomes less hazy around half a million years ago during the period known as the Middle Pleistocene. Hominid fossils of this age are known from a number of localities in the Old World—from Java, China, Europe and Africa. Doubtless men were living in other places too, although they are yet to be uncovered.

Like *Homo sapiens*, these men were apparently perfectly efficient upright walkers. Their brains however were smaller than ours; the average cranial capacity at this time was less than 1000 cm³. They were almost certainly less 'intelligent' than us, and had less highly developed cultures. This is reflected in the relative crudeness of their stone tools, compared with those of *Homo sapiens*. However, these men were efficient hunters who also knew how to use fire. They have been classified as members of the genus *Homo*, although they are usually put into another species, *Homo erectus* separate from *Homo sapiens*.

Now, we should be very careful when we say that *Homo erectus* evolved into *Homo sapiens*. What we are really doing is taking the last one million years or so of the hominid line and chopping it into two pieces with a dividing line somewhere between one-quarter and one-half million years ago. We have divided an evolutionary continuum in a quite arbitrary way (see Fig. 2). The latest *Homo erectus* populations will obviously be virtually identical in structure to the earliest *Homo sapiens*. The import-

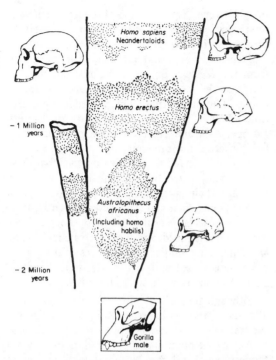

FIG. 2. An idealized representation of Pleistocene hominid evolution, the stippling representing known fossils. The pictures on the right are those of listed species; top left is a Neandertal from Western Europe. The distinct hominid lineage represented by the column on the left is not mentioned in the text. It became extinct half a million years ago.

ant point to remember is that we are dealing at any one time-level with just one species of hominid, distributed through most of the Old World. This species has evolved through time, and has changed so much between the middle and late Pleistocene that we need to use different names to describe the different segments of the lineage. Unfortunately, giving different names to different segments of a lineage immediately creates a sharp difference where none, of course, exists.

In fact, the *erectus sapiens* boundary has been decided by the historical accidents of discovery. The hominid line has been fairly well sampled in fossil terms for the period back to about 150,000 years, and for the period around one-half million years ago, and there has been little in between. So it has been easiest to draw the boundary in that gap. Had the gap in the record occurred elsewhere, we would have had different boundaries and consequently different limits for our species.

You can no doubt imagine the arguments that will follow when we find intermediate fossils. Are these the last of *Homo erectus* or the first *Homo sapiens*, or even a new species? As long as we can be sure that the new fossils are part of the single lineage which is evolving from the *erectus* to the *sapiens* level, it really matters very little what they are called. Of course, these arguments also apply to hominid fossils before *Homo erectus*.

Early Pleistocene hominids

Until 1925 no hominids were known from deposits of early Pleistocene age, that is the geological period between approximately one and two million years ago. It was claimed that the discoveries which had been made at Piltdown in Sussex in 1911 and 1912 represented an early Pleistocene type having a brain-case very close to that of modern man, although with a jaw like that of an ape. In the 1950's the Piltdown discoveries were shown to be fakes.[20] The evidence for the existence of modern-looking *Homo sapiens* before 40,000 years ago is now practically non-existent.

In 1925, a South African anatomist, Raymond Dart, described a new type of early Pleistocene hominid, called by him *Australopithecus africanus*.[4] The first specimen came from Taung in South Africa. Since 1925, a large number of specimens of this species has been recovered from other sites in South Africa, and today we know quite a lot about its anatomy.

When Dart first published his description of *Australopithecus*, only the skull was known. He noted that the brain size was small, only 500 cm^3. You will remember that volumes of this order are found in the living apes, and that they are never found in modern man, nor in the more primitive *Homo erectus*. However, Dart also observed that the teeth were man-like rather than ape-like. He believed that certain other features of the skull were also more typical of hominids than of pongids. But at this time Dart, along with many other anthropologists, believed that a large brain was the most distinctive hominid trait, and that since *Australopithecus* had an ape-sized brain, it could not be a hominid. However, he did place it in a new family, intermediate between the pongids and the hominids.

The reaction of the European anthropological establishment to Dart's discovery was sceptical in the extreme, and it was written off as just another

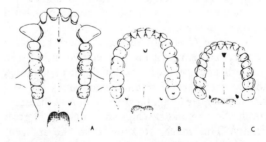

FIG. 3. The palate and upper teeth of (A) a male gorilla, (B) *Australopithecus* and (C) an Australian aboriginal. Note that in the curved contour of the dental arcade, the small canine teeth (worn down flat from the tip), and the absence of gap (diastema) between the canine and incisor teeth, the total morphological pattern consistently presented by the australopithecine palate and dentition is fundamentally of the hominid type. (From W. E. Le Gros Clark, *History of the Primates*, British Museum (Natural History), by permission of the Trustees.)

ape.[11] Remember that at this time most anthropologists believed that early Pleistocene hominids, like Piltdown, resembled *Homo sapiens*. It was generally accepted that early hominids had large brains and ape-like jaws and teeth. In fact this is the complete opposite of the correct picture. Our early Pleistocene ancestors had small, ape-sized brains, and dentitions like later hominids.

Australopithecus africanus was a small, lightly-built hominid standing perhaps no more than 4 ft 6 in tall with an average brain volume of 500 cm³. However, the smallness of his brain does not make him an ape, any more than a horse with a cow-sized brain becomes a cow.[15] Unlike the apes, *Australopithecus* had a dentition which is essentially human (see Fig. 3). The incisors were small and vertically placed in the jaws, the canines small and incisor-like, and the premolars and molars, although large, were similar to those of *Homo erectus* and *Homo sapiens*.

In apes, particularly the males, the canines are large and projecting teeth, important in display behaviour and in fighting. The incisors, particularly in the fruit-eating chimpanzee and orang-utan, are relatively very large indeed. This impressive battery of front teeth is used for cutting and chewing the tough fruits and shoots which cannot be prepared with the hands. Of course, it is still true that apes do use their hands in a wide range of activities, including the collection and preparation of a variety of food material.

The man-like structure of the dentition of *Australopithecus* implies that this early hominid did not use its teeth in the way in which pongids do. This point was in fact noted by some early workers, who inferred that *Australopithecus* probably used tools, both as weapons for offence and defence and as cutting and digging implements for obtaining food.[1] In more recent times, further discoveries have strengthened this view.

Archaeological evidence suggests that *Australopithecus* made and used stone and bone tools. To what end? Dart collected very carefully from caves the animal bones associated with these hominids and was able to show that, in all probability, these were remains of animals hunted, killed and eaten by *Australopithecus*.[5] It is difficult to visualize how *Australopithecus*, with his unimpressive front teeth, could have hunted and killed on this scale without using stone and bone tools.

A number of bones of the pelvis and leg show that *Australopithecus* almost certainly did not move in a quadrupedal—four-footed—or modified quadrupedal fashion like the monkeys and apes. In a number of basic ways, the pelvis and the leg resemble those of later hominids. *Australopithecus* was probably a bipedal animal, although not as efficient an upright walker as ourselves. Nonetheless, he was well on the way to being an efficient biped, and he was therefore probably a very

mobile animal, covering a good deal of territory.

Finally, the geological setting of the fossils shows that these early hominids were essentially open-country, savannah dwellers, unlike the basically forest-living apes.

The original South African *Australopithecus* specimens came from deposits which, unfortunately, cannot be dated with absolute accuracy. It is possible, though, that the oldest remains may be as much as two and a half million years old, or more. Recently, more early Pleistocene hominids have been recovered by Dr. and Mrs. Louis Leakey from the magnificient East African deposits at Olduvai Gorge in Tanzania.[13] The earliest of these finds are almost two million years old. Other fossils from the Gorge provide a series which runs right through to the middle Pleistocene with specimens of *Homo erectus* dated at around one-half million years.

The early Pleistocene hominids from Olduvai have been described by Leakey, Tobias and Napier as a new species of the genus *Homo*, *Homo habilis*.[14] Like *Australopithecus africanus* this species contains hominids with small, ape-sized brains and man-like teeth and skeletons. One particularly fine specimen is that of a set of fossil foot bones, which show quite clearly that *Homo habilis* was an upright biped and not a quadruped.

He was also a tool-maker, producing a surprising variety of stone implements. The Leakeys are fortunate enough to have excavated complete campsites with tools and animal remains preserved, as well as evidence that *habilis* built shelters at his campsites. This last is a discovery of great significance, suggesting that, by two million years ago, hominid bands were spending periods of time in one place, hunting from and living at a single camp.

Now, there has been a great deal of argument about the exact position of *Homo habilis* in human evolution. My own view is briefly as follows. Middle Pleistocene and later hominids are found throughout much of the Old World, and it is not unreasonable to assume that the immediate ancestors of these hominids would also have been widespread. The South African early Pleistocene *Australopithecus africanus* fossils are sampled from this ancestral species. So too are the *Homo habilis* specimens from East Africa. I believe that both *Australopithecus africanus* and *Homo habilis* are simply geographically separate populations sampled from one species. No doubt early Pleistocene populations of this species from other parts of the Old World are still waiting to be uncovered.[18]

In summary, the early Pleistocene hominids, living one and a half to two and a half million years ago, were quite efficient bipedal runners. This method of locomotion seems to have enabled them to hunt with some success, to cover a large amount of ground in pursuit of prey. Generally, it seems they inhabited open country in the tropics. In spite of their small 'ape-sized' brains, they must have been capable of quite a high level of co-operative behaviour, and they were able to make quite a variety of simple tools.

It was quite a struggle for Dart and others to gain acceptance for the view that these early forms were in fact hominids. We have noted already one of the objections to this view; that hominids anatomically more like modern man were living at the same time as *Australopithecus*. This objection is no longer tenable. The exposure of the Piltdown forgery has exploded what we can call the 'early *sapiens*' theory.

The geological picture too is being modified. When Sir Arthur Keith (President of the Association at the Leeds Meeting in 1927) was writing in 1931 he believed *Australopithecus* to be about 400,000 years old, not as we now know more than two million years; he thought that *Homo erectus* was 300,000 years old, not one half or three quarter million years.[12] This 'stretching out' of the Pleistocene gives us more time into which to fit our fossils, and more time for leisurely evolution from primitive to more advanced men.

There was another reason for the general reluctance to accept *Australopithecus* as an ancestor—brain size. We have noted already the evidence indicating that a number of rather human anatomical and behavioural features seem already to have been well established two million years ago. Yet these behavioural characters are found in animals with only ape-sized brains. Let me quote here from the 1947 edition of a work first published in 1931.[10] This book was a major, if not the major, text for American and English anthropologists for many years.

Australopithecus 'lacked the brain overgrowth that is specifically human and perhaps should be the ultimate criterion of a direct ancestral relationship to man . . . Because they lacked brains, they remained apes, in spite of their humanoid teeth.'

Presumably, we must once have had ancestors with brains smaller than our unusually large ones. It is becoming increasingly clear that our ancestors were hominids below the neck (and indeed above if teeth be included) long before our heads were graced with well-filled and lofty brows. It is surely illogical to call any small-brained hominid an ape, if at the same time one inevitably rules out of human ancestry any such 'ape-like' creature! We now realize, of course, that the early hominids were not 'apes' in any meaningful sense of the word.

Finally, we have what might be called, after the canon's wife, the Worcester syndrome—a horror at the idea of having any subhuman ancestors at all.

The value of primate field studies

The apes, I think, have had rather a bad deal. The Victorians seem to have thought of them as brutish creatures. This view is certainly not held by those who have actually studied primate behaviour. Since the 1950's, there has been a great rebirth of interest in living primates. Of special interest to us are the studies of chimpanzees and gorillas in their natural habitats in Africa. (We should never forget that the behaviour of animals in zoos is not necessarily typical of their normal behaviour.) Of the field studies, the most important for us is the work of Jane Goodall (now Baroness von Lawick-Goodall). Miss Goodall has been studying a group of chimpanzees in Tanzania, on and off, since 1960.[8]

The social behaviour of these apes is extremely complex. Individually, they are highly intelligent animals. They live in small, rather loosely-constituted bands of varying composition. Thus one finds groupings of females with infants and juveniles, of males and females, of juveniles, and of males. The composition of these small groups is fluid; an individual may leave one and join another at any time, without interference.

A wide range of relationships are clearly recognized; mothers and offspring greet one another affectionately when reunited, and interactions within and between these small bands are generally very friendly. As in human groups, facial expressions and body postures are important in social intercourse.

In Tanzania, where the animals live in open woodland, 50 or so chimpanzees may range over 10 or more square miles searching for food. Some students believe that it is this larger grouping of animals which makes up the chimpanzee 'troop', rather than the small bands. Within the 'troop', the social structure is constantly in flux, yet its overall coherence is maintained because individuals are able to recognize relationships with a large number of other animals, with whom they are not necessarily always in contact.

Chimpanzees sleep in the trees in nests which they make up each night. A new feeding and a new sleeping area are chosen each day as the troop moves on; unlike human hunters, chimpanzees are not tied to one home base for long periods of time. The all-male bands are the most adventurous, travelling widely in search of food. When a new source is found, males will often drum on trees or on the ground, their noise forming a focus for other chimpanzees in the area.

Yet this amazingly complex social structure, and the multitude of very flexible inter-individual relationships, are all possible with an ape-sized brain. So, at least as far as this very general point is concerned, the study of chimpanzees in the wild can help us in palaeoanthropology.

Australopithecus, the early Pleistocene hominid, had a brain somewhat larger than that of the chimpanzee, particularly if body size is considered; there is no reason to believe that the social behaviour of this early hominid was any less complicated than that of the chimpanzee. This is not to say that chimpanzees behave like *Australopithecus*! Of course, the difference between ape and human brains is not just a matter of size. Brain cells in man are larger than those of apes, and are more complex. New tracts of cells have been added and the internal organization of the human brain re-modelled. So although early hominids may have had ape-sized brains, these brains probably functioned in rather different ways from those of apes and produced different behavioural patterns.

As I have already noted, the apes are mainly forest-dwelling vegetarians, while *Australopithecus*, like later hominids, was a hunter living in open country. He was probably not as efficient a hunter as *Homo erectus*, nor would his social behaviour have been as highly developed. However, it seems probable that these early hominids were already occupying campsites for a few days at a time, and there might well have been some division of labour between the more mobile hunting males and the females who remained in camp caring for the young and gathering and preparing vegetable foods.

Tools and hominid evolution

I have mentioned briefly, almost in passing, the phenomenon of tool-making in hominid social life. Tool-making in fact has had far more than a passing importance in human evolution. Most authorities now accept the idea that tools have, so to speak, made man. There has been, to use fashionable terms, a constant feed-back between an increasingly complex cultural, tool-making environment and, via an enlarging brain, increasingly complex behaviour.

Now, man is one of the few social mammals in which the social group is organized to obtain food. The food which is obtained, particularly animal food, can only be utilized if natural objects like stones are used to prepare it. With a dentition which is not designed for slashing and cutting, tools become vital for dismembering carcasses, and, for instance, for smashing bones to obtain the edible marrow.

Tool-using and tool-making have therefore been important catalysts in human evolution. Object manipulation is one component of the play of young humans not found in the play of other primates. As juveniles and adults we generally exhibit a high degree of manual dexterity, and this dexterity has become built into our brains over several millions of years of evolution—tool-making evolution.

One of the most startling discoveries made by Jane Goodall during her field studies has been the fact that chimpanzees prepare tools to aid themselves in obtaining food. They will, for example, pick a grass stalk and poke this into a hole in a ter-mite mound. Withdrawing the stalk covered with termites, they will then pass it between their lips, stripping off the termites. Small twigs are also used, in which case leaves and small twiglets are removed beforehand, leaving a single trimmed tool. These tools may be carried for some distance

and time before being used. Chimpanzees have also been observed using a previously chewed leaf as a sponge to mop up water from a tree hollow. Tool-use, however, is not a vital aspect of chimpan-zee survival. For hominids though, tools *must* be used for individuals and groups to survive.

Meat-eating has also been observed by Miss Goodall. She has seen a number of male chimpan-zees occasionally band together to trap, kill and eat Red Colobus monkeys. The meat is also shared out to other chimpanzees who have 'begged' for a share. Although some other primates do catch and eat animal food, this is nevertheless very rare; the sharing out of animal food has not been reported in any other primates except chimpanzees. Food-sharing does of course occur in social carnivores like wolves or Cape Hunting Dogs. We, too, are social carnivores.

It should be noted that these behavioural patterns have been observed only in chimpanzees living in open woodland, and have not so far been reported for animals living in forests. This may be because of insufficient work on forest-living chimpanzees, or because vegetable food is not so plentiful in open woodland.

The late Professor Hall has recently suggested that the most important uses of objects by primates are as weapons rather than as tools in purely economic circumstances (for obtaining and pre-paring food).[9] Let us consider again the teeth of *Australopithecus*, *Homo erectus* and *Homo sapiens* (see Fig. 3). The canines are small, just like the incisors. Compare these to the dagger-like canines of male apes and monkeys. Why do hominid males *not* possess these dental weapons? Most anthro-pologists would argue that other objects were available for personal and group defence. These 'other objects' are tools, used as weapons.

The apes do occasionally use objects in their display behaviour, when they are aggressive or excited. Males may often pick up and hurl stones, clods of earth, sticks, or handfuls of vegetation. If these sorts of behavioural patterns were present in the very earliest hominids, it is not difficult to understand how regular club-using or spear-throwing might have developed. Unlike those primates that are vegetarians, a social hunting primate would soon learn to integrate the economic and the aggressive use of tools.

It seems that tools must have been used for some time before the early Pleistocene because the front teeth of *Australopithecus* are already reduced in size and are human-like in shape. Inanimate objects must have played an important part in hominid life long before the Pleistocene.

Now, let us summarize some of the points I have made. I said earlier that we should not worry too much about what names we are going to give to the various stage of hominid evolution. Instead, we should concentrate on the various trends in that evolutionary sequence.

If we look at the Pleistocene hominid fossils from oldest to youngest, from *Australopithecus* to present day *Homo sapiens*, we can see that bipedal walking and running became steadily more efficient. Hominids also became taller—from an average of perhaps 4 ft 6 in to one of over 5 ft 6 in; their brain size increased—from an average of about 500 cm³ to over 1300 cm³. Teeth became smaller, and with this change the face also shrank, the skull becoming rounded rather than elongated fore and aft.

Technological advance is also marked. Tool-making becomes more refined, and the tool-kits become more complex. In the middle Pleistocene the use of fire appears in northern latitudes. The size of the animals hunted increases; from middle Pleistocene time on, the remains of large mammals in large numbers are found at campsites.

This increasing technological competence is one reflection of a general improvement in behavioural, social, or culture efficiency. Other features of society, such as religious and political institutions and language, would have been developing too. Unfortunately, these are not preserved as archaeological fossils. Nevertheless, we have noted that the Neandertaloids buried their dead with ceremony 50,000 years ago and more, which implies belief in an after-life. Paintings and sculpture appear in the latest Pleistocene.

Many anthropologists would like to use the first appearance of manufactured tools as a sign of the first appearance of the genus *Homo*—the first sign that hominids had become human.[16] There are a number of objections to this. Unfortunately, stone tool-making is only one restricted facet of human behaviour. Also, as we go further and further back in time, manufactured tools become more difficult to recognize, and adequate sites more difficult to find. Finally, whichever hominid features we study, whether they are anatomical or behavioural (inferred from anatomy and archaeology), we see that these features change gradually through time. To draw a meaningful line across one or several of these trends is impossible. If arbitrary boundaries must be drawn, I believe that they should be rigid, time boundaries. For example, we might agree to draw the boundary between *Australopithecus africanus* and *Homo erectus* at exactly one million years ago.

Pre-Pleistocene hominids

I said before that we should not make the mistake of thinking that chimpanzee social behaviour can be used as a replica of early hominid behaviour. However, Vernon Reynolds has recently suggested that the social structure of the living apes may not be so very different from that of the very earliest hominids.[19] He argues that the behaviour of the three species of living ape is similar in a number of basic features and that these features are likely to be ancient, possibly shared with the very earliest hominids when these branched off from the line leading to the apes. His ideas are as follows.

Groups of exploratory males might have become converted into hunting parties, and the general peacefulness of social interactions would facilitate the development of co-operative behaviour between these male bands. Hominids would begin to live less in forests and more in open country where hunting is easier. Gradually, bipedalism would have become the most important mode of locomotion. During this time, too, the use of tools as weapons must have developed. As it concentrated on hunting in one particular area, the hominid group would tend less and less to move its campsite every night.

I want now to describe very briefly some of the exciting work which has been done during the past eight years with pre-Pleistocene hominids and pongids.[17] The majority of these fossils are between 10 and 20 million years old and probably cover at least part of the period during which these important behavioural changes mentioned above occurred.

There is definite evidence for the existence of a hominid in the late Miocene and early Pliocene, between 10 and 15 million years ago. This hominid is *Ramapithecus*; the evidence consists of just a handful of jaws and teeth from India and Kenya (see Fig. 4). Unfortunately no skeleton has been recovered. What is preserved shows that the canines and incisors were already reduced in size 14 million years ago. Like those of the early Pleistocene, these much older hominids did not possess large canines. In fact, in the parts preserved, *Ramapithecus* and *Australopithecus* are surprisingly similar. We have no record of any stone, bone, or wooden objects associated with *Ramapithecus*, although it is unlikely that he could have lived successfully without tools.

So we have now pushed back our knowledge of the earliest hominids from two or three million years ago to more than 10 million years. Clearly, long before the appearance of *Homo sapiens*, or even of the genus *Homo*, the hominids had been in existence as a lineage separate from the apes. This

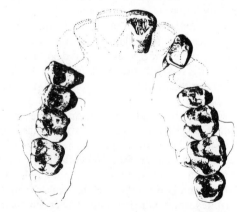

FIG. 4. A composite reconstruction of *Ramapithecus punjabicus* using specimens from India and Kenya. The dental arcade is rounded as in later hominids (see Fig. 3), the canine small, and the incisor human-like in form. Age: approximately 14 million years.

discovery is, as I have said, quite a new one. Although a number of earlier workers have proposed similar hypotheses, for the first time we have fossil evidence to support our theories.

Living alongside *Ramapithecus* in India, 14 million years back, were animals ancestral to the living Asian great ape, the orang-utan. Both hominids and pongids moved from Africa to Eurasia, along with many other animals, when a connection between the two landmasses was formed in the Middle Miocene, say 16 million years ago.

African deposits a little older than this—of middle and early Miocene age, some 20 million years old—have yielded some very interesting fossil apes, species which are ancestral to the gorilla and to the chimpanzee. Dr. Leakey has recently suggested that certain fossils from the same deposits are hominids rather than pongids. I am unable to agree with him in this and I prefer to regard these particular specimens as ancestral orang-utans before that lineage left Africa.

However, we have noted that at this time—20 million years ago—three separate species of a genus called *Dryopithecus* were living which were most probably ancestral to the chimpanzee, the gorilla, and the orang-utan. I think that these ancient pongid species were already too specialized, already too committed to their ape-dom, to have produced the hominids.

Some day therefore we must expect to find hominids even earlier than *Ramapithecus*; it is possible that the hominid and pongid lines have been separate for 30 million years or more (see Fig. 5). One might ask why so few of these early hominids have been recovered. Possibly because there were so few of them about. Why so few? Perhaps because they were creatures with a very low population density, perhaps because they were already hunters.

Of course, this is the sheerest of sheer speculation. However, I think it more likely than not that in the years to come we shall learn that our hominid pecularities of behaviour and anatomy have very ancient origins indeed.

In this paper I have tried to cover, very briefly, a little of what is known of human evolution. When I began I quoted from a lady who could not bear to think about her animal origins. Let me finish by quoting in reply some of Darwin's own eloquent words:

'Man may be excused for feeling some pride at having risen, though not through his own exertions, to the very summit of the organic scale; and the fact of his having thus risen, instead of having been aboriginally placed there, may give him hope for a still higher destiny in the distant future . . . (However) . . . with all these exalted powers—Man still bears in his bodily frame the indelible stamp of his lowly origin.'

Like Darwin, I prefer to regard men as risen apes rather than as fallen angels.

References

1. ALSBERG, P. (1933): 'The Taung puzzle. A biological essay'. *Man*, **34**, 154–159.
2. ASHTON, E. H. and SPENCE, T. F. (1958): 'Age changes in the cranial capacity and foramen magnum of hominoids', *Proc. zool. Soc. Lond.* **130**, 169–181.
3. COON, C. S. (1963): *The Origin of Races*. London: Jonathan Cape.
4. DART, R. A. (1925): '*Australopithecus africanus*: the man-ape of South Africa', *Nature, Lond.* **115**, 195–199.
5. DART, R. A. (1957): 'The osteodontokeratic culture of *Australopithecus prometheus*', *Transv. Mus. Mem.* **10**, 105 pp.
6. DARWIN, C. (1879): *The Descent of Man, and Selection in Relation to Sex*, p. 155. London: John Murray.
7. DARWIN, C. (1879): *The Descent of Man, and Selection in Relation to Sex*, p. 619. London: John Murray.
8. GOODALL, J. (1965): 'Chimpanzees of the Gombe Stream Reserve'. in *Primate Behaviour*, ed. by I. Devore. New York: Holt, Rinehart and Winston.
9. HALL, K. R. L. (1963): 'Tool-using performances as indicators of behavioral adaptability', *Curr. Anthrop.* **4**, 479–487.
10. HOOTON, E. A. (1947): *Up from the Ape*. New York: Macmillan.
11. KEITH, SIR A. (1925): 'The Taung skull,' *Nature, Lond.* **116**, 11.
12. KEITH, SIR A. (1931): *New Discoveries relating to the Antiquity of Man*. London: Williams and Norgate.
13. LEAKEY, L. S. B. (1965): *Olduvai Gorge*, vol. 1. Cambridge University Press.
14. LEAKEY, L. S. B., TOBIAS, P. V. and NAPIER, J. R. (1964): 'A new species of the genus *Homo* from Olduvai Gorge', *Nature, Lond.* **202**, 5–7.
15. LE GROS CLARK, SIR W. E. (1967): *Man-apes or Ape-Men?* New York: Holt, Rinehart and Winston.
16. OAKLEY, K. P. (1961): *Man the Tool-maker*. London: British Museum (Natural History).
17. PILBEAM, D. R. (1967): 'Man's earliest ancestors', *Science J.* **3**, 47–53.
18. PILBEAM, D. R. and SIMONS, E. L. (1965): 'Some problems of hominid classification', *Am. Scient.* **53**, 237–259.
19. REYNOLDS, V. (1966): 'Open groups in hominid evolution,' *Man.* new ser. **1**, 441–452.
20. WEINER, J. S., OAKLEY, K. P. and LE GROS CLARK, W. E. (1953): 'The solution of the Piltdown problem', *Bull. Br. Mus. nat. Hist. Geol. Ser.* 2, no. 3.

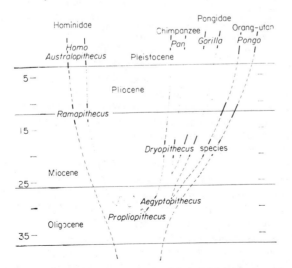

FIG. 5. A tentative scheme of hominid and pongid evolution during the past 30 million years.

19

Homo sapiens: 20 million years in the making

by William Howells

TODAY we can almost point to the first real "ancestor" of man. By this ancestor I mean a creature who, among the evolving primates of 20 million or more years ago, had just branched off from the group of our nearest relatives, the apes—a creature, still very much like an ape himself, whose descendants nevertheless evolved continuously in a different direction from that point on. We are quite sure we have the fossil jaws of such a creature—his name is *Ramapithecus* (named romantically for the Indian god Rama)—who lived about 14 million years ago, and the story of our knowledge of him is an interesting story about science itself.

We have realized for some time that man arose in this way, from animals leading to the apes on one side and to ourselves on the other. After Darwin's great book, "On the Origin of Species", had made inevitable the acceptance of evolution (including human evolution), Thomas Huxley almost at once showed how closely, in every way, we resemble the great apes. He said, in fact, that they, the apes, are closer to us than they are to monkeys.

This led to a lot of public jokes and private dismay, and the idea was resisted in many ways, by scientists as well as others. But now, after a hundred years, all the study of anatomy and, quite late, of such things as the molecular structure of proteins has

only shown more and more positively that Huxley was right. Indeed we can go a step beyond Huxley and say that apes of Africa, the gorilla and chimpanzee, are more closely related to man than is any of the three to the orang-utang of Indonesia.

After Huxley's time, some anatomists pointed to the fact that apes are adapted in body form for brachiating, or hanging and swinging from their arms. This is a particularly good and safe way for a large animal to move in trees. Pointing also to our own broad shoulders and flat, broad chests, as well as to details of our elbow and wrist joints, and arrangements of muscles, they argued that our ancestors were likewise adapted to a considerable degree for brachiation, and for life in trees. This was one more argument for close relationship to the apes.

Here again, other anatomists resisted the idea, arguing that the resemblances were not very significant, and perhaps had evolved in parallel with the apes. They preferred to think of an ancestral line which had been separate from apes, or even monkeys, for a very long time. (Always in the background there seems to have been an unconscious revulsion against relating ourselves to chimpanzees, by people who looked on them as "animals", not noticing how large-brained and intelligent these same animals really are.)

They had arguments: we do indeed stand upright, and our feet are very different from an ape's; and our jaws are now quite different, particularly with small eye teeth which do not project above the other teeth in the obvious way an ape's do. Could these larger teeth have evolved backwards to smaller ones? Could the hand-like

foot of an ape have been made over into a human foot?

These difficulties are not as great as they once seemed. Such changes are almost commonplace in animal evolution, with teeth being diminished or lost, and limbs modified in drastic ways. In addition, we must not try to picture our common ancestor as though he were a chimpanzee or gorilla; these animals have been evolving too. As study has gone on, and fact is piled on fact, most anthropologists have become convinced that our forebears did indeed use trees like the African apes, who actually live more on the forest floor than in trees.

Still later, fossil jaws of the ancestral ape *Dryopithecus* drew attention to the very close likeness of the molar teeth in ourselves and apes. Though the first specimen was found in France in 1856, it was during the early part of this century that such fragments were discovered in greater numbers, from fossil-bearing beds of Miocene and Pliocene age, and in the time range of about 20 million to 8 million years ago.

The fossils have come from other parts of Europe and from India, and later from East Africa, Georgia (U.S.S.R.) and China. With all this, the web of evidence has drawn tighter around our connexion with the apes. For *Dryopithecus* was evidently the ancestor of the large apes, and his remains are so widespread that we can now hardly expect to find a new and different fossil group in the future from which we ourselves might have come.

Another important fossil "ape", *Oreopithecus* of Italy and East Africa, who lived at the same time, became well known a few years ago. But,

WILLIAM HOWELLS, of the United States, is an international authority on prehistoric man. He is professor of anthropology at Harvard University and a past president of the American Anthropological Association. Associate editor of "Human Biology" and "American Naturalist", he is widely known for his books on the story of man's emergence, many of which have become best-sellers

108

After almost 30 years, however, L.S.B. Leakey found a very similar fossil at Fort Ternan in Kenya, which he could date as being 14 million years old.

It happened that at the same time, Elwyn Simons at Yale was looking once again at *Ramapithecus*. He was impressed with what Lewis had pointed to, and saw the same features in Leakey's new specimen.

Perhaps more important, Simons rescued other pieces of *Ramapithecus* from burial in museum drawers. He began examining old collections in various places from the U.S.A. to India, and recognized a few more fragments with the same special features, fragments which had previously been misnamed and ignored, but which he identified as fossils of *Ramapithecus*.

This careful sorting out made it easier to see the slight distinctions between *Ramapithecus* on one hand and *Dryopithecus*, ancestor of the apes, on the other. Thus we also see the beginnings of the separating paths of human and ape evolution, or between animals properly called pongids (apes) and those called hominids (anything on the human side of the same group). So palaeontology is not all looking for fossils in old river banks.

What brought the split about? Evolution has "reasons"—it follows lines of successful adaptation—but we know so little about *Ramapithecus* having only his jaws and teeth, that we cannot see the "reason". We cannot simply say that it is better or more successful to be "human", because that really means nothing, and *Ramapithecus* certainly resembled the ancestral apes far more than he resembled man. Like some chimpanzee populations he seems to have lived in an open wood and, again like chimpanzees, it is probable that he was still a tree-user.

Professors Simons and Keith Jolly, however, think he had begun to differ in diet from chimpanzees (who eat much coarse wild fruit) by using tough but nutritious foods like nuts, seeds and hard roots. This is because his teeth had thicker enamel than an ape's, and showed signs of heavy wear. He seems to have used his molars as grinders, more than his front teeth, and this would be related to his shorter face.

Ramapithecus lived from some time before 14 million years ago down at least as far as 8 million. Then, simply because no fossils have yet been found, there is a gap in knowledge until 5 million years ago. But surprising changes must have taken place: by this time much more obvious human ancestors had appeared, and they are fairly well known from the time between about 4 million and 1.5 million B.C. Here also, however, there was a long wait for recognition in the face of doubt.

It was in 1924 that Raymond Dart in South Africa saw the first skull, of a young child, in a box of fossils brought from Taung. He thought from its face and teeth that it stood halfway between man and ape, and he named it *Australopithecus* ("ape of the south"). But he had not found —and we never do find—a complete skeleton, adult, and exactly dated; and his colleagues rejected his idea, believing this juvenile, still with its milk teeth, to be merely an interesting new ape. Much later, and slowly, did the many finds arrive which showed that Dart himself had been too cautious. (The further fossils were found years ago by Dart and Robert Broom in South Africa. New ones are found every year, greatly added to by discoveries in East Africa by Dr. and Mrs. Leakey (at Olduvai Gorge) and their son Richard (in northern Kenya) as well as by Professors Camille Arambourg and F. Clark Howell.)

In the jaws of these australopithecines, the large (but human) back teeth also strongly suggest powerful chewing for tough foods. The front teeth (canines and incisors) were small and entirely hominid in nature, not something partly ape-like. For several million years there were two lines of these australopiths: *Australopithecus*, barely the size of a modern African pygmy, and *Paranthropus*, who was a little larger but had jaws as powerful as a gorilla's, though the jaws were short and deep (for grinding with the back teeth), not long, with a gorilla's large canines (for stripping forest vegetable food).

The australopiths, we know, were bipeds like modern man, capable of running in the open plains. Their hip and leg bones differ from ours today in some ways, showing that they were less efficient walkers. Nevertheless,

some time before 5 million years ago they had passed a major milestone of change, from tree-hanging, and from using the arms when walking on the ground (like apes), to a free upright gait on an arched foot with an erect torso. Apes can walk this way but poorly: their feet are flat, their great toes protrude and do not help in pushing forward, their knees will not straighten (except in orangs), and their long, high pelvic bones make them top-heavy.

SO we now know that definite hominids go back before 5 million B.C., while at the same time our strong likeness to the African apes means that we have a common ancestor at a time not too remote. *Ramapithecus* looks like the beginning of our line, and if he seems very ape-like we must remember that it is the human side, not the ape, which has been changing most rapidly. We can be sure our ancestors abandoned trees and a diet of fruit and coarse vegetable matter, perhaps only in the last 10 million years or less.

The reasons why we became bipeds are far from clear, though many have speculated. Even now we cannot run very fast: on uneven ground a gorilla, using the knuckles of his hands in running, can go as fast. We can, however, cover long distances in hunting, but could the first bipeds do so? Carrying food in the arms to a safe eating place might have encouraged uprightness: so might the need of a small animal to rise and peer over tall grass.

Perhaps, in our tree life, we became adapted to uprightness, as did apes, but not to such a degree that, as in apes, a heavy torso and long arms encouraged throwing part of our weight on our arms. Perhaps several such factors combined; we cannot say. But bipeds we were by about 5 million years ago, with important changes still going on in hip bones and feet to make this kind of gait more effective (see photos pages 42-43).

The australopiths are our undoubted ancestors at that time; there are no other possible candidates. Once again, there is controversy over the actual path of evolution. Some think there was only one varied species of australopith, not two distinct lines. And in former days it was assumed that there must have been a "cerebral rubicon", a magic brain size of about 750 cubic centimetres below which an ancestor could not be "human".

But simple stone tools, which are over two million years old, have now been found near Lake Rudolf in East Africa. They could have been made only by the australopiths since no more "advanced" men are known to have existed then; and the brains of these australopiths were not larger than a chimpanzee's. So shaped stone tools did not wait for "man" to make them, and it is thought likely that tools actually helped the australopiths to become "man", by accenting the evolutionary advantages of skilful hands and larger brains (1).

At any rate, this was the next major step, the advent of *Homo erectus*. His appearance, about 1 million B.C., probably follows another small gap in the record which might make the difference from *Australopithecus* more obvious. "Homo", a new genus, recognizes the difference, and the new group. Also *Homo erectus* is commonly spoken of as the first "true man", but it is not clear that such an expression is justified, since many of his traits were already present in the australopiths, who were also working tools at an earlier time.

These new men, however, must have presented an appearance more like our own. In body size, and in general features of the skeleton, they were much the same as ourselves. The head also would have looked more "human", with a smaller face and with jaws dominated at last by the braincase. However, this braincase was thick, and brain size had come only half the way from australopiths to modern man.

The first *Homo erectus* to be found was the famous Java man (originally named *Pithecanthropus*), of 1891. He caused a scientific explosion, as the first really primitive man to come to light, and even his own discoverer came to think that he was really a large tree-living ape. He reigned virtually alone (very recently five new examples of his skull have been found) until the Peking men of north

China were discovered, but *Homo erectus* is now recognized from East and North Africa, and in Hungary (Vertesszollos) and Germany (the Heidelberg jaw).

We know little about the transition to *Homo erectus*, or where it took place. Writers like to argue for either Africa or Asia as the "home of man", but this may not be important. *Ramapithecus* probably reached India from Africa 10 million years ago at least, and after that there must have been hominids in both continents, at the stage of *Australopithecus*. It happens that their remains so far have been found mostly in Africa, in favourable spots like Olduvai Gorge.

We have a few suggestions of what occurred. The large-jawed *Paranthropus* seems to have changed hardly at all during three million years or more. The site of Swartkrans, in South Africa, yielded many of his known fossil parts. It also provided two or three jaw fragments, of the same age, which Broom and Robinson twenty years ago believed to be different from *Paranthropus*, and more advanced in form. They christened the type "Telanthropus", though Robinson later decided that the parts belonged to *Homo erectus*. In either case, two different hominids were there together, one being *Paranthropus* and the other a more advanced kind. Here is a powerful argument for the real existence of two different forms at the same time.

A few years ago, by an almost magic piece of luck, three men were looking over these and other fragments in the collections in Pretoria when they noticed broken edges which could be fitted together to make larger pieces, where this had not been seen before.

They were able to join the "Telanthropus" upper jaw to much of a face, an ear region, and a bit of forehead. (Palaeontology, I said, is not just a matter of looking in river banks.) This gave most of the face and front of the skull, to which the lower jaw of "Telanthropus" would have been a fairly good fit. The whole thing suggests *Homo* even more strongly than before, but seems to be too small in size.

At about the same time Mrs. Leakey found a small crushed skull in the

lowest levels of Olduvai Gorge, below the well-known *Zinjanthropus* (a *Paranthropus*) and dated to not quite two million years. This was only the latest in a series of similar finds from Olduvai, all of which had been called *Homo habilis* by Leakey and his associates. Though fragmentary, they were obviously not *Paranthropus*, having higher skulls and smaller jaws, and to many they suggested the smaller South African form *Australopithecus*.

After a great deal of work, the new skull was put together. This and the reconstructed "Telanthropus" give us a better picture: they are somewhat more advanced than the known *Australopithecus* but are still very small for *Homo*. They may well be showing us the ancestor who had just begun to make stone tools and who, in the next million years, turned into *Homo*.

Again, controversy. Some prefer to call this little person *Homo habilis*, in the belief that both *Australopithecus* and *Paranthropus* became extinct, and that this graceful little creature developed directly into high-skulled, large-brained *Homo sapiens* without passing through the stage of low-browed, thick-skulled *Homo erectus*.

But this raises the problem of who might have been the ancestor of *Homo habilis*, unless it was *Australopithecus*, whom he greatly resembles; and also the problem of why remains of only *Homo erectus* have been found for the period immediately after. It seems safer to assume, for the present, that the *Australopithecus* line began making simple tools nearly 2 1/2 million years ago and, during a time from which we have almost no fossils, grew larger in size and advanced to the *erectus* stage, while *Paranthropus* continued contentedly munching coarse vegetable food with his great jaws, ignoring tools, until he became extinct.

If the first *Homo erectus* to be found, the Java Man, was considered in the 1890s to be very subhuman, we know better now. In Africa, and evidently in Europe, he made large stone hand-axes, or coups de poing, increasingly well-shaped in comparison with the earlier pebble tools.

We do not really know about how he used them. All we can say is that he occupied the warmer parts of the Old World for at least half a million years (and even some cool places in Europe and China), as the major

---

(1) *Some of these same australopiths, before the tools were found, had already been classed by Leakey and others as very early "men", or Homo and, following a suggestion of Professor Dart, were named Homo habilis, with the sense of being "good with the hands". We shall come back to this.*

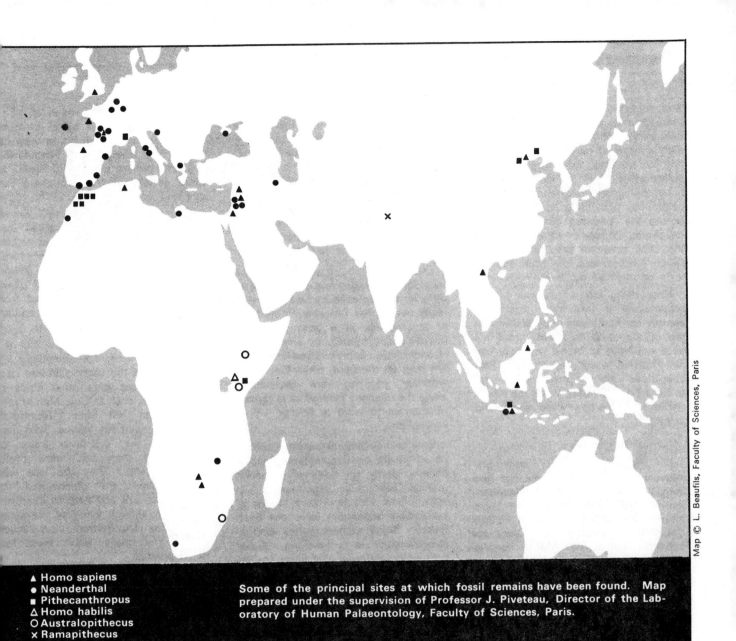

Map © L. Beaufils, Faculty of Sciences, Paris

▲ Homo sapiens
● Neanderthal
■ Pithecanthropus
△ Homo habilis
○ Australopithecus
× Ramapithecus

Some of the principal sites at which fossil remains have been found. Map prepared under the supervision of Professor J. Piveteau, Director of the Laboratory of Human Palaeontology, Faculty of Sciences, Paris.

glacial periods were beginning; and that in this time he showed some evolutionary progress in brains which became larger and skulls and jaws which became less massive.

At the moment, he may now seem more like a well-defined "stage" than he should, because we not only lack fossils from the period just before, but also have very few from the hundreds of thousands of years following the second (Mindel) glaciation. Change doubtless went on by small steps during these times, but we cannot see the steps just now.

The Swanscombe and Steinheim skulls, of the Second Interglacial, perhaps 250,000 years ago, and the new Tautavel skull from the early Third Glacial, are important. They are much advanced over the known *erectus* men, but they are still too few to help us much, or show what was happening

worldwide. It is only in the Third Interglacial and the last, or Fourth Glacial, mainly within the last 100,000 years, that we come again to a wealth of fossil men, and to the Neanderthal problem, the greatest controversy of all.

When the first of the Neanderthals was reported in 1856, he too was thought to be subhuman by some, but only an exceptional modern man, possibly a diseased person, by others (the first controversy, now forgotten). A Neanderthal skull is indeed exceptional, being very long and low, with a continuous protruding bony browridge across the forehead containing well-developed sinuses or air spaces. But the skull contours are not those of *Homo erectus*, and the brain was at least as large as our own.

Neanderthal man's face was equally remarkable; it was long, protruding

sharply forward in the midline from the top of the nose on down. Had his nose not been so broad we might call him "hatchet-faced", but modern "hatchet-faced" north Europeans are apt to be tall and slender, while the Neanderthals of Europe were short and stocky.

CONTROVERSY over primitiveness and antiquity did not last long. Today we know that Neanderthal man occupied Europe in the Third Interglacial and much of the Fourth Glacial periods (perhaps between 150,000 and 35,000 B.C.), and that he was the author of the Mousterian varieties of retouched flake stone tool, which were technically far advanced over something like a handaxe. These tools in some ways foreshadowed

111

those of the Upper Palaeolithic, which were made from bladelike flakes and were used by Cro-Magnon man among others.

For a hundred years now, discoveries of skeletons of the European Neanderthals have given rise to a conception of his "classic" form as I have described it. They have also reinforced the conclusion that he gave way, with seeming abruptness, about 35,000 B.C. to men who were entirely modern in physique, though robust, and who were in fact like living Europeans.

This is the heart of the modern controversy, with strong opinions on both sides. I have stated the distinctiveness of Neanderthal man too simply and sharply, in order to begin with a contrast. In North Africa there were other Neanderthal-like men, more modern, in some ways, lacking the typical facial projection of the Europeans. They too were followed by modern men of rugged build, apparently coming from the east about the same time (35,000 B.C.), or perhaps earlier.

The Near East is more puzzling. Men with Neanderthal faces, and with Neanderthal peculiarities of the skeleton, existed in the early Fourth Glacial, with Mousterian tools. But their skulls were not as "classic" as the Europeans, and some of them were remarkably tall, like the Amud man of Israel, found by Japanese excavators. (Here we must remember that modern men vary greatly—Scots and Eskimos might be compared to these Neanderthals in body size.)

The argument is over whether the Neanderthals, in Europe or elsewhere, were in fact replaced by invaders, with really new Upper Palaeolithic methods of tool-making, in a brief period (a few thousand years); or whether the Neanderthals simply evolved into modern man on the spot, while his stone-working, adopting new techniques, made the changes from what is termed Mousterian to what is termed Upper Palaeolithic.

It is a complex argument, and is based partly on assumptions (and, I believe, partly on tides of scientific opinion, like older arguments). In spite of all that is known, ways of convincing opponents have not been found. Some archaeologists emphasize transition in tool-making. Other archaeologists grant that there are important Mousterian survivals in the

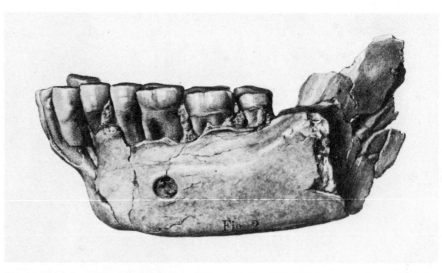

Big front teeth of Neanderthal man. Though now excluded by many from modern man's direct ancestry, Neanderthal man was much less of a brute than was first believed.

early Perigordian culture of the upper Palaeolithic of France. But they see a clear break with the coming of a second culture, the Aurignacian, which has different tool-making techniques and also a wealth of decorative objects previously lacking. This they view as something entirely new, an intrusion; and they cannot imagine a simple cultural evolution.

Similarly, some anthropologists cannot imagine biological evolution so swift as to produce a modern face and skull from that of Neanderthal Man in a few thousand years. Others are doubtful about the shortness of the period, and emphasize intergradation in shape between Neanderthal and modern man, especially in the east. They hold that evolution, not replacement, presents fewer difficulties. They note that if there was an invasion, the source of the "modern" Upper Palaeolithic men has not been found and that, if the European Neanderthals are rather special, the Near Eastern Neanderthals are more intermediate and "progressive".

These scholars would paint a rather simple picture of human history, probably too simple. They suggest that there was everywhere a "Neanderthal phase" of human evolution in the last glacial period, out of which all of us —Eskimos and Scots alike—emerged as modern man. This broad view assumes that there were Neanderthal men everywhere in the Old World, as there certainly were throughout Eur-

ope and apparently around its edges.

Carleton Coon, in a well known book, "The Origin of Races", has argued for another theory something like this one. Modern races appeared in different parts of the Old World. not from a single Neanderthal phase or Neanderthal population, but from different races of *Homo erectus* already present in these places.

There are difficulties here, but the theory does recognize something important which the other scholars neglect: that there were other kinds of Ice Age men, such as Solo Man of Java and Broken Hill Man ("Rhodesian Man") of southern Africa, who had some of the primitive traits of Neanderthal man but were really quite different. They are less well known: they are discoveries, or facts, which are still hard to interpret. Solo Man, though living at the same time as the Neanderthals, had a much thicker and cruder skull, more like *Homo erectus*.

There is a final chapter to all this. What *do* we know about modern man himself? Living races seem very different, some with very dark skin, some with blond hair, some with narrowed eye openings. But in form of skull (and this is what we can compare with early man) they are really much alike, with smaller faces and higher, narrower braincases. This is my own conclusion, after having worked with skulls from all parts of the globe. I believe, as do many colleagues, that all must have some common source. But where, and when?

HERE we are in a shadow-land lighted by too few discoveries. Outside of Europe, where we observe the disappearance of Neanderthal Man, remains are especially scanty. Nevertheless, striking recent finds seem to mean that *Homo sapiens* of our own kind existed elsewhere, in Africa and Asia, in the same period as the Neanderthals of Europe.

They are different from those "progressive" Neanderthals I spoke of. Several skeletons from Jebel Qafzeh, in Israel, have no radiocarbon date but come from cave levels in which the tools and the soils indicate a time fairly early in the last glacial period, probably well before 40,000 years ago. And the skulls are surprisingly modern —not completely so, but being quite different from Neanderthals. Only the large bony brows, and perhaps larger front teeth, in some of them, suggest Neanderthal Man, and others of the tribe had quite small teeth, and smaller, modern brows and faces as well

as far as is now known.

Two skulls found by Richard Leakey in Kenya, of modern form or close to it—and not Neanderthal—are surely older than 37,000 years. Some authorities think they may be very much older. For to the east a skull from the Niah Cave in Sarawak (Borneo) has been dated by two methods to about 40,000 BC, and it looks like a Melanesian or possibly an Australian.

MODERN men of the same general kind had made the difficult water crossings (difficult for early men) to Australia before 30,000 B.C., and many recent discoveries attest the presence of such people there and in New Guinea over the next ten thousand years. In the New World, recent finds prove the Indians were in South America about 20,000 years ago, much earlier than had been generally believed, so that men had come to the Americas from Asia probably several thousand years before. No American skeletons are as old as this, but we can only suppose that these earlier men were like the later.

Now here is the important thing. All the known skeletons I have mentioned were of modern form. In addition, the European Upper Palaeolithic people had the nature of later Europeans; the early Australians were recognizably like later Australians or Melanesians; and we can only suppose that the first Indians of America were the same kind of proto-Mongoloid we see in them today.

The Omo skulls of Africa cannot be recognized yet, and otherwise there are no African skulls quite so old. But the signs are that, by the time the Neanderthals vanished, or before, not only was modern man fairly widespread, but the races we see today had already taken shape.

We still cannot say how this happened. It is strange that we should know so little of our nearest ancestors. But we cannot expect to have the whole story after only one century of searching. There are blank parts of our history now, but they will be filled: we have hundreds of years of exploration ahead of us.

20

By Ralph S. Solecki

Neanderthal is not an epithet but a worthy ancestor

As research continues on some prehuman
remains from Iraq's Shanidar Cave,
the Neanderthals seem closer to us in spirit

The top of a skull was perched on the edge of the yawning excavation in the huge cavern. At first it was difficult to realize that we had before us an extreme rarity in human paleontology.

Except for its heavy brow ridge, the skullcap looked like a gigantic egg, soiled and broken. When fully exposed on the narrow excavation shelf, it was an awesome sight—obviously the head of a person who had suffered a sudden, violent end. The bashed-in skull, the displaced lower jaw and the unnatural twist of the head were mute evidence of a horrible death.

As we exposed the skeleton which lay under a heavy burden of stones, we had confirmation that this individual had been killed on the spot by a rockfall. His bones were broken, sheared and crushed on the underlying stones. A large number of rocks must have fallen on him within a split second, throwing his body backward, full-length down the slight slope while at the same time a block of stone severed his head and neck from his trunk.

Among his remains there were small concentrations of mammal bones, which might have been rodent nests. But it is equally possible these bones were dropped there as part of a funeral feast for the dead.

This was "Nandy," as we called him, a member of

Formerly with the Smithsonian, Dr. Ralph Solecki
is professor of anthropology at Columbia.

the species *Homo neanderthalensis* who had died about 48,000 years before. In the scientific literature he is referred to as Shanidar I, because his were the first adult human remains that we identified as Neanderthal from a cave near the village of Shanidar high in the mountains of Kurdistan in northern Iraq.

Large, airy, and conveniently near a water supply, Shanidar Cave is still a seasonal home for modern Kurdish tribesmen, as it has been for various groups of men for thousands upon thousands of years. I had led our expedition to Shanidar Cave in a search for cultural artifacts from the Old Stone Age in this part of Kurdistan, Iraq. Human remains, much less Neanderthal remains, were not the goal, yet altogether in four expeditions from 1951 to 1960 we uncovered nine Neanderthal skeletons.

Laboratory studies of these remains continue to this day and the results are bringing the Neanderthals closer to us in spirit and mind than we would ever have thought likely.

The Neanderthals have been a nettling problem ever since the first find was made more than 100 years ago. This was the famous faceless skull and other skeletal parts found during quarrying operations around a cave in the Neander Valley not far from Düsseldorf in Germany. Primarily through the writings of one man, Marcellin Boule, who was a greatly respected Frenchman in the field of human paleontology, the owner of the Neander skull was soon cast in the role of a brutish figure, slow, dull and bereft of sentiment.

Although we now know much more about Neanderthal man—there have been at least 155 individuals uncovered in 68 sites in Europe, the Near East and elsewhere—he still seems to hang in space on the tree of human evolution. Some anthropologists feel that he had reached a "dead-end" branch on this tree. In any case, his time span on Earth (about 80,000 years) was more than double that of modern man who replaced him, but roughly one-tenth of the time span of *Homo erectus* who preceded him.

An abundance of Neanderthals

The classical hypothesis, now abandoned, was that Neanderthal man was an ancestral stage through which *Homo sapiens* passed. A second theory is that Neanderthal man was a species apart from *Homo sapiens,* contemporary but reproductively isolated, as donkeys are from horses. The third is that Neanderthal man was a subspecies of early *sapiens,* forming a geographic race. On the whole, the evidence appears to indicate that the Neanderthal did not gradually change into *sapiens,* but was replaced by invading *sapiens.* The greatest difficulty for human paleontologists is that there is a real scarcity of skeletal finds to

Name: unknown. Alias: Shanidar I (Nandy). Cause of
death: rockfall. Place: Shanidar Cave, Iraq.
Date of death: 46,000 B.C. Nearest relative: Man.

which they can point with confidence as *sapiens* of an
age comparable to that of the Neanderthals.

There was, however, no scarcity of Neanderthals at
Shanidar Cave. Prior to the discovery of Nandy, or
Shanidar I, we had recovered the remains of an infant.
It was later identified as Neanderthal by our Turkish
colleague, Dr. Muzaffer Senyürek of the University of
Ankara. When it was found, we had little reason to
suspect that it was a Neanderthal child.

But not so with Nandy. "A Neanderthal if I ever
saw one," is the comment in my field notes for the day
of April 27, 1957, the day we found him. Although he
was born into a savage and brutal environment,
Nandy provides proof that his people were not lacking in compassion.

According to the findings of T. Dale Stewart, the
Smithsonian Institution physical anthropologist who
has studied all the remains of the Shanidar Neanderthals (except for the Shanidar child), Shanidar I lived
for 40 years, a very old man for a Neanderthal—equivalent to a man of about 80 today. He was a prime
example of rehabilitation. His right shoulder blade,
collar bone and upper arm bone were undeveloped
from birth. Stewart believes that his useless right arm
was amputated early in life just above the elbow.
Moreover, he must have been blind in his left eye
since he had extensive bone scar tissue on the left side
of his face. And as if this was not enough, the top right
side of his head had received some damage which had
healed before the time of his death.

In short, Shanidar I was at a distinct disadvantage
in an environment where even men in the best condition had a hard time. That Nandy made himself useful around the hearth (two hearths were found close

to him) is evidenced by his unusually worn front teeth. Presumably, in lieu of his right arm, he used his jaws for grasping. But he could barely forage and fend for himself, and we must assume that he was accepted and supported by his people up to the day he died. The stone heap we found over his skeleton and the nearby mammal food remains show that even in death he was an object of some esteem, if not respect, born of close association against a hostile environment.

The discovery of Shanidar I was for us a major, and unexpected, event. The discovery, about a month later on May 23, of Shanidar II was overwhelming.

The initial exposure was made by Phil Smith, then a Harvard University graduate student, who laid bare the great eye sockets and broken face of a new Neanderthal. My first impression was of the horror a rockfall could do to a man's face. The lower jaw was broken, the mouth agape. The eye sockets, crushed out of shape by the stones, stared hollowly from under a warped heavy brow ridge, behind which was the characteristic slanting brow of the Neanderthal.

From later reconstruction of the event, we determined that Shanidar II was killed by a relatively minor rockfall, followed closely by a major rockfall that missed the dead man. His demise did not go unnoticed by his companions. Sometime after the tumult, thunder and subsiding dust of the crashing rocks, they returned to see what had happened to their cave mate. It looks as though a small collection of stones was placed over the body and a large fire lit above it. In the hearth we found several stone points, and several split and broken mammal bones nearby that may have been the remains of a funeral feast. It appears that, when the ceremony was at an end, the hearth was covered over with soil while the fire was still burning.

As with the first two adults, Shanidar III was found in the course of cleaning and straightening the profile of an excavation. It was as if some Near Eastern genie was testing my alertness by tucking away the skeletons on the borders of the excavation proper.

Like the other two, Shanidar III had been accidentally caught under a rockfall and instantly killed. One of his ribs had a strange cut. X rays taken at Georgetown University Hospital revealed that he had been wounded by a rectangular-edged implement of wood and the wound had been in the process of healing for about a week when he died. Most likely, he had been disabled in a conflict with unfriendly neighbors and was recuperating when he was killed. Clearly, the dangers of the caveman's life were by no means shut out when he crossed the portal to his airy home.

On August 3, 1960, during our fourth and last season at Shanidar, we uncovered the fragile and rotted bones of Shanidar IV. While Stewart exposed these remains, I started to explore the stones and soil near the place where three years before we had found Shanidar III. Parts of his skeleton were missing and unaccounted for in our collection.

In my first trowelings, several animal bones turned up. One did not look like an animal bone; it looked human. Later I encountered a rib bone that Stewart authenticated as human, but it was not until I uncovered a human molar tooth that we confirmed the presence of Shanidar V. This was becoming too much.

Within four days we found several other bones of this fifth Neanderthal including the scattered fragments of the skull. It appeared that he too was killed by a rockfall, perhaps the same one that killed Nandy.

There was yet another discovery to be made. Stewart was clearing around the southern side of Shanidar IV when he encountered some crushed pieces of a humerus near the skull. "It doesn't make sense," said Stewart, "not in anatomical position." His immediate reaction was that he hated to think that there was yet another Neanderthal in the cave. Furthermore, there were already two humeri for Shanidar IV, the correct number, and now a third: Here was Shanidar VI.

In the space of only five days we had discovered three Neanderthal skeletal groups. Before us were the vast problems of preserving, recording and transporting the remains safely to the Iraq Museum in Baghdad. In the course of feverishly carrying out these activities, we discovered—in some loose material associated with Shanidar VI—more bones which later proved to be from yet another Neanderthal, Shanidar VII. These two, VI and VII, were females. We also retrieved some bones of a baby.

The skeleton remains of IV (a male), VI, VII and the baby (VIII) all appeared to lie in a niche bounded on two sides by large stone blocks. The nature of the soft soil and the position of the stone blocks leads me to believe that a crypt had been scooped out among the rocks and that the four individuals had been interred and covered over with earth. The child had been laid in first; the two females next, perhaps at a later time. The remains of these three were incomplete. Shanidar IV, the adult male, received the main attention of the burial. Probably, to make room for Shanidar IV, the bones of the others were disturbed.

As part of the archaeological routine, I had taken soil samples from around and within the area of Shanidar IV and Shanidar VI, as well as some samples from outside the area of the skeletal remains. These were sent for pollen analysis to Mme. Arlette Leroi-Gourhan, a paleobotanist in Paris.

Under the microscope, several of the prepared slides showed not only the usual kinds of pollen from trees and grasses, but also pollen from flowers. Mme. Leroi-Gourhan found clusters of flower pollen from at least eight species of flowers—mainly small, brightly colored varieties. They were probably woven into the branches of a pine-like shrub, evidence of which was also found in the soil. No accident of nature could have deposited such remains so deep in the cave. Shanidar IV had been buried with flowers.

Someone in the Last Ice Age must have ranged the mountainside in the mournful task of collecting flowers for the dead. Here were the first "Flower People," a discovery unprecedented in archaeology. It seems logical to us today that pretty things like flowers should be placed with the cherished dead, but to find flowers in a Neanderthal burial that took place about 60,000 years ago is another matter and makes all the more piquant our curiosity about these people.

Regarding their livelihood, we can certainly say the Neanderthals of Shanidar were hunters/foragers/gatherers. They most likely made a seasonal round of their wilderness domain, returning to shelter in Shanidar Cave.

The animals they hunted are represented in the cave by the bones of wild goat, sheep, cattle, pig and land tortoise. More rare are bear, deer, fox, marten and gerbil. It should be noted that the most common animals represented are the more docile type, the gregarious herbivorous mammals. It is likely that the Neanderthals caught them by running them over cliffs in herds or, conceivably, by running them into blind canyons where they could be slaughtered. There are several such canyons within easy striking distance of Shanidar Cave.

Communal life in a cultural backwater

The picture of the lone stalker cannot be ruled out in the case of the Neanderthal but, since these people lived in a communal setting, it would be more natural for them to have engaged in communal hunting. And the fact that their lame and disabled (Shanidar I and Shanidar III) had been cared for in the cave is excellent testimony for communal living and cooperation.

By projecting carbon 14 dates that we have received for certain portions of the cave, I estimate that its first occupation was at most about 100,000 years ago. For perhaps 2,000 generations, over a period of some 60,000 years, we think that groups of Neanderthals—probably numbering 25 members at a time—made their seasonal home in Shanidar Cave. Preliminary findings from the analysis of pollen samples show that, through the long history of their occupation of the cave, the climate vacillated from cool to warm.

Yet throughout the period, the Neanderthals changed little in their means of adapting to these climatic changes. Their tool kit remained much the same throughout: It included their flaked stone tools identified as a "typical Mousterian" industry of points, knives, scoopers and some perforators, all struck off from locally derived flint pebbles. Only a

few fragments of bone tools were found. With this meager tool kit Neanderthal man was able to survive and prosper in his own way.

Shanidar seems to have been a kind of cultural backwater, a "refuge" area bypassed by the stream of history because of the remoteness of the area—a condition still reflected in the Kurdish tribal compartmentalizations of today.

Then, around 40,000-35,000 B.C., the Neanderthals were gone from Shanidar Cave, replaced by a wave of *Homo sapiens* whom we have called Baradostians. We have no skeletal remains of these people but ample evidence that they possessed a brand new stone tool kit. Using the same raw materials available to their predecessors, the Baradostians used the Upper Paleolithic technique of flint-knapping, striking off blades which were used as blanks for tools. They had more stone tool types, a variety of bone tools and they also possessed a woodworking technology such as the Neanderthals never had. Probably they used elaborate wood-carving stone tools to fashion traps and more advanced kinds of hunting apparatus and with this equipment they pursued much the same kind of game animals (mainly goats) as their extinct Neanderthal predecessors had.

By 35,000 B.C., the Neanderthals seem to have disappeared from the world altogether and we may well ask, what did Upper Paleolithic *Homo sapiens* have that the Neanderthals did not have? To my way of thinking, there were probably two things that weighed heavily in the balance. One was language. Jacquetta Hawkes, the English student of language and prehistory, feels that although the Neanderthal was a skilled toolmaker, his tool kit shows a conspicuous lack of invention and adaptability. He was probably handicapped because he did not develop a fully articulate and precise language. This was the new weapon which we think his Upper Paleolithic replacement possessed and used to make a tool kit so diversified that in the graver category he had more working edges than master cabinetmakers are accustomed to working with today. With his greater articulateness, he was able to describe and demonstrate the details of the manufacture of these stone tools to his people, including the children who were to carry on the group's activities.

The second critical cultural achievement of Upper Paleolithic man, in my opinion, is his ability to keep track of events for the future. Alexander Marshack, a research fellow at Harvard, has provided us with this recent and powerful insight into prehistoric man. Thousands of notational sequences have been found on engraved bones and stones dating as far back as at least 30 millennia. These markings have been puzzled over or guessed about by archaeologists since the time they were first discovered more than 100 years ago. Marshack has determined that they served Upper

Paleolithic man as a kind of farmer's almanac tied in with a lunar notational count. Some are illustrated with the natural history of the events, giving the possessor of the object a mnemonic device reminding him when to expect the change of seasons and the movements and dispersal of game.

An ancestor of sympathetic character

In short, this was of tremendous economic advantage to Upper Paleolithic man, and it gave him a control over his environment and destiny such as was evidently denied to his predecessor, the Neanderthal.

So, men with these remarkable abilities and all that flowed from them overtook and presumably eliminated the Neanderthals. We have long thought of the Neanderthals as ultimate examples of the Hobbesian dictum that the life of a primitive man is "nasty, brutish and short." They have been characterized as having a near-bestial appearance with an ape-like face in profile, a thick neck, stooped shoulders and a shuffling gait. But now it appears that they were actually very similar to *Homo sapiens* in skeletal structure. Stewart's study of the Shanidar Neanderthals led him to the conclusion that below the head there was not too much difference between these early men and modern man. Of course, one cannot deny the bulging prominent eyebrows and the heavy coarse-featured face of the Neanderthal in general, though Anthropologist Earnest Hooton once said: "You can, with equal facility, model on a Neanderthaloid skull the features of a chimpanzee or the lineaments of philosopher."

His own biological evolution is something man really does not have conscious control over. But his culture, his social and religious life, is something else. In the millions of years of evolution that began with the ape-like hominids of Africa it is among the Neanderthals that we have the first stirrings of social and religious sense and feelings: the obvious care with

Ground plan of Shanidar Cave (inset) and skulls in excavation indicate approximate position of the nine Neanderthal finds and their time scale.

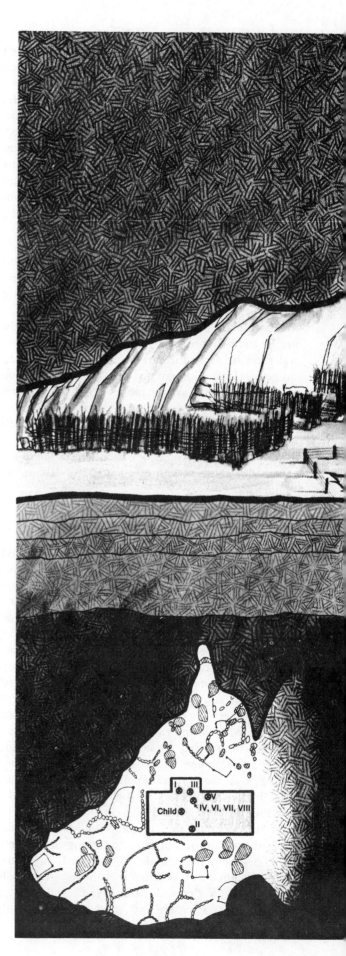

which the lame and crippled were treated, the burials —and the flowers. Flowers have never been found in prehistoric burials before, though this may simply be because no one has ever looked for them. And to be sure, only one of the burials in Shanidar Cave yielded such evidence. But the others buried there could have died during the wrong season for flowers, since death knows no season.

The Neanderthal has been ridiculed and rejected for a century but despite this he is still our ancestor. Of course we may still have the privilege of ridiculing him, but in the face of the growing evidence, especially in the light of the recent findings at Shanidar, we can not actually reject him. And what person will mind having as an ancestor one of such sympathetic character, one who laid his dead to rest with flowers?

VI. Problems in Interpretation

There are two parts to this section. Part A is concerned with two major issues in the interpretation of the hominid fossil sequence, while Part B addresses some ongoing controversies in the interpretation of archaeological remains.

A. Fossil Remains

The 1970s have been exciting years for paleontologists. A wealth of new finds has been brought to light, especially in East Africa. These have made the picture of human evolution considerably more complicated than it appeared to be at the end of the 1960s, but all scholars agree that they justify at least one major conclusion: We can now push back the emergence of full hominids that were directly ancestral to *Homo sapiens* millions of years further than had been thought a scant ten years ago—back at least to 5.5 million years B.P.

One of the major scholars to contribute to these findings is Richard Leakey, son of Louis and Mary Leakey, the famous researchers who first focused the world's attention on East Africa as a source of very ancient hominid remains in the course of their momentous work at Olduvai Gorge in Tanzania. In "Hominids in Africa" Leakey discusses the state of our knowledge with regard to hominid and human origins, starting with the first probable hominid (*Ramapithecus*) and focusing on controversial materials indicating a very early split between *Australopithecus* and *Homo* (of indeterminate species)—both fossil populations that are ancient and clearly hominid. Leakey takes a modest position, stressing the need for more data, but he strongly urges the view that australopithecines are side branches on the tree of human evolution. We should point out that many other scholars, such as David Pilbeam and Bernard Campbell, disagree. Some of the remains that Leakey calls *Homo* they include under *Australopithecus*—from which they envision the subsequent evolution of the other early *Homo* remains.

The selection by Brace tells the story of the "Neanderthal: Ridiculed, Rejected, but Still Our Ancestor." More accurately, it is the story of the early discovery of Neanderthal remains and the historical context that kept scholars from appreciating them for what they were. Brace also ties in the discovery and debate over other early fossil finds. An interesting picture emerges: The order of the discovery of hominid fossils was the reverse of their evolutionary sequence. In other words, the earliest finds were of our most recent ancestors, while subsequent finds were of more ancient populations. This has meant that with each new find human and hominid antiquity has had to be pushed back; and each time this has meant a fresh wave of heated debate, with earlier discoveries resisting the implications of new finds that undercut their claims to having found the "first" hominid. Indeed, history seems to be repeating itself at this very time, with Richard Leakey and the other fossil hunters in East Africa (and David Pilbeam in Pakistan) once more pushing back the date of the emergence of our direct ancestors.

B.   Cultural Remains

The first selection of this group is not controversial in itself. Rather, it represents a major recent thrust in archaeological interpretation, namely, focusing on the ways in which prehistoric cultures represent adaptive responses to environmental stresses. Klein's "Ecology of Stone Age Man at the Southern Tip of Africa" explores the relationships that can be observed between climate and stone tool technologies among prehistoric groups in southern Africa.

Tellefsen, on the other hand, offers in his discussion of "A New Theory of Pyramid Building" a new and exciting interpretation of materials that have challenged scholars for centuries. The great pyramids of Egypt were built without metal tools; and it has been assumed that perhaps hundreds of thousands of workers (or slaves) were necessary to erect them. Tellefsen, an engineer by profession, argues that the simple pulley systems the ancient Egyptians were known to have had could have been used to build the pyramids with relatively few laborers—and thus may have strained the human resources of Egyptian civilization to a much lesser degree than has been supposed before now.

Finally, Heyerdahl jumps right into the middle of a raging controversy as he discusses "Linking the Transoceanic Cultures." American archaeologists have tended to ignore the wild and speculative claims of the "hyperdiffusionists" who tried to trace the orgins of the mighty native American civilizations (including the Olmec, Maya, Aztec, and Inca) back to places such as Mesopotamia and Egypt (not to mention Atlantis, Mu, and other phantasmagorical home bases for the "chariots of the gods"). In the past two decades, however, professionally acknowledged scholars such as Betty Meggers have argued strongly—and increasingly convincingly—that many elements of the American civilizations did indeed originate elsewhere. Meggers herself traces Olmec origins back to the Shang civilization in China; others, such as Robert von Heine-Geldern, see China itself as the recipient of cultural elements from farther west and thus trace features of American (pre-Columbian) civilization back to the region of the Black Sea. In this context Heyerdahl has played a very controversial role. Having deduced transoceanic connections between cultures, he has set out to prove that they were possible using the technology available to the ancient peoples in question. His first exploit was the *Kon-Tiki* crossing from South America to Polynesia, which was intended to prove his hypothesis that the islands of the southern Pacific were populated from the Americas, not from Southeast Asia as is commonly accepted. He indeed proved that such voyages were possible, but he failed to convince scholars that they accounted for the peopling of Oceania. Here he argues that ancient Egyptians brought high civilization to the New World; and he details plans to prove the feasibility of such transatlantic crossings in the reed boats that the Egyptians had. In point of fact, what came to be known as the *Ra* expedition eventually was reasonably successful. But once again, proving that something *could* have happened is a far cry from proving that it *did* happen.

As of now, the controversy is still unresolved. No serious scholar, however, puts any credence in the wild and sensational popular accounts of extraterrestrial origins for New World civilizations. And we must emphasize here that all the so-called mysterious remains to be found in New World sites can be fully understood and explained in terms of the known capacities of the peoples of those times.

Richard E. Leakey

Views

Hominids in Africa

One of the world's foremost paleoanthropologists discusses recent finds from African sites that give evidence for very early differentiation among the Hominidae

The existing fossil evidence supports the contention that Africa was the crucible of human origins and development. African sites yield evidence illustrating many phases of the human story from the earliest stages. Fossils from early Miocene sites in Africa illustrate the very early differentiation of the Hominidae; from later strata there is evidence for more recent origin of the genus *Homo*. Asia and parts of Europe have also produced contemporary material of the earliest phases of development, but there is an absence of intermediate forms in Asia which could be held as possible evidence for migration of early *Homo* into Asia and the Far East. A growing interest in the field of prehistory and intensive work in Plio/Pleistocene sites (dating from 1 to 3 million years ago) of the Mediterranean region and Asia may yield data that will revise the present understanding. At present, however, the

Richard E. Leakey, Director of the National Museums of Kenya and well known for his fossil discoveries in East Africa, was born in 1944. He attended schools in Nairobi and received the education of experience by working with his parents in Olduvai Gorge and other parts of East Africa. Currently he is the leader of the East Turkana Research Project, a multinational, interdisciplinary investigation of the Plio/Pleistocene of Kenya's northern Rift Valley, where the group's discovery of many new fossil hominids has radically changed the thinking about human origins. Author of numerous publications, Mr. Leakey has received many honors for his research contributions and is Chairman of the Wildlife Clubs of Kenya Association and of the Foundation for Research into the Origin of Man. This article is based on an address given at the Sigma Xi National Meeting in November 1975. Address: National Museums of Kenya, P.O. Box 40658, Nairobi, Kenya.

earliest stage of the human family is represented by fossils of *Ramapithecus* from Ft. Ternan in Kenya (*1, 2*), with a date of between 12.5 and 14 million years ago. Slightly younger examples are known from the Siwalik sites (*3*), dated by their contained faunas at about 9 to 12 million, and closely allied material recently reported from Hungary (*4*) is thought to be dated at perhaps 11 million.

The case for *Ramapithecus* as a hominid is not substantial, and the fragmentary material leaves many questions open. There is general agreement that the dental morphology is of the hominid pattern; the canines were "reduced," or proportionately small. Because we have no cranial elements other than maxillary and mandibular fragments and as the postcranial skeleton is unrepresented, the arguments for the hominid status of this genus are severely limited. The survival of this unspecialized hominid is not documented at present, partly because late Miocene and Pliocene localities are not well represented in Africa and also perhaps because known sites in Eurasia have not been investigated in great detail.

The better documented nonprimate vertebrates in the Old World provide many instances of middle Miocene forms surviving into the Pliocene. It is conceivable that *Ramapithecus* maintained itself on the forest fringes and savannas and might be found to occur alongside the more specialized forms in the late Pliocene. In this connection it has been stated that KNM-ER 1482 (*5*), a mandible from the Koobi Fora Formation, at Lake Turkana

(formerly Rudolf), Kenya, shows certain traits that I believe distinguish it from the better documented *Australopithecus* and *Homo* of the same era, and perhaps it may be a *Ramapithecus*. Similarly, the recently reported finds from the Afar Valley in Ethiopia include a partial skeleton (called "Lucy" by its discovers) that may be considered a late *Ramapithecus*. The study of this material and publication of detailed descriptions will be extremely important.

The African record between the middle Miocene and Pliocene is sparse. Two isolated molars are recorded from the Baringo Basin— one from the Ngorora Formation (*6*) at 9 to 12 million and the other at Lukeino (*7*) at about 6 to 7 million years. These sites are within the Kenya Rift Valley and could well yield further specimens. A mandibular fragment with a single molar in place is known from Lothagam (*8*), where a date of 5.5 million has been reported. A nearby site, Kanapoi (*9*), has yielded a fragment of humerus, and an age of about 4 million years has been proposed. Both of these specimens have been provisionally attributed to the genus *Australopithecus*, although there are few morphological features to support this. It is extremely difficult to identify mandibular fragments with any exactness, and the material might equally represent a very early example of *Homo* or a late *Ramapithecus*. Consequently, the citations for *Australopithecus* earlier than 3 million years have to be regarded with caution and some doubt at this time. It would perhaps be useful to place the two isolated molars, the man-

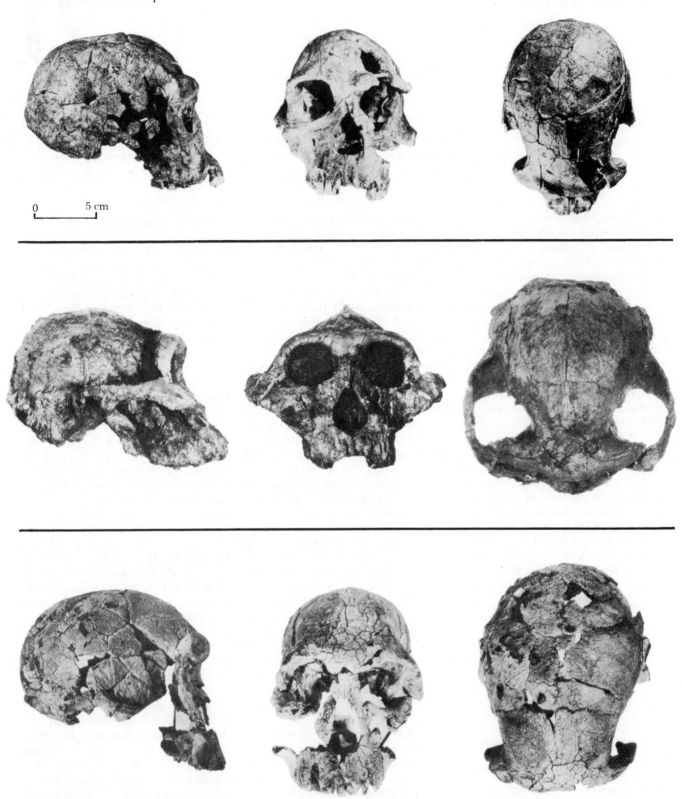

0   5 cm

Figure 1. *Top:* Lateral, frontal, and superior views show a small-brained, small-toothed hominid (KNM-ER 1813) that is proposed as *Australopithecus* cf. *africanus.* The specimen is from the Koobi Fora Formation, an extensive Plio/Pleistocene site that lies to the east of Lake Turkana in Kenya's northern Rift Valley. *Middle:* Compare the same three views of another *Australopithecus* (KNM-ER 406) found in the same area. It is also small-brained but has large cheek teeth. The apparent considerable breadth in the frontal and superior views is somewhat misleading, because it is influenced by the broad zygomatic arches, which flare in order to make room for the massive chewing muscles. The photo of the left side of the cranium has been reversed to make comparison easier. *Bottom:* Similar views of a large-brained *Homo* sp. (KNM-ER 1470), from levels of the Koobi Fora Formation that date between 2 and 3 million years, are given for comparison.

dibular fragment, and the humerus in a "suspense" category as "Hominidae indet." until further evidence is available.

There is a considerable collection of fossil hominid material from late Pliocene times onward. In the past two years new field work has been going on at sites that appear, mainly on faunal grounds, to date between 3 and 4 million years. The Hadar in the Afar Valley in Ethiopia is being investigated by a multidisciplinary international team under the joint leadership of M. Taieb, C. Johanson, and Y. Coppens (9). The results since 1973 have been spectacular, with reports of mandibular remains, maxillae, cranial fragments, postcranial elements, and the famous partial skeleton "Lucy." The latest news is of a site in northern Tanzania, some 50 kilometers south of Olduvai, known as Laetolil, where isolated teeth and several mandibles have been recovered from alluvial sediments that have a reported radiometric age of between 3.3 and 3.7 million years. This project is being led by Mary Leakey, who is also continuing field work at the Olduvai Gorge.

The material from Laetolil and the Afar has not been described in detail, and popular announcements in the media are far from satisfactory. It is stated that the bulk of the specimens are best accommodated within the genus *Homo,* and this presumably relates to specific morphological characteristics. There is an inherent problem in hominid taxonomy caused by the present lack of any precise diagnosis for fossil forms. I am reluctant to anticipate further new discoveries, but I would expect that the genus *Homo* will eventually be traced into the Pliocene at an age of between 4 and 6 million years, together with *Australopithecus.* At present, however, this has not been firmly established, and it is very unlikely that mandibular or dental morphology alone will be sufficient for positive identification.

The extensive Plio/Pleistocene sites in the Lake Turkana basin are well documented, and the two principal sedimentary formations are the Shungura Formation in the Omo Valley at the northern end of the lake and the Koobi Fora Formation lying to the east of the lake. Since 1968, major projects have been underway, and a wealth of data has been collected. The formations span approximately the same period of time—bracketed between 1.3 and 3.2 million years. While some time breaks are manifest, the successions offer what can be considered a continuous record over the period in one extensive geographical basin. *Australopithecus* is represented by cranial and postcranial fossils in varying degrees of completeness, and *Homo* is also represented by quite substantial data. There is the possibility of a late *Ramapithecus,* as has been mentioned, but this cannot be taken as established until further material is recovered.

Australopithecus species

The problem of species definition within *Australopithecus* is far from settled, but I am of the opinion that evidence for two species of this genus can be established with some conviction in the Koobi Fora Formation. The most obvious, *Australopithecus boisei* (10), is very distinctive, being characterized by hyper-robust mandibles, large molars and premolars relative to the anterior dentition, cranial capacity values less than 550 cc, and sexual dimorphism manifested in superficial cranial characters such as sagittal and nuchal crests. An example (KNM-ER 406) is shown in Figure 1. The known postcranial elements, such as the femur, humerus, and talus, are also distinctive. This widespread species has been reported from other localities, such as Chesowanja, Peninj, and Olduvai Gorge in the southern Rift Valley of East Africa. *A. boisei* may require reconsideration as a full species and should instead perhaps be ranked on a subspecific basis, as a deme of the South African form of *A. robustus.* Additional data are needed if we are going to solve the problems that are always associated with such refined systematics in vertebrate paleontology. Consequently the retention of two allied but spatially separate robust species seems desirable for the moment.

The case for a gracile East African species of *Australopithecus* is less secure, but there seems to be too great a degree of variation if all the material is included as a single species. The best example of the gracile form from East Africa would be the specimen from the Koobi Fora Formation—KMN-ER 1813 (11) (Fig. 1, *top*). Various mandibles and some postcranial elements might also be included, keeping in mind the difficulty of classifying mandibles. In addition, certain specimens from Olduvai, such as OH 13 and OH 24, might be reclassified as "gracile" *Australopithecus.* No detailed proposal for such a classificatory scheme for the East African fossils has been put forward, but the typical characteristics would include gracile mandibles with small cheek teeth, cranial capacity values at 600 cc or less, and sagittal crests rare or nonexistent. The postcranial morphology appears to be similar to that seen in *A. boisei,* although at a smaller and less robust scale. In both species, one of the most distinctive features is the proximal region of the femur: a long femoral neck is compressed from front to back, and there is a small, subspherical head. There are other features, but very little is known about variation, and the sample is not impressively large at present.

I consider this species to be closely allied to the gracile *A. africanus* from Sterkfontein in South Africa; it may be a more northern deme of that species. The innominate bone is known for *A. africanus* and for *A. robustus* in South Africa, and slight differences have been noted between the two forms. No innominate remains are attributable to *Australopithecus* from East Africa, but *Homo* is represented by two specimens that are time equivalent, and they illustrate marked differences between the two genera that are greater than would reasonably be expected for a single, albeit spatially extended, species.

Differentiation in *Homo*

The presence of *Homo* in late Pliocene and early Pleistocene deposits is still somewhat controversial, but I believe that relatively complete cranial and postcranial elements such as the femur and innominate are diagnostic and conclusive. The best examples are from the Koobi Fora Formation, with specific examples such as the crania KNM-ER 1470 (*12*) (Fig. 1, *bottom*) and 1590 (*11*). The femur KNM-ER 1481 and the innominate KNM-ER 3228 (*13*) are also explicit. The specimens referred to are from levels that date between 2 and 3 million years and from localities that have also yielded material that can be confidently attributed to *Australopithecus*.

The principal characters upon which the early species of *Homo* might be defined are relatively large anterior teeth, with equally large, although not buccolingually expanded cheek teeth; moderately robust and externally buttressed mandibles that have everted basal margins; cranial capacity values exceeding 750 cc; and a high-vaulted skull with minimal postorbital waisting and no sagittal crest. The postcranial morphology is very similar to the modern human. It is proposed that certain specimens from East African sites fall within this category; such examples would include OH 7 from Olduvai, the type specimen for *Homo habilis* (*14*). I have commented earlier on the specimens from the Afar and Laetolil, and their final taxonomic position remains an open question in my opinion.

Nomenclature at the species level in *Homo* is not settled, but I do believe that *Homo habilis,* as represented by the type specimen from Olduvai, OH 7, is the same as the more complete and slightly earlier material, such as KNM-ER 1470. On this basis, *Homo habilis* has priority. However, there are going to be difficulties when considering the various stages of a single evolving lineage, and it may be appropriate to use a somewhat arbitrary definition based upon absolute dates. An alternative scheme, which I would favor, is to retain *Homo erectus* as the only species of *Homo* other than *Homo sapiens* and to classify grades or stages of evolutionary development. This would require agreement only on the diagnostic characteristics of the genus. Under this system, the earliest examples of the genus would be Stage 1, and so on. Of course, difficulties arise when new and earlier finds are made after the scheme has been presented in detail. A further variation upon this approach might be to consider only two species, *sapiens* and *presapiens,* and to identify fossil variations at a subspecific level. In this way we could consider the form *erectus* as distinct but related to *habilis.*

Major differences between KNM-ER 1470 and examples of *Homo erectus* (*15*) may be the result of significant time separation since, at present, intermediate forms are unknown. During 1975, a complete cranium was recovered from the Koobi Fora Formation which does show a number of features that are perhaps to be expected in a transitional stage. The skull is awaiting preparation and description, and thus final comments must be postponed.

The South African fossil evidence is complicated by the absence of reliable dates and the uncertainty of relative dates for much of the material collected from the limestone quarry waste. Various suggestions have been based upon vertebrate faunas, and the collections probably range from late Pliocene to the Pleistocene, with an age bracket of between 1 and 3 million years. At least two species of *Australopithecus,* the robust *A. robustus* and the gracile *A. africanus,* are represented. There do not seem to be any compelling reasons to assume ancestral-descendant relationship between these two species; the East African evidence would support this view.

Tools and habitations

The most impressive record of tools and habitation sites is from Olduvai Gorge (*16*), where numerous localities have been excavated over the past 30 years. The progression from simple "pebble tools" to intricate and perfect bifacial implements is well documented in this one area. There are also inferences to be drawn on the probable social organization, in the sense of community size and hunting preferences. At one locality, remains of a stone structure—perhaps the base of a circular hut—were uncovered; there is an excellent date of 1.8 million years for this. The threshold of technological ability is difficult to pinpoint exactly, and at best one could only suggest that it occurred during the Pliocene, perhaps in relation to the adaptive response embodied by the differentiation of *Homo.*

During the early Pleistocene, circa 1.6 million years ago, bifacial tools such as crude handaxes make their appearance. This development can be traced in situ at Olduvai and is supported by findings from other East African sites. The first record of stone implements in Asia and Europe is of handaxes, but, unfortunately, no absolute dates are known for them at the present time. In my opinion, the evidence available could suggest a migration of the "handaxe" people—perhaps *Homo erectus*—from Africa into Europe, Asia, and the Far East during the early Pleistocene, or a little earlier. The subsequent development of stone implements is complex, with impressive late Pleistocene and Holocene records from most of the world. It is not proven but can be postulated that the post-Acheulean, or handaxe, technologies can be related to the emergence of *Homo sapiens* and the subsequent success of this species. The association of stone implements with early hominid remains is rare, and many mid-Pleistocene and subsequent sites contain only one or two specimens, with certain impressive exceptions. The earliest record of *Homo sapiens* remains a problem because of the limitations imposed both by the small samples and by the dating techniques that can be employed.

It is clear that extraordinary advances have been made in recent years in our data records, and continuing investigations will presumably provide further evidence. There is now obvious evidence for considerable morphological diversity in the Plio/Pleistocene hominids of Africa, which has been interpreted as a consequence of a Pliocene radiation with different evolutionary experiments persisting into the early Pleistocene. The presence of at least three contemporary species in East Africa may be established on both cranial and postcranial material, and any review must incorporate the analysis of the entire fossil collection. The problem of whether two closely related and competing species could live side by side will be better understood when further studies are completed on paleoecological evidence, including palynology and micropaleontology under closely documented stratigraphy. It is known that several closely allied and morphologically similar ceropithecoid monkeys live alongside one another in African forests today, with no suggestion of mutual exclusion.

Darwin seems to be vindicated for his prophesy on the African origin for man. Many great scientists—Robert Broom, Raymond Dart, and Louis Leakey among them—were pioneers in the field which today has so captured the popular imagination. As the ancient record builds up with each new fossil find, we are reminded that extinction is a common phenomenon in vertebrate evolution—and modern man may be no exception.

References

1. L. S. B. Leakey. 1961. A new Lower Pliocene fossil primate from Kenya. *Ann. Mag. Nat. Hist.*, ser. 13, 4:689–96.
2. E. L. Simons. 1969. Late Miocene hominid from Fort Ternan, Kenya. *Nature,* Lond. 221:448–51.
3. E. L. Simons and D. R. Pilbeam. 1972. Hominoid paleoprimatology. In *The Functional and Evolutionary Biology of Primates*, ed., R. H. Tuttle, Chicago:Aldine, Atherton, pp. 36–62.
4. M. Kretzoi. 1975. New ramapithecines and *Pliopithecus* from the Lower Pliocene of Rudabanya in northeastern Hungary. *Nature,* Lond. 257:578–81.
5. R. E. F. Leakey. 1973. Further evidence of Lower Pleistocene hominids from East Rudolf, North Kenya, 1972. *Nature,* Lond. 242:170–73.
6. W. W. Bishop and G. R. Chapman. 1970. Early Pliocene sediments and fossils from the Northern Kenya Rift Valley. *Nature,* Lond. 226:914–18.
7. M. Pickford. 1975. Late Miocene sediments and fossils from the Northern Kenya Rift Valley. *Nature,* Lond. 256:279–84.
8. B. Patterson, A. K. Behrensmeyer, and W. D. Sill. 1970. Geology and fauna of a new Pliocene locality in North Western Kenya. *Nature,* Lond. 226:918–21.
9. M. Taib, D. C. Johanson, Y. Coppens, R. Bonnefille, and J. Kalb. 1974. Decouverte d'hominides dans les series Plio-pleistocenes d'Hadar (Bassin de l'Awash; Afar, Ethipie). *C. R. Acad. Sc. Paris.*, Ser. D. 279:735–38.
10. P. V. Tobias. 1967. Olduvai Gorge, 2. *The Cranium and Maxillary Dentition of Australopithecus (Zinjanthropus) boisei.* Cambridge: Cambridge Univ. Press.
11. R. E. F. Leakey. 1974. Further evidence of Lower Pleistocene hominids from East Rudolf, North Kenya, 1973. *Nature,* Lond. 248:653–56.
12. R. E. F. Leakey. 1973. Evidence for an advanced Plio/Pleistocene hominid from East Rudolf, Kenya. *Nature,* Lond. 242:447–50.
13. R. E. F. Leakey. In press. New hominid fossils from the Koobi Fora Formation, Northern Kenya. *Nature,* Lond.
14. L. S. B. Leakey, P. V. Tobias, and J. R. Napier. 1964. A new species of the genus *Homo* from Olduvai Gorge. *Nature,* Lond. 202:7–9.
15. F. Weidenreich. 1943. The skull of *Sinanthropus pekinensis:* A comparative study on a primitive hominid skull. *Paleont. Sinica*, New Series D. 10:1–298.
16. M. D. Leakey. 1971. *Olduvai Gorge, 3. Excavations in Beds I & II 1960–1963.* Cambridge: Cambridge Univ. Press.

by C. LORING BRACE

22 Ridiculed, Rejected, But Still Our Ancestor NEANDERTHAL

Neanderthal: The word is now so familiar, and its implications of the archaic so clear, that it describes things quite unrelated to its original meaning. Modern writers refer to ultraconservative and moss-backed attitudes in social affairs as "Neanderthal," and occasionally call the holders of such views "Neanderthals"; likewise, so-called Neanderthals in politics are regarded as human fossils, with the further implication that they properly should have become extinct long ago.

As we shall see, this implication of extinction has been developed to a surprising degree by the majority of scientists who have studied the genuine human fossils called Neanderthals. But is this majority right? Did extinction of the Neanderthals come, as we are usually led to believe, because they were too different to qualify as our ancestors? If a Neanderthal existed today, if he appeared in a crowd of the rest of us, what would people say?

Would the robust bony structure, massive chest, and developed musculature be especially noticeable under a modern suit of clothes? Of course, clothes would not hide the broad, thick hands or the massive face beneath the heavy bony brow—particularly if this Neanderthal should smile and display the big front teeth that, more than anything else, hold the key to the difference between a Neanderthal and an average modern man. In his time, in a world where tools were crude, many manipulatory tasks had to be handled by that original built-in, the human dentition. Natural selection favored heavy-duty teeth that could withstand wear and tear; to support such teeth required a face somewhat larger than modern size.

The term Neanderthal itself refers to a valley in the heart of western Germany, through which flows a stream, the Düssel, which joins the Rhine at Düsseldorf. In the seventeenth century, this quiet valley was a favored place for picnics, and was particularly admired by the Düsseldorf organist and composer Joachim Neumann, who signed some of his works "Neander," the Greek translation of his name. After his death, local people began calling the secluded valley, then spelled *thal* in German, Neanderthal.

By the mid-nineteenth century, industrialism was transforming the Neanderthal with quarrying operations in the limestone cliffs that loomed above the stream bed. In 1856, quarrymen discovered a human skeleton buried in a small cave, the Feldhofer Grotto, but they did not recognize the bones as human; in fact, they unceremoniously shoveled them out of the cave while preparing it for blasting. However, the quarry owner preserved the bones, and their importance was recognized later by Johann Karl Fuhlrott, a science teacher at the local high school, who was an enthusiastic student of the region's natural history. Unfortunately, the bones were discovered so casually and unprofessionally that only the larger pieces of what must have been a complete human skeleton were preserved. None of the smaller bones, the fragile parts, or the teeth were saved.

Fuhlrott not only realized that the bones were human but also that they were of most unusual and possibly "primitive" form. Unlike certain more recent discoverers of important hominid fossils, he also realized that to study and interpret them required training he did not possess. So he enlisted the aid of Herman Schaaffhausen, professor of anatomy at Bonn. Both men then presented their evidence for discussion at a number of scientific society meetings, suggesting that the bones might have belonged to an individual of some antiquity. Actually, the antiquity they had in mind went back only to the pre-Celtic and pre-Germanic inhabitants of northern Europe hinted at in the writings of classical authors —a far cry from the forty thousand years and beyond that we now know must have been the case.

Unfortunately, respected and "competent" opinion on the significance of the Neanderthal skeleton was delivered before a basis existed for appreciating either the extent of human antiquity or the possibility of evolutionary changes and relationships in a biological sense. The relationship between ancient human remains and the course of man's development has always brought a heightened, emotion-laden concern, and even supposedly competent opinion has frequently been less than scientically objective. This is true even for recent exciting finds in Africa, but perhaps the most bizarre spectrum of opinion concerning a human fossil was that offered in supposed explanation of the original Neanderthal skeleton.

Suggestions that this ancient person had suffered from idiocy, lunacy, rickets, premature ossification of cranial sutures, and various other pathological manifestations came from a series of "experts." Others, reflecting the sense of superiority felt by denizens of such places as London, Paris, Berlin, reflected their prejudices when they compared the supposedly "inferior" traits of the Neanderthaler to features they assumed to be characteristic of people inhabiting various benighted places in the modern world—such as Holland or Ireland. One distinguished German anatomist dismissed the skeleton as that of an "old Dutchman"; an eminent French scholar referred to it as a robust Celt resembling "a modern Irishman with low mental organization."

Possibly the most amusing interpretation was based on the following data about the Neanderthaler: (1) evidently the left elbow had been broken early in life and had healed in such a way that movement was subsequently restricted; (2) the individual was presumed to have suffered from rickets, so it was suggested that pain from the elbow and the rickets had caused the person to knit his brows in a perpetual frown. This became ossified, producing what has become an outstanding characteristic in descriptions of Neanderthal form—the heavy ridge along the brow. Adding to this pathological "evidence," Schaaffhausen's anatomical colleague from Bonn, Professor Mayer, suggested that the bowed femurs might testify to a lifetime spent on horseback. Assembling all this, Mayer suggested the Neanderthal was a deserter from the Russian forces that chased Napoleon back across the Rhine in 1814 and, more specifically, a rickety Mongolian Cossack who had crawled into the cave for refuge.

The most significant opinion came from Rudolf Virchow, a German who was a recognized leader in cellular pathology and also highly respected as an anthropologist and liberal politician. This critical and uncompromising champion of the strict scientific principles of deduction and inference said that there was virtually no way of determining the antiquity of the find because with it were no associated tools or animal bones. After a detailed, careful review of the notable features of the skeleton, he pronounced it pathological. Naturally, few even thought to question the judgment of one of the world's leading pathologists.

To counter those who claimed great antiquity for the skeleton, Virchow pointed out that it was that of an individual who was past fifty years of age. This argued that the Neanderthaler had belonged to a civilization that cared for, and assured the survival of, the middle-aged and elderly, which would have been most unlikely in the remote prehistoric period that some had

suggested. With this logic Virchow increased the probability, so his readers believed, that unusual morphological features of the skeleton could be accounted for only by invoking some sort of pathological involvement. It was a cautious, critical, and skeptical approach; unfortunately, Virchow was using the right reasons to reach the wrong conclusion.

In 1858—two years after the Neanderthal discovery—a visit by British scholars to the site of Boucher de Perthes' archeological researches in northwest France led to the conviction that man must have been in existence for a substantial period of time prior to the dawn of written history. This conviction was confirmed by groups from both Britain and France in the succeeding year. And in November of the same year, 1859, appeared Darwin's book *Origin of Species*. It changed forever the entire frame of reference for appraising the significance of sequences of prehistoric animals—including the human animal. After a decade of debate, evolution by means of natural selection became a dominant aspect of natural science in both England and Germany.

In France, however, Darwin's reception was quite different. Twenty years after Darwin and A. R. Wallace (who had independently hit on the same ideas) published their preliminary essays, the term "evolution" was cautiously introduced to French biology. But in France, instead of meaning descent with modification by means of natural selection, the concept of evolution was so similar to the theory known as "catastrophism"—featuring extinctions, invasions, and successive creations, supported by Cuvier during the first third of the nineteenth century—that it largely amounted to a relabeling of the earlier view.

At any rate, Darwinian evolutionists were not yet able to do much about the initial Neanderthal interpretations. Still lacking was an adequate basis for appraising either the skeleton's antiquity or its evolutionary significance. And an aura of peculiarity has clung to the Neanderthals ever since. To this day, most professional anthropologists and paleontologists, with myself as one of

the unpopular exceptions, repeatedly refer to the Neanderthals as "extreme," "specialized," or "aberrant," and deny that they were ancestors of modern man.

Another decade passed. Then, exactly thirty years after the first Neanderthal discovery, vindication of the Schaaffhausen—Fuhlrott views came from the discovery of two more fossil skeletons, this time in the commune of Spy, in Belgium. Both resembled the original Neanderthal so closely that to claim that their characteristics, too, were explainable by idiocy or pathology was straining coincidence too much for most people, although Virchow continued to cling to his pathological judgment.

The excavation techniques this time had been more careful; the jaws, teeth, and many of the smaller bones were preserved. Not only did the Spy skeletons reinforce the view that the Neanderthal form characterized an entire prehistoric population; the Neanderthal population to which they evidently belonged could now be dated, relatively speaking, for the first time. This was because archeological research during the thirty years had provided a broad framework for the arrangement of prehistoric materials: the most recent of the Stone Age categories was the Neolithic, a period of crude crop tending and polished stone tools; most ancient was the Lower Paleolithic, characterized by heavy hand axes of chipped stone (bifaces) and a hunting mode of existence.

The Spy Neanderthals were fitted into a category one degree less ancient than the Lower Paleolithic, because they were found with tools of a type first recognized in excavations at the southern French village of Le Moustier. With today's radioisotope dating techniques we know that the cultural traditions of the Mousterian Neanderthals extended from about 35,000 B.C. back at least 50,000 years to somewhere between 80,000 and 100,000 years ago. In the 1880's, however, there was no way to make even rough estimates of antiquity other than to note that such-and-such cultural assemblage was older or younger than another one. Hence the Mousterian culture was considered a

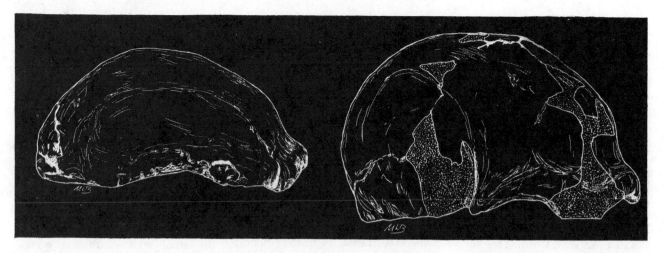

degree younger than the Lower Paleolithic hand axe cultures, but still much older than that of the earliest cultivators and herdsmen.

Since the Spy discovery, except for narrowing the dates and refining our knowledge of how the Neanderthals provided themselves with clothing and shelter, we retain pretty much the same picture of their life and times that was available by the end of the nineteenth century.

The Spy discovery, followed by others, provided a frame of reference for a few previously uncovered isolated fossils. One of these was a skull found on the north side of the Rock of Gibraltar in 1848. Although that was eight years before the "original" Neanderthal, its importance was not recognized until years later. The excitement over Darwin's book and the English translation of Schaaffhausen's memoir on Neanderthal focused a little belated attention on this Gibraltar skull, which, in the meantime, had been brought to England. After its brief appearance at a couple of scientific society meetings, it was consigned to the Museum of the Royal College of Surgeons in England, where it remained unappreciated until after the end of the nineteenth century. Not until a German anatomist made a detailed comparison with other Neanderthal skeletal material did the English become interested enough to initiate studies themselves.

The other fossils that could be placed in context because of the Spy discoveries were mandibles. The original Neanderthal lacked face, jaw, and teeth, and, although it was suspected that individual robust mandibles found in France, Belgium, and Czechoslovakia came from Neanderthal-like individuals, it remained only a suspicion until the Spy remains raised it to a substantial probability.

Meanwhile, the years between 1856 and 1886 saw the recovery of artifacts and skeletal remains from the period immediately following that of the Mousterian and Neanderthal. The artifacts were more finely made than those of the Mousterian, many more kinds of tools were represented, and tools of worked bone were found for the first time. Some

The evidence for human evolution can be arranged in four stages: Australopithecine, Pithecanthropine, Neanderthal, Modern. Proportions are not to scale; Neanderthal and Modern represent only 5 per cent of the two-million-year period.

	AUSTRALOPITHECINES	PITHECANTHROPINES	NEANDERTHALS	MODERNS
EUROPE		Heidelberg	Neanderthal / Spy / La Chapelle / Le Moustier / La Ferrassie / La Quina	Cro-Magnon / Grimaldi / Obercassel / Chancelade / Predmost
			Swanscombe / Steinheim / Fontéchevade Krapina	
MIDDLE EAST			Tabun / Shanidar	Hotu
				Skhul
ASIA		Pithecanthropus / Sinanthropus	Mapa	Upper Cave / Niah
			Solo Wadjak	
AFRICA	Sterkfontein / Makapansgat / Pre-Zinj	Olduvai Bed II	Rhodesia / Saldanha	Florisba

2,000,000 years   500,000   300,000   100,000   35,000

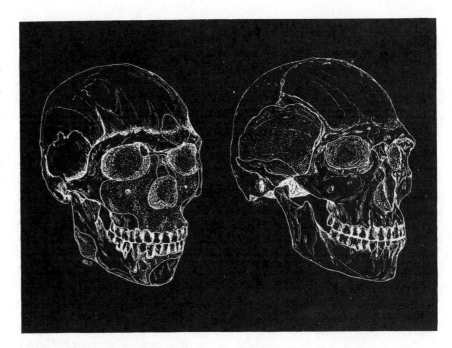

These skull casts show "recent" evolutionary gradation. From left: the original Neanderthal; Spy II, with higher forehead; Skhul V, a Neanderthaloid; Predmost III, a full modern (see chart below).

of them were decorated with graceful, realistic engravings showing many of the extinct animals whose bones occurred in the same deposits.

And for good measure, the human skeletal remains from those Upper Paleolithic levels, including the famous Cro-Magnon discovery, displayed aggregates of traits that allowed their describers to claim the creature had differed in no way from modern man. This depended on viewpoint. The skeletons indicated distinctly heavier musculature and larger faces, jaws, and teeth than the *average* modern man has. However, a small but sufficient number of living humans do attain this level of ruggedness. At any rate, the archeological record revealed the ancients were skillful hunters as well as talented artists. And, with their skeletal form suggesting they should be considered ancestors of contemporary Europeans, the modern interpreters studied and discussed the Upper Paleolithic men with an almost familial pride.

Next came an important discovery in the other direction of the time scale. The decade following 1886 brought the discovery and discussion of a very different and far older form —the famous *Pithecanthropus erectus* from Java. When the young Dutch physician, Eugene Dubois, found it in the Far East in 1891-92, opinions varied almost as much as those that greeted the first Neanderthal. By the turn of the century, however, a fair percentage of those qualified to judge had accepted the specimen as representing a true, if primitive, human being. Both *Pithecanthropus* and Neanderthal stood as erect as we do.

Then, at the very end of the nineteenth and for the first five years of the present century, came the discovery and description of the remains of between 14 and 15 Neanderthals from a Yugoslavian site at Krapina in Croatia. But there was not a complete long bone or reconstructible skull; the Krapina population is now known chiefly for adding to our knowledge about the human dentition. A total of 263 individual teeth was found.

It is evident that by the beginning of the twentieth century the modest collection of evidence concerning the course of human evolution was ripe for a thorough appraisal. This was done—in simple, logical, Darwinian fashion—by the Strasbourg anatomist and anthropologist Gustav Schwalbe in his book *Studien zur Vorgeschichte des Menschen* ("Studies on the Prehistory of Man").

He regarded Dubois' *Pithecanthropus* as representing the earliest known human population ancestral to all later men. Today, most scholars accept this part of his conclusions, although few now separate *Pithecanthropus* in a formal taxonomic sense from genus *Homo*. Consequently, *Pithecanthropus* becomes *Homo erectus*, but non-technically we can go on referring to members of this species as pithecanthropines.

Descended from the pithecanthropines are the Neanderthals. whom Schwalbe placed directly in the line

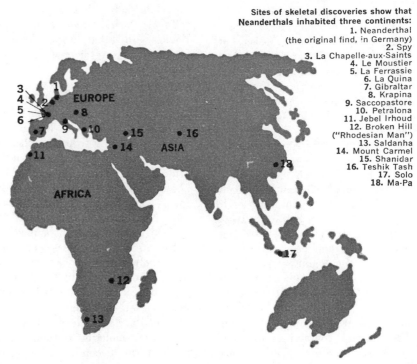

Sites of skeletal discoveries show that Neanderthals inhabited three continents:
1. Neanderthal (the original find, in Germany)
2. Spy
3. La Chapelle-aux-Saints
4. Le Moustier
5. La Ferrassie
6. La Quina
7. Gibraltar
8. Krapina
9. Saccopastore
10. Petralona
11. Jebel Irhoud
12. Broken Hill ("Rhodesian Man")
13. Saldanha
14. Mount Carmel
15. Shanidar
16. Teshik Tash
17. Solo
18. Ma-Pa

of human evolution, first as the separate species *Homo neanderthalensis* and later, for reasons not altogether clear, as *Homo primigenius*. Actually, the general scientific belief today is that the Neanderthals were so like modern men that, if some were alive today, they could interbreed with *Homo sapiens* to produce viable fertile offspring. In other words, most anthropologists now favor classifying the Neanderthals as *Homo sapiens*, the same as modern man; at most, they would only add the subspecific designation *neanderthalensis*. But this does not alter the basic situation. The same people retain the old belief that Neanderthal was too different to qualify as our ancestor.

Schwalbe had been more alert than that. Having classed Neanderthals as a separate species, he then claimed they became extinct, not because they left no descendants, but extinct in the sense that the world today no longer has a distinct population of Neanderthals. For his time, Schwalbe's was the most balanced and logical approach.

Contrast it with the general idea held by zoologists and anthropologists in 1968. Almost no vestige of Schwalbe's appraisal has survived. Instead one reads varying versions of a view that contrasts the Neanderthals with us. They are written off as victims of "specializations"— although just why it is disadvantageous to be extraordinarily robust and to possess heavy brow ridges, faces, and teeth is rarely spelled out. Ultimately these inhabitants of western Europe are said to have succumbed to the invasion of populations of fully modern form who had evolved somewhat mysteriously "in the east."

Why such a change in viewpoint? For an indicator, we turn to reminiscences by the late Sir Arthur Keith, the dominant physical anthropologist in the English-speaking world throughout the first half of the twentieth century: "I had supposed that man's ascent had been made by a series of succeeding stages [but] . . . discoveries were being made in France which indicated to my mind that Neanderthal man could no longer be regarded as an ancestor. The stratum containing his fossil bones was followed at once by one

containing the fossil bones of our type—the modern type. Apparently we moderns had invaded Europe and exterminated Neanderthal man."

He was referring to the Neanderthal skeletons found in 1908, one being the famous "old man" of La Chapelle-aux-Saints from Corrèze— the most complete, best-preserved Neanderthaler discovered up to then and for a long time thereafter. This find led to an overwhelming monograph published by paleontologist Marcellin Boule of the National Museum of Natural History in Paris. In sharp contrast to Schwalbe, he concluded that Neanderthal form was too divergent to represent a stage in the evolution of modern man. Every one of Boule's crucial points eventually turned out to be questionable, but in the meantime even Schwalbe inexplicably conceded that the Neanderthals had become extinct without issue. When Schwalbe died two years later, in 1916, his evolutionary views, with a few exceptions, died with him.

Then, fifteen years later, came the discovery of bones at the cave of Mugharet-es Skhul—on the slopes of Mount Carmel in what is now Israel. These bones showed a mixture of Neanderthal and modern traits in proportions so equal that the term Neanderthaloid was coined to acknowledge that here was no full-scale Neanderthal. It had been Boule's verdict that there could be no intermediaries, yet here was an intermediary.

Various hypotheses were offered in explanation. One of them was based on the idea that the Mount Carmel deposits were earlier in date than western Europe's "classic" Neanderthals, so perhaps here in the Middle East were the remains of the population that evolved into modern form—while the classic, or conservative, Neanderthals of the west remained isolated and unchanged.

Since such hypotheses were suggested, circumstances have changed. First, modern dating techniques place the Skhul remains at less than 40,000 years—in other words, right between the classic Neanderthals and the earliest moderns, in time as well as in form. Second, several good

classic Neanderthals in the full flower of brows, jaws, and teeth have been found at Shanidar cave in Iraq, the heart of the area "to the east." Also indicating that classic Neanderthals were not isolated in western Europe is the discovery of Neanderthals in Morocco, Greece, Israel, Uzbekistan, and even China—plus candidates for Neanderthal status that have existed for years in Java and Africa as well.

Certainly there is no longer any reason to regard the Neanderthals as an isolated European phenomenon. Nor is there any reason to reject their candidacy for status as the direct ancestors of more recent men. So, in an interpretive sense, we are right back where Gustav Schwalbe left us in 1906. Because the evidence with which Boule contradicted Schwalbe's relatively simple approach was faulty at that time, and has not been supported since then, it is reasonable to ask what impelled him to view the world as he did.

To begin with, we should realize that Marcellin Boule was trained in late nineteenth-century France, where the concept of "evolution" was far more akin to the catastrophism of Cuvier than to the Darwinian views in which Schwalbe and Keith were trained. Boule explained change in the human fossil record by extinctions and invasions with little concern for adaptive response and the mechanics of biological change. His view could be called "hominid catastrophism."

That it should have come to dominate thinking about the course of human evolution in general, and the Neanderthal's role in particular, is due in large part to the accidents of history. Prior to 1914, the most effective attempt to deal with human origins from an evolutionary point

A Neanderthal's physiognomy? The restorations at top left and bottom are generally acceptable versions of the "old man" from La Chapelle-aux-Saints; the third, based on a skull from Le Moustier, has been called a caricature of man's ancestor.

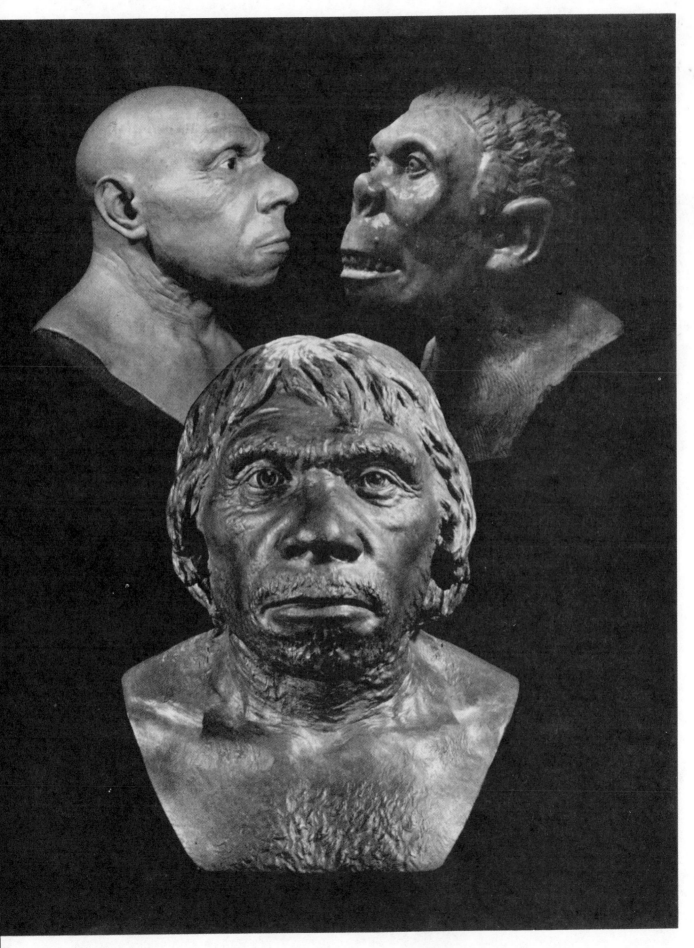

of view had been produced in a German academic context and had considerable influence elsewhere. But the invasion of Belgium and the burning of Louvain in 1914—in short, the initiation of World War I—seriously tarnished the civilized and scholarly image that German academia had previously enjoyed. From the point of view of the study of human evolution, it was particularly unfortunate that the tradition associated with Schwalbe should have been located at Strasbourg. Political control of Alsace-Lorraine, which had been in German hands since the Franco-Prussian war of 1870-71, returned to the French after World War I. They promptly fired the German faculty of the university at Strasbourg ending the tradition that had flourished there under Schwalbe.

Also after the war, major works summarizing our knowledge of human origins were published by Boule and Keith, among others; and two subsequent generations of professional students of human evolution have grown up schooled to believe that the prehistoric Neanderthals were a peculiar group, not because of anything pathological as Virchow once thought, but rather because of their assumed failure to adapt.

Our knowledge of the events that occurred in the remote past will always be incomplete, and proof for one or another interpretive hypotheses can never be final. Where the subject of our concern is as rare and fragmentary as Neanderthal skeletal remains, we have seen how the political and intellectual history of the past hundred years has, in some instances, played a more significant role in determining which points of view find favor than do the objective pieces of evidence themselves. From what we actually know, it is probable that if a properly clothed and shaved Neanderthal were to appear in a crowd of modern urban shoppers or commuters, he would strike the viewer as somewhat unusual in appearance—short, stocky, large of face—but nothing more than that. Certainly few would suspect he was their "caveman" ancestor.

B. Cultural Remains

23

It is now generally accepted that human origins are to be sought in the Old World tropics and subtropics, in time ranges to be measured in millions of years. Fossils which are almost universally assigned to the zoological family Hominidae ("human beings" in the broad sense) are known to occur in East Africa in deposits which are older than four million and perhaps even five million years. By at least two to three million years ago, one or more kinds of hominids had begun manufacturing stone tools and exhibiting the typically human

kind of behavior that results in the formation of "archaeological sites." By at least one million years ago, cultural and biological evolution had proceeded far enough to allow the colonization of temperate latitudes. Both theory and the actual discovery of very ancient artifacts, especially hand axes and associated stone tools, suggest that among the temperate areas that were colonized very early were the mountain ranges and adjacent coastal plains of the southern tip of Africa, in what is today the southern part of Cape Province of South

Ecology of STONE AGE MAN at the Southern Tip of Africa

By RICHARD G. KLEIN

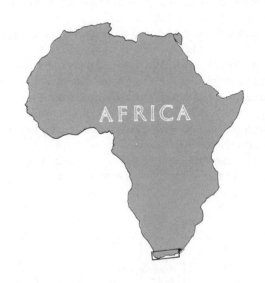

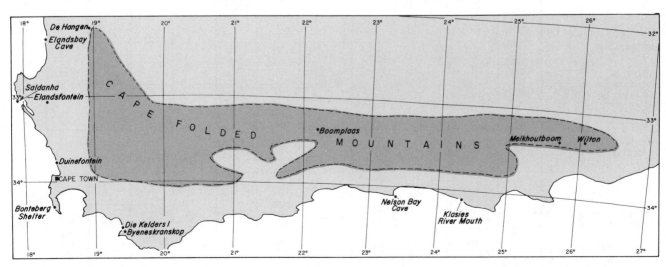

The approximate locations of southern Cape archaeological sites mentioned in the text. The shaded area indicates the rough extent of the Cape Folded Mountains.

137

Africa. At one important southern Cape site—Elandsfontein near Saldanha Bay—hand axes have been found in direct association with the remains of animals perhaps killed near ancient water holes by the hand-ax makers (so-called Early Stone Age or Acheulean peoples). Some of the animal bones belonged to ox-bodied, short-necked giraffes, giant baboons, saber-toothed cats and other creatures which became extinct in the Middle Pleistocene period, certainly more than 125,000 years ago. Elandsfontein has also provided a human skullcap belonging to an individual of the archaic species *Homo erectus,* which was widespread in the Middle Pleistocene period from Africa on the west to Java and China on the east. It was *Homo erectus* who probably made the Elandsfontein hand axes.

A great deal remains to be learned about the activities of hand-ax makers in the southern Cape. For the moment, detailed information on past lifeways is available only for their successors, particularly those who lived in the Upper or Later Pleistocene period, beginning roughly 125,000 years ago. In this article, I seek to summarize this information, with special emphasis on the ancient relationships between man and the animals in his environment.

The Upper Pleistocene period is ordinarily divided into two major episodes: the Last Interglacial, extending from roughly 125,000 to 75,000 years ago and characterized by climatic conditions more or less similar to modern ones; and the Last Glacial, spanning the interval between roughly 75,000 and 10,000 years B.P. (before the present) and generally characterized by temperatures considerably lower than modern ones. The Last Glacial period was followed by the Present Interglacial or Holocene period, in which man is still living.

Human occupation debris of certain or probable Last Interglacial age are known from several sites in the southern Cape, of which the most important is unquestionably Klasies River Mouth Cave I, excavated by John Wymer and Ronald Singer (both of the University of Chicago) in the middle 1960's. A layer of beach gravel lying directly on the bedrock floor of Klasies I records a high sea-level stand dating from the very earliest part of the Last Interglacial. When the sea retreated from this level, people making so-called Middle Stone Age artifacts moved into the cave and thereafter occupied it more or less continuously for several tens of thousands of years.

One of the exciting discoveries made at

		Klasies River Mouth Caves	Nelson Bay Cave	Boomplaas Cave	Die Kelders Cave I	Duinefontein MSA "Kill Site"	Elandsbay Cave	Saldanha Middle Stone Age Middens	Melkhoutboom Cave	Wilton Large Rock Shelter	Byeneskranskop Shelter	De Hangen Shelter	
	125,000												EARLY STONE AGE
LAST INTERGLACIAL	100,000	125,000-60,000/55,000? B.P.	125,000-60/55,000? B.P.			90/80,000? B.P.		90/80,000? B.P.					MIDDLE STONE AGE
	75,000												
LAST GLACIAL	50,000			125,000? B.P.- CA. 1500 B.P.	75,000-55,000? B.P.		75,000?-45,000 B.P.						CA. 40,000 B.P.
	25,000	Uninhabited	Uninhabited		Uninhabited		Uninhabited						
	10,000		Robberg 18-14,000 B.P. Albany 14-8000 B.P.				14,000-9000 B.P.						LATER STONE AGE
PRESENT INTERGLACIAL (HOLOCENE)	Present	5,000-1000 B.P.	Wilton 8000-400 B.P.		2000-1500 B.P.		Uninhabited 3500-1500 B.P.	16,000-2500 B.P.	12,000-2500 B.P.	12,000-2500 B.P.	A.D. 1800-1900	

Chart of remains of sites mentioned in the text. The Robberg, Albany and Wilton cultures appear at other sites than Nelson Bay but are not included in the chart.

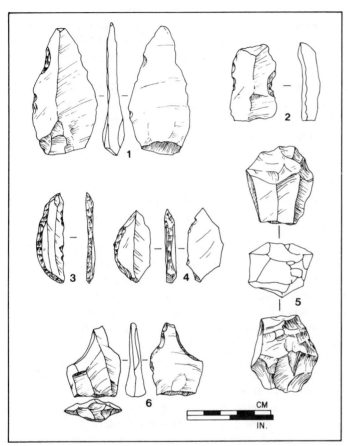

Middle Stone Age stone artifacts from Nelson Bay Cave (after original drawings by J. Deacon,). 1,2,6: flakes with varying amounts of retouching, possibly in part from utilization; 3,4: "crescents" or segments; 5: a core. Very similar artifacts occur in the Middle Stone Age levels of the Klasies River Mouth Caves and other sites in the southern Cape.

Klasies I was that its Middle Stone Age occupants had systematically utilized the food resources available along the nearby coast. The Klasies deposits contained abundant shells of limpets, mussels, winkels and other edible shellfish of the intertidal zone as well as numerous bones of seals and penguins. The remains of these animals, unquestionably associated with Middle Stone Age artifacts dating to beyond 100,000 years ago, so far constitute the oldest evidence for regular exploitation of marine resources known anywhere in the world. Recently, Middle Stone Age open-air shell middens of comparable (Last Interglacial) age have been found at Saldanha Bay, indicating clearly that Klasies I is not an

isolated occurrence. It will be interesting to see whether sites of like age as yet unexcavated or unreported in coastal situations elsewhere in the world provide similar evidence. Since the earlier mid-Pleistocene (Acheulean) sites in appropriate locations indicate only incidental use of seafoods, the Klasies and Saldanha sites may date from not long after the time when people first developed the technology to exploit coastal resources systematically.

The Klasies data are of additional interest because they suggest that Middle Stone Age cultural adaptations to coastal habitats were relatively incomplete. In much later, so-called Later Stone Age coastal sites in the southern Cape, which contain as many seal and penguin bones as the Klasies Middle Stone Age levels, bones of fish and of flying seabirds (cormorants, gannets and so on) are also very common. At Klasies I, they are very rare, suggesting that active fishing and fowling may have remained beyond the technological capabilities of the Klasies people.

Besides remains of marine creatures, the Klasies Middle Stone Age horizons provided thousands of bones of land animals, especially of antelopes and buffaloes. By far the most commonly represented antelope is the eland, which seems strange since it was almost certainly not the most numerous antelope in the vicinity. Furthermore, eland bones are not especially abundant in Later Stone Age sites in the southern Cape. Perhaps the eland's reputed docility, in combination with the relatively primitive level of Middle Stone Age subsistence technology, is responsible. In this context, I think it is relevant that remains of bushpig and warthog, both known to respond fiercely to predators, are very uncommon in the Klasies Middle Stone Age deposits, though individuals of one or both species were probably numerous nearby. At least the bushpig occurs in substantial numbers in comparable Later Stone Age sites.

One potentially dangerous animal that the Klasies people dealt with is the now extinct African giant buffalo. Adults of this species weighed between three and four thousand pounds, with shoulder heights of over six feet and horn spans often exceeding nine feet. Dozens of giant buffaloes are represented in the Klasies site, but it is interesting that the overwhelming majority of them are either fetal/newborn or fully adult animals. Older calves, yearlings and subadult specimens are virtually absent. I think the explanation may be that the Klasies people minimized their risk in hunting this particularly formidable creature by preying selectively on females in advanced pregnancy or even in the process of giving birth. The return in calories on the hoof would, of course, have been very great.

Middle Stone Age peoples continued to live near the Klasies River Mouth after the Last Interglacial had ended and the Last Glacial was under way, but the best evidence available for man-animal relationships during the early Last Glacial period comes from another coastal cave, Die Kelders I, excavated recently by Frank Schweitzer (South African Museum). Analysis of the Middle Stone Age sediments at Die Kelders I by A. J. Tankard (South African Museum) indicates clearly that they formed under cooler-than-present conditions, perhaps in the interval between 75,000 and 55,000 years ago. Although the sea level may have been significantly lower then than it is at present because of water locked up in the growing Northern Hemisphere ice sheets, the relatively steep offshore topography near Die Kelders ensured that the coast was never very far away. Indeed, as at Klasies, the Middle Stone Age peoples at Die Kelders made extensive use of marine resources. Once again, however, remains of seals and penguins are very common, while those of fish and flying birds are rare, corroborating my earlier suggestion that essentially modern adaptations to marine resources had not yet evolved.

The Die Kelders terrestrial fauna resembles the one from Klasies in that eland is the most common of the larger antelopes and pig remains are rare or absent. In contrast to the Klasies people, the Middle Stone Age occupants of Die Kelders focused their attention heavily on small animals. Tortoises, mole rats and hares, all barely represented at Klasies, occur by the dozens and even by the hundreds in some levels at Die Kelders. A tiny (20-25 pound) antelope known as the grysbok, which is not especially common at Klasies, is the dominant hooved creature at Die Kelders. The overall impression is that large terrestrial animals were far less numerous near Die Kelders than near Klasies, a contrast which characterized the two areas in historical times. But there may have

been a positive aspect to the Die Kelders concentration on such small mammals as mole rat and hare. Both are underrepresented in the deposits by foot bones as compared to other parts of the skeleton. It is possible that the Die Kelders people were especially interested in the animals for their pelts, with which the feet would have been removed. The fur of the mole rat in particular is of such high quality that some thought has recently been given to exploiting it commercially.

Besides Klasies and Die Kelders, there are other sites in the southern Cape which promise to provide important information on Middle Stone Age lifeways. One particularly interesting example, which so far has just been tested, is at Duinefontein near Cape Town. Here I found Middle Stone Age artifacts and associated animal bones on what appears to be an ancient land surface at a present depth of three to four feet. The environmental archaeologist Karl Butzer (University of Chicago), who has examined the geology of the site, tentatively suggests it may date from within the latter part of the Last Interglacial period, that is to perhaps 80,000 or 90,000 B.P. Among the animal remains, those of rhinoceros and elephant are quite prominent, a situation in direct contrast to that found at Die Kelders and Klasies. Perhaps the Duinefontein bones represent the remains of animals lying very near the place where the creatures were killed. Such large bones probably had very little chance of being transported from kill sites to camp sites located any distance away.

There are many problems which remain to be resolved about the Middle Stone Age in the southern Cape. One particularly outstanding question concerns the physical appearance of the people who made Middle Stone Age artifacts. At most sites in sub-Saharan Africa from which Middle Stone Age human remains have been reported, the true artifactual associations remain poorly documented, while at sites such as Klasies I and Die Kelders I, where the artifactual associations are not in doubt, the available human bones are very fragmentary. Further excavations in the southern Cape or some other portion of sub-Saharan Africa will soon provide, it is hoped, more complete Middle Stone Age skeletal material.

The time when the Middle Stone Age ended remains unestablished. All well-dated Middle Stone Age assemblages now appear to lie beyond 30,000 to 40,000 years B.P., the lower limit of the radiocarbon technique as practiced by most laboratories. Throughout all of sub-Saharan Africa, artifact assemblages which immediately postdate Middle Stone Age ones remain poorly known or described. In the southern Cape there is so far only one site where the artifactual remains of immediately post-Middle Stone Age peoples are known to occur. This is the cave of Boomplaas A, which is currently being excavated by Hilary Deacon (University of Stellenbosch). Bone preservation at this site is excellent, and in the very near future the cave should provide detailed information on man-animal relationships in the immediate post-Middle Stone Age period.

At Klasies I, Die Kelders I and virtually all other relevant cave sites in the southern Cape, the Middle Stone Age deposits are followed by a long interval of nonoccupation lasting tens of thousands of years. When a site is reoccupied, the new inhabitants are making the kinds of artifacts generally regarded as belonging to the Later Stone Age. Although much remains to be learned about the physical appearance of Later Stone Age peoples, sufficiently complete remains are known in reasonably well-documented contexts to indicate that they were anatomically modern, that is *Homo sapiens sapiens*.

So far the site where the gap between the Middle Stone Age and the Later Stone Age seems shortest is Nelson Bay Cave, where I

conducted excavations in 1970 and 1971. The oldest deposits in Nelson Bay Cave contain Middle Stone Age artifacts, but unfortunately the accompanying bones were long ago destroyed by acid ground waters. As at the Klasies River Mouth, the Middle Stone Age sequence at Nelson Bay begins in the Last Interglacial and extends upward to an indeterminate time within the earlier part of the Last Glacial. After Middle Stone Age people left the cave, there was a long period when no one lived there and only occasional roof-fall blocks accumulated on the floor. The level of these scattered blocks is covered by a sterile layer of gray silt whose origin is unclear. The first Later Stone Age occupation at Nelson Bay occurs directly on this silt and is dated to a little more than 18,000 B.P. by radiocarbon, probably at least 20,000 years after the last Middle Stone Age people inhabited the cave.

From 18,000 years onward, Later Stone Age occupation at Nelson Bay was more or less continuous, and all the Later Stone Age levels contain abundant animal remains. Three major Later Stone Age cultures are represented: the Robberg Culture between 18,000 and 14,000 B.P., the Albany Culture between 14,000 and 8,000 B.P., and various stages of the Wilton Culture from 8,000 years until very recently. People still making Wilton-style stone artifacts were occupying at least parts of the southern Cape before and after the first Europeans arrived in the fifteenth, sixteenth and seventeenth centuries.

The animal remains accompanying the Robberg artifacts at Nelson Bay belong

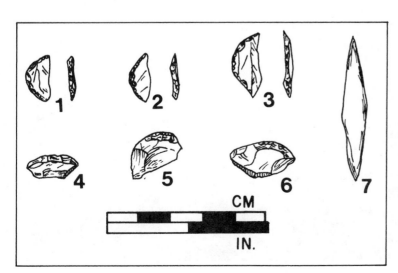

Later Stone Age (Wilton) artifacts from the Nelson Bay Cave (after original drawings by J. Deacon). 1-3: "crescents" or segments (stone); 4-6: "thumbnail scrapers" (stone); 7: a "fish gorge" (bone). Note the very small size of the stone artifacts compared to those in the illustration on page 139.

The mouth of the Nelson Bay Cave. The entrance has been choked by the buildup of immense shell middens in the last few thousand years. If the middens were removed, the height of the entrance would be closer to thirty or forty feet than the present five or six.

View east from the mouth of the Nelson Bay Cave along the coast of the Robberg Peninsula on which the cave is located. (*Center*) another large cave, so far only tested, is located roughly three-quarters of a mile away.

The modern evergreen forest near the Nelson Bay Cave as it appears along the side of a highway passing near the site.

Sable antelope grazing in the Matopos Hills of Rhodesia in a vegetational setting perhaps roughly comparable to that which existed near the Nelson Bay Cave 18,000 years ago. A grassy plain probably extended from Nelson Bay all the way to the coast, at the time some fifty miles distant owing to a sea level which was 400 feet or more below the present one.

143

overwhelmingly to grazing animals such as wildebeest, bastard hartebeest, "giant hartebeest," springbok, giant buffalo and guagga (a kind of zebra). When I first realized this, it seemed peculiar since the historic vegetation in the area was a closed evergreen forest in which none of these creatures lived or could live. The conclusion was inescapable that the vegetation in Robberg, or very late Pleistocene, times was quite different from that of the historic period, and in particular, that it included substantial areas of open grassland. The Nelson Bay Robberg fauna is further characterized by a total or near total absence of marine creatures, either vertebrate or invertebrate, a fact which is also unexpected since Nelson Bay Cave is presently located directly on the coast. But 18,000 to 14,000 years ago, the Last Glacial ice sheets in the Northern Hemisphere were at about their maximum extent and thickness, and as a consequence the sea level was four hundred feet or more below what it is today. Offshore topographic maps show that a drop in the sea level of four hundred feet or so near Nelson Bay would put the coastline roughly fifty miles away, much too far for people to have used the cave as a home base in their exploitation of seafoods.

The great Last Glacial ice sheets began to melt fairly rapidly around 14,000 years ago, and by roughly 12,000 B.P. the coastline was probably only a few miles from Nelson Bay. It is at about 12,000 B.P. during the Albany occupation of the site, that remains of shellfish, seals, seabirds and fish first appear in the deposits. Thereafter they are present in vast quantities, and in fact the beds formed during the last 10,000 years at Nelson Bay consist mainly of culturally accumulated shells, among which are found artifacts and vertebrate remains. In contrast to the Middle Stone Age horizons of Klasies and Die Kelders, the Albany and Wilton levels of Nelson Bay Cave and of other Late Stone Age coastal sites are always rich in bones of fish and flying birds. Unfortunately, it may never be possible to establish when active fishing and fowling came about in the area since the relevant sites, presumably all dating from the middle or later part of the Last Glacial, may now all be underwater.

Not only the coastline but also the vegetation around Nelson Bay changed during Albany times. The grazing animals which characterized the Robberg levels disappeared entirely, and such historically recorded creatures as the bushbuck, bushpig and grysbok either made their first appearance or increased dramatically in frequency. This indicates that closed vegetational communities, somewhat like the present ones, had replaced the previous stretches of open grassland. Faunal remains from like-aged deposits at other important sites such as Elandsbay Cave, excavated by John Parkington (University of Cape Town), Byeneskranskop Cave, excavated by Frank Schweitzer and Boomplaas and Melkhoutboom Caves, excavated by Hilary Deacon, indicate that similar, if not quite so dramatic, vegetational changes involving principally a reduction in the amount of grass land occurred 12,000 to 10,000 years ago over the entire southern Cape.

Some of the grazing animals undoubtedly affected by the shift in vegetation patterns during Albany Culture times are unknown in sites younger than 10,000 years old, and it seems likely they became extinct at or near the end of the Last Glacial period. Roughly contemporaneous large mammal extinctions have long been recorded in Europe and especially in North America. The animals involved in the southern Cape include the giant buffalo, "giant hartebeest," "giant Cape horse" and types of springbok, bastard hartebeest, wildebeest and reedbuck, all of which differed from the living forms. As in Europe and North America, the causes of extinction remain unclear. The coincidence of extinction with environmental changes suggests that the latter played a role, but they cannot be the sole cause, for the now extinct animals are known to have survived the comparable environmental changes that occurred at the end of the Glacial-before-Last, some 125,000 years ago. The one big difference between the end of the Glacial-before-Last and the end of the Last Glacial is the presence of more competent hunter-gatherer populations, as reflected in the contrasts between Middle Stone Age and Later Stone Age faunal remains. The hypothesis I favor is that vigorous attempts by Albany peoples to maintain a big-game hunting way of life in the face of rapid and dramatic reduction in herd sizes and distributions (which itself had been brought about by the reduction of suitable rangeland) led to the complete elimination of some of the prominent big-game species.

The transition from the Last Glacial to the Holocene did not put an end to environmental change in the southern Cape. Faunal remains from the Wilton levels of Nelson Bay indicate that the early Holocene was probably warmer than today. E. M. van Zinderen Bakker (University of the Orange Free State) and Karl Butzer have collected evidence that it was also drier, both on the coast and on the great interior plateau lying to the north of the southern Cape. The interior may have been so dry (and hot?) during the early Holocene period that habitation by hunter-gatherers was largely precluded. Janette Deacon (University of Cape Town) has recently analyzed the more than 225 radiocarbon dates available from southern African Later Stone Age sites. They exhibit a remarkable lack of horizons dated between 9,500 and 4,500 B.P. in the interior. In contrast, dates from sites in the mountains and coasts of the southern Cape indicate continuous occupation, and in fact, the early Holocene here witnessed the establishment of hunter-gatherer lifeways which persisted in some places to the time of European contact only a few hundred years ago.

Hilary Deacon's excavations in the Wilton deposits of Melkhoutboom Cave have provided a particularly rich record of Holocene lifeways in southernmost Africa. Not only do these deposits preserve animal bones (deriving as at other local Wilton sites mainly from nongregarious, browsing antelopes), but the relative dryness of the cave fostered the survival of identifiable plant remains in substantial quantities. Deacon's analysis of these has revealed a wide range of species, some of which were probably collected for food, some for oils and medicines, and yet others for the manufacture of arrow shafts, cordage and the like. Remains of probable food plants predominate. The principal food plant, so common throughout that it must have been a staple in Wilton times, is *Watsonia,* a member of the Iris family. The portion of the plant that was eaten was the corm (essentially a swollen subterranean stem); it is the harder, inedible

outer coverings and bases of the corms that are present in large numbers at the site.

The discovery of inflorescences of plants with restricted flowering seasons indicates beyond all doubt that Wilton people were present at Melkhoutboom in the spring and summer, which was probably also the optimum time to collect *Watsonia* corms and other plant foods on which they relied. The season in which plant collecting perhaps provided relatively little return for effort was winter. Although it cannot be proved at the moment, it seems very likely that the Wilton inhabitants of Melkhoutboom solved this problem by spending their winters at the coast where shellfish replaced plants as a reliable collectable dietary staple. That the Melkhoutboom Wilton people had coastal contacts is clear from the occurrence throughout the Wilton deposits of fragments of marine shell, apparently brought to the site for the manufacture of beads, pendants and possibly other artifacts. Still more significant is evidence that the Wilton inhabitants of coastal sites such as Nelson Bay Cave were there only in winter. In an ingenious application of oxygen-isotope ("paleotemperature") analysis to the growth increments of Wilton shells from Nelson Bay, Nicholas Shackleton (University of Cambridge) has shown that they were probably all collected when offshore waters were relatively cold, that is, in winter. Analogous to the levels at Melkhoutboom, the Nelson Bay Wilton levels contain ostrich eggshells, evidence that the world of the occupants included habitats very different from the surroundings of the cave. Ostriches are denizens of open country; during the Holocene period they probably occurred no closer to Nelson Bay than fifteen to twenty miles inland. Although it is very improbable that Melkhoutboom and Nelson Bay were ever stops on the seasonal round of a single people, taken together they still suggest that Wilton hunter-gatherers engaged in regular seasonal movements between the coast and inland areas. Further evidence for such movements in prehistoric times has been presented by John Parkington from material he excavated at the coastal cave of Elandsbay (a winter site?) and the inland shelter of De Hangen (a summer site?). Hilary Deacon has even uncovered ethnohistoric reports that some very late surviving hunter-gatherers practiced similar movements into the last century.

Hilary and Janette Deacon's detailed studies of the artifacts from the long Wilton sequences at Melkhoutboom and at the nearby Wilton name site indicate that the Wilton culture was not static. Rather, it was characterized by significant changes through time in the frequencies of raw materials used for stone tool manufacture and to some extent in the sizes and shapes of the tools. The most dramatic change, however, was the introduction of pottery at or shortly before the time of Christ. This event is particularly well recorded at Boomplaas, Nelson Bay, Die Kelders I and the Bonteberg Shelter. At Boomplaas, Nelson Bay and Die Kelders, there is evidence that the pottery was accompanied or closely followed by the introduction of domestic sheep. The sources of pottery and sheep are not clear, and the early dates for sheep (present at least as long ago as 2,000 B.P.), are particularly surprising since sheep bones have yet to be found in such early contexts in the areas farther north through which the animals must have passed. On evidence from Die Kelders it is possible to conjecture that cattle appeared at about the same time or shortly after the sheep. With the appearance of sheep and cattle, the stage was set for the complex situation which early European travelers discovered in the southern Cape. They reported that the land was shared by pastoralists who were known as Hottentots and hunter-gatherers who were known as Bushmen. Unfortunately, the lifeways of both kinds of aborigines were seriously disturbed before proper scientific observations could be made, and it is unclear precisely how they shared the land. Perhaps future archaeological research will show that, in some areas at least, people who would have been described as Bushmen at one time of the year became Hottentots at another. This is just one of many gaps in man's knowledge of southern Cape prehistory that archaeologists one day hope to fill.

My analyses of the faunal remains from Boomplaas, Byeneskranskop, Die Kelders, Elandsbay, Klasies River Mouth, Melkhoutboom, and Nelson Bay, as well as the excavations at Nelson Bay, were supported by the National Science Foundation. I thank H. J. Deacon, J. E. Parkington, F. R. Schweitzer, R. Singer, and J. J. Wymer for giving me the opportunity to study the faunal materials they excavated.

FOR FURTHER READING: E. M. van Zinderen Bakker and K. W. Butzer, "Quaternary Environmental Changes in Southern Africa," *Soil Science* 116 (1973) 236-248; K. W. Butzer, "Geology of Nelson Bay Cave, Robberg, South Africa," *South African Archaeological Bulletin* 111 and 112 (1973) 97-110; H. J. Deacon, "A Review of the Post-Pleistocene in South Africa," *South African Archaeological Society, Goodwin Series* 1 (1972) 1-26, *An Archaeological Study of the Eastern Cape in the Post-Pleistocene Period* (Ph.D. diss., University of Cape Town, 1974); J. Deacon, "Wilton, an Assessment after Fifty Years," *South African Archaeological Bulletin* 105 and 106 (1972) 10-48, "Patterning in the Radiocarbon Dates for the Wilton/Smithfield Complex in Southern Africa," *South African Archaeological Bulletin* 113 and 114 (1974) 3-18; R. G. Klein, "Geological Antiquity of Rhodesian Man," *Nature* 249 (1973) 311-312, "Environment and Subsistence of Prehistoric Man in the Southern Cape Province, South Africa," *World Archaeology* 5 (1974) 249-284; J. E. Parkington, "Seasonal Mobility in the Later Stone Age," *African Studies* 31 (1972) 223-243; F. R. Schweitzer, "Archaeological Evidence for Sheep at the Cape," *South African Archaeological Bulletin* 115 and 116 (1974) 75-82; N. J. Shackleton, "Oxygen Isotope Analysis as a Means of Determining Season of Occupation of Prehistoric Midden Sites," *Archaeometry* 15 (1973) 133-141; R. Singer and J. J. Wymer, "Archaeological Investigations at the Saldanha Skull Site in South Africa," *South African Archaeological Bulletin* 25 (1968) 63-74; A. J. Tankard and F. R. Schweitzer, "The Geology of Die Kelders Cave and Environs: A Palaeoenvironmental Study," *South African Journal of Science* 70 (1974) 360-369.

RICHARD G. KLEIN received a B.A. from the University of Michigan in 1962 and a M.A. and Ph.D. from the University of Chicago in 1964 and 1966, respectively. For the past seven years his major interest has been southern African prehistory, and he has spent more than three years in South Africa both excavating and analyzing faunal remains. He has taught at the University of Wisconsin-Milwaukee, Northwestern University and is currently an Associate Professor of Anthropology at the University of Chicago.

A NEW THEORY OF PYRAMID BUILDING

24

After 5,000 years
of speculation, a
fresh approach
eliminates the need
for a Cecil B.
deMille set and
a cast of 100,000

by Olaf Tellefsen

Egyptologists and engineers have been fighting over the great pyramids for years. The archeologists hold for a hundred thousand men hauling three-ton blocks up earthen ramps more mammoth than the pyramids themselves. The engineers produce pages of calculations to show there wasn't enough manpower in all Egypt to build such ramps, and further, that the Egyptians couldn't have gotten enough men on top of a pyramid, even with scaffolding, to heave the huge top piece into place.

The engineers have not come up

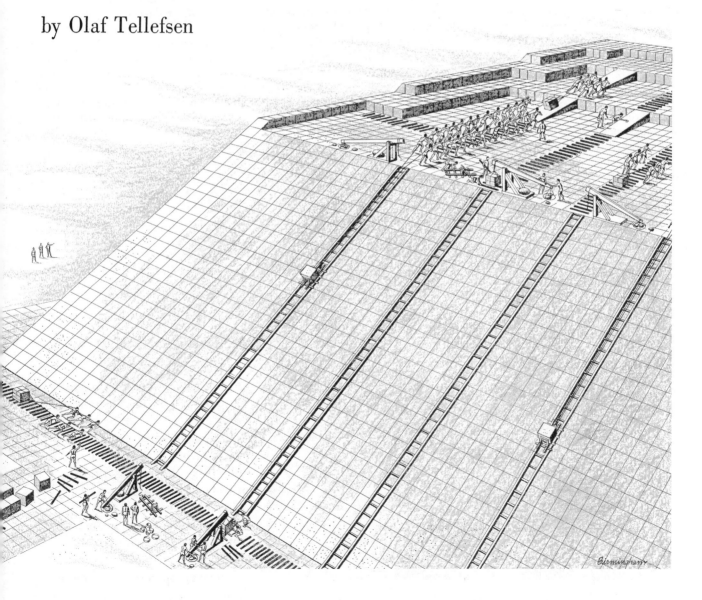

Birmingham

with anything to replace the ramp theory, however. The problem is simply stated: Devise a means of building a 480-foot-high monument out of more than two million 3-foot-square blocks of stone, without using any power other than human or animal strength. Based upon an accidental observation in present-day Egypt, I have an answer that involves the use of one simple tool easily accessible to the ancients and that does away with the need for a ramp and all but a few thousand of the postulated hordes of workers.

On a trip up the Nile some years ago, I saw three men moving large stones to the water's edge from a pile that could well have been the remains of some ancient structure. When I saw the size of the stones my engineering sense told me that I had run across a technological curiosity of note. The primitive piece of equipment the men were using was a triumph of elementary physics—a large weight arm, consisting of a heavy timber that pivoted on a sturdy, 6-foot-high fulcrum. The short arm was less than 3 feet long; the long arm 15 to 16 feet. A pallet was attached to the long arm, upon which rocks could be piled for counterweight. While the unit was roughly built, apparently with no tool other than an ax, it served its purpose admirably.

As I watched, the men slid a sling under one of the stones, looping the bight over the short end of the weight arm where one man held it in place while the other two piled rocks on the pallet. They piled on rocks until it almost balanced, then brought the beam down by adding their combined weight. That lifted the big stone about a foot, enough for the third man to place planks, rollers, and a pair of runners under it. With that done, the men at the pallet eased the stone down on the rollers and proceeded to dump the counterweight. The sling was removed, and the load was now ready for moving. Two men pushed with wooden levers while the third man shifted the rollers and leapfrogged the planks.

The block of stone must have weighed more than two tons, but the placing of it on the rollers had taken little more than ten minutes.

I felt sure the apparatus I had seen must have been based on an idea inherited from the past, where it had played a key role in the raising of the huge stone structures of the past, including the Great Pyramid. I could visualize a hundred weight arms being used on that great project, each serving several gangs of five or six men who, together, could easily place up to 600 of the regular building stones per day. This simple machine would reduce the manpower requirement from the assumed 100,000 to a few thousand men.

To substantiate what I intuitively felt to be true, I decided to eliminate what we positively know was nonexistent at the time, then determine what was left. The ancient master builders did not have power equipment, block and tackles, or hand winches, but they had everything else, including a firm grip of elementary physics.

The Egyptologists have concluded that, in the absence of aids more advanced than ropes, levers, and wooden rollers, the inclined plane in the form of a ramp was used "up which the blocks of stone were dragged by vast gangs of men to their position on the pile." In contrast, engineers have shown by cool figures that there was not manpower enough in the entire country to build such a ramp beyond the halfway mark. To double the height of a ramp, you must use eight times the amount of fill material and ten times the number of man days. Fifty feet or so is the practical limit. In addition, engineers have shown that the top piece could not have been elevated to the 480-foot level by manpower alone. There wouldn't be room for that many men on any scaffolding that could

In conventional explanations, the pyramid builders used giant ramps to raise the stone blocks up to the working area. The ramps either corkscrewed up the sides, as in this representation, or were built straight up to one face. Remains of ramps have been found at some pyramids, but many experts doubt that ramps were used all the way up to the 480-foot level.

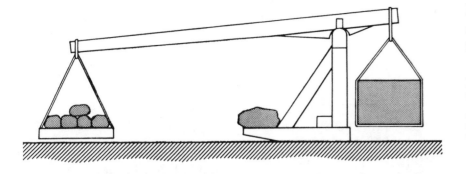

Built with nothing more than an ax, a weight arm enables two men to lift several tons. Counterweights are piled on a pallet hung from the long end; then the men simply pull down on that end, lifting the load with the short end.

be erected. It seemed obvious to engineers that the builders must have used some mechanical aid, but they were unable to agree on what it might have been. The Egyptologists clung to the ramp explanation, feeling they had no clear alternative. And from them it found its way into our school textbooks.

Although the situation looked discouraging, I remained confident because I had the winning ace in the hole—the missing apparatus.

Although it has been the workhorse of peoples ever since man learned to build with heavy stones, the weight arm is so completely out of use in our power-conscious age that it has virtually been forgotten. It isn't even mentioned in our college dictionaries. The more general term lever is defined and usually illustrated, but there are many forms of the lever. Each should be defined in accordance with its special characteristics. For example, the function of a pinch bar is pushing, while that of a weight arm is pulling. A pinch bar, or pry, can only push or tilt an object, while the weight arm can pull or lift it in a sling. And theoretically there is no limit to the capacity of a weight arm.

To push a heavy stone block onto rollers with pinch bars is a slow and awkward process, and to push it onto loose skids is nearly impossible. The block must be lifted so that skidway and skids can be positioned under it, exactly as I saw it done. The Egyptologists did not consider greased skids because they knew of no way such lifting could have been accomplished. But with the weight arm greased skids suggest themselves. They are particularly practical for moving heavy

loads up a steep incline, while rollers are preferable on the level. Thus, skidways of heavy planks, laid flat against the face of the pyramid from ground to working level, would be the ideal means for elevating the stone blocks. Several gangs of 25 to 30 men each would do the pulling, using a two-part tackle. Although they did not have pulleys as we know them, a rounded piece of hardwood, well greased and covered with a loose leather sleeve, would serve equally well.

For the lower half of the pyramid as many as 30 skidways would be necessary, each with a weight arm at top and bottom for transfer of the stones. Ten pulling gangs would be needed, each serving three skidways. At the halfway level, for example, each gang could pull three stones per hour or a total of 300 per day for all ten gangs. This quantity could easily be placed by 100 placing gangs of five or six men each. Then, assuming there were 100 delivery gangs, also of five or six men each, for pushing the blocks on rollers from the staging area to the skidways, and 200 masons with as many helpers for the passages and chambers, it would appear that 3,000 men could have raised the pyramid. In that figure are included masonry dressers, repairmen, and riggers.

The huge stones and slabs for the passages and chambers would be moved on timber skidways by banks of weight arms, rigged for lateral pull. The top piece would be hauled to its position by two banks of weight arms, which could move it about a foot with each bite. A scaffold on three sides of the pyramid top would accommodate the weight arms and their operators.

As to the regular masonry, it is most probable that three courses would be completed before each extension of the skidways. The blocks would be elevated to each second and third course by means of portable wooden ramps of easy incline, and placing gangs would double up for the short push uphill. The exception would be in the pull-up area itself where there would be no room for such ramps. There, the blocks would be lifted with dual weight arms—one to lift and one to pull sideways. Incidentally, Herodotus mentioned some such rig, calling it "a machine made of short planks." The full passage, in Rawlinson's translation, reads: "The Pyramid was built in tiers, battlementwise, as it is called, or, according to others, stepwise. When the Pyramid was completed in this form, they raised the remaining stones to their places by means of machines formed of short beams of wood. The first machine raised them from the ground to the top of the first step. On this there was another machine, which received the stone upon its arrival, and conveyed it to the second step, whence a third machine advanced it still higher. Either they had as many machines as there were steps in the Pyramid, or possibly they had but a single machine, which, being easily moved, was transferred from tier to tier as the stone rose—both accounts are given and therefore I mention both. The upper portion of the Pyramid was finished first, then the middle, and finally the part which was lowest and nearest the ground."

Herodotus is apparently referring here to the final dressing of the exterior of the pyramid. This is the only known reference to how

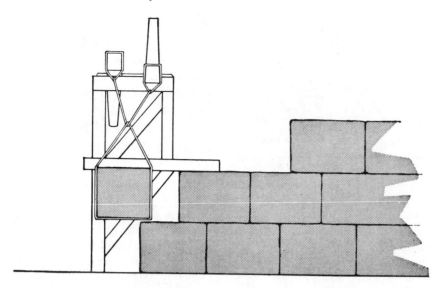

A double weight arm can work in tight places. The left arm raises a block in the normal way. Then the right arm is lowered and the sling attached. When it is raised, the block will move to the right as well as up.

the blocks were raised, and it points directly to the weight arm.

I have shown how the Great Pyramid could have been erected with only a few thousand men and without the use of a monstrous ramp. The capital question is, therefore, whether or not the engineers of the Fourth Dynasty could have succeeded without the devices I have mentioned.

Because there are no known records of on-the-spot observations or builders' perspectives, it is the popular verdict that we shall never know for sure. But we should be able to establish which is the most reasonable explanation.

Egyptologists have recently con-cluded, on the basis of new and more reliable evidence, that the manpower supply during the Fourth Dynasty was not as ample as previously believed. There were actually few slaves because foreign conquests were at a minimum. In-stead, seasonal farm workers, who otherwise would be idle during the growing season and during high

Certainly in planning a project as immense as the Great Pyramid, their foremost concern would have been that without numerous labor-saving devices the limited and fluc-tuating work force could not com-plete the bulky structure during the Pharaoh's reign. They needed a method of magnifying the power of a few men for lifting or pulling. I believe that the weight arm alone could have filled that bill. The de-vice—made entirely of wood—was quite within the possibilities of the Bronze Age. There is no physical reason why it could not have been used. It should be possible to deter-mine definitely whether it was or not. The determining factor is the manpower situation of the time be-cause, if it were in short supply, something like the weight arm must have been used.

At this point I must return the case to the Egyptologists. I hope I have convinced them that a drastic reconsideration of the entire pyra-mid question is in order.

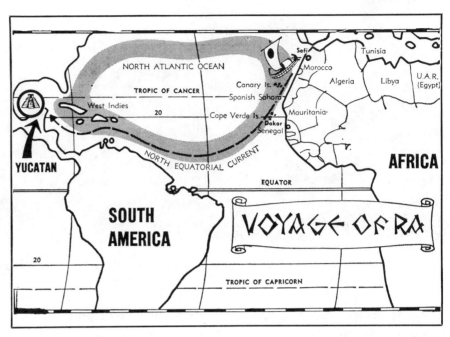

25

Twenty-two years after his historic Kon Tiki expedition across the Pacific, Thor Heyerdahl proposes to test another cultural migration theory. On a reed-boat, a phenomenon of marine architecture present in the Old and New Worlds, the Norwegian anthropologist is embarking on a three-month test of the proposition that the ancients of North Africa could have crossed the Atlantic, to land in Mexico. From Safi, on the Moroccan coast, Heyerdahl expects to catch the current and trade winds down the African coast, heading almost due west opposite Dakar. The craft, named Ra for the Egyptian sun god, will carry a crew of eight. This is Heyerdahl's account of Ra's genesis.

Linking the transoceanic cultures

by Thor Heyerdahl

The first man to die in America was born in Arctic Asia. He had no metal industry, his clothing was of animal hides or bark, he knew nothing about agriculture or architecture. He was a pure Stone-Age man. Science does not know when he arrived, or when the first descendants and followers of the Asians who crossed the Bering Straits started to spread southward from Arctic Alaska into North, Central and finally South America. Some believe this initial colonization started 15,000 years before the time of Christ; others are equally certain that this timespan can easily be doubled.

All agree, however, that the Arctic was man's initial gateway into America, and that only the simplest Stone-Age tools were known to the unorganized flocks of savages whose numerous descendants were to become known to the present world as the wide variety of aboriginal American Indians.

The narrow gap between Arctic Asia and Alaska was probably never closed for human crossings, and recent scien-

tific discoveries have shown that primitive migrants have apparently continued to leak back and forth across the local semi-frozen waters and the Aleutian chain of islands.

Nobody can ever take away from Columbus the honor of having put wide open for the first time the gates to America, thus revolutionizing history for men of all breeds and nations for all centuries to come.

Yet we must never forget that he did not arrive on an empty beach.

In the tropic jungle areas of Mexico, precisely where the perpetual tradewinds and the large transatlantic current had carried the early Spaniards who followed Columbus ashore, the conquistadores met people with organized communities and specialized occupations.

Their astronomical knowledge had reached the point that they had figured out the exact position of the equator and the equinox, and they distinguished the planets from the stars.

Their calendar system was more exact

than the Gregorian calendar, and their surgeons were able, not only to repair fractures or prepare mummies, but even to perform successful trepanation of the skull, something unheard of in Europe at that time.

Paved roads, enormous aqueducts and suspension bridges criss-crossed the landscape, and colossal monolithic monuments, pyramids and other architectural structures from quarried stones surpassed anything known in contemporary Europe in size and splendor.

Vast fields with intricate aqueducts, terracing and irrigation systems contained a wide variety of root-crops, vegetables, cereals, fruits, drugs and other cultivated plants, many of which were unknown to the European visitors.

The intruders marvelled at the fact that cotton was extensively cultivated also on this side of the Atlantic, and for the same purpose: the local cotton cultivators knew how to spin, dye and weave, and some of their materials were of a finer thread and technique than anything seen in Europe.

Heyerdahl's papyrus reed-boat set against the physical culture he will try to relate to both Mexico and Egypt.

Primitive craft built of reeds in the New World and papyrus in the Old could indicate a common heritage and an anthropological truth

With the European conquest of the Aztec and Inca empires the curtain fell on the aboriginal American civilizations, a curtain barely raised by Columbus only a few decades before. Today the science of archaeology and the deciphering of pre-Columbian inscriptions on stone and paper are our only means of reconstructing part of the broken picture.

What had happened in America before Columbus? Had the Stone-Age hunters from Siberia developed these splendid civilizations in Mexico, Central America and Peru independent of the outside world?

Or could it be that the tropic current reaching Mexico from North Africa had carried along some unidentified drift voyagers who had brought certain ideas to tropic America long before culture had spread from Africa and Asia Minor to the southern shores of Europe?

There was a time when the teachings of the so-called Vienna School of "diffusionism" had a firm grip on anthropological thinking throughout the world. Right into the 20th century it was a widely accepted theory that civilization had only one cradle, not too far from the Biblical lands, and from here culture spread across continents and oceans to every corner of the world wherever subsequently encountered by the medieval explorers from Europe.

Thus the existence of sun worship, pyramid-building, marriage between brothers and sisters in the royal families, mummification and the art of hieroglyphic writing among the American high-cultures were naturally seen as direct inheritance from ancient Egypt, and no ocean was considered wide enough to form a geographical barrier.

This theory of universal cultural diffusion was soon to be vigorously challenged by a rapidly growing group of more critical and exact American and European anthropologists, who refused to accept any such theory without a proof.

Gradually they became equally fanatic, guided by another emerging doctrine: All cultural parallels could be ascribed to the unity of the human mind. They justly pointed to the close mental and physical relationship among all subdivisions of human family which, they contended, made man react in a similar way to the same outer challenge as long as the environmental conditions were alike.

In other words, there was no need for the pyramid-builders of Mexico and Peru to have gotten their inspiration from across the ocean; after all, they had the same mind and body as the people of Egypt and could therefore have hit upon the same architectural ideas independently.

Reed-boats survive in Central Africa.

From then on modern anthropologists locked all gates to pre-Columbian America except the extreme Arctic north, and the Atlantic and Pacific oceans were considered total barriers to any human craft prior to the historic crossing of the three caravelles guided by Columbus. This frequently publicized doctrine gradually became an incontrovertible scientific axiom.

Nevertheless, a group of rebellious anthropologists at the American Museum of Natural History in New York began to point out striking similarities between southern Asia and Mexico in pre-Columbian times, and other leading authorities at the United States National Museum in Washington, D.C., followed suit by pointing to archaeological discoveries in coastal Ecuador that indicated to them contact with ancient Japan.

In 1966, I flew to Lake Titicaca in Peru-Bolivia to visit once more the remarkable bundle-boats of totora reeds which have navigated this stormy South American mountain lake since time immemorial. Their seaworthiness and carrying capacity struck me more than ever before as being quite astonishing.

At the International Congress of Americanists in Argentina that year, I had quoted an isolationist who had pointed to their remarkable similarity to the specialized bundle-boats of papyrus reeds which were in common use in ancient Egypt.

His conclusion was that, since nobody could have traveled from the Nile to Lake Titicaca, these peculiar reed-boats could be taken as proof that even a remarkable analogy such as this had to be the result of independent inventions in two continents.

The same isolationist had committed one serious error, however. He had overlooked the fact that similar bundle-boats of reeds and canes were formerly not restricted to Egypt and this isolated South American mountain lake.

At the arrival of the Spaniards they were in common use along a Pacific coastline of some 4,000 miles from California to Chile, and also on a number of lakes in Mexico.

Moreover, their Old World counterparts were not restricted to the Nile, but were used from Mesopotamia through Ethiopia, Chad, Niger and coastal Morocco. Morocco and Mexico were separated by nothing but a constantly westward-moving ocean current.

Was there anything that could prevent such an ingeniously constructed bundle-boat from drifting with the permanently westbound ocean current from the coast of northern Africa to the tropic areas around the Mexican Gulf?

I could no longer rid myself of the suspicion that the key to the whole problem might be the hitherto unexamined seaworthiness of such a pre-Columbian type of bundle-boat.

A reed is a tender water plant that can be bent by the hands of a child. A gust of wind along the swampy shores of a lake suffices to make the reeds wave like green grass in the field. A reed is a mere flower stalk unable to hold either a nail or a screw.

Yet, reeds have been used by man to navigate lakes and oceans, and pyramid-builders in two continents have

Pyramids and reed-boats could link New World and ancient Egyptian cultures.

floated tons of cargo on bundles of reeds tied together.

When the early European visitors crossed the Panama isthmus, the Indians of Panama had already told them of the existence of the Inca Empire with its wealth of gold and its sailing vessels which were reported to be as large as those of the Spaniards.

And true enough, a large vessel reported to carry sails and rigging like those of the Spanish ships, with a crew of men and women as well as 20 tons of precious cargo from the Inca Empire, was encountered and sacked by Pizarro's pilot before the Europeans reached Peru.

To the surprise and disgust of the Spaniards, the large Inca craft proved to be nothing but an open raft of light balsa wood which permitted the water to move freely up and down between the logs. The merchandise on board was kept dry on an elevated deck of plaited bamboo.

One after another of these sailing rafts of balsa logs were encountered by the Spaniards until they had passed the jungle coast of Ecuador and reached the desert coast of Peru. Here they found, side by side with the balsa log-rafts, a huge number of still stranger vessels, which from the distance looked like lofty ships with high and elegantly curved bow and stern.

The smallest of these reed vessels were nothing but tusk-shaped reed rollers on which one or two men could ride astride as on a horse, with their legs in the water. The larger ones, however, were reported to be as large

as a real sailing ship, with a crew of 24 men.

Any water pouring over the strange wash-through Inca reed-boats just ran through their bottom and out, making scooping or bailing unnecessary.

With the conquest of Peru and the introduction of European culture, these wash-through bundle-boats and raft-ships disappeared with the rest of the amazing Inca culture. To the modern generations they have become something symbolic of a primitive past, something leaking like a sieve, and therefore unfit for ocean travel.

Their non-European construction principles have been used to support the argument that the coastal population of Peru, although living almost entirely from off-shore fishing and coastal trade, had never discovered the secret of true boatbuilding: They had never learned how to build a watertight hull.

This is indeed a great misconception. In fact, the Inca boatbuilders knew very well how to make watertight canoes, but they used them only on calm rivers. In rough seas and in the open ocean they preferred something which was fully buoyant in itself, which surfs and stormy seas could never fill: a wash-through balsa raft or bundle-boat of buoyant reeds.

In the earliest pre-Inca ceramic art of Peru large reed ships with double deck and a great quantity of human passengers and cargo are commonly illustrated. And reed boats large enough to carry cattle across the stormy waters were still being built on the mountain lake of

In Lake Titicaca between Peru and Bolivia, Heyerdahl tries out a reed-boat.

Titicaca, in the high plateau of the South American Andes.

Whereas the reed-boats of Peru and Bolivia have survived to modern times, those of Mexico are known only from casual references in the literature. Various European travelers report having come across bundle-boats of reeds, bulrushes and canes in a number of isolated Mexican lakes as well as along the shoreline of the ocean.

My efforts at tracing any possible survivors of this type of watercraft north of the Panama isthmus led to my friendship with two Mexican traveler-adventurers and skindivers, Ramon Bravo and German Carrasco, who offered to be my pathfinders. Such boats had until recently been in use among the isolated Seris Indians in the Gulf of California, they said.

We flew to Hermosillo in northwestern Mexico and crossed the Sonora Desert to the barren local coast. Here, surrounded by gigantic candle-shaped cactus trees and flanked by rugged red mountains, a small tribe of colorful Seris Indians made their living from fishing in the open bay.

Against an adequate contribution from our side, however, it appeared that the past was not very far away. After an attempt to build an askam or reed-boat failed, an almost blind old former Seris chief rebuilt the ruins of one, and launched it from an ocean beach.

I realized that we were seeing perhaps the last bundle boat still preserved in Mexican waters. A proud tradition was ended in a country with a remarkable cultural history.

Since bundle-boats of reeds and canes have been widely used in adjacent parts of ancient America, the Seris Indians were hardly the original inventors.

But who were the original inventors? Peruvians? Mexicans? Or had the idea spread with the boat itself across the ocean from the Old World? Nobody has the answer yet.

When and where did the reed-boat evolve among Old World boatbuilders? Certainly long before man began to build similar vessels in Mexico and Peru. Rock carvings in the interior of Africa, identified by archaeologists as representing reed-boats, have been tentatively dated to 10,000 years ago. And the importance of reed-boats to ancient Egyptian culture is well documented in hierolyphics and drawings on the walls of Egyptian tombs.

We do not know if reed-boats spread with certain ancient cultures or these cultures spread by means of reed-boats, but such craft were used by pyramid-builders in Asia Minor as well as in Egypt.

That they were used in the open Mediterranean is indicated by their survival until modern times on the island of Sardinia, and it is directly shown by Isaiah who wrote in the Old Testament (Ch. 18.2) that ambassadors arrived from Egypt "in vessels of bulrushes upon the waters." What the former distribution was on the Atlantic seashore is not known. Reed bundle-boats, locally called madi, were in use at the mouth of Rio Lucus in Morocco until the beginning of our own century.

Very early in Egyptian history, before King Cheops built his famous pyramid, a vigorous oversea trade had developed between Egypt and Lebanon. From the swampy delta of the Nile, papyrus was shipped to Biblos, the oldest known port in the world, where papyrus was used to manufacture paper for regular books, locally called "bibles," an industry which gave the name to the old city.

From Biblos the return voyagers started to bring back to Africa cedar timber, a highly prized material in ancient Egypt. With a steadily increased access to cedar wood a sudden evolution, if not a sudden change, took place in Egyptian maritime architecture. The papyrus ships had great advantages, above all they could never be filled by breaking seas or bottom leakage, but the papyrus would gradually waterlog and rot, and the exposed cords were worn off against rocks and sand.

Inspired by other maritime people who had wooden ships that often lasted a lifetime, the Egyptians, too, began to cut planks and sew them together with stitches of cord. These wooden vessels, however, became strongly papyriform: The conservative Egyptian architects kept closely to the original outline of the ancestral papyrus vessel, although this shape was exceedingly awkward for the carpenter who had to imitate in the wood the elegantly bent bundles of reed with their curved flower-heads at the extremities.

Construction of the reed craft, Ra.

Today papyrus boats of any size are unknown in all of Egypt. The reason is obvious: papyrus no longer grows in this country where it once was a principal element in the culture.

To find papyrus today one has to travel far up the Nile beyond the borders of Egypt, or into the very heart of the African mainland. And in a few of these remote places the custom of building papyrus-boats has survived the millennia together with the plant itself. To get a first-hand impression of these ancient watercraft other than from wall paintings on plastered tombs, I decided to visit the village of Bol on remote Lake Chad in the Central African republic of the same name.

Bol, with its hundreds of beehive-shaped grass huts, was the principal town in the lake area, and the seat of the Sherif and the Sultan. In Bol we met Omar and Mussa, two of the numerous Buduma tribesmen who lived by fishing with papyrus-boats on the lake, precisely as on the Nile thousands of years ago.

Omar and Mussa built for us a papyrus-boat small enough to put on the roof of one of our jeeps, once we had tried it, together with a whole flotilla of larger papyrus vessels. Mussa was a professional papyrus-boatbuilder who was said to have once built a reed vessel that carried 80 cattle across the open lake to the opposite coast in neighboring Nigeria.

My meeting with the boatbuilders in the papyrus swamps of Chad sparked an idea that for some months had laid dormant in my mind. I asked Omar, the most active of the two brothers, if he would come to Egypt and build a large caday for me. He said yes, if his brother Mussa could come as well, and their friend Abdoullaye added on his own accord that he would come along as interpreter.

I had established my first contact with new friends in a hidden corner of our modern world where tradition kept alive an art developed to perfection before pharoanic times. Now I knew people who could build a real papyrus ship. I could test the possibility of contact between the ancient Old World and the New.

VII. Primates and Human Nature

Toward the end of his article, "Human Origins," which appears in Section V of this reader, Pilbeam provides the context in which physical anthropologists and other social scientists are devoting an increasing amount of time to the study of primates for insight into human behavior. The great apes are, after all, our closest living relatives, and even monkeys are our distant cousins. This section is divided into two parts. Part A presents some of the surprising facts that are emerging about primates. In Part B various scholars argue about what to make of these facts.

A. Living Primates

Fleming's "The State of the Apes" is a report on several research projects in which chimpanzees (of all the apes our closest relatives) are being taught to talk—well, almost. Chimps lack the throat and mouth equipment to produce the range of sounds that characterize human speech; but Washoe, Sarah, and other apes are being taught to communicate using various physical symbols such as plastic shapes and the gestures of sign language for the deaf. As the research results come in, it is becoming increasingly clear that apes (not only chimps but gorillas as well) have many—if not all—of the mental capacities for language, including open-ended grammatical structures.

Bernstein and Gordon's article is an analysis of the research that has been done on primate aggression. "The Function of Aggression in Primate Societies" is not yet well understood; in fact it is one of the subjects of debate in the next part of this section. However, it is clear that many of the stereotyped notions of rigid "pecking orders" that resulted from early research on primates in captivity and in crowded game parks are wrong. And the authors suggest that the concept of aggression itself needs rethinking; rather than seeing it in its usual negative sense, it may be useful to think of aggression as an important basis of social cohesion in groups.

B. A Human Biogram?

In the past decade the media have been swamped by movies, television shows, articles, and books that attempt in various ways to account for many social problems that resist solution in terms of innate patterns of behavior that the human species has inherited. This question of a human biogram—species-characteristic behavior that is genetically inherited—has thus become one of the "hot" issues in the social and behavioral sciences, with scholars lining up on both sides and criticizing not only each other's research and conclusions but each other's personal integrity as well.

A scholar who has been subjected to great personal harassment by some of his colleagues at Harvard and others who disagree with his views is Edward O. Wilson, whose recently published book *Sociobiology* has fanned the flames of controversy by suggesting that a broad range of human behavior might well be genetically controlled. In "The Origins of Human Social Behavior" Wilson lays out the bases of his reasoning. We follow this article with "A Dialogue on Man, the Killer," which takes place between the late Louis Leakey, one of the world's leading authorities on our early hominid ancestors, and Robert Ardrey, the former journalist and playwright who has published a number of popular books promoting the theories of Konrad Lorenz, specifically arguing that our inability to prevent warfare and violent crimes is due to our heritage as the descendants of meat-eating killer "man-apes." The dialogue covers a wide range of extremely controversial points. And whether or not you find yourself agreeing with its general thrust, insightful comments like Leakey's with regard to language—that is, that the beginnings of human aggression can be traced back to the origins of words that enabled people to plan and plot the undertaking of horrible deeds—will certainly provide you with stimulating reading.

In "An Idea We Could Live Without: The Naked Ape," Pilbeam attempts to place these issues in their proper perspective. He shows Ardrey's arguments to be simplistic and reductionist, adds new data to the discussion (note especially his comments on recent studies of baboons living in uncrowded conditions), and also discusses human social groups (which frequently—and mysteriously—are often left out of these debates altogether!). Indeed, Parr takes up the issue of real human groups and how people behave in "The Territories of Man," in which he cuts through the "nature" versus "nurture" argument and asks us to consider the subtlety and complexity of human behavior and worry less about "where" it comes from.

Finally, in "Roots of Human Behavior," Campbell addresses himself to the issue of human biological diversity (whereas the previous articles emphasized panhuman characteristics), and roots his discussion of our biological and social heritages in evolutionary terms that are refreshingly concrete: He states quite clearly and correctly that it makes no sense at all to argue that something has gone wrong in evolution—evolution is nothing more or less than adaptation, and its results at any given time simply *are*—they are not "good" or "bad," "right" or wrong." They simply exist.

We leave it up to you to draw your own conclusions. However, it is important that you recognize that those who leap to biological explanations for all the ills of human behavior have little or nothing to say about how we are to go about solving our problems. Indeed, biological reductionism is a frequent bedfellow of conservative political philosophy. But that is a topic to which we turn in the last section of this book.

MAN IS NOT UNIQUE; the belief that he is has been with us forever. The foreshadowing of the death of that belief is almost as old. It may have started when ancient physicians discovered the extensive similarity between the bodies of men and other animals. It certainly was evident when Darwin's theory of evolution attained general scientific acceptance. Now the end is in sight as man is forced to concede the last significant attribute that was his and his alone—language.

The animal reaching for our holy title, only user of language, is the chimpanzee. Not one that performs like a trained seal. Not one that dutifully repeats exactly what is taught. Not one at all, but a dozen chimps, in Reno, in Santa Barbara, in Norman, Oklahoma, and in Atlanta. They have vocabularies of substantial size. They combine symbols to produce appropriate combinations that they have never before seen. They use language to manipulate their environments. They mystify their experienced teachers with unexpected abilities and insights.

The Failure of the Spoken Word. For many years we believed that chimps must be smart enough to learn a language. Yet all attempts to teach them

to talk have been failures by even the most generous standards. The world's record for number of words spoken by a chimp is held by Viki, who managed to learn four words in the 1950s. Her problem was speaking. Chimpanzees cannot learn to talk, but they can learn to use a complex set of symbols to convey information. The symbols can be hand signals, pieces of plastic in different shapes and colors, geometric designs on typewriter keys; anything they can manipulate with their hands.

The record of failure turned to a record of success when Beatrice and Allen Gardner at the University of Nevada looked at communication among chimps in the wild, noticed that they used many more hand signals than vocal signals, and decided to try teaching a gestural language instead of a verbal one. They chose Washoe as their first pupil.

Washoe is a female chimpanzee who was born in the wild. She was about a year old when her language training began in June 1966. At this age her development and her needs were much like those of a human baby who is one or one and a half years old. She slept a lot, had just begun to crawl, did not have either her first canines or molars. During the first few months her daily routine was centered around diapers, bottles, and making friends with her human companions.

The Gardners chose a chimpanzee instead of one of the other higher

26

Field Report

THE STATE OF THE APES

by Joyce Dudney Fleming
One of humanity's last proud claims to uniqueness—the use of language—is in clear and present danger of dissolving. Psychologists in California, Nevada, Oklahoma and Alabama are teaching language to chimpanzees, and the conversations run both ways. Soon, the chimps may well begin to talk to each other.

primates because of the chimp's capacity for forming strong attachments to human beings. They believe that this high degree of sociability may be essential for the development of language. The language they chose for Washoe was American Sign Language (ASL).

ASL is a system of communication developed for deaf people and used extensively throughout North America. It is a set of hand gestures that corresponds to individual words. (The other system for the deaf, finger spelling, is not used in this research.) Many of the signs are iconic, visual representations of their meaning. For example:

drink—the thumb is extended from the fisted hand and touches the mouth,

up—the arms are extended upwards and the index finger may also point in that direction,

smell—the palm is held in front of the nose and moved slightly upward several times,

cat—the thumb and index finger come together near the corner of the mouth and are moved outward representing the cat's whiskers. This close association between sign and meaning makes it easy to learn to read some of the simple and frequently used messages.

Think Doctor. A wide range of expression is possible within this system. While learning to sign, the Gardners practiced translating songs and poems, and found that any material could be accurately signed. When technical terms and proper names present a problem they are designated by an arbitrary sign agreed upon by the community of signers. Washoe's teachers chose the signs *think doctor* and *think science* for the words psychologist and psychology.

Washoe invented *gimme tickle* to request tickling.

The fact that ASL is used by human beings allows for some comparison between Washoe's signing and that seen in deaf children of deaf parents. The Gardners report that deaf parents see many similarities between Washoe's early performance, some of which was filmed, and that of deaf children learning to sign.

Washoe lived in a fully-equipped house trailer. The Gardners designed her living arrangements to exploit the possibility that she would engage in conversations—ask questions as well as answer them, describe objects as well as request them. They gave her a stimulus-rich environment, minimal restraint, constant human

CHIMP AND FRIEND. Steve Temerlin, Lucy's human brother, is an animal caretaker at Lemmon's institute. When the feeding and cleaning are done, he gives the chimps a chance to do some of the things they like best.

companionship while she was awake, and lots of games that promoted interaction between Washoe and human beings. Her teachers used no language except ASL in her presence.

Flower and Smell. The results of combining this pupil and this language in this environment are remarkable. Her teachers taught her the sign for *more* in the context of tickling, a romping, wrestling game Washoe played with them. She generalized its use to all activities and all objects. They taught her the sign for *open* using only three particular doors in her house trailer. She transferred its use to all doors, containers, drawers, the refrigerator and, finally, to water faucets. They taught her the sign for *flower*. She used it for all flowers and for a number of situations in which an odor was prominent, such as opening a tobacco pouch or entering a kitchen where food was cooking. So they gave her the sign for *smell*. She differentiated the two signs and uses each appropriately, but the error she makes in odor contexts is frequently *flower*.

When she makes mistakes, Washoe often tells her teacher more about what she knows than when she signs correctly. The Gardners started using pictures of objects

to test Washoe's vocabulary after she spontaneously transferred her signs from objects to pictures of similar objects. However, if they used a photograph of a replica of the object, she made a lot of mistakes. She called them *baby*. In response to a picture of a cat she signed *cat* on almost 90 percent of the trials; to a picture of a replica of a cat she signed *cat* on 60 percent of the trials and *baby* on 40 percent. Her teachers used *baby* to refer to dolls and to human babies. To Washoe it meant something different, something like miniaturization, or replication in some artificial sense.

The First Sentence. In April 1967, less than a year after her training began, she produced her first combination of signs, a kind of sentence. Though no lessons on combinations had ever been given, her teachers had signed to her in strings. As soon as Washoe had learned eight or 10 signs she started putting them together in sets of two or three, much as small children learn to combine words. She learned some of her combinations from her teachers, but others she made up herself. For example, Washoe invented *gimme tickle* to request tickling and *open food drink* to ask that the refrigerator be opened. Her

teachers had always used the signs *cold box* for this appliance.

With just 10 signs there is a large number of possible two- and three-sign combinations, but Washoe did not make sentences from random groups of signs. The ones she used were usually the ones that made sense. The signs she used in front of a locked door included *gimme key, open key, open key please,* and *open key help hurry.* The Gardners analyzed Washoe's two-sign combinations using a method like the one Roger Brown, a psycholinguist from Harvard, developed for children. They found that her earliest combinations were comparable to the earliest combinations of children in terms of the meanings expressed and of the semantic classes used. These classes express relationships such as the agent of an action (*Roger tickle*), the location of a state, action or process (*in hat*), the experiencer of a state or emotion (*Washoe sorry*).

At the end of 21 months of training, she had 34 signs that met a rigorous set of accuracy and frequency criteria. The Gardners imposed these criteria to be sure she really knew a sign before they added it to her list. Not all of Washoe's early signs referred to objects or to actions. She used *hurt, sorry* and *funny* in appropriate situations. She acquired four signs during the first seven months of training, nine during the second, and 21 during the third. Instead of becoming bogged down by all of this new material, she processed it at a faster and faster rate. After three years of training, her total vocabulary was 85 signs. After another year, it had almost doubled.

Washoe probably could have gone on this way for ever, but her human friends had other plans. Several of her teachers were leaving the project. It would be difficult for Washoe to get used to a whole new set of teachers, so the Gardners chose another plan. In October 1970, they gave up Washoe and her 160-sign vocabulary to Roger Fouts, one of their most promising graduate students, who was going to Oklahoma to continue this research.

There is a new chimpanzee in Reno now. Mojo, who came to the Gardners on the second day of her life, is just over a year old. Some of her signing partners are deaf children and adults. Gardner says, "We're going to do it right this time."

The Well-Structured Sarah. Several other researchers are starting their second generation of chimp/language research. One of these is David Premack, a professor of psychology at the University of California, Santa Barbara. His approach to studying language in chimpanzees is as neat as his wavy black hair and well-trimmed beard. He is not very interested in either language or chimpanzees. He does not care if his animals ever have the opportunity to initiate a conversation, change the subject, or use language to control their environments. He is primarily interested in the nature of intelligence. Chimps are very intelligent; language is one important way of exercising intelligence. So he uses the chimp/language research as a means to another end.

Washoe did not make sentences from random groups of signs.

A computer would meet most of his requirements for a research subject as well as, or better than, a chimpanzee. Devising a training sequence for a chimp and writing a program for a computer have a lot in common. Either could be used to answer the question, "Can I develop a method for establishing language in this system?" But if the answer is yes, Premack wants to apply that method to human beings who have trouble learning language—autistic kids, retarded people, aphasics—and a method developed for a chimpanzee is more apt to work in these situations than one made for a computer.

In the meantime, he has learned a good deal about a chimp's linguistic abilities and admittedly is surprised by his findings. His first chimp, Sarah [see "The Education of S*A*R*A*H," PT, September 1970], was African-born and about six years old, almost an adolescent by chimpanzee standards, when the experiment began in 1968. Premack describes her as very active, highly dominant and inventive. Sarah did not live, like Washoe, in a language-rich, stimulating environment with daily invitations from human friends to play language games. She lived under standard laboratory conditions: wire cage, cement-block walls, a few toys. Her exposure to both human beings and her special language was largely limited to the one hour of language training she received five days a week.

Plastic Chips. Her symbols are a set of small pieces of plastic that vary in shape and color. Each piece stands for one word. After years of chewing and handling they are scuffed and worn like well-loved toys. A strip of metal on the back allows the pieces to be placed on a magnetized board that serves the same purpose as a blackboard in a classroom. The symbols are placed in a vertical line on the board to form sentences. Sarah often points to the symbols she is working on—thinking about? translating?—while composing her answer to a difficult sentence.

There are several advantages to using a language that is physically permanent, that is written instead of gestured or spoken. You can study language without worrying about the pupil's short-term memory. When Sarah answers incorrectly you know it is not because she forgot the question that is still on the board, right in front of her. You can make her lessons easier or harder by regulating the number and kind of symbols she has to use at a given time. You can avoid the situation of a chimp pretending not to see an unpopular command delivered via ASL. But you cannot use this language anywhere, anytime. Sarah is like a mute person whose ability to communicate depends on paper and pencil.

Sarah knows about the same number of symbols as Washoe, about 130, but the ways they use their languages are as different as the ways they acquired them. Washoe gained her signs through a combination of imitation, molding and prompting. Sarah learned her symbols through standard conditioning techniques. Her teacher presented a stimulus and she responded. If her response was the correct one she received a reward. She never was punished for incorrect responses, or for anything else. If the stimulus

ROGER, LUCY AND LUCY'S CAT.
All three enjoy
frequent outings
into the yard
around Lucy's
house. Trips in
Roger's VW Bus,
and visits with
friends in their
homes give Lucy
good opportunities
to sign, and
something to
sign about.

162

was the teacher holding up a piece of fruit, then Sarah had to write *Ann give apple Sarah*, using the proper order and the correct names for the teacher and the fruit to get the apple.

Sarah mastered this task easily and went on to harder problems. She learned the meaning of sentences like *Sarah insert apricot red dish, grape* [and] *banana green dish*. Her accuracy on these tasks was 80 to 90 percent. She learned the difference between *red on green* and *green on red*, a difficult discrimination because she had to look at the order of the symbols to answer correctly. As with most of her language performance, her level of accuracy was 80 to 90 percent after she mastered the problem.

Sarah's Staggering List. Like Washoe, Sarah transferred her knowledge to symbols and situations outside the context of her training. For example, though she learned *on* in the context of red and green she applied it to any pair of colors. She applied *same* or *different* to any pair of objects, not just the cups and spoons used to teach her these symbols. Premack usually employed new items when testing her, to be sure that her comprehension went beyond the materials used in training.

Sarah does not like to use all the language she knows.

Her language testing often required that she answer questions. Sometimes she would use the answers *yes* and *no* correctly. Sometimes she would change a question that required a negative answer to one that required a positive one, and then answer correctly. Sometimes she would steal the symbols from her teacher, form her own questions, and then answer them—correctly.

At the end of two and a half years of training, Sarah possessed a staggering list of language functions. She used words, sentences, the interrogative, class concepts, negation, pluralization, conjunction, quantifiers, the conditional, and the copula. Washoe's abilities cover only the first five on this list. There is no indication she could not learn the others; they were not taught. Unlike the Gardners, Premack deliberately set out to give Sarah many different parts of language.

However, when she has the chance, Sarah will gladly give some of them back to him. She does not like to use all the language she knows. The copula is a good example. The copula is the link between a subject and its predicate. In English it is

163

PRATTLING PRIMATES.
The human-chimp signing conversations go on all day in the yard, in the house, in the fields. This page shows Lucy and Bruno signing *toothbrush, go there, baby, shoe* and *hat*. The opposite page illustrates a conversation about tickling and signing.

164

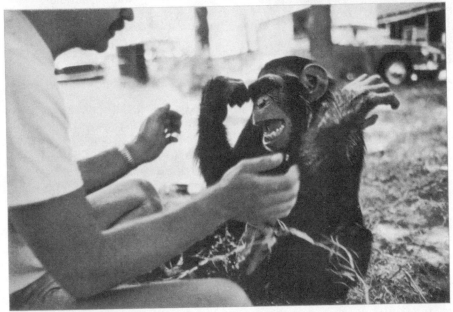

usually the word *is* or *are*. To Sarah *apple red* seems to mean the same as *apple is red*, so she omits the copula whenever she can get away with it. The Russians agree with her. Their language has no word for this linguistic function either.

Sarah Throws a Tantrum. Premack probably has fewer problems with Sarah's language than the Gardners have with ASL, but he doesn't have any fewer problems with his chimp. About two years ago Sarah started becoming difficult to handle. She was growing up and growing stronger. The temper tantrums she threw when she made a mistake became increasingly dangerous to her teachers. Her language training stopped. Right now she is sitting in a cage in the zoology building learning no language at all. Hopefully she won't be there long.

Premack is an energetic man who acts as if he is used to getting what he wants. What he wants is a new chimp compound where the animals will have more freedom, and the opportunity to wander into a special learning center where language lessons and the attendant rewards will be available whenever the chimps are interested. In the meantime Premack is replicating Sarah's training with two more chimpanzees.

Peony would rather beg for her rewards than work for them.

Elizabeth and Peony are five years old and each knows about 50 signs. In spite of these similarities, and the fact that they are both female chimps, they are as different as any two five-year-olds you have ever known. Elizabeth gets involved in her lessons. She seems to enjoy the routine. Peony does not. She would rather beg for her rewards than work for them. She performs the necessary tasks in order to win the approval of her teacher, who appears to be the most important element in Peony's life. Yet under Premack's highly structured training regime, both of the chimps acquire language at about the same rate.

Little Language-Making Machines. The structure leaves its mark. Working at their language board Elizabeth and Peony look like robots, little language-making machines. If you saw only these two it would be easy to conclude that chimpanzees with language are extraordinarily well-trained circus animals that repeat a complex routine with only a vague idea about what the plastic bits they are manipulating really mean. Only their testing data, or a look at Sarah's performance, would

change your mind. After hundreds of hours of training, the language is part of Sarah and she uses it with a kind of natural grace. With two years of training—one hour a day, five days a week—the younger animals still look as if they are doing someone else's work as they set out to perform their language tasks.

Chimpanzees that learn sign language do not go through this apparently mechanical stage. Because the language and the lessons are completely integrated into the daily routine, and because communication does not require equipment, their signing looks natural almost from the beginning. There are a lot of chimps signing their natural-looking language in Oklahoma. Roger Fouts has seven of them.

A Farm Full of Chimps. You remember Fouts. He completed his doctorate with the Gardners, and then took Washoe to the Institute for Primate Studies just outside of Norman, Oklahoma. The Institute, which is run by William B. Lemmon, is a little world of assorted, run-down buildings. Every building is filled with nonhuman primates except the house and the big barn that stables the cows, the peacocks, and the cats. The house is usually filled with people who divide their time between being outside talking to the primates and being inside talking about them.

The Institute seemed more like a farm to me and when I went there I asked myself why Fouts chose this place to continue his work. There must be half-a-dozen primate centers in this country that have more facilities for chimpanzees. After being on the farm only a couple of hours I could answer that question. There may be places that have more facilities, but there are few that have more chimps (the Institute has between 25 and 30), and none that treat the chimpanzees so much like human beings.

Here the chimps are partners in research, not subjects for experimentation. The treatment they receive reflects this attitude. Social needs get the same careful attention as dietary ones. The need for exposure to different kinds of stimulation is as important as the need for different kinds of medication. These features make Lemmon's Institute an excellent place to look at the problem Fouts wants to pursue, communication among chimpanzees using ASL.

She had seen another chimp only once, so she labeled other chimpanzees *bug*.

To get the program started, Fouts had to get Washoe accustomed to other chimps, and other chimps used to signing. Washoe was slowly introduced to the animals on the farm. She called the ducks *water bird*, a combination she invented. Fouts gave her the sign for duck but she preferred her own nomenclature. Since her capture during the first year of her life she had seen another chimp only once, so she labeled the other chimpanzees she met *bug*. It was going to take some time before she would be comfortable with her conspecifics.

Dirty Monkey. In the meantime Fouts reinstated Washoe's language training. He taught her a new sign, *monkey*. She was happy to use it for the squirrel monkeys and for the siamangs, but she concocted a different name for a rhesus macaque who had threatened her. She called him *dirty monkey*. When Fouts asked her the sign for the squirrel monkeys again she quickly went back to just plain *monkey*. But when they returned to the macaque, it was *dirty monkey*. Before this incident Washoe has used *dirty* to describe only soiled objects or feces. Since her meeting with the aggressive macaque, she has applied this sign to various teachers when they refuse to grant her wishes.

During the early stages of her repatriation Washoe often signed to the other chimpanzees. She frequently signed *come hug* when she wished to comfort one of the younger animals who was distressed. And she signed *tickle* when she wanted to play with one of the adults. When the chimps did not respond she pursued them until a general romping session began. She also signed *go drink*, indicating a nearby water faucet, to a chimp who was competing with her for some fruit that was being given out.

Washoe does not sign to the other chimps much anymore. After all, nobody ever answers. But that is going to change. Bruno and Booee are going to answer.

Bruno and Booee are six-year-old males. Both were born in captivity and lived in human homes for a couple of years before coming to the Institute. Eventually they will participate in an experiment with Washoe. They are learning to sign but their identical vocabularies are being carefully limited to 36 signs. Fouts hopes to induce Washoe to teach them more signs, some of the ones she knows but they do not. No one knows if she will play teacher, but Fouts's bright blue eyes twinkle at the very thought of it.

Salomé is two and a half years old. She has a human sister.

Bruno and Booee already are threatening to make linguistic history by becoming the first nonhuman animals to use an unnatural language—one not endemic to their species—to communicate with each other. They sign to each other in a number of situations Fouts devised to encourage them to do so. If they are playing and their teachers separate them, then they sign to each other. The signs are usually limited to appropriate combinations of *come, hug, hurry, Bruno* and *Booee.* The same signs appear if they are separated while one is being punished for some mischievous behavior by being made to sit in a chair. The only conversations, spontaneous two-way signing, occurred when they were required to sign *tickle* before they were allowed to romp together.

The exchanges were brief.

Bruno: *Tickle Bruno.*
Booee: *Tickle Booee.*
(Later) **Booee:** *Tickle.*
Bruno: *Booee come hurry.*
(Later) **Booee:** *Tickle Booee.*
Bruno: (Who was eating raisins): *Booee me food.*

But on the basis of such limited data neither Fouts nor any other careful researcher is going to conclude that the two chimpanzees definitely were communicating. Instead he is developing a set of complex procedures for testing their ability to exchange information via signs with no human beings in the immediate area.

In the meantime, Fouts is teaching ASL to three other chimpanzees, Salomé, Ally and Lucy. All were born in captivity and placed in homes a few days after birth where they are being raised like human children.

Salomé and Her Human Sister. Salomé is two and a half years old. She has a human sister, Robin, who is two, and a set of human parents. Robin is a cherub of a child with wispy blond hair, blue eyes, and a

LANGUAGE LESSONS. **In the top two pictures Roger holds up a book and signs *what this.* Ally signs *book* with his usual grandiose gestures. In the bottom two, Roger and Lucy discuss swallowing. Roger signs and Lucy repeats the sentence.**

167

shy but friendly smile. Salomé's face is just as friendly as Robin's, but there is little evidence of shyness. Her black eyes sparkle against her light skin as she comes out to greet me. She looks, and acts, like a bundle of innocent mischief. The two are great friends.

Salomé's motor skills are much more advanced than Robin's but the child is easily her superior when it comes to language. Robin uses about 50 words. Salomé uses about 20 signs. Both understand a lot of English. Salomé acquired her first sign, *drink*, when she was four months old. One study reports that deaf children begin to sign as early as five months. By the time she reached her first birthday, Salomé was producing sign combinations—*gimme drink, gimme food,* and *more food.*

Fouts plans to keep close tabs on the development of language in Salomé and Robin. Right now Salomé produces and comprehends some ASL, and understands a lot of English. Robin does not know ASL, but she speaks some English, and comprehends quite a bit more. She also produces and comprehends chimpanzeese. She has picked up all the natural chimpanzee vocal signals from Salomé and she uses them appropriately.

Ally is a great signer. His gestures are crisp, clear and deliberate.

Ally has no human siblings. He is four years old and lives alone with his human mother. His ASL vocabulary contains over 70 signs. Ally is a great signer. His gestures are crisp, clear and deliberate. It is easy to imagine him lecturing a class in a large auditorium, raising his voice and articulating each word carefully for the benefit of the students in the back. After only a few hours of exposure I could read most of his well-formed signs. It took longer to reach this point with the other chimps.

What That? Like all of the Institute's home-grown chimps, Ally comprehends a large number of English words. Fouts believes that a combination of English and ASL is the best system for teaching language to chimps and he has good evidence that information can be transferred between these two systems. Fouts selected 10 objects for which Ally knew the English word, but not the ASL sign, words like spoon, nut, water and leaf. Then he tried to teach him all 10 signs by only saying the word and signing at the same time. He did not refer to the object itself at any time during the training.

A person who did not know which objects Ally had learned the signs for tested

him. Without speaking, the tester held up various objects and signed *what that.* Ally successfully transferred the signs from the word to the object that the word stood for in all 10 cases. Transferring a gestural response from an auditory stimulus (word) to a visual stimulus (object), and from one language (English) to another (ASL) is an impressive feat. Neither Sarah nor Washoe could do it because each knows only one language. But Lucy might be able to.

Lucy is eight years old. Since she was two days old, she has lived with her human parents and a human brother who is 12 years older than she. Her informal training in English began as soon as she moved in and she knows a lot of it. Fouts started her ASL lessons—one or two hours per day, five days a week—a little over three years ago. With her knowledge of English and an ASL vocabulary of over 80 signs she might well be able to translate in the same way that Ally does, but she has not been tested on this kind of problem.

Instead, Fouts has been looking at the way she generalizes the application of a new sign and how the acquisition of a new sign affects the way she uses her other signs from the same class. For example, if

she learns *rabbit*, does she apply it to different kinds of small animals and does it change the way she uses signs like *cat* and *dog?*

Cry Hurt Food. The signs Lucy knew for different kinds of foods were *food, drink, fruit, candy* and *banana.* Fouts tested her use of these old signs with 24 fresh fruits and vegetables, then he taught her *berry* using a cherry as an example. Obviously, a cherry is not really a berry, but it was selected because of its similarity to other foods—strawberries, cherry tomatoes, radishes, etc. In the initial testing she called most fruits *fruit* and most vegetables *food.* After learning *berry* she did the same. She used *berry* just as she uses *banana*, to name only one specific kind of fruit. She did not even use it for frozen cherries.

In the initial testing she called most fruits *fruit* and most vegetables *food*.

During this experiment she developed great names for some of the testing items. She called a radish *food* until she happened to take a bite of it, experienced its sharp taste, and signed *cry hurt food.* After this she continued to use

SALOMÉ AND ROBIN. The differences between these two sisters are less apparent when they play in their yard than at any other time. They scramble up and down displaying the kinds of parallel play that are frequently seen in human playmates.

either *cry*, or *hurt*, or both with *food* to describe radishes. Lucy started out calling a cut watermelon *drink*, then switched to *candy drink* and *fruit drink*. These names show her ability to combine her signs in unique and appropriate ways. This ability, called productivity, is an important point in the debate about whether chimps can learn a language. The same is true of her ability to understand the difference between two sets of signs which are the same except for order, the difference between *Roger tickle Lucy* and *Lucy tickle Roger*. Washoe, Sarah, Ally and Lucy all have this ability, an important part of syntax.

In five years the number of chimps with some syntactical ability probably will be 25. A popularity explosion is about to hit. The number of labs teaching artificial language to chimps doubled in 1973. Everyone who can get his hands on a young chimpanzee, gorilla, or orangutan, is trying to teach it some language based on the manual manipulation of a set of symbols. The expense of obtaining and maintaining these animals is the only thing that keeps this research from replacing the rat in the Skinner box as America's favorite learning experiment.

Lana's Yerkish Typewriter. The most interesting of the new projects is the undertaking of a team of scientists headed by Duane Rumbaugh of Georgia State University. Other members of the team are E.D. von Glasersfeld and Pier Pisani from the University of Georgia, Timothy V. Gill and Josephine V. Brown from Georgia State University, and Harold Warner and C. L. Bell from the Yerkes Primate Research Center. Their pupil is a three-year-old chimpanzee, Lana, who operates a typewriter. But Lana's typewriter is no ordinary machine. It has 50 keys with a colored background and white geometric configuration on each. The configurations represent words in a special language called Yerkish, named for Robert M. Yerkes, the great primatologist.

The keyboard is attached to a set of projectors and a PDP-8E computer. The projectors flash the configurations Lana selects on a screen in front of her. The computer makes a permanent record of all interactions with Lana, analyzes the sequences she types, and rewards her when she performs correctly. Through this system Lana asks for all of her food and drink, a look outside, music, toys, movies, and human companionship.

Rumbaugh studied cognitive abilities in primates for years and believed that it should be possible to teach Lana to read the configuration sequences projected on the screen. He never got a chance to try.

Lana learned it by herself. She began pushing a few keys and checking the sequence on the screen. If her sentence was correct she finished it. If not, she pushed a key that erased it.

How can we recognize a language that is not exactly like human language?

When Rumbaugh saw her doing this he decided to test her ability to distinguish between correct and incorrect sequences. From a second keyboard he typed part of a sentence and waited to see what Lana would do. She completed the correct segment or erased the incorrect one on about 90 percent of the trials.

After only one year of training Lana has outstripped her teachers' expectations. Already they predict conversation with her. Perhaps this system—which allows a chimpanzee to demonstrate language abilities without any possibility of cues from a human being—will be instrumental in eliminating some of the doubts expressed by scientists about the possibility of chimpanzees learning language.

The Evidence Piles Up. The scientific community is justifiably skeptical about the idea of talking chimps. All reported attempts to teach them a verbal language have been failures. But little by little the all-important evidence is piling up.

The Gardners, who pioneered with Washoe, are very conscientious about distributing information to other psychologists. In the early years of Washoe's training they periodically sent out summaries of her linguistic development. The usual response was that it was all very interesting, but that her performance would not be scientifically important until she:

1 demonstrated an extensive system of names for objects in her environment;

2 signed about objects that are not physically present;

3 used signs for concepts, not just objects, agents and actions;

4 invented semantically appropriate combinations; and

5 used proper order when it is semantically necessary.

All of these are reasonable criteria. All are demonstrated by at least one chimp, most by several. But as the type of data demanded as evidence for language becomes more complex, it is increasingly difficult to decide which criteria are reasonable.

This difficulty arises because we have no definition that allows us to recognize language outside the context of vocal human communication. This is an unusual situation.

The definition for a particular function is usually a set of principles that are common to all the systems that perform that function. Reproduction is a good example. All animals have a system of reproduction. These systems are very different from each other, but all have some principles in common. These principles allow us to recognize, and correctly label, all the different systems. But the only naturally occurring system of language belongs to human beings. What can we compare it with? How can we recognize a language that is not exactly like human language?

There is no final answer to this question, but the possibility of one becomes stronger each time Booee signs to Bruno, or Peony solves another linguistic problem. Perhaps we will get our answer if Lucy becomes pregnant from the artificial insemination planned for her, and if she bears a healthy infant, and if she teaches that infant signs. I know this is a lot of ifs, but I would like to add another one. If it happens, it will be dynamite.

FOOLING AROUND. Graduate-student Sue Savage plays with Salomé. Tickling, wrestling, romping and general tomfoolery keep both the humans and the chimps in high spirits. They get high on signing, but mostly they are high on each other.

169

27

Irwin S. Bernstein
Thomas P. Gordon

The Function of Aggression in Primate Societies

Uncontrolled aggression may threaten human survival, but aggression may be vital to the establishment and regulation of primate societies and sociality

Beginning with the earliest studies, investigators of primate social behavior have been struck by the significance of primate aggressive potential and the consequent need for social control of such aggressive potential in socially living animals. Studies directed at describing aggressive behavior and the situations which elicit it, as well as the social mechanisms which control it, were therefore among the first investigations of primate social behavior.

Irwin S. Bernstein is Associate Professor of Psychology with an adjunct appointment in anthropology at the University of Georgia in Athens. In addition he maintains an adjunct appointment at the Yerkes Regional Primate Research Center, where he has studied the social organization of monkeys and apes since 1960. His work includes field studies in Malaysia, Thailand, Panama, and Colombia as well as studies of captive groups. Present interests in aggression and social change stem from long-term interests in role behavior and social mechanisms which regulate interactions in primate societies.
Thomas P. Gordon received graduate training in physiological psychology at the Universities of Delaware and Georgia. From 1966 through 1970 he was employed as a research psychologist at the U.S. Army Human Engineering Laboratory in Aberdeen, Maryland, in a multidisciplinary research program directed at measuring hormonal correlates of behavioral events in both nonhuman primates and humans. Since then he has continued to pursue these interests working with group-living primates at the Yerkes Primate Center Field Station in Lawrenceville, Georgia.
Research was supported by PHS grants MH-20483, MH-13864, and by the U.S. Army 17-696-9014 and PHS FR-00165. Address: I. S. Bernstein, Department of Psychology, University of Georgia, Athens, GA 30602.

The largest Old World monkeys—drills, mandrills, baboons, and geladas—have the longest and sharpest canine teeth literally rivaling those of the great cats. These monkeys are sexually dimorphic, the males often weighing two or three times as much as the females, and it is the males which have the well-developed canines. Furthermore, the elaborately evolved, lower first premolar and upper canine honing surfaces insure maintenance of a razor-sharp cutting edge. Even the casual zoo visitor cannot help but be awed by the yawning, canine-grinding displays of adult male monkeys, and primate colony managers can readily attest to the effectiveness of such teeth in fights involving adult males.

Competition theories

Quite naturally, then, the focus of many early studies was upon male aggression. Zuckerman (1932) described competitive interactions among hamadryas baboon males at the London Zoo when females were introduced to the colony. The subsequent severe fighting resulted in multiple deaths, primarily female, and Zuckerman analyzed these violent encounters in relationship to primate social structure. It seemed that sexual competition was such a powerful and pervasive social incentive that it might permeate every aspect of group living. As a consequence, the resultant aggressive competition and its control

must be central to the organization of primate groups.

Other competitive interactions were explored by Maslow and coworkers (1936, a, b, c, 1940) who noted the variety of expressions given to competitive interactions in different kinds of primates. Carpenter (1954), as a result of his pioneering primate field studies, suggested that the dominance hierarchy so apparent in many primate societies might have as its primary function the control of intragroup and even intergroup aggression. During the years that followed, many investigators worked to explicate the forms of primate aggression, the situations which elicit such aggression, and the social mechanisms which channel and control aggression. Chance and his colleagues (1967, 1970) focused on spatial control mechanisms; others took developmental approaches noting the special status of infants and the possible significance of natal coats as inhibitory cues. Attention which had earlier focused on sexual competition gradually shifted to consider the whole array of incentive situations which theoretically provoked primate aggression.

Because primates were considered to compete for any resource in the environment, it was expected that hungry monkeys would fight over food, thirsty monkeys would fight over water, sexually aroused males would fight over receptive females and, in general, any time more than one monkey sought the same incentive simultaneously, resolution of this conflict was expected to be through some form of aggressive expression. Theories were developed which relegated the function of aggression entirely to such conflict resolution, but the motivating force of competition for incentives began to be doubted when experiments involving the reduction of space or the withholding of food failed to produce more than temporary increases in intragroup conflict (Southwick 1967). Indeed, food deprivation not only failed to increase agonistic frequencies (Rosenblum 1969) but in some cases actually resulted in decreased frequencies of agonistic interactions (Marsden 1972). Studies of animals in the wild under conditions of extreme food deprivation likewise revealed that starving monkeys devoted almost all available energy to foraging, with little remaining for aggressive interaction or any social behavior (Hall 1963). Furthermore, evidence from a variety of primate taxa began to accumulate which indicated that one of the most potent stimuli for eliciting aggression was the simple introduction of an intruder into an organized group (Bernstein 1964b, 1969a, 1971; Kawai 1960; Southwick 1967). Such introductions resulted in far more serious aggression than had been produced in any laboratory experiments contrived to stimulate competition.

Introductions and group formation

These studies suggested that unfamiliar conspecifics introduced to one another for the first time showed considerable hostility because, in the absence of a social order, one had to be established to control interanimal relationships. When a new animal was introduced into an existing social organization, the newcomer met even more serious aggression. Whereas in the first case aggression established a social order, in the second case, resident animals mobbed the intruder, thereby initially excluding a new animal from the existing social unit. When several animals were introduced simultaneously, the ef-

fect was lessened, if only because the group divided its attention among the multiple targets. If, however, the several animals introduced to a group themselves constituted a social unit, it might be postulated that two social organizations in conflict would constitute the most potent situation. Indeed, in such cases each group may mass and fight the opposing group as a unit, but, again, no individual is subjected to the consequences of mass attack, and the very cohesion of the groups precludes prolonged

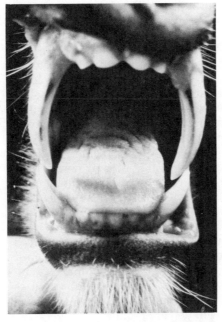

Figure 1. The dentition of the adult male mandrill reveals canine teeth which rival those of the great cats. However, these teeth are not required for obtaining food; females and youngsters without such teeth are successful in obtaining all the items for a typical mandrill diet.

individual combat as group members come to each other's aid and the focus of activities shifts from area to area. The defeat of one group is marked both by a reduction in aiding and by responding to further aggression solely with submissive signals. The submission of the defeated group, rather than unleashing unchecked aggression on the part of the victorious group, serves to reduce both the intensity and frequency of further attack. Monkey groups therefore seem to be organized primarily to maintain their established social order rather than to engage in hostilities per se.

Studies of introductory techniques in captive group formations (e.g. Bernstein and Mason 1963; Bernstein 1964b, 1969a, 1971; Vandenbergh 1967; Vessey 1971) have revealed certain uniformities among the variety of cercopithecine monkeys studied. Despite the intensity of initial strife and the occasional exclusion of some individuals, almost all of our attempts to form a social unit have proved successful and have revealed similar social mechanisms among these primate groups. Initial high levels of aggressive interaction decline sharply even within the first hour, and the expression of aggression gradually shifts from the most extreme forms of attack to more token expressions and threats. Furthermore, the age and sex of the animals introduced, the number of animals simultaneously introduced, and the age-sex composition of the resident group all clearly influence the original reception.

As part of a series of studies concerned with hormonal correlates of stress and aggression conducted in collaboration with Robert M. Rose, we instituted a systematic exploration of some of these variables. Nearly one hundred planned introductions, reintroductions, and group formations involving rhesus monkeys have clarified the nature of social mechanisms and have permitted us to obtain an understanding of the function of primate aggression in these and other situations (Bernstein et al. in press, a, in press, b).

Moreover, examination of field study literature and our own field work reassured us that these situations and phenomena were not merely the results of the artificial conditions of captivity. To be sure, spatial restriction precludes effective use of some social mechanisms and enhances aggressive encounters. We thus might see more extreme aggression more frequently than under conditions where escape is possible, but severe fighting does sometimes occur under the same sets of circumstances in natural habitats. Whereas troop-to-troop fighting in the wild may routinely follow ritualized patterns as in territorial disputes or similar encounters (Bernstein 1968; Carpenter 1938; Ellefson 1968; Mason 1966), when spatial mechanisms fail, other more violent forms of interaction may prevail (Southwick et al. 1965). Furthermore, inasmuch as the exchange of males is the principal means of genetic exchange among the semiclosed social units common to so many of the primates, the use of confined groups and deliberate introductions only serves to exaggerate natural response patterns and allows specification of their operation.

Considering the well-earned reputation of rhesus monkeys as nearly intractable laboratory animals and the frequency with which they engage in agonistic displays, the choice of subject for study may also be challenged. Fortunately, studies of sooty mangabeys, geladas, green monkeys, and a variety of macaques under the same laboratory conditions produced very similar results (Bernstein 1970).

Aggressive restraints

It was with some trepidation that we approached our first introduction of thirty-six adult male rhesus monkeys into a single enclosure. The vigor of initial encounters seemed to justify our fears, but it soon became apparent that there was an element of restraint even in the most intensive male-to-male fighting. From the onset it was clear that many males selectively displayed submissive behavior to other males even on first encounters. Positive social behavior, such as combining to form mutually supportive alliances, was in evidence even in the first minutes and played a significant role in the establishment of a social order.

Initial fighting seemed unrestrained, but later investigation of the wounds actually inflicted, and consideration of the damage that unmodified canine teeth can inflict, led us to conclude that the male aggression witnessed was not uninhibited. No animal died of wounds,

and all the wounds healed spontaneously, without sign of infection. Furthermore, the location of wounds—and their absence on the throat or abdomen—suggested that conspecific male-to-male fighting in rhesus monkeys was in some way limited. The areas injured—shoulders, face, haunches, brows, tails, and even back areas—can all sustain injuries without damage to vital organs. The most vulnerable areas—throat and abdomen—were uninjured, although opportunity for such injuries certainly existed as animals were sometimes rolled over and appeared helpless to defend themselves against further attack.

The apparent helplessness of a victim in fact appeared to inhibit further attack. Thus, animals no longer attempting to defend themselves were soon subjected to only token aggressive responses. Species-typical responses communicating a submissive role include passive crouching and turning away from the attacker. Such signals combined with the obvious helplessness of a defeated animal to exert an inhibitory influence against further attack. The inhibition is reinforced by the tendency of even the most passive submissive animals to resume resistance when subjected to further real injury. Thus, we have seen defeated males passively accept incisor bites, emitting only grimaces and squeals in response to each nip, but abruptly wheel about and slash when canine teeth were also used in further biting. The sudden turnabout from passive to active defense, albeit still mixed with grimacing and squealing, seemed difficult to explain until analysis of photographic records clearly indicated the use of a canine in bites preceding such defense.

A suggestion of ritualization of fighting was reinforced by watching the fighting patterns of males attacked by females in later studies. Male aggression was so controlled in these cases that at times a small number of females succeeded in completely overpowering male opponents twice their physical size and possessing vastly superior dental armament.

Female monkeys proved themselves formidable opponents in agonistic interactions and, in undisturbed groups, demonstrated more frequent aggressive responses than did males (Bernstein 1970). This difference could be demonstrated for a variety of species and was especially clear when noncontact forms of aggression, such as threatening and chasing, were considered. This suggests that concern for understanding male aggression and the emphasis on its importance has been based more on the consequences of male aggression than its frequency. In undisturbed groups, males may rarely be involved in fighting, but when they are, the results may be apparent for weeks. More important perhaps is the fact that male aggression, both in frequency and intensity, does exceed female aggression in crucial situations. Thus, during group-to-group introductions and group formations, males accounted for almost all the aggression displayed in the first twenty minutes, which included the most serious forms of contact aggression. By the end of the first hour female participation in agonistic episodes had increased, rivaling or exceeding male rates, and forms of contact aggression were superseded by chases, threats, and other noncontact expressions of aggression (Bernstein et al. in press, a, in press, b).

Control roles

When an intact natural group is challenged by some external source of disturbance, one or more particular animals in the group will respond in predictable fashion, identified as the "control animal role," most often played by a male (Bernstein 1964a, 1966). This individual may be the last group member to retreat or may otherwise place himself between the source of disturbance and the group. Deliberate challenges to captive groups have revealed that this role behavior is dependent on the presence of the group and also is "expected" by group members who will seek out the control animal when subjected to attack or harassment.

This was experimentally verified by separate testing of the control animal in the presence and absence of his group and by testing the group with the control animal physically restricted in space (Bernstein 1966). Naturally there are limits to any such behavior pattern, and we may regard the headlong flight of all baboons when chased by a lion as not in contradiction to the bluffing behavior of baboon males when confronted by less capable predators (DeVore and Washburn 1963; Rowell 1973).

The same animals which serve control role functions when a troop is threatened by external disturbance are most likely to respond to intragroup sources of disturbance as well. In the event of prolonged or intensive fighting within the group, the control animal may intervene by attacking either participant, attacking a neutral third party, or otherwise making a display of aggression. In any case, the control animal's aggression usually supersedes all other aggression in the group, thus terminating the original fight. The intervention of the control animal thus appears to be part of a role pattern—not truly "aggressively motivated"—whose functions can be satisfied with only a few token gestures.

Eliciting aggression

But what of the initial fighting within the group? What situations provoke such fighting and what function does such aggression serve? Is aggression ordinarily only a disruptive force that requires elaborate control mechanisms, including the use of aggression to control aggression? Is the "natural" aggression of primates a socially centripetal force that tends to destroy primate societies? Is primate society and sociality only possible when social mechanisms are capable of suppressing this "naturally" disruptive force? Or is it possible that this "excessive" primate aggression is the very force which bonds primates to one another and maintains their primate societies? Before dismissing the last question as

heresy, let us look at the evidence and examine some supporting views.

First, although there is irrefutable evidence that primates are at times predators, they are more often prey. For most primates, ultimate safety lies in the trees, but many of the larger species are often on the ground and sometimes far from trees. Although vigilance and rapid flight may still serve a primate well, more active defense against the smaller predators is possible. In these circumstances, one or more of the large troop males, upon discov-

Figure 2. A defeated group is subjected to token attack by members of a victorious group. Note the male in the foreground has bitten at the base of the tail rather than a

ering a potential predator, may engage in aggressive displays that seem to drive the predator off (DeVore and Washburn 1963).

It should not be inferred that a baboon male, or a coalition of several males, can really defeat an animal such as a leopard in combat, but it is only necessary to postulate that they would inflict injury upon the leopard in a fight. Such injuries can

prove fatal for an animal that requires maximum ability every few days to obtain his next meal. There has surely been selection against predators who risk serious injury routinely and, likewise, selection against baboon males who recklessly attack predators such as leopards—for the baboon risks more than just a wound. The net result is a carefully balanced stalemate with a premium placed on alertness and the communication of aggressive threat for the baboon, and on stealth and the search for easier prey on the part of the leopard. By contrast, a lion, at three to five

more vulnerable area, and the female in the rear is participating in attacking physically dangerous, larger animals despite the presence of her tightly clinging ventral infant.

times the body weight of a leopard, can probably dispatch a fair number of male baboons with little personal risk—thus there is no need for a lion to be cautious about attacking boisterous baboons and no gain for baboons who try to bluff lions.

Concerted group aggression against an outside threat thus may serve to preserve the group, and any mechanisms making the expression of such directed aggression more effective would have positive value. In this case at least, it is the expression of outward-directed aggression, rather than its inhibition, which unites and preserves the society. We might similarly analyze the effect of extragroup aggression directed against conspecifics. Once again, a noisy bluffing display rather than actual combat would be the more desirable expression of spacing mechanisms or the means for resolution of conflict. Bluffing certainly kills fewer members of a species than does intraspecific fighting.

But what of intragroup aggression? How can this ever be anything but disruptive to normal social relations? First, let us examine the circumstances under which we see intragroup agonistic behavior, and simultaneously consider how "normal" social relations are established. Beginning with one of the most common experimental procedures, we might study aggression by throwing one piece of food between two monkeys in a group. At times one monkey may quietly retrieve and eat the food; at other times we may see one monkey aggress against the other. Before assuming this aggression to be competitive aggression, we should realize that it is almost invariably unidirectional—i.e. one animal aggresses and the other flees or otherwise submits. We may explain the absence of aggression in the one case by postulating that dominance hierarchies exist to control aggressive competition. The aggression that does occur thus reflects a failure of the rank structure to completely suppress aggression.

At times, however, we may note that a social "inferior" may take the offered food and do so with apparent impunity. Infants, young juveniles, and favored females may be exceptionally bold in feeding in the immediate proximity of a large male who will not tolerate another male anywhere in the area while he is feeding. Surely his dominance rank must be more securely established with regard to the immature animals, and yet it is they that fail to respect it by the same deference the male's peers show. Rather than invoke special mechanisms to protect females and infants taking such liberties, it might be more parsimonious to explain why intragroup aggression in a wide variety of circumstances is most frequently directed to animals of adjacent rather than distal ranks. Stated another way, we might say that the greater the social rank disparity between two animals, the less frequently we see aggressive encounters.

By way of illustration, a group of juvenile rhesus monkeys instantly deferred to a single large adult male introduced to their group, and the male seldom directed even the mildest forms of aggression against the immature animals while maintaining his alpha rank absolutely (Bernstein and Draper 1964). His superiority was such that the juveniles represented an insignificant threat to his alpha status. Animals of more equal abilities and of near-equal rank are the ones most likely to challenge an established social relationship, and aggression against these potential usurpers may be used to ward off any perceived threat to existing social relationships.

Aggression may, therefore, at times function to curb the upward social mobility of individuals whose success can only be at the expense of those of the next highest ranks in an agonistic dominance hierarchy. Greater frequencies of agonistic interactions among animals of adjacent rather than distal rank have been reported in a variety of primates studied under diverse conditions. It is most readily recognized by significantly higher scores along the diagonals of agonistic matrices organized to reflect a dominance hierarchy (Christopher 1972, Plotnik et al. 1968).

The significance of this mechanism was revealed in a sequence of events leading to the spontaneous reorganization of a pigtail monkey group after years of relatively stable rank relationships. A young male who had achieved third rank in the hierarchy was repeatedly attacked by the second ranking male, who ceased in his attacks as the young male successfully defended himself. However, no reversal in agonistic roles was seen. Instead, the young male was challenged to several fights by the alpha male, who subsequently died of infection. The second male assumed the alpha position, but, because he avoided all agonistic confrontations with the young male, two months later the young male claimed the alpha position and attacked the second male each time he failed to conform to his newly subordinate role. Although the young male had not previously *initiated* any aggression, he now enforced his new position by repeated attacks against his former superior, showing less and less frequent aggression as his former superior showed more and more submission (Bernstein 1969b, 1969c).

Aggression would therefore seem to be motivated *primarily* by efforts to preserve established social position and to enforce expected patterns of social behavior, rather than resulting from active competition leading to conflict. An individual will fight to maintain his social position and warn all potential usurpers of his readiness to fight. A group of animals will use aggression to preserve an established social order and to maintain role relationships. A society will mobilize all of its aggressive resources for self-preservation.

Maintaining social order

If the difference between a society and an aggregation lies in the interrelated network of roles in the former, and if these roles are characterized by typical patterns of responses for individuals under specified conditions of social interaction, we may correctly ask how the rules of primate societies are developed and maintained. What enforces these codes of conduct?

The late Professor K. R. L. Hall put it very succinctly when he wrote that one of the most potent stimuli eliciting primate aggression was a perceived violation of the social code (1964). Aggression is then used to maintain the very fabric of primate society. Rather than disrupting social relationships, aggression serves to enforce regulated social interactions which maintain primate societies.

One other point in Professor Hall's statement should be considered and appreciated. He stressed that it was the *perceived* rather than the *actual* violation of the social code which elicited aggressive response. Thus, no particular response will invariably provoke aggression; it must first be perceived as a challenge to a social relationship. For example, in food competition tests, the alpha male need show little response to group members showing proper deference, he need show no aggression to insignificant juveniles feeding on scraps in his area, but he may be motivated to respond strenuously should it appear that some individual is contesting him for a piece of food he has claimed as his own. The perception of challenge can result from the mere proximity of an animal to the morsel the dominant individual is moving towards. Thus, a rolling piece of food approaching a stationary animal may cause that animal to flee. This apparent paradox of hungry animals fleeing choice food is better understood when one realizes that the animals are avoiding a situation which in the past has provoked the wrath of superiors. When the more dominant individuals no longer seek food, then it is safe for the more subordinate animals to feed freely on the same food previously avoided.

Socialization and social roles

How then are these social relationships established? Newborn infants enjoy extraordinary toleration and are objects of active interest in primate societies. As the infant grows, its behavior is slowly shaped by the requirements of its group. We may think of this as the socialization process. An infant's weaning experiences certainly will vary in accordance with species membership as

well as with the personalities of mothers, but most weaning includes some of the earliest experiences with punishment—"punitive deterence." Such punishment was at first thought to drive the infant from the mother, thus aiding in the separation of mother and child. It was therefore surprising to learn that mother-infant attachment appeared greater in species with more punitive mothers, and that the most punitive mothers within a species had the most dependent offspring (Kaufman and Rosenblum 1969; Jensen et al. 1967). It seemed that baby monkeys sought their mothers for protection and comfort when distressed, even if the mother was the source of the distress.

Longitudinal studies of several groups of Old World monkeys in our laboratory have demonstrated that the bond between mother and infant is not severed at weaning, or even at full maturity. This long association with mother results in close association with siblings, and mother's relationships as well; matriarchal groups can be recognized by persisting high frequencies of social interaction even when as many as four generations are represented. Furthermore, in the pigtail monkey at least, even in the event of the matriarch's death, the association of siblings is not diminished—we still see regular association between the now-adult offspring of several deceased females. It is perhaps noteworthy that strong bonding is particularly evident in our pigtail monkey group—the very species which Kaufman and Rosenblum (1969) had described as so punitive in comparison with bonnet macaque groups.

The use of aggression in establishing social bonds is not limited to infant socialization studies. In fact, the same "bizarre" response of approaching the attacker was reported by Kummer as the mechanism by which hamadryas male baboons maintain their females in close proximity (1968). A straying female is attacked by her male unit leader, who subjects her to a ritualized neck bite. Instead of fleeing the male, the female may then be

embraced and comforted by the male, the punishment clearly having been in response to her failure to maintain proper social proximity, not distance. Aggression here establishes and maintains a social bond.

In a series of field experiments, Kummer introduced strange hamadryas and anubis females to a troop of hamadryas baboons. The rapid integration of the hamadryas females was not surprising, but anubis females ordinarily live in troops with no particular bond between individual males and females. Although in anubis troops, females usually avoid actively aggressive males, the hamadryas males were successful in training at least some of the anubis females to approach and to maintain proximity in response to male aggressive display. To be sure, there were modifications of the typical hamadryas patterns, but primates are capable of great behavioral plasticity and anubis females could learn the appropriate responses to a hamadryas male's aggressive signals.

Perhaps as an indicator that the male hamadryas behavior is not a unique species attribute, but rather only an extreme form of a common pattern, we should recognize that even in the familiar rhesus monkey, consort pairs make frequent use of aggression to maintain close proximity and stimulate reproductive behavior. Whereas the pair generally shows mutual support in outwardly directed aggression (at times with no apparent target visible), the initial response may be an ambiguously directed threat by the female or the male.

Primate societies are characterized by relatively stable social relationships. However, as animals grow and individuals age and pass from one category to another, their roles in a society change, and social relationships are dynamic. The rules governing social relationships are in part typical of the species and in part determined by past individual histories. The enumeration and etiology of rules governing social conduct in the variety of extant primate societies remain a future challenge. For the present, however, we may predict that a change in social relationships and "expected" social responses will be accompanied by aggressive interactions as individuals resist the change and/or enforce the new rules of behavior governing the relationship. Since a change in relative position is enforced by aggression, one might expect that every illness and injury would represent an opportunity to overthrow a social superior, but animals living in a society depend more on alliances and coalitions rather than on individual fighting skills to maintain their social position. Thus a scrawny old female supported by many generations of offspring and long associations with other females and adult males may maintain a position of unquestioned superiority over young males of much greater fighting ability. So, too, may an old male retain his high rank, eventually losing to a challenger not because of his failing fighting abilities but because of the successful recruitment of support from group members by the challenger. After such a defeat, a new order is established incorporating all animals into a society that recognizes the new relationships (Bernstein 1969b, 1969c).

Infants born into a group are newcomers and intruders, but they represent little direct threat to anybody. The infant's position in the group is entirely dependent upon its alliances, usually consisting of the mother and the coalition of animals who support the mother. These allies of the mother are among the first to contact the new infant and, when the infant begins to move independently, both they and the mother will protect the infant in social conflicts. The infant's socialization then consists of learning its mother's position relative to all others in the group, and in learning which responses will provoke a superior and which will be tolerated. Representing so little challenge to an adult animal in and of itself, it enjoys an initial toleration which gradually declines as the infant matures.

An adult inserted into a group, however, is an immediate challenge. The more capable the individual, the greater the threat it represents to the existing social structure. In the face of this threat, a society can dissolve and allow the newcomer to reorder the group and its social relationships, or it can attack and subdue the threat. Under most circumstances, a group will coalesce to meet such a threat, members supporting one another in repelling the intruder. The group members most threatened will likely be of the same age-sex class as the intruder, but they can usually enlist the rest of the group. An adult male is thus met by resident adult males supported by females and even the immature members of a group. Adult females are challenged by adult females backed by resident adult males and immatures. Immature animals, however, represent little threat to adults, and resident immature animals are so dependent on adult support to maintain their own social position that they seldom attempt direct challenge to gain social position. Thus, very young animals may be incorporated into a group with little incident, sometimes being rapidly adopted by a group member or otherwise accepted into the group (Bernstein et al. in press).

Genetic exchange

What of the introduction of a female to an all-male group? Such a female represents little threat to adult males in and of herself, and females introduced to all-male groups in our laboratory have suffered little attack. A female, however, may ally herself with a high-ranking resident male and thus achieve even second-ranking position in a group of adult males, all of which outweigh her and are better equipped for combat. Nonetheless, the female allied to an alpha male will enforce her position by repeated aggression against all lower-ranking males, at first heavily dependent upon her male ally, but gradually acting more and more independently. The full weight of the alliance can thus be brought to

bear by any party to an alliance in monkey societies where the individuals have had ample opportunity to learn which animals support which other animals.

In contrast, a male introduced to a group of females is an immediate challenge to all. He may be successful in claiming alpha position and possibly reorganizing the group, or the resident females may resist. In our laboratory groups, the outcome seemed dependent on the breeding season, with males attaining success far more readily then than at other times of the year. It should be remembered that primate societies are only semiclosed breeding units and that species integrity is maintained by genetic exchange between troops, principally by the transfer of males during the breeding season. Thus, the mechanism of genetic exchange runs counter to social mechanisms preserving and protecting social orders by isolation and exclusion.

The net result of these two social mechanisms appears to be that male mobility for the rhesus monkey is largely restricted to the breeding season (Lindburg 1969; Neville 1968), which is also the period of most significant male wounding (Vandenbergh and Vessey 1968; Wilson and Boelkins 1970). Therefore adult males may be wounded during the breeding season not because of direct competition for receptive females but rather as a consequence of their mobility—from one troop to another. The stimulus for changing troops is imperfectly understood; fully adult prime males with little competition from other males, and with estrous females present, may abandon a troop only to show up later attaching themselves to another troop. Because such males may have been of any previous rank position, we cannot claim that they were "driven out" of their natal troops, nor can we claim that only newly adult or very old males leave, for it appears that adult males may transfer from troop to troop on an average of every three years (Neville 1968). The male joining a new troop need not suffer immediate group attack, for under natural conditions he may follow at a distance and gradually make contact with troop members before being integrated into the troop. The presence of a brother already in the new troop has been shown to appreciably ease acceptance into the troop, thus demonstrating the long-term relationships between siblings and the influence of alliances in troop structure (Sade 1968).

Conclusions

Aggression can certainly produce damage to an individual, and uncontrolled aggression can destroy a society. It may at times run counter to other biological mechanisms, but aggression is itself a biological mechanism shaped by natural selection into an adaptive force which helps to establish and maintain primate societies. The development of extraordinary male aggressive potential in certain Old World monkeys may function to protect the group from some predators, thus preserving the individual male and other individuals most likely sharing his genetic heritage.

The same aggressive displays may be used in conspecific group competition, or other sources of social disruption, to preserve the group. Minor altercations within a group can be rectified with little effort and, indeed, fighting within a group should result in minimum injury if the group is not to suffer in its ability to survive. With adult males responding to external threats, there is little need for females and juveniles to develop lethal fighting abilities for intragroup aggressive encounters. Indeed, such abilities in females and juveniles may be contraindicated for group survival, especially because there may be ample opportunity for aggression among group members, and severe wounding of genetically related individuals would surely be rapidly selected against.

But what of the adult males and their fighting potential? Granted their abilities may have evolved as

protection against external threats where there is clear positive selective pressure for increased fighting ability in conflicts with genetically unrelated animals. Can we therefore ignore the damage such males may inflict in intragroup fighting? Indeed not, and we may readily recognize a number of independent mechanisms which control primate male intragroup aggression. Some primate groups are organized into one-male units or societies wherein the unit leader faces no serious challenge to his social position from females and juveniles. On the other hand, many primates are organized into multimale units wherein not only may male-to-male fighting occur but the system of alliances may pit females against males. The full expression of male fighting potential could be disastrous to a society in such cases, and numerous checks are apparent, such as ritualization and inhibition in response to social communication. In fact, many communication responses are specifically related to communication of threat and submission, thereby averting direct physical contest. Male fighting potential is thus limited within the group by established relationships and specific control mechanisms. Its full expression is released primarily in response to serious challenges to the survival of the male or his group.

All this is not to say that the sole function of aggression is to maintain a society, nor is it to be taken as implying that aggression is the primary mechanism maintaining primate societies. Certainly primates are attracted to one another and live as members of social groups as a result of multiple motivational systems, and aggression may be elicited in a variety of situations, at times driving animals apart. In its extreme expression, aggression may threaten the survival of a group or a species, but it is because of the many positive facets of primate aggression that selection has been for control and not for elimination. Ritualized fighting within groups limits the consequences of aggressive encounters, and social mechanisms controlling

aggression between groups of conspecifics clearly helps preserve the species. Even with regard to extraspecific aggressive encounters, we have seen that bluffing and display may be positively selected.

Uncontrolled aggression is certainly disastrous to primate societies, but the complete absence of aggression may be equally disastrous. We require a new perspective to view aggression in terms of its biological and sociological functions rather than simply in terms of its extreme direct outcomes. It may not be possible to have a primate society totally devoid of aggression, but by studying its function, expression, and control, we may be better able to limit the undesirable side effects.

References

Bernstein, I. S. 1964a. Role of the dominant male rhesus in response to external challenges to the group. *J. Comp. Physiol. Psychol.* 57:404–06.
———. 1964b. The integration of rhesus monkeys introduced to a group. *Folia Primatologia* 2:50–63.
———. 1966. Analysis of a key role in a capuchin (*Cebus albifrons*) group. *Tulane Studies in Zool.* 13(2):49–54.
———. 1968. The lutong of Kuala Selangor. *Behaviour* 32:1–16.
———. 1969a. Introductory techniques in the formation of pigtail monkey troops. *Folia Primat.* 10:1–19.
———. 1969b. Spontaneous reorganization of a pigtail monkey group. In *Proc. Sec. Int. Cong. Primat.* Vol. 1, C. R. Carpenter, ed. Basel: S. Karger, pp. 48–51.
———. 1969c. Stability of the status hierarchy in a pigtail monkey group (*Macaca nemestrina*). *Animal Behaviour* 17:452–58.
———. 1971. The influence of introductory techniques on the formation of captive mangabey groups. *Primates* 12:33–44.
———. 1970. Primate status hierarchies. In *Primate Behavior: Development in Field and Laboratory Research*, Vol. 1, L. A. Rosenblum, ed. Academic Press, pp. 71–109.
Bernstein, I. S., and W. A. Draper. 1964. The behavior of juvenile rhesus monkeys in groups. *Animal Behaviour* 12:92–96.
Bernstein, I. S., T. P. Gordon, R. M. Rose. Aggression and social controls in rhesus monkey [*Macaca mulatta*] groups revealed in group formation studies. *Folia Primatologia*, in press, a.
———. Factors influencing the expression of aggression during introductions of rhesus monkey groups. In *Primate Aggression, Territoriality and Xenophobia*, R. Holloway, ed. Academic Press, in press, b.
Bernstein, I. S., and W. A. Mason. 1963.

Group formation by rhesus monkeys. *Animal Behaviour* 11(1):28-31.

Carpenter, C. R. 1954. Tentative generalizations on the grouping behaviour of nonhuman primates. *Human Biology* 26(3):269-76.

Chance, M. R. A. 1967. Attention structure as the basis of primate rank orders. *Man* 2(4):503-18.

Chance, M. R. A., and C. J. Jolly. 1970. *Social Groups of Monkeys, Apes and Men.* Dutton, p. 224.

Christopher, S. B. 1972. Social validation of an objective measure of dominance in captive monkeys. *Behav. Res. Meth. Instrum.* 4:19-20.

DeVore, Irven, and S. L. Washburn. 1963. Baboon ecology and human evolution. In *African Ecology and Human Evolution,* F. Clark Howell and Francois Bourliere, eds. Aldine, pp. 335-67.

Ellefson, John O. 1968. Territorial behavior in the common white-handed gibbon, *Hylobates lar Linn.* In *Primates,* Phyllis C. Jay, ed. Holt, Rinehart and Winston, pp. 180-99.

Hall, K. R. L. 1964. Aggression in monkey and ape societies. In *The Natural History of Aggression,* J. D. Carthy and F. J. Ebling, eds. Academic Press, pp. 51-64.

Jensen, G. D., R. A. Bobbitt, B. N. Gordon. 1967. Sex differences in social interaction between infant monkeys and their mothers. *Recent Adv. Biol. Psychiat.* 9:283-93.

Kaufman, I. C., and L. A. Rosenblum. 1969. The waning of the mother-infant bond in two species of macaque. *Determinants of Infant Behavior* 4:41-59.

Kawai, Masao. 1960. A field experiment on the process of group formation in the Japanese monkey (*Macaca fuscata*) and the releasing of the group at Ohirayama. *Primates* 2(2):181-253.

Kummer, Hans. 1968. *Social Organization of Hamadryas Baboons.* University of Chicago Press, p. 189.

Lindburg, D. G. 1969. Rhesus monkeys: Mating season mobility of adult males. *Science* 166:1176-78.

Marsden, H. M. 1972. Effect of food deprivation on intergroup relations in rhesus monkeys. *Behav. Biol.* 7:369-74.

Maslow, A. H. 1936. The role of dominance in the social and sexual behavior of infrahuman primates: I. Observations at Vilas Park Zoo. *J. Genet. Psychol.* 48:261-78.

———. III. A theory of sexual behavior in infrahuman primates. *J. Genet. Psychol.* 48:310-36.

———. IV. The determination of heirarchy in pairs and in a group. *J. Genet. Psychol.* 49:161-98.

Maslow, A. H., and S. Flanzbaum. II. An experimental determination of the behavior syndrome of dominance. *J. Genet. Psychol.* 48:279-309.

Mason, W. A. 1966. Social organization of the South American monkey, *Callicebus moloch:* A preliminary report. *Tulane Stud. Zool.* 13:23-28.

Neville, M. K. 1968. Male leadership change in a free-ranging troop of Indian rhesus monkeys (*Macaca mulatta*). *Primates.* 9:13-27.

Plotnik, R., F. A. King, L. Roberts. 1968. Effects of competition on the aggressive behavior of squirrel and cebus monkeys. *Behaviour* 32:315-32.

Rosenblum, L. A. 1969. Interspecific variations in the effects of hunger on diurnally varying behavior elements in macaques. *Brain Behav. Evol.* 2:119-31.

Rowell, T. 1973. *The Social Behavior of Monkeys.* Penguin Books, p. 203.

Sade, D. S. 1968. Inhibition of son-mother mating among free-ranging rhesus monkeys. *Sci. and Psychoanal.* 12:18-37.

Southwick, C. H. 1967. An experimental study of intragroup agonistic behavior in rhesus monkeys (*Macaca mulatta*). *Behaviour* 28:182-209.

Southwick, C. H., M. A. Beg, M. R. Siddiqi. 1965. Rhesus monkeys in North India. In *Primate Behavior: Field Studies of Monkeys and Apes,* Irven DeVore, ed. Holt, Rinehart and Winston, pp. 111-59.

Vandenbergh, J. G. 1967. The development of social structure in free-ranging rhesus monkeys. *Behaviour* 29:179-94.

Vandenbergh, J. G., and S. H. Vessey. 1968. Seasonal breeding of free-ranging rhesus monkeys and related ecological factors. *J. Reprod. Fert.* 15:71-79.

Vessey, S. H. 1971. Free-ranging rhesus monkeys: Behavioural effects of removal, separation and reintroduction of group members. *Behaviour* 40:216-27.

Wilson, A. P., and R. C. Boelkins. 1970. Evidence for seasonal variation in aggressive behaviour in *Macaca mulatta. Animal Behav.* 18:719-24.

28

The origins of human social behavior

One of the founders of a new discipline—sociobiology—examines the inborn responses and behavioral tendencies that adapt human beings to social life.

by Edward O. Wilson

For the past twenty years biologists and anthropologists have been cooperating in an attempt to trace human social evolution. The task is one of the most difficult in science, because the human species has leaped forward in a way that all but denies self-analysis.

On anatomical grounds we are certainly primates, and our closest living relative is the chimpanzee. But the extraordinary mental evolution that characterizes *Homo sapiens* has distorted even the most basic primate social qualities into nearly unrecognizable forms. Individual species of monkeys and apes have plastic social organizations, easily modified by learning to adapt societies to particular environments; man has extended the trend into an endlessly varying ethnicity. Monkeys and apes are able to adjust their aggressive and sexual interactions somewhat to fit the needs of the moment; in man this adjustment has become multidimensional, culturally dependent, and almost endlessly subtle. The formation of close bonds and the reciprocation of favors among individuals are rudimentary behaviors in other primates; man has expanded them into great contractual networks in which individuals consciously alter roles from hour to hour as if changing masks.

The biologists and anthropologists are constructing a new discipline, comparative sociobiology, to trace these and other human qualities as closely as possible back through time. Besides adding perspective to our view of humankind and perhaps offering some philosophical ease, the exercise will help to identify the behavior and rules by which individual human beings increase their Darwinian fitness through the manipulation of society.

In a phrase, we are searching for the human biogram—the set of inborn responses and behavioral tendencies that adapt human beings to social life. One of the key questions is, to what extent is the biogram an adaptation to the more or less civilized existence of the past ten

thousand years and to what extent is it a useless vestige of earlier social evolution? Our civilizations were jerry-built around the biogram. How have they been influenced by it? Conversely, how much flexibility is there in the biogram, and in what portions of it particularly? Experience with other animal species has shown that when an organ or a behavior pattern is as grossly changed as human behavior has been, evolutionary reconstruction is very difficult. This is the crux of the problem in the historical analysis of human behavior.

In pursuing this matter I believe that we can safely discard two extreme interpretations that have attracted a great deal of attention in recent years. Human beings are not thinly clothed instinct machines. For example, we are not in the grip of a basic aggressive instinct that must be relieved periodically by war or football games, as suggested by Konrad Lorenz. Our aggressive tendencies are real, and predictable to a large extent, but they are finely adjusted to circumstances and capable of remaining dormant for indefinite periods in the right environments. Nor are men stimulus-response machines molded by reward, punishment, and a few basic learning rules, as suggested by B. F. Skinner and the extreme behaviorists. The truth is much more complicated and interesting than either of these two alternatives. The human mind is something in between—a kind of palimpsest, from which the codes of several key periods in evolution will eventually be deciphered. This is why the study of human prehistory is so important to the understanding of modern psychology.

Modern man can be said to have been launched by a two-stage acceleration in mental evolution. The first occurred during the transition from a larger arboreal primate to the first man-apes (*Australopithecus*). If the primitive manlike creature *Ramapithecus* is in the direct line of ancestry, as current opinion holds, the change may have required as much as ten million years. *Austra-*

lopithecus was present five million years ago, and by three million years ago it had divided into several forms, including probably the first primitive *Homo*, or "true" man. The evolution of these intermediate hominids was marked by an accelerating increase in brain capacity. Simultaneously, erect posture and a striding, bipedal locomotion were perfected, and the hands were molded to acquire the unique human precision grip. These early men undoubtedly used tools to a much greater extent than do modern chimpanzees. Crude stone implements were made by chipping, and rocks were pulled together to form what appear to be the foundations of shelters.

The second, much more rapid phase of acceleration began about 100,000 years ago. It consisted primarily of cultural evolution as opposed to a genetic evolution of brain capacity. The brain had reached a threshold, beyond which a wholly new, enormously more rapid form of mental evolution took over. This second phase was in no sense planned, and its potential is only now being revealed. The study of man's mental and social origins involves two questions that correspond to the dual stages of mental evolution.

What challenges in the environment caused the human ancestors to adapt differently from other primates and started them along their unique evolutionary path?

Once started, why did the human line go so far?

Scientists have concentrated on two indisputably important facts concerning the biology of *Australopithecus* and early *Homo*. First, the evidence is strong that the "gracile man-ape," *Australopithecus africanus*, the species closest to the direct ancestry of *Homo*, lived on the open savanna of Africa. The wear patterns of sand grains taken from the Sterkfontein fossils suggest a dry climate, while the pigs, antelopes, and other animals found in association with the fossils are of the kind usually specialized for existence in grasslands. The australopithecine way of life came as the result of a major habitat shift. The ancestral *Ramapithecus* or an even more antecedent form lived in forests and was adapted for progression through trees by arm swinging. Only a very few other large-bodied primates have been able to join man in leaving the forest to spend most of their lives on the ground in open habitats (see diagram below). This is not to say that bands of *Australopithecus africanus* spent all of their lives running about in the open. Some of them might have carried their game into caves and even lived there in permanent residence, although the evidence pointing to this often-quoted trait is still far from conclusive. Other bands could have retreated at night to the protection of groves of trees, in the manner of modern baboons. The important point is that much or all of the foraging was conducted on the savanna.

The second peculiar feature of the ecology of early men was the degree of their dependence on animal food, evidently far greater than in any of the living monkeys and apes. The *Australopithecus* were catholic in their choice of small animals. Their sites contain the remains of tortoises, lizards, snakes, mice, rabbits, porcupines, and other small, vulnerable prey that must have abounded on the savanna. The man-apes also hunted baboons with clubs. From an analysis of 58 baboon skulls, Raymond Dart estimated that all had been brought down by blows to the head, fifty from the front and the remainder from behind. The *Australopithecus* also appear to have butchered larger animals, including the giant sivatheres, or horned giraffes, and dinotheres, elephantlike forms with tusks that curved downward from the lower jaws. In early Acheulian times, when true men of the genus *Homo* began employing stone axes, some of the species of large African mammals became extinct. It is reasonable to suppose that this impoverishment was due to excessive predation by the increasingly competent bands of men.

What can we deduce from these facts about the social life of early man? Before an answer is attempted, it should be noted that very little can be inferred directly from comparisons with other living primates. Geladas and baboons, the only open-country forms, are primarily vegetarian. They represent a sample of at most six species, which differ too much from one another in social organization to provide a baseline for comparison. The chimpanzees, the most intelligent and socially sophisticated of the nonhuman primates, are forest-dwelling and mostly vegetarian. Only on the infrequent occasions when they kill and eat baboons and other monkeys do they display behavior that can be directly connected with ecology in a way that has meaning for human evolution. Other notable features of chimpanzee social organization, including the rapidly shifting composition of subgroups, the exchange of females between groups, and the intricate and lengthy process of

This simplified evolutionary diagram of the Old World primates shows that only three existing groups have shifted from the forest to the savanna. They are the baboons (Papio), *the gelada monkey* (Theropithecus gelada), *and man.*

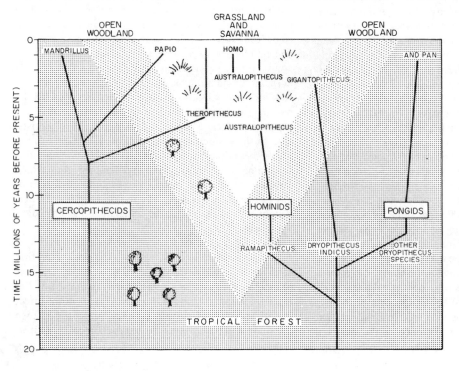

Social traits of living hunter-gatherer groups and the likelihood that they were also possessed by early man

Traits that occur generally in living hunter-gatherer societies	Variability of trait category among different species of monkeys and apes	Reliability of concluding early man had the same trait
Local group size: Mostly 100 or less	Highly variable but within range of 3-100	Very probably 100 or less but otherwise not reliable
Family as the nuclear unit	Highly variable	Not reliable
Sexual division of labor: Women gather, men hunt	Limited to man among living primates	Not reliable
Males dominant over females	Widespread although not universal	Reliable
Long-term sexual bonding (marriage) nearly universal; multiple wives general	Highly variable	Not reliable
Exogamy universal, abetted by marriage rules	Limited to man among living primates	Not reliable
The size and composition of subgroups change often	Highly variable	Not reliable
Territoriality general, especially marked in rich gathering areas	Occurs widely, but variable in pattern	Probably occurred; pattern unknown
Game playing, especially games that entail physical skill but not strategy	Occurs generally, at least in elementary form	Very reliable
Prolonged maternal care; pronounced socialization of young; extended relationships between mother and children, especially mothers and daughters	Occurs generally in advanced species of monkeys and apes	Very reliable

socialization, may or may not have been shared by primitive man. We cannot argue either way on the basis of our perception of ecological adaptation. It is often stated in the popular literature that the life of chimpanzees reveals a great deal about the origin of man. This is not necessarily true. The manlike traits of chimpanzees could be due to their having converged toward the human species in evolution, rather than sharing ancestral traits, in which case their use in evolutionary reconstructions would be misleading.

The best procedure to follow, and one that I believe is relied on implicitly by most students of the subject, is to extrapolate backward from living hunter-gatherer societies. In the table above this technique is made explicit. From the anthropological literature, I have listed the most general traits of hunter-gatherer peoples. Then I have evaluated the degree to which each behavioral category is subject to evolution by noting the

amount of variation in the category that occurs among the nonhuman primate species. The less variable the category, the more likely that the trait displayed by the living hunter-gatherers was also displayed by early man.

What we can conclude with some degree of confidence is that primitive people lived in small territorial groups, within which males were dominant over females. The intensity of aggressive behavior and the ways in which its expression varied according to circumstances remain unknown. Maternal care was prolonged, and the relationships were at least to some extent based on ties between mothers and their offspring. Speculation on the other aspects of social life is not supported either way by the variability data and is therefore more tenuous. It is likely that the early hominids foraged in groups. To judge from the behavior of baboons and geladas, such behavior would have conferred some protection from large predators. By the

time *Australopithecus* and early *Homo* had begun to feed on large mammals, group hunting almost certainly had become advantageous and even necessary, as in the case of the African wild dog. But there is no compelling reason to conclude that men did the hunting while women stayed at home. This occurs today in hunter-gatherer societies, but comparisons with other primates offer no clue as to *when* the trait appeared. It is certainly not essential to conclude a priori that males must be a specialized hunter class. Among chimpanzees males do the hunting, which may be suggestive. But among lions, the females are the providers, often working in groups and with cubs in tow, while the males usually hold back. In the case of the African wild dog both sexes participate. This is not to suggest that male group hunting was not an early trait of primitive man, but only that there is no strong independent evidence to support the hypothesis.

This brings us to the prevailing theory

of the origin of human sociality. It consists of a series of interlocking hypotheses that have been fashioned from bits of fossil evidence, extrapolations back from extant hunter-gatherer societies, and comparisons with other living primate species. The core of the theory can be appropriately termed the "autocatalysis model." Autocatalysis is a word used in biology to denote a process in which the product of a reaction speeds up the rate at which the reaction occurs, causing the reaction to accelerate. The theory holds that when the human ancestors became bipedal as part of their terrestrial adaptation, their hands were

freed, the manufacture and handling of artifacts were made easier, and intelligence grew as part of the improvement of the tool-using habit. With mental capacity and the tendency to use artifacts increasing through mutual reinforcement, the entire materials-based culture expanded. Cooperation during hunting was perfected, providing a new impetus for the evolution of intelligence, which in turn permitted still more sophistication in tool using, and so on through cycles of causation. At some point, probably during the late *Australopithecus* period or the transition from *Australopithecus* to *Homo*, this autocatalysis carried the

evolving populations to a certain threshold of competence, at which the hominids were able to exploit the antelopes, elephants, and other large herbivorous mammals teeming around them on the African plains. Quite possibly the process began when the hominids learned to drive big cats, hyenas, and other carnivores from their kills. In time they became the primary hunters themselves and were forced to protect their prey from other predators and scavengers. The autocatalysis model usually includes the proposition that the shift to big game accelerated the process of mental evolution. The shift could even

At the threshold of autocatalytic social evolution two million years ago, a band of early men (Homo habilis) forages for food on the African savanna. In this speculative reconstruction the group is in the act of driving rival predators from a newly fallen dinothere. The great elephantlike creature had succumbed from exhaustion or disease, its end perhaps hastened by attacks from the animals closing in on it. The men have just entered the scene. Some drive away the predators by variously shouting, waving their arms, brandishing sticks, and throwing rocks, while a few stragglers, entering from the left, prepare to join the fray. To the right a female saber-toothed cat and her two grown cubs have been at least temporarily intimidated and are backing away. As they threaten the men, they reveal the extraordinary gape of their jaws. In the left foregound, a pack of spotted hyenas has also retreated but is ready to rush back the moment an opening is provided. The men are quite small, less than five feet in height, and individually no match for the large carnivores. According to prevailing theory, a high degree of cooperation was therefore required to exploit such prey; and it evolved in conjunction with higher intelligence and the superior ability to use tools. In the background can be seen the environment of the Olduvai region of Tanzania as it may have looked at this time. The area was covered by rolling parkland and rimmed to the east by volcanic highlands. The herbivore populations were dense and varied, as they are today. In the left background are seen three-toed horses (Hipparion), while to the right are herds of wildebeest and giant horned giraffelike creatures called sivatheres.

The drawing is by Sarah Landry and was prepared in consultation with F. Clark Howell. The reconstruction of the saber-toothed cats was based in part on an Aurignacian sculpture.

have been the impetus that led to the origin of early *Homo* from their australopithecine ancestors two or more million years ago. Another proposition is that males became specialized for hunting. Child care was facilitated by close social bonding among the males, who left the domiciles to hunt, and the females, who kept the children and conducted most of the foraging for vegetable food. Many of the peculiar details of human sexual behavior and domestic life flow easily from this basic division of labor. But these details are not essential to the autocatalysis model. They are added because they are displayed by modern hunter-gatherer societies.

Although internally consistent, the autocatalysis model contains a curious omission—the triggering device. Once the process started, it is easy to see how it could be self-sustaining. But what started it? Why did the earliest hominids become bipedal instead of running on all fours like baboons and geladas? Clifford Jolly has proposed that it happened in order to allow them to feed more efficiently on grass seeds. Because the early pre-men, perhaps as far back as *Ramapithecus*, were the largest primates depending on grain, a premium was set on the ability to manipulate objects of very small size relative to the hands. Man, in short, became bipedal in order to pick seeds. This hypothesis is by no means unsupported fantasy. Jolly points to a number of convergent features in skull and dental structure between man and the gelada, which feeds on seeds, insects, and other small objects. Moreover, the gelada is peculiar among the Old World monkeys and apes in sharing with man the following anatomical traits used in sexual display: growth of hair around the face and neck of the male and conspicuous fleshy adornments on the chest of the female. According to Jolly's model, the freeing of the hands of the early hominids was a preadaptation that permitted the increase in tool use and the autocatalytic concomitants of mental evolution and predatory behavior.

Autocatalytic reactions in living systems never expand to infinity. Biological processes normally change in a manner that slows growth and eventually brings it to a halt. But almost miraculously, this has not yet happened in human evolution. The increase in brain size and the refinement of stone artifacts indicate a gradual improvement in mental capacity for at least five million years. With the appearance of the Mousterian tool culture of Neanderthal man some 75,000 years ago, the trend gathered momentum, giving way in Europe to the Upper Paleolithic culture of modern man about 40,000 years ago. Starting about 10,000 years ago, agriculture was invented and spread, populations increased enormously in density, and the primitive hunter-gatherer bands gave way locally to the relentless growth of tribes, chiefdoms, and states. Finally, after 1400 A.D., European-based civilization shifted gears again, and knowledge and technology grew at an accelerating pace.

There is no reason to believe that during this final sprint there has been a cessation in the evolution of either mental capacity or the predilection toward special social behaviors. The theory of population genetics and experiments on other organisms show that substantial changes can occur in the span of less than 100 generations, which for man reaches back only to the time of the Roman Empire. Two thousand generations, roughly the period since typical *Homo sapiens* invaded Europe, is enough time to create new species and to mold them in major ways. Although we do not know how much mental evolution has actually occurred, it would be false to assume that modern civilizations have been built entirely on capital accumulated during the long haul of the Pleistocene. The investigation of the genetic constraints on human behavior and their true meaning has just begun. As it proceeds we can hope to acquire a much deeper and more useful understanding of man's capacity to adapt to his relentlessly changing environment.

29

LOUIS S.B. LEAKEY and **ROBERT ARDREY** in a dialogue on **MAN, THE KILLER**

ROBERT ARDREY   LOUIS S. B. LEAKEY

Robert Ardrey: Jean Jacques Rousseau first asked such questions as "How did man come about?" and "If we behave, or misbehave, how much has this to do with our origin from a state of nature?" Unfortunately, Rousseau did not have any evidence to support his answers. Over the past few decades you have supplied some of the evidence man needs to conduct an inquiry into his own past. Quite literally you have uncovered the skeletons in our ancestral closet. Do you have any idea why man behaves so badly toward his fellow man? Animals don't. Why is man different from other animals? When did the violence begin?

Louis S. B. Leakey: I would like to make a distinction first. Lions eat zebras, but that is not aggression. That is hunting food. You are asking me about organized killing. I am not a specialist on living primates, but as far as I know, wild primates as a whole have not reached the stage where they organize attacks against each other—for food or for any other reason.

Down at the Gombe Stream Reserve,

Jane Goodall set up bunches of bananas to attract the chimpanzees to an area near her camp, so that she could get certain pictures. From time to time some baboons came to the place where the bananas were and began to fight the chimpanzees for the bananas. But that was a situation contrived by humans. In the ordinary course of events, I have not seen primates competing against other species of primates for food.

Ardrey: There are a few species of primates that organize battles, but they turn into charades. Every morning, certain vervets and langurs come out and have a fight with the group next door. But they're just having a little fun. There's nothing serious about it—nobody ever gets killed. The howling monkeys go out and screech at each other worse than delegates at the United Nations. This is a primate exercise that some species seem to enjoy and others don't. I sometimes say that animals make sense, but that men don't. This becomes especially clear when you observe the way some animals defend territory. Not all species are territorial. An elephant is not, the gorilla is not, chimps are not. They all have their range. There are in-between species, like the baboons, who don't defend their territory, because no one intrudes. Baboons make sense. Somewhere in their history they learned that it's a lousy idea to intrude. If something is advantageous, an animal will do it; if it is not advantageous, the animal will not do

it. I sincerely hope that after our experience in Vietnam, Americans will learn that it is not advantageous to intrude.

Leakey: In a similar vein, I have never seen sexual instinct play a part in animal aggression. Animals and birds defend territory, but they are not sexually jealous. Jane Goodall reported that Flo, one of the sexiest, most attractive chimpanzees in her group, was sometimes mated by seven or eight different males in one day. Frequently, the younger chimpanzees, or those who were not as dominant, would take the field first.

Ardrey: The problem, then, is to identify at what point man became different from the animals, and what factors contributed to that evolutionary step.

Leakey: I look at man and man's ancestors as creatures which, until they became what Sir Julian Huxley and I call psychosocial men, were purely animal men. This includes the early *Homo sapiens*, their predecessors *Homo habilis*, and hominids such as the australopithecines that R. A. Dart found in South Africa and that we are finding in East Africa. And before that, *Kenyapithecus wickeri*. These men and manlike creatures were like the animals themselves, and were not, as far as I can see, aggressive or violent toward each other. For one thing, they did not have the time, the opportunity or the means to attack their own species. There were so very few of them on the ground that there was enough territory for every-

Persons familiar with the laws of the quest know that there are gates in the wall of the world that open only for certain individuals. The hero passes through the gate into a realm to test his skill, strength and luck. If he is successful, he will discover the secret that he was destined to learn.

Olduvai Gorge in Tanzania, south of Nairobi, Kenya, is one such gate; it opens onto the realm of prehistoric man. The man who entered that world, and who is uncovering the secret of the origins of mankind, is Louis S. B. Leakey.

Kikuyu. He was born on August 7, 1903 at Kakete, a tiny village near Nairobi. His parents were English missionaries who worked among the Kikuyu, Kenya's largest tribe. Leakey grew up among these people who taught him their customs and the skills of the hunt. When he was 13, be became an initiate of the Kikuyu. The elders named him Wakaruigi, "Son of the Sparrow Hawk."

Leakey speaks and dreams in Kikuyu. He is as much an African as he is a European. Chief Koinange, of the Kikuyu, calls him "the black man with a white face." Leakey attributes his success as a fossil hunter to the training he received as a Kikuyu youth. In a recent *National Geographic* article he said it taught him "two things, patience—especially patience—and observation. In Africa, survival depends upon your reaction to irregularities in your surroundings. A torn leaf, a paw print, a bush that rustles when there is no breeze, a sudden quiet—these are the signals that spell the difference between life and death.

"The same instant recognition of something different—a glint of white in the face of a cliff, an odd-shaped pebble, a tiny fragment of bone—leads to the discovery of fossils. And patience. I can still hear the Kikuyu elders telling the boys of my age over and over, 'Be patient, be careful, don't hurry. Try again and again and again.' "

Also when he was 13, Leakey received for Christmas a copy of H. R. H. Hall's *Days Before History* and immediately began to search the African hills for arrowheads and axheads, and began to

LEAKEY
Son of the Sparrow Hawk

evolve a belief. He recalls: "Even then I believed Darwin's theory: that the mystery of man's past would be unraveled here in Africa. So, long before my parents packed me off to school in England, I had . . . prepared myself to hunt here on my home grounds, not only for prehistoric man, but for the complete picture of his world."

Leakey entered school in England when he was 16; two years later he became a student at Cambridge.

In his second year at Cambridge, Leakey suffered a head injury during a rugby game. Ordered to take a year off, he joined a British expedition bound for East Africa. W. E. Cutler, a Canadian paleontologist, sought fossil reptiles and was glad to have someone along who was familiar with Africa. In turn, he instructed Leakey in the care and preservation of fossils.

Leakey returned to Cambridge and passed examinations for a degree in archeology and anthropology.

In 1926, in a farm near Lake Nakuru in Kenya, he discovered a Stone Age burial site. In 1929, at Kariadusi, Kenya, he spied a hand ax jutting out of the face of a cliff and uncovered the living area of a paleolithic nomad who had lived some 200,000 years earlier.

In 1913, a German geologist, Professor Hans Reck, had found animal fossils at a place called Olduvai Gorge, which is in present-day Tanzania. Leakey visited Reck, and asked if he had found stone tools among the animal fossils. Leakey believed that the fossil bed at Olduvai Gorge was the same age as the beds at the Kariadusi River, and that he might find signs of human culture there. Reck disagreed, saying that he had searched for tools but had found none. Leakey invited Reck to go to Olduvai. He made a bet with Reck that he would find stone implements the first day on the site. (He discovered a hand ax within eight hours of arriving and won the bet.)

Factory. In 1933 at a London lecture, Leakey met a young archeology student, Mary Nicol. Two years later she accompanied him on an expedition to Olduvai, as one of four students on his staff. A short time later, they were married. They have worked side by side ever since, and Mary Leakey made several important discoveries on her own.

World War II interrupted Leakey's work at Olduvai. He served in army intelligence, while Mary Leakey continued digging alone at Olorgasaille, southwest of Nairobi. In 1942, Louis visited her there on a three-day pass, and they discovered a Stone Age tool factory that contained over 3,000 hand axes.

In 1952 the Leakeys led a full expedition to Olduvai, where they began to find fossils of early men—some of them lying among the scattered tools and bones of living sites. They slowly worked their way back through time, filling the gaps in man's evolutionary history. One by one, *Proconsul, Kenyapithecus, Zinjanthropus,* and finally two-million-year-old *Homo habilus* silently testified for Leakey's thesis—that the cradle of mankind was Africa.

—James Petersen

one. They did not normally live in close contact with one another, and there was no need to squabble. We became violent when we became psychosocial men—when we invented fire, speech, abstract thought and religion, magic. This change occurred probably 30,000 to 40,000 years ago. Since then we have developed a way of life that throws us together into great masses of people and gives us more and more leisure to think up things like jealousy, hatred, and malice, and then indulge in them.

Ardrey: There are exceptions to your hypothesis. Peking man, or *Homo erectus*, evidently was a headhunter and cannibal. You find no body bones at Chou-k'ou-tien, but you do find heads with the underside of the skull hollowed out to extract the brains. He lived over 300,000 years ago. The Vértesszöllös man that was found in Hungary—the first known *Homo sapiens*—also lived 300,000 to 400,000 years ago. He was definitely killed by one of the stone implements that lay beside him. His head was caved in. You can find Monte Circeo men and Neanderthals with their heads cut off, their brains scooped out, and their skulls mounted in circles of stone. In other words, you find a great deal of mayhem throughout the history of developing man. Personal violence seems part of human nature. Today, two thirds of all murders are committed between people who know each other. I think we had the same instincts in the old days. It is perfectly natural for a man to get mad at his wife and hit her over the head and kill her, or vice versa. We have always been dangerous animals. Didn't the first *Homo habilis* that you found show signs of a violent death?

Leakey: Yes, our first *Homo habilis*, an 11-year-old youngster, had a hole in the top of his head. As far as I'm concerned, that was definitely a sign of death by violence. Whether it came from falling out of a tree or being hit accidentally by a fellow schoolboy (if you can call it that) or whether it was a deliberate killing, I don't know. I personally do not think that people were killing each other seriously at that stage because they were angry with each other. It is true that there is some evidence of cannibalism at the Chou-k'ou-tien site, but you must realize that Peking man is an exception to the rest of mankind. They were already living in caves and they had fire. When you start living side by side in the small area of one cave with a lot of different families, then jealousies and hostilities between each other are going to start. My argument is that if you go back to *Homo habilis* or to early

Homo sapiens, you find that he was not in a position really to be hostile. He was living in very small groups and did not have the leisure in which to develop hostilities.

Ardrey: I agree. He was too busy surviving. As hunters they had to live quite far apart. They could not have had next-door neighbors because there wouldn't have been enough animals. What happened when the rest of mankind caught up with Peking man?

Leakey: The cave dwellers at Dordogne are good examples of the next step. These caves in southwestern France, which include the famous painted cave at Lascaux, provided shelter from the wind and the cold that the hunters had never had when they were in the open. At that point, men lived in much closer communities, but they also were going farther out to hunt. I put that down to the discovery that man could make fire himself. Long before fire was made and before man could control and have continuous fire, man from time to time captured wildfire as he might capture a wild animal, took it home and domesticated it temporarily. When for some reason or another—because he didn't feed it, or because he was away when the rain came—the fire died and he couldn't remake it. Peking man had fire spasmodically—then no fire at all for a time—then another fire. He knew fire, but he couldn't make it.

Ardrey: With fire came the next step?

Leakey: Yes. Have you ever thought about the significance of the making of fire in relation to human speech? I have been out on a number of occasions with hunting tribes in Tanganyika. To my great surprise they were mostly silent from dawn to dark because they were hunting. After they made a kill, they were still silent because they might make a second kill—it might be their lucky day. When they got back to camp they talked. I thought that the women of the tribe, because they were food-gathering, would chatter, chatter, chatter all day long, because the nuts, berries and fruits would not run away. But I had overlooked the fact that they, too, always had their eyes open for any meat that they could find.

Ardrey: The women didn't talk?

Leakey: They were like the hunters. They would not talk during the day, for fear of scaring away game. They would come around a bush and there would be a baby Grant's gazelle or Thomson's gazelle lying on the grass. They had bifocal vision. They could see game that other animals would miss. A dog would go right past if he wasn't on the right side of the wind. But humans, no. At night both the

Australopithecus,

a small-brained hominid, roamed the dry savannah of Africa between one- and four-million years ago. Anthropologists have found fossil remains of *Australopithecus* in South Africa, Tanzania, Kenya and Ethiopia. Current theory holds that the creature ate meat scavenged from natural predators to supplement a vegetable diet. Many prehistorians place *Australopithecus* at the head of a direct line of hominids that culminated in modern man. Recently though, L. S. B. Leakey has uncovered the remains of *Kenyapithecus*, a protohominid more than 13-million-years old that bears a strong resemblance to *Australopithecus*. He suggests that if *Australopithecus* is the grandfather of man, *Kenyapithecus* is the great-grandfather.

Prepared in collaboration with Clark Howell, Professor of Anthropology, University of California, Berkeley.

men and the women talked. Once they could make fire, they would come home, cook the meal, then talk around the fire late into the night. And *that* to me is the beginning of our real aggression: to invent words for and begin to think about horrible things like hatred and malice and war—things that have never been in our consciousness.

Ardrey: This reminds me of a joke—

that the Aswan Dam in Egypt was going to light up all the villages and reduce the birth rate. All the people would have something else to do. Supposedly talk or play dominoes, or something. But I agree, the fire makes a focus at night that you wouldn't have otherwise, and encourages you to communicate and tell the story of what happened during the day.

Leakey: And thus get speech. And with

the arrival of real speech, although it has done a great many beautiful things, it certainly has done awfully bad things. It gave us time and leisure to invent ideas. Some of those ideas were the causes of our aggression (language, names for our enemies—but the biggest enemy is the name, and not the person).

Ardrey: So much communication is *this* kind of communication. And so

much of language has made it absolutely impossible to understand what somebody else thinks. This is part of our problem today. Speech is not all fine. You hear some beautiful things from anthropologists about how it makes mankind one. I don't see any part of it.

Leakey: I don't think speech was present at all early. The proto-men, hominids, and the early things like *habilis* may have had some form of speech. I think they had more words than the chimpanzees do. Jane Goodall has now, with the help of one of our sound machines, identified about 80 different sounds. I imagine our ancestors had three or four times that number, but not speech in my sense.

Ardrey: I disagree. I think speech—not elaborate, but in moderately grammatical form—emerged at a fairly early date, let's say, before the big brain, in your *Homo habilis* stage, because of the necessity of transmitting the social wisdom—the wisdom of the hunter—to the young. I don't think the hunter needed it so badly, but I do think there was a tremendous necessity for the young hunter, the hunter-to-be, to learn verbally from his elders the ways of the wild animals of different forms. So I have a feeling that speech

189

started at a very early date, but perhaps it did not become too sophisticated until later on.

Leakey: *Homo habilis* definitely had the *potential* for speech of a far greater quality than any chimpanzee or any near-man had—even more than the australopithecines. *Homo habilis* had a speech potential created by the muscles of the root at the lower jaw. This was two-million years ago. I don't think he had developed that potential because he didn't have the leisure to do so. I cannot see that men or women, until they had fire, were able to develop speech to any degree—at least not abstract speech. Until you have fire, when you come home in the evening you just sit. And those who are not cooking or cutting up the meat and getting ready to go to bed, are listening, listening. Elephants can stampede past; snakes can come wiggling up where they lie.

Ardrey: Man developed the capacity for articulate violence along with articulate speech?

Leakey: Yes. Between man and man. This happened just about 40,000 years ago—with the mastery of fire. I can't see it any earlier. Once you had fire at will, you moved into caves, and once you moved into caves, you had freedom and leisure. But with that came concentrated groups. The number of caves in the Dordogne valley was limited. And for the first time I think the people went in large numbers in one and the same place to sleep and to live, although not to hunt. They had to hunt separately. I think that was the last milestone in human evolution.

Ardrey: I would take it back farther than the Dordogne, because that is not so long ago. I have great difficulty with my wife; she gets mad sometimes because when I say *recent*, I mean 50,000 years and she means last Tuesday. Dordogne is really recent. That's 15,000 to 20,000 years ago. It's very difficult for me to believe that the proliferation of languages—all based on essential unified grammatical structure—occurred as recently as 40,000 years ago. I feel that it must have started much earlier to have reached the last ends of the earth that it has. This, however, is a very speculative argument.

Leakey: Robert, do you think I have overstressed the importance of speech?

Ardrey: It's a very important *contributing* factor. It's a cultural thing that happened to us, which is a contributing factor of no end of importance. But I think that other things are going on in the meantime. Man was a dangerous animal from way back into the hominid days. He was a dangerous animal in the sense that a wolf

or a lion is a dangerous animal. We were hunters for a very long time. By selective necessity, hunting encouraged a desire not to flee, a desire to attack, a pleasure in the chase. You had to be adjusted entirely toward attack. Through most of our history as hunter, we were not better armed than any other hunter—wolf, or whatever. We carried a stone, wood club, whatever weapons we had, to defend ourselves, or to attack with. But they were hand-held weapons. The long-distance weapon came into being in just about the same period you're talking about—the fire thing of 40,000 years ago. The very last of Neanderthal man in the Sahara Desert invented the long-distance weapon. At this time, in between the Atlas Mountains and Algiers, you find the Aterian culture that developed the very first thong weapons with a little notch at the bottom like an American arrowhead. *Tanged* we call it. This meant the weapon could be fastened to a shaft. If it was light, it could be a bow and arrow. A heavy one would make a throwing spear.

Before that we had been simply animals among animals. If we killed for a living, we killed no differently from the lion or the hunting dog, or the hyena or the wolf. We killed in close quarters, taking all the risks. But the day we had a weapon that could kill at 50 or 100 yards (there is a record of a Samoan chief who could knock over an animal at 257 yards with a bow and arrow), we got into the new era that culminated with the nuclear bomb.

Now we started talking about violence. Language meant that we could share the knowledge on how or why to do violence—or we could kid ourselves into why we should do violence—because those guys are terrible and we are fine. We could say these things to each other. We couldn't do it when we were like the wolves.

With language came the possibility of the mob, of the organized group, of organized killing that we now call war, or simply violence on the streets. It is all the same thing. The violent group. The vast change in the quality of the weapon in the hands of a dangerous animal, which we were and which we remain, seems to have introduced a qualitative change in our evolving life. It didn't, in fact, have a great effect on human existence for some time. The glaciers still covered Europe. It was quite a long time, maybe 12,000 to 15,000 years ago, before these long-distance weapons began to come around.

Early settlers to the American continent brought them over here and killed with them. But it seems to me this is

Homo erectus

was the earliest member of the genus *Homo* (of which modern *Homo sapiens* is the only surviving member). This creature lived between 400,000 and 700,000 years ago. Anthropologists have found fossil remains in Java and China and in North and East Africa. The species show a more efficient adaptation for fully erect posture and bipedal gait than do earlier hominids; the brain is larger and the teeth smaller than those of prehistoric apes. Evidence uncovered at Chou-k'ou-tien, China, indicates that *Homo erectus* used fire, lived in cave communities, and was a cannibal. (In 1960, Leakey and his assistants found the remains of a 1.75-million-year-old hominid that seems to fall between the australopithecines and *Homo erectus*. They named the creature *Homo habilis*.)

Prepared in collaboration with Clark Howell, Professor of Anthropology, University of California, Berkeley.

Among the products of the Anthropology Department at the University of Chicago are an unusual trio—Saul Bellow, Kurt Vonnegut Jr., and Robert Ardrey. All three studied there under Robert Redfield, and the experience shaped their later work. All three have produced what might be called anthropological art.

In the late '50s playwright Ardrey renewed his interest in anthropology. He turned his talents to a tour of the natural sciences and produced in quick succession three best sellers: *African Genesis, The Territorial Imperative* and *The Social Contract.* Some critics call his work "fictional anthropology" and describe it as the effort of a talented but shamelessly inaccurate opportunist. Some admirers hail Ardrey as a prophet of ethology—the study of the relationship of animal behavior to human behavior—agent provocateur for the revolution now sweeping anthropology, biology and psychology.

Paradox. When he emerged from the six years of research that preceded *African Genesis,* Ardrey had prepared a disclaimer of sorts:

"Why a dramatist should have become the accountant and interpreter of a scientific revolution is a paradox that need not divert us here . . . a dramatist is a specialist, in a sense, in human nature. In another sense, however, he is a specialist in nothing, and therefore, a generalist. And while the generalist may be the most suspect of creatures in the view of the modern specialized human animal, a generalist was what a revolution of specialists demanded."

Later in the same work he proclaimed that "Hollywood knows more about the inner nature of *Homo sapiens,* viewed as a species, than any political, philosophical, or scientific school on earth." Statements such as these are guaranteed to offend specialists, but Ardrey was speaking directly to a huge audience whose special interest was *Homo sapiens,* and whose primary source of information had been television and movies. Ardrey singlehandedly exposed these persons to a wealth of scientific data and created a new awareness of our evolutionary inheritance.

Remains. In 1955 Ardrey went to Africa to scout articles for *The Reporter* magazine. There he met two anthropologists—Louis S. B. Leakey and Raymond A. Dart—who claimed to have found fossil remains of a primate ancestor of man.

ARDREY
Prophet of the Ethologists

Since this ran against the accepted theory that Asia was the birthplace of man, Ardrey's news instincts impelled him to examine their evidence closely.

Dart showed Ardrey the skull of an infant creature that he had found in 1924. *Australopithecus africanus* seemed to have been halfway between a man and ape—four feet tall, erect, bipedal, with a brain the size of a gorilla's. Because the creature lacked the prominent canine teeth of other primates, Dart concluded that *Australopithecus* was a carnivore, who hunted or scavenged for food.

Dart told Ardrey how his theory had been received—anthropologists either rejected it or ignored it. Some told Dart that his creature was a freak of nature, perhaps a mongoloid idiot. And anyway, orthodoxy held that man evolved a big brain *before* he was able to develop weapons or hunting tactics.

Weapons. Ardrey became convinced that man had evolved from terrestrial apes on the African savannah, and cheerfully appropriated the controversy for his own use. But it was not just the pre-hominid fossils that captured his fancy.

Dart told Ardrey that he believed *Australopithecus* had used bones as weapons to kill animals, and that man had

emerged from this species of killer ape. Big-brained *Homo sapiens* did not invent weapons; weapons invented man. Dart's theory struck Ardrey with the force of a religious revelation. In *African Genesis* Ardrey wrote:

"The mightiest of predators had come about as the logical conclusion to an evolutionary transition. With his big brain and his stone handaxes, man annihilated a predecessor who fought only with bones. And if all human history from that date has turned on the development of superior weapons, then it is for very sound reason. It is for genetic necessity. We design and compete with our weapons as birds build distinctive nests."

And then:

"Man emerged and triumphed over his rival primates for this single reason—he was a killer."

Reach. The apostasy was complete, and Ardrey began the long and difficult task of documenting his new faith. He read obscure journals in zoology and biology, interviewed scientists in several nations, and made extensive field trips to Africa.

Ardrey had to reach into other disciplines because there was not enough anthropological evidence to prove his thesis. He studied reports on territorial drives, social hierarchies, and sexual relationships among animals. He subsequently proposed (in the *Territorial Imperative*) that man possessed an inherited drive to acquire and defend property, not unlike the birds who build nests and defend them against intruders. He also claimed (in *The Social Contract*) that man has an instinctive drive for power and status—the same drive that causes animals who live in groups to form dominant-subordinate hierarchies.

At 62, Robert Ardrey defends a territorial nest in Rome, with his wife Berndine Grunewald, a South African actress. He turns down frequent invitations to write screenplays for Hollywood. He lectures for professional societies, and the BBC is working on a series of 13 hour-long films based on his books. He may write a book on the nature of sex.

As for the controversy surrounding his work, Ardrey says: "If I have climbed out on every limb in sight, it has been to scout out the human utility of biology's findings; although I must confess that I can think of no furniture other than limbs on which a man can rest comfortably."

—James Petersen

where the predator came into his own. I believe that the hunting way coupled with the growth of weapon-making is the essential necessity or the genetic background of human propensity for violence (not that we are *all* violent, but enough of us are violent to make the rest of us have to go around with steel vests). It may have started way back in the days of your friends at the bottom of Olduvai, or your son Richard's friends near Lake Rudolf, in northern Kenya.

Leakey: I disagree. I don't believe the earliest man—even up until *Homo habilis*—was anything more than a scavenger. I don't think he was killing in general. The remains we find on these very early sites at Rudolf and Olduvai are never the remains of a complete animal. We usually find front legs or back legs. Richard and I once tested this hypothesis. We went out naked, picking up some giraffe limb bones and jaws to act as rudimentary weapons, but not such as we could attack or kill anybody with, just protect ourselves a little. We drove off the vultures and the hyenas when they came in to the kill, but we couldn't drive off the lions. We watched them and the vultures watched them and the hyenas watched them, and then we rushed in as scavengers. I think for a very long time—almost until the very point of discovery of fire—we were scavengers and not weapon-makers, and therefore not offensive.

Ardrey: I don't agree. I see no reason on earth why an animal should have been afraid of us before we had a weapon that killed at a distance. The scavenging hypothesis holds that we went in and were able to frighten off animals, or that we went in and other animals did not quarrel with us. Hugo van Lawick and Jane Goodall have come to the conclusion that nowhere in the human past would we have been capable of scavenging regularly. We certainly swiped what we could, there is no question about that. But then, lions swipe from hyenas. This goes on all the time in the predatory community. The question is, can you live off it? I don't believe that we could have. The farther back you go, the more poorly were our feet developed, the slower could we run, the more inadequate we were. And I see no reason why we could have competed with natural predators and scavengers. They all hunt and they all scavenge from each other. How could we have won in a competition with a hyena? A hyena would have eaten us.

Leakey: Richard and I went and were able to keep the hyenas off for 10 minutes—they were furious. And after 10 min-

utes I signaled to my son, "Get out, it's not safe any longer. They're going to kill us now." But we got a little zebra meat. And I think that the evidence at the sites does show that men were getting legs here and there, and of course they were supplementing it by killing small game—juvenile animals—which can be done very easily, and what I call "slow game"—tortoises, frogs, baby birds, rodents.

Ardrey: Louis, you forget you are talking about modern man who has been shooting animals with bow and arrow, guns, clobbering them in one way or another for so long that they have developed flight distance to get out of our way. They're scared stiff of us. They've been scared ever since the long-distance weapon, when we were separated from all other animals. You can go out today and scare hyenas off with a lot of noise or you may even bother lions; you can do it because they associate you with sudden death. But why in the old days, when we were only four feet tall and weighed 85 pounds, and had nothing more to kill with than a stone in the hand, a piece of wood, or whatever—why should such animals have been afraid of us then? I just don't think we were capable of killing them.

Leakey: But you can scavenge. Many times I've seen a kill with vultures and jackals and no bigger animals on the kill at all. Early men didn't scavenge all the time; they'd kill other things, and they had nuts and berries as well. They were omnivorous, but I don't believe in the earlier days we were anything but scavengers, insofar as we would eat meat at all.

Ardrey: Well, it's a big difference, but in a way it doesn't all matter that much, because we're going back so far. We're talking now about one to two million years ago. This isn't even recent in my terms. If we go back 500,000 years ago to *Homo sapiens*, the big-brain man, there isn't much question about what went on. They were definitely hunters. This heritage has had an immense effect on us in terms of natural selection. Those men who had an efficient capacity for violence, who enjoyed violence, were the men who survived and passed on their genes. If you didn't like to go out and hunt, you wouldn't get the girl, and you wouldn't get any food—you'd just be an extra mouth to feed. And I would assert that we didn't live on spinach. This is a fashionable point of view much promoted in American anthropology. Lettuce is great for diets, but not for men who have to work for a living. We had to live off meat. We undoubtedly scavenged whenever we could, but we could not survive 365 days

Neanderthal man,
numerous, earliest member of the species *Homo sapiens*, best known of prehistoric people, inhabited Europe and the lands around the Mediterranean before and during the early part of the last Ice Age. Anthropologists have discovered several remains in coastal caves in the limestone massif of Monte Circeo, south of Rome. In one cave they found a complete skull, resting upside down in a ring of stones, with broken animal bones nearby. The manner in which the base of the skull was broken off suggests that Neanderthal man was a cannibal and that he removed his victim's brain ritually.

Prepared in collaboration with Clark Howell, Professor of Anthropology, University of California, Berkeley.

Cro-magnon man

replaced Neanderthal man in Europe and is the immediate ancestor of historic man. In 1868 anthropologists discovered the remains of Cro-magnon man in a cave near the village of Les Eyzies, in the Dordogne region of southern France. Evidence suggests that he practiced human burial in a ceremony involving animal remains, sea shells, stone artifacts, and decoration of the corpse. In addition, Cro-magnon invented art and made the first museum—he is responsible for stone engravings, carved figures, and the famous cave paintings at Lascaux, France. Cro-magnon man was a nomad— he wandered across the earth, spreading the seeds of human civilization. When he learned how to farm and domesticate animals, Cro-magnon man became modern man.

Prepared in collaboration with Clark Howell, Professor of Anthropology, University of California, Berkeley.

of the year hoping someone would leave some meat around. So we had to be able to hunt and kill. Unhappily, about 10,000 years ago we domesticated cereals and we domesticated cattle, goats, sheep and so on—I say "unhappily" because in the new book *The Imperial Animal*, Lionel Tiger and Robin Fox go back to the date when we got control of our food supply and say, *Was it good or was it bad? We have sure had enough trouble since.* Suddenly we had much more food and many more children. Overpopulation produced scarcity, and scarcity produced conflict.

This is where your idea and mine link together so interestingly. Three points add up: language made inordinately irrational beliefs possible; weapons made violence possible at inordinate distances; and efficiency and, finally, food made possible too inordinately many people. The foundations of violence were there in front of us to be perfected, and we have perfected them as no other species of the living world has done.

I recently spent a day with P. D. MacLean who is a director of the National Institute of Mental Health. He believes that we too frequently refer to the brain as we do the heart, as if it were an organ. It is an evolved organ with various areas, and MacLean's point is that the reptilian brain still exists, circled by the early mammalian brain, and then finally by the immense cortical development of the human being. He feels that this cortical development is so recent that we haven't developed proper connections yet. We don't have the entire switchboard installed. And this means that the old animal brain (which is a delightful phrase, because it means that nature never throws anything away) still operates, but without the inhibition we'd like to believe the cortex could give. The problem is that we have somehow to work on the communication from the cortex that tells us that something isn't going to do. That the violent life, for example, is simple annihilation in the end. But the trouble is that we have one of those Spanish postal systems when it comes to dropping a message into the box and getting it down to the old brain. We don't know how soon the message will get there, if at all. And so we are fighting against something that is very tough. But you can't take your eye off it— you have to work on it all the time. You can't believe that the old brain is angelic in any sense.

Leakey: This brings us to a most terribly important thing. Our talk suggests that we have become so violent now that there is no hope for the future. I person-

ally don't believe this at all. I think we have reached a point where we certainly have a very short time in which to make up our minds what we are going to do. We can, because we're the only animal (and I say "animal" advisedly) who amongst his evolutionary developments developed a

"We became violent when we invented fire, speech, abstract thought and religion."

thinking brain and a precision grip. And, if we do not want to destroy ourselves in the very near future, we can and we must today set to work jointly and all together— over the whole world—say to each other and to our leaders, we are not prepared to allow man to destroy himself and the whole beauty of the arts, of the music that we have inherited from our forefathers. We insist on changing direction, now.

Ardrey: I have never known an evolutionist who was a pessimist. It's very curious. Part of the reason is that life has a way of solving its own problems. Now, you may have to go through dreadful things to get to the solution. You know, "Things have to get worse before they get better"—that sort of thing. It's never going to be easy.

But there is an idea that has come up in recent years that I think is marvelous. The man responsible is David Hamburg, a clinical psychiatrist at Stanford University. The Hamburg hypothesis is quite simply this: forget about instinct when you get up into the higher animals in which learning is so important. Never have the idea that people go by learning and animals by instinct. It grades so gradually—read Jane Goodall's book, *In The Shadow of Man*, about the chimpanzees. The greatest book ever written on animal

193

observation. And you will see how much the chimp has to learn. Why it takes so long to grow up, because it has so much to learn. Ten years of observation before it becomes an adult.

Evolution makes easy to learn that which has survival value. Evolution

❝Those men who enjoyed violence were the men who survived and passed on their genes.**❞**

makes difficult to learn that which has no survival value. Think how quickly you learn language and how long it takes to learn the multiplication tables, which have no survival value in our evolutionary history. But language has. So we learn—bingo!—between the age of two and three.

Hamburg also says that it is pleasurable to learn those things that are of survival value. During more than 99 percent of his time on earth violent ways came easily to man, because they were of survival value. The violence of the hunt was pleasurable. Now it is maladaptive. It's murder. You can learn to be inimical.

Kids can wind up in trouble or kids can wind up angels. But you have got to work on them, because it is easier to learn to be a murderer than it is to be a peacemaker. Now we have to do an about-face and say *no*. We must be nonviolent. Yes, we can do it—but are we going to have to work at it. We must not applaud the violent. We must even think twice before we applaud the motives of the violent. Successful violence merely breeds more violence. We have to face this in America where we have so many groups that have just grievances. But that which is accomplished by violence will only mean an extension of violence, until finally you have a violent end in which the violent figure rises above

and suppresses all violence, meaning takes a monopoly on violence. This is the only end result.

Leakey: I entirely agree, and consequently we have to take steps now. We know the potential of men; either we will be destroyed by overpopulation, pollution, etc., or we are going to save the world for our future generations—for our children and grandchildren and great-grandchildren. One or the other. I would encourage more and more mixing of people from different backgrounds, until mankind realizes that we are all one and the same. We think differently, our colors may vary, our hair may be different, but, nevertheless, we are all men and women. We must work together for better things. As soon as people of different races and backgrounds start mixing they begin to find so much in common with each other that the other things that are different fall apart. This is heresy in some circles, but I am certain it is true.

Secondly, I think you have to distinguish, in teaching the young, between what I call a "faith" as distinct from "religion." Today, as I see it, we are losing all faith—the faith that man has grown to a point where he has some awareness, some consciousness of right and wrong. But because of the destructive influence of dogmas and doctrines, as distinct from faith, we are letting our young people lose faith, which they don't need to lose. And having lost faith, because they confuse faith with religion, they are not willing to abandon violence. You can't really kill people if you have a real feeling that they also have a faith and are meaningful in this life and the world.

Some years ago I selected a random sample of dossiers of people who had committed violence in this country. Out of 100 random files that I was allowed to see, only three individuals admitted to any faith. All the others had no faith. If you have no faith of any kind, if you think you are just body, hair, skin, flesh, and nothing more, then obviously if I snuff you out today instead of letting you go on, it doesn't matter. But if you believe that a person is something worthwhile, you don't snuff him out.

And I believe that you have to differentiate with the young people between real faith and false religion.

Ardrey: It's interesting, but 40,000 years ago, when man discovered fire, speech, and dangerous weapons, he also discovered religion. He buried his dead with red ochre, painted on the bones. A blood symbol. A life symbol. Something to believe in.

30

An Idea We Could Live Without—
The Naked Ape

David Pilbeam

Last fall CBS Television broadcast a National Geographic Special, in prime time, called "Monkeys, Apes, and Man." This was an attempt to demonstrate how much studies of primates can tell us about our true biological selves. In a recent *Newsweek* magazine article, Stewart Alsop, while discussing problems of war, stated that nations often quarrel over geopolitical real estate when national boundaries are poorly defined: his examples were culled from areas as diverse as the Middle East, Central Europe, and Asia. One of his introductory paragraphs included the following:

"The animal behaviorists—Konrad Lorenz, Robert Ardrey, Desmond Morris—have provided wonderful insights into human behavior. Animals that operate in groups, from fish up to our ancestors among the primates, instinctively establish and defend a territory, or turf. There are two main reasons why fighting erupts between turfs—when the turfs are ill-defined or overlapping; or when one group is so weakened by sickness or other cause as to be unable to defend its turf, thus inviting aggression."

Here Alsop is taking facts (some of them are actually untrue facts) from the field of ethology—which is the science of whole animal behavior as studied in naturalistic environments—and extrapolating directly to man from these ethological facts as though words such as *territoriality, aggression,* and so forth describe the same phenomena in all animal species, including man.

Both these examples from popular media demonstrate nicely what can be called "naked apery" or the "naked-ape syndrome." When Charles Darwin first published *The Origin of Species* and *The Descent of Man*, over 100 years ago, few people believed in any kind of biological or evolutionary continuity between men and other primates. Gradually the idea of man's physical evolution from ape- or monkey-like ancestors came to be accepted; yet the concept of human behavioral evolution was always treated with scepticism, or ever horror. But times have changed. No longer do we discriminate between rational man, whose behavior is almost wholly learned, and all other species, brutish automata governed solely by instincts.

One of the principal achievements of ethologists, particularly those who study primates, has been to demonstrate the extent to which the dichotomy between instinct and learning is totally inadequate in analyzing the behavior of higher vertebrate species—especially primates. Almost all behavior in monkeys and apes involves a mixture of the learned and the innate; almost all behavior is under some genetic control in that its development is channelled—although the amount of channelling varies. Thus, all baboons of one species will grow up producing much the same range of vocalizations; however, the same sound may have subtly different meanings for members of different troops of the same species. In one area, adult male baboons may defend the troop; those of the identical species in a different environment may habitually run from danger. Monkeys in one part of their species range may be sternly territorial; one hundred miles away feeding ranges of adjacent groups may overlap considerably and amicably. These differences are due to learning. Man is the learning animal par excellence. We have more to learn, take longer to do it, learn it in a more complex and yet more efficient way (that is, culturally), and have a unique type of communication system (vocal language) to promote our learning. All this the ethologists have made clear.

Studies of human behavior, at least under naturalistic conditions, have been mostly the preserve of social anthropologists and sociologists. The anthropological achievement has been to document the extraordinary lengths to which human groups will go to behave differently from other groups. The term "culture," a special one for the anthropologist, describes the specifically human type of learned behavior in which arbitrary rules and norms are so important. Thus, whether we have one or two spouses, wear black or white to a funeral, live in societies that have kings or lack chiefs entirely, is a function not of our genes but of learning; the matter depends upon which learned behaviors we deem appropriate—again because of learning. Some behaviors make us feel comfortable, others do not; some behaviors may be correct in one situation and not in another—forming a line outside a cinema as opposed to the middle of the sidewalk, for example; singing rather than whistling in church; talking to domestic animals but not to wild ones. The appropriate or correct behavior varies from culture to culture; exactly which one is appropriate is arbitrary. This sort of behavior is known as "context dependent behavior" and is, in its learned form, pervasively and almost uniquely human. So pervasive is it, indeed, that we are unaware most of the time of the effects on our behavior of context dependence. It is important to realize here that although a great deal of ape and monkey behavior is learned, little of it is context dependent in a cultural, human sense.

In the past ten years there has been a spate of books—the first of the genre was Robert Ardrey's *African Genesis* published in 1961—that claim first to describe man's "real" or "natural" behavior in ethological style, then go on to explain how these behaviors have evolved. In order to do this, primate societies are used as models of earlier stages of human evolution: primates are ourselves, so to speak, unborn. *African Genesis, The Territorial Imperative, The Social Contract*, all by Ardrey, *The Naked Ape* and *The Human Zoo* by Desmond Morris, Konrad Lorenz's *On Aggression, Men in Groups* by Lionel Tiger, and, most recently, *The Imperial Animal* by Lionel Tiger and Robin Fox, plus Antony Jay's *Corporate Man,* approach the bestseller level. All purport to document, often in interminable detail, the supposedly surprising truth that man is an animal. Also they argue that his behavior —particularly his aggressive, status-oriented, territorial and sexual behavior—is somehow out of tune with the needs of the modern world, that these behaviors are under genetic control and are largely determined by our animal heritage, and that there is little we can do but accept our grotesque natures; if we insist on trying to change ourselves, we must realize that we have almost no room for maneuver, for natural man is far more like other animals than he would care to admit. Actually, it is of some anthropological interest to inquire exactly why this naked apery should have caught on. Apart from our obsessive neophilia, and the fact that these ideas are somehow "new," they provide attractive excuses for our unpleasant behavior toward each other.

However, I would describe these general arguments as rubbish, and pernicious rubbish; they are based upon misinterpretation of ethological studies and a total ignorance of the rich variety of human behavior documented by anthropologists. At a time when so many people wish to reject the past because it has no meaning and can contribute nothing, it is perhaps a little ironic that arguments about man's innate and atavistic depravity should have so much appeal. The world *is* in a mess; people *are* unpleasant to each other; that much is true. I can only suppose that argument about the inevitability of all the nastiness not only absolves people in some way of the responsibility for their actions, but allows us also to sit back and positively enjoy it all. Let me illustrate my argument a little.

Take, for example, one particular set of ethological studies—those on baboons. Baboons are large African monkeys that live today south of the Sahara in habitats ranging from tropical rain forest to desert. They are the animals that have been most frequently used as models of early human behavior; a lot of work has been done on them, and they are easy to study—at least those living in the savannah habitats thought to be typical of the hunting territories of early man. They are appealing to ethologists because of their habitat, because they live in discrete and structured social groups, and because they have satisfied so many previous hypotheses.

Earlier reports of baboon behavior emphasized the following. Baboons are intensely social creatures, living in discrete troops of 30 to 50 animals, their membership rarely changing; they are omnivorous, foraging alone and rarely sharing food. Males are twice as big as females; they are stronger and more aggressive. The functions of male aggression supposedly are for repelling predators, for maintaining group order, and (paradoxically) for fighting among themselves. The adult males are organized into a dominance hierarchy, the most dominant animal being the one that gets his own way as far as food, grooming partners, sex, when to stop and eat, and when and where the troop should move are concerned. He is the most aggressive, wins the most fights, and impregnates the most desirable females. Females, by the way, do little that is exciting in baboondom, but sit around having babies, bickering, and tending to their lords. Adult males are clearly the most important animals—although they cannot have the babies—and they are highly status conscious. On the basis of fighting abilities they form themselves into a dominance hierarchy, the function of which is to reduce aggres-

sion by the controlling means of each animal knowing its own place in the hierarchy. When groups meet up, fighting may well ensue. When the troop moves, males walk in front and at the rear; when the group is attacked, adult males remain to fight a rearguard action as females and young animals flee to safety in the trees.

Here then we have in microcosm the views of some men—and it is a very male view—of the way our early ancestors may well have behaved. How better to account for the destructiveness of so much human male aggression, to justify sex differences in behavior, status seeking, and so forth. I exaggerate, of course, but not too much, for the main damage is done because I have telescoped the argument—though not, I'm afraid, its intellectual content—into such a small space. But what comments can be made?

First, the baboons studied—and these are the groups that are described, reported, and extrapolated from in magazine articles, books, and in CBS TV specials—are almost certainly abnormal. They live in game parks—open country where predators, especially human ones, are present in abundance—and are under a great deal of tension. The same species has been studied elsewhere—in open country and in forest too, away from human contact—with very different results.

Forest groups of baboons are fluid, changing composition regularly (rather than being tightly closed); only adult females and their offspring remain to form the core of a stable group. Food and cover are dispersed, and there is little fighting over either. Aggression in general is very infrequent, and male dominance hierarchies are difficult, if not impossible, to discern. Intertroop encounters are rare, and friendly. When the troop is startled (almost invariably by humans, for baboons are probably too smart, too fast, and too powerful to be seriously troubled by other predators), it flees, and, far from forming a rearguard, the males—being biggest and strongest—are frequently up the trees long before the females (encumbered as they are with their infants).

When the troop moves it is the adult females that determine when and where to; and as it moves adult males are not invariably to be found in front and at the rear. As for sexual differences, in terms of functionally important behaviors, the significant dichotomy seems to be not between males and females but between adults and young. This makes good sense for animals that learn and live a long time.

The English primatologist Thelma Rowell, who studied some of these forest baboons in Uganda, removed a troop of them and placed them in cages where food had to be given a few times a day in competition-inducing clumps. Their population density went up and cover was reduced. The result? More aggression, more fighting, and the emergence of dominance hierarchies. So, those first baboons probably were under stress, in a relatively impoverished environment, pestered by humans of various sorts. The high degree of aggression, the hierarchies, the rigid sex-role differences, were abnormalities. In one respect, troop defense, there is accumulating evidence that male threats directed toward human interlopers occur only after troops become habituated to the observers, and must therefore be treated as learned behavior too.

Studies on undisturbed baboons elsewhere have shown other interesting patterns of adult male behaviors. Thus in one troop an old male baboon with broken canines was the animal that most frequently completed successful matings, that influenced troop movements, and served as a focus for females and infants, even though he was far less aggressive than, and frequently lost fights with, a younger and more vigorous adult male. Here, classical dominance criteria simply do not tie together as they are supposed to.

The concept of dominance is what psychologists call a unitary motivational theory: there are two such theories purporting to explain primate social behavior. These are that the sexual bond ties the group together, and that social dominance structures and orders the troop. The first of these theories has been shown to be wrong. The second we are beginning to

realize is too simplistic. In undisturbed species in the wild, dominance hierarchies are hard to discern, if they are present at all; yet workers still persist in trying to find them. For example, Japanese primatologists describe using the "peanut test" to determine "dominance" in wild chimpanzees by seeing which chimp gets the goodies. Yet what relevance does such a test have for real chimp behavior in the wild where the animals have far more important things to do—in an evolutionary or truly biological sense—than fight over peanuts? Such an experimental design implies too the belief that "dominance" is something lurking just beneath the surface, waiting for the appropriate releaser.

Steven Gartlan, an English primatologist working in the Cameroons, has recently suggested a much more sensible way of analyzing behavior, in terms of function. Each troop has to survive and reproduce, and in order to do so it must find food, nurture its mothers, protect and give its young the opportunity to learn adult skills. There are certain tasks that have to be completed if successful survival is to result. For example, the troop must be led, fights might be stopped, lookouts kept, infants fed and protected; some animals must serve as social foci, others might be needed to chase away intruders, and so on. Such an attribute list can be extended indefinitely.

If troop behavior is analyzed in such a functional way like this, it immediately becomes clear that different classes of animals perform different functions. Thus, in undisturbed baboons, adults, particularly males, police the troop; males, especially the subadults and young adults, maintain vigilance; adult females determine the time and direction of movement; younger animals, especially infants, act as centers of attention.

Thus a particular age-sex class performs a certain set of behaviors that go together and that fulfill definite adaptive needs. Such a constellation of behavioral attributes is termed a role. Roles, even in nonhuman primates, are quite variable. (Witness the great differences between male behaviors in normal baboon troops and those under stress.) If dominance can come and go with varying intensities of certain environmental pressures, then it is clearly not innately inevitable, even in baboons. Dominance hierarchies, then, seem to be largely artifacts of abnormal environments.

What is particularly interesting in the newer animal studies is the extent to which aggression, priority of access, and leadership are divorced from each other. Although a baboon may be highly aggressive, what matters most is how other animals react to him; if they ignore him as far as functionally important behaviors such as grooming, mating and feeding are concerned, then his aggression is, in a social or evolutionary sense, irrelevant.

I want to look a little more closely at aggression, again from the functional point of view. What does it do? What is the point of a behavior that can cause so much trouble socially?

The developmental course of aggressive behavior has been traced in a number of species: among primates it is perhaps best documented in rhesus macaques, animals very similar to baboons. There are genetical and hormonal bases to aggressive behavior in macaques; in young animals males are more aggressive, on the average, than females, and this characteristic is apparently related to hormonal influences. If animals are inadequately or abnormally socialized, aggressive behaviors become distorted and exaggerated. Animals that are correctly socialized in normal habitats, or richly stimulating artificial ones, show moderate amounts of aggression, and only in certain circumstances. These would be, for example, when an infant is threatened, when a choice item is disputed, when fights have to be interrupted, under certain circumstances when the troop is threatened, and occasionally when other species are killed for food.

Under normal conditions, aggression plays little part in other aspects of primate social life. The idea that the function of maleness is to be overbearingly aggressive, to fight constantly, and to be dominant, makes little evolutionary sense.

How about extrapolations from primates to man that the "naked-apers" are so fond of? Take, for example, dominance. Everything that I have said about its shortcomings as a concept in analyzing baboon social organization applies to man, only more so. Behaviors affecting status-seeking in man are strongly influenced by learning, as we can see by the wide variation in human behavior from one society to another. In certain cultures, status is important, clear-cut, and valued; the emphasis placed on caste in Hindu society is an obvious example. At the opposite extreme, though—among the Bushmen of the Kalahari Desert, for example—it is hard to discern; equality and cooperativeness are highly valued qualities in Bushman society, and hence learned by each new generation.

I've used the term "status-seeking" rather than "dominance" for humans, because it describes much better the kind of hierarchical ordering one finds within human groups. And that points to a general problem in extrapolating from monkey to man, for "status" is a word that one can't easily apply to baboon or chimp society; status involves prestige, and prestige presupposes values—arbitrary rules or norms. That sort of behavior is cultural, human, and practically unique.

As we turn to man, let's consider for a while human groups as they were before the switch to a settled way of life began a mere—in evolutionary terms—10,000 years ago. Before that our ancestors were hunters and gatherers. Evidence for this in the form of stone tool making, living areas with butchered game, camp sites, and so on, begins to turn up almost 3 million years ago, at a time when our ancestors were very different physically from us. For at least 2½ to 3 million years, man and his ancestors have lived as hunters and gatherers. The change from hunting to agricultural-based economies began, as I said, just over 10,000 years ago, a fractional moment on the geological time scale. That famous (and overworked) hypothetical visiting Martian geologist of the 21st century would find remains of hunters represented in hundreds of feet of sediments; the first evidence for agriculture, like the remains of the thermonuclear holocaust, would be jammed, together, in the last few inches. Hunting has been a highly significant event in human history; indeed, it is believed by most of us interested in human evolution to have been an absolutely vital determinant, molding many aspects of human behavior.

There are a number of societies surviving today that still live as hunters; Congo pygmies, Kalahari Bushmen, and Australian Aborigines, are three well-known examples. When comparisons are made of these hunting societies, we can see that certain features are typical of most or all of them, and these features are likely to have been typical of earlier hunters.

In hunting societies, families—frequently monogamous nuclear families—are often grouped together in bands of 20 to 40 individuals; members of these hunting bands are kinsmen, either by blood or marriage. The band hunts and gathers over wide areas, and its foraging range often overlaps those of adjacent groups. Bands are flexible and variable in composition—splitting and reforming with changes in the seasons, game and water availability, and whim.

Far from life being "short, brutish, and nasty" for these peoples, recent studies show that hunters work on the average only 3 or 4 days each week; the rest of their time is leisure. Further, at least 10% of Bushmen, for example, are over 60 years of age, valued and nurtured by their children. Although they lack large numbers of material possessions, one can never describe such peoples as savages, degenerates, or failures.

The men in these societies hunt animals while the women gather plant food. However, women often scout for game, and in some groups may also hunt smaller animals, while a man returning empty-handed from a day's hunting will almost always gather vegetable food on his way. Thus the division of labor between sexes is not distinct and immutable; it seems to be functional, related to mobility: the women with infants to protect and carry

simply cannot move far and fast enough to hunt efficiently.

Relations between bands are amicable; that makes economic sense as the most efficient way of utilizing potentially scarce resources, and also because of exogamy—marrying out—for adjacent groups will contain kinsmen and kinsmen will not fight. Within the group, individual relations between adults are cooperative and based upon reciprocity; status disputes are avoided. These behaviors are formalized, part of cultural behavior, in that such actions are positively valued and rewarded. Aggression between individuals is generally maintained at the level of bickering; in cases where violence flares, hunters generally solve the problem by fission: the band divides.

Data on child-rearing practices in hunters are well known only in Bushmen, and we don't yet know to what extent Bushmen are typical of hunters. (This work on Bushman child-rearing, as yet unpublished, has been done by Patricia Draper, a Harvard anthropologist, and I am grateful to her for permitting me to use her data.) Bushman children are almost always in the company of adults; because of the small size of Bushman societies, children rarely play in large groups with others of their own age. Aggression is minimal in the growing child for two principal reasons. First, arguments between youngsters almost inevitably take place in the presence of adults and adults always break these up before fights erupt; so the socialization process gives little opportunity for practicing aggressive behavior. Second, because of the reciprocity and cooperativeness of adults, children have few adult models on which to base the learning of aggressiveness.

Thus, the closest we can come to a concept of "natural man" would indicate that our ancestors were, like other primates, capable of being aggressive, but they would have been socialized culturally in such a way as to reduce as far as possible the manifestation of aggression. This control through learning is much more efficient in man than in other primates, because we are cultural creatures—with the ability to attach positive values to aggression-controlling behaviors. Thus Bushmen value and thereby encourage peaceful cooperation. Their culture provides the young with non-violent models.

Other cultures promote the very opposite. Take, for example, the Yanomamö Indians of Venezuela and Brazil; their culture completely reverses our ideals of "good" and "desirable." To quote a student of Yanomamö society: "A high capacity for rage, a quick flash point, and a willingness to use violence to obtain one's ends are considered desirable traits." In order to produce the appropriate adult behaviors, the Yanomamö encourage their children, especially young boys, to argue, fight, and be generally belligerent. These behaviors, I should emphasize, are learned, and depend for their encouragement upon specific cultural values.

Our own culture certainly provides the young with violent, though perhaps less obtrusive, models. These I should emphasize again, are learned and arbitrary, and we *could* change them should we choose to do so.

So far we have seen that fierce aggression and status-seeking are no more "natural" attributes of man than they are of most monkey and ape societies. The degree to which such behaviors are developed depends very considerably indeed upon cultural values and learning. Territoriality likewise is not a "natural" feature of human group living; nor is it among most other primates.

As a parting shot, let me mention one more topic that is of great interest to everyone at the moment—sex roles. Too many of us have in the past treated the male and female stereotypes of our particular culture as fixed and "natural": in our genes so to speak. It may well be true that human male infants play a little more vigorously than females, or that they learn aggressive behaviors somewhat more easily, because of hormonal differences. But simply look around the world at other cultures. In some, "masculinity" and "feminity" are much more marked

than they are in our own culture; in others the roles are blurred. As I said earlier, among Bushmen that are still hunters, sex roles are far from rigid, and in childhood the two sexes have a very similar upbringing. However, among those Bushmen that have adopted a sedentary life devoted to herding or agriculture, sex roles are much more rigid. Men devote their energies to one set of tasks, women to another, mutually exclusive set. Little boys learn only "male" tasks, little girls exclusively "female" ones. Maybe the switch to the sedentary life started man on the road toward marked sex role differences. These differences are learned though, almost entirely, and heavily affected by economic factors.

So much of human role behavior is learned that we could imagine narrowing or widening the differences almost as much or as little as we wish.

So, what conclusions can be drawn from all this? It is overly simplistic in the extreme to believe that man behaves in strongly genetically deterministic ways, when we know that apes and monkeys do not. Careful ethological work shows us that the primates closely related to us—chimps and baboons are the best known—get on quite amicably together under natural and undisturbed conditions. Learning plays a very significant part in the acquisition of their behavior. They are not highly aggressive, obsessively dominance-oriented, territorial creatures.

There is no evidence to support the view that early man was a violent status-seeking creature; ethological and anthropological evidence indicates rather that pre-urban men would have used their evolving cultural capacities to channel and control aggression. To be sure, we are not born empty slates upon which anything can be written; but to believe in the "inevitability of beastliness" is to deny our humanity as well as our primate heritage—and, incidentally, does a grave injustice to the "beasts."

ACKNOWLEDGMENTS. I would like to thank the following for helpful discussions and/or assistance in translating the manuscript into American English: Patricia Draper, Zelda Edelson, Fredericka Oakley, and Carol Pilbeam.

David Pilbeam is British, and was educated at Cambridge and Yale, where he received his Ph.D. After teaching at Cambridge, he returned to Yale in 1968 and he is now Associate Professor of Anthropology and Associate Curator of Anthropology in the Peabody Museum. His interests are mainly in primatology and human evolution; he has done field work in Spain, Egypt, Uganda, and Kenya, and is hoping to start work soon on a project involving study of the pygmy chimpanzee in the Congo (Zaire Republic).

31

The Territories of Man

Albert Eide Parr

The current debate about the sources of aggressiveness in the naked ape conjures up the image of doctors embroiled in medical dispute over the name and antecedents of the disease, while the patient dies unattended. David Pilbeam [*Discovery* 7(2), 1972] has effectively squelched the argument for the hereditary inevitability of nastiness in man, but has, in so doing, also laid the foundations for fresh and equally futile controversies about natural versus unnatural behavior in man and beast.

What we inherit, or acquire from the conditions under which we develop from egg to adult, is not a behavior, but a mechanism for behaving—for converting our input of stimuli into an output of responses. Our reactions will vary according to the behavioral machinery with which we respond. In the totality of its structure this equipment is as unique to each individual as are the fingerprints, but it is unavoidable that it will also resemble the corresponding equipment of other people in most of its basic features, whether because of inheritance, or because similarities in the physical parts and functions of all members of the same species insure a certain degree of likeness of experience in the progress through life from ovum to old age. By the same reasoning we must also expect to find many parallelisms extending across the animal kingdom, and particularly within the circle of the mammals and their relatives among the vertebrates.

Our responses, and those of all other living things, will also vary according to the circumstances to which, and in which, we react. Pilbeam's comments on ''game-park'' baboons, and Thelma Rowell's observations on caged forest baboons [as quoted by Pilbeam], confirm for yet another ilk what is already well known for rats and man, namely that aggressiveness generally increases with increasing population density. To speak of normal responses to certain living conditions as ''abnormalities'' is hardly enlightening. Neither do we learn anything from references to ''unnatural'' and ''disturbed'' conditions, when such, or suchlike, ''disturbances'' may well be produced by completely natural processes, as ''over-population'' can result from biological reproduction in man or lemming. Such terms can merely serve to confuse the issues.

Actually ''territoriality'' is not a much better word, unless we simply think of it as a label attached to the hub of a wide circle of manifestations radiating in all directions. I have, in other connections [A. E. Parr: The City as Habitat. *The Centennial Review* XIV(2), 1970] spoken of the privacy-territoriality syndrome, but no workable inflation of terminology could possibly cover the entire range of related phenomena, except by arbitrary definition. ''Territoriality'' does not mean much more than the name of the ship in a discussion of where it may, or ought to, take us.

"WHAT WE INHERIT, OR ACQUIRE FROM THE CONDITIONS UNDER WHICH WE DEVELOP FROM EGG TO ADULT, IS NOT A BEHAVIOR, BUT A MECHANISM FOR BEHAVING — FOR CONVERTING OUR INPUT OF STIMULI INTO AN OUTPUT OF RE-SPONSES."

One nearly always finds an assumption of such strong ties between territoriality and aggression that the two expressions some-times seem to be used interchangeably. Actu-ally a sense of territory can just as well be associated with attitudes of hospitality as with those of hostility, although the latter seem to be gaining predominance in the state of the world today. One does not have to go back farther than to the days of my own child-hood, less than three quarters of a century ago, to recall a hospitable territoriality in rural districts that seems almost unbelievable now. Traveling by horse and buggy, or on foot, one was welcomed everywhere, whenever a need for rest, refreshment, or even overnight accommodation in barn or bedroom arose. The host's pleasure in extending the hospital-ity was definitely, and usually quite obvi-ously, in part an aspect of pride of domain. This hospitable form of territoriality was also obviously related to low population density and small community size. The living condi-tions of the Congo Pygmies, the Kalahari Bushmen, and the Australian aborigines listed by Pilbeam as examples of territorial friendliness, also fit this description, and not a single example of more crowded people in larger settlements has been mentioned.

There was, of course, also a mutually advantageous or enjoyable functional rela-tionship involved in the state of hospitable territoriality that I have described. The guest was a bearer of tidings from the world beyond the host's daily range of contact. And the slow speed of movement made the traveler

dependent upon a density of hospitality along the route, that inns and other commercial establishments could not economically main-tain.

The electronic mass media have practically eliminated the traveler's news value, and with the speed of the motor car he easily covers the distances between service stations and motels without much need for hospitality in between. The former underexposure to direct human contact has now become overex-posure.

The automobile has also brought changes for the worse in the relationship between resi-dents and strangers for many other reasons than mere speed of movement, but the com-plexities of this subject would take us far afield at this point.

Our feelings for locale are not confined to a single size or concept or domain, but embrace an entire hierarchy of realms of vari-ous dimensions and definitions. Important among these are: the exclusive private niche of each individual; the domestic family ter-ritory; group territories such as "our street," "our neighborhood," "our turf;" and the larger territories of community, region and country, among many others.

There is also a special sense of territory such as a servant is likely to feel towards the domain of the master. Perhaps it might be described as vicarious territoriality. It was undoubtedly an important factor in baronial days, and it is still with us in many forms.

In my own early years as a seaman, sharing the forecastle with the rest of the crew before

"ACTUALLY A SENSE OF TERRITORY CAN JUST AS WELL BE ASSOCIATED WITH ATTITUDES OF HOSPITALITY AS WITH THOSE OF HOSTILITY, ALTHOUGH THE LATTER SEEM TO BE GAINING PREDOMINANCE IN THE STATE OF THE WORLD TODAY."

> "COULD THE DOWN-GRADING OF THE SEXUAL FUNCTIONS, AND THE GRADUAL EQUALIZATION OF MALE AND FEMALE ROLES, NOW IN PROGRESS AMONG OURSELVES, POSSIBLY BE A SOCIO-ECOLOGICAL ADAPTATION OF OUR SPECIES TO HIGH POPULATION DENSITIES?"

the age of sailor's cabins, I had opportunity to become intimately familiar with several levels of territoriality. The private territory of each individual was limited to his bunk and his sea chest. Group territoriality was very strongly developed in relation to the division of the forecastle between the "deck gang" on the starboard side, and the engine room crew to port. While the sense of group domain was always intense, the degree in which it expressed itself as hostile or hospitable fluctuated from ship to ship and from time to time. But on the wrong side of the forecastle you were always very conscious of being an intruder, whether you were among friends or among enemies. Finally, there was a sense of territoriality embracing the entire vessel, which might be considered vicarious or communal, or a little of each. Such feelings were most strongly developed on a "good ship" and might be totally lacking on a really bad one, which may tell us something about our past history, when master and servant identification with the same domain was more important than it is today.

The forecastle also showed that a dichotomous classification into hostile or hospitable territorialities is too simplistic. Between the two extremes there is a wide range of defensive territorial behavior of potentially enormous value to society in keeping peace and order in the precincts of our habitat (See Parr: The City As Habitat) but currently rather feebly manifested in our cities.

In the broadest possible terms, defensive territoriality may be said to differ from open hospitality by not requiring the host to adjust to the needs and habits of the guests, but by demanding instead that the stranger conform, or, at least, does no sudden harm to the accustomed way of life, and by enforcing such demands if necessary. Hostile territoriality, on the other hand, rejects any stranger out of hand, simply because he is an alien. The state of affairs in a peaceful forecastle was one of defensive territoriality.

One striking lesson to be learned from the old crew's quarters was how enormously individual territorial needs are reduced in a single-sex population. A person among members of his own sex seemed to require much less than half the space needed by two individuals paired in sexual roles. Armies, monasteries, all–male or all–female colleges, and similar establishments confirm the observation for both sexes. It is also interesting to note that the same thing applies to many of our fellow vertebrates, when sex differences become operational.

The closely packed flock of migratory birds breaks up into widely dispersed nesting families, often showing very hostile territoriality even towards fellow members from the same flock. Even among fishes the same thing happens to the European Stickleback which shows the male coloration only during the breeding season [A. E. Parr: Sex Dimorphism and Schooling Behavior among Fishes. *American Naturalist* 65(697), 1931] while the poor herring that goes through life

> ". . . THERE IS A WIDE RANGE OF DEFENSIVE TERRITORIAL BEHAVIOR OF POTENTIALLY ENORMOUS VALUE TO SOCIETY IN KEEPING PEACE AND ORDER IN THE PRECINCTS OF OUR HABITAT . . . BUT CURRENTLY RATHER FEEBLY MANIFESTED IN OUR CITIES."

without ever having opportunity to tell one sex from the other, never breaks up its densely crowded schools, but indiscriminately ejects its eggs and sperm into the sea, without knowing either mate or brood.

Of course, one must not blandly extrapolate from beast to man, but if it seems almost universally true that sexual roles in a bisexual relationship greatly increase the spatial demands per member of the species, one may be permitted to speculate upon what significance this may have for a breed now in the process of cramming its habitat by a population explosion.

The greatest population densities among settled and home-building higher organisms are those that obtain in a beehive or an ant hill. In these overcrowded communities, sexual differentiation and functions are confined to a very small fraction of the total population, such as queens and drones. Could the downgrading of the sexual functions, and the gradual equalization of male and female roles, now in progress among ourselves, possibly be a socio-ecological adaptation of our species to high population densities? It would not be the same solution as that evolved by the insects, and, of course, the insects cannot tell us anything about ourselves. But whether you get an idea from looking into a sunset or into a beehive has nothing to do with its merits and possiblities. It is only that, for better or for worse, the beehive seems much more likely to be thought-provoking on the subject at hand.

In settled populations beyond a certain density there seems to be a very real need to identify with nest and habitat on several different levels. Whether the craving is inherited or acquired in other ways hardly matters. What is important, is the manner in which the need expresses itself in our behavior. To become the object of identification the environment must have identifiably unique characteristics. The increasing uniformity of surroundings and impermanence of location combine to reduce the opportunities for identification with home base. If sound patriotism represents the top stratum of an ascending hierarchy of territorialities, could chauvinism be defined as patriotism distorted by an upward sublimation of frustrated cravings for territorial identification on home and neighborhood levels, aided by the electronic injection of the images of broader domains into the home sanctuary?

These are only questions. I have very few answers. But this is certainly no time to sweep the problems of aggression and hostile territoriality under the rug by simplistic references to either heredity or abnormalities of behavior.

Albert Eide Parr, Director Emeritus of the American Museum of Natural History, headed that institution from 1942 to 1959 and prior to that was Director of the Peabody Museum of Natural History from 1937 to 1942. He is a former president of the American Association of Museums and a former member of the United States Commission to UNESCO. His wide-ranging and distinguished writings include studies on marine biology, physical oceanography, museology, and diverse works on man and his relation to his environment.

32

Roots of human behaviour

An understanding of the animal roots of Man's anatomy and behaviour can help us to understand the nature of human variability, and to realize the social and natural environment in which mankind can flourish. Biological anthropology will have an important contribution to make in stabilizing Man's ecosystem—in making Man's behaviour more adaptive to a finite world

Bernard Campbell was recently visiting professor in anthropology at Harvard University and is author of *Human Evolution* (Heinemann)

Hair styles establish sexual dominance and effect sexual attraction in men and women. Both head and facial epigamic hair patches vary in form and appearance among the living races of Man: **A.** Eastern European; **B.** West African; **C.** New Guinean; **D.** North American. *Courtesy* Hans Friedenthal and Gustav Fischer

As soon as we come to realize fully that Man is a product of evolution and therefore a kind of animal, the relevance of biology to an understanding of Man and his works becomes clear. The success of recent books which attempt to make inferences from animal to human behaviour suggests that the realization of Man's place in Nature is at last close to our way of thinking. An article in the *New York Times* (13 October, 1968) included this sentence: "Modern anthropology teaches that nationalism and imperialism are deeply rooted in animal pasts and, perhaps like our own, the foreign policy of the Kremlin may sometimes derive from remote instincts first noted among wolves, horned owls or lions patrolling their preserves for sustenance." This comment (which is dangerously misleading) suggests what the job of the biological anthropologist is: to study the relevance of biological knowledge to the human condition.

Three things have occupied biological anthropologists: first they have been elucidating the path of human evolution by the interpretation of hominid fossils and their archaeological contexts. Second they have been studying biological variation in modern populations of different races. Third and most recently they have been examining the biology and observing the behaviour of their nearest relatives in the animal kingdom, the higher primates. From these three sources, they have been painstakingly gathering data which throw much light on human anatomy and physiology, on human behaviour and ecology.

Of these three sorts of biological study, the elucidation of the path of human evolution is the most central to our quest. Man's present nature and his variability are a product of it, and our studies of living primates, valuable in themselves, also throw light upon the fossil discoveries. Digging up fossil bones is not a glamorous occupation. It takes many years of patient work, often with very small reward, and yet its fruits are priceless. Hundreds of skulls and bone fragments from throughout the world are beginning to give us a broad idea of the course of Man's prehistory. In the early days the bones were collected without much regard to their context, unless it consisted of stone tools. Today archaeologists study the artifacts, fauna and flora associated with the human fossils, and try to distinguish those which can be taken as a key to the environment and climate of the times from those which were brought on to a living floor by the people themselves. The most famous example of this kind of work is that of the Leakeys at Olduvai, who had the good fortune and foresight to select one of the richest sites in the world, and to apply to it modern methods of excavation.

From this and many other sites we have learnt the following facts: early hominids, usually called *Australopithecus,* lived in East Africa and made stone tools to a regular pattern as much as 2.5 million years ago. Their bones are fossilized in a fairly continuous sequence from nearly 5 million years. Other fossils from 8 to 14 million years of age, known as *Ramapithecus,* may be their ancestors. These creatures had more in common with the chimpanzee than we have, and yet they had certain distinct characters of their own: they were successful bipedal runners, they had more or less human teeth (without large canines) and they hunted a certain amount of game in the open woodland and savannah areas of Africa. We also know that about one million years ago, as Man moved north into the temperate zones, his society became complex, and he probably developed some linguistic ability; his brain expanded, and he became more dependent on meat during the winters. Since we know that chimpanzees and most monkeys eat some animal food in a varied diet, it follows that Man is *not* naturally a vegetarian, nor incidentally is he a carnivore. Like other primates he has always had a varied diet, and been very adaptable in this respect.

Various studies of wild primates, and especially apes, have thrown some light on the nature of these early hominids. But we must be careful not to jump too hastily to conclusions. The fossils which we have are not the fossils of chimpanzees; they belonged to an entirely different genus. They were very like chimpanzees in certain features, and yet they may have had a long independent history. At present this is an area of some discord among anthropologists. Those who, like Professor S. L. Washburn of the University of California at Berkeley, emphasize the similarities between Man and the chimpanzee claim a common ancestor must have existed as recently as 8 to 10 million years ago and consider *Ramapithecus* a side-branch which became extinct. Those who stress the peculiar characters of early Man feel justified in pushing back that common ancestor to the lower Miocene, as much as 25 million years before present. Yet this disagreement does not seriously alter our interpretation of the fossils themselves, nor does it lessen the authority of biological anthropologists in this field. Science moves forward by the presentation and testing of alternative hypotheses, and the one characteristic which a scientist must possess is the ability to change his mind when new evidence becomes available.

As we examine the evolution of humanity from an animal ancestry, we can understand the meaning of the existing variability and distribution of human populations and races. We are neither surprised nor disturbed by racial differences and find them to be a usual characteristic of animal species: differences adapted to different environments in which the races evolved (not necessarily those in which they now live).

Just as one environment is not better or worse than another (unless it is your own) so one racial adaptation is not better or worse. Value judgments are irrelevant, and the differences are extremely superficial (in a literal sense). The genes which bring about differences among racial groups affect appearances: it is the outer boundary of the body tissues which is altered through intra-specific selection. The total of genetic differences involved in these superficial characters is probably far less than the amount of difference between people of the same breeding population. But the racial differences are superficially rather striking because they are unfamiliar. It is therefore not scientific to make value judgments about racial differences (but it may be socially meaningful). Values are social tools. Biologists only recognize one "good": evolutionary success. A biologist sees racial diversity as a priceless pool of genetic variation which should be maintained because it is enriching and irreplaceable. Variablity is one of the characteristics essential for species survival.

A number of authors have recently popularized a view of Man which seems to throw a powerful light on his nature. Desmond Morris describes him as a *Naked Ape,* while Robert Ardrey sees him as a carnivorous killer-ape with a *Territorial Imperative.* The ethologist Conrad Lorenz has interpreted his nature in the light of his studies of bird behaviour (*On Aggression*). There is a tendency in all these books to stress the animal nature of Man and the power of instincts and drives in the development of his personality. If indeed the roots of Man's behaviour are to be found in the animal kingdom, then it follows that our animal inheritance might account for our failures to be "fully human". This is an appealing idea, and is in some ways a useful balance to another popular notion which sees the environment and family background as the sole determinants of Man's nature. But it is a dangerous idea, and as we shall see, simplistic in the extreme. If our failures are built in, is there any hope at all? This point of view has been developed by Arthur Koestler in his book *The Ghost in the Machine* and a number of articles, which have been published widely throughout the United States and the United Kingdom in reputable journals, and deserve serious consideration. In the April issue of *Chemistry in Britain,* Koestler argues that "during the last explosive stages of the evolution of *Homo sapiens,* something has gone wrong; that there is a flaw, some subtle engineering mistake built into our native equipment which would account for the paranoid streak running through our history". This flaw Koestler refers to as a "congenitally disordered mental condition": he sees man as suffering from a "biological malfunction", a "species-specific disorder of behaviour". Although this is not science, I like Koestler's discussion in so far as he bases it on a consideration of uniquely human behaviour patterns, and I agree with him that in the search for an understanding of Man we should not neglect those characters which are uniquely human and not shared by other animals. Man is not in fact an ape, nor is he a carnivore, and the determinants of his behaviour are unlikely to be paralleled among birds. But when Koestler adds to his diagnosis that Man's neocortex "has evolved too fast for the good of its possessor" he again displays a surprising misapprehension of the process of evolution. The idea that something can go wrong in evolution is meaningless.

We can project upon the natural world our own value systems (cows are good and useful, tapeworms bad and revolting), but these judgments relate to our needs, and are not scientific. To say that something went *wrong* during Man's evolution is without meaning. Each evolutionary product (Man included) has survived because it has become adapted to its particular environmental niche. In the process of adaptation Man has evolved peculiar behaviour patterns, as so many other animals have. The female spider kills the male; birds desert their nests; dogs eat their young; lions kill lions, *in certain circumstances.* The subjective beauty and richness of the animal and plant worlds, as well as their occasional obscenity, is the product of evolution. Evolution does not "make mistakes": evolution is the most creative process in the universe, and the extinction of certain species is just part of that creative process. Any species is, by definition, a success—its replacement another success: this is the mode of creation.

Man's condition is not and cannot be accounted for by postulating an inbuilt flaw: the hypothesis of congenital defect sounds like the doctrine of the Fall, but it is more dangerous because the defect is irreversible. (Christianity has at least taught us that Man can become whole.) Koestler's man can only be rendered harmless—a horrible thought. Writers like Koestler cling to the more lurid findings of anthropology and dwell on such behaviour as human sacrifice, modern warfare, and so on. But what are the facts? Anthropology teaches us clearly that Man lived at one with Nature until, with the beginnings of agriculture, he began to tamper with his ecosystem: an expansion of his population followed. It was not until the development of the temple towns (around 5000 BC) that we find evidence of inflicted death and warfare. This is too recent an event to have had any influence on the evolution of human nature. For millions of years early Man had enjoyed, with other primates, a stable and peaceful adaptation. Modern bands of hunters and gatherers, such as Bushmen, are small self-contained groups that live in peace with their neighbours, and a similar situation existed throughout the vast span of human prehistory. For a long time now, anthropologists have recognized that the principal means of Man's adaptation has been cultural: *those beliefs, customs and practices that are learned.* Man is not programmed to kill and make war, nor even to hunt: his ability and desire to do so are learned from his elders and his peers when his society demands it. All Man's varied activities arise from the flexibility of his cultural behaviour, and it is this flexibility which allows him to colonize such a variety of habitats throughout the world.

What, in this case, is the point of studying Man's biology? In the first place, a study of evolution shows us clearly the nature of animal adaptation. There are no flaws, no mistakes, no good and no evil. Animals which survive are adapted to their environment. Man has enlarged his environmental niche by the evolution of culturally determined behaviour. This kind of behaviour can be extremely flexible and variable, and will contain facets which other societies may or may not judge to be evil. The Aztecs who sacrificed their young men and women, and the crusaders who went to war, did not recognize the evil of their actions, and today those who pollute our environment do not apparently yet recognize the much greater evil of theirs. Let us say merely that some behaviours are non-adaptive: it is non-adaptive to destroy your environment (this is so obvious, yet sadly uncomprehended): it is non-adaptive to live so close together that stress and its attendant symptoms result from overcrowding (another obvious fact). If you want to preserve your environment without overcrowding then you must reduce your population. So overpopulation is also non-adaptive. If we don't act on these facts, we shall destroy ourselves without much delay. If our errors are cultural, not biological, this is grounds for optimism: but it also means we cannot blame anyone but ourselves. To blame the state of affairs on our biology is not only dangerously irresponsible; it has no basis in fact. A simplistic comparison of Man with any animal misses the point of everything that anthropology has learned about Man.

The biological anthropologist is qualified to take a stand on such issues, and to condemn inaccurate popularization of biological research. The significance of the animal roots of human behaviour is not unimportant; indeed, this area of research is of pressing relevance. But the interpretation of these data is complex. The animal roots of human nature determine Man's potential: his culture realizes it. The neural mechanism of learning, including speech production, is inherited and genetically determined: the actual form of the resulting behaviours is determined by an individual's social context, and is called culture. Our evolutionary history, our biology, makes culture possible, but the biological mechanism is distinct from the cultural behaviour because the former is genetically determined, and subject to natural selection; the latter is socially transmitted, and socially selected. Though culture is a product of biology, of Nature, it is distinct from it in its mode of transmission and of adaptation. There is no good reason to doubt that our political and moral difficulties arise primarily from self-perpetuating features of child-rearing which result from, and at the same time maintain, some of the particular conditions of modern society. The human condition is not the result of a biological "flaw", and its "cure" does not involve adjustment of brain chemistry. The vicious circle is cultural; it follows that it can be broken by cultural means.

VIII. The Road to Civilization

Civilization is something that most of us take for granted. But what, really, is civilization? In many people's minds the term connotes a superior way of living—although superior to *what* is not necessarily clear. This is certainly not what anthropologists mean by civilization, nor is it a useful approach to the subject.

Civilization is a way of life. It is neither inherently better nor worse than any other way of life, but it is distinctive. Although social scientists have yet to agree on an exact definition, the following one is serviceable and reasonably well accepted. Civilization, then, consists of all social forms that embody four of the following five elements: (1) agriculture, (2) urban living, (3) a high degree of occupational specialization and social differentiation, (4) social stratification, and (5) literacy (at least for favored or elite groups). Thus, for example, Early Dynastic Egypt qualifies as a civilization even though it was not urban, as do the pre-Columbian civilizations of the Americas that lacked writing.

Virtually all of the spectacular advances in human skills and knowledge have been spawned in the context of civilized society. But many thoughtful people question the price of these accomplishments, especially with regard to the apparently inevitable social stratification and exploitation of subordinate groups that seem to characterize all civilizations thus far. However, whatever one's evaluation of the benefits and costs of civilization, one thing is clear: The process of civilization emerging—once it gets under way—is irreversible, and groups that attempt to resist the process are either pushed into the marginal and undesirable regions of the world, destroyed, or absorbed in spite of their opposition. Hence, in this section we consider the road that has led to civilization.

Civilization as we know it is inconceivable without the prior emergence of food production techniques—that is, plant and animal domestication (sometimes called the agricultural revolution). Hence, this section consists of three parts. Part A contains selections about preagricultural society; Part B is about the emergence of food production; and in Part C we focus on various aspects of the flowering of civilization in the Old World. (Because this book is aimed primarily at a North American audience, the next section is devoted to developments in the New World.)

A. Foraging Societies

Pfeiffer's article "Man the Hunter" begins the narrative of the remarkable human success story—which saw a marginal primate emerge as the dominant life form on this planet some 20 million years ago. Pfeiffer argues that by adopting hunting as a major subsistence strategy our ancestors locked themselves into a causal chain that led to the development of intrinsically human social patterns, including the cooperative division of labor between males and females. These patterns, then, became the base on which all subsequent developments of human sociocultural evolution rest.

Smith's "Stone-Age Man on the Nile" moves from the general to the particular and takes a close look at a specific ecological niche; it views the nature of the adaptations that human groups developed in the Nile region for coping with its challenges. These adaptations are shown to have underlain the civilization that emerged in this region after the local introduction of agriculture.

B. Food-Producing Societies

Scholars still debate the question of where, when, and how people invented agriculture. Although we may never know the exact causes of the emergence of food production, we do know that it was a very successful subsistence strategy. It spread rapidly from the few centers where it was independently invented and became the foundation of all ancient—and modern—societies. In "The Origins of Agriculture" Darlington traces its emergence in three relatively autonomous areas: the Middle East, the Far East, and the Americas. This is followed by Harris' "The Origins of Agriculture in the Tropics," which makes a strong ecological case for the tropics—not semiarid hilly regions—as the environment where the earliest agricultural experiments were attempted and mastered.

C. Civilization in the Old World

Like civilization itself, most of us take cities for granted. But what is a city? Although intuitively the answer may seem clear, scholars disagree. While some stress the concentration of people in a relatively confined space as the defining feature of cities, others suggest that it is not crowding in itself that makes cities unique but, rather, the concentration of a large number of diverse social processes within a relatively confined population. A definition that we think you will find useful is an attempt at a middle course in the debate. We suggest that a city is defined by (1) the presence of a substantial population living in (2) a confined area with (3) a considerable portion of the population consisting of nonagricultural occupational specialists.

Just as the adoption of a hunting subsistence mode was critical in setting the course of human evolution, and just as the "agricultural revolution" was an irretrievable turning point in the development of society, so too the emergence of cities marks a qualitatively new stage in human existence. Pfeiffer considers "How Man Invented

Cities'' and some of the unintended consequences of their rise; as he suggests, we are both the beneficiaries and the victims of the process.

In "Wheels and Man" de Borhegyi explores the history and consequences of another fundamental invention on which society as we know it rests; and that article together with Wertine's "Pyrotechnology: Man's First Industrial Uses of Fire" will provide you with a view of the processes through which the principal technological elements of modern civilization developed.

A. Foraging Societies

MAN THE HUNTER 33

By JOHN PFEIFFER

Five million years ago a small band of hominids called australopithecines
abandoned a vegetarian diet in favor of meat. From them, man the
hunter evolved—with all his predatory instincts, his distrust of strangers,
and his notions of family and friends

In this reconstruction, our first hunting ancestor, the australopithecine, chases game on the African plains.

Whatever one happens to think about the future of man, and the pessimists seem more vocal than the optimists nowadays, we have certainly enjoyed a spectacular past. Indeed, viewed in broad biological perspective, the past has been a success story without precedent. The first "hominid," the first member of the family of man, started out as nobody in particular, as a face in the crowd. He was one species among a wide variety of primates, and not a particularly distinguished species at that. Most of his fellow primates had been around a long time before he arrived on the scene and were more fully adapted to life in the trees.

That was some fifteen to twenty million years ago, only yesterday in evolutionary terms, and a great deal has happened since then. A near ape confined to narrow stretches in and around tropical forests has developed into the most widespread of all primates. We live practically anywhere—in treeless polar regions, in bare and bone-dry desert places, in the thin atmosphere of mountain slopes more than three miles high—and our eyes are currently on the stars, on the possibility of settling elsewhere in the solar system or beyond. We, the descendants of a minor breed, have become dominant with a vengeance, the only species with the power to remake or ruin a planet.

There can be no simple explanation for the phenomenon of man. But considerable evidence supports the notion that one of the major forces in prehistory, in the process that led to human beings, was the rise of hunting. Hunting represented a significant break with deep-rooted primate traditions. All primates but man live predominantly on plant foods, and if our ancestors had followed established feeding patterns and remained vegetarians, the odds are that we would still be more apish than human, still be wild animals foraging in the wilderness.

Hunting was no exception to the general rule that far-reaching changes in human evolution—in the evolution of all species, for that matter—come at a slow pace rather than in melodramatic bursts. In the beginning it was simply a case of stopgap measures calculated to obtain a somewhat larger supply of food than could be provided by plants alone, an activity that apparently could be pursued without radical changes in living habits. But there were changes as hunting became more and more prevalent, until it resulted in the reshaping of hominids both biologically and socially, and to such an extent that important aspects of our behavior today reflect the persisting influence of events that took place during the distant prehistoric past.

According to continuing research, much of it not yet published, this development included the three following stages:

Individual hunting. A stage during which hominids went chiefly after small game and probably did some scavenging; starting perhaps 5,000,000 or more years ago.

Group hunting. This stage was marked by an increasing emphasis on big game, sharing, and sexual division of labor, and began about 1,500,000 years ago.

Corporate hunting. The final stage probably featured the exploitation of great migratory herds on a large-scale, systematic basis, with long-range planning and food storage, and started some 40,000 to 50,000 years ago.

For a glimpse of the earliest hunting hominids, imagine that you are a spectator transported by a time machine to a world long since vanished, an African savanna world that still belongs to zebras and giraffes and vast antelope herds and their predators. Some strange and yet half-familiar animals are squatting not far from a rocky ledge, feeding on grass and roots. They look rather like small chimpanzees, except that when one of them hears a rustling sound, he stands upright like a man and listens intently, with a surprisingly human expression on his face.

Suddenly he sees what made the

noise, a hare moving near a low thorn-bush, and is off after it. The chase ends quickly. The hare darts away in a swift zigzag path, easily outdistancing its pursuer for fifty yards or so, and seems well on its way toward a successful escape. But then it leaps over a log and freezes in its tracks on the other side, crouching against the ground as though being stone-still would make it invisible. The hominid comes running up to the log, reaches over to grab the hare, and kills it with one neck-wringing motion. Picking up a sharp rock, he proceeds to dismember his victim and eat it raw on the spot.

This brief and hypothetical encounter is based partly on studies of fossil remains found in Africa during the past forty-five years and partly on observations of the behavior of living primates in the wild. The first hunters weighed fifty pounds or so on the average, stood about four feet tall, and belonged to a breed known as "australopithecines," or "southern apes," although the name does not do them justice. They were rather less than humans, to be sure, but considerably more than apes.

The australopithecines were a product of ten million years of evolution. Their predecessors had begun shifting from fruits and other forest foods to such open-savanna fare as grasses and roots and grains, perhaps because of population pressure in the trees, and not long before, the australopithecines had lived on a similar diet. Now they were vegetarians in the process of being corrupted. Not that meat eating is remarkable for primates. Contemporary savanna-dwelling baboons will eat vervet monkeys, hares, and fauns that happen to lie in their paths, but only occasionally, and more than 99 per cent of their food is plant food.

But baboons eat larger quantities of meat during droughts, and the australopithecines may have had to do the same. For them, however, it was not a matter of occasional dry-season emergencies. Dry conditions were spreading over wide continental areas, producing a permanent "emergency," which is probably the chief factor that brought about meat eating on a regular basis. The practice started at least two or three million years ago, the age of the oldest known stone tools (bashing and cutting tools found during the past year near Lake Rudolf in Kenya), and may well have started two to three million years before that.

We can make some educated guesses about the hunting techniques of remote prehistory. For example, like the aborigines of the Australian Western Desert, our ancestors may have erected blinds near water holes, piles of rocks behind which they could hide until their prey came within striking distance. They were probably capable of building such simple structures. Excavating in the Olduvai Gorge—one of the world's richest sites for hominid remains—Louis Leakey, director of the Center for Prehistory and Paleontology in Nairobi, has found traces of a stone wall or windbreak in deposits nearly two million years old.

Then as now, survival required an intimate knowledge of the ways of other animals, particularly an ability to take advantage of their instincts, their built-in escape tactics. The sight of a potential meal moving away at top speed can be a highly discouraging experience for a relatively sluggish predator, and it takes a special kind of wisdom to keep up the chase, confident that sooner or later the prey will go into a freeze-and-crouch pattern. Hares do this, as do certain birds, including a type of partridge whose bones have been found at some of the oldest Olduvai campsites.

Stalking is another ancient and effective technique. But as Leakey has learned from years of practice, it demands a measure of patience rarely found among hunters who are not playing for keeps, whose lives do not depend on hunting. Once, near a lake outside Nairobi, he camouflaged himself with leafy branches stuck in his belt and started stalking a gazelle

ADAPTED FROM *Vertebrate Paleontology* BY ROMER, THIRD EDITION

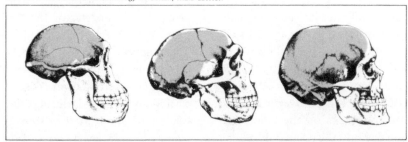

The skulls and brains of the australopithecine, Neanderthal man, and Cro-Magnon man are shown left to right. A big-game hunter, Neanderthal man had a human-sized brain, but lacked the cerebral development of the fully human Cro-Magnon man.

about 250 yards away. He advanced slowly as long as the gazelle had its head down to graze. But whenever it stopped grazing and raised its head to look around, he stopped too. He was always one move ahead of the animal. For example, he anticipated the instant of head-raising: "Just before the gazelle looks up, it seems to raise one shoulder a bit higher than the other. That's my signal to stop moving."

Leakey kept on the alert, observing the positions of other gazelles and nearby birds that might call out in alarm at a sudden movement and give him away. He noted possible sources of food in case his prey should escape, such things as a large snail, birds' nests, and an anthill. At last, after two long hours of stalking, he found himself poised only six feet from the gazelle. The hunt ended when he brought it down with a flying tackle, perfected during his university rugby days.

Hunting resulted in a breakdown, or rather, a partial breakdown, of rugged individualism. As far as getting food is concerned, each member of a troop of nonhuman primates is strictly on its own. That even includes infants after their first year: if a mother is feeding and her infant reaches for some of her food, she will push the child away. But hunting involves sharing, apparently from the very beginning. The existence of australopithecine base camps suggests that they established places where they could await the return of hunters with meat for the troop.

Inevitably, as the hunters became more ambitious, there was more to share. Small game predominated at the oldest Olduvai living sites—hares, tortoises, rats, lizards, and migratory birds, as well as the young of various antelopes. But excavations at later sites in Africa and Europe indicate a gradually increasing preference for a diet that included a higher proportion of big game, a change dictated largely by economics. It may take many hours of intensive small-game hunting to yield the amount of food represented by the killing of a single large antelope. Two or three men hunting together for big game in abundant savanna lands can obtain far more than two or three times as much meat as a lone man in search of small game.

Such tactics were important not only as a way of obtaining meat in large packages. From the standpoint of survival, they were not strictly necessary. Our prehistoric ancestors could, and often did, get along quite adequately, if less efficiently, on a diet consisting solely of small game and various kinds of plants. The shift to the hunting of big game is noteworthy mainly for its social impact. In fact, it helped trigger the most significant chain of developments in the evolution of hominids since they came down from the trees and took up meat eating in the first place.

This trend probably began gathering momentum between 2,000,000 and 1,000,000 B.C., and was certainly well established by about 300,000 years ago.

The oldest known prehistoric site outside Africa, the Vallonet cave located on a Mediterranean cliff in France, contains a few chopping tools that were used nearly a million years ago and a museumful of large-animal fossils, including those of rhinoceros, hippopotamus, brown bear, wild boar, and deer. A somewhat more recent site near the village of Torralba in north-central Spain, excavated by Leslie Freeman and Clark Howell of the University of Chicago, has yielded, among other things, the remains of some forty horses and as many elephants, most of which seem to have been deliberately driven into a swamp.

The fossil record hints at the full evolutionary impact of this sort of activity. The period that saw the rise of big-game hunting also saw a notable expansion, and probably a basic reorganization, of the hominid brain and the coming of creatures who had definitely crossed the borderline region between pre-man and man. The most advanced australopithecines had brains with a volume of some 600 cubic centimeters, about the size of a small grapefruit. Estimates based on a study by David Pilbeam of Yale University suggest that within a million years their descendants had brains averaging more than half again as large—and in some cases twice as large, which is almost comparable to the brains of people today.

Pilbeam and other investigators point to a direct relationship between big-game hunting, the development of more complex brains, and the appearance of the first men, members of the species Homo erectus. Natural selection went to work on the hunters. Bands that happened to include individuals with larger-than-average brains tended to outhunt and outlive bands made up of smaller-brained individuals. The inference is that the former were better able to think things through beforehand—preparing ambushes and pitfalls, arranging schedules and signals, using and improving whatever crude form of language they had at the time, and making better tools, a development that seems somehow to have been closely connected with the development of language.

Another advance contributing to the hunting way of life was the use of fire, the earliest known traces of which have been found in a cave not far from Vallonet. The lights went on about 750,000 years ago. Little spots of fire appeared in valleys that had always been dark at night. Fire, originally brought into caves for warmth, acquired another function, that of keeping animals away; and later it was used as an offensive weapon to stampede animals. Signs of burned grass indicate that fire may have been used at Torralba to drive big game into bogs.

Fire also brought a longer day. Hominids, like most forest and savanna animals, had always lived sunrise-to-sunset lives. Now they had extra time to gather at firesides when the hunt was done and review the day's successes and the day's failures, the big ones that got away. The hearth became the first family circle. We have no archaeological proof of ritual activities during this period, but it is quite possible that legends and hunting ceremonies, accompanied by dancing and rhythmical noisemaking, originated around early hearths. Flame and the crackling of burning wood and the moving shadows on cave walls aroused a variety of emotions, and may have served as a kind of stimulant.

Life was becoming more and more complicated, even in those days. The expansion of the brain itself, the most human thing about human beings, introduced a host of difficulties and confronted nature with a bio-engineering problem that has never been solved to everyone's satisfaction. The birth of bigger-brained babies called for an enlarged female pelvic opening and wider hips. But there are limits in that direction, one of them being the fact that wider hips result in an undesirable decrease in running speed and general mobility. So evolution achieved a compromise: hips became a little wider, while babies were born with brains designed to do most of their growing after birth.

The compromise was in line with an established trend in primate evolution; the repercussions have been enormous. The brain of a newborn rhesus monkey has already attained 75 per cent of its final adult size, and the infant is ready to forage for itself at the age of one. But Homo erectus infants came into the world with brains only about a fourth of adult size; the infants were helpless for four or five years, and more completely helpless than the offspring of any other primate. Incapable of either following or clinging to their mothers, they evolved special ways of actively attracting and summoning grownups, notably with the smile and an entire repertory of cries.

Bigger brains affected the habits of mothers as well as those of infants. Prolonged infant dependency meant prolonged maternal dependency. Just as infants needed a mother's care longer, so mothers relied more than ever before on males for defense, help in obtaining food and firewood, and more active participation in the rearing of offspring. The psychoanalyst Erik Erikson of Harvard speaks of the fear of being abandoned as "the most basic feminine fear, extending over the whole of a woman's existence," and that fear may have developed during Homo erectus times, along with new ways of attracting and holding males.

The typical pattern for female primates, for all female mammals, is to be sexually receptive during a brief period of the month only. They come into estrus, or sexual heat, at or immediately following ovulation, tending to be indifferent and unreceptive during the rest of the month. The human female is the only female in which estrus has disappeared, and according to one theory, the evolutionary advantage of the disappearance was that she could become sexually receptive throughout the month and thus improve her chances of tying the male, and eventually a particular male, more securely to her and her offspring.

Developments like these marked the beginnings of monogamy, and an early phase in the prehistory of the human sort of love. They also marked changes in males, changes emphasized in an important study by Lionel Tiger of Rutgers University. Male-male ties were becoming stronger, along with male-female ties. Hunting gave a new meaning to the feelings of man for man. Relationships became closer, more emotionally charged, in the excitement of the chase and the kill, the satisfaction of working as a team, and the sharing of intense experiences and nights at remote camps.

Larger brains, prolonged infant and maternal dependency, changes in sexual behavior—these were some of the consequences of the new kind of primate co-operation that came when a few men began making a regular practice of going out together to kill meat on the hoof. But the story of hunting has another, a final, chapter. The shaping of modern man may have been related to further advances in the technology of killing big game and may have involved events following the appearance of Neanderthal man about 100,000 years ago.

Neanderthal man was a full-fledged member of our species, Homo sapiens, which had appeared more than 150 millenniums earlier with the passing of Homo erectus. His forehead was lower and more sloping than ours, and he had heavier limbs and heavy bone ridges over his eyes. Contrary to popular opinion, however, he was neither brute nor savage; he stood fully erect and is known to have been a highly accomplished hunter. Investigators who have spent time among the Eskimos still do not understand how he managed to live through the long and bitter glacial winters of western Europe.

His fate was determined not by climate but by the evolution of a superior breed. Neanderthal man represented a special kind of Homo sapiens, a subspecies that never made it, but came very close. He lived always on the verge of becoming fully human, or at least as human as we are. For example, judging by a few recent finds of shapes scratched on bone, he was groping to express something and had a vague feeling for pattern and design.

One region of special interest in the study of Neanderthal man lies at the eastern end of the Mediterranean, along the slopes of mountain ranges running roughly parallel to the coastline of Israel, Syria, and Lebanon. This region includes three sites on which traces of a transitional people have been found, people who were definitely Neanderthals, but not like those typical of western Europe. In a cave and nearby rock shelter on the slopes of Mount Carmel, for example, investigators have excavated the remains of individuals with less massive brow ridges, somewhat more rounded skulls, more prominent chins, and smaller faces. The remains date back 40,000 to 50,000 years.

Sally Binford of the University of New Mexico, an archaeologist who has excavated in the Near East, has a theory about why the change occurred in that region and at that time. For one thing, the climate was becoming slightly drier, producing a pattern of seasonal rainfall and affecting the behavior of wild cattle and other herd animals. During the summer the animals grazed on the relatively damp coastal plains, and during the fall, when grasses became scarce, they moved up along green wooded valleys into the foothills, where highland meadows were watered by late fall rains.

Up to this point in human evolution most hunters probably killed one animal at a time, the idea being to stalk a herd and go after a particular individual, often an individual weakened by advanced age or injury. Lions, wild dogs, and other carnivores use similar tactics, which are well suited for groups of three or four hunters. But conditions were ripe for a change along the slopes of the Near Eastern mountains, and according to Miss Binford, late Neanderthal people had the wits to take advantage of their opportunities.

This was the beginning of corporate hunting, with its emphasis, as it were, on "mass production" methods. Large groups of hunters, perhaps as many as twenty to thirty, gathered to wait, not at places where the game was, but at places where their prey could be expected to come in the near future—at narrow passes and natural blinds along the traditional routes of migratory herds. Certain sites in the area are located at such points and include what may be interpreted as further evidence for the Binford theory, a sharp increase in the proportion of wild-cattle bones. Incidentally, the animals did not behave like the docile, mild-eyed creatures of contemporary pastures; the bulls measured more than six feet at the shoulder and were probably fierce, fast on their feet, and well built for fighting back.

Corporate hunting, the most advanced stage of prehistoric food gathering, may have provided the main stimulus for the coming of the most advanced of the hominids. New tactics presumably brought a new need for the ability to look ahead and devise increasingly sophisticated plans. Great quantities of tools would have to be manufactured beforehand, and individuals assigned to special tasks in preparing ambushes and killing, in large-scale butchering, and finally in sharing the meat. These and other organized activities would have favored the development of the brain, not so much in its over-all size, since Neanderthal man had a brain as large as ours, but in certain areas—especially those areas located at the front and sides of the brain and concerned with language and long-range planning.

The record is clear on one basic point. About 35,000 to 40,000 years ago the heavy-browed Neanderthal man of western Europe was replaced by Cro-Magnon man, and prehistory's golden age had begun, an age that culminated in the magnificent cave art of southern France and Spain. The general opinion is that the newcomers originated in the Near East and adjacent areas, and that they were people essentially like us. Or, to put it another way, we have a great deal in common with them psychologically and socially, which is perhaps the most important reason for the current interest in human evolution among scientists and laymen alike.

The past is not something over and done with. It is alive in man, in the sense that some of the things he does most easily, the things that come most naturally, are hang-over responses considerably less useful and relevant today than they once were. We have been wild animals roaming the wilderness for more than 15,000,-000 years, hunters for perhaps 5,000,000 years, and civilized —or rather, partially and intermittently civilized—for the last few millenniums only. So it is hardly surprising that upon occasion we behave inappropriately.

According to one estimate, the world's total hominid population two or three million years ago was about 125,000 individuals, all of them in Africa. Man has been a minority species so long that he reacts to "ghost" circumstances, circumstances that no longer exist, like the punch-drunk ex-prize fighter who the instant he hears a bell is up and on his feet in fighting stance. The sight of a stranger in a small town may arouse the precise feelings of hostility and distrust that the

PAINTING BY Z. BURIAN, COURTESY OF PAUL HAMLYN LTD.

Neanderthalers drive ibexes over a cliff, exemplifying the most advanced stage of hunting: highly organized mass roundups of game.

sight of a stranger aroused long, long ago, when hominids spent their entire lives as members of small hunting bands and anything new was a shock and a threat.

Being frightened by novelty is only part of man's instinctive small-band psychology, only one sign that he lives partly in a vanished world. His capacity to care for others tends to be limited. Generally speaking, a person feels deep love for a few close relatives only, and perhaps for a few close friends. Beyond that, there is a rather rapid falling off of concern; he is not really moved by the problems and frustrations of people across the street or across the hall. This is fundamentally a hunter's behavior, the psychology of one who lives his life among a few of his fellows, rarely seeing anyone else.

Man's instinct is to take, and to take right now while the taking is good. After ages of living on his own among more numerous species, hunting and being hunted, learning to get his share of food and shelter, he has become a master exploiter. Now he has made a world that no longer has a place for exploiters, and yet his relationship to the land and to other animals continues to be primarily one of exploitation. He continues to behave as though the world were still a place of savannas and virgin forests that covered continents.

The existence of such instincts does not mean that man is doomed, that he is innately a killer and must sooner or later wipe himself out. Of all species Homo sapiens is by far the most adaptable. But change is never easy, and it demands a real effort—an act of creation—to control and modify behavior rooted in the past. The problem is to design environments as appropriate for modern man as the wilderness was for prehistoric man.

Studies of contemporary hunters, like the Bushmen of Africa's Kalahari Desert, indicate that man has lost certain important things in the process of becoming civilized. In most hunting societies men and women live on equal terms with one another, and murder and warfare are extremely rare.

Class distinctions and mass killing come with the passing of the hunt. Furthermore, hunters generally have an easy life. Travelers from affluent societies are responsible for the myth that primitive peoples are, and have always been, engaged in a bitter struggle for survival. Richard Lee of Rutgers reports that the Bushmen require no more than two or three days to obtain a week's supply of food, even in a semi-desert environment. They spend the rest of the time talking, playing games, and visiting friends and relatives. Man has never known true leisure since the end of his hunting days.

These facts do not call for a return to the hunt, a "return to nature." But they provide insights into current efforts to recover the desirable features of a past way of life, equality and nonviolence and leisure, as well as to modify the undesirable features, such as the distrust of strangers and novelty in general. Man today is what he has always been, a creature in transition—and, despite the pessimists, a creature with a future.

John Pfeiffer writes on a wide range of scientific topics and most recently has concentrated on the areas of archaeology and anthropology. His book The Emergence of Man *was published in 1970.*

34

Stone-Age Man on the Nile

Thousands of years before the first pharaohs, hunters and gatherers lived along the great river. Their adaptations to their environment underlay the later development of agriculture and high civilization

by Philip E. L. Smith

In Egypt today the annual rainfall south of Cairo, if any, is measured in millimeters. This has been true since the days of the pharaohs. In earlier times, however, the level of the Nile was much higher. The great river and its seasonal tributaries watered a countryside that was fertile and temperate in climate even though it was surrounded by inhospitable desert. This combination of circumstances makes prehistoric Egypt virtually a laboratory microcosm for the study of human adaptations.

When did men first inhabit the Nile Valley? Only in recent years has much been learned about Nilotic prehistory; even today knowledge is spotty. We do have proof that people representative of two general stages of human techno-cultural development, the Lower and Middle Paleolithic periods, were present in Lower (or northern) Egypt from about a million to 30,000 years ago. Apart from the evidence to be gleaned from stone tools, however, little is known about those early inhabitants of Egypt. For example, not a single human fossil from these periods has been found.

As we come to within some 22,000 years of the present, in the latter part of the Upper Paleolithic, a more detailed picture of Egyptian prehistory comes into view. We can begin to speak with some conviction of the way people lived, of their settlement patterns, economic activities and technological proficiencies, and of the environmental and climatic conditions that prevailed. It is of more than passing interest because

the Old World during the Upper Paleolithic has traditionally been seen against the background of the harsh glacial environment of Europe at that time, when small groups of hunters pursued such cold-climate animals as the woolly mammoth and the reindeer. A greater contrast in settings can scarcely be imagined than that between the chill, art-rich caves of the Pyrenees and the Dordogne on the one hand and the lush green sloughs and side channels of the Nile on the other, where the hippopotamus, the hartebeest and the gazelle took the place of the reindeer, the bison and the wild horse.

Most of our new knowledge about prehistoric Egypt is a by-product of the dam construction at Aswan in Upper (or southern) Egypt in the 1960's. The Egyptian and Sudanese governments, in association with the United Nations Educational, Scientific and Cultural Organization, invited many foreign archaeologists to salvage monuments and sample as many as possible of the sites that would eventually be submerged by the enlarged Nile reservoir. Some of those who responded, mainly prehistorians from Canada, the U.S. and the U.S.S.R., concentrated their efforts on sites that had been inhabited by early man. Their work, undertaken in collaboration with colleagues in such related fields as geology and paleontology, has greatly enhanced our understanding of the preagricultural populations of the Nile Valley at the time when the last glaciers were beginning to retreat in Europe.

Not all the early-man sites investigated during the 1960's were in danger of flooding. The area where my group from the National Museum of Cana-

KOM OMBO PLAIN, on the east bank of the Nile some 500 kilometers south of Cairo, is where the author and his colleagues inves-

224

da conducted excavations in 1962 and 1963 was threatened in a different way. The Kom Ombo Plain ("kom" is the Egyptian equivalent of the Near Eastern "tell" or "tepe," mound), about 50 kilometers north of Aswan, is an extensive area of ancient alluvial silts, which, although they are now desiccated, need only water pumped from the Nile to transform them into fertile farmland. Reclamation of this kind had begun at the turn of the century, when European promoters established pumping stations and developed sugar plantations on the plain. Now the Egyptian government decided to follow suit and resettle most of the population that would be flooded out of Egyptian Nubia in the remainder of the plain.

Many valuable Paleolithic sites at Kom Ombo had already been planted with sugarcane. My group, sponsored by the Canadian government, and a group from Yale University undertook to salvage or sample a fair number of those that were still undisturbed. In so doing we were following in the footsteps of a French engineer and amateur archaeologist, Edmond Vignard, who worked in a Kom Ombo sugar refinery in the early 1920's and made many useful observations at a time when the early-man sites of the plain were still relatively intact.

Other advantages in addition to Vignard's reconnaissance were available to us at Kom Ombo. One was that the stratigraphy, and thus the chronology, of the geological formations there has been worked out in considerable detail by Karl W. Butzer of the University of Chicago (together with his student Carl L. Hansen) and also by R. J. Fulton of the Geological Survey of Canada. These studies made it possible to match the various prehistoric sites with the geological record of fluctuations in the level and course of the Nile and also with changes in the local tributary streams that reflect past changes in local rainfall. The second major advantage was that whereas animal remains from the Paleolithic are both scarce and poorly preserved in most of Egypt, large quantities of bones are present at the Kom Ombo sites. The bones, of course, provide the investigator with invaluable clues to the early inhabitants' subsistence activities.

The environment in late Paleolithic times at Kom Ombo was the product of a complex interplay of factors. The behavior of the Nile itself—its long-term cyclical fluctuations, annual inundations, volume and velocity—was determined by climatic events far off in East Africa. Moreover, the local rainfall, the temperature and the behavior of the tributary streams flowing across the plain from their headwaters in the Red Sea Hills some 150 kilometers away were products of patterns of atmospheric circulation in the Northern Hemisphere, where the European glaciers were still influential. Both factors interacted further with the geomorphology of the plain and of adjoining areas. The result was a mosaic of microenvironments and habitats in a restricted geographical zone. In such an unstable ecosystem rapid shifts in the inventory of plants and animals, and in the exploitative methods of the human cultures subsisting on them, might be expected to occur as one or another variable was altered.

In the Nile Valley immediately north and south of Kom Ombo the river and its floodplain have long been confined to a narrow corridor that runs between sandstone cliffs and high terraces. At Kom Ombo, however, a series of geological faults has caused the cliffs to retreat eastward, so that a wide depression, extending over 500 square kilometers, lies along the east bank. From the prehistorian's viewpoint the most interesting features of the local geology are the sediments—silts, sands and pebbles—that were deposited between

tigated a series of Stone Age living sites dating back to between 15,-000 and 10,000 B.C. The site being excavated here belongs to cultures designated Sebekian and Silsilian, dating back to between 13,-000 and 12,000 B.C. In it the investigators found stone tools characteristic of the cultures and bones of animals hunted by inhabitants. Cliff in the background is part of the northern boundary of the plain.

15,000 and 10,000 B.C. by the Nile and its tributary streams. The Nilotic silts, the products of soil erosion far to the south in Ethiopia, were laid down when the river was considerably higher and more vigorous than it is today. They stand some 15 meters above the modern floodplain. It is in and on these silts, known as the Gebel Silsila Formation, that the late Paleolithic sites are found, in some places buried deep and revealed only by erosion or artificial cuts and in others lying exposed on the surface where the desert wind has blown away the concealing silt.

The plain today, with miles of green sugarcane plantations, vegetable fields and irrigation canals surrounding the new town of Kom Ombo, is very different from the arid, dusty wasteland of less than a century ago. It is also very unlike the plain of the late Paleolithic period. Archaeologists no longer accept the notion that before agriculturists transformed the Nile Valley in Neolithic times it was hostile jungle and swamp, difficult to reach, inhabited by dangerous animals and holding little attraction for man. We now know that on the contrary the valley was a zone of fairly open terrain where hunters, gatherers and fishermen had access to a biomass of aquatic and terrestrial resources that could support a considerable population. Moreover, the Kom Ombo Plain was a better than average segment of the Nile Valley, and its inhabitants must have been among the best-nourished people in the late Paleolithic world.

The climate in Upper Egypt at that time was only slightly less arid than it is today. We may guess at an annual precipitation of 10 or 20 millimeters, falling mainly in the Red Sea Hills during the winter months. The permanent river and the seasonal tributaries flowing westward from the Red Sea uplands, however, largely canceled out the effects of inadequate rainfall at Kom Ombo. The range of temperatures was lower than it is today by perhaps 10 degrees Celsius, and in winter there could be frost.

By that time the Nile had long established its modern regime of summer flooding, induced by the monsoon rains in East Africa. From August to October the river rose to inundate areas that today lie far beyond its shrunken floodplain. At its height the swollen Nile cut long, meandering side channels across the Kom Ombo Plain, creating what were in effect islands until the waters ebbed late in the fall. The floodplain was probably about five kilometers wide. The human settlements were concentrated along the levees of the seasonal overflow channels when the Nile was

high and were shifted to the lower floodplain as the river receded. The banks of the tributaries, now dry wadis, have yielded few campsites; perhaps they were less attractive for settlement.

Little concrete paleobotanical evidence has been recovered at Kom Ombo, but it is possible to gain an overall impression of the vegetation, generally subtropical, that grew on the plain. In the low floodplain, in addition to a grassy mat that covered much of the area, a gallery forest of acacia, tamarisk, sycamore and Egyptian willow probably stood beside the main stream. Less dense growths of the same trees would have occupied the channel levees. Thorn trees probably grew in the larger tributary valleys, and the higher water table outside the zone of annual flooding probably supported a semidesert vegetation of low scrub or brush with dry grassland on the hills and scattered desert shrubs farther east. We can also assume a rich growth of aquatic flora—reeds, sedges, lotuses and papyrus plants—along the river, the side channels and the sloughs.

C. S. Churcher of the University of Toronto has analyzed the animal remains from our excavations. His work has revealed a surprisingly wide range of vertebrates: at least a dozen taxa of mammals, 22 of birds, three of fishes and one taxon of reptiles. Prominent among the mammals are a now extinct large wild ox (*Bos primigenius*), the bubal hartebeest (*Alcelaphus buselaphus,* a species still living in the Sudan) and several species of gazelle. These and the hippopotamus were the most important game animals. There were in addition hares, hyenas, a species of canine, bandicoot rats and possibly the so-called Barbary sheep (the aoudad, *Ammotragus lervia,* still found in North Africa).

In the streams and pools lived the large Nile catfish, the Nile perch and the African barbel, as well as clams, the Nile oyster and a species of soft-shelled turtle. Many of the bird bones are representative of migratory species; the Nile Valley was probably then, as it is now, an important flyway between Europe and Africa. Wading and diving birds included numerous goose and duck species, the cormorant, the heron, the flamingo, the spoonbill, the crane and the curlew. Apparently the elephant, the gi-

MAP OF THE NILE shows the course of the river from the Sudan (*bottom*) to the Mediterranean (*top*). Some 15 years ago the Egyptian and the Sudanese governments invited many foreign scholars to investigate archaeological sites, actual or potential, along the river that later were flooded by the new reservoir or were destroyed by land reclamation.

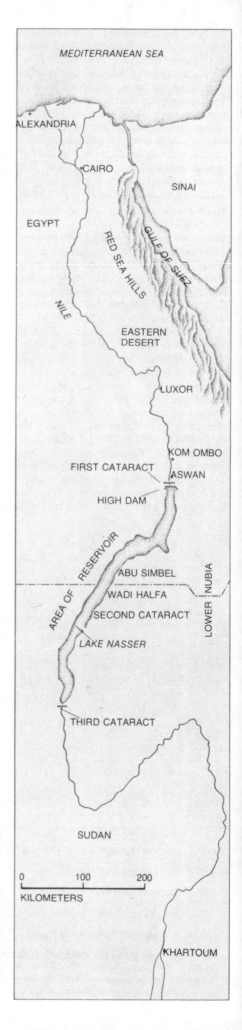

raffe, the rhinoceros and large carnivores such as the lion and the leopard were not present. The ostrich, the wild pig, the zebra and the crocodile may well have existed there, but we found no trace of them among the animal bones.

Such an abundant concentration of plant and animal resources must have made Kom Ombo one of the most attractive human habitats available anywhere in late Paleolithic times. An economy at once river-oriented and diversified was to emerge at Kom Ombo and flourish for at least 5,000 years. Even though much archaeological evidence has been destroyed and precise information on the vegetation is meager, we can to some extent plot the seasonal flow of food energy through the plain and attempt to show how human activities were accommodated to long- and short-term fluctuations in the energy flow.

The earliest of the Upper Paleolithic sites at Kom Ombo are about 17,000 years old. There were probably people on the plain before that time, but either their sites have not been preserved or they remain undiscovered. In any event in the centuries immediately preceding 15,000 B.C. rainfall at Kom Ombo was minimal, there was little seasonal runoff in the tributaries and vegetation and game were probably sparse away from the Nile. From about 15,000 to 10,000 B.C., however, rain was generally more plentiful and tributary runoff was greater. The climatic change evidently contributed to rich and varied cultural developments. The same general phenomenon, although differing in detail, has been reported by other excavators who have worked recently in Lower Nubia and Upper Egypt. Evidence of a cultural flowering up and down the Nile Valley has caused prehistorians to revise the traditional view that the later Paleolithic of the area was impoverished. At Kom Ombo alone during this 5,000-year interval we find emerging a series of styles in the manufacture of stone tools (which prehistorians call industries or sometimes, as a convenient fiction, cultures); they vary considerably in the form of the tools, the methods of manufacture and the kinds of stone the toolmakers preferred. We are still not entirely certain how this unexpected and seemingly anarchic diversity in tool production should be interpreted, but it is surely one of the most intriguing new aspects of the prehistory of Egypt.

The majority of the stone tools are small and light. Small flakes and blades were struck from a stone "core" and then chipped into tools. We find no implements that can be interpreted as axes or adzes, and only a small number of heavy tools (usually roughly split or chipped pebbles) appear to have been used for smashing or chopping. Some of the tools are only a few centimeters in length, small enough to be characterized as microliths. One can only assume that most of the stone artifacts were associated in one way or another with the subsistence activities of their makers; unfortunately, as is usually the case in Paleolithic studies, it is hard to ascertain the precise function or functions of an artifact with any degree of certainty.

The first late Paleolithic stone-tool industry recognized on the Kom Ombo Plain is called the Halfan. Carbon-14 determinations at several small campsites place the Halfan industry around 15,000 B.C. It is a curious industry com-

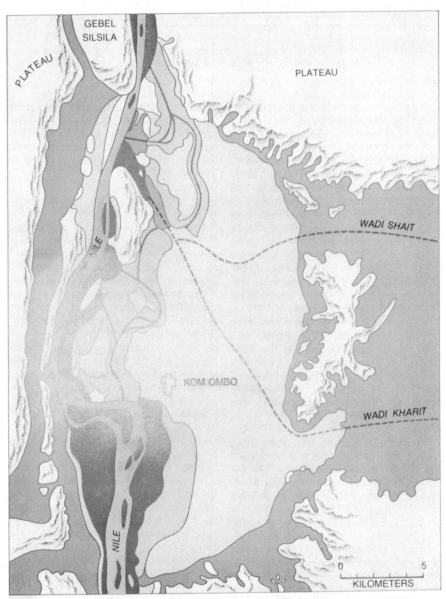

NILOTIC DEPOSITS BEFORE 15,000 B.C. (MASMAS FORMATION)

NILOTIC DEPOSITS 15,000–10,000 B.C. (GEBEL SILSILA FORMATION)

POST-10,000 B.C. NILE AND WADI DEPOSITS

MODERN NILE FLOODPLAIN ALLUVIUM   ROCK OUTCROPS AND HILLS

PREHISTORIC NILE CHANNELS

PREHISTORIC WADI TRIBUTARIES

MAP OF THE KOM OMBO PLAIN shows the prehistoric Nile channels, wadi streams and geological deposits. In the period between 15,000 and 10,000 B.C. the river was considerably higher and more vigorous and the climate somewhat less arid than today. Map is based on studies undertaken by Karl W. Butzer of the University of Chicago and his student Carl L. Hansen.

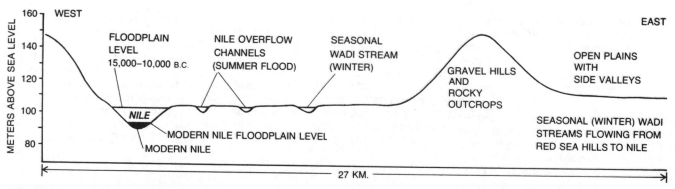

SCHEMATIC CROSS SECTION OF THE PLAIN on a line running east and west in the period between 15,000 and 10,000 B.C. shows height of the Nile, overflow channels and wadi streams. Annual flood of river covered a much greater area than it does today.

bining relatively archaic and relatively advanced technological features. The archaic feature is what prehistorians call the Levallois method of removing large flakes from a specially prepared core. The method was known in Egypt, in Europe and elsewhere for hundreds of thousands of years before the Upper Paleolithic period. The advanced feature is the fabrication of small flakes with lightly retouched edges.

Only a few Halfan sites have been found. Perhaps the Kom Ombo Plain was not densely occupied at the time. Indeed, it is not until about 13,000 B.C., following a phase when the volume of the Nile had decreased somewhat and its annual inundations were lower, that sites on the plain become fairly abundant.

A second industry, which we have called the Silsilian, and a third, known as the Sebekian, appear roughly between 13,000 and 12,000 B.C. The Silsilian industry specialized in microlithic tools: many small "backed" blades (that is, blades blunted on one edge) and even tiny triangles and trapezoids made on blades of such exotic multicolored stone as agate, jasper and quartz. The Sebekian industry featured longer, narrower blades with the edges lightly retouched by "nibbling," usually near the base; the makers showed a preference for gray or buff-colored flint. Beginning about 11,000 B.C. and continuing for several millenniums thereafter, a fourth industry, the Sebilian (identified and named by Vignard half a century ago), is found at Kom Ombo. Here the old Levallois technique of core preparation reappears: many of the flakes struck from the core were broad and thin. They were then chipped into geometric shapes, including large triangles and trapezoids as well as microliths. More or less contemporaneous with the Sebilian, and sharing certain of its traits, is a fifth group of artifacts we have named the Menchian industry. Many of the Menchian tools are made on rather thick, heavy flakes

and blades; they may have been used for scraping. Both the Sebilian and the Menchian artifacts seem to be associated with sandstone slabs and handstones that were evidently used for grinding or pulverizing.

To what extent these variations in stone-tool industries reflect distinct sociocultural groupings, or specialized subsistence activities, or the evolution of one or more traditions over a period of time, it is still difficult to say. The long-term cyclical oscillations of the Nile may well have had some impact on the cultural situation. When the level of the river dropped, as it periodically did for centuries or millenniums, many of the valley zones outside the Kom Ombo Plain where the floodplains were narrower would have been adversely affected as the annual inundations were more restricted. The total biomass of the plants and animals in such areas would have been reduced for long periods, and under such conditions there might have been a tendency for the human groups living in them to move into larger and stabler zones such as the Kom Ombo Plain. The migrations, whether temporary or permanent, of outside groups to the Kom Ombo Plain may help to explain some of the rapid cultural changes and replacements the stone-tool industries seem to reflect between 15,000 and 10,000 B.C.

The exploitable part of the Kom Ombo Plain, which includes the former Nile floodplain, the wadis and the groundwater zones but excludes the modern floodplain (then largely submerged) and isolated rocky outcrops, was probably about 400 square kilometers, or about 150 square miles. It is not easy to calculate the density of Paleolithic populations, but a very approximate figure, based on recorded populations of recent and still living nonagricultural peoples with diversified patterns of subsistence, is about one person per square mile. Thus it is likely that the

Kom Ombo Plain could have supported at least 150 people and perhaps as many as 300 under optimum conditions. It is of course unlikely that the population density was constant over the 5,000-year period.

Analyses of the animal remains, together with what we can infer of the river regime and the vegetation patterns, strongly suggest that the plain was capable of supporting human life not just seasonally but all year round. It is nonetheless highly unlikely that the population of the plain could have remained together as a single group throughout the year, or could have remained permanently in a single locality. Probably at any one time the population was split into a number of small bands, perhaps composed of related families who tended to hang together in a loose kind of organization. Each band probably moved in an annual cycle related to the seasonal availability of different food resources. Each of the bands may even have been identified with a certain territory on the plain, although these territories were probably not exclusive. Whether the entire population, or only those who recognized themselves as being culturally related, periodically came together for economic or social purposes we do not know, but judging by the behavior of living hunting peoples it is not unlikely.

The settlement system and subsistence strategy that prevailed were undoubtedly fluid, since they would have had to be correlated with seasonal variations in the abundance of food, just as biomass output itself was linked to short- and long-term pulsations in rainfall and river height. The output was probably spread fairly evenly over most or all of the year, although winter and spring (approximately from November through April) would have been the seasons of abundance. Much of the aquatic biomass, including fish, clams, oysters, waterfowl, turtles and hippopotamus, and such edible plants as water lily, wa-

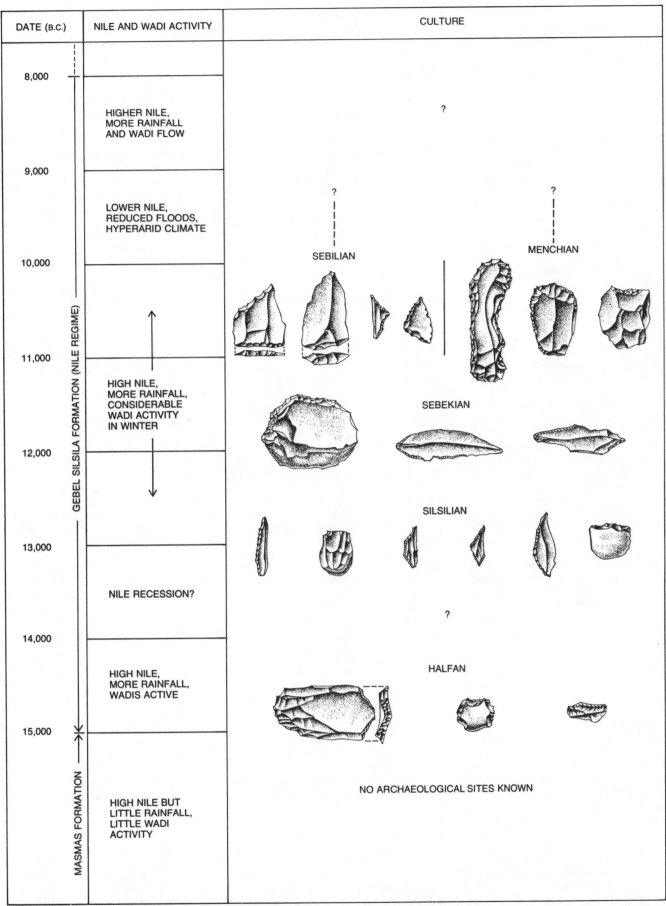

DATE (B.C.)	NILE AND WADI ACTIVITY	CULTURE

The chart columns read:

DATE (B.C.): 8,000 — 9,000 — 10,000 — 11,000 — 12,000 — 13,000 — 14,000 — 15,000

GEBEL SILSILA FORMATION (NILE REGIME)

MASMAS FORMATION

NILE AND WADI ACTIVITY:
HIGHER NILE, MORE RAINFALL AND WADI FLOW

LOWER NILE, REDUCED FLOODS, HYPERARID CLIMATE

HIGH NILE, MORE RAINFALL, CONSIDERABLE WADI ACTIVITY IN WINTER

NILE RECESSION?

HIGH NILE, MORE RAINFALL, WADIS ACTIVE

HIGH NILE BUT LITTLE RAINFALL, LITTLE WADI ACTIVITY

CULTURE:
?

SEBILIAN ?   MENCHIAN ?

SEBEKIAN

SILSILIAN

?

HALFAN

NO ARCHAEOLOGICAL SITES KNOWN

CHRONOLOGY OF CLIMATES AND CULTURES on the Kom Ombo Plain shows the relations between the two. The stone tools of the Halfan culture are characterized by flakes struck from a specially prepared core and by small blades with lightly retouched edges. The Silsilian culture specialized in microlithic tools, many of which are "backed," or blunted on one edge. The Sebekian culture featured long, narrow blades with edges lightly retouched by "nibbling." The Sebilian flakes, like the Halfan, were struck from a specially prepared core and were then often chipped into geometric shapes. The Menchian tools are heavy; many may have been used for scraping.

229

ter chestnut, water lettuce, water plantain, papyrus and other reeds, was probably available in all seasons. These foods would have been exploited along the side channels during the flood period from August through October and along the main stream at other seasons. Dry-land provender, including fruits, berries, nuts and edible gums from the acacia, the palm, the sycamore and other trees, and perhaps melons, cucumbers, the "Abyssinian banana" (*Ensete edula*) and various wild grass seeds, would have been most abundant in winter and spring, during and just after the rains. These plants would have been most common along the wadis but would also have grown on the desert steppe beyond them. Roots and bulbs should have been available throughout the year.

Most of the large mammals, particularly the wild ox and the hartebeest (the principal sources of meat), would also have been hunted in winter and spring. One hunting area was the marshy floodplain with its natural pastures beside the lowered river. The wadis and the grassy hills and plains to the east of Kom Ombo were a second area. The herds of wild cattle, unable to go for long periods without water, were almost certainly never far from the channels, pools and pastures of the floodplain and might even have been systematically culled by the hunters all year long. The hartebeests would have ranged more widely, and in the winter, when the tributary streams were flowing, they were probably found along the wadis. Remains of gazelles and asses and perhaps Barbary sheep suggest hunting forays into the drier open grasslands, hills and the fringes of the desert. Fowling was probably in the main a winter activity; many of the birds identified by the bones unearthed at Kom Ombo (for example the crane, smew, goosander and several other species of duck and goose) are migratory.

Late spring and early summer (from April through June) was probably a more difficult period of subsistence. As the heat and aridity increased, the Nile shrank to its lowest level, the grassy vegetation diminished and some of the game dispersed. At this time of year the hunting bands may have been forced to split up into smaller units, each perhaps consisting of a few nuclear families, and to spread out more widely in order to exploit the less abundant food resources of the plain until the summer floods resumed.

In terms of reconstructing seasonal activities on the Kom Ombo Plain, one of the most informative sites we exca-

vated was Gebel Silsila III, near the northern end of the plain about four kilometers east of the present Nile. The site stands near a side channel of the Nile that 15,000 years ago ran a few hundred meters from a range of sandstone cliffs. When we found the site in 1962, it was almost entirely buried under an accumulation of hard, carbonate-rich Nilotic silt as much as a meter thick, deposited by river floods soon after the site was abandoned. Only a scatter of flints and bones exposed on the wind-eroded surface betrayed the site's existence. With the aid of Robert Fulton, my assistant Morgan Tamplin and I spent several months excavating here in the winter of 1962–1963. The site proved to be stratified in two main levels: a rich Sebekian occupation, containing many stone tools and animal remains, overlay a somewhat poorer Silsilian one.

Between 13,000 and 12,000 B.C. the prehistoric inhabitants of the plain had settled near a small depression, some 10 meters in diameter, that held water during at least part of the year. Here they lived and ate, built their fires and made their stone artifacts. The large quantity of flint tools manufactured and discarded on the spot, the great number of broken animal bones and the overall size of the area occupied indicate that, at least for the Sebekian people who lived there last, this may have been an important base camp. They hunted cattle, hartebeest and gazelle (a variety of game that reflects the exploitation of several distinct microenvironments), ate an occasional hippopotamus, caught turtles, catfish and perch and killed at least 14 different kinds of birds. It is possible that the Sebekian group occupied the site during more than one season of the year, although not necessarily the year round or even for very long at any one time. For example, the bones of migratory birds suggest that the Sebekian group was at the site at some time between September and April. The bones of immature gazelles, which presumably, like their modern counterparts, were born either in January or in late July and August, show that the group was present at one or both of these times. The bones of immature hartebeests, born at any time between May and December, also point to summer and/or fall occupancy.

In addition to stone tools and animal bones two more intimate relics of human presence have come from the Gebel Silsila III site. One, found in the lower level, is a milk tooth from a Silsilian child less than seven years old. This evidence that children were among the early occupants of the site lends weight to the view that we are dealing here with a

family group rather than, say, a temporary encampment of adult hunters. The other relic is a lump of hardened mud from the upper, Sebekian level. It clearly shows impressions from the palm of a human hand, probably an adult's, and is one of the rare examples of a skin impression from the Paleolithic.

Putting together the data from all the sites at Kom Ombo, we are able to reach certain tentative conclusions about other aspects of the inhabitants' lives. First, there are no caves or sheltering rock overhangs in the surrounding cliffs, and so all the living sites on the plain were in the open. At none of the sites have we found traces of permanent dwellings: stone or mud construction or postholes that would indicate substantial wood shelters. We can assume that the inhabitants built brush huts, windbreaks or light tents, shelters that would have left few traces, much as the modern Bushmen and Australian aborigines do.

Second, tools made of bone or horn are rare. Wood was probably used more generally, but no trace of wood implements has survived. The inhabitants of the plain did not have pottery, so that it also seems likely that they used containers made of skin, basketry, bark or wood. They probably made nets and lines for fishing and perhaps fowling. Again, however, none of these artifacts have survived. Whether the bow and arrow were present is not known, but the small stone points of several industries may well have served as arrowheads. Small flint blades may have been set into wood knife handles or fish spears. Dugout or reed canoes and rafts would have been useful during the flood season, and perhaps for crossing to the west bank of the Nile, but again no evidence of such craft has survived.

Like most of the other Paleolithic peoples of the Nile Valley (but unlike many contemporaneous groups elsewhere), the inhabitants of Kom Ombo seem to have shown no interest in beads, pendants, bracelets or other personal adornments. Perhaps the red and yellow ocher found in some of the sites was used for body decoration. It is also possible that the spectacular plumage of such birds as the golden eagle, the osprey and the black kite, whose bones are found at the sites, were used for decorative purposes. We have no good evidence that any of the inhabitants engraved or sculptured bone and stone, as their Magdalenian contemporaries in Europe did. Their art, if they had any, may have been expressed in more perishable materials. Interesting scenes of wild animals, including cattle and hippopotamus, are engraved on the cliffs near our Gebel Silsila sites, but no one

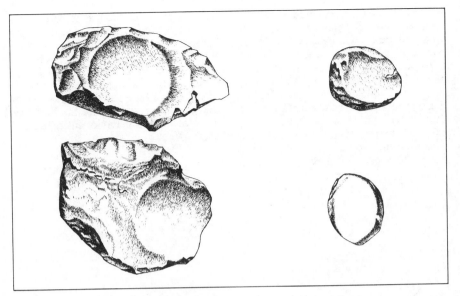

GRINDING STONES are associated with Sebilian and Menchian artifacts. Some were possibly used to process wild plant foods. Stones at left are grinding slabs; those at right are rubbers.

can prove they were the work of a late Paleolithic group. Physically the Paleolithic inhabitants of the Kom Ombo Plain were fully modern representatives of *Homo sapiens* and were apparently rather robust in build.

With the benefit of hindsight we can now see that many late Paleolithic peoples in the Old World were poised on the brink of plant cultivation and animal husbandry as an alternative to the hunter-gatherer's way of life. The new livelihood had its formal beginnings around the start of postglacial times in southwestern Asia and perhaps elsewhere as well. One current hypothesis about the origins of agriculture is that it was related to late Pleistocene population growth and increased pressure on food resources. This, the hypothesis contends, led in some cases to the greater exploitation of foods that up to that time had been comparatively neglected, particularly plants, smaller animals, birds, fish and mollusks.

J. Desmond Clark of the University of California at Berkeley and others have recently argued that some evidence for this trend may be seen at Kom Ombo and elsewhere in the lower Nile Valley. Between 13,000 and 10,000 B.C. there appears to have been a general tendency toward population increase and more numerous and larger settlements. At some sites, particularly those of the Menchian and Sebilian cultures on the Kom Ombo Plain, we find many grinding stones: artifacts that suggest the processing of plant foods, perhaps even wild seed-bearing grasses. None of these grasses has yet been identified with certainty, although millets, sorghum

and even barley have been postulated. At similar sites elsewhere in Egypt flint blades with a gloss or polish resembling that found on much used stone sickle blades have been reported. It has also been suggested that there may have been some tentative efforts at controlling or taming wild cattle, gazelles and other animals at about this time.

If there was such a trend toward the manipulation and domestication of plants and animals in Egypt at the end of the Ice Age, it would seem to have been a false dawn. We do not know much about human activities at Kom Ombo during the interval after 10,000 B.C. that is sometimes called the Epipaleolithic or Mesolithic. We do know, however, that a complex series of small-scale climatic and environmental changes took place. Contrary to earlier hypotheses, although there was a warming trend in Egypt at the end of the Pleistocene, it was not accompanied by either a sudden or a continuous period of desiccation. From about 10,000 B.C. until 3000 B.C. conditions fluctuated between the semiarid and the hyperarid. But no catastrophic drought, as some earlier archaeologists had believed, forced the hunter-gatherers out of the hills and plains into the narrow confines of the Nile Valley, where all at once, in propinquity with the appropriate plants and animals, they "invented" agriculture. Indeed, local rainfall seems actually to have increased for a time after 9000 B.C. and again about 5000 B.C.

Nevertheless, even though the tributaries continued their seasonal flow, the hydrological budget of the Nile itself now tended to be reduced as a result of

climatic changes in East Africa. The river's floods were more restricted, the water table was lowered and the wetlands shrank in extent. Although there were still periodic fluctuations in the size of the Nile, conditions were never quite the same again at Kom Ombo. The plain seems to have become a marginal zone, unable to support a population as large as that of the late Paleolithic. Over the next few thousand years most of Kom Ombo slowly reverted to near-desert conditions; the ephemeral wadi waters gradually faded away, and sometime late in the third millennium B.C. the present hyperarid climate of Egypt became established.

We know that in other parts of Upper Egypt after 10,000 B.C., and in Lower Nubia as well, a hunting and fishing way of life continued for at least 4,000 years more, although its practitioners appear to have been reduced in numbers. At Kom Ombo too some hunting-gathering-fishing groups probably still lived on the western edge of the plain near the river. The general reaction of the inhabitants of the Nile Valley to the changing environmental conditions seems to have been to place a greater emphasis on fishing and the procurement of other riverine foods in order to supplement the increasingly scarce supply of game animals and land plants. Possibly some of the brief hyperarid periods after 10,000 B.C. led to a rapid reduction in the populations of these plants and animals. Unlike certain groups in southwestern Asia, however, the early Egyptians had not developed a sedentary way of life based on villages and on the collection of wild plants, which under conditions of demographic or ecological stress would have promoted the plants' domestication. If an indigenous trend toward plant and animal domestication developed in the Nile Valley at all, it apparently never passed the incipient level. Such a trend may, however, have helped to preadapt the Egyptians to a ready acceptance of food production later.

When diversified food production finally arose in Egypt, perhaps around 5000 or 4000 B.C., or at least 2,000 years after its development in western Asia, it was evidently introduced from outside and utilized the familiar animals (goats, sheep and pigs) and cereals (wheat and barley) domesticated long before in Asia. The imported plants quickly took the place of those indigenous to Egypt because they were more productive, particularly after the advent of irrigation. They and the imported animals provided the economic base for Pharaonic civilization, which emerged about

3000 B.C. Nevertheless, it is interesting to note that in the earliest Pharaonic era, that of the Old Kingdom, the Egyptians showed a lively interest in domesticating local animals—wild cattle, gazelles, antelopes and even hyenas—and continued to make use of cranes, geese and ducks in sacrifices and for food. The roots of this practice may lie in the preagricultural traditions of the Nile Valley.

In recent years prehistorians working in many areas of both the Old World and the New have uncovered a great diversity of human specializations and adaptations that developed in the closing phases of the Pleistocene. Our knowledge of the riparian hunters, fishermen and gatherers of the Nile Valley provides a valuable addition to the data on these processes of local adaptation. Although we should not exaggerate the role of environmental change in our attempts to explain cultural change, no one denies that there are close, if still poorly understood, articulations between the two, particularly at the hunting-gathering level of cultural evolution. What is being learned from the work on the Kom Ombo Plain and at other localities along the Nile should be of value to all prehistorians in search of the principles underlying the development of human behavior in the distant past.

35

THE ORIGINS OF AGRICULTURE

The earliest grain farmers began to cultivate the wild ancestors of our crop plants about 10,000 years ago. Their unforeseen harvest was the transformation of human life

by C. D. Darlington

According to the notions of our forebears, early man first learned to forge and smelt iron to make his weapons and his tools. Then he tamed his beasts and tilled the earth, sowed the seeds of the plants he had collected for food, and so raised his crops. Finally, years of cultivation improved these crops to a standard that came to support agriculture. Man could now provide better fodder for his stock, and could, therefore, breed improved beasts. These developments had occurred in many parts of the world with different kinds of crops and stock on which the different civilizations were based.

This view of agriculture's origins had been reasonably supported by the European discovery of the American civilizations. and it was still generally held at the beginning of the nineteenth century. It showed man progressing almost inevitably by his own efforts, his own skill and intelligence, and in a way that commended itself well to the thought of the nineteenth century.

But in the middle of that century all these ideas were rudely shaken by a series of unforeseen discoveries. It was then that archeology began to show that agriculture had long preceded the smelting of metals. History and language began to indicate that crops had been carried far away from the places where they were first grown. And two naturalists, Darwin and De Candolle, argued that it was not cultivation in itself, but selection by the cultivator—the choice of species and the choice of variations to sow and propagate—that had played the decisive part in improving cultivated plants.

Darwin and De Candolle thus advanced our understanding of the origins of agriculture for the first time in two thousand years. In the hundred years that have followed them, however, a far greater upheaval of ideas has occurred. It has been set off from two directions. One was the study of how plant breeding and selection actually work among primitive farmers. This we owe largely to the Russian geneticist and plant breeder Nikolai Vavilov. The other was Willard Libby's 1947 discovery of the use of radiocarbon. This led to the physical dating of prehistoric remains and settled the arguments of earlier centuries. What happened when these two fields of inquiry, so utterly remote from one another, came together?

To see how these great advances transformed the problem of the origins of agriculture, we have to look at the world as it was when agriculture began, the world of 10,000 years ago.

First, consider the people. There were about five million people in the world. They were divided into thousands of tribes, all living by various kinds of hunting or collecting, mostly by both. Like their surviving descendants, these people often had special skills for dealing with foods and fibers, drugs and poisons, weapons and boats. The tribes also included some individual artists and craftsmen, as well as men with special knowledge of trade, especially trade in minerals—tools and ornaments, for example, made from obsidian, amber, and precious stones. But, in general, these people had a vast and accurate knowledge of what they could do with the plants, the animals, and the earth on which they depended for their living.

There was, however, one factor in their surroundings on which the main masses of mankind could not depend. This was the climate, for the climate at that time was changing unusually fast. The last Ice Age was in full retreat. The snow was melting all around what is now the temperate Northern Hemisphere. Mountain ranges were becoming passable. The oceans were rising and cutting off islands. Inland seas were drying up. In short, vast new regions were being opened or closed to human habitation.

In these circumstances it is evident that movements of people must have been taking place on a greater scale than ever before. Inevitably the greatest movements of all, and the greatest meeting and mixing of peoples, would be concentrated in those necks of land that join the three continents of the Old World and the two continents of the New. Significantly, therefore, the first evidences of settled agriculture are found close to these necks of land.

Over the last twenty years, radiocarbon dating of the organic remains in a great number of early agricultural settlements has shown beyond doubt that agriculture began at different times in different regions. And it has shown the order in which it actually began in these different regions. The use of radiocarbon has corrected many slight —and a few big—misconceptions.

First, agriculture began, not exactly in what the American Egyptologist James Breasted called the Fertile Crescent, not in the fertile valley bottoms, but rather on the hillsides and tablelands adjoining them. This nuclear zone, as it has been called, is a three-pronged area stretching from the headwaters of the Euphrates, west through Anatolia into the Balkans, south into the Jordan Valley, and east along the foot of the Zagros Mountains toward the Persian Gulf. Later there was a fourth prong crossing Persia south of the Caspian Sea. In other words, the nuclear zone was just at the neck, or the crossroads, of the Old World.

Secondly, we find that this zone of original settlement did not expand—apart from seaside intrusions into Egypt and the Crimea— until about 4000 B.C. There are three or four silent millennia between the beginning of agriculture 10,000 years ago and the great transformation and expansion that followed it. To be sure, during this period pottery was invented. Artists and traders were attracted by the security of the permanent settlements and put their skills and goods at the service of the new, rich, settled communities. But the great technical and biological discoveries of bronze and writing, the wheel and the horse, lay ahead.

These discoveries were made only at the end of the silent millennia, when the great geographical expansion was beginning. In the fourth millennium B.C. the tribes of

The World After Agriculture

grain cultivators began to move out of the nuclear zone and to settle or colonize the wild lands of the hunters and collectors, which lay around them. They moved in four main directions: into Europe, into Africa, into India, and into China. They had waited a long time to make these journeys, and they took a long time, more than a thousand years, to accomplish them. Why? The answer depends mainly on the crops they were cultivating. And, as

we shall see, these crops give us the answers to several other questions.

That we know exactly what crops were cultivated by the earliest farmers is the result of the work of the Danish botanist Hans Helbaek. The foundation of their agriculture was wheat, and its two main forms continued to live and were cultivated side by side in the nuclear zone for the nine succeeding millennia. The first of these, known as emmer, existed and still exists there wild. The

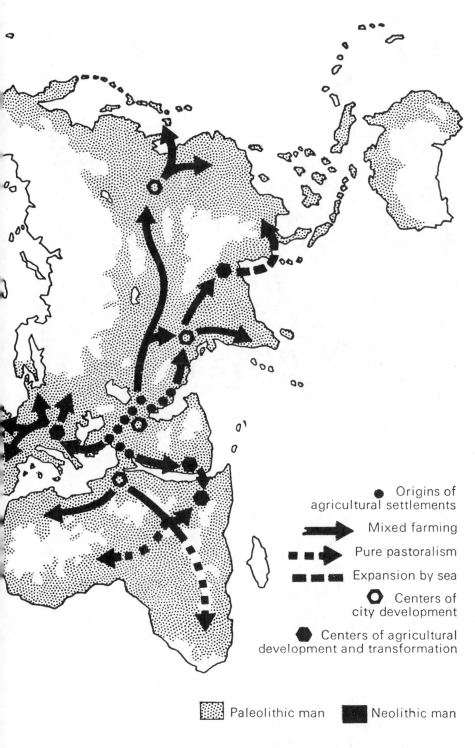

● Origins of
   agricultural settlements

➤ Mixed farming

⇢ Pure pastoralism

⇛ Expansion by sea

⬡ Centers of
   city development

⬣ Centers of agricultural
   development and transformation

▨ Paleolithic man   ■ Neolithic man

rope a new grain, oats, appeared beside the wheat. In India, cotton took the place of wool and flax. In Central Asia the native buckwheat displaced wheat and barley. On the Upper Nile, sorghum displaced the other grains. And almost everywhere various kinds of new light grains, the millets, began to take the place of the heavy-grained wheat and barley.

Some of these later displacements were no doubt due to conscious selection. But some, it seems, were quite unconscious. In 1916 a German geographer, Engelbrecht, attempted to account for these displacements. As a crop is taken into a new territory or habitat, it is apt to be invaded by new weeds. Rye appears as a weed of wheat and displaces the wheat as the crop moves north or moves higher into the mountains. This happens today with cultivated rye, and originally wild rye would have done the same.

No doubt this transformation of crops was exceedingly slow, and indeed its speed was probably the limiting factor in allowing the expansion of agriculture from the nuclear zone. The cultivator had to wait for an evolutionary change, which depended on processes of selection of which he was quite unconscious.

The idea of unconscious selection was Darwin's, but he had no idea how far it would go. It turns out to be the key to the understanding of the development of agriculture. The decisive changes undergone by cultivated plants are not, as one might suppose, in the visible yield, but in properties of behavior which, to the layman or nonfarmer, would seem unimportant.

The discovery of this principle was the main contribution of Vavilov, who found that nearly all cultivated plants had gone through certain parallel transformations. In cultivation they had lost the faculty of distributing their seeds, which was necessary for their survival in nature. And, at the same time, they had acquired a new faculty of submitting to convenient harvesting of fruits and threshing of seed, which was necessary for their survival in the hands of the cultivator.

second does not exist wild. It is derived, as we know by experimental breeding and by looking at its chromosomes. from hybridization between emmer and a wild grass also still found growing in this region. This second grain is bread wheat, and today it is still the most important of all man's food crops.

Along with the two wheats, a variety of other food plants were cultivated, a variety that increased with the passing of time: peas and lentils for porridge, barley for beer, linseed for oil, and the vine for wine. Doubtless many unidentified fruits and vegetables were also collected, without at first being bred and cultivated.

But when men passed to the new lands the picture changed. In warmer Egypt linseed began to be grown, not for oil, but for fiber; it was retted and spun for flax and was used to make linen, the first substitute for wool. In colder Eu-

Take the crowning instance of Vavilov's principle. The ear of wild emmer, when it is ripe, shatters into its separate parts, each containing one grain protected by its coat, the chaff, and armed with a beard that will catch in the coat of any passing animal. When the grain falls to the ground it will dig itself in. But the ear of cultivated emmer or bread wheat does not shatter when ripe. It can be cut and carried unbroken. Only when it is threshed does it gently shed its naked grain into the farmer's bushel or bin.

This extraordinary transmutation, it might be thought, could be the result of conscious selection. It could, if the selector were one who knew all that we know thousands of years later. But how could those first farmers have known what evolutionary changes were possible? And how could they have foreseen how the rich harvests that lay ahead of them might be won?

There is, however, an even more striking example of the scope of unconscious selection. In general, the wild ancestors of crop plants have built-in mechanisms of self-incompatibility: genetic devices that prevent the pollen from growing in the styles and fertilizing the ovules of the same plant. These devices are necessary for the evolutionary success of all wild species for they insure that a proportion of the seed will be crossbred. In cultivation these devices cease to matter. They confer no immediate advantage; indeed they can only impair the yield. And, sure enough, they are nearly always lost in cultivation. For example, wheat and barley, peas and beans, which all allowed cross-fertilization in their wild ancestors are regularly self-fertilized in their modern cultivated forms. This change was made by selection, but it was not made by conscious selection, for until the last century no one knew it had happened; no one even knew that it could happen.

The cultivator who improved his crops did so, therefore, not by his intelligent practice of plant breeding, but by his intelligent practice of cultivation. And this was a capacity for which, we cannot doubt, the cultivator himself was continually being selected.

Modern agriculture. Furrow irrigation of grain using stilling basins for take out from head ditch.

The contrast, indeed the conflict, between the tiller of the soil and the keeper of cattle, between the peasant and the herdsman, between Cain and Abel is so ancient and obvious that we naturally think of the domestication of plants and of animals as belonging to separate and opposed problems. But this is misleading. Out of the grain farmer came the ancient civilizations. Around the grain farmer assembled every kind of agricultural and civilized activity. Before grain farming, there was the collecting and even the cropping of roots in many parts of the world. Long before the grain farmer, there was the use of the dog for hunting, for food in time of famine, and later, for herding sheep and goats. But none of these activities led to a more complicated life, which in turn meant a more complicated, a stabler, and ultimately, a more productive society. No great development came about until the grain farmer had, during his four silent millennia, laid the foundations of the future.

The various kinds of stock and stockmen were therefore bound to have had different histories because of their different relations with the grain farmer. What these relations were are still partly obscure. The early settlements mostly contain bones of cattle, pigs, and sheep; but to what extent had these been bred and fed by the farmer and to what extent had he taken them by hunting? Did the early herdsman allow his domesticated female animals to mate with wild males or males that had gone wild? This is the practice of Nagas in India with their gaur cattle today. It is also the practice in mating dogs with wolves. The distinction between what is wild and what is domesticated is therefore harder for the archeologist to draw with stock than with crops.

Allowing for these uncertainties, we may say that sheep and pigs were probably the first to be taken under man's care, probably during the seventh millennium B.C. Later, in the sixth or fifth millennium, came the cattle. Whether their first use was for sacrifice in religious ritual will take us a long time to discover. But certainly this first introduction was quickly followed by their diversified uses for plowing, for milk, for meat, and later, in the salt-hungry regions of Africa, for blood.

When we come to the means of improving domesticated animals along their different lines, we can think of them together and we can see them in contrast with crop plants. The herdsman, it is clear, has from the beginning understood something of the purpose and practice of selection. Indeed we may say that the first herdsmen could never have improved their lot until they understood that better animals could be raised by choosing and setting apart better parents. It is a principle that is suitably and elaborately commemorated by the story of Jacob and Laban in the Book of Genesis.

The processes of animal breeding have thus been more conscious than those of plant breeding, and this has been true at every stage. For example, when the cultivators came into India in the third millennium B.C., they allowed their cattle to hybridize with the native humped cattle. This was no doubt an unconscious and merely traditional practice. But in the Indus city of Mohenjo Daro they also deliberately domesticated new species, notably the native water buffalo. Man's dependence on conscious purpose in dealing with animals as opposed to plants is further indicated by the length of time—five thousand years after the beginning of cultivation—that it took him to acquire the initiative, skill, and audacity to domesticate the most difficult animals, the horse and the camel.

If early farmers were sometimes aware of their effects on crops and stock, it is certain that they were wholly unaware of any effects their crops and stock were having on them (that is, beyond feeding, clothing, or working for them). But those who have observed peasants and pastoralists most closely have seen that between these two great classes of men, there is a genuine and profound contrast, a contrast

related to their work. The record goes back, as we saw, to the legend of Cain and Abel, which takes its root in the conflict between the desert and the sown, between the Bedouin shepherds and their peasant neighbors. But on the way, it fills a large part of our history. It is the story of the borderland struggle between the English farmers and the Welsh drovers during the Middle Ages. It is also the story of the struggle between the farming Kikuyu and the grazing Masai in Kenya today.

How are we to describe it? In the first place it should be noted that each class is of many kinds. The nomadic pastoralist may sow crops for a quick harvest during his summer grazing, while the settled peasant may breed cattle or horses to till his land, a practice that has transferred the main labor of farming from the woman with a hoe to the man with a plow. The basic contrast remains however. It is one of character, behavior, and belief.

O n the one hand, the peasant is a man who knows and loves his soil and crops. He even worships them. His life, like the lives of his ancestors for two or three hundred generations, has depended on his prudence and industry in handling the soil and crops. He is therefore deeply attached to them, and he and his women will accept serfdom rather than be separated from their land. As a consequence, they are inbred—conservative and traditional, stubborn but peaceful.

How different is the pastoralist! He is correspondingly attached to his animals, but his animals can move and usually have to move in search of pasture. He is therefore mobile, alert, and aggressive. He will steal the cattle and the women of his neighbors. Consequently, he is relatively outbred. And the most mobile of his animals, the horse and the camel, are kept by the most mobile and alert, aggressive and warlike, of herdsmen.

How, then, did this contrast arise? In part, of course, the differences were there in the ancestors, the collectors and the hunters from whom each was partly derived. But it developed during those long silent millennia because the earliest men who chose to adopt these different ways of life were themselves from the beginning dependent for survival on the crops or the stock they were raising. They were therefore dependent on their different abilities to cope with different ways of life. The croppers were in fact being unconsciously selected by their crops, and the stockmen by their stock. Each way of life was tied up together in one related and adapted system.

To put it in another way, man thought himself to be consciously in control of his destiny, but he was in fact unconsciously having his destiny, his evolutionary destiny, thrust upon him. It is a situation from which we can see he has not yet by any means escaped.

The greatest of all human experiments was man's invasion of the New World. Whether it happened fifteen or twenty thousand years ago does not much matter. What matters is that mankind had put himself into two separate boxes between which there was effectively no exchange of people or ideas, of plants or animals, or even of their diseases. That was the situation for over ten thousand years. And during that time, agriculture arose and developed independently in the two boxes. This was, as we may say, an experimental situation, for it goes a long way in showing us what matters and what does not matter for the whole process of developing agriculture.

Looking first at the similarities between the Old World and the New, it can be seen that in the New World, cultivation began around a kind of central or nuclear zone. It began about 7000 B.C., when the ice was melting at its fastest. And it began with a grain crop that the Europeans called Indian corn or maize. A variety of other crops—beans and potatoes, gourds and peppers, cotton and tobacco—slowly assembled around this early crop. But the processes of improvement and distribution show us a number of rule-breaking novelties. Several of these concern maize.

Unlike any of the other important grains, maize has its male and female flowers, the tassels and silks, on different parts of the plant. This has meant that the ordinary evolution toward inbreeding could not occur. Maize remained, and was bound to remain, crossbred. For that reason, it ultimately became the object of the most remarkable of all crop improvements: the American hybrid corn industry of the twentieth century turned an old shortcoming into a controlled advantage.

But maize is also unique with respect to its origin. No botanists would believe that maize was derived from a slender, wild Mexican grass, teosinte. Indeed they had put the two plants into different genera, *Zea* and *Euchlaena*. Yet when the hybridization is tried, the two species are found to cross readily. Their chromosomes pair in the hybrid. And, as Dr. Paul Mangelsdorf found, the hybrid is fertile, yielding the expected recombinations of characters in the second generation. Evidently the selection of mutations, probably conscious selection in this case, has produced the most remarkable evolutionary plant transformation known. All in the course of 9,000 years of cultivation.

There is another American crop, the sweet potato, to which we owe an equally important piece of enlightenment. This plant, coming from Mexico or Peru, was already being cultivated across the Pacific all the way to New Zealand at the time of Columbus. The Maoris had brought it there from the mid-Pacific one or two hundred years earlier, and it had since become the main crop in the North Island. They knew it as *kumara*, the same name that it had borne in Central America. By their languages, their blood groups, their canoes, and their other crops, we know that the Maoris, like other Polynesians, came originally from Indonesia. It is the sweet potato that tells us that at some earlier time other people traveling westward from America had joined them. The two boxes of which I spoke had been almost entirely closed. But not quite.

The great difference between the Old World and the New, however, had nothing to do with these or any other crop plants. In the first place, the nuclear zone of America, instead of being a single, broad, and well-connected area, was split into two by the narrow, twisted 1,500-mile neck that runs from Tehuantepec to Panama, a track that had to be followed by everyone passing from North to South America. In the second place, stock raising was absent in America. In the previous five millennia the American Indian hunters had killed off what could have been the farmer's stock. Horses and mammoths were no longer available for domestication. All that were left were llamas and turkeys.

These two differences, together with the lesser area and resources of the New World, slowed down the development of agriculture and of civilization. The silent millennia were longer. When the two worlds were brought together in 1492, the civilizations of the New World were found to be about three millennia behind those of the Old World. Mexico and Peru proved to be not unlike the Egypt of Hatshepsut and Thutmose in 1500 B.C. The consequences of this difference in evolution, the submergence of the Amerindians, are with us now, but they are beyond our present inquiry. They show us, however, in a practical way, the overwhelming importance for us today of what happened during the distant years when men and women first began to hoe the earth and sow the seed.

36

David R. Harris

The Origins of Agriculture in the Tropics

Ecological analysis affords new insights into agricultural origins and suggests a fresh evaluation of the limited archaeological evidence

The late V. Gordon Childe, whose conceptualization of the so-called "Neolithic revolution" in the Near East crystalized for a generation ideas about the beginnings of food production, spared few thoughts for the origins of tropical agriculture. The archaeological record in the tropics, and indeed in the whole of the New World, was, he maintained, so meager and so late by comparison with the Near East that it was only of peripheral interest. The mainstream of cultural progress, which, as he saw it, led inexorably from the nomadic hunters and gatherers of Paleolithic and Mesolithic times through settled Neolithic farming communities to the initiation of trade and urban life in the Bronze and Iron Ages, issued from the lands of the Fertile Crescent, flowed vigorously west and north around the Mediterranean and up the Danube, and ultimately reached the far confines of Atlantic Europe (Childe 1936, 1942, 1958).

Dr. Harris's research is concerned with man's modification of ecosystems in the historic and prehistoric past, and focuses on the evolution of agricultural systems and on related problems of plant and animal domestication. After taking his B.A. at Oxford University, he did graduate work first at Oxford for the B.Litt. degree and then at the University of California, Berkeley, where he took his Ph.D. He has since held posts in the University of London and visiting professorships at the universities of California, New Mexico, and Toronto. He has carried out field work principally in the American tropics, has published widely in geographical and other journals, and is the author of Plants, Animals, and Man in the Outer Leeward Islands, West Indies *(University of California Press, 1965) and co-editor of* Africa in Transition *(Methuen, 1967). The present article is based on a guest lecture he delivered at Berkeley in November 1970. Address: Department of Geography, University College London, Gower Street, London WC1E 6BT, England.*

This diffusionist model of the origins of European sedentary society had the elegance of simplicity, and, with the advent of carbon-14 dating, its relative chronology was satisfyingly confirmed by a large number of absolute dates (Clark 1965). But the Childean interpretation reinforced and perpetuated a mid-latitude, European-eyed view of prehistory. One of the drawbacks of the classical education enjoyed by most European archaeologists in the past has been that they suffered such prolonged immersion in the glory that was Greece and the grandeur that was Rome that they became obsessed with the search for the antecedents of those maritime thalassic civilizations in the potamic lands around the eastern Mediterranean. The fact that the archaeological richness of those lands was, in part at least, due to the excellence of their arid and semi-arid climates for the preservation of artifacts, especially organic remains, was frequently overlooked. And the belief that the Near East was the primary Neolithic hearth, from which cultural innovations radiated outward successively into other parts of the Old World, was gradually transformed from hypothesis into dogma.

As long as the attention of most archaeologists remained focused on the Fertile Crescent and its hilly borderlands, this orthodoxy went substantially unchallenged, even though some biologists and geographers, notably Nicolai Vavilov of the Leningrad Plant Breeding Institute, Oakes Ames of Harvard, and Carl Sauer of the University of California at Berkeley, had long regarded it as a gross oversimplification. But in the last few

decades work undertaken outside the Near East, particularly by American archaeologists and paleobotanists working on early cultural phases in Mexico and South America, has produced such fundamental advances that the Near East has lost much of its apparent preeminence as the scene of man's earliest achievements in agriculture and plant and animal domestication. From the vantage point provided by new findings in American prehistory, the Near East has yielded its claim to uniqueness as the stage on which the main events of the Neolithic revolution were enacted.

Indeed the very concept of a revolution has had to be rejected as evidence has accumulated in both the Old World and the New to show that the crucial transition from food-gathering to food-producing took place only gradually over long periods of time and that it followed different courses in different geographical areas. This emerges most clearly from the evidence recovered in Mexico by Richard MacNeish, Kent Flannery, and others which indicates that there the transition from hunting and gathering to food production occupied over eight millennia and that the beginnings of agriculture were not associated with sedentary village life, pottery, polished stone artifacts, and other traits that Childe regarded as integral components of the Neolithic revolution (MacNeish 1964; Flannery et al. 1967; Byers 1967).

My purpose here, however, is not to review available evidence on the origins of agriculture in the subtropical dry lands of Mexico and the Near

East, but to explore the more problematical question of agricultural beginnings within the tropics and to present an ecological interpretation that I believe has some explanatory power.

Complex and simple ecosystems

One variable of great significance to the understanding of both natural and artificial ecosystems is species diversity. It is often expressed as the relationship between the number of species and of individual organisms in an ecosystem (Odum 1963). Thus complex ecosystems contain many different species, each of which exists in relatively small numbers, whereas simple ecosystems contain fewer species, each of which tends to be represented by a relatively large number of individuals. Biotically complex ecosystems are also struc-

Figure 1. A swidden plot "cleared," burned, and planted with manioc. Guayaba, Casiquiare, southern Venezuela.

Figure 2. World distribution of tropical seasonal climates showing extent of the intermediate tropical zone (based on Troll and Paffen 1963).

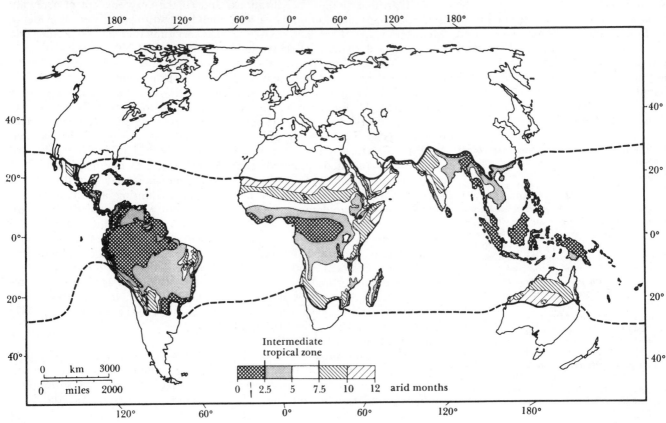

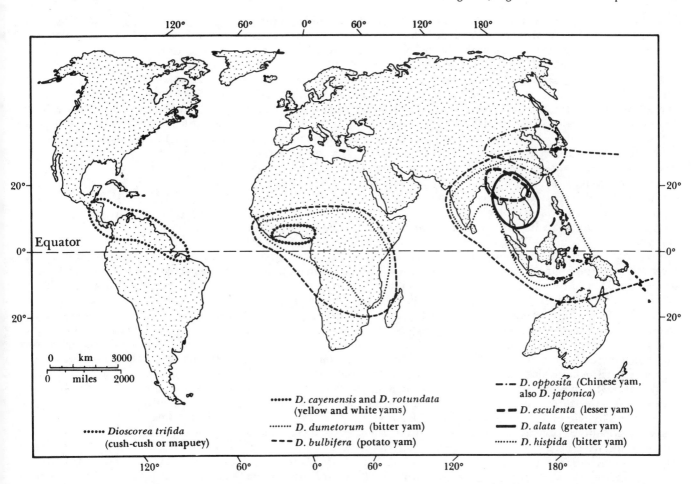

Figure 3. Approximate areas of origin of cultivated yams (modified from Coursey 1967, Fig. 1).

turally and functionally diverse and inherently more stable than simpler systems: equilibrium or homeostasis is maintained more effectively because a variety of ecological niches are available to species at all trophic levels in the food web and environmental changes, such as the reduction, removal, or introduction of an organism by man, have less effect on the system as a whole when alternative paths for energy flow and greater genetic diversity exist within it.

These characteristics attain their most impressive manifestation in the tropical rain forest, which is the most complex and stable of major terrestrial ecosystems. Conversely the tundra, the boreal forest, and the mid-latitude grasslands are among the most simple and least stable of major terrestrial ecosystems. Within the tropics there is a gradient, which correlates broadly with climate, from the most complex and stable equatorial evergreen rain

forest, through the seasonal semi-evergreen and deciduous forests where species diversity is lower and plant growth limited by a winter-dry season of latitudinally increasing length and severity, to the floristically simpler xerophytic shrub communities of the perennial deserts.

The criterion of species diversity, which has proved valuable in the analysis of natural ecosystems, can also aid understanding of agricultural systems (Harris 1969). It is clear that the artificial ecosystems created by modern "neotechnic" agriculture are relatively simple: they exist to produce maximum numbers of optimum-sized individuals of one or two preferred plant or animal species. In other words, modern agriculture tends toward monoculture, or, in economic terms, toward simplification for efficiency. Some "paleotechnic" agricultural systems of the traditional world, such as wet-padi farming, also incorporate relatively few species of cultivated plants and domestic animals, but most traditional agricultural systems are more complex, raising

diverse assemblages of crops in polycultural patterns of structural and functional interdependence and sometimes integrating livestock into the system as both consumers and fertilizing agents. Shifting, or swidden, cultivation and fixed-plot horticulture, both still widely practiced in the tropics, are examples of such ecologically complex, polycultural systems, whereas the European tradition of mixed farming based on crop combinations of grains, roots, and livestock, constitutes a somewhat less complex system that has evolved progressively more specialized techniques for exploiting a limited range of cultivated plants and domestic animals.

Ecological manipulation and transformation

The contrast between ecologically simple and complex agricultural systems suggests two broadly contrasted ways in which the advent of cultivation changes natural ecosystems. Agricultural utilization may—and, if sufficiently intensive, usually does—

lead to the transformation of a natural into a largely artificial ecosystem: the replacement of tropical forest by plantation, of temperate woodland by wheat fields, or of desert shrubland by irrigated oases. But agriculture may also proceed by a process of manipulation which involves the alteration of selected components of the natural system rather than its wholesale replacement—a method of cultivation which involves substituting certain preferred domesticated species for wild species in equivalent ecological niches and so simulates the structure and functional dynamics of the natural ecosystem. This mode of change is most clearly exemplified today by tropical swidden cultivation and fixed-plot horticulture. Both entail the cultivation of mixed plant assemblages of trees, shrubs, climbers, herbs, and root crops which take over spatial and functional roles similar to those fulfilled by wild species of equivalent life forms in the natural forest ecosystem.

In the past, prior to the development of ecologically simplified and specialized agricultural systems, manipulation would have been the dominant mode of agriculturally induced ecological change, although the precise pattern of manipulation would have varied widely with time and place; it would have included, for example, the substitution of free-ranging pigs for wild scavengers in the forests of Medieval Europe and of small-grained cereal crops for wild grasses in the woodlands and grasslands of the prehistoric Near East. The emergence of ecologically simple and specialized agricultural systems implies ample prior time for the genetic amelioration of the relatively few highly productive crops and domestic animals on which such systems depend and for the elaboration of complex societies adapted to their maintenance.

In all probability man manipulated natural ecosystems for agricultural production long before he succeeded in transforming them into simplified and specialized agricultural systems. On ecological grounds, therefore, we can postulate that a long initial phase of cultivation by ecosystem-manipulation preceded the emergence of agriculture in the strict sense of the word. This hypothetical phase may be thought of as corresponding to the cultural stage of "incipient agriculture" formulated by archaeologists for the Near East, Mexico, and elsewhere. But rather than adopt this somewhat deterministic epithet, the fundamental contrast between early ecosystem-manipulation and later agricultural transformations may be better expressed by distinguishing an initial phase of "proto-cultivation" from the later development of "specialized agriculture" in its various forms.

If cultivation originated by ecosystem-manipulation the question arises as to which of the major natural ecosystems were most readily manipulated. Neither inference nor evidence suggests that early cultivators manipulated the simpler ecosystems. Apparently very few cultivated plants and domestic animals originated from wild ancestors native to relatively simple ecosystems such as the boreal forest and the mid-latitude grasslands—the reindeer and the horse may be exceptions— and within such areas there is little archaeological evidence of early agriculture. It is both more plausible and more probable that cultivation began by the manipulation of complex ecosystems in which a wide variety of wild plants and animals were used for subsistence, some of which became so closely involved with man, as items in a seasonally scheduled pattern of wild food procurement (Flannery 1968), or perhaps in some cases as objects of ritual significance, that they were gradually domesticated and ultimately incorporated into an organized system of agricultural production. Such complex ecosystems would have been available principally in the forested and wooded lands of low- and mid-latitudes, particularly within the tropics.

Progenitors of plant domestication and cultivation

We may next ask what type of subsistence economy may have pre-adapted nonagricultural peoples to become cultivators. Judging from ethnological and archaeological evidence, simple natural ecosystems have been most usually and effectively occupied by mobile hunting groups who became intimately adapted to the exploitation of a principal food source, usually seasonally migrant herds of game, such as the bison and guanaco pursued by the mid-latitude grassland hunters of North and South America, or the caribou and sea mammals hunted by the Eskimo of the Nearctic boreal forest and tundra.

Figure 4. Aerial view of freshly cleared and burned swiddens near Puerto Ayacucho, upper Orinoco, southern Venezuela. Recently abandoned swiddens are in the background.

Such specialized hunters make relatively little direct use of wild plants for subsistence, and, on account of their highly mobile, game-dependent way of life, they may be precluded as progenitors of plant domestication and cultivation—a conclusion that accords with the lack of archaeological evidence for early agriculture in the simple ecosystems they occupied.

Complex natural ecosystems, on the other hand, have characteristically been occupied by less specialized populations of gatherers, fishermen, and hunters of small and slow game. These forager groups exploit a broader spectrum of plant and animal resources than the specialized hunters; they move less far and less frequently and are normally organized in small bands localized within a circumscribed territory. Historically they have occupied mainly forested and wooded areas and their less mobile existence, coupled with an intimate familiarity with the varied plant life of a limited area, suggests them as the most likely progenitors of plant domestication and cultivation.

If this crucial innovation did originate among such forager bands, the most propitious areas may have been marginal transition zones, or ecotones, between major ecosystems. Biological productivity tends to be high at both primary and secondary levels in these contact zones, and they offer maximum local and seasonal variation in the availability of plant and animal species. They are therefore likely to have been the preferred habitats of forager populations because they provide optimum access to the most diverse and assured supply of wild plants and animals. Upland-lowland margins, and forest- and woodland-edge habitats where tree cover gives way to more open country, are likely to have been preferentially selected for occupation. Here, where forest or woodland abuts on grassland, swamp, river, or coast, it would have been easier than elsewhere for foragers to combine the gathering of wild plants with the cropping of animal protein by hunting and fishing.

The more adequate and assured diet thus afforded would have increased opportunities for sedentary settlement, which would in turn have facilitated

the selection of advantageous mutations through many generations of wild and semi-domesticated plants and favored the transition from gathering to harvesting to planting and full domestication. Furthermore, the existence of semipermanently or permanently occupied living sites would have intensified human disturbance of the local ecosystem and led readily to the creation of the open habitats that provided optimum sites for colonization by the weedy ancestors of later cultigens (Hawkes 1969, 1970).

On the basis of ecological inference, therefore, we may postulate that optimum conditions for ecosystem-manipulation leading to plant domestication and cultivation existed among those forager bands who established relatively permanent settlements along forest and woodland margins and who created open habitats within the territories they occupied.

Tropical vegeculture

With these suppositions in mind we may now turn specifically to the question of agricultural origins within the tropics. It has long been recognized that a fundamental contrast exists within traditional agricultural systems between those that are primarily dependent upon seed-reproduced plants and those that de-

Figure 5. "Open canopy" maize plot beside the upper Orinoco near Esmeralda, southern Venezuela.

pend mainly on the reproduction of crops by vegetative propagation. In modern times this contrast was first observed and commented on by European naturalists visiting the tropics and its significance has since been stressed particularly in the work of Carl Sauer (1952, 1959), Jacques Barrau (1965), and Desmond Clark (1962, 1967). Today the distinction between seed-culture and vegeculture is most evident in the ecologically complex paleotechnic agricultural systems of the tropics, where it recurs in Asia, Africa, and the Americas. Seed-culture appears to represent the indigenous mode of cultivation in the drier subtropics of both the Old and New Worlds, specifically in Southwest Asia and Middle America where archaeological and biological investigations have shown conclusively that the beginnings of seed-crop domestication date back over eight millennia (Flannery 1969; Renfrew 1969; Mac-Neish 1964; Byers 1967).

No such antiquity has yet been demonstrated for seed-culture in other areas that invite investigation, such as ecotone habitats, especially along upland-lowland margins, in West Africa, Ethiopia, Southwest Arabia, the Indian subcontinent, China, and the less humid parts of Southeast Asia, al-

tween 6000 and 8000 B.C. (Gorman 1969, 1971).

Vegeculture is most clearly established as an indigenous mode of cultivation in the humid tropical lowlands of America and Southeast Asia. It is also widespread in the African tropics, although there it has largely depended, at least through the historic period, on vegetative cultigens introduced from Asia and America. Starch-rich culti-though from one site in the latter area—Spirit Cave in northwest Thailand—remains of twelve genera of exploited, mainly seed-reproduced plants, some of which may represent cultigens, have recently been recovered and radiocarbon-dated to begens with enlarged roots or stems in the form of tubers, corms, and rhizomes, for example manioc (*Manihot esculenta*), sweet potato (*Ipomoea batatas*), taro (*Colocasia esculenta*), and the yams (*Dioscorea* spp.), together with many lesser known cultigens of little commercial importance today, comprise the basic crops of humid tropical vegeculture. In South America there is a uniquely developed highland tradition of vegeculture based on the cultivation of white potato (*Solanum tuberosum*) and several minor root crops, together with seed crops such as maize (*Zea mays*) and quinoa (*Chenopodium quinoa*). This tradition has analogies, less fully developed and on a smaller scale, in other tropical highlands, specifically in the southern part of the Ethiopian massif, where ensete (*Ensete edule* = *Musa ensete*), a vegetatively reproduced banana-like plant, is a traditional staple (Smeds 1955; Simoons 1960), and in the highlands of central New Guinea where vegecultural systems exist based on taro, yam, the introduced sweet potato, and a minor root crop, *Pueraria lobata* (Watson 1964, 1968; Strathern 1969).

Figure 6. Ocumo (*Xanthosoma sagittifolium*), a local root crop, growing beneath banana in a polycultural swidden. Rio Ocamo, upper Orinoco, southern Venezuela.

As an indigenous system of cultivation, vegeculture is associated chiefly with tropical lowlands, but ecological inference suggests that it is unlikely to have originated in areas of humid tropical evergreen rain forest. Tropical root crops, with their underground organs specialized for starch storage, are adapted to survive dry seasons and to grow quickly to maturity once the rains return. It may be assumed that their wild ancestors were native to areas of pronounced dry season and that man's earliest selection of shallower-rooting forms with larger tubers, corms, or rhizomes took place in such areas rather than in the humid tropical rain forest zone, which may be defined, following Troll and Paffen's classification (1963), to include those areas with fewer than $2\frac{1}{2}$ dry months in the year. At the other extreme the tropical dry lands, which experience more than $7\frac{1}{2}$ dry months in the year, may also be excluded as a homeland of these cultigens because aridity there is too severe and prolonged. It is to the intermediate tropical zone between the hot deserts and the humid rain forests that the tropical lowland root crops are best adapted (Fig. 2). And within this large zone areas with a shorter dry season of $2\frac{1}{2}$ to 5 dry months and a dominant vegetation cover of semi-evergreen and deciduous forest are the probable native habitat of those root crops, such as yams, that have climbing stems adapted to growth under a light tree canopy. In contrast, more drought-resistant, upright-stemmed root crops, such as manioc, have greater ecological tolerance and a wider habitat range, which extends into areas with a longer dry season of 5 to 7¹/₂ dry months and a vegetation cover of rain-green deciduous woodland and xerophytic shrubs.

At present little detailed botanical or archaeological evidence is available on the origins of particular tropical root crops, but where a considerable body of data does exist, as for example for the yams, it tends to confirm ecological expectation. Thus current views on the homelands of cultivated yams in both Southeast Asia and West Africa point to their having originated in areas with dry seasons of intermediate length, *Dioscorea alata*, the greater yam of Southeast Asia, being attributed to northwest Indochina, and the West African yams, *D. cayenensis* and *D. rotundata*, being attributed respectively to forest and savanna areas of shorter and longer dry season in the yam zone that stretches from the central Ivory Coast to southeastern Nigeria (Fig. 3) (Coursey 1967; Alexander and Coursey 1969). Similarly, recent work on manioc ascribes its origin to one or more areas of intermediate tropical climate in Middle America and northern South America (Rogers 1965; Renvoize 1970, 1972).

In the search for the origins of tropical lowland vegeculture ecological inference thus directs attention toward areas of tropical climate with dry seasons of intermediate length, and particularly toward riparian, coastal, swamp- or savanna-edge situations along the margins of semi-evergreen and deciduous tropical forests. Such inference must allow for evidence of past climatic and environmental change in the areas concerned, but, with that qualification, it does provide a useful analytic approach to the problem of the origins of tropical vegeculture. If account is also taken of present knowledge of the probable taxonomic relationships and areas of origin of the cultigens themselves, then it is possible to suggest several regions within the tropics that appear to hold the greatest promise for future investigation: in Southeast Asia, the margins of the Ganges lowland and

the Indochinese peninsula from Burma to southern China; in Africa, the Guinea coast from west of Accra to east of Lagos together with its hinterland stretching east along the northern margins of the Congo rain forest; and in South America, the Orinoco basin and coastal lowlands of Venezuela and Colombia with possible extensions into Middle America.

At the present time insufficient archaeological evidence is available from

these areas to allow any firm conclusions to be drawn as to the absolute antiquity of tropical vegeculture, but it is possible to examine the temporal and spatial relations of vegeculture and seed-culture in the light of both ecological and archaeological data and by so doing to illuminate the whole question of the origins of agriculture in the tropics. Therefore, I shall now discuss the relationship between vegeculture and seed-culture in ecosystematic terms and then test the resultant inferences against cur-

Figure 7. Yanomamö (Waica) Indian girls expressing hydrocyanic acid from the pulp of grated tubers of bitter manioc. Upper Orinoco, southern Venezuela. (Courtesy of *The Geographical Magazine*.)

rently available archaeological evidence.

The ecology of vegeculture and seed-culture

It has already been suggested that paleotechnic agricultural systems in the tropics tend to be polycultural and to raise diverse assemblages of crops in structural and functional interdependence. There are, however, significant differences in the planting patterns that commonly characterize vegecultural and seed-cultural systems. Both systems widely employ the techniques of shifting, or swidden, cultivation (Harris 1972) (Figs. 1 and 4), but in vegecultural plots plant diversity tends to be greater, plant stratification more intricate, and the canopy of vegetation more nearly closed; in other words they represent floristically, structurally, and functionally more complex ecosystems than do seed-cultural plots (Figs. 6 and 8). Vegeculture thus has greater inherent ecological stability than seed-culture, a tendency which is enhanced by the fact that under vegeculture opportunities for soil erosion are less because the ground is more completely and continuously shielded by plant cover.

Still more significant are the contrasted demands on soil fertility that the two systems exert. Because under vegeculture productivity is focused upon predominantly starch-yielding root and tree crops—many of which have, under domestication, partially or completely lost their capacity to set seeds—it makes smaller demands on plant nutrients than do the protein-yielding seed crops, particularly cereals and legumes. This contrast is accentuated at harvest, when the seed-crop cultivator removes from his plot for consumption highly concentrated nutrients in the form of, for example, cereal grains or beans, whereas the vegeculturalist removes a smaller fraction of fertility in his harvest of tubers, corms, or rhizomes. The period of time for which a plot may be cultivated without excessive decline of yields tends therefore to be longer under vegeculture. Conversely, seed-cultural systems are less conservative of soil resources and more readily get out of ecological equilibrium. The preeminence of cereals, beans, and other nutrient-demanding crops, the less intricate stratification, and the more open canopy (Fig. 5) which increases opportunities for both soil erosion and weed invasion, all combine to make seed-culture less durable and more prone to relatively rapid shifts from one temporary clearing to another.

Recent field work I carried out among vegecultural swidden cultivators in the upper Orinoco area of Venezuela (Figs. 4–8) suggests that the ecological contrast between vegeculture and seed-culture may be further enhanced by differences in techniques of clearance and tillage (Harris 1971). Here it was observed that manioc swiddens were customarily cleared and burned very incompletely, the stem-cuttings being planted among tangled and rotting debris (Figs. 1 and 8), whereas maize swiddens were cleared and burned more thoroughly and the seeds planted in open ground. Analysis of soil samples from manioc and maize plots revealed that, whereas in the latter organic carbon showed an expected decrease following clearance and burning, in the former it actually increased.

A possible explanation of this anomaly is that the techniques of partial clearance and deep soil disturbance at harvest that are associated with manioc cultivation allow decaying surface organic matter to become incorporated into the soil and thus raise the level of organic carbon in the upper part of the horizon. This phenomenon would have the effect of accentuating the ecological stability of vegecultural as opposed to seed-cultural plots, and it may help to explain the persistence of vegeculture in the tropical evergreen rain forest of northern South America. Here, as the dry season diminishes in duration, intensity, and regularity toward the equator, so the cultivation of manioc and other root crops by partial clearance and burning and the addition of organic debris to the soil becomes relatively more rewarding.

Ecologically, therefore, we can postulate that seed-culture, particularly when practiced as shifting or swidden cultivation, should exhibit a greater tendency than vegeculture to expand into new areas. This inference is strengthened if the dietary effectiveness of the two systems is also considered. It is well known that seed crops, especially cereals, provide relatively large amounts of protein as well as carbohydrates and fats, whereas root crops provide minimal amounts of protein. Vegeculturalists who lack staple seed crops are therefore dependent on alternative sources of protein to achieve a balanced diet. In the tropics protein from wild terrestrial and aquatic animals and fish normally provides this want, although some vegeculturalists also obtain considerable amounts of protein from domestic livestock. Dependence on supplies of wild animal protein ensures the persistence of hunting and fishing as major subsistence activities among tropical vegeculturalists and thus enhances the inherent stability of the system by limiting its adaptability to those habitats with assured supplies of animal protein, particularly river-bank, seashore, savanna-edge, and other ecotone situations. Seed-culture on the other hand, by providing a better balanced vegetable diet, frees communities from major dependence on hunting and fishing and allows expansion into new habitats where little animal protein is available.

In the light of these ecological and dietary contrasts between the two systems of cultivation we might therefore predict an evolutionary development whereby seed-culture would gradually gain spatial ascendancy over vegeculture by territorial expansion. I will conclude by briefly examining the currently available archaeological evidence to see whether such a pattern of seed-culture expanding into areas of vegeculture can be verified in the prehistoric record. To do so we will take a summary look at the evidence for tropical America, Southeast Asia, and West Africa.

The archaeological record

In the New World tropics (Fig. 9) at the time of European discovery seed-culture predominated over vegeculture in the greater part of Middle

America, although in both Central America and the Antilles staple seed and root crops coexisted. In South America seed-culture was well established in the river valleys of the dry west coast and coexisted with vegeculture both along the southern coasts of the Caribbean and in the Andes. The main area of vegeculture comprised the tropical lowlands of the Orinoco and Amazon basins and the forested eastern uplands.

Archaeologically the great antiquity of seed culture in the Tehuacan Valley of southern Mexico has been convincingly demonstrated by MacNeish and his co-workers, and he has now begun to probe the origins of food production in the Ayacucho area of the Peruvian Andes, where, in the first two seasons' work, he has recovered evidence suggesting that seed-reproduced plants such as gourd (*Lagenaria* sp.), maize, squash, and possibly beans were being cultivated by 2500 B.C. if not earlier (MacNeish 1969; MacNeish et al. 1970; Pickersgill 1971). No definite evidence of vegeculture has been recovered by MacNeish in the Andes, but artifacts resembling hoe blades, which occur late in the preceramic sequence, may possibly indicate the cultivation of root crops (MacNeish et al. 1970).

In the lowlands of northern South America, on the other hand, there is some evidence from two sites—Momíl in northern Colombia and Rancho Peludo in northwestern Venezuela—to suggest that vegeculture may have preceded seed-culture in this area. At these sites *metates* and *manos*, which imply the preparation of flour from seed crops such as maize, occur stratigraphically above pottery griddles, or *budares*, associated with the baking of cassava bread from bitter manioc, thus suggesting an intrusion of maize cultivation into an area in which vegeculture was already established. Direct and indirect dating of these sites indicates that vegeculture may have given way to seed-culture in this part of northern Colombia and Venezuela some time after 500 B.C. (Reichel-Dolmatoff 1957; Rouse and Cruxent 1963; Bischof 1969). It has also been suggested by Rouse and Cruxent that the distribution of a distinctive type of painted pottery (Saladoid series) may be correlated with the putative early phase of vegeculture in this area and that, accordingly, vegetative planters may have migrated to the north coast from the Venezuelan interior, probably by way of the lower Orinoco, whence they would have carried vegecultural crops and techniques through the Lesser and into the Greater Antilles. A strong inferential case for the development of manioc-based vegeculture in the northern interior of tropical lowland South America has also been presented recently by Lathrap (1970).

Meager though the archaeological evidence is, it accords well both with the ecological case for regarding the Orinoco basin and southern Caribbean coast as a probable hearth area of South American tropical lowland vegeculture and with the ecological expectation that vegeculture would tend to give way before an intrusive and nutritionally more effective seed-crop complex. It is quite probable that maize-dominated seed-culture gradually spread into lowland South America from the west and north during prehistoric times, modifying or replacing vegecultural traditions of cultivation as it did so. However, the greater ecological fitness of vegeculture over seed-culture in the tropical humid environment, which is evident today in the upper Orinoco area (Harris 1971), may have curtailed the penetration of maize and other seed crops into the evergreen rain forests of the Orinoco basin, the Amazon basin, and the eastern uplands during prehistoric and historic times.

A similar pattern of seed-culture expanding into areas of vegeculture is apparent in tropical Southeast Asia, where an intrusive rice culture appears progressively to have replaced an indigenous form of vegeculture, based primarily on yam and taro cultivation (Fig. 10). Joseph Spencer (1966) has demonstrated the historical retreat of taros and yams eastward through the Indonesian archipelago, and both I. H. Burkill (1951) and Jacques Barrau (1965) have stressed the formerly greater importance and wider distribution of root crops in the subsistence economies of Southeast Asia.

Figure 8. The edge of a polycultural swidden plot. The canopy layer consists mainly of banana with occasional papaya and other fruit trees; beneath and between these are shrubs such as bush cotton. The ground layer consists of root crops and other useful herbaceous plants. Rio Ocamo, upper Orinoco, southern Venezuela.

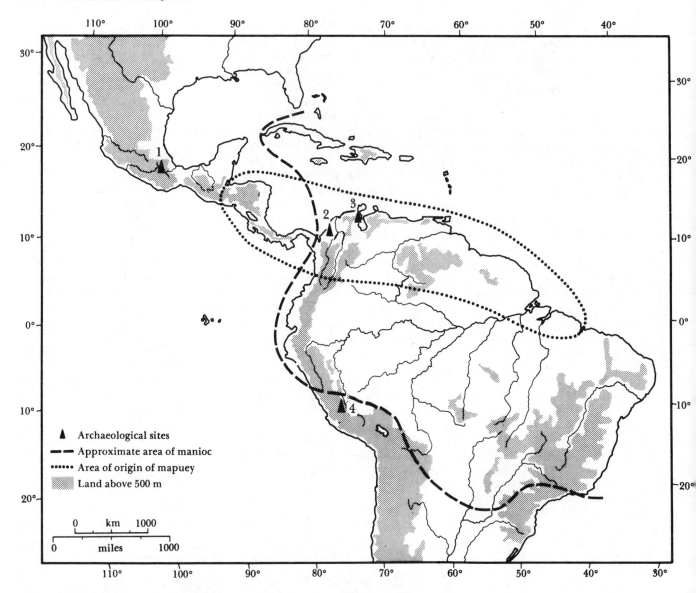

Figure 9. Tropical America. The area of both bitter and sweet varieties of manioc as a staple crop in historical times (after Renvoize 1970, Fig. 18) and the area of origin of the mapuey yam. Archaeological sites: (1) Tehuacan, (2) Momíl, (3) Rancho Peludo, and (4) Ayacucho. (Modified from Coursey 1967, Fig. 1.)

The source region of this expansive seed-culture probably lay north of the Indochinese peninsula in north and east China. The earliest available evidence of agriculture in China comes from sites of the "Neolithic" Yang-shao culture on the loess-mantled hills and terraces bordering the valleys of the Hwang-ho and its tributaries in western Honan. This north Chinese nuclear area became an early focus of seed-culture—possibly during the sixth or fifth millennium B.C.—in which foxtail millet (*Setaria italica*) appears to have been the most important staple crop, cultivated probably by swidden methods (Chang 1968; Ho 1969; Wheatley 1971).

During the succeeding Lungshanoid period, cultures of Neolithic type spread through northern, eastern, and southeastern China, and it has recently been suggested by Kwang-chih Chang (1970) that this expansion was associated with the southward diffusion of a seed-crop tradition of cultivation based on foxtail millet, broomcorn millet (*Panicum miliaceum*), and rice (*Oryza sativa*).

The postulated southward diffusion of seed-culture may also relate to recent discoveries at Spirit Cave in northwestern Thailand. There Chester Gorman has found evidence of an introduced complex of stone tools and

pottery dated to approximately 6000 B.C. (Gorman 1971). The tools include ground stone knives which, by analogy with ethnographically known Indonesian examples, are interpreted as rice-harvesting knives. It is suggested that they indicate the introduction of rice, which is itself associated in Southeast Asia with a shift in foci of settlement from upland sites to lowland plains where early agricultural villages developed, such as Non Nok Tha, which has yielded indirect evidence of rice and is provisionally dated to about 3000 B.C. (Bayard 1971; Solheim 1971; Higham 1972), and Ban Kao, dated to about 1500 B.C. (Sørensen and Hatting

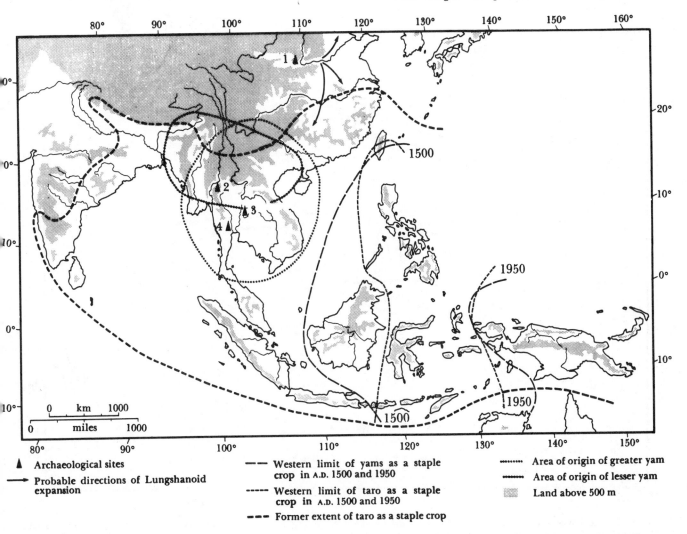

Figure 10. Tropical South and East Asia. The limits of taro and yams as staple crops (after Spencer 1966, Figs. 4 and 5) and areas of origin of the greater and lesser yams. (*D. alata* and *D. esculenta*). Archaeological sites: (1) Yang-shao, (2) Spirit Cave, (3) Non Nok Tha, and (4) Ban Kao. (Based on Coursey 1967, Fig. 1.)

▲   Archaeological sites

⟶   Probable directions of Lungshanoid expansion

— —   Western limit of yams as a staple crop in A.D. 1500 and 1950

- - -   Western limit of taro as a staple crop in A.D. 1500 and 1950

– – –   Former extent of taro as a staple crop

·········   Area of origin of greater yam

▬▬▬   Area of origin of lesser yam

▨   Land above 500 m

1967). Thus, although much of China and Southeast Asia remains archaeological terra incognita, it may be argued that what little data is available broadly supports ecological expectation of a gradual intrusion of seed-culture into tropical areas of vegeculture.

In the African tropics the outlines of a similar pattern are also beginning to emerge out of archaeological obscurity. Most of the limited evidence relates to West Africa and adjacent areas of the southern Sahara and Congo basin, and my comments are restricted to that part of the continent. West Africa is, as we have seen, the homeland of a distinctive group of cultivated yams (Fig. 11), and three minor tuberous crops grown in West Africa—*Coleus dysentericus* = *Soleno-*

stemon rotundifolius, *Plectranthus esculentus*, and *Sphenostylis stenocarpa*—may also have originated there (Harlan 1971). Vegecultural techniques are deeply interwoven with the ceremonial traditions of peoples living in the "yam zone" (Coursey 1967), and this and other indirect evidence suggests that vegeculture may be of considerable antiquity in West Africa despite the fact that no archaeologically preserved remains of root crops have so far been recovered there.

It is possible that some of the stone artifacts found in Mesolithic and Neolithic contexts in western and central Africa represent the blades of vegecultural planting-sticks or hoes rather than wood-working tools or the points of digging-sticks used for collecting wild vegetable foods. Davies

(1960, 1967, 1968) has used such evidence to argue for a "protoagricultural" stage in West Africa based on the collection and planting of tubers. Botanical, linguistic, and ethnological evidence has also been adduced in support of the early domestication of root crops in West Africa. For example, Coursey (1967) has argued strongly for the ancient cultivation of indigenous yams, suggesting that the existence of prohibitions on the use of iron tools for digging yams that are to be used in "new yam" festivals implies that yam cultivation predates the beginning of the West African Iron Age; and Posnansky (1969) has suggested that yam cultivation may have begun in West Africa between 2500 and 1500 B.C.

The traditional seed-cultural complex

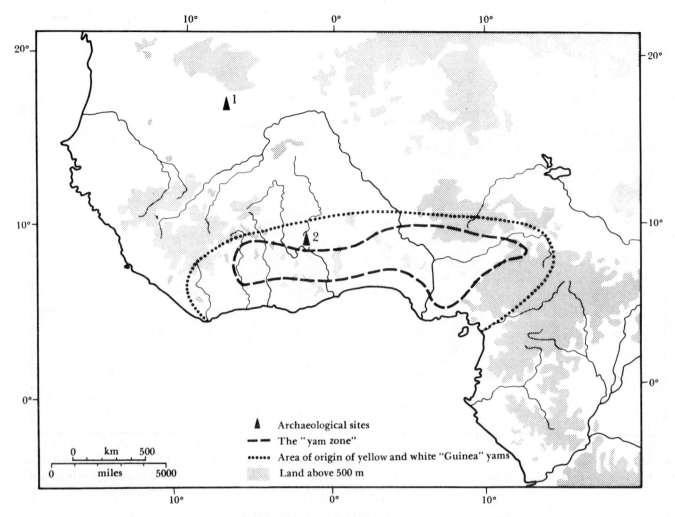

Figure 11. Tropical West Africa. The area of origin of yellow and white "Guinea" yams (*D. cayenensis* and *D. rotundata*) and the "yam zone." Archaeological sites: (1) Tichitt-Walata and (2) Ntereso. (Based on Coursey 1967, Figs. 1 and 3.)

of West Africa includes certain cereals, such as sorghum (*Sorghum bicolor*) and bullrush or pearl millet (*Pennisetum typhoideum = P. americanum*), which probably originated within the Sudanic zone north of the Congo basin, and others, such as fonio and black fonio (*Digitaria exilis* and *D. iburua*), the millet *Brachiaria deflexa*, and African rice (*Oryza glaberrima*), which are more definitely thought to be of local West African origin (Baker 1962; Portères 1962; Harlan 1971). Direct evidence of seed plants, usually in the form of pottery impressions, has so far been recovered archaeologically at only a few West African sites: for example, impressions of pearl millet and *Brachiaria deflexa* at Tichitt-Walata in southern Mauritania dated to about 1100 B.C. (Munson 1968, 1970) and possibly of pearl millet at Ntereso in northern Ghana dated to the second millennium B.C. (Davies 1968), although

at the latter site both the identification and the dating are uncertain. Such finds, together with indirect evidence in the form of possible sickle blades from Nigeria which may indicate grain cultivation (Shaw 1969), suggest that seed-culture was being practiced in West Africa at least by 1000 B.C., and perhaps considerably earlier in view of the fourth millennium dates attributed to several "Neolithic" sites in the western Sahara (Clark 1967).

Whether or not knowledge of seed-culture was initially transmitted across the Sahara from the north, possibly during the putative subpluvial period of moister climate (Harris 1967; Butzer 1964; Clark 1962), there is some evidence to suggest that northern seed cultivators first occupied much of the drier savanna and deciduous forest zone of West Africa and later expanded southward into parts of

the more humid evergreen forest zone. For example, African rice, which probably originated in the area of the "inland delta" of the Niger, appears to have moved gradually south from its center of origin, eventually reaching the rain-forest zone in present-day Ivory Coast (Portères 1950, 1955, 1962). Evidence of the penetration of the more humid forest zone by other staple crops of West African seed-culture is less clear, but there is little doubt that the process has occurred through historic times and is continuing at present (Coursey 1967; Vermeer 1970). Thus, despite the inadequacy of the data, it appears that a pattern of seed-culture progressively expanding into areas of vegeculture can be discerned in West Africa, just as it can in the Asian and American tropics.

Much remains to be learned about

how, where, and when agriculture originated in the tropics. We are still only at the beginning of the quest for answers to this threefold problem, but if the arguments I have presented are well-founded, ecological inference and archaeological evidence appear now to be converging. A pantropical model of agricultural origins may be suggested that shows vegeculture anciently established in parts of all three continental tropical lowlands, but as an ecologically stable, localized, and nutritionally unbalanced system of food production unsuited to territorial expansion, whereas seed-cultural systems, which appear to have ancient origins in drier tropical and warm temperate lands, are seen as inherently unstable and expansive complexes progressively intruding into the homelands of vegeculture.

References

Alexander, J., and D. G. Coursey. 1969. The origins of yam cultivation. In *The Domestication and Exploitation of Plants and Animals*, P. J. Ucko and G. W. Dimbleby, Eds. London: Duckworth, pp. 405–25.

Baker, H. G. 1962. Comments on the thesis that there was a major centre of plant domestication near the headwaters of the River Niger. *J. African History* 3:229–33.

Barrau, J. 1965. L'humide et le sec. An essay on ethnobiological adaptation to contrastive environments in the Indo-Pacific area. *J. Polynesian Soc.* 74:329–46.

Bayard, D. T. 1971. Excavations at Non Nok Tha, Northeastern Thailand. *Asian Perspectives*. In press.

Bischof, H. 1969. Contribuciones a la cronología de la Cultura Tairona. La Cultura Tairona en el Area Intermedio. *Verhandlungen des XXXVIII Internationalen Amerikanistenkongresses Stuttgart-München* (Munich), Vol. 1, pp. 259–80.

Burkill, I. H. 1951. The rise and decline of the greater yam in the service of man. *Advancement of Science* 7:443–8.

Butzer, K. W. 1964. *Environment and Archeology*. London: Methuen, pp. 44–53.

Byers, D. G., Ed. 1967. *The Prehistory of the Tehuacan Valley*. Vol. 1: *Environment and Subsistence*. Austin & London: University of Texas Press.

Chang, K. 1968. *The Archaeology of Ancient China*. Second ed. New Haven and London: Yale University Press, pp. 85–92.

Chang, K. 1970. The beginnings of agriculture in the Far East. *Antiquity* 44: 175–85.

Childe, V. G. 1936. *Man Makes Himself*. London: Watts.

Childe, V. G. 1942. *What Happened in History*. Harmondsworth: Penguin Books.

Childe, V. G. 1958. *The Prehistory of European Society*. Harmondsworth: Penguin Books.

Clark, J. D. 1962. The spread of food production in Sub-Saharan Africa. *J. African History* 3:211–28.

Clark, J. D. 1967. A record of early agriculture and metallurgy in Africa from archaeological sources. In *Reconstructing African Culture History*, G. Creighton and N. R. Bennett, Eds. Boston: Boston University Press, pp. 3–24.

Clark, J. G. D. 1965. Radiocarbon dating and the expansion of farming culture from the Near East over Europe. *Procs. Prehistoric Soc.* 31:58–73.

Coursey, D. G. 1967. *Yams*. London: Longmans, Green, pp. 5–27, 143, 197–203.

Davies, O. 1960. The neolithic revolution in tropical Africa. *Trans. Hist. Soc. Ghana* 4:14–20.

Davies, O. 1967. *West Africa before the Europeans: archaeology and prehistory*. London: Methuen.

Davies O. 1968. The origins of agriculture in West Africa. *Current Anthrop.* 9:479–82.

Flannery, K. V. et al. 1967. Farming systems and political growth in ancient Oaxaca. *Science* 158:445–54

Flannery, K. V. 1968. Archeological systems theory and early Mesoamerica. In *Anthropological Archeology in the Americas*, B. J. Meggers, Ed. Washington, D.C.: Anthropological Society of Washington, pp. 67–87.

Flannery, K. V. 1969. Origins and ecological effects of early domestication in Iran and the Near East. In *The Domestication and Exploitation of Plants and Animals*, P. J. Ucko and G. W. Dimbleby, Eds. London: Duckworth, pp. 73–100.

Gorman, C. F. 1969. Hoabinhian: a pebble-tool complex with early plant associations in Southeast Asia. *Science* 163:671–3.

Gorman, C. F. 1971. The Hoabinhian and after: subsistence patterns in Southeast Asia during the late Pleistocene and early Recent periods. *World Archaeology* 2:300–20.

Harlan, J. R. 1971. Agricultural origins: centers and noncenters. *Science* 174:468–74.

Harris, D. R. 1967. New light on plant domestication and the origins of agriculture: a review. *Geographical Review* 57:90–107.

Harris, D. R. 1969. Agricultural systems, ecosystems and the origins of agriculture. In *The Domestication and Exploitation of Plants and Animals*, P. J. Ucko and G. W. Dimbleby, Eds. London: Duckworth, pp. 3–15. (This paper represents my first attempt to formulate the general ecological argument developed here.)

Harris, D. R. 1971. The ecology of swidden cultivation in the upper Orinoco rain forest, Venezuela. *Geographical Review* 61:475–95.

Harris, D. R. 1972. Swidden systems and settlement. In *Man, Settlement and Urbanism*, Peter J. Ucko, Ruth Tringham, and G. W. Dimbleby, Eds. London: Duckworth, pp. 245–62.

Hawkes, J. G. 1969. The ecological background of plant domestication. In *The Domestication and Exploitation of Plants and Animals*, P. J. Ucko and G. W. Dimbleby, Eds. London: Duckworth, pp. 17–29.

Hawkes, J. G. 1970. The origins of agriculture. *Economic Botany* 24:131–3.

Higham, C. F. W. 1972. Initial model formulation *in Terra Incognita*. In *Models in Archaeology*, D. L. Clarke, Ed. London: Methuen. In press.

Ho, P. 1969. The loess and the origin of Chinese agriculture. *American Hist. Rev.* 75:1–36.

Lathrap, D. W. 1970. *The Upper Amazon*. London: Thames and Hudson, pp. 45–67.

MacNeish, R. S. 1964. Ancient Mesoamerican civilization. *Science* 143:531–7.

MacNeish, R. S. 1969. *First Annual Report of the Ayacucho Archaeological-Botanical Project*. Andover, Mass.: R. S. Peabody Foundation.

MacNeish, R. S. et al. 1970. *Second Annual Report of the Ayacucho Archaeological-Botanical Project*. Andover, Mass.: R. S. Peabody Foundation, p. 39.

Munson, P. J. 1968. Recent archaeological research in the Dhar Tichitt region of south-central Mauretania. *West African Archaeological Newsletter* 10:6–13.

Munson, P. J. 1970. Corrections and additional comments concerning the "Tichitt Tradition." *West African Archaeological Newsletter* 12:47–8.

Odum, E. P. 1963. *Ecology*. New York: Holt, Rinehart and Winston, pp. 28–35.

Pickersgill, B. 1971. Personal communication. Department of Agricultural Botany, Reading University, England.

Portères, R. 1950. Vieilles agricultures de l'Afrique intertropical. *L'Agronomie Tropicale* 5:489–507.

Portères, R. 1955. Historique sur les premiers échantillons d'*Oryza glaberrima* St. recueillis en Afrique. *J. d'Agric. Trop. et de Bot. Ap.* 2:535–7.

Portères, R. 1962. Berceaux agricoles primaires sur le continent africain. *J. African History* 3:195–210.

Posnansky, M. 1969. Yams and the origins of West African agriculture. *Odu* 1:101–7.

Reichel-Dolmatoff, G. 1957. Momíl: a Formative sequence from the Sinú Valley, Colombia. *American Antiquity* 22:226–34.

Renfrew, J. M. 1969. The archaeological evidence for the domestication of plants: methods and problems. In *The Domestication and Exploitation of Plants and Animals*, P. J. Ucko and G. W. Dimbleby, Eds London: Duckworth, pp. 149–72.

Renvoize, B. S. 1970. Manioc (*Manihot esculenta* Crantz) and its role in the Amerindian agriculture of tropical America. Unpublished thesis submitted for the degree of M.Phil. in the University of London.

Renvoize, B. S. 1972. The area of origin of manioc (*Manihot esculenta* Crantz) as a tropical American crop plant—a review of the evidence. *Economic Botany*. In press.

Rogers, D. J. 1965. Some botanical and ethnological considerations of *Manihot esculenta*. *Economic Botany* 19:369–77.

Rouse, I., and J. M. Cruxent. 1963. *Venezuelan Archaeology*. New Haven and London: Yale University Press, pp. 5–6, 53–54.

Sauer, C. O. 1952. *Agricultural Origins and Dispersals*. New York: American Geographical Society.

Sauer, C. O. 1959. Age and area of American cultivated plants. *Actas del XXXIII Congreso Internacional de Americanistas* (San José, Costa Rica) 1:215–29.

Shaw, T. 1969. The Later Stone Age in the Nigerian forest. *Actes du Premier Colloque International d'Archéologie Africaine* (Fort Lamy), pp. 364–73.

Simoons, F. J. 1960. *Northwest Ethiopia. Peoples and Economy*. Madison: University of Wisconsin Press, pp. 89–99.

Smeds, J. 1955. The ensete planting culture of Eastern Sidamo, Ethiopia. *Acta Geographica* 13:1–39.

Solheim, W. G. 1971. Northern Thailand, Southeast Asia, and world prehistory. *Asian Perspectives*. In press.

Sørensen, P., and T. Hatting. 1967. *Archaeological excavations in Thailand*. Vol. 2: *Ban Kao*. Copenhagen: Munksgaard.

Spencer, J. E. 1966. Shifting cultivation in Southeastern Asia. *Univ. California Publics. in Geography.*, Vol. 19. Berkeley and Los Angeles: University of California Press, pp. 111–14.

Strathern, M. 1969. Why is the Pueraria a sweet potato? *Ethnology* 8:189–98.

Troll, C., and KH. Paffen. 1963. Map 5. Seasonal climates of the earth. In H. E. Landsberg et al., *Weltkarten zur Klimakunde*. Berlin-Heidelberg-New York: Springer-Verlag.

Vermeer, D. E. 1970. Population pressure and crop rotational changes among the Tiv of Nigeria. *Annals Assoc. American Geographers* 60:299–314.

Watson, J. B. 1964. A previously unreported root crop from the New Guinea highlands. *Ethnology* 3:1–5.

Watson, J. B. 1968. Pueraria: names and traditions of a lesser crop of the Central Highlands, New Guinea. *Ethnology* 7:268–79.

Wheatley, P. 1971. *The Pivot of the Four Quarters: A Preliminary Enquiry into the Origins and Character of the Ancient Chinese City*. Edinburgh: Edinburgh University Press, pp. 23–25.

How Man Invented Cities

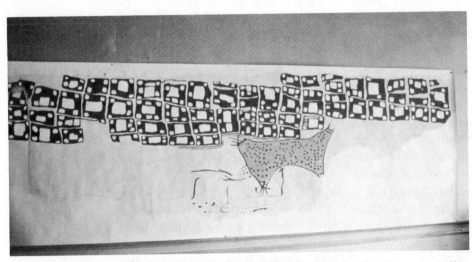

Possibly the first cityscape ever painted was a mural found at Çatal Hüyük, an Anatolian community that flourished during the seventh millennium B.C. As can be seen in this copy drawing, the mural shows a cluster of houses, and behind them, an erupting volcano.

The wonder is not that man could live without civilization but that he could learn to tolerate it. Why and how he went against his nature as a foot-loose primate is only beginning to be understood

By JOHN PFEIFFER

The most striking mark of man's genius as a species, as the most adaptable of animals, has been his ability to live in cities. From the perspective of all we know about human evolution, nothing could be more unnatural. For over fifteen million years, from the period when members of the family of man first appeared on earth until relatively recent times, our ancestors were nomadic, small-group, wide-open-spaces creatures. They lived on the move among other moving animals in isolated little bands of a few families, roaming across wildernesses that extended like oceans to the horizon and beyond.

Considering that heritage, the wonder is not that man has trouble getting along in cities but that he can do it at all—that he can learn to live in the same place year round, enclosed in sharp-cornered and brightly-lit rectangular spaces, among noises, most of which are made by machines, within shouting distance of hundreds of other people, most of them strangers. Furthermore, such conditions arose so swiftly, practically overnight on the evolutionary time scale, that he has hardly had a chance to get used to them. The transition from a world without cities to our present situation took a mere five or six millenniums.

It is precisely because we are so close to our origins that what happened in prehistory bears directly on current problems. In fact, the expectation is that new studies of pre-cities and early cities will contribute as significantly to an understanding of today's urban complexes as studies of infancy and early childhood have to an understanding of adolescence. Cities are signs, symptoms if you will, of an accelerating and intensive phase of human evolution, a process that we are only beginning to investigate scientifically.

The first stages of the process may be traced back some fifteen thousand years to a rather less hectic era. Homo sapiens, that new breed of restless and intelligent primate, had reached a high point in his career as a hunter-gatherer subsisting predominantly on wild plants and animals. He had developed special tools, special tactics and strategies, for dealing with a wide variety of environments, from savannas and semideserts to tundras and tropical rain forests and mountain regions. Having learned to exploit practically every type of environment, he seemed at last to have found his natural place in the scheme of things—as a hunter living in balance with other species, and with all the world as his hunting ground.

But forces were already at work that would bring an end to this state of equilibrium and ultimately give rise to cities and the state of continuing instability that we are trying to cope with today. New theories, a harder look at the old theories, and an even harder look at our own tendencies to think small have radically changed our ideas about what happened and why.

We used to believe, in effect, that people abandoned hunting and gathering as soon as a reasonable alternative became available to them. It was hardly a safe or reliable way of life. Our ancestors faced sudden death and injury from predators and from prey that fought back, disease from exposure to the elements and from always being on the move, and hunger because the chances were excellent of coming back empty-handed from the hunt. Survival was a full-time struggle. Leisure came only after the invention of agriculture, which brought food surpluses, rising populations, and cities. Such was the accepted picture.

The fact of the matter, supported by studies of living hunter-gatherers as well as by the archaeological record, is that the traditional view is largely melodrama and science fiction. Our preagricultural ancestors were quite healthy, quite safe, and regularly obtained all the food they needed. And they did it with time to burn. As a rule, the job of collecting food, animal and vegetable, required no more than a three-hour day, or a twenty-one-hour week. During that time, collectors brought in enough food for the entire group, which included an appreciable proportion (perhaps 30 per cent or more) of dependents, old persons and children who did little or no work. Leisure is basically a phenomenon of hunting-gathering times, and people have been trying to recover it ever since.

Another assumption ripe for discarding is that civilization first arose in the valleys of the Tigris, Euphrates, and Nile rivers and spread from there to the rest of the world. Accumulating evidence fails to support this notion that civilization is an exclusive product of these regions. To be sure, agriculture and cities may have appeared first in the Near East, but there are powerful arguments for completely independent origins in at least two other widely separated regions, Mesoamerica and Southeast Asia.

In all cases, circumstances forced hunter-gatherers to evolve new ways of surviving. With the decline of the ancient life style, nomadism, problems began piling up. If only people had kept on moving about like sane and respectable primates, life would be a great deal simpler. Instead, they settled down in increasing numbers over wider areas, and society started changing with a vengeance. Although the causes of this settling down remain a mystery, the fact of independent origins calls for an explanation based on worldwide developments.

An important factor, emphasized recently by Lewis Binford of the University of New Mexico, may have been the melting of mile-high glaciers, which was well under way fifteen thousand years ago, and which released enough water to raise the world's oceans 250 to 500 feet, to flood previously exposed coastal plains, and to create shallow bays and estuaries and marshlands. Vast numbers of fish and wild fowl made use of the new environments, and the extra resources permitted people to obtain food without migrating seasonally. In other words, people expended less energy, and life became that much easier, in the beginning anyway.

Yet this sensible and seemingly innocent change was to get mankind into all sorts of difficulties. According to a recent theory, it triggered a chain of events that made cities possible if not inevitable. Apparently, keeping on the move had always served as a natural birth-control mechanism, in part, perhaps, by causing a relatively high incidence of miscarriages. But the population brakes were off as soon as people began settling down.

One clue to what may have happened is provided by contemporary studies of a number of primitive tribes, such as the Bushmen of Africa's Kalahari Desert. Women living in nomadic bands, bands that pick up and move half a dozen or more times a year, have an average of one baby every four years or so, as compared with one baby every two and a half years for Bushman women living in settled communities—an increase of five to eight babies per mother during a twenty-year reproductive period.

The archaeological record suggests that in some places at least, a comparable phenomenon accompanied the melting of glaciers during the last ice age. People settled down and multiplied in the Les Eyzies region of southern France, one of the richest and most-studied centers of prehistory. Great limestone cliffs dominate the countryside, and at the foot of the cliffs are natural shelters, caves and rocky overhangs where people built fires, made tools out of flint and bone and ivory, and planned the next day's hunt. On special occasions artists equipped with torches went deep into certain caves like Lascaux and covered the walls with magnificent images of the animals they hunted.

In some places the cliffs and the shelters extend for hundreds of yards; in other places there are good living sites close to one another on the opposite slopes of river valleys. People in the Les Eyzies region were living not in isolated bands but in full-fledged communities, and populations seem to have been on the rise. During the period from seven thousand to twelve thousand years ago, the total number of sites doubled, and an appreciable proportion of them probably represent year-round settlements located in small river valleys. An analysis of excavated animal remains reveals an increasing dietary reliance on migratory birds and fish (chiefly salmon).

People were also settling down at about the same time in the Near East —for example, not far from the Mediterranean shoreline of Israel and on the border between the coastal plain and the hills to the east. Ofer Bar-Yosef, of the Institute of Archaeology of Hebrew University in Jerusalem, points out that since they were able to exploit both these areas, they did not have to wander widely in search of food. There were herds of deer and gazelle, wild boar, fish and wild fowl, wild cereals and other plants, and limestone caves and shelters like those in the Les Eyzies region. Somewhat later, however, a new land-use pattern emerged. Coastal villages continued to flourish, but in addition to them, new sites began appearing further inland— and in areas that were drier and less abundant.

Only under special pressure will men abandon a good thing, and in this case it was very likely the pressure of rising populations. The evidence suggests that the best coastal lands were supporting about all the hunter-gatherers they could support; and as living space decreased there was a "budding off," an overflow of surplus population into the second-best back country where game was scarcer. These people depended more and more on plants, particularly on wild cereals, as indicated by the larger numbers of flint sickle blades,

mortars and pestles, and storage pits found at their sites (and also by an increased wear and pitting of teeth, presumably caused by chewing more coarse and gritty plant foods).

Another sign of the times was the appearance of stone buildings, often with impressively high and massive walls. The structures served a number of purposes. For one thing, they included storage bins where surplus grain could be kept in reserve for bad times, when there was a shortage of game and wild plants. They also imply danger abroad in the countryside, new kinds of violence, and a mounting need for defenses to protect stored goods from the raids of people who had not settled down.

Above all, the walls convey a feeling of increasing permanence, an increasing commitment to places. Although man was still mainly a hunter-gatherer living on wild species, some of the old options no longer existed for him. In the beginning, settling down may have involved a measure of choice, but now man was no longer quite so free to change locales when the land became less fruitful. Even in those days frontiers were vanishing. Man's problem was to develop new options, new ways of working the land more intensively so that it would provide the food that migration had always provided in more mobile times.

The all-important transition to agriculture came in small steps, establishing itself almost before anyone realized what was going on. Settlers in marginal lands took early measures to get more food out of less abundant environments—roughing up the soil a bit with scraping or digging sticks, sowing wheat and barley seeds, weeding, and generally doing their best to promote growth. To start with at least, it was simply a matter of supplementing regular diets of wild foods with some domesticated species, animals as well as plants, and people probably regarded themselves as hunter-gatherers working hard to maintain their way of life rather than as the revolutionaries they were. They were trying to preserve the old self-sufficiency, but it was a losing effort.

The wilderness way of life became more and more remote, more and more nearly irretrievable. Practically every advance in the technology of agriculture committed people to an increasing dependence on domesticated species and on the activities of other people living nearby. Kent Flannery of the University of Michigan emphasizes this point in a study of one part of Greater Mesopotamia, prehistoric Iran, during the period between twelve thousand and six thousand years ago. For the hunter-gatherer, an estimated one-third of the country's total land area was good territory, consisting of grassy plains and high mountain valleys where wild species were abundant; the rest of the land was desert and semidesert.

The coming of agriculture meant that people used a smaller proportion of the countryside. Early farming took advantage of naturally distributed water; the best terrain for that, namely terrain with a high water table and marshy areas, amounted to about a tenth of the land area. But only a tenth of that tenth was suitable for the next major development, irrigation. Meanwhile, food yields were soaring spectacularly, and so was the population of Iran, which increased more than fiftyfold; in other words, fifty times the original population was being supported by food produced on one-hundredth of the land.

A detailed picture of the steps involved in this massing of people is coming from studies of one part of southwest Iran, an 880-square-mile region between the Zagros Mountains and the Iraqi border. The Susiana Plain is mostly flat, sandy semidesert, the only notable features being man-made mounds that loom on the horizon like islands, places where people built in successively high levels on the ruins of their ancestors. During the

past decade or so, hundreds of mounds have been mapped and dated (mainly through pottery styles) by Robert Adams of the University of Chicago, Jean Perrot of the French Archaeological Mission in Iran, and Henry Wright and Gregory Johnson of the University of Michigan. Their work provides a general idea of when the mounds were occupied, how they varied in size at different periods—and how a city may be born.

Imagine a time-lapse motion picture of the early settling of the Susiana Plain, starting about 6500 B.C., each minute of film representing a century. At first the plain is empty, as it has been since the beginning of time. Then the pioneers arrive; half a dozen families move in and build a cluster of mud-brick homes near a river. Soon another cluster appears and another, until, after about five minutes (it is now 6000 B.C.), there are ten settlements, each covering an area of 1 to 3 hectares (1 hectare = 2.47 acres). Five minutes more (5500 B.C.) and we see the start of irrigation, on a small scale, as people dig little ditches to carry water from rivers and tributaries to lands along the banks. Crop yields increase and so do populations, and there are now thirty settlements, all about the same size as the original ten.

This is but a prelude to the main event. Things become really complicated during the next fifteen minutes or so (5500 to 4000 B.C.). Irrigation systems, constructed and maintained by family groups of varying sizes, become more complex. The number of settlements shows a modest increase, from thirty to forty, but a more significant change takes place—the appearance of a hierarchy. Instead of settlements all about the same size, there are now levels of settlements and a kind of ranking: one town (7 hectares), ten large villages (3 to 4 hectares), and twenty-nine smaller villages of less than 3 hectares. During this period large residential and ceremonial structures appear at Susa, a town on the western edge of the Susiana Plain.

Strange happenings can be observed not long after the middle of this period (about 4600 B.C.). For reasons unknown, the number of settlements decreases rapidly. It is not known whether the population of the area decreased simultaneously. Time passes, and the number of settlements increases to about the same level as before, but great changes have occurred. Three cities have appeared with monumental public buildings, elaborate residential architecture, large workshops, major storage and market facilities, and certainly with administrators and bureaucrats. The settlement hierarchy is more complex, and settlements are no longer located to take advantage solely of good agricultural opportunities. Their location is also influenced by the cities and the services and opportunities available there. By the end of our hypothetical time-lapse film, by the early part of the third millennium B.C., the largest settlement of all is the city of Susa, which covers some thirty hectares and will cover up to a square kilometer (100 hectares) of territory before it collapses in historical times.

All Mesopotamia underwent major transformations during this period. Another city was taking shape 150 miles northwest of Susa in the heartland of Sumer. Within a millennium the site of Uruk near the Euphrates River grew from village dimensions to a city enclosing within its defense walls more than thirty thousand people, four hundred hectares, and at the center a temple built on top of a huge brick platform. Archaeological surveys reveal that this period also saw a massive immigration into the region from places and for reasons as yet undetermined, resulting in a tenfold increase in settlements and in the formation of several new cities.

Similar surveys, requiring months and thousands of miles of walking, are completed or under way in many parts of the world. Little more than a millen-

nium after the establishment of Uruk and Susa, cities began making an independent appearance in northern China not far from the conflux of the Wei and Yellow rivers, in an area that also saw the beginnings of agriculture. Still later, and also independently as far as we can tell, intensive settlement and land use developed in the New World.

The valley of Oaxaca in Mexico, where Flannery and his associates are working currently, provides another example of a city in the process of being formed. Around 500 B.C., or perhaps a bit earlier, buildings were erected for the first time on the tops of hills. Some of the hills were small, no more than twenty-five or thirty feet high, and the buildings were correspondingly small; they overlooked a few terraces and a river and probably a hamlet or two. Larger structures appeared on higher hills overlooking many villages. About 400 B.C. the most elaborate settlement began to appear on the highest land, 1,500-foot Monte Albán, with a panoramic view of the valley's three arms; and within two centuries it had developed into an urban center including hundreds of terraces, an irrigation system, a great plaza, ceremonial buildings and residences, and an astronomical observatory.

At about the same time, the New World's largest city, Teotihuacán, was evolving some 225 miles to the northwest in the central highlands of Mexico. Starting as a scattering of villages and hamlets, it covered nearly eight square miles at its height (around A.D. 100 to 200) and probably contained some 125,000 people. Archaeologists are now reconstructing the life and times of this great urban center. William Sanders of Pennsylvania State University is concentrating on an analysis of settlement patterns in the area, while Rene Millon of the University of Rochester and his associates have prepared detailed section-by-section maps of the city as a step toward further extensive excavations. Set in a narrow valley among mountains and with its own man-made mountains, the Pyramid of the Sun and the Pyramid of the Moon, the city flourished on a grand scale. It housed local dignitaries and priests, delegations from other parts of Mesoamerica, and workshop neighborhoods where specialists in the manufacture of textiles, pottery, obsidian blades, and other products lived together in early-style apartments.

The biggest center in what is now the United States probably reached its peak about a millennium after Teotihuacán. But it has not been reconstructed, and archaeologists are just beginning to appreciate the scale of what happened there. Known as Cahokia and located east of the Mississippi near St. Louis, it consists of a cluster of some 125 mounds (including a central mound 100 feet high and covering 15 acres) as well as a line of mounds extending six miles to the west.

So surveys and excavations continue, furnishing the sort of data needed to disprove or prove our theories. Emerging patterns—patterns involving the specific locations of different kinds of communities and of buildings and other artifacts within communities—can yield information about the forces that shaped and are still shaping cities and the behavior of people in cities. But one trend stands out above all others: the world was becoming more and more stratified. Every development seemed to favor social distinctions, social classes and elites, and to work against the old hunter-gatherer ways.

Among hunter-gatherers all people are equal. Individuals are recognized as exceptional hunters, healers, or storytellers, and they all have the chance to shine upon appropriate occasions. But it would be unthinkable for one of them, for any one man, to take over as full-time leader. That ethic passed when the nomadic life passed. In fact, a literal explosion of differences accompanied the coming of communities where people lived close together in permanent dwellings and under conditions where

moving away was not easy.

The change is reflected clearly in observed changes of settlement patterns. Hierarchies of settlements imply hierarchies of people. Emerging social levels are indicated by the appearance of villages and towns and cities where only villages had existed before, by different levels of complexity culminating in such centers as Susa and Monte Albán and Cahokia. Circumstances practically drove people to establish class societies. In Mesopotamia, for instance, increasingly sophisticated agricultural systems and intensive concentrations of populations brought about enormous and irreversible changes within a short period. People were clamped in a demographic vise, more and more of them living and depending on less and less land—an ideal setting for the rapid rise of status differences.

Large-scale irrigation was a highly effective centralizing force, calling for new duties and new regularities and new levels of discipline. People still depended on the seasons; but in addition, canals had to be dug and maintained, and periodic cleaning was required to prevent the artificial waterways from filling up with silt and assorted litter. Workers had to be brought together, assigned tasks, and fed, which meant schedules and storehouses and rationing stations and mass-produced pottery to serve as food containers. It took time to organize such activities efficiently. There were undoubtedly many false starts, many attempts by local people to work things out among themselves and their neighbors at a community or village level. Many small centers, budding institutions, were undoubtedly formed and many collapsed, and we may yet detect traces of them in future excavations and analyses of settlement patterns.

The ultimate outcome was inevitable. Survival demanded organization on a regional rather than a local basis. It also demanded high-level administrators and managers, and most of them had to be educated people, mainly because of the need to prepare detailed records of supplies and transactions. Record-keeping has a long prehistory, perhaps dating back to certain abstract designs engraved on cave walls and bone twenty-five thousand or more years ago. But in Mesopotamia after 4000 B.C. there was a spurt in the art of inventing and utilizing special marks and symbols.

The trend is shown in the stamp and cylinder seals used by officials to place their "signatures" on clay tags and tablets, man's first documents. At first the designs on the stamp seals were uncomplicated, consisting for the most part of single animals or simple geometric motifs. Later, however, there were bigger stamp seals with more elaborate scenes depicting several objects or people or animals. Finally the cylinder seals appeared, which could be rolled to repeat a complex design. These seals indicate the existence of more and more different signatures—and more and more officials and record keepers. Similar trends are evident in potters' marks and other symbols. All these developments precede pictographic writing, which appears around 3200 B.C.

Wherever record keepers and populations were on the rise, in the Near East or Mexico or China, we can be reasonably sure that the need for a police force or the prehistoric equivalent thereof was on the increase, too. Conflict, including everything from fisticuffs to homicide, increases sharply with group size, and people have known this for a long time. The Bushmen have a strong feeling about avoiding crowds: "We like to get together, but we fear fights." They are most comfortable in bands of about twenty-five persons and when they have to assemble in larger groups—which happens for a total of only a few months a year, mainly to conduct initiations, arrange marriages, and be near the few permanent water holes during dry seasons—they form separate small groups of about twenty-five, as if they were still living on their own.

Incidentally, twenty-five has been called a "magic number," because it hints at what may be a universal law of group behavior. There have been many counts of hunter-gatherer bands, not only in the Kalahari Desert, but also in such diverse places as the forests of Thailand, the Canadian Northwest, and northern India. Although individual bands may vary from fifteen to seventy-five members, the tendency is to cluster around twenty-five, and in all cases a major reason for keeping groups small is the desire to avoid violence. In other words, the association between large groups and conflict has deep roots and very likely presented law-and-order problems during the early days of cities and pre-cities, as it has ever since.

Along with managers and record keepers and keepers of the peace, there were also specialists in trade. A number of factors besides population growth and intensive land use were involved in the origin of cities, and local and long-distance trade was among the most important. Prehistoric centers in the process of becoming urban were almost always trade centers. They typically occupied favored places, strategic points in developing trade networks, along major waterways and caravan routes or close to supplies of critical raw materials.

Archaeologists are making a renewed attempt to learn more about such developments. Wright's current work in southwest Iran, for example, includes preliminary studies to detect and measure changes in the flow of trade. One site about sixty-five miles from Susa lies close to tar pits, which in prehistoric times served as a source of natural asphalt for fastening stone blades to handles and waterproofing baskets and roofs. By saving all the waste bits of this important raw material preserved in different excavated levels, Wright was able to estimate

A French archaeological team here surveys part of the ruins of ancient Susa in Iran.

This site and surrounding ones are yielding new evidence about the origins of urban life.

fluctuations in its production over a period of time. In one level, for example, he found that the amounts of asphalt produced increased far beyond local requirements; in fact, a quantitative analysis indicates that asphalt exports doubled at this time. The material was probably being traded for such things as high-quality flint obtained from quarries more than one hundred miles away, since counts of material recovered at the site indicate that imports of the flint doubled during the same period.

In other words, the site was taking its place in an expanding trade network, and similar evidence from other sites can be used to indicate the extent and structure of that network. Then the problem will be to find out what other things were happening at the same time, such as significant changes in cylinder-seal designs and in agricultural and religious practices. This is the sort of evidence that may be expected to spell out just how the evolution of trade was related to the evolution of cities.

Another central problem is gaining a fresh understanding of the role of religion. Something connected with enormous concentrations of people, with population pressures and tensions of many kinds that started building up five thousand or more years ago, transformed religion from a matter of simple rituals carried out at village shrines to the great systems of temples and priesthoods invariably associated with early cities. Sacred as well as profane institutions arose to keep society from splitting apart.

Strong divisive tendencies had to be counteracted, and the reason may involve yet another magic number, another intriguing regularity that has been observed in hunter-gatherer societies in different parts of the world. The average size of a tribe, defined as a group of bands all speaking the same dialect, turns out to be about five hundred persons, a figure that depends to some extent on the limits of human memory. A tribe is a community of people who can identify closely with one another and engage in repeated face-to-face encounters and recognitions; and it happens that five hundred may represent about the number of persons a hunter-gatherer can remember well enough to approach on what would amount to a first-name basis in our society. Beyond that number the level of familiarity declines, and there is an increasing tendency to regard individuals as "they" rather than "we," which is when trouble usually starts. (Architects recommend that an elementary school should not exceed five hundred pupils if the principal is to maintain personal contact with all of them, and the headmaster of one prominent prep school recently used this argument to keep his student body at or below the five-hundred mark.)

Religion of the sort that evolved with the first cities may have helped to "beat" the magic number five hundred. Certainly there was an urgent need to establish feelings of solidarity among many thousands of persons rather than a few hundred. Creating allegiances wider than those provided by direct kinship and person-to-person ties became a most important problem, a task for full-time professionals. In this connection Paul Wheatley of the University of Chicago suggests that "specialized priests were among the first persons to be released from the daily round of subsistence labor." Their role was partly to exhort other workers concerned with the building of monuments and temples, workers who probably exerted greater efforts in the belief that they were doing it not for mere men but for the glory of individuals highborn and close to the gods.

The city evolved to meet the needs of societies under pressure. People were being swept up in a process that had been set in motion by their own activities and that they could never have predicted, for the simple reason that they had no insight into what they were doing in the first place. For example, they did not know, and had no way of knowing, that settling down could lead to population explosions.

There is nothing strange about this state of affairs, to be sure. It is the essence of the human condition and involves us just as intensely today. Then as now, people responded by the sheer instinct of survival to forces that they understood vaguely at best—and worked together as well as they could to organize themselves, to preserve order in the face of accelerating change and complexity and the threat of chaos. They could never know that they were creating what we, its beneficiaries and its victims, call civilization.

38

WHEELS and MAN

Stephan F. de Borhegyi

One of man's most important inventions, one that dramatically altered his way of life, was the abstraction of the idea of rotary motion and its subsequent use in the wheel. Man has been making tools for some 500,000 years, but his use of wheels, pulleys and wheeled vehicles is barely 6,000 years old. Rotary motion in the form we know it in machines and vehicles is therefore a comparatively recent addition to man's equipment. Although the development of such machines, as in the case of any other human tool, has been cumulative and progressive, rotary motion was probably discovered independently by many human societies living in far different parts of the globe. Once a society was able to conceptualize a circle, it was on the road to discovering the principle of rotary motion and its many applications, such as the spinning wheel, the spindle whorl, the fire drill, the rotary quern, the pulley, the potter's wheel and the vehicular wheel.

The vehicular wheel, which revolutionized transportation, is basically a disc equipped with bearings to allow it to spin freely. The manufacture of a disc requires in itself the performance of another rotary motion, namely tracing a circle. Tracing a true circle can be accurately executed only with an appropriate instrument. A length of string, one end of which is fixed, or by a forked stick or bone, one prong of which is rotated on the other as a fixed point can serve as such an instrument. As a matter of fact, the wishbone of a bird may well have been the first, accidentally discovered "compass," which many used successfully to draw a perfect circle in the sand. Once the concept of a free-spinning disc was developed, the next step toward the invention of the wheel and its application to vehicular transport was logical.

The earliest known vehicular wheels were probably made of horizontal cross-sections of fallen tree logs. In the Near East the use of solid spokeless wooden wheels most probably coincided with the domestication of draft animals: the oxen, the mule and the horse. The first wheeled vehicles were clumsily built four-wheeled wagons or two-wheeled carts. Each wheel consisted of three wooden discs, held together by wooden, copper or bronze clamps. The existence of such disc-wheeled vehicles is known to us primarily through pictographic symbols and miniature terracotta replicas. Such replicas, employed probably in magico-religious contexts, are first found in Mesopotamian tombs and burials and would indicate that massive wheeled wagons and carts were used as early as 3250 B.C. by the Sumerians, and were soon followed and imitated by other cultures between the Tigris and Euphrates Rivers, on the Indus River and in Anatolia. Then their use gradually diffused into North Africa and through the Caucasus to Europe, the Middle Danube area, and to northern and western Europe. By 1500 B.C. wheeled vehicles were used as far east as China.

Meanwhile, by 3000 B.C., lighter and fast-moving two-wheeled mule and horse drawn chariots made their appearance in Mesopotamia, Anatolia and Egypt. They changed the military history of the Middle East, spurring nations to conquer foreign lands and establish far-reaching empires. The first spoked wheels appeared around 2000 B.C. in Mesopotamia, and then in Egypt. By 1000 B.C. they were universally in use around the shores of the entire eastern Mediterranean. Meanwhile, the earlier wooden wheels and wooden chariots were rapidly being

Hollow, jointed-limb terracotta figurine, from Teotihuacan, Mexico. Classic Period, a.d. 600-900. Height, 17 cms.; Milwaukee Public Museum inventory number 53382/18733.

wheeled miniature animals were found in tombs and burials at many archaeological sites in Mexico and El Salvador. Among the animals represented are the deer, jaguar, dog, alligator, spider monkey and small rodent. They are known since 1880 when the explorer-archaeologist, Désiré Charnay, dug some up at the site known as Tenenpango, on the slopes of the volcano Popocatepetl, just southeast of Mexico City. Since this first discovery several more wheeled figurines have been excavated at archaeological sites located in nothern and central Veracruz on the Gulf Coast of Mexico (Panuco, Pavon, Tres Zapotes, Remojadas, Cerro de las Mesas, etc.) at the Mexican Highlands (Atzcapotzalco, Valley of Teotihuacan, Culhuacán, Santiago, Ahuixotla, Chalco, etc.), at Oaxaca, and on the west coast of Mexico (Lake Chapala, Cojumatlán, Tepachtitlán, Guerrero, Iguala, Nayarit), and also at the Lempa River, in eastern El Salvador. Of these, the Salvadorean pieces seem to be the oldest (dating possibly to the end of the Late Pre-Classic period, around 200 b.c. to a.d. 200), while the rest of the known wheeled zoomorphic and anthropomorphic figures and whistles from Mexico are the products of Classic times (a.d. 200 to a.d. 900).

Precolumbian wheeled figures are still considered rarities and collectors' items. The Milwaukee Public Museum is fortunate enough to possess several miniature disc-shaped wheels from the Valley of Mexico (catalog numbers 14323 to 14325 and 52910 *a* and *b*) and three complete miniature Classic period four-wheeled effigy whistles from central Veracruz, on the Gulf Coast of Mexico. One whistle represents a jaguar; the other two represent a deer and a spider monkey. All three were donated to the Museum in 1968 by the Northwestern Mutual Life Insurance Company of Milwaukee, to enhance the Museum's exhibit on "Inventions."

Toys usually mirror the world of grown-ups. How

replaced by more durable ones plated with or made entirely out of metal, first of bronze, and later on of iron. And so the wheel was rolling on its way to revolutionary success all over the Old World.

The ultimate success of equipping wheels with comfortably bouncing rubber tires or tubes was not possible until after the sixteenth century, when the discovery of the New World brought inventors of wheels and horse- and oxen-driven vehicles face to face with the discoverers of solid and liquid rubber in Mexico. The natives of Mesoamerica were first stunned by the unfamiliar horses and vehicles. The Spaniards were awed by the Indians' bouncing rubber balls. The Indians soon took to the horses, mules and carts while the Spaniards began experimenting with rubber. And so, the rubber covered wheel came into use, to the mutual benefit of the Old and New World.

Until recently it has been a generally accepted fact that the principle of the wheel and the use of wheeled vehicles were unknown in the New World up to the time of European contact. Nor were any of the draft animals known to the people of the New World until they stood eye to eye with the mounted conquistadors of Spain. For this reason it is especially important to realize that small clay figurines and effigy whistles equipped with four wheels, representing animals, were known and used in ancient Mesoamerica long before the arrival of the Spanish conquistadors. As in ancient Mesopotamia, these four-

Creamish white, terracotta chariot with solid wheels. Hurrite culture, Mesopotamia, 1850 b.c. Height, 13 cms.; Milwaukee Public Museum inventory number N-13754.

Red colored, two-wheeled clay cart and draft animals from Mohenjo-Daro, Indus River. 2200 b.c. Height of cart, 6 cms.; Milwaukee Public Museum collection, inventory number 13230 (replica).

ever, although the people of Mexico had miniature vehicles, they were apparently still far from having full-sized wheeled vehicles. Except for the Incas of South America, who had admirable roads and highway systems for pedestrians and their domesticated beasts of burden, the llama and alpaca, the rest of the native population of the Americas had neither paved roads nor pack animals. To be sure, the dog was used by some of the Plains Indians to pull loads and *"travois,"* and the Maya Indians did build some paved roads (*saché*). The latter were most likely used only for ceremonial processions and for the convenience of pilgrims flocking to the ceremonial centers for prescribed celebrations. Therefore, the general lack of good roads and animals for transportation may be the reason why the prehistoric inhabitants of the New World never developed wheeled vehicles. That they knew the basic principles of rotary motion is clear, not only from the miniature wheeled animals, but, as in the Old World, from numerous other archaeological objects of clay or stone which involved some form of rotary motion. The many circular spindle whorls (*malacates*), hollow roller seals, jointed limb figurines, pump and bow drills, just to mention a few, are all mute testimonies to the inventive and mechanical genius of Precolumbian man.

While he unquestionably knew how to put rotary motion and wheels to other uses, he never had developed a need for wheeled vehicles. Perhaps heavy stone blocks or objects could more easily be transported with the aid of log rollers than carts. Lacking pack animals, human porters wearing tumplines and/or specially designed wooden carrying boards such as the *cacaxté* had free use of both of their hands so they could cut the jungle growth on their path or climb narrow and winding mountain trails where no carts could be used. So when the "toy" wheel was invented in Mesoamerica around 100 B.C., there was no need for it to be used for transportation. The four-wheeled miniature animal figures and effigy whistles here described were perhaps used by their makers not as movable toys but for some now obscure religious ceremonies, probably in connection with the rotation of the sacred calendar or with the movement of celestial deities. They were never developed for vehicular transport. As with Leonardo da Vinci's many inventions in Renaissance Europe, in the New World the age was not ripe for this truly great human invention. But the Mesoamerican wheeled "toys" whatever they were used for will forever attest the historical and sociological facts that any human society is capable of discovering independently the basic mechanical principles underlying technical progress. Whether such principles will be developed and applied to practical or ceremonial uses depends entirely on the timeliness, the practicability and the orientation and needs of the culture which made their initial discovery.

39

Pyrotechnology: Man's First Industrial Uses of Fire

The Neolithic Revolution introduced man to the new energy resources to be had from agriculture and those to be gained by applying fire to fuels and earths

Theodore A. Wertime

Men have been using fire for light and heat for at least a million years. Anthropologists agree that in such settings as the Escale Cave in southern France—which has fire-reddened areas up to a yard in diameter (1)—man began that great shift to domesticity that brought him in time within the orbit of civilization. Cooking marked his emancipation from the daily rhythms of the hunt and taught him the first rudiments of the chemical and physical transformations in materials to be wrought by fire.

If the cooking of food has been a consistent art for at least 100,000 years, the fire-hardening of spears for perhaps 80,000 years, and the annealing of stones for chipping perhaps 25,000 years, the consistent cooking of earthy materials is at best 10,000 to 15,000 years old. Indeed, it was only in the late Mesolithic or early Neolithic—with the advent of sedentary community life—that men were caught up in the disciplines of firing clay or earths in an orderly fashion. Beginning with fertility figurines and graduating to pots, they learned in

Theodore A. Wertime has recently served as Cultural Officer in the American Embassy in Athens and the American Embassy in Tehran, and while in these posts he brought to fruition twenty-five years of research in the history of metals and of fire. Also a Research Associate at the Smithsonian Institution, he has led seven expeditions for the National Geographic Society and the Smithsonian Institution in search of man's Neolithic applications of fire to earth. His findings are summed up in this article. Currently Deputy Director of USIA's Information Center Service, Mr. Wertime looks to the future of man's technology as well as its past. Address: 5919 4th Street North, Arlington, VA 22203.

the cooking hearth to dry gypsum to plaster, to anneal native copper and eventually to cast it, to smelt copper and lead from their ores, and ultimately to turn slaggy silicates into glazes and glass.

The domestication of earths through fire was one of the last great irretrievable steps in the domestication of man. Although they might have been launched as innocent and isolated skills, the pyrotechnic crafts in the years between 10,000 B.C. and 2000 B.C. became formidable industrial "disciplines," entailing the most severe chemical controls on daily operations. No woman at her bread oven or stewpot was as much in the grip of formularies as her husband, as he learned from working copper and lead how to confect bronze and iron.

Pyrotechnology came in time to embrace a temperature range from 100°C to 1500°C. At 100°C men roasted gypsum to get plaster of paris. At 1100°C they cast copper, slagged most metals, and vitrified pots to a kind of glaze. At a little above 1500°C they extracted iron from its ores and turned silica into glass. All this happened through a rising scale of chemical sophistication about all kinds of earthy substances—not as a straight line extrapolation but through the early attainment of the casting temperature of copper (1083°C).

The discovery of the industrial uses of fire thus had an intimate connection with man's larger revolution in his approach to sources of energy (2). On the one hand, population increases and densening settlement were unthinkable without the ex-

panded human energy gained from the collection and the cultivation of foodstuffs. On the other, the rendering of materials through fire to make new tools, containers, and buildings involved both new fuels and new chemical and mechanical uses of fire. There is no easy way of characterizing the range of transformations. One can say that oxidation and reduction are at the basis of photosynthesis, animal respiration, and the making of fire; they can be called the means of energy transfer common to both the revolution in food production and that involving fire.

At the same time, oxidation and reduction are susceptible to several definitions. While they account for fire itself ($C + O_2 = CO_2$), they do not account for all the manifold reactions in materials brought on by the application of the heat of fire to them. Metals are separated from their various ores and from each other by a process that is generally reductive: a glassy slag is yielded. But the making of actual glass involves a substitution reaction rather than oxidation and reduction.

The late Neolithic and the Bronze Age thus introduced expanding human populations simultaneously to necessary new energy sources, to new materials, and to complex chemical and physical changes in these materials. Plants and animals

Figure 1. The working of clay and native copper appeared with the first sedentary mud-brick villages in the Taurus-Zagros and evolved into pyrotechnology in the cooking hearth. Here a contemporary mud-brick village in Afghanistan features an advanced pottery kiln in the foreground.

gave man his carbohydrates for movement and proteins for growth; desert brush, wood, and dung gave him his fire; water sorted his materials. Given his acquaintance with matter in such a variety of forms, it is no longer proper to say that man moved from the Age of Stone to the Age of Metal. Native metals were

tools, such as one finds in the traditional blacksmithy, is fully reflected in Iron Age Gordion (to be published by Rodney Young), and also in Assyria, as material from Nimrud shows (to be published by J. E. Curtis).

The archaeological record suggests that pottery is the oldest branch of

the most straightforward processes, from the point of view of the early pyrotechnologist. In effect, one turns clay back to stone by dehydrating it and heating it to a high enough temperature to aggregate the fine mineral particles. There are many possibilities as to the origins of ceramics, such as accidental burning in conflagrations or deliberate baking of fertility figures and case-hardening or sun-drying of bricks in the fireplace. In his new book on Aegean civilization, Renfrew carries the baking of clay figurines back to the Gravettian culture of Czechoslovakia, more than 20,000 years ago (9).

Figure 2. This traditional iron furnace of clay and stone, in the desert near Anarak and Sialk in Iran, differs little from copper and lead furnaces still extant in this ancient mining zone in the early 20th century.

Anarak has a history of metal-working going back 8000 years and linking the technologies of pure native copper, cast native copper, lead and silver, and the ultimate derivative technology, that of iron.

The most obvious clue for pyrotechnologists who have studied hearths is the cooking or baking hearth itself. The early hearth was in many cases already a semipot, baked in the mud or clay by continuous fire. Its walls were a self-registering pyrometer showing in their colors and hardness the degrees of temperature attained as well as the oxidizing or reducing atmospheres. The hearth was clearly man's first laboratory in the industrial use of fire.

discovered in the course of working cherts, flints, obsidian, turquoise, lapis, steatite, and jade and in the development of overlapping trading zones in these materials (3). But the mass production of metals through smelting of ores by fire seems to have begun in the fifth and fourth millennia, *after* plaster and pottery and fired bricks had been in production as adjuncts to expanding community life.

Until the late third millennium, metals were mainly employed for warfare (axes, arrowheads, knives, daggers, swords) and for decoration or sumptuary purposes. It is mainly at Sumer, in the Third Dynasty of the Ur, that one finds men branching out into more commonplace bronze objects such as nails, agricultural implements, chisels, files, spatulas, and the like (4). A full range of tools to produce other

pyrotechnology. In some cases, it may be older than organized food production, though pottery was intimately linked with food preparation and storage in its origins. We shall not attempt a recapitulation of earliest finds. Wilhelm Solheim and K. C. Chang have been pushing pottery horizons in the Far East back to the region of 10,000 B.C. (5). Isolated pottery in a Stone Age setting has appeared in Lepenski Vir, Yugoslavia (6). In the Turkana district of Africa, Lawrence H. Robbins has found pottery beginnings at around the mid-seventh millennium B.C.—before men were producing food for consumption—in a region in which the tradition of shaping Stone Age tools goes back to early man (7). Tepe Ganj-Dareh in Iran offers pottery finds in the eighth millennium B.C. (8).

Pottery-making represented one of

An exceedingly varied set of mechanical and chemical reactions was elicited from that hearth in the millennia 7000–1500 B.C. Plasters (and later cements), pots, and bricks were the products of the dehydration of matter. The removal of water improved bonding qualities, with variable effects on microcrystalline structure. Plasters and cements were rehardened to a stonelike condition with the addition of water (hydration), whereas pots and bricks were partially vitrified in the fire. Metals underwent both chemical reduction from ores and a liquefaction in the fire, recrystallizing into the familiar atomic patterns of metal cooled through the eutectic. Glass, as we shall see, is vitrification carried to the ultimate of a complete reshaping of the mineral crystals of silicates into the fourth state of matter.

One could not possibly argue that this medley of disciplines, ranging in space from Yugoslavia to Thai-

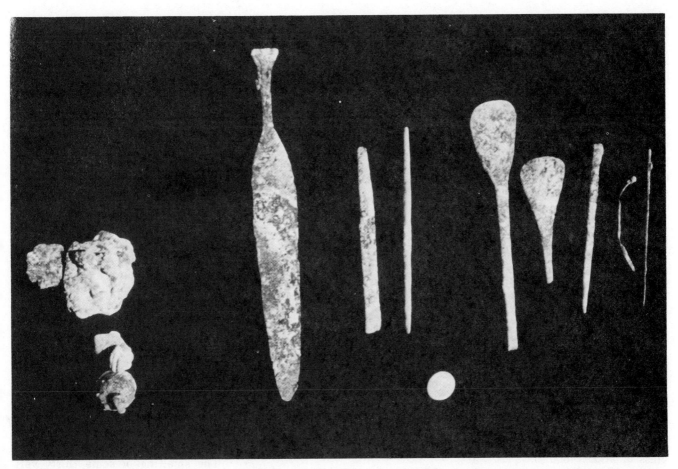

Figure 3. Tepe Yahya, overlooking the Persian Gulf in southeastern Iran, is now seen as an important trading center with Mesopotamia. Excavated by Clifford Lamberg-Karlovsky, it has yielded evidences of being both an entrepot in steatite and an entrepot in metals, directly linking the so-called Stone Age and the early stages of copper fabrication.

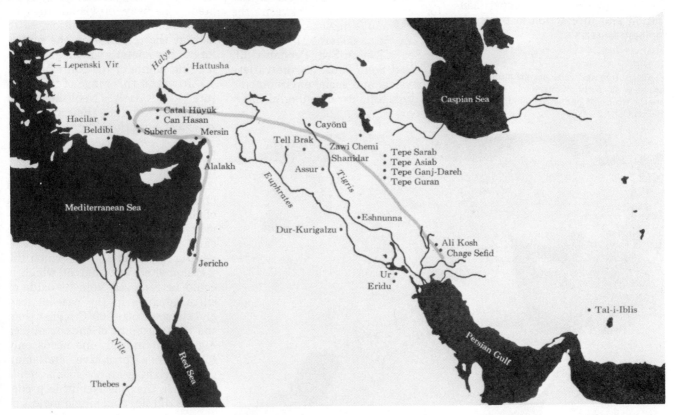

Figure 4. For reasons given on page 270, southwestern Asia became the premier zone of early experimentation with varying industrial uses of fire. The colored line indicates the interacting technologies of obsidian, copper, and fired clay from approximately 8000–6000 B.C. which set the stage for the later consolidation of the metallurgic and vitric traditions.

land and over more than five millennia in time, could have had a common single origin. Today, archaeology describes for us a multitude of beginnings in native metals and pottery over the Old and New Worlds, reflecting the urge of human communities to maximize their food, energy, and material resources as well as man's natural inquisitiveness about earth and fire.

But technical history seems to have conspired to yield two major interconnected pyrotechnological traditions in the arc of the Black Sea, Red Sea, and Persian Gulf (southwestern Asia–Egypt) between 2100 and 1500 B.C. One we identify as the metallurgic tradition, which culminated in the use of iron in Anatolia ca. 2100–1800 B.C. The other was the vitric tradition, starting with faïence technology about 4000 B.C. and expressing itself in old Babylonian formularies and in cored Mesopotamian and Egyptian glass of about 1500 B.C. (*10*). We venture several tentative hypotheses as to why the zone of southwestern Asia–Egypt became the premier area of human experimentation and interaction in pyrotechnologic materials:

Figure 5. Iron and glass are the culminating products of early pyrotechnology, arriving on the scene as industrial products about 1500 B.C.

1. A variety of crucial raw materials ranging from obsidian and turquoise to native copper were drawn into the complex patterns of interregional trade, noted by Gary Wright, Clifford Lamberg-Karlovsky, and James Muhly (*11*).

2. The nature of the urbanizing process was broad and intense, marked as it was by a high level of tribal migration, animal transhumance, and the extensive shifting of plant and animal species and raw materials from their normal niches to places where they were not at home (*12*).

3. Southwestern Asia was relatively versatile in the application of fire making (*13*). The area appears to have witnessed the first smelting of ores to metals; the first shaping of metals into a wide variety of useful forms; the application of burnt clay to a spectrum of uses for building materials, containers, and ultimately writing and numerology; and an early appearance of plasters.

4. There were unique opportunities for communication between the Lower Danube regions, Black Sea, Aegean Sea, eastern Mediterranean Sea, Caspian Sea, Persian Gulf, and Red Sea. Thus, a wide variety of physical and social environments was brought into meaningful interaction.

The metallurgic pyrometer

Although ceramics and plasters were the first earthy products to be yielded by fire, metals set the parameters of pyrotechnology. This was true for three reasons:

1. Metals gave the first inklings of the range of chemical transformations associated with the application of oxidation and reduction to materials.

2. Metallurgy and glassmaking are back-to-back manifestations of the single phenomenon of reducing a metal from its oxide or carbonate or sulfide states and removing its silicate gangue.

3. It was through working with bright glittery metals that men came to have some scientific understanding of the physical forms of materials.

The smelting of some thirty varieties of common ores ranging from lead to iron therefore set the frame in which all of pyrotechnology operated. One way of visualizing the pyrotechnological revolution is to look at the readings on the metallurgic pyrometer, which gives the melting points of the common metals. It was in this range of temperature that early Neolithic men learned to conduct their pyrotechnological operations.

Figure 7 is of course very much a modern scientific conception and as such has given many scholars and archaeologists a misleading notion of the phenomena that the Neolithic tribesmen worked with. For the early craftsmen the effective temperature was not that at which the metal melted but that at which it could be removed from its oxide or silica gangue—in the case of lead and tin some 500–700°C higher than the melting point of the metal (see Figure 12). Indeed, one needs only to watch a primitive craftsman today weighing an ore in his hands to realize that his Neolithic predecessors did not find single metals or ores in isolation but in polymetallic deposits, in which ores of copper, lead, and iron are generally found

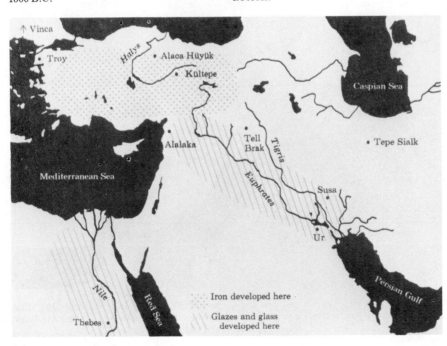

↑ Vinca

• Troy   Halys   • Alaca Hüyük
                    • Kültepe
                                        Caspian Sea

Alalaka   Tell Brak   Tigris   • Tepe Sialk

Mediterranean Sea   Euphrates

Susa

Ur

Nile   Red Sea   Persian Gulf

Iron developed here

Glazes and glass developed here

Thebes •

in confusing juxtaposition (14).

Metallurgy emerged only very slowly as men learned to flux ores with each other (lead with iron, or copper with limestone), to separate metals by cupellation or liquation, and to work with deliberate alloys. They learned the properties of metals only in juxtaposition to each other, to impurities that affected their smelting or casting qualities, and to glass and other ceramics. An understanding of glass as a new kind of matter came only after long experience with metals.

We assume from archaeological finds at such sites as Catal Hüyük, Cayönü Tepesi, Zawi Chemi Shan-

Figure 6. Both metallury and pottery reached an apogee in the early civilizations of the Greek world. This squat jug, tripod stand, and tankard are examples of geometric ware from Greece.

Figure 7. Melting points of pure metals set the parameters of all of pyrotechnology, but they do not accurately describe oxidation and reduction.

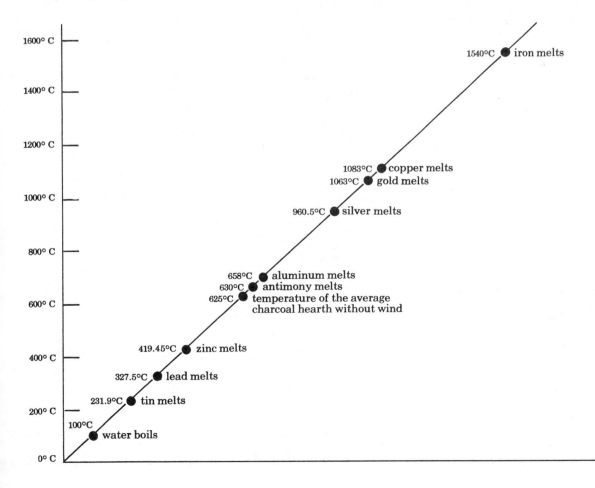

idar, and Ali Kosh that men in the Taurus-Zagros arc were working native copper from about 8000 B.C. (*15*). There is good reason to believe that during the next 3,000 years they learned to anneal copper and to cast it, even before they learned to smelt ores extensively. It appears that the average cooking hearth can reach 625°C and with a good wind, 940°C. Dung and desert woods give an even hotter fire.

The evidence from both archaeology and technology suggests that artisans in southwestern Asia and the Old Copper Culture of North America—and possibly on the west coast of South America—were introduced to metallurgy by annealing native copper in a cooking fire; and long before southwestern Asian workers had reduced other metals in substantial quantities, they had thoroughly explored the parameters of copper by puddle-casting it in the hearth at 1083°C (*16*). There was not, then, an even progression of discovery up the temperature scale from lead to iron, as one would expect from Figure 7, but an early concentration on copper and an introduction of lead and silver metallurgies in the fifth millennium and of iron in the third.

In the fifth millennium, artisans found themselves involved in the complex chemistry of separating ores from their earthy gangues, an operation that occurs at a quite different temperature from the melting point of the pure metal, but in most cases not much less than the melting point of copper. Indeed fire unloosed a series of conflicting chemical reactions in materials from one temperature to the next.

Perhaps the crucial temperature was that at which silicates began to fuse—a temperature slightly above 1000°C. At this temperature, men discovered they could readily "slag" the silica gangue off metals as a kind of glass. They came to identify calcium-sodium alkalis and such metal oxides as hematite as the best aids or fluxes in the process. In so doing they accidentally produced iron and began to learn of its complex role in both metallurgy

and ceramics. As importantly, the art of fluxing silicates with alkalis or metallic oxides carried over into the pottery furnace, taking artisans beyond terra cottas to real glazes and glass—for one could not escape the calcium or iron oxides that are constantly present in most pottery clays and which lower the vitrifying point of the clay.

Figure 8. This painted glass vessel was excavated at Begram, Afghanistan, in the 1930s and is now in the National Museum of Afghanistan. It is thought to have been made in Alexandria, Egypt, between A.D. 100 and 250. The piece is enameled with an ancient lead-containing pigment that was baked on. It belongs with soda-lime-silica glasses common to ancient Mesopotamia and Egypt (*26*).

If Figure 7 expresses the general temperature range in which pyrotechnology occurred, Table 1 tells how it evolved in fact, culminating in the nearly simultaneous appearance of iron manufacture in Anatolia and of glass manufacture in Mesopotamia and Egypt (*17*). Both births were belated, given the fact that the technology of working iron was substantially more diffi-

cult than the technology of working copper and lead. Glass, too, came about through smelting operations, albeit through an intermediate stage of the manufacture of faïence, glazes, and Egyptian blue. Undoubtedly there were psychological impediments to the acceptance of iron and glass as other than slag or throwaway materials. The technologies of producing both were sufficiently different from the usual operations of the pottery kiln and copper or lead metallurgical furnace to warrant a great deal of mind twisting before they could be brought into general acceptance as products. But iron and glass, both yielded in the same temperature range, are true heirs of a single, complex pyrotechnic tradition.

Ceramic temperature scale

The materials for the potter are diverse and somewhat random, however carefully he selects his clays. There are a large variety of clays, mixed with amounts of quartz, flint, feldspar, calcite, biotite, and iron oxides, as well as minor minerals such as serpentine, augite, muscovite, and hornblende, with salts as frequent intruders from the water. Possibly the plasterer, metalworker, and glassmaker were able to make a more precise selection of specific earths than was the potter (*18*).

There seem to have been a variety of prototypes for the earliest pottery—reed baskets, palm-leaf containers, stone bowls, the hearth pit. Primeval clay vessels were coiled, stacked, molded by thumb, laid over basket molds; they were incised, impressed with corded designs; and in time they were overlaid with painted figures (Fig. 6). David French has shown for Turkey and Greece how pottery technologies may have been narrowly localized to zones of varying clays, expanding as trade grew (*19*).

The conceptual possibilities of clay as a plastic medium are suggested by pellets found at the Spirit Cave in Thailand, which were used with bows for killing birds, a kind of primeval slingshot (20). At Beldibi Rock Shelter, Tepe Asiab, Tepe Ganj-Dareh, and several other sites, geometrical clay forms were incised with an early numerology—foreshadowing by 6,000 years wedge-shaped writing in clay (21). Because clay lent itself to making containers, to building walls, to shaping spindle whorls, to making mousetraps, and to inscribing numbers and figures, it was Neolithic man's prime instrument for storage and shelter.

The baking of clays begins somewhere above 500°C, and continues to 1100°C, a temperature at which copper melts and most clays are in an advanced state of fusion. The ceramic experience seems to have

been the first in pyrotechnology, largely because it relates most closely to the daily activity of the cooking hearth.

Regrettably there is no one study of all the various types of hearths and ovens. Coghlan, Tylecote, Smith, Pleiner, and Wertime have scrutinized metallurgical furnaces, and Shepherd, Matson, and Lucas those for ceramics; but the two arts have rarely joined forces. The closest approach was the expedition of 1966 to Tal-i-Iblis in southeastern Iran, where a team experimented with both prototypal metallurgical furnaces and pottery kilns, but without applying the pyrometer to the kilns (22).

Quite apart from this modern ne-

glect, ceramics and metallurgy were at some odds over purposes, if only because the potter seeks restraint. He does not bring his material to a melting, fusing, or total reducing point. Only the early iron founder was under such restraint in metallurgy. The potter has two subtle basing points in his operations—the temperature of near 600°C, at which the clay permanently loses its chemically combined water and its plasticity and at which its crystals interlock; and the much less critical temperature of around 850°C, at which vitrification begins in earnest. These, in a sense, defined the zones of soft and hard ceramic ware.

However, metallurgic chemistry is constantly at work in pots and bricks. Iron is present in most clays and, under oxidizing conditions, yields the red color associated with early Sialk ware, for example. Under reducing circumstances it can turn the dark grey or black of magnetite, such as one sees in early Susa ware (black is also produced by residual carbon as in Vinca ware). Because iron is basic, it tends to inhibit the yellow coloring effect of lime in clay till about 900°C, at which temperature the lime begins to fuse with the clay to produce calcium silicates; but in most clays the maximum coloring effect of iron lies at about 900°C. In causing silicates to fuse, calcium pushes the pot-maker toward a direct awareness of glazing and glass (if only through defective "pips" in his brick or pot). Calcium is also the basis of slagging in metals through additions of limestone or oyster shells. As metathesis comes into play, ceramics and metallurgy become one.

The ceramic tradition had its similarities and differences with that by which the hydrated "binders" of pyrotechnology—plaster, lime begins to fuse with the clay to (23). Plaster and lime begin with the fundamental ceramic operation of drying, but with diametrically opposed purposes in mind. Gypsum ($CaSO_4 \cdot 2H_2O$) can be calcined mildly (below 100°C) to remove most of the water of crystallization.

Figure 9. The contemporary primitive glassblower at Herat, Afghanistan, prepares his barely molten material for blowing. His process, as scrutinized by Dr. Robert H. Brill of the National Geographic–Smithsonian Pyrotechnological Expedition of 1968, helps to throw light on ancient processes as well as on the Assyrian glass texts from Mesopotamia.

Figure 10. At this Kurdish Village in western Iran, one still sees the stacks of straw or dung adjacent to the houses. Similar storage of fodder or fuel may have been the cause of some of the great fires of prehistory.

When it has disintegrated to a fine powder, the addition of water (hydration) causes it to set in the hard, smooth, whitish finish familiar to the users of plaster of paris.

A similar incompatibility existed between ceramics and lime ($CaCO_3$), though as we have seen, lime plays a central role in turning silica to glass or slag. Above 840°C, it fluxes a clay, adding the typical yellow colors of fusion and, at higher temperatures, the progressively darker green. Either as whitewash or in conjunction with alumina, as cement, lime requires water to be slaked and harden.

I have observed the intimate pyrotechnic relationship of lime-making to ceramics in a primitive pottery kiln that was also a lime kiln at desert Anarak (Iran). The two operations were conducted simultaneously at well above 800°C, leaving a powdery lime amidst the pots. Where the two had come into contact, the lime had fused the pots to a dark green. The lime introduced a chemical variable into pot-making, whereas normal kilning was mainly dependent on the vagaries of the fire.

The pyrotechnologic arts did not, then, live in a kind of immaculate isolation, and still less did they live in isolation in the mind of the artisan. As Cyril Smith has well shown in his essay dedicated to Joseph Needham, the Chinese bronze-casters of the Shang and Chou dynasties built on an advanced ceramic technology whose outstanding features seem to have been the mold-making properties of loess soils and the tradition of carved decoration (*24*). The very deficiencies of the two-piece molds led to the aesthetic triumphs of the bronze, such as the flanges. But there were other instances of mutual interconnections of ceramics to metallurgy, not least the employment of metallurgical crucibles first noted by Caldwell at fifth-millennium Tal-i-Iblis and used for the smelting or casting of copper (*25*).

The temperature range of glass

Yet the cross-fertilization produced by tinkering with materials and by raising temperatures into the zone of 1000–1600°C was not sufficient to bring on glassmaking at an early phase as a logical extension of both ceramics and metallurgy, as one might infer from Figure 12. The sudden and nearly simultaneous efflorescence of the art of cored vessels

Figure 11. A burned room at the Kültepe site, which was devastated by fire approximately 1830 B.C.

in two such separate civilizations as Mesopotamia and Egypt has been the subject of considerable speculation. Why are there so few evident antecedents? Leo Oppenheim, in his study of glass texts largely from the library of Assurbanipal, has provided an answer: it seems that the late Assyrian tablets derived from a tradition that goes back to the Ur III period in Sumer (at the end of the third millennium B.C.). The tradition was not written down until the Middle Babylonian period at the end of the second millenium B.C. (*26*).

Assyrian tablets thus were a distillation, not of contemporary glass technologies, but those of an earlier period. What these technologies were involves some difference of in-

terpretation between Oppenheim and Brill. But two lumps of glass respectively from Eshnunna of the Sargonid period (twenty-third century B.C.) and Eridu of the Third Dynasty of Ur (twenty-first century B.C.) seem to be identifiable glass. And a tradition of faïence and glazing was present in Mesopotamia from the fifth millennium, possibly of Syrian or Anatolian origin. The metals trade at Ur III was in process when glass came on the scene.

Faïence and Egyptian blue are the progenitors of true glass. Faïence usually consists simply of silica with a small mixture of soda and impurities—again an alkali working to fuse the silica. The sodium carbonate was applied moist to finely powdered quartz, and the mixture was fired. The quartz grains took on a glassy coating where the soda attacked the silica, thus holding the grains together when the mix-

ture cooled. At higher temperatures than the usual 840–870°C, glass could eventuate. The vitreous, colored glaze covering the white body could have been applied in several ways, one of which was rediscovered by Hans Wulff at Qom in Iran.

Similarly, Egyptian blue—a specific compound of copper, lime, and silica—was a man-made material which could be molded and fired into lovely blue beads or figures. In time, other glazes which would adhere to clay bodies came into existence as men added ground materials from copper and lead slag heaps, PbO being a notable example.

Glass proper exhibits a relatively simple chemistry dependent on highly varied combinations of silica—the main ingredient—and alkali or lime or their substitutes, with vitrification occurring in the relatively high zone of temperatures between the melting point of native copper and that of wrought iron. Glass is defined not by its chemical content—beyond silica—but by its physical state, which Brill calls a fourth state of matter. This means that it possesses the disorganized molecular structure of a liquid and the mechanical rigidity of a solid. Glass is characterized both by the relatively high temperature at which it is made and the conditions of sudden cooling which make its essentially noncrystalline character quite different from the orderly arrangements of atoms in crystals in metals or of the mineral crystals in pots.

Metallurgy did, however, make momentous contributions to glassmaking, not least the art of applying color to glass. Indeed, one can reflect that glass may not have achieved a respectable status till the art of coloring was perfected. The earliest Egyptian glasses incor-

porate the following colorants: blue transparent—copper or cobalt; purple transparent—manganese; yellow opaque—lead-antimony compound ($Pb_2 Sb_2 O_7$); white opaque —calcium-antimony compound ($Ca_2 Sb_2 O_7$); red opaque—cuprous oxide (Cu_2O); and green—mixture of blue and yellow. As early as the seventh century B.C., antimony was used as a decolorizer, to be replaced in the first century A.D. by manganese. Iron produces a green color in glass, a dual coloration reflecting the presence of both ferrous ions (blue) and ferric ions (yellow). Manganese helps to remove the green color due to iron, but by itself it lends an amethyst color. These observations are naturally subject to the modifying circumstances of oxidizing and reducing conditions.

All the states of matter thus fell within the domain of pyrotechnology. The potter eschewed fusion in order to protect the crystals of minerals; the metallurgist sought it in order to achieve the orderly crystals of the metal through application of heat, proper cooling, and hammering, while eliminating a glassy slag.

The iron-worker did not want complete fusion, for that gave him the largely worthless cast iron. Unlike the metallurgist, the glassmaker wanted something very much like the slaggy castoff and wanted it to harden suddenly as a permanent transparent liquid. The plasterer or cement-maker wanted a partially dehydrated powder that would rehydrate and harden to a stonelike state on the addition of water. They were all dealing in one way or another with oxidation, reduction, metathesis, and changes in physical state on heating and cooling.

Dawning of pyrotechnic materials

The student of prehistory can no longer tolerate the myth that human civilization in the late Neolithic moved from stone and bone to metals. The myth was fostered by the Greek poets Hesiod and Aeschylus and was brought to bloom by the Roman naturalist Lucretius and the Chinese scribe Yuan Kang (Han Dynasty) (27). Metals, it is true, established the norms of weight and value and monetary

Figure 12. Reducing points of oxides set the chemical and physical terms on which all of pyrotechnology became a unified art.

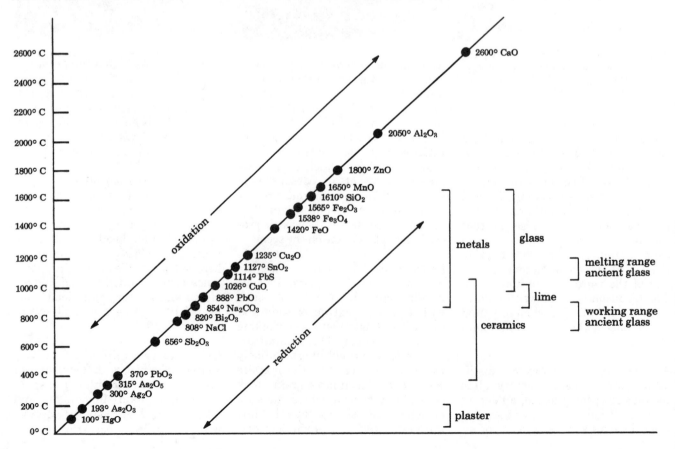

trust for urban life as well as standards of utility for cutting, thrusting, digging, and killing. They became catalysts of social life for men even as they had been catalysts of energy exchanges for cells in the biological organism.

But the thrusts of settled life were many, and as they converged on fire as the main agency for transforming materials, they decreed that civilization would begin its march toward a varied field of substances. Such natural polymers as wood and dough figured prominently in the technologic revolution. But simply by experiencing plaster, bricks, lime, glazes, and metals, man added to his ken of the varieties of matter as well as to his capacity to make flexible and versatile things, from razors to ziggurats.

Wood is an unsung hero of the revolution, for it became both the chief fuel and the chief material of construction. Whatever is said of mudbrick, adobe, or *pisé*, of plasters and stones, or of copper, gold, and iron, wood remained the central structural and energic element in Neolithic technology, even that of the mudbrick house. At such sites as Tepe Guran, it helped to give stone a larger plasticity. One cannot think of energy equations without conjuring up wild pistachio, almond, or *haloxylon amodendron,* or of shipbuilding or early monuments without the Cedars of Lebanon.

And with wooden timbering, fire remained an everpresent danger—manifested by the great conflagrations that burned at one time or another at Tepe Ganj-Dareh and Tal-i-Iblis, Kültepe, Hasanlu, Knossos, Pylos, and Persepolis (28). In this area of pyrotechnics, accidental incendiarism was abetted by the tendency of late Neolithic men to store straw, dung, hay, and wood at the sides of their houses and oil within (Figs. 10–11).

One can say, then, that by about 1500 B.C., when Thebes, Hattusha, Knossos, and Mycenae were the centers of competing empires, pyrotechnology had become a rea-

sonably coherent if not always integrated body of crafts. It incorporated the urge to reshape materials by new energy forms and an understanding of the ways in which hearths, kilns, or unexpected conflagration could do so.

Southwestern Asia, Egypt, and Greece present the focal locale for the great transformations that united the personalized energy resources of food for man with the impersonalized energy of fire for his containers, shelter, and tools. Har-

Table 1. Although ceramics, metallurgy, and glassmaking have been treated as separate disciplines, history makes clear that they evolved in close interconnection between the ninth and the second millennium B.C.

Metallurgy	Ceramics and glass
1800–1200 B.C.	
In Anatolia, iron asserted itself as a dominant metal and spread gradually to Assyrian, Ugaritic, Iranian, Egyptian, Palestinian, and Minoan peoples.	The first cored glass vessels were made simultaneously in Mesopotamia and Egypt, appearing about 1500 B.C. and involving lead-antimony as a colorant.
2300–1800 B.C.	
The earliest manifestations of iron capped the first period of industrial metallurgy. This was marked by the extensive production of copper, silver, and lead in Anatolia and trade by Assyrian and Babylonian merchants in copper and tin.	Old Babylonian glass formularies were coterminous with the first true pieces of glass at Eshnunna and Eridu.
Anatolia—swords of Alaca Hüyük were of terrestrial iron. Iron slag was present in a copper furnace at Alaca Hüyük. The export of metoric iron was forbidden by Kültepe tablets.	
Late fourth and third millennia	
The invasion of the sulfide zone of copper ores accompanied the birth of the Bronze Age and marred the full advent of polymetallism.	Faïence and Egyptian blue came into vogue as by-products of glazing. Pottery production showed an increasing awareness of reducing conditions.
Fifth and fourth millennia	
Smelting of a variety of metals from their ores and casting of copper introduced men to arsenic, antimony, bismuth, and tin as impurities. Iron, silver, and zinc were major by-products of smelting.	Glassy slags provided one introduction to glazes, which found their origin in Anatolia and Syria and spread to Mesopotamia. Glazes, like slags, reflected a new sophistication in vitrifying silicates by adding an alkali.
Sixth millennium	
Annealing of copper led men to 1083°C, the temperature at which copper could be cast. Experiments with smelting other ores proceeded apace.	Ceramics was a widespread art in Eurasia and parts of Africa, but especially where the cooking hearth and trade in stones had reached an apogee.
Ninth–seventh millennium	
Copper was first hammered as a stone, then annealed and hot worked, drawing on a tradition of annealing obsidian and other stones as a way of working them.	Plasters and clay bricks and pots became widespread in Southwest Asia, taking over an ancient tradition of cooking figurines and other clay materials in the fire.

lan's studies of the centers of plant domestication and Protsch and Berger's analyses of animal domestication show that from the eighth to the fifth millennium food production was becoming a reality over a wide zone of Europe, Asia, and Africa, centering in the eastern Mediterranean (*29*). It was in the eastern Mediterranean and Middle East that fire came into its own as an instrument of cookery—of both foods and materials. The high-energy technologies of change first came to fruition here.

Ali Kosh was an early locus classicus of emerging high-energy technologies (*30*). Starting with its assemblage of obsidian blades, the new materials and technologies are here in abundance. There was rapid movement from preceramic to ceramic, the surprisingly early advent of native copper, bitumen as an important patching and tarring agent, the early presence of gypsum plaster. It can almost be said from this kind of array that we have here the zone of innovation in early pyrotechnology.

In general, one finds the earliest appearances of clay ceramics in southwestern Asia on an arc extending from Jericho and Mersin through the Beldibi Rock Shelter, Catal Hüyük, Hacilar, Cayönü Tepesi, Suberde, Tepe Sarab, Tepe Ganj-Dareh, Tepe Asiab, Tepe Guran, and Ali Kosh—where sedentary life had begun. The technology of native copper appeared at Catal Hüyük, Suberde, Can Hasan, Zawi Chemi Shanidar, Cayönü Tepesi, Tepe Zage, Chage Sefid, and Ali Kosh, and mutated into smelting throughout Anatolia and Iran. After a long history of glazes, true glass appeared at Eshnunna and Eridu in the late third millennium B.C., followed in the mid-second millennium by an impressive array of sandcore-formed glass bottles from Assur, Nuzi, and Tell Brak in Assyria, Ur, Babylon, and Dur-Kurigalzu in Babylon, and Al-alakh in Syria. The spread of glassmaking followed the old lines of the tin trade.

Whether such other potential set-

tings as the lower Danube, Thailand, the Huang Ho in China, or the Oaxaca valley of Mexico exhibited equal versatility in trade and pyrotechnical communication is a moot question. Many factors were present in the coming of the new energy systems and technologies to southwestern Asia—a favorable geography, the challenges of cross-fertilizing trade, the span of visible biotechnic and pyrotechnic resources, and tribal movement between ecological niches.

To sum up, pyrotechnology took its cue from Tubal Cain, even as agriculture took its cue from Cain, and herding and nomadism their cue from Abel. The early *industries à feu* operated within the temperature range 100°C to 1500°C, yielding fusion, dehydration, and rehydration of materials, and mechanical alteration in them through heat. The great technologies that began 10,000 years ago can still be found in altered form in the bazaars and workshops of Afghanistan, Iran, Turkey, Ceylon, India, Thailand, and China—but their modern effects are evident in the cities of concrete and steel and the age of plastics that surrounds us (*31*). They have also bequeathed us problems of environmental pollution and shortages of energy that are only now being measured for their effects.

Notes

1. J. E. Pfeiffer. 1972. *The Emergence of Man.* Harper & Row, pp. 112, 167–68.
2. F. Hole, K. V. Flannery, James A. Neely. 1969. *Prehistory and Human Ecology of the Deh Luran Plain.* University of Michigan. P. 342 ff. affords a useful discussion of the revolution and its relationship to population growth and expanded use of materials.
3. G. Wright. 1969. *Obsidian Analyses and Prehistoric Near Eastern Trade.* University of Michigan. C. C. Lamberg-Karlovsky. 1972. Trade mechanisms in Indus-Mesopotamian interrelations. *J. Amer. Orien. Soc.* 92:222–29. James Muhly. 1973. Tin trade routes of the Bronze Age. *Amer. Sci.* 61:404–13.
4. H. Limet. 1960. *Le Travaille du Métal au Pays de Sumer.* Paris: Université de Liège, pp. 190–236.
5. W. Solheim. 1972. An earlier agricultural revolution. *Sci. Amer.* 226(4):34–42. K.

C. Chang. 1968. *The Archaeology of Ancient China.* Yale University Press, p. 87.
6. D. Srejovic. 1972. *Europe's First Monumental Sculptures: New Discoveries at Lepenski Vir.* London: Thames and Hudson, p. 134. R. Tringham. 1971. *Hunters, Fishers, and Farmers of Eastern Europe, 6000–3000 B.C.* London: Hutchinson University Press, pp. 104, 108.
7. L. H. Robbins. 1972. Archeology in the Turkana district, Kenya. *Science* 176:359–66.
8. P. E. L. Smith. 1971. Iran: 9000–4000 B.C.: the Neolithic. *Expedition* 13(3):9.
9. C. Renfrew. 1972. *The Emergence of Civilization: The Cyclades and the Aegean in the Third Millennium B.C.* Methuen, pp. 308–14.
10. A. L. Oppenheim, et al. 1970. *Glass and Glassmaking in Ancient Mesopotamia.* Corning Museum of Glass, pp. 4ff, 76ff, 105ff, 181ff.
11. See note 3.
12. Kent Flannery. 1965. The ecology of early food production in Mesopotamia. *Science* 147:1256.
13. T. A. Wertime. In press. The beginnings of metallurgy: A new look. *Science.*
14. For example, see C. W. Ryan. 1957. *A Guide to the Known Minerals of Turkey.* United States Operations Mission to Turkey, pp. 6ff.
15. J. Mellaart. 1967. *Catal Hüyük: A Neolithic Town in Anatolia.* London: Thames and Hudson, p. 218. H. Cambel and R. J. Braidwood. 1970. An early farming village in Turkey. *Sci. Amer.* 222(3):50–56. R. Solecki. 1969. A copper mineral pendant from northern Iraq. *Antiquity* 43:311–14. See also notes 2 and 3.
16. The issue of the early annealing and casting of native copper is explored by the author elsewhere. See especially C. Renfrew. 1969. The autonomy of the east European Copper Age. *Proc. Prehist. Soc.* 35(2):12–47. Arnold Friedman, Edward Olson, Junius Bird. 1972. Mochican copper analyses: early New World metal technology. Read in manuscript. Swarna Kamal Bhowmik. 1969. Investigations of an unpublished metal image. *Bull. Mus. and Picture Gallery of Baroda* 21:53–60.
17. Iron appears in several Alaca Hüyük swords ca. 2100 B.C. C. Conophagos has analysed a piece, finding no nickel—meaning that the iron was terrestrial. We have also found pieces of iron in the slags of a copper smelter from Alaca Hüyük dated 1800 B.C. While formal production of a wide variety of tools first appeared in Gordion of the 8th century B.C., iron was being consciously produced in Anatolia after 1500 B.C. The subject will be covered by Radomir Pleiner in one of his forthcoming monographs on the coming of the age of iron.
18. Consult F. R. Matson. 1943. Technologic notes on pottery. In N. Toll, ed. *The Excavations at Dura Europas,* Fasc. 1, pp. 81–95. Yale University Press. 1955. Ceramic archeology. *Amer. Cer. Soc.*

Bull. 34(2):33–34. 1963. Some aspects of ceramic archeology. In D. Brothwell and Eric Higgs, eds. *Science in Archeology.* London: Thames and Hudson, pp. 488–98.

19. D. French. Unpublished. Prehistoric pottery groups from central Greece.

20. Solheim, 1972, p. 37.

21. Two remarkable unpublished articles by Denise Schmandt-Besserat constitute the most complete record of the developing uses of clay in the Neolithic that I know. They are entitled The beginnings of the use of clay in the Zagros (December, 1970) and The beginnings of the use of clay in Anatolia (May, 1971). She finds the first extensive exploitation of clay in small objects beginning at Tepe Asiab, Tepe Ganj-Dareh, and Karim Shahir in the Zagros, and Beldibi Cave, Asikli Hüyük, and several other sites in Anatolia. Strangely, figurines, human or animal, do not comprise the most extensive early use of clay. It is rather geometric figures—small spheres, cores, tetrahedrons, discs, and cylinders, which Schmandt-Besserat has now conclusively shown were three dimensional records of transactions, and

were later codified into a one dimensional numeralogy in *bullae* in Mesopotamia.

22. J. Caldwell. 1967. *Investigations at Tal-i-Iblis.* Illinois State Museum, p. 368.

23. Plasterlike substances appear at a variety of sites in the eastern Mediterranean-southwestern Asian area. Classic examples are Cayönü Tepesi and Ali Kosh. In some cases, possibly including Cayönü, lime plasters may have been used in the Neolithic, although gypsum is much easier to make.

24. C. S. Smith. 1973. Bronze technology in the East: A metallurgical study of early Thai bronzes, with some speculation on the cultural transmission of technology. In M. Teich and R. Young. *Changing Perspectives in the History of Science.* London: Heinemann, pp. 21–32.

25. Caldwell, 1967, pp. 17–21.

26. For this discussion of glass, see Oppenheim et al. 1970. Esp. p. 83. Also R. Brill. 1962. A note on the scientists' definition of glass. *J. Glass Studies* 4:127–38. 1968. The scientific investigation of ancient glasses. *Proc. 8th Int. Congress on Glass,* pp. 47–68. For Figure 8, an illustration of Begram glass: 1972. A

laboratory study of a fragment of painted glass from Begram. *Afghanistan* 15 (2): 75–81. I thank Brill for his helpful assistance with this manuscript.

27. Summed up in T. A. Wertime. 1964. Man's first encounters with metallurgy. *Science* 146:1257.

28. The author has inspected all these sites except Tepe Ganj-Dareh. For the latter see P. E. L. Smith, 1971, p. 9.

29. J. Harlan. 1971. Agricultural origins: centers and non-centers. *Science* 174:467–74. Reiner Protsch and Reiner Berger. 1973. Earliest radiocarbon dates for domesticated animals. *Science* 179:235–39.

30. See note 2.

31. T. A. Wertime. The National Geographic–Smithsonian pyrotechnological reconnaissance of Afghanistan, Iran, and Turkey, August-Sept. 1968: A Report. In press by the National Geographic Society. Thanks are due to the Society for the several grants that have made this research possible.

IX. Developments in the New World

New World archaeology covers a much shorter time span than does the archaeology of the Old World. At the very outside, human beings peopled the Americas between 50,000 and 70,000 years ago, and maybe even more recently than that. However, since their arrival as hunters of the large game that roamed the bleak plains in the course of the last glacial period, these "native" Americans displayed tremendous ingenuity in adapting to the wide range of environments they came to occupy. Before their obliteration at the hands of invading Europeans in the course of the past four centuries, native American populations had evolved a vast array of diverse cultures and an almost bewildering diversity of languages. They had also developed some of the most spectacularly sophisticated and politically refined civilizations in the history of the preindustrial world.

But "Where Did the First Americans Come From?" asks Comas. He reviews some of the mistaken beliefs about the origins of New World populations and examines some theories held by eminent scholars that have not become widely known among the lay public. We should note, however, that in spite of Comas' attempt to credit some of these theories, the vast majority of scholars believe that the Americas were peopled through Alaska by small bands of Siberian hunters who crossed the Bering Strait. It is not necessary to postulate other population sources to account for the physical and cultural diversity of pre-Columbian native American peoples.

In high school most of you probably heard about—or even briefly studied—the famous pre-Columbian civilizations of Mesoamerica: the Mayas and the Aztecs. But did you ever wonder where they came from, how they arose? Coe demonstrates that these famous civilizations really evolved from "The Shadow of the Olmecs," the first true civilization in the Americas. But the origin of the Olmecs themselves is poorly understood—for they both appeared and disappeared with shocking suddenness. This article gives you a glimpse of archaeologists at work trying to unlock the riddle of the Olmec civilization.

The Mayas, the Aztecs, the Incas—these are the civilizations that the layperson knows about. But right here in the United States native Americans built their own civilization—and a remarkably advanced one at that, as you will read in Pfeiffer's article describing "America's First City."

It is impossible, of course, to do justice here to the tremendous wealth of archaeological finds in the New World. We hope that the selections in this section will whet your appetite and give you a feel for the tremendous accomplishments of the prehistoric aboriginal inhabitants of the Americas. But since this is merely an introductory survey we must move on, after lingering here briefly, to the final section of the book.

40

ANTARCTICA, SIBERIA OR ACROSS THE PACIFIC...

Where did the first Americans come from?

by Juan Comas

WHERE did the first inhabitants of America come from? At what time in history did their immigration to the American continent begin? These are the first questions we must ask ourselves before seeking to determine the biological and cultural traits of the first settlers in America.

I have used the terms "immigration" and "settlers" on purpose, thereby explicitly rejecting the belief commonly held at the end of the last century and in the first decades of the present century, according to which the New World saw man evolve independently from earlier forms as in the Old World, and hence that early forms of man existed in the Americas many hundreds of thousands of years ago.

This is the theory held by the so-called "autochthonists" who based their beliefs on the discovery of bone remains on the American continent attributed—erroneously—to hominids less evolved than *Homo sapiens* and unearthed in geological strata judged to be—also erroneously—much older than has since proved the case.

JUAN COMAS, *born in Spain and now a citizen of Mexico, is internationally known for his work as an anthropologist. He is head of the department of anthropology of the University of Mexico, and editor of the authoritative "Anales de Antropologia", published by the university in Spanish. He was for many years vice-president of the International Union for Anthropological and Ethnological Sciences, and was a member of both committees of experts on racial questions set up by Unesco in 1949 and 1955.*

Going counter to this belief is the fact that only the less evolved primates, that is, lemuroid fossils corresponding to the Eocene period at the beginning of the Tertiary Era (some 55 million years ago) have ever been found in America. As to the present-day living species, the New World comprises only the simpler types of simians, known scientifically as platyrrhines, but there is no trace of the higher types of primates, called catarrhines, which include apes and the anthropoids.

As for the ancestors of *Homo sapiens*, such as the pre-hominids and hominids, they are completely unknown to the Americas though they have been found in Africa, Asia and Europe. All of the prehistoric bone remains found on the American continent indisputably belong to modern man and hence are much much more recent than any of the more primitive forms such as *Homo erectus* or Neanderthal Man discovered elsewhere.

Many suppositions have been advanced over the years (and passionately argued) to explain where the first settlers in America came from. The list includes the Phoenicians, Hebrews, Etruscans, Egyptians, Sumerians and Aryans, but no scientifically valid proof for any of these suppositions has been forthcoming, nor, for that matter, for the existence of the imaginary, fabulous Atlantis as the birthplace of the first Americans.

Certain writers in the 19th century

and even in the present century took it for granted that all the Indians of America stemmed from a common biological stock. This gave rise to the common saying that: "all Indians are alike in colour and other features. When you've seen an Indian from one region you have seen them all."

This was based on the idea that all the migrants to the New World were Mongols of Asian origin who had crossed the Bering Straits at different epochs going back no earlier than 20,000 to 25,000 years ago. According to this hypothesis, the physical and cultural differences observed among the Indians of the Americas can be explained in two ways: partly by the different degrees of biological evolution of the migratory groups that crossed north-east Asia in the course of thousands of years; partly by the differing environments of the various regions of America the settlers established themselves in.

Other scientists, however, are of the opinion that from remote antiquity there coexisted on American soil human groups of different physical characteristics and of different origins. All the scientists who support this "multi-racial" thesis nonetheless unanimously agree that the Mongoloid element that crossed the Bering Straits from Siberia at different periods of migration by far dominates all other groups.

According to Paul Rivet, former director of the Paris Musée de l'Homme, the populations of pre-Columbian America are the result of migrations to the continent of four racial groups: Mongols and Eskimos via the Bering Straits, Australoids and Malayan-Polynesians across the Pacific. Rivet based his conclusions not only on the findings of physical anthropology by studying data on physical and other characteristics of Indian groups from southern South America and those of Indians from certain areas in Brazil, Baja California and Ecuador, but also on cultural and linguistic analogies with population groups in Oceania.

A. Mendes Corrêa, of Portugal, advanced the theory that an Australo-Tasmanian human element populated America not by sailing across the Pacific but by marching across Antarctica, island-hopping across the string of archipelagos between Tasmania and Tierra del Fuego at the southern tip of South America!

Mendes Corrêa has indeed demonstrated that between 15,000 and 6,000 B.C., Antarctica was free of glacial ice and actually had a temperate climate at the time. Obviously, no archaeological proof exists to confirm this Antarctic migration hypothesis, and it will be extremely difficult, not to say impossible, to uncover any evidence with the permanent ice cap now covering all of the Antarctic continent.

According to Jose Imbelloni of Argentina, one cannot truly understand the racial and cultural history of early America without taking into account the contribution of the peoples of south-east Asia. Imbelloni concludes that seven distinct racial groups migrated to America : Tasmanoids, Australoids, Melanesianoids, proto-Indonesians, Indonesians, Mongoloids and Eskimos. In his works he describes and delineates a total of 11 types of Amerindians.

More recently (1951) Joseph Birdsell of the U.S.A. sharply criticized the contradictory views concerning the population of the Americas put forward by various multi-racial exponents such as G. Taylor, R.B. Dixon, H.S. Gladwin, E.A. Hooton, E.W. Count, F. Weidenreich and J. Imbelloni. He advanced his own hypothesis that America had been settled by a mixture of two racial groups, Mongols and "Amurians" or archaic Caucasoids who had also reached the New World via north-east Asia.

As proof of this dual origin, Birdsell claims to have found "Amurian" traits in contemporary American Indians, among the Cahuillas of the interior of Lower California and among the Yuki and Pomo of the northern Californian coast. But if the Indians of North and

South America were indeed the result of the mixture of only the two Mongoloid and Amurian strains, there ought to be a much greater similarity in blood groups than has actually been observed, particularly as regards the A-B-O and M-N groups.

There have been repeated efforts to establish similarities and indeed possible contacts between the "redskins" of the Atlantic seabord of the United States and the prehistoric Caucasoid man of the Cro-Magnon type who peopled western Europe at the beginning of the Upper Palaeolithic or Old Stone Age. Such claims cannot be dismissed since they do contain an element of possibility but no proof of any kind has yet been forthcoming.

FROM the above we can summarize our conclusions concerning the first inhabitants of the American continent as follows:

1) No authochtonous human population ever existed in America.

2) Never was there nor is there now any biologically homogeneous Amerindian type.

3) The overwhelming population migration consisted of Mongoloids.

4) There is still doubt and debate as to what and how many other human types also populated America, the most widely accepted hypotheses being 2 (Birdsell), 4 (Rivet) and 7 (Imbelloni).

The advocates of each of these hypotheses naturally explain the physical and other differences between the various types of Amerindians in different ways, and no definite conclusion can, of course, be reached until more extensive data is obtained. However, the large number of archaeological explorations carried out in recent years in various parts of the Americas has unearthed a rich store of stone implements and other objects as well as, to a lesser extent, fossilized human remains which, with our modern dating techniques including Carbon-14 now permit us to establish with relative certainty when man first appeared in America and a chronological time-table of his presence there.

Thus we now know that man was present in the United States, for example, as early as 38,000 B.C. at a site found at Lewisville, Texas. Other prehistoric sites have been clocked at 27,650 B.C. (Santa Rosa, California); 19,500 B.C. (La Jolla, California); 8,505 B.C. (Gypsum Cave, Nevada); 7,883 B.C. (Plainview Site, Texas); and 6,274 B.C. (Allen Site, Nebraska). In each case we must allow a few hundred

years or more plus or minus as is customary for C-14 readings. The people who lived in this area between 40,000 years ago and 8,000 years ago were all hunter-gatherers.

The oldest human settlement in Mexico has been found to be Tlapacoya in Mexico State where a disc-shaped file and an obsidian knife have been unearthed dating back to 20,200 B.C. (plus or minus 2,600 years) and 21,150 B.C. (1,950 years) respectively. Later prehistoric sites are also known, of course, which show that they too belonged to hunter-gatherers.

Here are a few examples of datings from South America (plus or minus years are omitted): crude stone tool industries in Venezuela (14,375 B.C. and 12,275 B.C.); cultural remains in Lagoa Santa, Brazil (8,024 B.C.); pre-ceramic lithic culture in Lauricocha, Peru (7,566 B.C.); Inithuasi Grotto at San Luis, Argentina with a pre-ceramic lithic industry (6,068 B.C.); a cultural complex on the high terraces of the Gallegos river in southern Patagonia dating from between 10,000 and 7,000 B.C.; excavations in Chile (9,380 B.C.) and elsewhere in southern Patagonia (8,760 to 6,700 B.C.).

From the above examples a very interesting observation can be made, namely, that as we proceed southward the datings of the hunting and gathering cultures are less ancient. Is this a confirmation of the thesis that the settlers of America came exclusively by way of the Bering Straits and that South America was therefore peopled many millenia later than North America? I believe it is still too early to say and we must wait for further research and investigations.

IT is generally agreed, for the moment, that the oldest date of 38,000 to 40,000 years ago corresponds to the beginnings of the warming-up period of the last Ice Age in North America (known as the Wisconsin glaciation) when it was possible to cross from eastern Siberia to Alaska and thereby reach the more temperate regions of southern North America.

Culturally, the first hunter-gatherers evolved until they became sedentary groups after learning to cultivate plants and domesticate animals. This was a slow and gradual process, but we have evidence of prehistoric sites where hunter-gatherer tribes were simultaneously engaged in the cultivation of squash, chile beans and later, maize.

Such agricultural sites have been found at Tamaulipas, Mexico, dating back to between 7,500 and 5,500 B.C., at Sierra Madre, Mexico (4,500 - 2,500 B.C. and 5,000-3,000 B.C.). In the Tehuaca area of the State of Puebla in Mexico several prehistoric sites have been unearthed offering definite proof of the existence of agriculture between 6,000 and 5,500 B.C.

In New Mexico (USA) agricultural levels have been found at a site known as Bat Cave dating back to about 3,300 B.C. while in the Peruvian Andes agricultural complexes dating between 4,700 and 3,000 B.C. have been found at Huaca Prieta, Nazoa, Paracas, Chilica, and other sites.

The evolution from the hunter-gatherer stage to agriculture occurred in America independently of the same development in the Old World. Research in plant genetics, ecology and ethno-history as well as chronological datings have effectively demonstrated this, thus refuting the thesis that agriculture was introduced into America from Asia.

The initial phases of an agricultural economy are known to have occurred in different parts of America, first with seasonal sedentary settlements and then year-round permanent agricultural sites. Central America and the Peruvian-Bolivian area are at least two of the centres on the continent which originated the cultivation of certain species of plants. Graded terraces and *Chinampas* (incorrectly called "floating gardens") are two typical techniques used here in early intensive agriculture.

From this point we see the beginning of a new process of development, the so-called "high cultures" based on what Gordon Childe has termed the "urban revolution", depending on extensive cultivation of maize, yucca, potato, beans and squash as well as the manufacture of ceramics, the use of polished stone implements and the beginning of the textile industry, etc.

In Meso-America (Mexico, Guatemala, parts of Honduras and El Salvador) the high cultures began around 1,500 B.C. in the highlands. This was the case with the Toltec, the Aztec and Zapotec civilizations which ended with the arrival of the Spaniards in the 16th century. The Olmec, Maya and Totonec civilizations emerged in the lowlands a little later than 1,500 B.C.

In the Peru-Bolivia area, both along the coast (Huaca Prieta, Cupisnique, Paracas, Mochica, Nazoa, Pachacamac, Chuncay and Inca civilizations) and in the Andean uplands (Chavin, Cajamarca, Huaylas, Huilca, Qalassaya, Tiahuanaco and Inca civilizations) the high cultures began to develop about 1,600 B.C. until their decline at the end of the 15th century A.D.

Alongside these great civilizations there also existed much less advanced cultural groups, hampered no doubt by the rigours of their surroundings and habitat. Notable amongst these were the populations living in the great river valleys of the Amazon, Orinoco and Parana as well as their many tributaries.

From the 16th century, with the conquest, colonization and acculturation stemming from the arrival of European immigrants, the original Indian population of America underwent the following three major modifications:

1) The Indians have dwindled to the point of extinction, as in Uruguay, Cuba, Haiti, Dominican Republic and Puerto Rico; or a reduced number are confined to reservations, as in the United States.

2) The Indian population still exists but has little contact with the rest of the country, living within its own self-sufficient economy, virtually untouched by the process of acculturation. Such populations are found in the Amazon and Orinoco river basins, eastern Peru, Bolivia, Ecuador, etc.

3) Large-scale intermingling of races has taken place to the extent that the majority of the inhabitants are biologically and culturally mixed, though small pockets of Indian populations, where less intermingling and acculturation have taken place, continue to exist, as in Mexico, Guatemala, the Andean plateau regions of Ecuador, Peru and Bolivia.

41

THE SHADOW OF
THE
OLMECS

Who were these mysterious forerunners of the Mayas and the Aztecs?

More than one hundred years ago, in 1862, a Mexican scholar named José Maria Melgar set out from a sugar-cane hacienda on the lower slopes of the Tuxtla Mountains, in southern Veracruz, Mexico, to look into a report of a gigantic inverted "kettle" the natives had discovered buried in the soil. Instead of the "kettle," he found a ten-ton basalt head, the "Ethiopic" features of which led him to believe that African Negroes had settled here in remote antiquity. His subsequent article describing this stone, one of a dozen such "Colossal Heads" now known, was the first published account of an object typical of what is called the Olmec civilization.

Just who were the Olmecs?

They were the first American Indians to achieve a level of social, cultural, and artistic complexity high enough for them to be called civilized. As such, they were precursors of

This statue of a ball player, with ratcheted sockets for movable arms, was deliberately decapitated.

the later Mexican and Central American cultures, whose great achievements could not have been realized without them.

Though we are familiar with the Aztec empire, and know something of the Mayas, the name "Olmec" probably means little to most of us. Yet today Olmec archaeology is laying bare one of the most exciting chapters in the history of our continent. Imagine a people capable of carving human heads on a gigantic scale and exquisite figurines from blue-green, translucent jade. Imagine an art style based on the combined features of a snarling jaguar and a human infant. Then transport these people back beyond all known Indian civilizations, to a distance in time of more than three thousand years, and put them down in the inhospitable, swampy jungles of Mexico's Gulf Coast.

The extraordinary discovery Melgar made in these jungles went largely un-

By MICHAEL D. COE

noticed until the first decade of this century, when the stone was visited by the German scholar Eduard Seler. Then it was again forgotten by the archaeological world. Forgotten, that is, until the 1920's, when the pioneer archaeologists Frans Blom and Oliver La Farge discovered the great, swamp-bound site of La Venta. There they found another Colossal Head, along with a number of other great stone sculptures in a style they mistakenly ascribed to the Mayas.

La Venta intrigued several other scholars, who quickly noted that this style, while highly sophisticated, was very different from that of the Classic Mayas, who flourished in the Yucatán Peninsula and farther south from about A.D. 300 to 900. They also noticed that some figurines and ceremonial axes of jade and other fine stones that had been turning up in museums and private collections were stylistically similar to the objects found at La Venta. They christened the unknown, non-Mayan civilization that had produced them "Olmec," after the mysterious tribe (whose name meant "Rubber People" in the Aztec tongue) that dominated the southern Gulf Coast of Mexico on the eve of the Spanish Conquest. But who were the *archaeological* Olmecs? How old was their civilization, and what was its relationship to the other civilizations of Mexico and Central America, for example, the Mayan or Toltec? Only in recent years has enough attention been paid to these questions to provide at least partial answers.

The foundations of scientific archaeology in the Olmec area were laid by Matthew W. Stirling of the Smithsonian Institution during his expeditions between 1938 and 1946. The first task Stirling set for himself was that of excavating Tres Zapotes, the site of Melgar's Ethiopic head. There he came

upon an Olmec-type carved stone, the now-famous Stela C, which bore a date in the Mayan system that seemed to match a day in the year 31 B.C.—over three centuries earlier than the most ancient date then known for the Mayas. This and other leads suggested to Stirling, as it did to leading Mexican archaeologists, that the Olmec civilization was probably the most ancient high culture yet known for the New World. After 1940 Stirling moved to La Venta, in neighboring Tabasco, and continued to make spectacular Olmec discoveries, particularly tombs of extraordinary richness.

One group, however, remained skeptical; the Mayan specialists. It seemed heresy to these American and British archaeologists to believe that the upstart Olmec civilization could have predated—and according to Stirling and his Mexican colleagues, even fore-

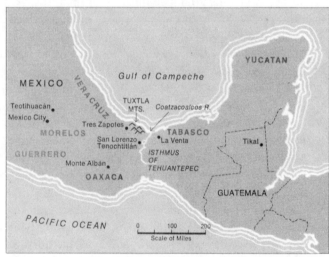

The Isthmus of Tehuantepec was the Olmecs' heartland, but their influence spread west into Mexico and south into Central America.

shadowed—Classic Mayan culture, which in many respects represented the highest achievement of the American Indian. Since 1840 the world had known and appreciated the splendid achievements of the ancient Mayas in writing, astronomy, calendrical science, art, and architecture. It was inconceivable that the Olmecs could have flourished before A.D. 300. Few Mayan buffs were ready to admit that Stela C at Tres Zapotes was a date to be read in the Mayan system.

The controversy over the Olmecs could not be settled until the advent of radiocarbon dating. In 1955 a University of California team under Dr. Robert F. Heizer opened a series of trenches at La Venta and secured a large number of charcoal samples. Most of the radiocarbon dates turned out to be far older than anyone would then have thought possible: 800–400 B.C. Incredibly, Olmec culture seems to have been at its height *seven to eleven* centuries before that of the Classic Mayas. La Venta—with its gigantic basalt monuments, mosaic pavements of serpentine blocks, a hundred-foot-high earthen pyramid, caches of carved jade and serpentine, and other wonders—was not a town or city in the usual sense but a mysteriously remote center for ceremonies and politics, isolated on its swamp-bound island. Why did it exist at all? And where did its builders come from?

There was no easy answer to the second question. Olmec sculptures had been found along the Gulf Coast as far north as the city of Veracruz, Olmec reliefs carved on a cliff had been located in the state of Morelos, and Olmec jades had turned up in puzzling profusion in the western state of Guerrero. The frequency of such finds prompted Miguel Covarrubias, the talented artist-archaeologist and long-time proponent of Olmec antiquity, to suggest Guerrero as the Olmec homeland, on the theory that they must have learned to carve small figures before moving to Veracruz and Tabasco, where their gigantic monuments are concentrated.

But many archaeologists, including myself, were convinced that Olmec origins would some day be found in the Olmec "heartland," the crescent-shaped, low-lying region along the Gulf Coast. Since the highest development of the culture was surely there, then why couldn't its beginnings, perhaps as far back in the pre-Classic period as 1500 B.C., also be there?

My own quest for Olmec origins—and for the conditions, ecological or otherwise, that may have stimulated the rise of native American civilization—led me, in December, 1964, on a trip of exploration up the sluggish, meandering Coatzacoalcos River, which drains the northern part of the Isthmus of Tehuantepec, to a riverside village called Tenochtitlán. A few miles south of the village lies a jungle-covered mesa known as San Lorenzo. In 1945 Matthew Stirling had been taken there by local Indians who had seen a great stone eye staring up from the dirt of a trail crossing the mesa. The eye turned out to belong to a new Colossal Head, one of a number of basalt monuments that Stirling found and excavated that season and the next. Some of these multi-ton heads, with their "football" helmets, flat faces, and staring eyes, have traveled as far afield as Leningrad and are the best-known examples of Olmec achievement in sculpture.

Two mysteries had immediately presented themselves to Stirling at San Lorenzo. First, the basalt from which the heads and other stones were carved did not occur anywhere around the site, the nearest source lying some fifty miles to the northwest.

The second mystery concerned the final disposition of the sculptures. Almost all of them were found either lying on the bottoms or the slopes of the deep, jungle-filled ravines that cut into the San Lorenzo mesa. Stirling guessed that some non-Olmec invaders had smashed or otherwise mutilated the monuments and then pushed them into the ravines. If so, there would be little chance of dating the Olmec occupation of San Lorenzo by associating the sculptures with archaeological layers.

The idea of mounting a major archaelogical effort at San Lorenzo came

to me during my trip in 1964. By the end of the next year I found myself, aluminum camera case in perspiring hand, standing in the grass-covered "street" of Tenochtitlán looking in vain for a sympathetic face. The natives were decidedly *not* friendly. Those Colossal Heads that had gone around the world had been removed by Veracruz archaeologists without the villagers' approval, and they were angry. Even so, I felt sure that a little diplomacy would make it possible to work there, and my optimism proved to be justified. We eventually claimed the majority of the local villagers as our friends and colleagues.

In 1966 Yale University, with financial backing from the National Science Foundation, began three years' work at the site. Our first step was to build a camp. In southern Mexico there are supposed to be two climatic seasons: a winter dry season, when it almost never rains, and the very wet summer. But in southern Veracruz some kind of moisture—drizzle, rain, or torrential downpour—is almost always falling. Shivering in our leaky tents, we found that

fierce northers sweep down the Gulf Coast in winter, bringing cold drizzle and rain for days at a time. Until we put up houses with thatched roofs, we were a very soggy camp.

Our next job was to get San Lorenzo mapped. The picture that emerged after two seasons of surveying was very different from the one we had first imagined: San Lorenzo turned out to be one of the world's strangest archaeological sites.

The mesa, rising some 150 feet above the surrounding grass- and swamp-covered plains, was originally considered to be a naturally formed plateau, the ravines being the result of erosion. Indeed, it must in large part be the result of geologic uplift by tectonic forces, most likely one of the deeply buried salt domes that are common in the northern half of the Isthmus of Tehuantepec. But San Lorenzo as we see it today has clearly been altered by the hand of ancient man. Reaching out like fingers on its north, west, and south sides are long, narrow ridges divided by the ravines. A pair of ridges on the western side exhibit bilateral symmetry, that is, every feature on one ridge is matched mirror-fashion by its counterpart; another such pair, divided by an asymmetric ridge, can be seen on the south side. This is hardly consistent with a natural origin.

Our excavations over three years demonstrated that the ridges are artificial, consisting of fill and cultural debris to a depth of at least twenty-five feet. Presumably, the first inhabitants—the Olmecs or their predecessors—took advantage of an already existing sand- and gravel-covered hill to carry out their plans. What could they have had in mind? As our map began to take shape, my first thought was that they might have been trying to construct a running or reclining animal on a titanic scale, three-quarters of a mile long, with its legs stretching north and south. But a subsequent mapping of the entire zone by aerial photography revealed much more of the total plan of San Lorenzo than our field map did. It showed a gigantic bird flying eastward, its extended wing feathers forming the ridges on the north and south, with its tail trailing to the west.

This may sound like poppycock, since such a grandiose plan could only have been appreciated from the air. Yet similar effigy mounds were erected by the early Adena and Hopewell cultures of our own midwestern states, and the tremendous hilltop markings above the Peruvian deserts cannot be fully grasped from ground level either. My own guess is that some ancient Olmec ruler or priest (or both), inspired by cosmological ideas, ordered this construction on such a scale to impress the gods and men but that the plan was never completed.

There are several hundred earth mounds on the flat surface of San Lorenzo, but the site is not very impressive compared with such Mesoamerican giants as Teotihuacán or Tikal. At the center stands a very modest pyramid, probably once the substructure for a thatched-roof temple. Extending north and south of it are pairs of long mounds with narrow plazas between them. Presumably this was the focal point of San Lorenzo.

But was it an "empty" site, as we guess La Venta to have been, inhabited only by priestly bureaucrats and their entourages? Apparently not, for most of the two hundred structures are what we call house mounds: low, rectangular or ovoid platforms of earth designed to raise the pole and thatch houses of the commoners above the discomforts caused by summer (and winter) rains. A reasonable estimate of the ancient population might be a thousand persons, thus making Olmec San Lorenzo far from "empty."

When we arrived, there was no archaeological chronology for San Lorenzo, and we had to work one out for ourselves. This meant digging at least a dozen stratigraphic trenches and pits, peeling off layer by layer as we descended and segregating all broken pottery, stone tools, and other artifacts from each stratum. Having done this before at pre-Classic sites in coastal Guatemala, I was familiar with very early Mesoamerican pottery, but I was appalled by the number of potsherds—several hundred thousand in all—that accumulated in our three seasons at San Lorenzo. This material has now been analyzed, and I have worked out a pre-Classic sequence consisting of seven distinct phases, or cultures, followed by a long period of abandonment (from around the time of Christ to about A.D. 900), and finally, a very late reoccupation by another, Toltec-like people.

But it is the pre-Classic period that concerns us here, for in that time span lies the story of the Olmecs at San Lorenzo. This is a story with dates, too, for we were fortunate enough to find well-preserved hearths or cooking fires with ample charcoal for radiocarbon analysis. It now seems that the first people to inhabit the San Lorenzo plateau arrived about 1500 B.C. They were not Olmecs, since their finely made pottery showed no signs of Olmec influence, but they may have been their ancestors. Two and a half centuries later, around 1250 B.C., there are signs that the people at San Lorenzo were beginning to take on Olmec characteristics: beautiful figurines of white clay show the unmistakable baby faces of the Olmecs, and there is much of the white-rimmed black pottery distinctive of the culture. Most important, we found a stone fragment that must have been part of a monumental carving of basalt.

The height of civilization in the area was reached in what we call the San Lorenzo phase, reliably dated to 1150–900 B.C. Here we are faced with remains that are undeniably Olmec, and it is also apparent that the site itself had reached its present form by that time. Olmec figurines of all sorts are found, some showing ball players wearing the heavy, padded belts and gloves typically used in that sacred game. Neither we nor Stirling found jade at San Lorenzo, which is curious since the Olmecs of La Venta were master jade carvers.

We are confident that the bulk of the fifty-eight known monuments at San Lorenzo were carved during the San Lorenzo phase. How do we know this? Remember that Stirling found most of his stones lying in or near the ravines, obviously not in their original positions. One morning in March, 1967, I spotted a rough stone slab, or stela, sticking out of the ground in one of the western ridges and ordered that it be dug up. It was this modest excavation that enabled us to date the Olmec sculptures of San Lorenzo and to solve the riddle of their final disposition.

The stela in question appeared to be in its original position, and I wanted to establish its relationship to whatever strata might exist in the ridge. It soon became clear, however, that the workman I had set at this task could not do

his job within the limited excavation square I had measured off. Slightly to the north on the east-west ridge we started a new square, with the idea of enlarging the total work area. To my astonishment and delight we hit upon another sculpture, totally buried.

This turned out to be Monument 34, a magnificent, larger than life-size statue of a half-kneeling man in pure Olmec style. Like almost all other known Olmec monuments, this one had been mutilated before burial, in this case by having its head knocked off. At each shoulder was a disk, perforated in the center, to which movable arms could be attached; whether they were of wood or stone we had no way of knowing.

Here, then, were two monuments, one just north of the other. If we continued to excavate along the ridge in the same direction, mightn't we find a whole line of buried monuments? My guess was right. For weeks we dug on, uncovering one mutilated sculpture after another. And while following the same kind of lead west along another ridge, a second line of stones appeared, this time oriented east-west. Both "collections" produced a great variety of representations, ranging from a gigantic column embellished with a relief of a horrific werejaguar-god to a tiny carving of a fantastic spider. We now had strong evidence that a single monumental act of destruction had been inflicted on the Olmec sculptures of San Lorenzo. The iconoclasts had begun by smashing some monuments and pitting the features of others, sometimes by grinding axes on them. They had then dragged the objects of their fury onto specially prepared floors running along the ridges of the site, placed them carefully in long lines, and covered them with a special fill. Clearly, the stones found by Stirling in the ravines had *not* been pushed there by ancient hands but had slipped down, as the slope eroded, from their original positions in the ridges. This opened up the possibility that there might be a great many more stones still to be discovered.

Once we could associate the sculptures with archaeological strata, we were able to date them—or rather, date their final placement. From our study of the pottery and other artifacts lying on the floors and in the covering fill we learned that the great act of destruction took place no later than 900 B.C. But here again, we had settled one problem only to raise another: until now no archaeologist would have believed the Olmec sculptural style to be any older than 800 B.C. In the period 1150–900 B.C., when we are positive our monuments were carved, the rest of Mesoamerica had not yet shown the first glimmerings of civilized life. Only at San Lorenzo did civilization burn brightly, with no antecedents yet discovered. Where did these people come from, with their culture already in full development?

The mysteries of San Lorenzo were tied up with more than the monuments. In one of the ridges we uncovered a troughlike stone, U-shaped in cross section. In his 1946 explorations Stirling had found a number of these lying jumbled at the bottom of one of the ravines, along with a like number of flat, rectangular stones, also of basalt. He surmised that the latter were covers for the troughs, which had once been fitted end to end to form a drain. He was right. On the edge of that same ravine, on the southwestern border of the San Lorenzo plateau, one of my laborers pointed out to me the end of just such a drain, still in place and deeply buried.

We excavated the drain completely during the final season, no simple task as it was covered with twelve to sixteen feet of overburden. A very remarkable system it was: a "main line" sloping down in an east-west direction and measuring 558 feet in length, with three subsidiary lines, totaling 98 feet, meeting the main line at a steep angle. From loose stones lying on the surface elsewhere, we are reasonably sure that another system, the mirror image to this one, lies on the southeast edge of the site.

What was the purpose of this drain, which represents no less than thirty tons of hard basalt? At its upper end there are openings for water to enter. Nearby, on the surface of the site, are several artificial ponds constructed by the Olmecs. We have good reason to believe that during the San Lorenzo phase, when the drain system was put down, its starting point lay beneath the center of a large pond that was later covered up. Thus, it appears that the drain had no other function than to draw off water from the pond.

Since irrigation is unnecessary in the wet local climate, the ultimate function of this strange water-control system must have been purely ceremonial, perhaps connected with ritual bathing by the ancient Olmec leaders. Near the head of the drain we uncovered a remarkable statue of the Olmec rain god, complete with snarling, werejaguar face, while near its other end was a curious stone receptacle in the shape of a duck. The latter, discovered by Stirling, has an opening into which a trough-stone would fit perfectly.

What kind of a world did the Olmec leaders of San Lorenzo look out upon from their lofty plateau? Who owed them allegiance? Was theirs a tribal polity, ruled by chiefs, or a pristine state, dominated by kings? Since the Olmecs of those times left no writing, we must rely on other lines of inquiry to answer these questions. But first let us consider the magnitude of the Olmec achievement at San Lorenzo three thousand years ago.

The site itself represents hundreds of

The rain god appears as a werejaguar, part human, part snarling beast. Concave at the back, the statue probably belonged to a system of water drains found at San Lorenzo.

thousands of tons of material—gravel, soil, sand, and rock—carried in by basketloads on men's backs. Similarly, the monuments must have required an army of laborers. Geological analysis has shown that the source of the basalt used in almost all the San Lorenzo monuments is the Cerro Cintepec, an extinct volcano some fifty miles north-northwest of San Lorenzo. The Colossal Heads average about eighteen tons, and one of the so-called altars weighs even more than that.

The Olmecs must have selected boulders of a suitable shape from the slopes of the volcano, somehow transporting them to the nearest navigable stream (no small distance) and then floating them to the mouth of the Coatzacoalcos River on balsa rafts. From there they would have been poled and pulled up the river to a point near San Lorenzo. Finally, each boulder

would have been hauled up 150 feet, probably with ropes and simple rollers, to their final destination. We ourselves had some experience using simple materials and methods to move the monuments, and I can attest to the enormous effort required to move a ten-ton stone just one foot! It took fifty men with ropes and poles to set one Colossal Head upright. Thus, moving the larger monuments must have involved using more than a thousand workmen at a time.

Then there is the testimony of the persons represented by the stones. Scholars seem to agree that the Colossal Heads are portraits of Olmec rulers. Likewise, the seated figures in the niches of the "altars," shown either with ropes holding captives or carrying the characteristic werejaguar infants, seem to depict real men. Great leaders, or their descendants, must have ordered the carving and setting up of these monuments—at what cost can only be imagined. Surely, then, we can postulate the existence of a polity that was more powerful than a mere tribal state.

But there is more. The existence of a political state implies a government with territorial jurisdiction not over a single tribe but over many. Whether an Olmec state can be postulated under this definition can never be fully determined, any more than it can be for *any* of the later civilizations of Mexico, other than the documented civilization of the Aztecs. Nevertheless, there is good reason to believe that the San Lorenzo Olmecs exerted an influence, political or otherwise, upon regions as distant as the highlands of central and western Mexico, where Olmec pottery and even Olmec rock paintings have been discovered during the past few years.

But the most compelling evidence for San Lorenzo's high cultural and political status under the Olmecs comes from what at first glance might be thought an unlikely line of inquiry:

ecology. Working within a sample area of about thirty square miles, centering on San Lorenzo, we are now trying to arrive at some idea of what the upper limit of human population may have been three thousand years ago. The extent of the sample area is probably that which would have been controlled by an agricultural tribe. If our population figure turns out to be much lower than the number of persons presumably involved in the construction and maintenance of the Olmec center, then San Lorenzo would have to have drawn labor and tribute from an area far greater than that of our sample.

Our calculation is based on the number of mouths that native systems of cultivation could have fed. It is not an easy one to make. Our preliminary studies strongly suggest, however, that the local population could never have constructed the artificial plateau and set up the monuments unaided. We may assume, then, that the Olmec rulers held sway over more than one tribe, and that they may, indeed, have exercised authority over much of southern Mexico.

One significant outgrowth of our study has been the work of Dr. Elizabeth S. Wing of the Florida State Museum, who has managed to identify scraps of bone contained in our Olmec rubbish heaps. The Olmecs were more finicky in their culinary habits than the present-day natives, who eat almost any kind of fish or game they can get their hands on. Olmec preferences, however, are curious, since the most common animals represented are snook (a large and good-tasting fish), man, marine toad, and turtle! We are not particularly bothered by the human remains, since cannibalism is well attested for the rest of Mesoamerica, but the toads are a puzzle, as they cannot be skinned without an extremely dangerous poison getting into the meat. We are now looking into the possibility that the Olmecs used them for a hallucinogenic substance called bufotenine, which is one of the active ingredients of the poison.

Far more significant, however, has been our research into local farming practices. The Olmecs, like all Mexican Indians, were basically corn eaters. Here we think that we may have hit upon the secret of the very early rise of native civilization in the San Lorenzo area. As in most of the world's tropical lands, the basic system of agriculture is of the shifting, or slash-and-burn, type, which means that a farmer will fell the trees or bush on a plot of land, burn them when dry, and continue to plant and harvest on the plot until declining yields or other factors force him to abandon it and search for another patch of forest.

One must also remember that there is a dry season and a rainy one. Most Mesoamerican farmers have only one major crop, planted with the first rains and harvested in the fall. On the gently rolling upland soils of the San Lorenzo area, however, there are *two* major crops, thanks to the winter northers, which keep the soil moist. Furthermore, in summer, when the rainstorms sweep daily across southwest Mexico, the winding, sluggish Coatzacoalcos River rises rapidly and covers all of the low-lying land with great sheets of water. San Lorenzo becomes a world afloat. As the rains taper off and the floods recede, the gift of the river is revealed: fresh mud and silt, deposited along the broad natural levees that flank the river.

These levees are classed by the natives as "prime land." While the upland areas tend to be communally owned, the levees are pretty much in private hands. Even though it is possible to cultivate only one crop on them, during the dry season, their production is incredibly high for indigenous corn farming. As might be expected, those who bid for economic—and political—power in the village must gain effective control of the levee lands.

Was this, then, how the Olmecs rose to power and civilization more than three millenniums ago? We are reminded of ancient Egypt, so obviously tied to the rise and fall of its one great river. It is hardly a coincidence that most of the world's early civilizations have arisen in major river basins, and our Olmecs of San Lorenzo seem to have been no exception.

Every story has an end, or at least an epilogue. Olmec civilization did not come to a close after the massive destruction of San Lorenzo around 900 B.C. Curiously enough, La Venta seems to have reached the summit of its achievement immediately *after* this brutal event, and it may be that the overthrow of San Lorenzo's rulers was instigated by the leaders of that island citadel. Thereafter, the Olmec character of San Lorenzo was lost, for the pre-Classic reoccupations that continued until the beginning of the Christian Era lack the art style that is the Olmec hallmark.

Eventually, even La Venta was destroyed, and perhaps its successor, Tres Zapotes. But Olmec civilization became transformed into some of the other brilliant civilizations of Mesoamerica's Classic period. The farther back we trace the Classic cultures of Mexico and Central America, the more characteristic of the Olmecs they seem to become.

The most clear-cut case for an Olmec heritage is presented by the famous Mayan civilization of the Classic period. It may seem a far cry from the earth or adobe constructions of the Olmecs to the towering pyramid-temples of the Mayas, but a closer look at Mayan art and learning reveals much in common. Take the day-to-day calendar system called the Long Count. Although for many decades scientists considered this a Mayan invention, Stirling and others have shown that it had far earlier roots in Olmec country. There is now good reason to believe that the well-known writing system of the Mayas may be of Olmec origin as well. Based on what we know of the earliest Classic Mayan art and culture, the Mayas themselves may, indeed, once

A brooding male figure here cradles the symbolic werejaguar. This statue was recently stolen from a Mexican museum by art thieves.

have been Olmec, moving in the centuries before the Christian Era eastward into the jungles of Yucatán and Guatemala.

Strong Olmec influence may also be detected in the Oaxaca highlands of Mexico, where the Zapotec people held sway. Kent Flannery of the University of Michigan has recently identified a local Oaxaca culture that was either importing Olmec products or making very good imitations of them, and Olmec artistic traits are to be found in the well-known Danzante reliefs, the strange stone carvings of slain men erected at the great Zapotec site of Monte Albán.

The list could be expanded to encompass most early civilizations of Mexico and Central America. The Olmecs seem to be behind all of them—an ancient, shadowy, "mother culture" whose own origins remain shrouded in mystery even to this day.

Professor of anthropology at Yale, Michael D. Coe is the author of several books on pre-Columbian civilizations and has made a number of important archaeological discoveries in the field as well.

42
America's First City

Monks Mound (top right in this 1964 photograph) dominated central Cahokia. In a temple located on smaller, flat-topped Fox Mound (in the foreground), the dead were prepared for burial in the cone-shaped mound to the left.

A thousand years ago,
Mississippi Valley Indians built a metropolis
—complete with high-rise
mounds, overpopulation, and bread and circuses

By JOHN PFEIFFER

In the heart of the Midwest, on the Illinois side of the Mississippi River, is the site of a great prehistoric city. It lies in a perfectly ordinary suburb that has little use for times past: commuters have been passing through it day after day for years, never realizing what happened there, just six miles east of St. Louis. Known as Cahokia, the city has vanished without a trace, except for a number of mounds that still remain and could easily be mistaken for natural hills.

Things were different some eight centuries or so ago. Imagine that all the marks of what passes for civilization have faded away—the four-lane highways and gas stations and hamburger joints and drive-in theatres and smog—and you stand in another age, another America. You are at Cahokia as it appeared in its prime, at about the time of the signing of the Magna Carta.

You stand in the midst of a bustling scene in the center of a wide plaza. An earthen skyscraper looms before you, a terraced mound about ten stories high, with a platform overlooking the plaza, and ramps and stairways leading to a large, decorated building at the top. Surrounding you are other buildings, a dozen smaller mounds, and two smaller plazas, all enclosed in a stockade of heavy logs a mile and a half long.

There is more to see beyond the stockade. The plaza and its associated buildings make up only the inner part of the city. The rest consists of more than five square miles of bottom land laced with waterways—a maze of meanders and oxbows and streams and winding creeks. There are barges and canoes on the waterways, farmsteads and cornfields, groves of hickory and cottonwood and willow trees, thousands of thatch-roofed houses, and at least a hundred more mounds.

The city dominates an even wider area, a fertile and abundant valley some thirty miles long, with more waterways and cornfields. Beyond central Cahokia is a system of satellite communities: half a dozen towns and perhaps fifty villages and hamlets, and a six-mile line of mounds extending to the banks of the Mississippi, with

clusters of other mounds on both sides of the river. More than seventy-five thousand people live in Greater Cahokia, about a third of them in the city itself.

Cahokia, by its very presence, represents one of the most spectacular challenges confronting New World archaeologists. Indeed, it has a wider significance, because what we learn there is helping to promote a fuller understanding of urban evolution in other parts of the world. The sheer size of the city is all the more striking when you realize that no other site of comparable dimensions exists in the United States; the runners-up boast a mere two dozen mounds and a few thousand inhabitants at most. A seasoned excavator put it this way recently: "Cahokia is overwhelming. It's one of those sites that kills you. You can spend years working on a single mound." And indeed, the

High atop Monk's Mound there stood a thatched and stockaded building (here in an artist's reconstruction) that was used for religious ceremonies and also as a residence for the paramount chief of Cahokia.

site proved so overwhelming during the early nineteenth century when it first attracted attention that it inspired a variety of fanciful theories. Some observers believed that the mounds were too massive to have been made by mere men and claimed that the structures were features of the natural landscape. Others recognized the mounds for what they were but refused to believe that they could have been the work of native "savages," crediting instead everyone from the Vikings, Welsh, and Phoenicians to De Soto's men (Benjamin Franklin's notion) and the Lost Tribes of Israel.

Serious studies did not start until the 1920's, however, and intense work was begun only little more than a decade ago, when about half the site had already been destroyed to build housing developments and other commercial enterprises. It was the building of an interstate highway just north of Cahokia's central plaza that finally prompted a program of salvage, preservation, and reconstruction involving archaeologists from the University of Illinois, the Illinois State Museum, the University of Wisconsin at Milwaukee, Washington University, and Beloit College in Wisconsin.

The program calls, above all, for hard physical labor, the sort that few people except archaeologists and a scattering of other hardy souls will endure routinely and of their own free will. During recent summers, from seventy-five to a hundred students and professional investigators have spent eight to ten hours a day digging in the hot Mississippi Valley climate, with the humidity as well as the temperature frequently in the nineties. The evidence gathered to date includes tens of thousands of potsherds, animal and human bones, soil and pollen samples, shell beads, a large assortment of flint artifacts, and virtually a libraryful of aerial photographs, maps, and diagrams.

The site is the result of a basic process in the rise of cities—the evolution of raw power, of ways of controlling people in the mass. Cities arose by necessity, in response to changes that put a severe strain on man's abilities to live with other men. At Cahokia we are just beginning to catch glimpses of what happened as people came together along the Mississippi—the consequences they faced when things became too crowded and they could not or would not move away.

The story of Cahokia starts nearly thirteen hundred years ago when the largest sites in the Midwest were only about four or five acres, with a valley of little villages and a threatened food shortage. People had been living very much as their ancestors had lived for thousands of years, on a diet made up chiefly of wild resources such as deer, fish, seeds and nuts, and perhaps a few cultivated native plants. The population had grown slowly but steadily and now the pressure was on. So people turned to a familiar plant. Corn had been grown in the Midwest for a millennium or so, but only in small quantities, perhaps to be used as a ceremonial food or delicacy. Now, for the first time, corn was cultivated on an intensive basis, and the population continued to increase. If each house could be seen at night, marked by an individual hearth fire, the settlement pattern would begin with scattered clusters of fires and then, as time passed, more fires in each cluster, and finally new clusters appearing on the once-dark landscape.

Similar developments took place elsewhere at nearly the same time, but special conditions account for all the explosive events about to happen at Cahokia. The valley was, and still is, one of the nation's most fertile farmlands. Furthermore, it was superbly located at the junction of a system of natural "superhighways," where the waters of the Missouri and Illinois rivers flow into the Mississippi. All the forces that were shaping society throughout the Midwest came into sharp focus at this continental crossroads.

The change occurred swiftly and suddenly, and the most vivid mark of it is that mammoth ten-story mound in the central plaza of Cahokia. Named Monks Mound after members of a holy order who lived nearby more than 150 years ago, it covers some sixteen acres, which makes it the largest mound in the United States and the third largest in the New World (two mounds in Mexico are bigger: the great pyramid at Cholula, and Teotihuacán's Pyramid of the Sun).

Monks Mound is a complicated structure with four terraces. Seven years ago Nelson Reed, John Bennett, and James Porter of Washington University used a truck-mounted drilling rig and hydraulic ram to drive steel tubes into various parts of the mound, obtaining a set of soil samples that indicate the nature of deposits at various depths. An analysis of the samples, test excavations, and radiocarbon dating suggest that the building of the mound was carried out in fourteen stages,

its height starting at about twenty feet and ultimately reaching a hundred feet during the period from A.D. 900 to 1150.

The view from the top of this man-made prominence must have been magnificent, looking down across the plains and over the people and the city. Even today the prospect is impressive, particularly when skies are clear and one can see all the way to St. Louis, with its stainless-steel Gateway to the West. But the increasing height may be a hint of the increasing problems and the increasing complexity of life in Cahokia: the Cahokians needed to impress people more and more forcibly with the superior qualities of their leaders and simultaneously bolster their own egos.

We have a number of clues to what went on at the summit of Monks Mound. Excavating on the uppermost terrace, Washington University archaeologists have uncovered traces of a small-scale Vatican or White House, or both—fragments of floor timbers, walls three feet thick, and circular patches of dark, loose earth where posts as big around as telephone poles had supported a large roof. The building itself stood at least fifty feet high and occupied an area about the size of three tennis courts. It was almost certainly a temple, and may have included the residence of the paramount chief of Cahokia.

Monks Mound represented the focal point of power, the grand symbol of the Establishment. The apparatus of leadership was concentrated in the central plaza and stockaded inner city, an area of about two hundred acres, and lesser chiefs and administrators perhaps lived on the tops of the smaller mounds surrounding the plaza, somewhat as feudal knights lived within the walls of the king's castle. The plaza may have served primarily as a great market area, and also as a kind of show place, a combination outdoor theatre and church where people gathered on "Saturday nights" and holidays.

What sort of ceremonies took place here? Part of the answer comes from a low, inconspicuous mound located half a mile to the south. Started not long after work had begun on Monks Mound and finished in a relatively short period, pos-

sibly a decade or so, it is identified only as No. 72 on detailed maps. But Melvin Fowler of the University of Wisconsin at Milwaukee is convinced there are two notable points about this otherwise undistinguished pile of earth.

For one thing, Mound 72 lies on the city's major north-south axis, which also runs through Monks Mound. Even more significant, it is long, ridge-shaped, and rectangular at the base—and the architects of Cahokia often designed such "hayrick" structures as monuments indicating places of outstanding importance. For example, mounds of this sort were built at the south end of the north-south axis and at the west end of the east-west axis. In 1967, after studying maps and aerial photographs, Fowler hypothesized that city planners had placed a special marker at a particular spot on the eastern edge of the mound, and a crew under the direction of James Anderson, now head of the Illinois State Museum field station at Cahokia, began digging in the designated area.

For a while Mound 72 seemed like a dead end. The crew unearthed nothing but a few potsherds and nondescript rocks until Fowler rechecked his maps, detected a mistake in arithmetic, and pinpointed another area about a yard away. Not long afterward excavators found the predicted marker, a circular black stain more than three feet in diameter, where a huge pole had been driven into the ground.

In focusing on Mound 72, Fowler had hit the jackpot, or rather, several jackpots. An early find was a mound inside a mound, a buried earthwork whose small, domed top enclosed a wealth of material. It included the skeleton of a man of rank, perhaps the paramount chief himself, resting on more than ten thousand mussel and conch shell beads that had apparently once decorated a cape or blanket. Also in the same area were two rolled sheets of copper, about two bushels of mica, fifteen "chunkey" stones used in a game something like horseshoes, and two caches of arrowheads. Excavating the caches was a major operation, which took more than two weeks. During most of that time,

Anderson slept nearby in his car to guard against looters—a necessary precaution, since about eight hundred beautiful arrowheads were eventually uncovered.

Not only grave goods were buried with the chief in this domed mound. Surrounding him were the bodies of half a dozen servants, at least one of whom may not have joined his master willingly, if his sprawled-out, face-down remains are any indication. This single structure has already yielded two dozen bodies and is still only two-thirds excavated. Two hundred additional burial sites have been found in other parts of Mound 72, including those of four men with heads and hands removed and a pit containing the bones of more than fifty young women.

All of which brings us back to Saturday night at Monks Mound, for the ritual killing of people was very likely a featured part of the activities on the first terrace overlooking the central plaza. The ceremonies called for science as well as sacrifice, as Warren Wittry, then of the Illinois State Museum, discovered more than a decade ago. Noting the pattern of large post holes in an area west of the plaza, he suggested that the posts had been laid out to form at least two great circles—and that the structures were "sun circles," crude astronomical observatories.

Subsequent work has confirmed this theory. Cahokia's "Woodhenge" was a circle 410 feet in diameter with forty-eight logs arranged around the circumference and an observation post near the center. As a matter of fact, Cahokia had a number of woodhenges at various times, perhaps as many as ten. They were, in effect, horizon calendars, used to indicate the seasons by sightings of the rising and setting sun and to determine the timing of planting and harvesting and associated festivals.

To make those days come alive we can turn to historical records. The builders of Cahokia are still unknown, but people who lived and thought very much as they did were flourishing when Europeans discovered the New World. In 1542 De Soto's expedition encountered the Natchez Indians of Mississippi, who lived in a clus-

"Chunkey" stones (used with long sticks in playing a game that resembled horseshoes) were highly prized by the Cahokians.

ter of villages not far from the present town of Natchez and, like the Cahokians, used corn as a staple and built mounds with temples at the top.

They also turned out to be sun worshipers, as the Spanish explorer learned in due course when he claimed to be a younger brother of the sun. The Indians were not particularly impressed, mainly because they already had in their midst a younger brother of the sun—their paramount chief, known as the Great Sun. They proceeded to attack De Soto instead of bowing down to him.

Eyewitness accounts of their way of life come from Frenchmen who lived among them as traders and missionaries between 1698 and 1732. For example, a report by the Jesuit priest Maturin Le Petit suggests that the Natchez's high temple mounds served to bring the Great Sun and the celestial sun closer together: "The great chief of this nation, who knows nothing on earth more dignified than himself, takes the title of brother of the Sun, and the credulity of the people maintains him in the despotic authority which he claims ... Every morning the great chief honors by his presence the rising of his elder brother, and salutes him with many howlings as soon as he appears above the horizon ... Afterwards, raising his hands above his head and turning from the east to the west, he shows him [the sun] the direction which he must take in his course."

According to another observer, the chief was exalted above his fellow men, including his closest kin, "when he gives the leavings of his dinner to his brothers or any of his relatives, he pushes the dishes

to them with his feet." His was the major role at harvest festivals and mock war ceremonies. When he died all fires were extinguished, except the perpetual flame that burned in the antechamber of the temple—and there was an orgy of public sacrificing. The retainers, guards, and wives of the late Great Sun were duly killed and buried after much dancing and feasting. A number of commoners were also killed rather less ceremoniously. Monks Mound, the great plaza, and Mound 72 are probably mementoes of such activities.

Less spectacular features indicate the sort of work that made the pomp possible, the daily grind of running a city. Housing at Cahokia is one concern of Charles Bareis of the University of Illinois. He and his students are currently digging near a department store where the mound marking the city's western limit once stood. Part of their job is to make sense of a jackstraw pattern of intersecting and overlapping wall foundations and trenches, the remains of houses built and rebuilt many times. Bareis is also working on the first terrace of Monks Mound, excavating a complex buttress structure, which indicates, among other things, that the ancient builders were soil experts.

There are hundreds of additional features, explained and unexplained: traces of specialized workshops for the making of pottery, drilled shell beads, copper jewelry, and arrowheads; at least one large, square enclosure with small, circular houses that may have been primitive saunas; and a keyhole-shaped structure more than 1,200 feet long that can be seen faintly on aerial photographs.

All the evidence suggests that the lifeblood of Cahokia was trade. Traffic must have been heavy along the big rivers and their tributaries, and representatives of the city were well known over a wide area. No traces remain of the paraphernalia of travel, the boats and barges and docks and shipyards, but excavated materials indicate that Cahokians ranged far afield. The grave goods found in Mound 72, for example, include marine shells from the Gulf of Mexico (a round trip of more than 1,300 miles), copper from pits in the Lake Superior region, mica from the Carolinas, and cherts and flints from Oklahoma and Wisconsin.

People needed stone hoes to break up tough prairie soils, and Cahokia probably acted as the manufacturing and distribution center for mass-produced hoes made of slabs of tan chert from a quarry in a tiny valley a hundred miles to the south. There was also a rising demand for bracelets and necklaces and pendants, ornaments made of copper and other imported materials. Such items, at one time designed mainly for personal decoration, served increasingly as marks of identification, status symbols to help distinguish those who gave the orders from those who took them.

Extra labor was recruited from outlying areas: from villages located high on the bluffs to the east, for example. At first, most of the workers probably returned home when the day's chores were done. Later, however, they came to stay, as indicated by the settlement-pattern studies of Patrick Munson of Indiana University and Alan Harn of the Dickson Mounds Museum. Crowds seem always to have attracted crowds, and increasing traces of the bluff-dwellers' characteristic houses and pottery are found within the city limits. By about 1100, when Monks Mound had reached its maximum height, sites on the bluffs were abandoned. The people from the boondocks had been drawn into the big city.

The decline of Cahokia was imminent even at this peak stage. Trouble really began a century or so later. Population pressure was almost certainly a major factor. Things may have gone too far and too fast, for the technology of the times was not equal to the task of feeding and organizing the people. The subsistence demands of a rapidly increasing work force, and perhaps an even more rapidly increasing bureaucracy, exceeded the capacity of the land as it was used by people in those days. Apparently, even a meat shortage was also involved.

At the same time, there are signs that people were getting out of control. Cahokia became a fortified city with inner and outer stockades at about the time of the completion of Monks Mound. The inner stockade, a wall twelve feet high built of some fourteen thousand logs with raised platforms at seventy-foot intervals, offered a formidable deterrent to unwelcome people—although the identity of the enemy is open to argument. The general assumption is that the structures were built for defense against the raids of displaced people, outsiders in need of food and land. But the danger may have been greater from within, from local looters and commoners dissatisfied with their lowly positions. Whatever the source of unrest, it was a regional as well as a local problem, for the same period saw the building of stockades around large settlements throughout the Midwest.

The solution was a redistribution of people and power, and Cahokia lost most because it had most to lose. By the early fifteenth century it was still of respectable size but no longer a city, merely one of a number of towns with estimated populations of three to five thousand. When French explorers entered the valley some three hundred years later, the site had been abandoned.

As so often happens, we are confronted at Cahokia with more questions than answers. A host of projects and subprojects offers enough work for many lifetimes of research. The phenomenon of Cahokia, however, can never be accounted for by excavations at Cahokia alone. It demands regional archaeology and a great deal of work at other places in the valley and beyond. According to James Porter, "the answers are down river; that's where to test your ideas"—the point being that important information can come from small and undisturbed sites in the hinterlands, indicators of where people lived in quieter times and of the ways they had to change with the rise and fall of the city.

Porter sees the entire valley as the center of a widespread trade network. The system involved ceremonies intended, among other things, to awe visitors and workers (some of whom may have been slaves), organized "caravans" carrying goods along waterways according to care-fully worked-out schedules, and merchants busily accumulating wealth. In a search for the origins and impact of such developments, Porter, with Glen Freimuth of the University of Illinois, is digging in an area twelve miles southwest of Cahokia, at three sites that span a period from about 500 B.C. to A.D. 1200 and that have not been completely chewed up and destroyed by advancing bulldozers.

Archaeological evidence shows that the city of Cahokia established outposts far beyond the valley. There is a site by a small river in southern Wisconsin, for example, with a stockade and two pyramidal mounds (miniatures of Monks Mound), and Cahokia-type pottery. There are also signs of what Bareis calls "a preoccupation with death," the dismembered remains of many persons, possibly captives, and split long bones hinting at cannibalism. Since the site lies about halfway between Cahokia and Lake Superior, it may have been a subcenter for the copper trade. Other outposts are known in Kansas, Oklahoma, Georgia, and Arkansas.

At the broadest level Cahokia must be seen in a New World context, and that raises some of the most intriguing questions of all. Long-range as well as local forces were at work in A.D. 900 when people in the valley started constructing a city. That development was connected in some way with events to the south, in the Lower Mississippi Valley, for example, where corn agriculture and an increase in the density of the population had started several centuries earlier.

The precise nature of the relationship, however, is still unknown. Some investigators see migrants from the south, overflow populations, moving up the Mississippi and settling in Cahokia among other places, bringing advanced ideas and technology with them. Supporting this notion is the fact that everything seems to have happened rapidly around the year 900: the appearance of new kinds of pottery and new ways of building houses and the building of the city itself—all implying a sudden influx of newcomers.

A good case also exists for the opposite viewpoint, namely that the city was essentially a "home grown" product, the work of Indians who had been living in the valley all along. Confronted with the need to reorganize their world, they borrowed from outsiders. But they drew chiefly from their own rich Midwestern traditions of ancient and extensive trade networks and the construction of earthen monuments.

Mound-building peoples have left their marks over a wide region. Some two thousand years before the appearance of Cahokia, people in the Mississippi and Ohio river valleys began piling earth high over the remains of their dead. The practice became an outstanding feature of the so-called Hopewell culture, which seems to have started in Illinois, flourished throughout the Midwest from about 200 B.C. to A.D. 400, and eventually inhabited an area from Pennsylvania to Kansas and from the Great Lakes to the Gulf of Mexico. An estimated 100,000 mounds were raised in Illinois and Ohio alone, the largest measuring several hundred feet long and approximately forty feet high.

And what about influences south of the Rio Grande? In Mesoamerica, major events were taking place during the period of Cahokia's rise and decline. At about the time intensive corn production started in the valley of Cahokia, around A.D. 700, the largest city yet to appear in the New World—the Mexican center of Teotihuacán with its 125,000 inhabitants—collapsed for reasons as yet unknown.

The first phase in the development of Cahokia as a city, including the first work on Monks Mound, occurred about two centuries later and coincided with the collapse of Mayan civilization. But the relationships among these and other beginnings and endings have not been determined. Mesoamerica's most definite contributions include corn, beans, and other subsistence items, and perhaps such architectural features as plaza layouts, large pyramidal mounds, and certain art motifs and associated ceremonies.

Cahokia was not an isolated or remote phenomenon in its time, nor is it today. Having moved rapidly and not long ago from village to urban status, it provides an invaluable case history of a city in the process of being formed. And it has much to tell us about the formation of cities everywhere. The same fundamental elements seem to have been involved in the Near East, Mesoamerica, Peru, and Southeast Asia—populations on the rise, threatening food shortages, people clustering in larger and larger groups, and concentrations of pomp and power in a continuing effort to keep people under control.

After a surprisingly long period of indifference, urban planners are beginning to show an interest in the origins and evolution of cities like Cahokia. For forces set in motion a long time ago bear directly on the future of our own cities, by far the most complex and subtle of man's artifacts.

X. Contemporary Issues

Every discipline has both a body of data and a set of questions that it regards—rightly or wrongly—as being settled, as being beyond dispute. There are also facts and issues that are at the center of debate. Frequently these debates lead to a reexamination of "settled" issues, and suddenly new light is shed on them. And the dialogue continues. The lay public often confounds this process with disarray in the ranks of a discipline's practitioners, with anarchy, with a state of existence in which nothing, really, is "known." But that view is false; for it is precisely from such internal dialogue that new insights arise.

In this concluding section we focus on three areas that currently are the subject of a great deal of debate in the disciplines of physical anthropology and archaeology. Part A is concerned with human variation (or "race," as it used to be thought of); Part B raises the issue of biological determinism; Part C asks how "new" the new archaeology really is.

A. Human Variation

You will recall from the first article in this reader ("Stones and Bones") that the study of human variation was one of the main undertakings of the emerging discipline of physical anthropology. The early concern was to note the distribution among the world's populations of selected physical characteristics and to use these features to classify the world's populations into distinct and discrete categories—called races. Unfortunately this taxonomic approach has failed to yield any clarity: Exceptions to any classificatory scheme seem to be as prevalent as elements that "fit," and no two researchers have managed to agree totally with regard to (1) which physical features should determine "race" and (2) how many—and what kind—of "races" there are. This has led the current generation of physical anthropologists virtually to abandon use of the concept of race altogether and to focus instead on the relationship(s) that can be discovered to obtain between physical traits and the environment(s) in which they are found. This explicit concern with adaptation rather than classification is much more evolutionary in perspective, and allows for the systematic study of the origins of physical attributes and their ongoing functions.

"Early Man and the Emergence of Races," by Yakimov, represents the traditional approach to human variation, and seeks to answer the question of the origin of modern "races." We will let the article speak for itself. However, it seems to us that Yakimov makes one error that is sufficiently large to warrant a dissenting note. He dates the emergence of coordinated and collective social behavior far too late, arguing that it arose among modern *Homo sapiens* and thus stabilized the development of the species. The overwhelming bulk of data, however, clearly indicate that such behavior is millions of years old—quite probably already in operation among australopithecines—and indeed that it was a causal factor in the molding of human evolution.

In "Race: A Four Letter Word That Hurts," Fried summarizes the substance of the current rejection of the concept of "race" and argues that this is not just a minor academic matter. Rather, this is a debate of great social and political significance.

B. Biological Determinism

Both of the selections in this section attack biological determinism. This is one of those issues that seemed to have been "settled" but has recently risen again. Its proponents have flooded the mass media and indeed seem to have gained the upper hand in government policy-making circles. Because these views are so widely circulated, we have not bothered to reprint them here (although you will find them represented at least partially in Wilson's "The Origins of Human Social Behavior" and Leakey and Ardrey's "A Dialogue on Man, the Killer" in Part B of Section VII). Rather, two articles by critics of this movement are presented. Gould's "The Nonscience of Human Nature" looks at the issue broadly, exploring the validity of the basic assumptions of the biological reductionists, or determinists, as he calls them. Lewontin's "The Fallacy of Biological Determinism" reviews the history of biological determinist thought, then focuses quickly on the issue of the extent to which intelligence is (or is not) genetically inherited. Both Gould and Lewontin are affiliated with Harvard University, which seems to have become one of the main arenas for this dispute. It was the *Harvard Educational Review* that first gave a prestigious public forum to Arthur Jensen's theories with regard to the "racial" inheritance of intelligence, and Edward Wilson (a leader of the sociobiology movement) is a member of the Harvard University faculty with his own committed group of followers. Apparently this dispute has polarized the Harvard community, and it has become a major political issue within the American Anthropological Association as well. Both of the articles reprinted here indicate why the issue of biological determinism is so politically loaded.

C. The New Archaeology

We end this book with a less strident but no less real dispute. As we have indicated with regard to some articles that appear earlier in this reader, archaeology in the Americas has emerged within the context of social science in general and anthropology in particular. Adams' "Archaeological Research Strategies" (Section III) indicates that in recent years American archaeologists in particular have been concerned with systematizing research strategies and tactics, and have taken a strong interest in using the perspective of cultural ecology to build explanatory models. It has become the practice in the past decade or so for these archaeologists to refer to what they do as the "new archaeology." In doing so they wish to differentiate what they do from the (more European) practice of emphasizing the classification of tools, assemblages, industries, and cultures in what they consider to be a static manner analogous to butterfly collecting. Weiss introduces "The New Archaeology" and shows its ecological and process-oriented concerns. Hogarth dissents. Calling for "Common Sense in Archaeology," he accuses the self-proclaimed "new archaeologists" of pompousness. He suggests that what they do is hardly novel but, rather, represents the development of a self-serving and mystifying system of terminology that obscures the fact that nothing really new is going on. We invite you to draw your own conclusions.

43

Early man and the emergence of races

by Vsevolod P. Yakimov

THE 3,500 million humans on our planet comprise an astonishing conglomeration of peoples. Amid this vast variety, anthropologists distinguish between groups of people having a common origin, living, or having lived, in certain defined regions, and possessing differing characteristic features in their facial structure, skin colour and colour and type of hair.

Scientists call these groups races, but we should remember that there are no strict lines of demarcation between races. All these groups blend imperceptibly into one another with intermediate types possessing various combinations of physical characteristics.

It can readily be seen that distinctions between individual groups do not affect the basic traits that all people have in common—an upright posture, well-developed hands and feet, an intricately structured brain encased in a big skull with a straight, high forehead, absence of a bony eyebrow ridge, the presence of a prominent chin and a common structure of the speech organs. All humans have the

VSEVOLOD P. YAKIMOV, of the U.S.S.R., is internationally famous for his work on prehistoric man. He has written over 100 studies on primates and the evolution of man. He is director of the Research Institute for Anthropology and the D.N. Anuchin Anthropological Museum of Moscow State University, and is a member of the Executive Committee of the International Union for Anthropology and Ethnology.

same number of chromosomes (46) in the cell nucleus; primates have 48 and the lower simians between 54 and 78.

Thus modern man is biologically uniform in basic features and polymorphous as regards many secondary features, and scientists consider all human beings as belonging to the single species, Homo sapiens. The variations found in groups living in different geographical areas reflect only a differentiation within the single species due to a host of biological, social and other factors.

The emergence of the earliest Homo sapiens was preceded by the stage of the "oldest" (palaeoanthropus) and the "old" (late palaeoanthropus) people, though it is important to note that late palaeoanthropus co-existed with early Homo sapiens in adjoining territories.

The genetic relationship between various groups of palaeoanthropus and Homo sapiens is a matter of considerable controversy. The question on which anthropologists are divided is whether all groups of palaeoanthropes can be considered as the ancestors of modern man and whether modern man developed in one or several regions.

In modern anthropology there are two schools of thought on the origins of man and the major races—the polycentric and the monocentric schools.

The founder of the polycentric theory, the American anthropologist Franz Weidenreich, assumes that modern man evolved in several regions, relatively independent of one another, and that people developed at different rates. His theory claims that modern man evolved from the "oldest" and "old" people in each region and that this gave rise to the formation of the major races—Europoid, Negroid, Australoid, Mongoloid, etc.

Anthropologists of this school, such as G. Debetz and V. Alekseev of the U.S.S.R. and Carleton Coon and C. Loring Brace of the U.S.A., point out that representatives of the modern races still possess traits typical of the fossil remains found in territories where these races once lived.

ON the other hand, monocentrists, Henri-Victor Vallios and G. Olivier in France, Francis Howell in the U.S.A., Kenneth Oakley in Britain, Victor Bunak, M. Nesturkh, Y. Roginsky and myself in the U.S.S.R., among others, consider that modern man evolved in a single region. Professor Roginsky believes that *Homo sapiens* emerged in a relatively wide area covering west Asia, parts of central and south Asia, and north-east Africa. Here various groups of palaeoanthropes interbred, enriching the genetic stock and triggering off the development of modern man.

The ancient *Homo sapiens* who evolved there did not possess clearly distinguished traits of any of the modern races. In a certain sense he was "neutral" in racial aspects, and characteristics of the modern races were present in him in the most diverse combinations.

It was only when human groups spread geographically and settled in definite territories that racial types evolved. That is why the races of modern mankind resemble one another so closely. This resemblance is a sign of their common origin, of their emergence in a single region.

The monocentrists, who believe that mankind passed in its evolution through the palaeoanthropus stage, do not, however, maintain that every local group of ancient people formed part of the ancestry of modern man. For historical and natural reasons some groups did not participate in the formation of modern man, or participated in that process through subsequent blending with already existing *Homo sapiens*.

Some researchers, including myself, believe the late Neanderthals, the so-called classic Neanderthals, who lived in the Early Würm glacial period some 50,000 to 35,000 years ago, to be one of these groups. They differed greatly from *Homo sapiens* in physical respects; they were short (150 to 166 cm.), massive, with big heads and big, coarse faces, and they also differed in their brain and hand structure.

The late Neanderthals of Europe, however, did not go up an evolutionary blind alley. They too made considerable progress in the development of culture, society and speech. Yet certain of their characteristics, their inordinate physical strength and structural ungainliness, hindered and complicated their transformation into modern man.

This hypothesis is borne out by the palaeoanthropus fossils of the more progressive "sapient" type found in central and west Asia—in the Teshik-Tash caves, in the U.S.S.R. and the Skhul, Tabun and Qafzeh caves, in Israel. It is highly significant that they are older (about 60,000 B.C.) than the "classic" Neanderthals.

Fossils of ancient representatives of *Homo sapiens* displaying some palaeo-anthropic traits have been found in the Crimea and the Caucasus, in the Mousterian culture sites generally linked with Neanderthals. This can be taken to indicate that the ancient "sapiens" spread from the area of their origin to the west, where "classic" Neanderthals still existed at that time.

Quite recently the Soviet scientists A. Zubov and V. Alekseev expressed the view that *Homo sapiens* emerged in two centres—north-east Africa and south-west Asia. This is a variant of the polycentrist viewpoint, based mainly on the differences between the specific dental structures of ancient and modern man, and can in a sense be regarded as a compromise between extreme polycentric and monocentric views. Moreover, both centres fall territorially within the fairly extensive area the monocentrists regard as the cradle of *Homo sapiens*.

The most likely hypothesis, therefore, as to who modern man's ancestors were and where and when they emerged seems to be as follows.

Modern man's ancestors were the palaeoanthropes who possessed a set of "sapient" traits and inhabited west and south Asia and north-east Africa. From this one area groups of *Homo sapiens* spread to neighbouring territories. As these *Homo sapiens* populations, morphologically "neutral" in relation to modern races, were migrating, settling and integrating, the modern races formed. *Homo sapiens*

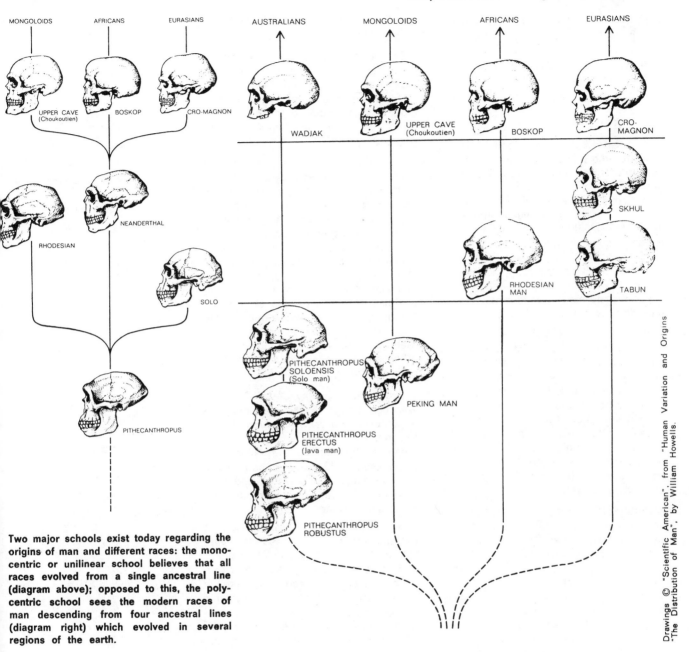

Two major schools exist today regarding the origins of man and different races: the monocentric or unilinear school believes that all races evolved from a single ancestral line (diagram above); opposed to this, the polycentric school sees the modern races of man descending from four ancestral lines (diagram right) which evolved in several regions of the earth.

Drawings © "Scientific American", from "Human Variation and Origins "The Distribution of Man", by William Howells.

probably emerged in the ancient "homeland" some 50,000 to 45,000 years before our time.

This view is confirmed in particular by data furnished by the British anthropologist, Kenneth Oakley. He established that the skeletons from Jebel Qafzeh were 70,000 years old. Morphologically "Qafzeh man" was a transitional form from palaeoanthropus of the "sapient" type to *Homo sapiens*. Radioactive carbon datings fix the age of *Homo sapiens* fossils in Europe at 35,000 to 38,000 B.C. The oldest fossil of modern man, the skull found at Niah, on Kalimantan Island (Indonesia), displaying all the traits of fully formed

Homo sapiens, is about 39,000 years old.

Many original theories have been advanced concerning the factors responsible for the development of *Homo sapiens*. At the beginning of this century the French archaeologists Gabriel and Adrien de Mortillet considered changes in climate (from humid, sub-tropical to a dry climate) and the change from an arboreal existence (which they believed Neanderthal man to have led) to life on the ground to be the main reasons for his transformation into modern man. Later, H. Weinert (Fed. Rep. of Germany) and V. Gromov (U.S.S.R.) and some other scientists asserted that the colder climate, caused by the advance of the glaciers, had been the main factor in the progressive evolution of the ancestors of *Homo sapiens*.

STILL other scientists believe that the evolution of Neanderthal man into *Homo sapiens* was due largely to the change from in-breeding within small scattered palaeoanthropic groups to breeding between different groups, which thus put an end to the negative consequences of incestuous breeding. Naturally, every one of these factors was important, but it is doubtful whether they alone could have transformed Neanderthal man into *Homo sapiens*.

In 1949 I expressed the view (it was also arrived at independently by Francis Howell of the U.S.A. in 1951) that selection in the severe conditions of the pre-glacial period prevented rather than promoted the evolution of the classic Neanderthals towards *Homo sapiens*. The colder climate did not promote mankind's progressive development and the severe living conditions made the Neanderthal's physique even more rugged.

Refuting the above theory, the polycentrists point out that classic Neanderthals have been found in areas far from the glaciers, notably in Iraq (The Shanidar cave) and in Israel (the Wadi el-Amud site). But they ignore the fact that these were not pure classic Neanderthals since they possessed some "sapient" traits in the structure of the brain-case and the shape of the cerebral hemispheres as shown by moulds of the inner skull surface.

The formation of "sapient" features proceeded more actively on territories free of glaciers. When we discuss "sapient" features, less importance should be attached to morphological traits than to those traits of *Homo sapiens* which substantially distinguish him from his direct predecessor, palaeoanthropus.

Researchers have always been struck by the relatively high development of the culture of *Homo sapiens*, as compared with that of Neanderthal man, by his ornaments and his flair, which his ancestors did not possess, for various forms of graphic art (sculp-ture, stone and bone carving, polychromic mural painting, etc).

This testifies to a qualitative change in man's thinking, to a growing complexity in the relations between people and hence to a progressive development of social organization and forms of communication—the emergence of speech.

Comparative studies of moulds made of the inner brain-case of palaeoanthropus and *Homo sapiens* fossils show that in the latter the areas of the brain connected with purposeful labour, that is physical activity, speech and the regulation of the individual's social behaviour, underwent considerable changes. Hence we can assume that emerging *Homo sapiens* acquired qualities important to man as a social being. Groups of ancient people who attained such qualities more rapidly found themselves better placed than other socially less organized palaeoanthropic groups.

Professor Roginsky of the U.S.S.R. was one of the first to advance this hypothesis. He drew attention also to the relative stability of the features displayed by man as a species from the moment of his emergence down to our own times, along with the astoundingly rapid advance of techniques and social development.

At the same time the replacement of the Mousterian culture, associated with Neanderthal Man, by the late palaeolithic culture, generally associated with *Homo sapiens*, proceeded against the background of great changes in man's physical type, so important to environmental adaptation. During the transition from palaeoanthropus to man with his present bodily structure, an evolution of the species took place—a transformation of one type of man into another. It can be assumed that, in primeval society, selection, which guided the evolution of the ancients, stimulated their development into *Homo sapiens*.

ONCE *Homo sapiens* had evolved, social tendencies neutralized and weakened the action of the species-forming selective mechanisms, and thus assumed paramount importance. Modern men began to resolve the problems facing them, not so much by adapting themselves to new environmental conditions which had resulted in anatomical and physiological changes in their ancestors, but by relying on and utilizing the fruits of collective labour.

For this reason the physical type of *Homo sapiens* underwent no major changes during many millenia, whereas the range and complexity of his activities developed enormously. Although the morphological changes that took place in *Homo sapiens* during the formation of the major races were partly adaptational, they did not change any of man's traits as a species.

According to this viewpoint, *Homo sapiens* is a supreme stage, in specific qualitative terms, of man's evolu-

tion, a stage characterized by a high level of social organization. In this development of man as a social being, speech has played a major role by passing on the experience and wisdom accumulated by many generations and making possible their integration, along with new individual experience, in a collective store of knowledge.

Academician N. Dubinin, the Soviet geneticist, has aptly pointed out that *Homo sapiens* is unique, since, with his advanced social awareness, he has developed, in addition to the hereditary programme possessed by all organisms, a second, non-genetic, non-hereditary programme—"a programme of social heredity" as Dubinin calls it, which makes for man's progress in every new generation.

44

Race: A Four Letter Word That Hurts

Morton H. Fried

Taking the great white race away from today's racists is like taking candy from a baby. There are sure to be shrieks and howls of outrage. But it will be very hard to take away this piece of candy, because, to drop the metaphor, nothing is harder to expunge than an idea. The white race is not a real, hard fact of nature; it is an idea.

In 1959 a young anthropologist named Philip Newman walked into the very remote village of Miruma in the upper Asaro Valley of New Guinea to make a field study of the Gururumba. It was late that first afternoon when it began to dawn upon his native hosts that he had made no move to leave. Finally a man of some rank plucked up his courage and said, "How long will you stay, red man?"

Most people are probably amused, but a few will be puzzled and chagrined to know that what passes in our own culture as a member of the great white race is considered red by some New Guineans. But when did anyone ever really see a *white* white man? Most so-called white men are turned by wind, rain, and certain kinds of lotion to various shades of brown, although they would probably prefer to be thought bronze. Even the stay-in who shuns the sun and despises cosmetics would rarely be able to be considered white in terms of the minimal standards set on television by our leading laundry detergents. His color would likely be a shade of the pink that is a basic tint for all Caucasoids. (That, like "Caucasian," is another foolish word in the service of this concept of race. The Caucasus region, as far as we know, played no significant role in human evolution and certainly was not the cradle of any significant human variety.)

Actually, even the generalization about pink as a basic skin tint has to be explained and qualified. In some people the tint of the skin is in substantial measure the result of chemical coloring matter in the epidermis; in others there is no such coloring matter, or very little, and tinting then depends on many factors, including the color of the blood in the tiny capillaries of the dermis. Statistically, there is a continuous grading of human skin color

from light to dark. There are no sharp breaks, no breaks at all. Since nobody is really white and since color is a trait that varies without significant interruption, I think the most sensible statement that can be made on the subject is that there is no white race. To make this just as true and outrageous as I can, let me immediately add that there never *was* a white race.

While at it, I might as well go on to deny the existence of a red race, although noting that if there was such a thing as the white race it would be at least esthetically more correct to call it the red race. Also, there is not now and never has been either a black race or a yellow race.

To deny that there are differences between individuals and between populations is ridiculous. The New Guineans spotted Dr. Newman as an off-beat intruder as soon as they clapped eyes on him. Of course, they were noticing other things as well and some of those other things certainly helped to make the distinctions sharper. After all, Newman was relatively clean, he had clothes on, and, furthermore, he didn't carry himself at all like a Gururumba—that is to say like a human being. I was spotted as an alien the first time I showed up in the small city of Ch'uhsien, in Anhwei province, China, back in 1947. Even after more than a year in that place, there was no question about my standing out as a strange physical type. During the hot summer, peasants who had never seen anything like me before were particularly fascinated by my arms protruding from my short-sleeved shirt, and I almost had to stop patronizing the local bath house. I am not a hirsute fellow for someone of my type, but in Ch'uhsien I looked like a shaggy dog, and farmers deftly plucked my hairs and escaped with souvenirs. Another time, a charming young lady of three scrambled into my lap when I offered to tell her a story; she looked into my eyes just as I began and leaped off with a scream. It was some time before I saw her again, and in the interval I learned that in this area the worst, bloodthirsty, child-eating demons can be identified by their blue eyes.

Individual differences are obvious, even to a child. Unfortunately, race is not to be confused with such differences, though almost everybody sees them and some people act toward others on the basis of them. I say "unfortunately," because the confusion seems so deeply embedded as to make anyone despair of rooting it out.

Most laymen of my acquaintance, whether tolerant or bigoted, are frankly puzzled when they are told that race is an idea. It seems to them that it is something very real that they experience every day; one might as well deny the existence of different makes and models of automobiles. The answer to that analogy is easy: cars don't breed. Apart from what the kids conjure up by raiding automobile graveyards, and putting the parts together to get a monster, there are no real intergrades in machinery of this kind. To get a car you manufacture parts and put them together. To get our kind of biological organism you start with two fully formed specimens, one of each sex, and if they are attracted to each other, they may replicate. Their replication can never be more than approximate as far as either of them, the parents, is concerned, because, as we so well know, each contributes only and exactly one-half of the genetic material to the offspring. We also know that some of the genetic material each transmits may not be apparent in his or her own makeup, so that it is fully possible for a child to be completely legitimate without resembling either side of the family, although he may remind a very old aunt of her grandfather.

The phenomenon of genetic inheritance is completely neutral with regard to race and racial formation. Given a high degree of isolation, different populations might develop to the point of being clearly distinguishable while they remained capable of producing fertile hybrids. There would, however, be few if any hybrids because of geographical isolation, and the result would be a neat and consistent system.

Much too neat and consistent for man. Never in the history of this globe has there been any species with so little *sitzfleisch*. Even during the middle of the Pleistocene, way down in the Lower Paleolithic, 300,000 or more years ago, our ancestors were continent-hoppers. That is the only reasonable interpretation of the fact that very similar remains of the middle Pleistocene fossil *Homo erectus* are found in Africa, Europe, and Asia. Since that time movement has accelerated and now there is no major region of this planet without its human population, even if it is a small, artificially maintained, nonreproductive population of scientists in Antarctica.

The mobility so characteristic of our genus, Homo, has unavoidable implications, for where man moves, man mates. (Antarctica, devoid of indigenous population, is perhaps the only exception.) This is not a recent phenomenon, but has been going on for one or two million years, or longer than the period since man became recognizable. We know of this mobility not only from evidence of the spread of our genus and species throughout the world, but also because the fossils of man collected from one locality and representing a single relatively synchronic population sometimes show extraordinary variation among themselves. Some years ago a population was found in Tabun Cave, near Mt. Carmel, in Israel. The physical anthropologists Ashley Montagu and C. Loring Brace describe it as "showing every possible combination of the features of Neanderthal with those of modern man." At Chouk'outien, a limestone quarry not too far from Peking, in a cave that was naturally open toward the close of the Pleistocene geological period, about 20,000 years ago, there lived a population of diverse physical types. While some physical anthropologists minimize them, those who have actually pored over the remains describe differences as great as those separating modern Chinese from Eskimos on one hand and Melanesians on the other. All of this, of course, without any direct evidence of the skin color of the fossils concerned. We never have found fossilized human skin and therefore can speak of the skin colors of our ancestors of tens of thousands of years ago only through extrapolation, by assuming continuity, and by assuming the applicability of such zoological rules as Gloger's, which was developed to explain the distribution of differently pigmented birds and mammals.

The evidence that our Pleistocene ancestors got around goes beyond their own physical remains and includes exotic shells, stones, and other materials in strange places which these objects could have reached only by being passed from hand to hand or being carried great distances. If our ancestors moved about that much, they also spread their genes, to put it euphemistically. Incidentally, they could have accomplished this spreading of genes whether they reacted to alien populations peacefully or hostilely; wars, including those in our own time, have always been a major means of speeding up hybridization.

Even phrasing the matter this way, and allowing for a goodly amount of gene flow between existing racial populations through hundreds of thousands of years of evolution, the resulting image of race is incredibly wrong, a fantasy with hardly any connection to reality. What is wrong is our way of creating and relying upon archetypes. Just as we persist in thinking that there is a typical American town (rarely our own), a typical American middle-class housewife (never our wife), a typical American male ("not me!"), so we think of races in terms of typical, archetypical, individuals who probably do not exist. When it is pointed out that there are hundreds of thousands or millions of living people who fall between the classified races, the frequently heard rejoinder is that this is so now, but it is a sign of our decadent times. Those fond of arguing this way usually go on to assert that it was not so in the past, that the races were formerly discrete.

In a startlingly large number of views, including those shared by informed and tolerant people, there was a time when there was a pure white race, a pure black race, etc., etc., depending upon how many races they recognize. There is not a shred of scientifically respectable evidence to support such a view. Whatever evidence we have contradicts it. In addition to the evidence of Chou-k'outien and Tabun mentioned above, there are many other fossils whose morphological characteristics, primitivity to one side, are not in keeping with those of the present inhabitants of the same region.

Part of the explanation of the layman's belief in pure ancestral races is to be found in the intellectually lazy trait of stereotyping which is applied not only to man's ancestry but to landscape and climate through time as well. Few parts of the world today look quite the way they did 15,000 years ago, much less 150,000 years ago. Yet I have found it a commonplace among students that they visualize the world of ages ago as it appears today. The Sahara is always a great desert, the Rockies a great mountain chain, and England separated from France by the Channel. Sometimes I ask a class, after we have talked about the famous Java fossil *Pithecanthropus erectus,* how the devil do they suppose he ever got there, Java being an island? Usually the students are dumbfounded by the question, until they are relieved to discover that Java wasn't always cut off from the Asian mainland. Given their initial attitudes and lack of information, it is not surprising that so many people imagine a beautiful Nordic Cro-Magnon, archetypical White, ranging a great Wagnerian forest looking for bestial Neanderthalers to exterminate.

Once again, there is no evidence whatsoever to support the lurid nightmare of genocide that early *Homo sapiens* is supposed to have wreaked upon the bumbling and grotesque Neanderthals. None either for William Golding's literary view of the extirpation of primitive innocence and goodness. The interpretation that in my view does least damage to the evidence is that which recognizes the differences between contemporary forms of so-called Neanderthals and other fossil *Homo sapiens* of 25,000 to 100,000 years ago to have been very little more or no greater than those between two variant populations of our own century. Furthermore, the same evidence indicates that the Neanderthals did not vanish suddenly but probably were slowly submerged in the populations that surrounded them, so that their genetic materials form part of our own inheritance today.

Then, it may be asked, where did the story come from that tells of the struggle of these populations and the extinction of one? It is a relatively fresh tale, actually invented in the nineteenth century, for before that time there was no suspicion of such creatures as Neanderthals. The nineteenth century, however, discovered the fossils of what has been called "Darwin's first witness." After some debate, the fossil remains were accepted as some primitive precursor of man and then chopped off the family tree.

The model for this imaginary genealogical pruning was easily come by in a century that had witnessed the hunting and killing of native populations like game beasts, as in Tasmania, in the Malay peninsula, and elsewhere. Such episodes and continuation of slavery and the slave trade made genocide as real a phenomenon as the demand for laissez-faire and the Acts of Combination. It was precisely in this crucible that modern racism was born and to which most of our twentieth-century mythology about race can be traced.

In the vocabulary of the layman the word "race" is a nonsense term, one without a fixed, reliable meaning, and, as Alice pointed out to Humpty Dumpty, the use of words with idiosyncratic meanings is not conducive to communication. Yet I am sure that many who read these words will think that it is the writer who is twisting meaning and destroying a useful, common-sense concept. Far from it. One of the most respected and highly regarded volumes to have yet been published in the field of physical anthropology is *Human Biology,* by four British scientists, Harrison, Weiner, Tanner, and Barnicot (Oxford University Press, 1964). These distinguished authors jointly eschewed the word "race" on the ground that it was poorly defined even in zoology, *i.e.,* when applied to animals other than man, and because of its history of misunderstanding, confusion, and worse, when applied to humans.

Similar views have been held for some time and are familiar in the professional literature. Ashley Montagu, for example, has been in the vanguard of the movement to drop the concept of human race on scientific grounds for twenty-five years. His most recent work on the subject is a collation of critical essays from many specialists, *The Concept of Race* (Free Press, 1964). Frank B. Livingstone, a physical anthropologist at the University of Michigan, has spoken out "On the Non-existence of Human Races" (*Current Anthropology,* 3:3, 1962). In the subsequent debate, opinions divided rather along generational lines. The older scientists preferred to cling to the concept of race while freely complaining about its shortcomings. The younger scientists showed impatience with the concept and wished to drop it and get on with important work that the concept obstructed.

Quite specifically, there are many things wrong with the concept of race. As generally employed, it is sometimes based on biological characteristics but sometimes on cultural features, and when it is based on biological traits the traits in question usually have the most obscure genetic backgrounds. The use of cultural criteria is best exemplified in such untenable racial constructs as the "Anglo-Saxon race," or the "German race" or the "Jewish race." Under no scientifically uttered definition known to me can these aggregates be called races. The first is a linguistic designation pertaining to the Germanic dialects or languages spoken by the people who about 1,500 years ago invaded the British Isles from what is now Schleswig-

Holstein and the adjacent portion of Denmark. The invaders were in no significant way physically distinct from their neighbors who spoke other languages, and in any case they mated and blended with the indigenous population they encountered. Even their language was substantially altered by diffusion so that today a reference to English as an Anglo-Saxon language is quaint and less than correct. As for the hyperbolic extension of the designation to some of the people who live in England and the United States, it is meaningless in racial terms—just as meaningless as extending the term to cover a nation of heterogeneous origin and flexible boundaries, such as Germany or France or Italy or any other country. As for the moribund concept of a "Jewish race," this is simply funny, considering the extraordinary diversity of the physical types that have embraced this religion, and the large number that have relinquished it and entered other faiths.

The use of cultural criteria to identify individuals with racial categories does not stop with nationality, language, or religion. Such traits as posture, facial expression, musical tastes, and even modes of dress have been used to sort people into spurious racial groups. But even when biological criteria have been used, they have rarely been employed in a scientifically defensible way. One of the first questions to arise, for example, is what kind of criteria shall be used to sort people into racial categories. Following immediately upon this is another query: how many criteria should be used? With regard to the first, science is still in conflict. The new physical anthropologists whose overriding concern is to unravel the many remaining mysteries in human evolution and to understand the role that heredity will play in continuing and future evolution are impatient with any but strictly genetic characters, preferably those that can be linked to relatively few gene loci. They prefer the rapidly mounting blood factors, not only the ABO, Rh, MNS, and other well-known series, but such things as Duffy, Henshaw, Hunter, Kell, and Kidd (limited distribution blood groups named for the first person found to have carried them). Such work has one consistent by-product: the resultant classifications tend to cross-cut and obliterate conventional racial lines so that such constructs as the white race disappear as useful taxonomic units.

Some scientists argue that a classification based on only one criterion is not a very useful instrument. On the other hand, the more criteria that are added, the more abstract the racial construct becomes as fewer individuals can be discovered with all the necessary characteristics and more individuals are found to be in between. The end result is that the typical person is completely atypical; if race makes sense, so does this.

That racial classification is really nonsense can be demonstrated with ease merely by comparing some of the most usual conceptions of white and Negro. What degree of black African ancestry establishes a person as a Negro? Is 51 per ecnt or 50.1 per cent or some other slight statistical preponderance necessary? The question is ridiculous: we have no means of discriminating quantities of inherited materials in percentage terms. In that case can we turn to ancestry and legislate that anyone with a Negro parent is a Negro? Simple, but totally ineffective and inapplicable: how was the racial identity of each parent established? It is precisely at this point that anthropologists raise the question of assigning specific individuals to racial categories. At best, a racial category is a statistical abstraction based upon certain frequencies of genetic characters observed in small samples of much larger populations. A frequency of genetic characters is something that can be displayed by a population, but it cannot be displayed by an individual, any more than one voter can represent the proportion of votes cast by his party.

The great fallacy of racial classification is revealed by reflecting on popular applications in real situations. Some of our outstanding "Negro" citizens have almost no phenotypic resemblance to the stereotyped "Negro." It requires their acts of self-identification to place them. Simultaneously, tens of thousands of persons of slightly darker skin color, broader nasal wings, more everted lips, less straight hair, etc., are considered as "white" without question, in the South as well as the North, and in all socioeconomic strata. Conversely, some of our best known and noisiest Southern politicians undoubtedly have some "Negro" genes in their makeup.

Why is it so hard to give up this miserable little four-letter word that of all four-letter words has done the most damage? This is a good question for a scientific linguist or a semanticist. After all, the word refers to nothing more than a transitory statistical abstraction. But the question can also be put to an anthropologist. His answer might be, and mine is, that the word "race" expresses a certain kind of unresolved social conflict that thrives on divisions and invidious distinctions. It can thrive in the total absence of genetic differences in a single homogeneous population of common ancestry. That is the case, for example, with the relations between the Japanese and that portion of themselves they know as the Eta.

In a truly great society it may be that the kinds of fear and rivalry that generate racism will be overcome. This can be done without the kind of millenarian reform that would be necessary to banish all conflict, for only certain kinds of hostilities generate racism although any kind can be channeled into an already raging racial bigotry. Great areas of the earth's surface have been totally devoid of racism for long periods of time and such a situation may return again, although under altered circumstances. If and when it does, the word "race" may drop from our vocabulary and scholars will desperately scrutinize our remains and the remains of our civilization, trying to discover what we were so disturbed about.

45

B. Biological Determination

The Nonscience of Human Nature

by Stephen Jay Gould

"We have been deluged during the past decade by a resurgent biological determinism, ranging from 'pop ethology' to outright racism"

When in the seventeenth century a group of girls simultaneously suffered seizures in the presence of an accused witch, the justices of Salem explained the girls' behavior as demonic possession. In 1971, when the followers of Charles Manson attributed occult powers to their leader, no judge took them seriously. During the nearly 300 years separating the two incidents, we have learned quite a bit about the psychological determinants of group behavior. A crudely literal interpretation of such events now seems ridiculous.

An equally crude literalism has prevailed in the past in interpreting human nature and the differences among human groups. Human behavior was simply attributed to innate biology. We do what we do because we are made that way. The first lesson of an eighteenth-century primer stated the position succinctly: In Adam's fall, we sinned all. A progressive advance from this biological determinism has been a major trend in twentieth-century science and culture. We have come to see ourselves as a learning animal; we have come to believe that the influences of class and culture far outweigh the weaker predispositions of our genetic constitution.

Nonetheless, we have been deluged during the past decade by a resurgent biological determinism, ranging from "pop ethology" to outright racism.

With Konrad Lorenz as godfather, Robert Ardrey as dramatist, and Desmond Morris as raconteur, we are presented with the behavior of man, "the naked ape," descended from an African carnivore, innately aggressive and inherently territorial.

Lionel Tiger and Robin Fox try to find a biological basis for outmoded Western ideals of aggressive, outreaching men and docile, restricted women. In discussing cross-cultural differences between men and women, they propose a hormonal chemistry inherited from the requirements of our supposed primal roles as group hunters and child rearers.

Carleton Coon offered a prelude of events to come with his claim (*The Origin of Races*, 1962) that five major human races evolved independently from *Homo erectus* ("Java" and "Peking" man) to *Homo sapiens*, with black people making the transition last. More recently, the I.Q. test has been (mis)used to infer genetic differences in intelligence among races (Arthur Jensen and William Shockley) and classes (Richard Herrnstein)—always, I must note, to the benefit of the particular group to which the author happens to belong.

All these views have been ably criticized on an individual basis; yet they have rarely been treated together as expressions of a common philosophy—a crude biological de-

terminism. One can, of course, accept a specific claim and reject the others. A belief in the innate nature of human violence does not brand anyone a racist. Yet all these claims have a common underpinning in postulating a direct genetic basis for our most fundamental traits. If we are programmed to be what we are, then these traits are ineluctable. We may, at best, channel them, but we cannot change them, either by will, education, or culture.

In various guises, the political function of biological determinism has been to serve the supporters of class, sex, and race distinctions at home and of conquest or domination of supposedly inferior peoples abroad. In the context of Western history, this means that biological determinism has served as a tool of state and commercial power.

If we accept the usual platitudes about "scientific method" at face value, then the coordinated resurgence of biological determinism must be attributed to new information that refutes the earlier findings of twentieth-century science. Science, we are told, progresses by accumulating new information and using it to improve or replace old theories, but the new biological determinism rests upon no recent fund of information and can cite in its behalf not a single fact. Its renewed support must have some other basis, most likely social or political in nature.

Science is always influenced by

society, but it operates under a strong constraint of fact as well. The Church eventually made its peace with Galilean cosmology. In studying the genetic components of such complex human traits as intelligence and aggressiveness, however, we are freed from the constraint of fact, for we are sure of practically nothing about these traits. In these questions, "science" follows (and indirectly exposes) the social and political influences of the time.

What, then, are the nonscientific reasons for the resurgence of biological determinism? They range, I believe, from pedestrian pursuits of high royalties for best sellers to pernicious attempts to reintroduce racism as respectable science. Their common denominator must lie in our current malaise. How satisfying it is to fob off the responsibility for war and violence upon our presumably carnivorous ancestors. How convenient to blame the poor and the hungry for their own condition—lest we be forced to blame industry or government for our abject failure to secure a decent life for all people. And how convenient an argument it is for those who control government and, by the way, provide the money that current science requires for its very existence!

The deterministic arguments divide neatly into two groups—those based on the supposed nature of the human species in general and those based on presumed differences among "racial groups" of *Homo sapiens* (see my column of March, 1974). I shall treat the first subject here and reserve the second for my next column.

Summarized briefly, mainstream pop ethology contends that two lineages of hominids inhabited Pleistocene Africa. One, a small, territorial carnivore, evolved into us; the other, a larger, presumably gentle herbivore, became extinct. Some carry the analogy of Cain and Abel to its full conclusion and accuse our ancestors of fratricide. The "predatory transition" to hunting established a pattern of innate violence and engendered our territorial urges: "With the coming of the hunting life to the emerging hominid came the dedication to terri-

tory" (Ardrey, *The Territorial Imperative*).

According to this view, although clothed, citified, and civilized, we carry deep within us the genetic patterns of behavior that served our ancestor, the "killer ape." In *African Genesis* Ardrey champions Raymond Dart's contention that "the predatory transition and the weapons fixation explained man's bloody history, his eternal agression, his irrational, self-destroying, inexorable pursuit of death for death's sake."

Tiger and Fox extend the theme of group hunting to claim a biological basis for the differences between men and women that Western cultures have traditionally valued. Men did the hunting; women stayed home with the kids. Men are aggressive and combative, but they also form strong bonds among themselves that reflect the ancient need for cooperation in the killing of big game and now find expression in touch football and rotary clubs. Women are docile and devoted to their own children. They do not form intense bonds among themselves because their ancestors needed none to tend their homes and their men: sisterhood is an illusion. "We are wired for hunting. . . . We remain Upper Paleolithic hunters, fine-honed machines designed for the efficient pursuit of game" (Tiger and Fox, *The Imperial Animal*).

The pop ethology story has been built on two lines of supposed evidence, both highly disputable:

1. Analogies with the behavior of other animals (abundant but imperfect data). No one doubts that many animals (including some, but not all, primates) display innate patterns of aggression and territorial behavior. Since we exhibit similar behavior, can we not infer a similar cause? The fallacy of this assumption involves a basic difference in evolutionary theory between homologous and analogous features. Homologous aspects of two species are due to a common descent and a common genetic constitution. Analogous traits evolved separately.

Comparisons between human beings and other animals can yield causal assertions about the genetics

of our behavior only if they are based on homologous traits. But how can we know whether similarities are homologous or analogous? It is hard to differentiate even when we are dealing with concrete structures, such as muscles and bones. In fact, most classic arguments in the study of phylogeny involve the confusion of homology and analogy, for analogous structures can be strikingly similar (we call this phenomenon evolutionary convergence). How much harder it is to tell when the similar features are only the outward motions of behavior!

Baboons may be territorial; their males may be organized into a dominance hierarchy—but is our quest for Lebensraum and the hierarchy of our armies an expression of the same genetic makeup or merely an analogous pattern that might be purely cultural in origin? And when Lorenz compares us with geese and fish, we stray even further into pure conjecture; baboons, at least, are second cousins.

2. Evidence from hominid fossils (scrappy but direct data). Ardrey's claims for territoriality involve the assumption that our African ancestor *Australopithecus africanus*, was a carnivore. The evidence is based on accumulations of bones and tools at the South African cave sites and on the size and shape of teeth. The bone piles are no longer seriously considered; they are more likely the work of hyenas or leopards than of hominids.

Teeth are granted more prominence, but I believe that the evidence is equally poor if not absolutely contradictory. The relative size of grinding teeth (premolars and molars) is the basis of the argument. Herbivores need more surface area to grind their gritty and abundant food. *A. robustus*, the supposed gentle herbivore, possessed grinding teeth relatively larger than those of the presumed carnivore, our ancestor *A. africanus*.

But *A. robustus* was the larger of the two species. As size increases, an animal must feed a body growing as a cube of length by chewing with tooth areas that would increase only as the square of length if they maintained the same relative size. This will not do, and larger mammals must have differentially larger teeth than smaller relatives. I have tested this assertion by measuring tooth areas and body sizes for species in several groups of mammals (rodents, piglike herbivores, deer, and several groups of primates). Invariably, I find that larger animals have relatively larger teeth—not because they eat different foods, but simply because they are larger.

Moreover, the "small" teeth of *A. africanus* are not at all diminutive. They are *absolutely larger* than ours (although we are three times as heavy), and they are about as big as those of gorillas weighing nearly ten times as much! The evidence of tooth size indicates to me that *A. africanus* was primarily herbivorous.

The issue of biological determinism is not an abstract matter to be debated within academic cloisters. These ideas have important consequences, and they have already permeated our mass media. Ardrey's dubious theory is a prominent theme in Stanley Kubrick's film *2001*. The bone tool of our apelike ancestor first smashes a tapir's skull and then twirls about to transform into a space station of our next evolutionary stage. Kubrick's next film, *Clockwork Orange*, continues the theme and explores the liberal dilemma inspired by claims of innate human violence. (Shall we accept totalitarian controls for mass deprogramming or remain nasty and vicious within a democracy?) But the most immediate impact will be felt as male privilege girds its loins to battle a growing women's movement. As Kate Millett remarks in *Sexual Politics*: "Patriarchy has a tenacious or powerful hold through its successful habit of passing itself off as nature.

46

The Fallacy of Biological Determinism

There's no good evidence suggesting that IQ is inherited

by R.C. Lewontin

Even the most superficial look at the history and present state of human societies shows an immense inequality in status, wealth and power both between individuals within societies and between nations and continents. This manifest inequality is in sharp contrast to the leading value in Western ideology since the 18th century, a value that characterizes the national myths of all the states of the world, the value of equality. If it is really "self-evident" that "all men (but apparently not women) are created equal" and that the political structure of states is designed to eliminate artificial barriers to equality and to promote general welfare, then how are we to explain those manifest inequalities in wealth and power between individuals and nations?

One possibility, of course, would be to assert that the political economy of most nations is not such as to promote equality in status, wealth and power, but, on the contrary, is carefully designed by the possessors of these attributes to keep themselves in possession. The idea that inequalities are a structural element of our social organization is not a popular one and not surprisingly is regarded with hostility by the governmental, educational and information-producing agencies of our society. The alternative, which has proved more palatable and, of course, more serviceable, is that our society is pretty much as fair as any society can be and that the inequalities we observe are the irreducible differences resulting from basic biological differences between people. This is, in effect, the ideology of *biological determinism*. It asserts that although some minor improvements may still be possible in spreading status, wealth and power, there is a limit to how closely equality can be approached—a limit set by the nature of the human species.

Biological determinism as an ideology has two seemingly contradictory facets, both of which are complementary and necessary to the complete argument. First, biological determinists claim that differences in status, wealth and power among individuals and among groups are the result of genetic differences in abilities, personalities and behaviors. Thus, some people are more aggressive, more intelligent, more creative, more skillful because, it is asserted, their genes make them so; if one nation or race has a greater preponderance of these superior genotypes, then that group will dominate as a whole. As Arthur Jensen puts it,

R. C. Lewontin, Alexander Agassiz Professor of Zoology at Harvard University, is a population geneticist engaged in both theoretical and experimental research in evolutionary genetics. In 1970, Dr. Lewontin resigned from the National Academy of Sciences in protest against its conducting classified research for military purposes. This article is based on a New York Academy of Sciences public lecture.

some people can paint houses while others can paint pictures. "We have to face it: the assortment of persons into occupational roles simply is not 'fair' in any absolute sense. The best we can hope for is that true merit, given equality of opportunity, act as a basis for the natural assorting process."(*Harvard Educational Review 39*: 1-123, 1969)

But the ideology requires more than the view that differences in ability and personality are innate. It can be argued, as Dobzhansky did in *Social Biology* (20: 280-288, 1973), that the fact of biological diversity in abilities does not in itself necessitate social inequalities. We might simply organize our society so that both house painters and picture painters would receive the same psychic and material compensations. It is at this point that the second facet of biological determinism enters the argument.

Biological determinists argue that superimposed on the biological differences between individuals in ability is a tendency towards biological uniformity in behavior. Together, these biological qualities guarantee, in the determinists' view, that societies will always be hierarchical. The argument of a biologically based *human nature* holds that man tends to be "by nature" aggressive (Lorenz, 1963), territorial (Ardrey, 1966), entrepreneurial, genocidal, indoctrinable, male dominated (Wilson, 1975). That biological differences in ability between individuals must inevitably be turned into a hierarchical system of differential status and wealth is nowhere better stated than in Wilson's description of the characteristic political economy of the human species: "The members of human societies sometimes cooperate closely in insectan fashion, but more frequently they compete for the limited resources allocated to their role-sector. The best and most entrepreneurial of the role-actors usually gain a disproportionate share of the rewards, while the least successful are displaced to other, less desirable positions." (*Sociobiology: The Modern Synthesis,* Harvard University Press, Cambridge, Massachusetts, 1975)

This description, it must be noted, is not regarded as a historically contingent phenomenon in market societies, but as arising out of the biological nature of the human species. A human society like that envisaged by Dobzhansky, in which genetic differences in ability are not converted into status and wealth differences, would be biologically "unnatural" for Wilson and therefore either impossible or maintainable only under the most rigid totalitarian rule.

The attempt to justify the status quo by a resort to biological arguments has a long history. Before the middle class revolutions of the 18th century, aristocrats claimed superior "blood." In the 19th and 20th centuries, such arguments became more sophisticated, first turning to anatomy and then to DNA as a basis for the biological distinction. Thus, in the 19th century Lombroso founded an influential school of "criminal anthropology" with his claim that "criminal types" could be recognized by the conformation of their ears, noses, skulls, lips, etc. No less a personage than Louis Agassiz, the greatest of 19th century American zoologists, claimed that the skull sutures of black children closed earlier than those of whites. Consequently, it was dangerous to teach blacks too much for their brains would swell up and burst inside their rigid crania. Although this may seem absurd, it is typical of the claims of 19th century physical anthropology and comparative anatomy, which found blacks, criminals and women to be either more childlike, more primitive, or less developed anatomically than northern European men.

migrants proportional to the numbers of those nationalities in the United States as of the 1890 census, when the overwhelming majority of Americans had come from northern Europe. The Immigration Act of 1924 was the greatest political consequence of biological determinism until that time, but it was soon to be surpassed by the deaths of "biologically inferior" millions in eastern Europe.

Although the shock produced by Nazi racism resulted in a disappearance of biological determinist arguments from respectable intellectual circles for twenty years, these arguments have now come back into fashion among academics, albeit in more sophisticated and "scientific" forms. The latest versions include the claims that 1) differences between individuals in school and socio-

Louis Agassiz claimed that it was dangerous to teach blacks too much for their brains would swell up and burst inside their rigid crania.

After the rediscovery of Mendel in 1900, the gene took over as the biological basis for human differences. At about the same time, intelligence testing was founded in France by Binet and was imported into the United States and popularized by Terman; his 1916 Stanford-Binet test was the prime tool of the mental testing movement in the United States. The idea that intelligence could be measured quantitatively and the rapid advances in Mendelian genetics came together to produce the single most powerful and popular form of biological determinism, the eugenics movement. It was asserted that the health and welfare of society were dependent upon the more intelligent people, that intelligence was determined chiefly by genes, that the less intelligent were producing too many children and that, by both law and custom, this degeneration of the population should be stopped and reversed.

A racist version of the eugenics doctrine held that blacks, orientals and southern and eastern Europeans were genetically inferior mentally and morally, as demonstrated by intelligence testing. This aspect of the eugenics movement culminated in the U.S. Immigration Act of 1924. Until that act was passed, immigration of Europeans had been unrestricted. It was argued by mental testers, including such founders of American educational psychology as Terman, Yerkes and Goddard, that IQ tests, especially tests administered at Ellis Island and the Army classification tests given to those inducted during the first World War, had shown most southern and eastern European immigrants to be mentally inferior. Supported by the overwhelming testimony of the American academic community, with virtually no dissenting voice from geneticists, an immigration act was passed by Congress setting national quotas for im-

economic success are chiefly the result of genetic differences and are therefore unchangeable (Jensen, 1969); 2) differences in average scholastic and socioeconomic levels among races (chiefly black and white) are mostly genetic and therefore unchangeable (Jensen, 1969, 1975); 3) differences between social classes are mostly the result of genetic and unchangeable differences in intelligence (Herrnstein, 1971); 4) differences in status and roles of men and women are largely biological, a result of the evolution of our species, and are therefore natural and unchangeable (Tiger and Fox, 1971; Wilson, 1975); 5) as mentioned earlier, the human species has built into its genes as a result of its evolutionary history such traits as aggression, territoriality, conformism, indoctrinability, entrepreneurship, etc.

The arguments about innate differences between sexes and about "human nature" are of a speculative and loose form appealing chiefly to common sense notions and prejudices, to analogies with non-human animals, and to carefully selected data from paleontology, archeology and ethnography. There is not a great deal that can be said about them except to remind the unwary reader that they are purely imaginative invention and speculation, even though they are often presented as demonstrated fact. The arguments about genetic differences in ability among individuals and groups, however, have a much greater appearance of "objectivity," since they use statistical analyses, cite masses of evidence from quantitative tests of intelligence of relatives of various degrees and, in general, bring into play what appears at first sight to be an unchallengeable apparatus of statistical-genetical theory and observation. "Facts are facts," we are told, "and even though we may not like the conclusions, we must be objec-

The gathering and presentation of the "facts" from which the heritability of IQ has been calculated have been so scandalously bad as to constitute a veritable Watergate of human behavioral genetics.

tive about them."

It turns out that on close examination the concepts on which the determinist position is based prove to be incorrect, the theoretical arguments offered do not stand up logically, and the "facts" in some important cases have been cooked. Therefore, for the remainder of this article, I shall look at that particular brand of biological determinism embodied in the claims of hereditarians that differences in performance on IQ tests are chiefly genetic and unchangeable, and that differences between races and social classes in performance on these tests are also genetic and unchangeable.

I will leave aside the questions of whether performance on IQ tests measures anything that can be called "intelligence" in an important sense and whether performance on such tests is, in fact, a good predictor of eventual socioeconomic success. The first of these questions seems to me entirely metaphysical, and the answer to the second depends upon what one means by a good predictor. The gross correlation between IQ and eventual socioeconomic success, as measured on the scores used by sociologists, is rather poor (only about 25 per cent of the variation in socioeconomic success is explained by variation in IQ) and that correlation decreases considerably if such variables as family background and years of schooling are held constant. In fact, these latter variables explain much more of the variation in socioeconomic success than does IQ, but at present no set of variables gives very high predictability. (Bowles and Nelson, 1974, *Review of Economics and Statistics, 56:* 1) I pass over this point lightly because my main concern is with the misuse of biology.

The main *conceptual* error in the biological determinist argument stems from an incorrect understanding of the relation of gene, environment and organism. The error appears in different forms, sometimes naive and simplistic, sometimes sophisticated. Jensen's 1969 paper in *Harvard Educational Review* (39: 1-123) contains all the forms. The title of the paper is "How much can we boost IQ and scholastic achievement?" The answer given in the paper is "not much" and the reason given for the answer is that IQ differences are mostly inherited. This is the first and most elementary fallacy of biological determinism.

It is totally incorrect to equate "inherited" or "genetic" with "unchangeable," although this equation is often made. The plasticity of a morphological or physiological or behavioral trait is not made greater or less by the fact that genes influence it. If "inherited" meant "unchangeable,"

then human clinical genetics would be a largely fruitless enterprise, limited only to counseling parents about the risks of having defective children. But that is not the case. Inherited disorders can be treated and corrected as easily (or with as much difficulty) as those arising from birth traumas, accidents or environmental insults. To cure a disorder, we need to know what the metabolic or anatomical lesion is, not whether it is the result of being homozygous for a gene.

It is irrelevant whether "blue babies" suffer from a genetic or accidental development disorder; the cure is the same—surgical intervention to close off the short circuit in the circulation. Wilson's disease is characterized by progressive degeneration of nervous and other tissues resulting in death in late childhood or early adulthood. It is the result of being homozygous for a single recessive mutant gene, which, as it turns out, causes the sufferer to retain too much copper in his body. This knowledge of the metabolic lesion has led to prevention of the degenerative process through the use of a simple drug that removes excess copper ions.

What is true for extreme disorders is also true for the normal. Whether behavior is modified by social influences depends upon events that long postdate the original action, if any, of genes influencing the growth of neurons. Genes do not mediate processes that are somehow sealed off from the rest of the universe. As Jacob and Monod showed long ago, even the primary transfer of information from gene to protein is directly modifiable by information from the environment. The opposition of "inherited" and "modifiable" is a relic of 19th century thought.

A more sophisticated form of the erroneous view of gene and organism is that of "genetic potential," also found in the writings of Jensen and especially in those of Herrnstein. Although the concept admits that gene and environment interact, the description of that interaction incorrectly assumes that the genes set the limit or the maximum of a character, while the environment determines how much of that "limit" will be realized or fulfilled. It is as if we were empty buckets at birth, some larger than others. If the environment is poor, even the large buckets will be only partially filled; if the environment is enriched, every genotype will reach its maximum and the large buckets will contain more than the small ones. But there is nothing in developmental genetics to sustain this idea of differing genetic potentials.

To understand the situation, we must look at the concept of the *norm of reaction,* the most basic concept of developmental genetics. For a particular genetic type, there is some functional relationship between the environment experienced by the developing organism and the resulting morphology, physiology or behavior that is developed, the so-called phenotype. The norm of reaction of a given genotype is the relation between its phenotypic expression and the environment in which it has developed. Different genotypes have different norms of reaction. Figure 1 shows two hypothetical genotypes with different norms of reaction—one, G_1, in which the phenotype, say weight, increases with the environmental variable, say temperature, while the other, G_2, has a decreasing weight with increasing temperature.

In order to draw the norms of reaction for different genotypes, it is necessary to allow each genotype to develop in a series of different environments and to observe the

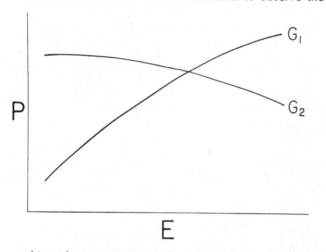

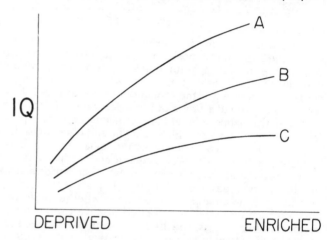

plication is that the genetically superior types will be even more superior as the environment is made better. The conclusion one is supposed to draw is that spending more money and effort in general improvements in education will only produce greater inequalities than already exist between genotypes. But there is not a shred of evidence for such a proposition as Figure 2. It is simply a convenient hypothesis arranged to suit an erroneous preconception.

The third, and most sophisticated, form of hereditarian error is the use of the concept of *heritability* in describing the degree to which genes influence behavioral traits. It is not possible to ascribe a particular fraction of an individual's phenotype to genes and the rest to environment—it is an obvious absurdity to say that of my 5 feet 11 inches of height, I owe 5 feet to my genes and 11 inches to my environment. It is possible, however, to divide up the *variation in a population* into a variation that results from genetic variation and one that results from environmental variation. The propor-

resulting phenotypes. But such an experiment is quite impossible for any human trait, especially any human behavioral trait, because it is simply impossible to produce a large number of human beings, all of whom have the same genetic constitution, and then to raise each one in a different controlled environment. We would need large numbers of groups of "centuplets" and dictatorial power to put each in a different environment, obviously an absurdity. For that reason, *no one has ever been able to characterize human norms of reaction for any behavioral trait* (or for any human trait at all). Where norms of reaction for different genotypes have been determined in experimental animals, they tend to look like Figure 1. That is, they cross each other, with one genotype having a larger phenotype in some environments and another genotype having a larger phenotype in other environments. Thus, it is clearly impossible to speak of one genotype having a higher "potential" than the other which is "fulfilled" in a "better" kind of environment.

Despite the fact that the norms of reaction that are known tend to look like Figure 1, and despite the fact that human behavioral norms of reaction are *totally unknown* , Jensen in his 1969 paper discusses the concept of norm of reaction using the lines shown in Figure 2. These hypothetical lines correspond to the erroneous notion of genetic potential. Genotype A is better than B, which is better than C in all environments. Thus, enriching the environment will not help C relative to A. On the contrary, the lines are drawn so as to fan out in the "enriched environment." The obvious im-

tion of all the variation that is genetic is called the heritability of the trait, H^2, in the population. Symbolically, H^2 = genetic variation/genetic variation + environmental variation.

As defined H^2 applies only to a particular population at a particular time, since another population at another time will have different genotypes and different environments. Thus we cannot say that "the heritability of weight is 43 per cent," but only that "in the population of New York, in 1976, the heritability of weight is 43 per cent." Yet in discussing IQ, biological determinists repeatedly refer to the heritability of IQ as a constant, usually giving 80 per cent as their best estimate. What they fail to understand (or willfully ignore) is the fact that the per cent heritability applies *only* to the set of environments in which the determination was made and cannot be extrapolated to other distributions of environments.

More important than the error of supposing the heritability of IQ to be a universal constant is the incorrect implication drawn from the figure. If the heritability of IQ is 80 per cent, it is asserted, this means that IQ is "mostly genetic" and therefore not very changeable, or at least that the variation among individuals in IQ cannot be reduced by more than about 20 per cent since 80 per cent of the variation is genetic. But, as I have pointed out, this is totally incorrect. The heritability of a trait gives us no hint as to how malleable or plastic the trait may be. Before the discovery of the faulty copper metabolism that underlies Wilson's disease, it was 100 per cent heritable. It is simply a non sequitur to claim that if the heritability of IQ were 80 per cent, then only 20 per cent of the variation could be removed by varying the environment.

The error is compounded by biological determinists, who go on to claim that the heritability of IQ *within* populations is a basis for concluding that the differences *between* groups are also genetic. Jensen commits this error with respect to black-white differences and Herrnstein does it with respect to social class differences. But there is neither a logical nor empirical relationship between the heritability of a trait within a population and the causes of differences between populations. Differences within and between populations arise from quite separate causes on quite different time scales and one cannot be judged from the other. So, for example, the difference in skin color among New Yorkers classified as "white" can reasonably be attributed to heredity, since the Finns, Italians, Slavs, Puerto Ricans and so on clearly differ in skin pigmentation genetically. Yet no one would assert that the difference in skin color between New Yorkers who stay in New York all winter and their better-off relatives who spend the winter in Miami is genetic.

Differences within populations are a manifestation of the genetic history of the population in recent times, especially of migrational mixture, and of environmental differences of a local nature having to do with the internal organization of the society. Differences between populations reflect long term genetic divergence and major environmental differences associated with the clear identification and separation of the groups. There is simply no way to judge the causes of between group differences from genetic variation within groups. Although this point has been made over and over since Jensen published his paper in 1969, it does not seem to have been understood, since the error reappears in his 1975 book. (*Educability and Group Differences*, Harper and Row)

Finally, let us turn to the "facts" from which the heritability of IQ has been calculated. It is worth looking at the status of some of these facts, not because they themselves are relevant to any social issues, but because the gathering and presentation of these facts have been so scandalously bad as to constitute a veritable Watergate of human behavioral genetics.

The study of genetics is the study of relatives. If genes influence a trait, then closer relatives should resemble each other, on the average, more than distant relatives. This study of relatives presents no problem in experimental organisms, where related individuals can be placed randomly in different environments. In the human species, the problem is to distinguish similarities that arise from genetic relationships from similarities that arise from environmental correlations, since close relatives tend to share environments as well as genes. Any estimate of heritability will then be upwardly biased by an unknown amount, unless the relatives being compared have been randomized across environments. That is, we must place children of the same biological parents with adopting parents who will represent a random sample of the population with respect to various socioeconomic variables that might influence intelligence.

Despite this elementary consideration, the first lesson in any course in biometrical genetics, *the great bulk of estimates of heritability of IQ come from a comparison of relatives raised together in the same family*. Thus, these estimates are completely useless. Although this kind of error is so elementary that no student in an animal breeding course could make it without being called to account, behavioral geneticists continue to publish such estimates of heritability in the leading journals of their field with the approval of the editors and referees who are their colleagues.

But gross experimental errors are only a part of the story. Realizing the importance of adoption studies, those who have attempted to estimate heritability of IQ from published studies of identical twins raised apart and together have relied heavily on four such studies. The largest of the four studies comparing twins raised apart and together was the series carried out by Cyril Burt and his colleagues; the Burt studies are a major source of the 80 per cent heritability of IQ so often quoted. It now appears, however, that Burt's "data" are not part of the corpus of science at all, but of science fiction. In 1973, Kamin, addressing the American Psychological Association, showed so conclusively that Burt had cooked his data in at least two ways that Jensen was forced to conclude that they could not be relied upon. (*Behavior Genetics*, 4:1-28, 1974) Kamin has since published his brilliant detective work as *The Science and Politics of IQ*. (Lawrence Erlbaum and Associates, Potomac, Md., 1975)

First, it appears that Burt did not use actual test scores in his comparisons, but made "final assessments" subjectively and altered the numerical scores to be more in accord with his hypothesis of genetic determination. Not content with these adjustments, Burt further "adjusted" his statistics to give the following remarkable results: in 1955, with 21 twin pairs raised apart and 83 pairs together, the correlation for twins raised apart was .771 while for those raised together it was .944. In 1958 with more twin pairs added to the tests, the correlations were again .771 and .944. In 1966, with still more pairs—53 raised apart and 95 together—the correlations were still .771 and .944! Sir Cyril Burt must have been a remarkable experimenter indeed.

Nor is Burt the only sinner. Kamin's book reveals several other instances of the plotting of non-existent data points, the suppression of others, etc. Ignorance and inadvertance cannot be pleaded here.

How are we to explain the scandalous state of investigations in this field? It is hard to come to any other conclusion than that it is the result of the explicitly political position of the advocates of biological determinism. Not content with making conceptually incorrect and contradictory assertions about what might be the case if IQ were highly heritable, they have tried to force the data to fit their preconceptions. In this act of supererogation they have given themselves away.

All of science, of course, has an ideological component. No research is entirely free of the social and political views of its practitioners. The very act of engaging in experimental science in an academic context carries with it a host of political presuppositions about the allocation of labor, resources and power in society. But occasionally ideology becomes so overriding and political advocacy so potent as to completely dominate the mode of scientific production.

As we look back at the discredited versions of biological determinism in the 19th century and in the first half of the 20th, they seem to us crude and sometimes absurd. Who would be so foolish as to believe that one could tell a murderer from the shape of his skull? Yet we are asked seriously to believe in 1976 that the possession of an extra Y chromosome predisposes people to criminal acts. The arguments for the heritability of IQ are just another instance of the same old ideology in modern and respectable guise. Nothing is known in biology that dictates the limits of human social organization or individual fulfillment. Claims to the contrary must be regarded with extreme suspicion, for they usually turn out to benefit their authors.

47

DIGGING UP THE GOOD, OLD, OLD DAYS

by Brian Weiss
THE NEW ARCHEOLOGY

Pots and arrows are not enough anymore. Now archeologists use computers, statistics and logic to tell how folks centuries dead, lived, loved, ate and fought.

ONCE UPON A TIME the people living in farmer Theodore Koster's cornfield near Kampsville, Illinois, helped themselves to 15 kinds of waterfowl, 35 types of fish, basketsful of hickory and other wild nuts, a plentiful supply of edible plants, and an occasional deer or wild turkey. They ate in beautiful surroundings, protected from cold winds by the neighboring bluffs, and quenched their thirst at a clear, flowing spring. For all this affluence, they probably worked about 20 hours a week, or half the time most people in our industrial society must labor to put food on their table.

Those were the good old days. They currently lie 12 feet and 4,500 years below the surface of Mr. Koster's farm, yet archeologists who are exploring this village, and others that are thousands of years further away, routinely discuss the family structure, community ideals, and esthetic inclinations of the original inhabitants. Archeologists, who were once satisfied to find stones, bones, and bits of pottery, are now looking for human behavior when they dig.

Until recently, archeological reconstructions were about equal parts data and conjecture. It once took a strong back *and* a vivid imagination to be an archeologist. After digging the potsherds and other remnants out of the ground, you assembled them in your laboratory and hoped for an insight, a vision, or a similarity to the items used by some group of live people previously described by an ethnographer.

Today, aided by new methods, archeologists recover more data when they dig. More important, they now ask different questions of their data, and do it in a way that allows them to decide how good the answers are. Twenty years ago, an archeologist complained that "the stereotype of the American archeologist has somehow come to be a pretty dull sort of clod, with most of his gray matter under his fingernails." Today, many archeologists come equipped with computers, advanced training in statistical analysis, and a working knowledge of deductive and inductive logic. For these scientists it is only a slight inconvenience that the people they study are dead.

"I think we can use potsherds to get at psychological behavior in the past." UCLA archeologist Jim Hill was describing for me some of his recent attempts to obtain more information about *individuals* from the decorated clay remains of pots. Archeologists have tended to talk about populations or entire cultures, rather than individuals, since there were no data to support conclusions such as "John Doe slept here."

Even when painting the same design, potters unconsciously vary in their patterns of movement, and these individual differences appear as variations in the thickness, angle, and other details of the lines used in forming a decoration. Hill developed a method for measuring this variation, and felt it would be possible to identify individual potters when looking at archeological remains.

Similar Sherds. To test his idea, Hill and some students drove to Tijuana, Mexico and had each of five potters make and paint 15 pots. Two of the potters had been trained by the same person, and three of the five were brothers. Hill asked them to paint the same designs on all the pots.

After explaining his cargo to an incredulous and skeptical Customs officer, Hill and the students returned to their lab and broke the pots into pieces, which were labeled to identify their maker, and then mixed together. Other students then set about taking measurements of line widths and angles, and a variety of other information, all of which were fed into a computer program that grouped the sherds according to their similarity. Almost without fail, the computer grouped sherds of the same potter together, showing that in spite of the similarities resulting from painting the same design, or being trained by the same person, differences arise from idiosyncratic habits of movement.

Hill also thinks it is possible to know when there was stress on either an individual or an entire group. He and his students have examined pottery from Eastern Arizona, searching for "errors" in the decorative patterns, such as corners that don't meet or lines that cross unintentionally. These errors, the archeologist says, may well be evidence of psychological or physiological stress. Preliminary analysis suggests that there is a much higher frequency of these errors during times of environmental stress, when food was in short supply, and social tension increased.

"I don't know if archeology wants to get at individual hangups, but we could do it," Hill says. "I think we've hit on something that may force me to go back and take some psychology."

Questions about individuals inevitably lead to questions about the way these individuals were organized. When Hill dug the site of Broken K Pueblo in East-Central Arizona, he found the artifacts left by people who had died almost 700 years before. Yet, in addition to describing such mundane matters as what they ate and how long they occupied Broken K, Hill can also say that the 120 or so prehistoric residents were divided into five residence groups, and that the men came to live with their wives' group after marriage.

This kind of information again comes from the study of pottery remains. In modern pueblos, women are the potters, and the major designs are passed on as a mother teaches her daughter to make and decorate pottery. At Broken K pueblo, there were five

Archeologists study stress by picking up the pieces.

living areas. Each of these had a distinctive style of ceramic decoration, and each had been occupied for at least 65 years. The pattern of postmarital residence that would have most likely produced such a distribution of artifacts was one in which the men went to live with their new wives, near the woman's maternal relatives. If the women had gone to live with their husbands, taking their designs to a

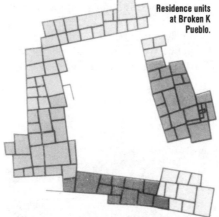

Residence units at Broken K Pueblo.

different area of the pueblo, decorative motifs would have been distributed evenly and randomly throughout the village. Hill found further confirmation in the nonrandom distribution of fire pits, storage pits, and other evidences of female activities.

A Relaxed Struggle. Archeologists, unlike other social scientists, have an opportunity to study human behavior over long spans of time, and to look for similarities and differences in the way populations change, adapt or perish. There is a disquieting sort of comfort in knowing that many other people, at many other times, have faced problems such as overpopulation, resource depletion, environmental change, and warfare. This long view gives archeologists the chance to look for regularities in the way cultures function. "If we can explain the

past, we can predict the future," says Hill.

One of the most elaborate attempts to take this long view of cultural processes is occurring back in Mr. Koster's cornfield. For the last six years, Northwestern University professor Stuart Struever has supervised excavation of the Koster site, from which he and legions of student and public helpers have extracted an 8,000-year record of life in the Lower Illinois Valley.

Many of the things Struever has found are forcing a substantial change in our view of early man. For example, most textbooks paint a picture of life in 6000 B.C. as a constant struggle for existence, with insufficient leisure time to develop culture to a higher level of refinement. Yet the evidence from Koster shows that early man lived amidst plenty. By concentrating on a limited number of abundant foods, the earliest residents of Koster probably fed themselves with fewer hours of daily labor than most factory workers today. "The Koster site" says Struever, "is going to change our whole idea of adaptations to the environment."

Struever, like Hill, feels that stress plays a major role in the changes that occur over time. Because the early populations of Koster were small, they placed little or no strain on the available resources. Among later groups, as populations grew, the residents had to abandon the hunting

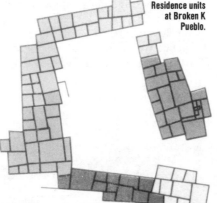

The Koster Site, 6000 B.C.

and gathering strategy that had served them for thousands of years and utilize the greater productivity available from agriculture.

Although people began raising corn near Koster about 200 B.C., there was no full-scale use of agriculture until 1,000 years later, when an expanding population made it necessary for survival.

This latter conclusion also contradicts the traditional textbook wisdom which states that people immediately incorporate any change that offers them greater productivity. Koster's inhabitants had the means for engaging in agriculture; however, they chose not to invest the time. If leisure time is a prerequisite for the development of culture, the preagricultural inhabitants of this area should have started the Renaissance rolling.

Struever has found evidence of at least

15 distinct occupations of the Koster site. One of these occurred around 2500 B.C. At that time, the people occupied Koster the entire year, spreading their village over about two acres of land. They built houses of branches, twigs and grass, using mud as mortar. There is evidence of community cooperation in the form of large, limestone-lined pits that were used to roast game for the entire village.

Cross-Disciplinary Cooperation. Neither famine, violence nor war seems to have intruded on the rather comfortable life of these people, who depended largely on hickory nuts for food. They also used deer, fish and waterfowl.

Among the many bone tools found from this time period were some ornate, engraved bone pins that may have been hairpins. These people also buried their dead in a graveyard at the edge of the village. This is further evidence that early man had both time and the esthetic inclinations usually thought to be the exclusive property of later cultures.

In reconstructing the behavior of Koster's previous residents, Struever utilizes data from a wide variety of other disciplines. Malacologists study snail and other mollusk remains for information they yield about climatic change, while other specialists examine fossil pollen, fish and animal bones, soil samples, carbonized plant remains, and the trace elements in various artifacts. This cross-disciplinary cooperation is essential to get the kind of data archeologists need to answer questions about the processes of culture change. This

archeological search for the general laws of human behavior comprises what is usually referred to as the "new archeology."

Archeology underwent—some say suffered—an intellectual upheaval in the 1960s. Like an amoeba, the field developed a cleft in the middle, and split into opposing parts dubbed "Old" and "New" archeology. It got a bit unpleasant for awhile, with partisans on both sides suggesting that the opposition not be allowed to dig with anything sharper than a wooden spoon, lest they hurt themselves. The differences were intellectual, methodolog-

Looking for behavioral remains at Mr. Koster's farm.

ical and, in some cases, generational. The "New" archeologists came armed with advanced statistical techniques, electronic computers, and an insistence on a rigorous framework of deductive logic. Their goal was to find the laws of human behavior (what one archeologist called "the law-and-order" approach), or to look for the regularities that human and other complex systems shared ("the Ex-Lax approach"). Mutual sniping prevailed for several years,

aided and abetted by a cast of participants who varied from eccentric to eclectic, and some of whom avoided confinement only because they were college professors. The "Old" archeologists were understandably displeased at being informed that they were going about their business all wrong, especially when the gibes came from people who seemed to spend more time writing computer programs than shoveling dirt.

Stylistic Differences. Peace broke out unexpectedly, leaving most of the archeologists with a new set of questions and with new ways of seeking the answers. Many of the Old archeologists now do New archeology, and many of the New archeologists now speak of psychology, cosmology and individuals, all topics that a few years ago were thought of only at night, after all the lights were off.

One of the archeologists pursuing the concrete evidence of what was on prehistoric man's mind is Meg Fritz, at the San Jose campus of California State University. Fritz has spent hundreds of hours in museums and caves throughout Europe. She studied the paintings, the engravings on bone and the other efforts of man to record, and perhaps control, the world of the Magdalenian period, which extended from about the years 15,000 to 10,000 B.C.

These efforts, Fritz says, were not simply the daubings and dabblings of people with time on their hands, but an important part of the cultural repertoire that helped these early members of our own species to adapt to their environment, and to each other. "I'm trying to see the ways in which these human groups were adapting to their environment by symbolic means, by encoding and classifying information and dealing with the world as they saw it and as they conceived it" she says.

"My hypothesis is that many of these groups were having to deal with their neighbors, having to deal with each other, having to deal with their environment, and one of the ways of dealing with this was through their material culture. I think they were engraving these bones to differentiate among themselves on a stylistic basis, so that they could recognize their own group, and recognize other groups when they came in contact with them."

Just as science gives us a concrete, if limiting, way to look at the environment and other people, these stone and bone forms may well have been an earlier means for understanding and ordering an otherwise chaotic universe. These items were a means for recording information about the plants, animals and environment on which early man depended for his subsistence. Far from being frivolous, much of the art from this period may have had a direct relation to the subsistence success of a group.

These data, like Struever's, make it abundantly clear that early man lacked neither time nor talent for the production of items requiring a knowledge of the world and a sense of the esthetic. These images, like our current movies and photographs, contained very condensed and very effective messages about how to organize and conceptualize the world, and how to organize people for dealing with it.

The study of symbolic behavior promises to shed light on the question of what it is to be human, since the capacity to routinely attach arbitrary meaning to form distinguishes man from the other primates. Like microfilm, these engraved and painted representations are a condensed form for storing information; and the information load and the number of storage devices increased as culture became more complex. The capability to acquire, manipulate, store and transmit information, gave some groups an advantage in the evolutionary race.

Neither Castles Nor Hovels. Centuries later, the capacity to understand and use symbols made possible the social organization and cooperation needed to build the town that is now Salmon Ruin, in Northwestern New Mexico. For the last several years, Cynthia Irwin-Williams of Eastern New Mexico University has supervised excavation of this site, which she says is "one of the first planned communities in North America.

"Essentially the entire town was planned and laid out as a single design. Although it has been abandoned to decay for nearly 800 years, it is still a very imposing structure. Built in the form of a great C, it stands two to three stories high, and extends 450 feet along the back and 175 feet along the arms."

One of the things Williams found about the behavior of the Salmon Ruin occupants is that, judging from their housing, they did not have an economically based class system. "There are neither castles nor peasant hovels at Salmon" she says. "Rather, there is a planned community, suited to relatively uniform comfort." Yet the ability to carry out great public-works projects, involving the mobilization of the entire society, usually means a class of rulers, and a class of ruled.

Seeking an explanation, Williams turned to contemporary Pueblo societies for a starting point. She found that there are two categories of societal membership, but the differences have to do with access to certain sacred and secular knowledge, rather than differences in economic status. While the group with access to this knowledge also has the authority over certain vital community activities, such as irrigation, this knowledge can be used only on behalf of the community. Pueblo architects and engineers do not turn into a Cadillac class, and those who try it face ostracism and exile.

This ethnographic information does not *necessarily* hold true for the occupants of Salmon Ruin. What it does do is provide a starting point for asking a series of questions about the material remains that *should* be found *if* the model is correct. By explicitly formulating these questions, the archeologist states what will and won't be acceptable evidence for a particular model of how a society functioned. This approach, which is one of the theoretical cornerstones of the New archeology, also makes it possible to test any set of proposals about a prehistoric population, including ones for which there are no living equivalents. Archeologists thus hope to escape the limitation of knowing about the past only in terms of what is known about the present.

At the same time, an increasing number of archeologists seek to refine their method and theory by the further study of contemporary groups. Since 1969, University of New Mexico archeologist Lewis Binford has spent thousands of hours in the field studying the way in which modern Eskimos kill and butcher animals, and the material remains of those activities.

Child's Play. Binford did "archeology-on-the-spot" by recording the entire butchering sequence, and then returning after the site was abandoned and mapping all the remains. He also excavated a series of archeological sites for which the Eskimos, through accounts passed from father to son, could provide information on the time of year the site was used, the number of people using it, and other data that would be comparable to what had been gathered for the current sites.

By holding factors such as season of use constant, Binford was able to see what was responsible for the differences in artifact and animal remain patterns between the old and new sites. These differences might result from changes in behavior, such as different hunting strategy, or changes in technology, such as the use of firearms. Where there was a similar distribution of

artifacts and animal remains in old and new sites despite changes in technology, he found it was determined by "economic anatomy" such as where fats localized in an animal's body, how the fat content changed seasonally, and the ratio of muscle mass to bone.

Binford was looking for archeological evidence of behavior that responded to technological change, and simultaneously trying to find out why other types of behavior persisted in the face of an altered technology.

For example, methods of killing caribou might change as new weapons become available, but the seasons when the animals are killed and the way meat is cut up for distribution might not be changed, since migratory patterns determine the former, and economic anatomy dictates the latter.

As a result of his research, Binford can now specify what combinations of social, environmental and other factors result in certain decisions regarding the use of animal resources, and thus determine the pattern of remains that will be found archeologically. He hopes to use this information to test new ideas about organization, behavior and change in the Paleolithic period.

Binford also found that the play habits of children can have a significant effect on what gets left behind for archeologists. Among the Eskimos he lived with, 15 percent of the features that an archeologist would later have recovered were a result of children's play.

Eskimo children monitor and mimic adult behavior in much of their play, in what Binford calls a "culturally organized educational system" that teaches basic skills. In many ways, he says, you could tell more about what was going on by examining the artifacts children left behind, since they tended to "play and abandon," while adults tended to recycle their implements.

Increased Stress. Binford recently did similar research in Australia, and found that among the Aborigines less than one tenth of one percent of the features resulted from children's play. The difference, he says, reflects a behavioral difference between the two cultures. The play of Aborigine children, until the age of puberty, consists primarily of roughhousing and chasing, rather than the learning of skills that involve the use of material items, as among the Eskimos.

The type of children's play, Binford says, relates to the nature of the adult culture. "The more information being carried by the cultural system, the earlier and

VACATION WITH A MISSION ARCHEOLOGY SITES YOU CAN SEE AND DIG

A guide to where the dirt flies and what you can learn there. Some archeologists will even let you help.

With pain and toil, we move the soil,
We sift the dirt to find the chert.
When things get dull, we find a skull,
So dig on while you hurt.
—work song of archeologists at the Koster site

The past is close at hand for nearly everyone. Museums, reconstructed and preserved sites, and ongoing excavations offer opportunities to take part in the study of prehistoric human behavior. This summer you can roll down the Interstate net to spend from a few moments to several weeks learning and seeing how people lived tens of thousands of years ago.

Awe and excitement comingle in most people as they view the delicate jewelry and pottery or the monumental architecture of our not-so-primitive predecessors. Whether visiting a local museum or touring ruins throughout the country, a look at the past can provide a valuable perspective from which to view the present.

Archeologists welcome public interest. Material remains from the past are a national resource that archeologists hope to see widely understood and wisely used. Simultaneously, there is a strong effort to prosecute those responsible for destroying that resource by removing artifacts from sites. There are now stringent Federal, state and local statutes that make it illegal to disturb sites. "Pothunting" is illegal and ignorant. The price of this depredation is the irretrievable loss of information, since material removed from its resting place is almost worthless to an archeologist.

This map, together with the accompanying information, will provide ideas on where you can presently see the past. *Museums* (●) display artifacts and information on how prehistoric people lived. Many of these museums are part of *pre-*

Here are some of the accessible and important archeological sites and museums.

National Monuments (N.M.) and National Parks (N.P.) are administered by the National Park Service.

Washington: Lake Lenore Caves (1). Dry Falls Interpretive Center (2). Washington State University Anthropology Museum (3). Roosevelt Petroglyphs (4).

Idaho: Nez Perce National Historical Park, Spalding (16). Alpha Rockshelter, Shoup (17). Idaho State University Museum, Pocatello (18).

Montana: Madison Buffalo Jump (19). Pictograph Cave State Monument (20). Museum of the Plains Indians (21).

Wyoming: Mammoth Visitor Center, Yellowstone N.P. (22). Wyoming State Museum (23).

Colorado: Mesa Verde N.P. (24). Lowry Pueblo Ruins (25). Denver Museum of Natural History (26).

Oregon: University of Oregon Museum of Natural History (5). Winquatt Museum (6).

California: Calico Mountains Archaeological Project (7). Joshua Tree N.M. (8). Big and Little Petroglyph Canyons, (9). Lowie Museum of Anthropology, Berkeley (10). Los Angeles County Museum of History and Science (11). San Diego Museum of Man (12). Huntington Beach (13).

Nevada: Rocky Gap Site (14). Lost City Museum of Archeology (15).

Utah: Hovenweep N.M. (27). Arch Canyon Indian Ruin (28). Canyonlands N.P. (29). Natural Bridges N.M. (30). Anthropology Museum, University of Utah (31).

Arizona: Navajo N.M. (32). Canyon de Chelly N.M. (33). Sunset Crater N.M. (34). Casa Grande Ruins N.M. (35). Arizona State Museum, Tucson (36). Navajo Tribal Museum, Window Rock (37).

North Dakota: Slant Indian Village (38), State Historical Society Museum (39).

South Dakota: Badlands N.M. (40), Over Dakota Museum (41).

Nebraska: University of Nebraska State Museum (42).

Kansas: Indian Burial Pit (43), Pawnee Indian Village Museum (44), University of Kansas, Museum of Anthropology (45), El Quartelo Pueblo (46).

Oklahoma: Indian City, U.S.A. (47), Museum of the Great Plains (48), Philbrook Art Center (49).

Minnesota: Pipestone N.M. (60), Minnesota Historical Society Museum (61).

Iowa: Effigy Mounds N.M. (62), Pikes Peak State Park (63), Iowa State Museum (64).

Missouri: Graham Cave (65), Lyman Archaeological Research Center and Hamilton Field School (66), Museum of Science and Natural History (67).

Wisconsin: Aztalan State Park (68), Devils Lake State Park (69), Sheboygan Mound Park (70), Wisconsin State University Museum of Anthropology (71), Clevedon Site (72).

Illinois: Koster Site, Kampsville (77), Cahokia Mounds State Park (78), Field Museum of Natural History (79), Dickson Mounds Museum of the Illinois Indian (80), Orendorf Site, Peoria (81).

Michigan: Fort Michilimackinac Museum (82), Norton Mounds (83), University of Michigan Exhibit Museum (84).

Indiana: Mounds State Park (85), Angel Mounds State Memorial (86), Indiana University Museum (87).

Kentucky: Mammoth Cave N.P. (88), Adena Park (89), Pikeville-Elkhorn City (90).

Ohio: Mound City Group N.M. (97), Serpent Mound State Memorial (98), Fort Hill State Memorial (99), Fort Ancient State Memorial (100), Cincinnati Museum of Natural History (101).

Virginia: Peaks of Otter Visitor Center (102), Jamestown Festival Park (103), Norfolk Museum of Arts and Sciences (104).

Pennsylvania: Carnegie Museum (105), North Museum, Franklin and Marshall College (106), Meadowcroft Rockshelter (107), Fort Gaddis (108), Clarion (109).

West Virginia: Grave Creek Mound State Park (110), University of W. Virginia Archeology Museum (111).

New York: American Museum of Natural History (118), Museum of the American Indian, Heye Foundation (119), Rochester Museum and Science Center (120), Jamaica (121), Upper Susquehanna Valley (122).

Maryland: Maryland Academy of Sciences Museum (123), Museum of Natural History (124).

Maine: Wilson Museum (125).

Vermont: University of Vermont, Robert Hall Fleming Museum (126), Daniels Museum (127).

New Hampshire: Dartmouth College Museum (128).

Massachusetts: Bronson Museum (133), Peabody Museum of Archaeology and Ethnology, Harvard University (134).

Rhode Island: Rhode Island Historical Society (135), Haffenreffer Museum, Brown University (136).

Connecticut: Peabody Museum of Natural History, Yale University (137), Fort Stamford (138).

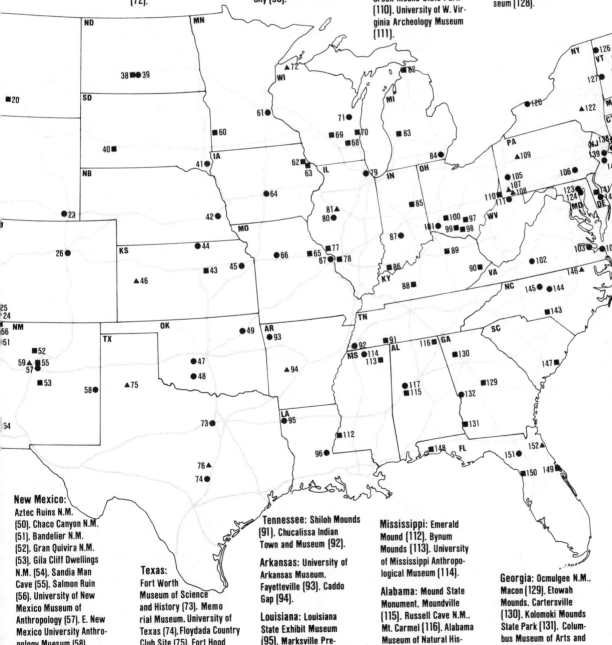

New Mexico:
Aztec Ruins N.M. (50), Chaco Canyon N.M. (51), Bandelier N.M. (52), Gran Quivira N.M. (53), Gila Cliff Dwellings N.M. (54), Sandia Man Cave (55), Salmon Ruin (56), University of New Mexico Museum of Anthropology (57), E. New Mexico University Anthropology Muesum (58), Cerrillos Mine Site (59).

Texas:
Fort Worth Museum of Science and History (73), Memorial Museum, University of Texas (74), Floydada Country Club Site (75), Fort Hood Site (76).

Tennessee: Shiloh Mounds (91), Chucalissa Indian Town and Museum (92).

Arkansas: University of Arkansas Museum, Fayetteville (93), Caddo Gap (94).

Louisiana: Louisiana State Exhibit Museum (95), Marksville Prehistoric Indian Park (96).

Mississippi: Emerald Mound (112), Bynum Mounds (113), University of Mississippi Anthropological Museum (114).

Alabama: Mound State Monument, Moundville (115), Russell Cave N.M., Mt. Carmel (116), Alabama Museum of Natural History, Tuscaloosa (117).

Georgia: Ocmulgee N.M., Macon (129), Etowah Mounds, Cartersville (130), Kolomoki Mounds State Park (131), Columbus Museum of Arts and Crafts (132).

New Jersey: Princeton University Museum of Natural History (139), New Jersey State Museum (140).

Delaware: Island Field Site, Dover (141), Delaware State Museum (142).

North Carolina: Town Creek Indian Mound (143), University of North Carolina, Research Laboratories of Anthropology (144), Greensboro Historical Museum (145), Halifax (146).

South Carolina: Sewee Mound Archaeological Area, Francis Marion National Forest (147).

Florida: Temple Mound Museum and Park, Fort Walton Beach (148), Turtle Mound Historical Memorial, New Smyrna Beach (149), Crystal River Historical Memorial (150), Florida State Museum, Gainesville (151), St. Augustine (152).

329

served and reconstructed sites (■), where it is possible to view the dwellings and other major features that remain. In a few cases, digs (excavations in progress) (▲) offer the opportunity to participate directly in archeological work; volunteer assistance is sometimes welcome.

GENERAL INFORMATION

Most major cities display archeological materials from the state or region in a science or natural-history museum, and this is an excellent starting point. The curator or other museum personnel can provide information on specialized museums, sites that are open to the public, and perhaps the name of the local amateur archeological society.

In many states, there is a state archeologist. Inquire of the Parks Department at your state capitol, or write to an archeologist at the state university.

SITES

Many sites are opened to the public after excavation, and there is often a museum or guide to explain what was found. Some of these areas, particularly in the Southwest, have been declared national monuments and are now under the care of the National Park Service. You can get descriptive folders about Park Service sites by writing to The Office of Public Inquiry, National Park Service, Department of the Interior, Washington, D.C. 20240.

Few archeologists are prepared to receive visitors at a site while work is in progress, but there are exceptions, such as the Koster site in Kampsville, Illinois, where archeology students conduct tours of the work.

DIGS

Getting your hands dirty in archeological work is an experience that few people ever forget. Archeological sites are almost unfailingly in hot, humid locations that are short on water and long on things that bite. Work normally begins at daybreak, and often continues far into the night as the seemingly meager finds from tons of dirt are washed and catalogued. Just to make the entire proposition attractive, you will usually pay money for the joys of laboring like a coal miner.

Most digs make extensive use of an apparently inexhaustible supply of inexhaustible undergraduate students who have had classroom training. However, some digs do use green volunteers, who get on-the-job training.

Current lists of 1975 field-work opportunities may be obtained from the Archaeological Institute of America, 260 West Broadway, New York, N.Y. 10013

(send $1.00) and from the Society for American Archaeology, 4242 Piedras Drive East, University of Texas, San Antonio, Texas 78285. The Archaeological Institute's bulletin also includes information about opportunities in other countries, and how to inquire further.

Educational Expeditions International (68 Leonard St.—PTA–1, Belmont, Massachusetts 02178) offers several digs, foreign and domestic, as part of a program in which laymen join working scientists on their projects. They will provide a catalog upon request.

The Archaeological Institute of America, the American Museum of Natural History and many other institutions and private companies offer tours that include archeological sites.

AMATEUR SOCIETIES

There are amateur archeological societies in every area of the country. These groups meet regularly for discussions and lectures, and frequently undertake excavations under the supervision of a professional archeologist. Inquire of the curator at the state or local museum, or of an archeologist at your state university.

JOURNALS

Archaeology magazine ($8.50/year, issued quarterly by the Archaeological Institute of America) and *Popular Archaeology* ($7.00 for 12 issues from the Editor, Box 4211, Arlington, Virginia 22204) both offer material for interested amateurs. *Natural History, Scientific American* and other special-interest magazines occasionally carry archeology articles. *American Antiquity* is the professional journal, but it's fairly heavy going for the uninitiated. Try a copy at a university library before requesting a membership blank from the Society for American Archaeology, 1703 New Hampshire Ave. N.W., Washington, D.C. 20029.

FURTHER INFORMATION

America's Ancient Treasures (Rand McNally, $2.95) offers a readable and extensive guide to archeological sites and museums throughout the country.

Archeology and Archeological Resources (40 cents per copy from the Society for American Archaeology) is a brief introduction to the problems of preserving and recovering prehistoric materials.

Should you get really hooked, the Archaeological Institute of America offers a free reprint of the article "Archaeology as a Career," and a catalog ($2.50) of colleges and universities that offer training in archeology. —Brian Weiss

more structured children's play becomes." With one eye again on the Paleolithic, Binford suggests that with this type of information in hand archeologists can begin to look for the point in time where learning began to be culturally organized.

Binford, like Struever and Hill, could identify stress from the archeological remains he studied. There are parts of the animals being used by the Eskimos that yield a very small amount of food for the amount of time needed to process them. "For example, there is a little bit of grease underneath the teeth in the lower jaw. Now, you have to be pretty pushed to go after that systematically" he says. When the archeological record shows that a population was using such marginal resources, it's a good sign that they were under stress, and Binford says there is archeological evidence of increasing stress as the relatively mild climatic conditions of an interglacial period gave way to the glaciation.

As archeologists continue to refine their abilities to look for prehistoric human behavior, they have more opportunities for examining the regularities of culture, and the social mechanisms that come into use for coping with various sets of circumstances. Many archeologists and anthropologists believe that there is an ordered set of "coping mechanisms"; if one solution fails, another applies, and on until there is either equilibrium or extinction.

The population bomb, resource exhaustion, and warfare are familiar concerns to archeologists and readers of the daily newspaper. Many archeologists want to join sociologists and political scientists in their discussion of how to make decisions about contemporary problems. If Jim Hill is right in his belief that the ability to explain the past implies insight into the future, other archeologists who dig deep into cornfields may come to the surface to help us look at the horizon.

Brian Weiss pursues the study of human behavior both above and below the ground. Although his doctoral research involved a group of living Miskito Indians in Nicaragua, he has, by his own estimate, moved at least 16 tons of dirt on various archeological digs ranging from a search for some of California's early residents to a historic fort in Michigan. Weiss received his undergraduate degree in anthropology from UCLA, and did graduate work at the University of New Mexico and the University of Michigan.

48

Common sense in archaeology

A. C. HOGARTH

A. C. Hogarth is Head of the Department of Latin and Archaeology at Chatham House Grammar School, Ramsgate. He excavated in three seasons from 1969 to 1972 the Anglo-Saxon cemetery at St Peter's, Broadstairs. He is a member of the committee of 'Rescue'. His modest, clear-headed article—written as he says 'from the sidelines of the professional game'—will stimulate many of our readers. He would preface it with this sentence from G. E. Moore: 'It is foolish to doubt, or to pretend to doubt, commonsense propositions.'

The recent discussion of the New Archaeology, certain manifestations of its ostensible practitioners, Professor Charles Thomas's 'Ethics in archaeology, 1971' (*Antiquity*, XLV, 268–74) are, I suppose, indicative of the directions in which some archaeological thinking seems to be moving. As an active worker in the field, and as a teacher of archaeology at secondary school level, I am prompted to make a response from, as it were, the sidelines of the professional game. I find disturbing the fashionable claim to shift archaeology into more and more exclusively scientific domains, and no less alarming the counter claims of those who would force it into purely historical context.

The New Archaeology has been held before our eyes, by proponents and adversaries alike, with portentous fanfares, as if to say 'Look! And be amazed/dismayed.' Yet after the initial *thauma*, when the senses recompose themselves, what is there either so wondrous or so novel about it? That the most modern developments of science can and should be applied to the study of the past is no new idea. One seems to have heard of Meadows Taylor, of Pitt-Rivers, of Crawford, all applying enthusiastically the methods and discoveries of science. Did not Piltdown succumb to fluorine? Have not resistivity, magnetometry and a plethora of other field techniques been welcomed? Are not specialist metallurgical, mineralogical and micro-analytical reports part of the standard contents of site publication? Palaeo-botany, palaeo-pathology and palaeo-almost-every-other-natural-science have been avidly grasped by archaeologists eager to squeeze the last droplet of evidence from their excavations. I recall no Neo-Luddites thirsting for Libby's blood. Suess's work has aroused no vehement rejection, though the recent mass-media lobby

on behalf of his calibration would seem to suggest so. Even *Analytical archaeology* has hardly sparked thunderous denunciation from the steely pulpits of orthodoxy, albeit stimulating some mirth at its idiosyncratic version of the English language.

The fact is, of course, that there is no such thing as the New Archaeology. It is merely Newspeak Archaeology, tricked out in a whole wardrobe of new vocabulary apparently designed more to impress than to enlighten. 'Hypothesis generation and validation', 'locational analysis', 'time-space episodes' and the like are all names comparatively new to archaeology, to be sure. But the ideas which they express, or rather fail to conceal, are not. One might as well describe (and in so doing, perhaps, 'dramatically rehabilitate'?) fieldwork as the 'operation of simultaneous location determinative, detectional and status-analytical programs relative to primary source material data retrieval contributive to reconstructive syntheses of pre-current socio-cultural entities'; but it would still be fieldwork, and a lot easier to say, and possibly to do, under its old name. The coiners of new words for old should realize that we recognize the ratcatchers, even when they dress as 'rodent eliminators'. Archaeologists, of all people, ought to call a spade a spade.

To be fair, the new vocabulary causes no real problems when it is used as part of the technical jargon of computer studies by D. L. Clarke and others of his calibre. Behind the hedge of esoteric nomenclature their approach is discernibly scholarly and their grasp of the realities secure. It is more hazardous when ridden as a modish band-wagon by others less at home in the language of statistics and computers. And some surprising people are to be found falling into error about analytical methods.

331

Professor Thomas hails the 'revulsion from pure typology', and is expressly contradicted by Clarke in so doing. Of the twenty-two examples of statistical and computer-aided studies in Chapter 13 of *Analytical archaeology,* no less than fifteen are studies in—of all things—pure typology, only the name being changed to protect the novelty. The two volumes of *Beaker pottery* are massive monuments to typology, even if its techniques and results are mathematically based. No revulsion here.

Much more disturbing, however, have been talks on BBC Radio 3 during December 1971, when, on successive programmes, Dr Ammerman and Professor Binford became so enmeshed in the complexities of their own language that they produced, the one a facile and distortedly simplified exposition of the Stimulus Bow Wave Diffusion model, the other a banal and pretentious regurgitation of principles expressly stated by Pitt-Rivers and part of the most elementary thinking of anyone who dares to call himself an archaeologist. Such extreme examples tend to foster the suspicion that the new archaeology may be seen by a few of its adherents as some mystery religion, which will give, by initiation and revelation, a seat on the summit of Parnassus to which they are unable or unwilling to attain by the slower and less dramatic climb up the path of genuine academic discipline.

A less unworthy, though no less depressing, explanation may lie in the system of education, common in America and becoming more prevalent here, which insists that children, instead of being given directly the immediate benefit of the knowledge of their elders, should be allowed and encouraged, sometimes to the exclusion of other methods of learning, to 'discover' things for themselves. As one in the general range of educational techniques this is a valuable exercise; but elevated into a 'method' it has inherent in it the risk that what a child discovers for himself he may be allowed to think he has discovered for all mankind. Clearly, there are some archaeologists who are subject to that delusion, *nam nova quae sibi sint omnibus esse putant.*

Significantly, Clarke does not make this error. Indeed, he is at pains to point out that what he calls 'construction of models' and 'generation and validation of hypotheses' have under their former names been the very essence of archaeological interpretation since Thomsen, albeit within a less formalized logic, and perhaps less explicitly, than he would require. What he describes is a range of new and more potent aids to more accurate analysis and more precise typology, leading to improved models susceptible not only to more rigorous testing but also to more realistic theoretical modification. He is providing access to mechanisms for just such

synthesis as was foreseen by Professor Atkinson (*Archaeology, history & science,* 1965), and to which Professor Grahame Clark's successive books have pointed the way, and for which Dr Daniel (*PPS,* XXXVII, Pt. II) looks today. Because computers are new to most of us, *Analytical archaeology* is in effect a handbook for potential users, in which are described the sort of pre-digestive processes needed to feed machines which cannot take the strong meat of raw information, and which are incapable of understanding even the most basic logical foundations of archaeological method unless these are made explicit and cumbrously self-explanatory. Its main drawbacks are, first, the lack of a suitable sub-title: 'The understanding, care and diet of the family computer' and, second, the lack of detailed recipes. The error of some seems to be to regard the computer as a sort of super-nanny which will understand, care for and cook for the archaeologist; and that of others to talk to a human audience in the same electronic baby-talk which is necessary for addressing a computer. The error of D. L. Clarke is that though he realizes that 'scientific aids no more make archaeology a "science" than a wooden leg makes a man into a tree', he fails to stress that no more do mathematical aids make it a mathematical discipline.

Mathematics, even when they help in the creation of a total framework of flawless logic within which to archaeologize, no more convert either the discipline or the objects of study into mathematical processes and entities than does the National Grid convert either map-reading or the ground itself. The Grid, like the map, is an aid to location and movement: it is a precise and logical frame within which certain aspects of study may be made more precise: but it has no intrinsic value beyond its usefulness, and is an arbitrary technique for helping study, superimposed upon the map by geographers. One does not expect to find it as a series of canals or rocky outcrops on the ground. Nor have mathematical frameworks in archaeology any greater intrinsic merit. Mathematical analysis will have come of age when the conceptual and constructional complexities of fitting it to assist archaeological work have been so mastered by its technicians that its use becomes as simple a matter of course as the use of the National Grid.

The new archaeology, then, is new only to those unfamiliar with the old. Certainly the fears that modern analytical techniques will remove the responsibility for interpretation from the human archaeologists are groundless. Science and mathematics are essentially concerned with recovery and presentation of evidence, not with its interpretation. The onus of decision on a judge is not lifted by the activities of police or counsel. Traditionally archaeologists have been doing both the detection and the presentation of evidence for themselves, but to complain because help is now at hand is to forget that the whole purpose of those activities has always been to arrange material for the exercise of judgment. It is still the same baby, though the bath-water may have been changed; and who knows, perhaps the fresh water may help to wash cleaner?

There is, however, considerable danger not in the new techniques themselves but in both the cult of novelty which exaggerates their contribution and the excessive conservatism which denies and ignores their value. Of the two, the former is currently the more prevalent error, but both are to be resisted, since they both spring from an abandonment of the faculty for discrimination and critical evaluation, on the one hand indiscriminately accepting and on the other obstinately rejecting the new *ipsius causa*. Statistics, the new geography, electronics and computers have enormous contributions to make to archaeology; but they must be treated to a healthily sceptical and painstaking assessment. Some types of material are unsuited to statistical treatment: some new geographical methods are by no means universally accepted among geographers with access, theoretically at least, to total evidence, and are the more fraught with problems when applied to the incomplete data of the past: most of all is caution needed when adopting techniques from America.

There is great risk that in incautious acceptance of American methods the predispositions of American archaeologists may be adopted along with them. European archaeology is, in at least one essential, different from that of the United States. Domestic periods of study in the United States are exclusively prehistoric, and there has been consequently an overwhelming bias towards prehistory and an almost complete dependence on it, both in the home training of American archaeologists and in the creation of domestic professional posts. It is hardly surprising, therefore, that Americans have come to equate archaeology with prehistory; that the techniques, which have necessarily been developed to recover evidence for societies about which nothing is known except their material remains, should have been applied also to archaeological problems overseas with the same attitude and in the same science-based spirit as characterized their own domestic successes. For Europe, however, with nearly 3,000 years of (albeit interrupted) literate civilizations, their earlier barbaric societies in contact with the civilizations of the Near East, and with constant contact between literate and non-literate societies within the continent, archaeology has inevitably developed from a historical base. The successive discoveries of science have been employed towards solving essentially historical problems. In Britain, the present strength of this tradition is to be seen in every period, but nowhere more clearly than in the post-war contributions of Medieval, Post-Medieval and Industrial archaeology to progressively better-documented historical periods. There is for us a need for both historical and scientific attitudes, and they are complementary. Between them there should be no dichotomy and certainly no hostility.

American archaeology, then, has developed to suit American circumstances, and ours to suit ours. It is sensible to compare notes and to ask whether each may not have things of value to the other; but it is not sensible to suppose that their archaeological thinking, any more than their political or economic, is necessarily apposite to our situation. We should be happy selectively to adopt such techniques as are appropriate or modifiable to our requirements, but in rejecting those that are not we should suffer no feeling, and tolerate no jibes, of being 'not with-it'.

Finally, one of the greatest merits of archaeology has been that it forms a bridge across the great gulf, fixed between the sciences and the the humanities. The study of human societies is explicitly the study of total human activity within a total ecology, with the emphasis on 'human'. Our professed intent is to reveal *logos* in the remains of antiquity, and *logos* is, by definition, a human characteristic. Of our study the principle ethos is that it should 'train upon the problems of man's history the full armament of his science'. The new archaeology is merely the bringing to bear upon those problems the weaponry of the latest research to supplement the existing armoury. This is in the best tradition of commonsense archaeology. It is hardly fortuitous that archaeology, as an inter-disciplinary study, has always attracted its best brains from a wide range both of academic specialities and of occupations, and that all have had a contribution to make. It has developed as the happy hunting ground of all those independent spirits who seek a field wider than the constraining frontiers of any specific subject discipline, and whose cry is still *nihil humanum alienum a me puto*. It would be the height of folly to abandon this position, and to have archaeology identified with one or other side of the 'Snow' line. Archaeology confined within the narrow cage of either history or science (or mathematics, for that matter) would be a sad and shackled beast. We should include in our 'genetic conscience syndrome' (*absit omen*) some concern for the protection of the intellectual habitat of archaeology. It will do better there than in captivity.

GLOSSARY

Abbevillean (or Chellean) culture The earlier of two stages in the handax (bifacial core tool) tradition, lasting approximately 600,000 to 400,000 B.P.; found across southerly and medium latitudes of the Old World, radiating out from Africa to southwest Europe and as far east as India; associated with *Homo erectus.*

Absolute dating Physical-chemical dating methods which tie archaeologically retrieved artifacts into clearly specified time ranges calculated in terms of an abstract standard such as the calendar.

Acclimatization The process by which an organism's sweat glands, metabolism, and associated mechanisms adjust to a new and different climate.

Acheulian culture The second stage of the handax bifacial core tool tradition; associated primarily with *Homo erectus;* found in southern and middle latitudes all across the Old World from India to Africa and West Europe; lasting *in toto* from about 400,000 to 60,000 B.P.

Adaptation Generally, the ways in which individuals become fitted, physically or culturally, to particular environments. More specifically, adaptation is a two-way process in which changes in physiological and social mechanisms are made in order to cope successfully with environments; but organisms are also constantly changing their environments, making them more "livable."

Adaptive grade A level of primate social organization representing a particular complex of behavioral features that are adapted to those aspects of the environment that form major selection pressures.

Aegyptopithecus An especially important Oligocene ape form, dated to 28 million years ago, and found in the Fayum area of Egypt. It represents a probable evolutionary link between the prosimian primates of the Paleocene and Eocene, and the apes of the Miocene and Pliocene. *Aegyptopithecus* probably was ancestral to *Dryopithecus,* and thus to modern apes and humans.

Agonistic interactions Behavior that is aggressive or unfriendly, including the behavior of both the initiator and the recipient of aggression.

Agriculture Domesticated food production involving minimally the cultivation of plants, but usually also the raising of domesticated animals. More narrowly, plant domestication making use of the plow (versus horticulture).

Alleles Alternative forms of a single gene.

Alveolar ridge Thickened portions of the upper and lower interior gums in which the teeth are set.

Amino acid The building blocks of proteins, of which there are 20 different kinds.

Anagenesis The evolutionary pattern in which a given species evolves into a different species.

Androgens Hormones, present in relatively large quantities in the testes, which are responsible for the development of the male secondary sex characteristics.

Angular gyrus An area of the brain crucial to human linguistic ability that serves as a link between the parts of the brain that receive stimuli from the sense organs of sight, hearing, and touch.

Anthropoidea Suborder of the order of Primates that includes monkeys, apes, and humans.

Anthropology The systematic investigation of the nature of human beings and their works, past and present.

Anthropometry A subdivision of physical anthropology concerned with measuring and statistically analyzing the dimensions of the human body.

Anthropomorphism The ascription of human characteristics to objects not human—often deities or animals.

Antigens Proteins with specific molecular properties located on the surface of red blood cells.

Ape A large, tailless, semierect primate of the family *Pongidae.* Living species include the gibbon, orangutan, gorilla, and chimpanzee.

Aphasia Loss or distortion of speech.

Archaeology The systematic retrieval, identification, and study of the physical and cultural remains that human beings and their ancestors have left behind them deposited in the earth.

Archaeomagnetic dating Absolute dating technique that uses as its basis temporal variations in the direction and intensity of the earth's geomagnetic field.

Arcuate fasciculus The large bundle of nerve fibers in the human brain, connecting Broca's area with Wernicke's area. A crucial biological substratum of speech in humans.

Artifact Any object manufactured, modified, or used by human beings as an expression of their cultural values and norms.

Assemblage All the industries at one prehistoric site considered together.

Associated regions Broad regions surrounding the three geographical centers where agriculture was invented. Here different plants and animals were domesticated, and then spread individually throughout the whole area.

Aurignacian culture Upper Paleolithic culture that some scholars claim may represent a separate Middle Eastern migration into Europe. Flourished in western Europe from 33,000–25,000 B.P. The Aurignacians began the European tradition of bone carving. The skeletal remains associated with this culture are the famous Cro-Magnon fossils.

Aurochs A European wild ox, now extinct.

Australopithecine An extinct grade in hominid evolution found principally in early to mid-Pleistocene in central and southern Africa, usually accorded subfamily status.

Australopithecus africanus The original type specimen of australopithecines discovered in 1924 at Taung, South Africa, and dating from approximately 3.5 million years ago to approximately 1.6 million years ago. Belongs to the gracile line of the australopithecines.

Australopithecus boisei One of two species of robust australopithecines, appearing approximately 1.6 million years ago in sub-Saharan Africa.

Australopithecus habilis Fossil form contemporaneous with *A. boisei* whose evolutionary status is disputed. Although the Leakeys designated the form *H. habilis,* most physical anthropologists regard it as an advanced form of gracile austropithecine, separate from its smaller South African relative, *A. africanus.* This is the only australopithecine with which stone tools have been found in unambiguous relationship.

Australopithecus robustus One of two species of robust australopithecines, found in both East and South Africa, first appearing about 3.5 million years ago.

Aztec civilization Final Postclassic Mesoamerican civilization, dated from about 1300–1521 A.D., when Cortes conquered and destroyed the empire. The Aztec capital at Tenochtitlán (now Mexico City) housed some 300,000 people. Aztec society was highly stratified, dominated by a military elite.

Baboon Large, terrestrial Old World monkey. Baboons have long, doglike muzzles, short tails, and are highly organized into troops.

Band The simplest level of social organization; marked by very little political organization and consisting of small (50–300 persons) groups of families.

Bifaces Stone artifacts that have been flaked on two opposite sides, most typically the hand axes produced by *Homo erectus.*

Binomen The genus and species names for any living form. The binomen for all modern humans is *Homo sapiens.*

Biological anthropology See *physical anthropology.*

Bipedalism The ability to walk consistently on two legs.

Blade tool A long and narrow flake tool that has been knocked off a specially prepared core.

Blood groups (types) Biochemical variations of blood, identified on the basis of the presence or absence of particular antigens.

Brachiation A method of locomotion, characteristic of the pongids, in which the animal swings hand over hand through the trees, while its body is suspended by the arms.

Breeding population In population genetics, all individuals in a given population who potentially, or actually, mate with one another.

Broca's area An area of the brain located toward the front of the dominant side of the brain that activates, among other things, the muscles of the lips, jaw, tongue, and larynx. A crucial biological substratum of speech.

Brow ridge A continuous ridge of bone in the skull, curving over the eyes and connected across the bridge of the nose.

Burins Chisel-like Upper Paleolithic stone tools produced by knocking small chips off the end(s) of a blade, and used for carving wood, bone, and antlers to fashion spear and harpoon points. Unlike end scrapers, burins were used for fine engraving and delicate carving.

Call systems Systems of communication of nonhuman primates, consisting of a limited number of specific sounds (calls) conveying specific meanings to members of the group, largely restricted to emotional or motivational states.

Capsian culture Upper Paleolithic culture of North Africa, descended from Oranian culture, and based on a subsistence strategy of shellfish gathering.

Carotene A yellowish pigment in the skin.

Catarrhini Old World anthropoids. One of two infraorders of the suborder of *Anthropoidea,* order of Primates. Includes Old World monkeys, apes, and humans.

Catastrophism A school of thought, popular in the late eighteenth and early nineteenth centuries, proposing that life forms became extinct through natural catastrophes, of which Noah's flood was the latest.

Cenezoic era The geological era comprised of six separate epochs that began some 70 million years ago and lasted until about 10,000 years ago.

Cephalic index A formula for computing long-headedness and narrow-headedness:

$$\frac{\text{head breadth}}{\text{head length}} \times 100$$

A low cephalic index indicates a narrow head.

Cercopithecoidea One of two superfamilies of the infraorder Catarrhini, consisting of the Old World monkeys.

Cerebral cortex The "grey matter" of the brain, associated primarily with thinking and language use. The expansion of the cortex is the most recent evolutionary development of the brain.

Ceremonial center Large permanent site that reveals no evidence of occupation on a day-to-day basis. Ceremonial centers are composed almost exclusively of structures used for religious purposes.

Chavin culture Highland Peruvian culture dating from about 1000–200 B.C. It was the dominant culture in the central Andes for some 700 years.

Cheek pouches Folds of cheek skin that can expand to hold large amounts of food stuffed into the mouth, a feature frequently found in terrestrial or semiterrestrial Old World monkeys.

Chellean handax A bifacial core tool from which much (but not all) of the surface has been chipped away, characteristic of the Abbevillean (or Chellean) culture. Produced by *Homo erectus*.

Chiefdom A term used to refer to a society at a level of social integration a stage above that of tribal society, characterized by a redistributive economy and centralized political authority.

Chimpanzee *(Pan troglodytes)* Along with the gorilla and the orangutan, one of the great apes; found exclusively in Africa; one of *Homo sapiens'* closest relatives.

Choppers Unifacial core tools, sometimes called pebble tools, found associated with *Australopithecus habilis* in Olduvai sequence, and also with *Homo erectus* in East Asia.

Chou dynasty Period in Chinese history, dating from 1122 B.C. to 221 B.C. Various Chou rulers built much of the Great Wall of China in the fourth and third centuries B.C.

Chromosomal sex The sex identity of a person determined by the coded message in the sex chromosome contributed by each parent.

Chromosome Helical strands of complex protein molecules found in the nuclei of all animal cells, along which the genes are located. Normal human somatic cells have 46.

Circumscription theory Theory of the origins of the state advanced by Carneiro and others which emphasizes the nature of the environment as a major factor in producing the state.

Civilization Consists of all those life styles incorporating at least four of the following five elements: (a) agriculture; (b) urban living; (c) a high degree of occupational specialization and differentiation; (d) social stratification; and (e) literacy.

Cladogenesis (divergent evolution) The evolutionary pattern by which two different, but closely related species evolve from a common ancestor.

Classical archaeology A field within archaeology that concerns itself with the reconstruction of the classical civilizations, such as Greece, Rome, and Egypt.

Classic period Spectacular and sophisticated Mesoamerican cultural period dated from 300–900 A.D., and marked by the rise of great civilizations and the building of huge religious complexes and cities. By 500 A.D., the Classical city of Teotihuacán housed some 120,000 people.

Classifications Groups of organisms (or *taxa*) organized into a series of levels that reflect varying degrees of relationship or affinity.

Cline Minor variations in a genetic trait within a species.

Comparative linguistics (historical linguistics) A field of linguistics that attempts to describe formally the basic elements of languages and the rules by which they are ordered into intelligible speech.

Continental drift Hypothesis introduced by Wegener in the early twentieth century of the breakup of a supercontinent, Pangaea, beginning around 225 million years ago, and resulting in the present positions of the continents.

Convergent evolution The evolutionary pattern in which two forms that are distantly related evolutionarily and are classified into separate taxonomic orders evolve functionally (but not structurally) similar adaptations to the same environment.

Core tool A rough, unfinished stone tool shaped by knocking off flakes, used to crush the heads of small game, to skin them, and to dissect the carcasses.

Cranial index Anatomical measure computed on skeletal material, otherwise similar to the cephalic index.

Cranium The skull, excluding the jaw.

Creation myth A myth, unique to each culture, in which ancestors become separated from the rest of the animal kingdom, accounting for the society's biological and social development.

Cro-Magnon A term broadly referring to the first modern humans, from 40,000–10,000 B.P. Specifically refers to humans living in southwest France during the same period.

Cultural anthropology The study of the cultural diversity of contemporary societies. It can be divided into two aspects: ethnography and ethnology.

Cultural components (of a site) All the different divisions that can be found in a site.

Cultural ecology (of a group) The ways in which a group copes with and exploits the potentials of its environment.

Culture The patterned behavior that individuals learn, are taught, and practice within the context of the groups to which they belong.

Cuneiform Wedged-shaped writing developed by the Sumerian civilization.

Cytoplasm The living matter in a cell, except that in the nucleus.

Darwinism The theoretical approach to biological evolution first presented by Charles Darwin and Alfred Russel Wallace in 1858. The central concept of the theory is natural selection, referring to the greater probability of survival and reproduction of those individuals of a species having adaptive characteristics for a given environment.

Demographic study Population study, primarily concerned with such aspects of population as analyses of fertility, mortality, and migration.

Dendrochronology See TREE-RING DATING.

Dental formula The number of incisors, canines, premolars, and molars found in one upper and one lower quadrant of a jaw.

Deoxyribonucleic acid (DNA) The hereditary material of the cell, capable of self-replication and of coding the production of proteins carrying on metabolic functions.

Diachronics The comparison of biological, linguistic, archaeological and ethnographic data within a limited geographical area through an extended period of time.

Differential fertility A major emphasis in the modern (or synthetic) theory of evolution, which stresses the importance of an organism actually reproducing and transmitting its genes to the next generation.

Diffusion The spread of cultural traits from one people to another.

Diluvialism The theory that Noah's flood accounted for the earth's geological structure and history.

Diploid number The number of chromosomes normally found in the nucleus of somatic cells. In humans, the number is 46.

Divergent evolution See CLADOGENESIS.

DNA See DEOXYRIBONUCLEIC ACID

Domesticants Domesticated plants and/or animals.

Dominance hierarchy The social ranking order supposed to be present in most or all primate species.

Dominant allele The version of a gene that masks out other versions' ability to affect the phenotype of an organism when both alleles co-occur heterozygotically.

Dryopithecus The most common Miocene ape genus, known from Africa, Europe, and Asia, and dated from 20–10 million years ago. A forest-dwelling ape with about six or seven species, *Dryopithecus* was most probably ancestral to modern apes and humans.

Ecological niche Features of the environment(s) that an organism inhabits, which pose problems for the organism's survival.

Ecology The science of the interrelationships between living organisms and their natural environments.

Emics The perspective of the people being investigated.

Environment All aspects of the surroundings in which an individual or group finds itself, from the geology, topography, and climate of the area to its vegetational cover and insect, bird, and animal life.

Eocene epoch Second of the six epochs that comprise the Cenezoic era. Dates from about 60–35 million years ago.

Estrogens The hormones, produced in relatively large quantities by the ovaries, which are responsible for the development of female secondary sex characteristics.

Estrous cycle The approximately four-week reproductive cycle of female mammals.

Estrus Phase of the approximately four-week cycle in female mammals during which the female is receptive to males and encourages copulation.

Ethnocentrism The tendency of all human groups to consider their own way of life superior to all others, and to judge the lifestyles of other groups (usually negatively) in terms of their own value system.

Enthnographic analogy A method of archaeological interpretation in which the behavior of the ancient inhabitants of an archaeological site is inferred from the similarity of their artifacts to those used by living peoples.

Ethnography The intensive description of individual societies, usually small, isolated, and relatively homogeneous.

Ethnology The systematic comparison and analysis of ethnographic materials, usually with the specification of evolutionary stages of development of legal, political, economic, technological, kinship, religious, and other systems.

Etics The perspective of Western social science in general, and anthropology in particular.

Eutheria The most advanced of the three subclasses of mammals. These are the placental mammals.

Evolution The progress of life forms and social forms from the simple to the complex. In Spencer's terms, evolution is "change from an indefinite, incoherent homogeneity to a definite, coherent heterogeneity; through continuous differentiations and integrations." In narrow terms, evolution is the change in gene and allele frequencies within a breeding population over generations.

Evolutionary progress The process by which a social or biological form can respond to the demands of the environment by becoming more adaptable and flexible. In order to achieve this, the form must develop to a new stage of organization that makes it more versatile in coping with problems of survival posed by the environment.

Excessive fertility The notion that organisms tend to reproduce more offspring than actually survive; one of the principal points in Darwin's theory of organic evolution.

Female husband A form of gender role alteration found in some African societies in which a woman assumes the social role of a husband within a socially recognized marriage.

Field study The principal methods by which anthropologists gather information, using either the participant-observation technique to investigate social behavior, excavation techniques to retrieve archaeological data, or recording techniques to study languages.

Flake tool A tool made by preparing a flint core, then striking it to knock off a flake, which then could be further worked to produce the particular tool needed.

Flourine dating A technique for the dating of fossils that relies on the principle that bones and teeth buried in soil gradually absorb flourine from the groundwater in the earth. Flourine intake varies with soil conditions, so flourine dating is useful only to determine whether a fossil has been in the soil as long as other remains found in the same site.

Foraging society A society with an economy based solely on the collection of wild plant foods, the hunting of animals, and/or fishing.

Foramen magnum The "large opening" in the cranium of vertebrates through which the spinal cord passes.

Fossil The mineralized remains of an organism.

Gametes The sex cells which, as sperm in males and eggs in females, combine to form a new human being as a fetus in a mother's womb.

Gender identity The attachment of significance to a self-identification as a member of a sexually defined group, and the adopting of behavior culturally appropriate to that group.

Gender roles Socially learned behaviors that are typically manifested by persons of one sex and rarely by persons of the opposite sex in a particular culture.

Gene The unit of heredity. A segment of DNA which codes for the synthesis of a single protein.

Gene flow (Admixture) The movement of genes from one population into another as a result of interbreeding in cases where previous intergroup contact had been impossible or avoided due to geographical, social, cultural, or political barriers.

Gene frequency The relative presence of one allele in relation to another in a population's gene pool.

Gene pool The sum total of all individuals' genotypes included within a given breeding population.

Genetic drift The shift of gene frequencies as a consequence of genetic sampling errors that come from the migration of small subpopulations away from the parent group, or natural disasters that wipe out a large part of a population.

Genetic load The number of deleterious or maladaptive genes that exist in the gene pool of a population or entire species.

Genetic plasticity A characteristic of the human species that allows humans to develop a variety of limited physiological and anatomical responses or adjustments to a given environment.

Genotype The genetic component that each individual inherits from his or her parents.

Geographic center One of three regions in the world—in the Middle East, East Asia, and the Americas—where agriculture probably was invented independently.

Gigantopithecus Miocene-Pliocene ape form consisting of two species, dating from 8 million to possibly less than one million years ago. The largest primate that ever existed, it stood some 8–9 ft tall and weighed about 600 lbs. Found in China and India.

Glottochronology (Lexicostatistics) A mathematical technique for dating language change.

Gonadal sex Refers to the form, structure, and position of the hormone-producing gonads (ovaries located within the pelvic cavity in females and testes located in the scrotum in males).

Gondwanaland The southern portion of Pangaea.

Gorilla *(Gorilla gorilla)* The largest of the anthropoid (Great) apes and of the living primates; found exclusively in Africa.

Gracile australopithecines One of two lines of australopithecine development, first appearing about 3.5 million years ago; usually refers to the fossil forms *Australopithecus africanus* and *Australopithecus habilis,* which are widely thought to be directly ancestral to humans.

Grid system A method of retrieving and recording the positions of data from an archaeological "dig."

Habitation site A place where whole groups of people spent some time engaged in the generalized activities of day-to-day living.

Han dynasty Period of Chinese history, dating from about 221 B.C. to 220 A.D. Under Han rulers, all of China was unified and Confucianism was declared the state philosophy.

Handax An unspecialized flint bifacial core tool, primarily characteristic of the Lower and Middle Paleolithic, made by chipping flakes off a flint nodule and using the remaining core as the tool; produced by *Homo erectus,* later by *Homo sapiens neanderthalensis.*

Handax tradition A technological tradition developed out of the pebble tool tradition, occurring from about 600,000 to about 60,000 years ago during the Lower and Middle Paleolithic; primarily associated with *Homo erectus.* Also called Chelloid tradition.

Haploid number The number of chromosomes normally occurring in the nucleus of a gamete (sex cell). For humans the number is 23 (one-half the diploid number).

Harappan civilization Civilization in the northwest corner of the Indian subcontinent (roughly, in present-day Pakistan), which reached its peak about 2000 B.C. Its major cities were Mohenjo-Daro and Harappa.

Hardy-Weinberg law The principle that in large breeding populations, under conditions of random mating, and where natural selection is not operating, the frequencies of genes or alleles will remain constant from one generation to the next.

Hemoglobin Complex protein molecule that carries iron through the bloodstream, giving blood its red color.

Heritability The proportion of the measurable variation in a given trait in a specified population estimated to result from hereditary rather than environmental factors.

Heterozygote The new cell formed when the sperm and egg contain different alleles of the same gene.

Heterozygous A condition in which there are two different alleles at a given locus (place) on a pair of homologous (matched pair of) chromosomes.

Historical archaeology The investigation of all literate societies through archaeological means.

Historical linguistics The study of the evolutionary tree of language. Historical linguistics reconstructs extinct "proto" forms by systematically comparing surviving language branches.

Holism The viewing of the *whole* context of human behavior—a fundamental theme of anthropology.

Holocene The most recent geologic epoch that began about 10,000 years ago.

Homeostasis The process by which a system maintains its equilibrium using feedback mechanisms to accommodate inputs from its environment.

Home range (of a primate species) An area through which a primate habitually moves in the course of its daily activities.

Hominid The common name for those primates referred to in the taxonomic family *Hominidae* (modern humans and their nearest evolutionary predecessors).

Hominidae Human beings, one of *Hominoidea,* along with the great apes. See also HOMINID.

Hominoidea One of two superfamilies of *Catarrhini,* consisting of apes and human beings.

Homo erectus Middle Pleistocene hominid form that is the direct ancestor of *Homo sapiens*. It appeared about 1.9 million years ago, flourished until about 200,000–250,000 years ago. *H. erectus* was about 5 ft tall, with a body and limbs that were within the range of variation of modern humans and had a cranial capacity ranging from 900–1200 cm³.

Homo habilis See AUSTRALOPITHECUS HABILIS.

Homo sapiens neanderthalensis The first subspecies of *Homo sapiens* appearing some 300,000 years ago and becoming extinct about 35,000 B.P. Commonly known as Neanderthal man.

Homo sapiens sapiens The second subspecies of *Homo sapiens,* including all contemporary humans, appearing about 60,000 years ago. The first human subspecies was the now extinct *Homo sapiens neanderthalensis.*

Homologous A matched pair; usually refers to chromosomes, one from each parent, having the same genes in the same order.

Homozygote The new cell formed when the sperm and egg contain the same allele of a particular gene.

Homozygous A condition in which there are identical genes at a certain locus on homologous (matched pair) chromosomes.

Hopewell period Middle Woodland period in North America, dated from 2500–1500 B.P. Enormous earthenworks were built during this period.

Horizon (archaeological) The similarity in a series of cultural elements over a large geographical area during a restricted time span.

Horizontal excavation An approach to the excavation of a site that involves the excavation of relatively large areas of a site.

Hormonal sex Refers to the hormone mix produced by the gonads.

Horticulture The preparation of land for planting and the tending of crops using only the hoe or digging stick; especially the absence of use of the plow.

Human paleontology See PALEONTOLOGY, HUMAN.

Hunting and gathering society A society that subsists on the collection of plants and animals existing in the natural environment.

Hybrid vigor The phenomenon that occurs when a new generation, whose parent groups were from previously separated breeding populations, is generally healthier and larger than either of the parent populations.

Hydraulic theory A theory of the origins of the state advanced by Wittfogel that traces the rise of the state to the organization, construction, and maintenance of vast dam and irrigation projects.

Hylobatidae The so-called lesser apes (gibbon and siamang).

Hypothesis A tentative assumption, that must be tested, about the relationship(s) between specific events or phenomena.

Inca Empire Empire of the Late Horizon period of Peruvian prehistory, dated about 1438–1540 A.D.

Indus Valley civilization See HARAPPAN CIVILIZATION.

Intelligence The ability of human beings and other animals to learn from experience and to solve problems presented by a changing environment.

Interglacial Periods during which glaciers retreat and there is a general warming trend in the climate.

Intersexual A person whose genitals are neither clearly male nor female.

Invention The development of new ideas, techniques, resources, aptitudes, or applications that are adopted by a society and become part of its cultural repertoire.

Involution Evolution through which a biological or social form adapts to its environment by becoming more and more specialized and efficient in exploiting the resources of that environment. Sometimes called specific evolution.

Irrigation The artificial use of water for agriculture by means of human technology when naturally available water (rainfall or seasonal flooding) is insufficient or potentially too destructive to sustain desired crop production.

Ischial callosities Bare, calloused areas of skin on the hindquarters, frequently found in terrestrial or semiterrestrial Old World monkeys.

Jomon culture Upper Paleolithic Japanese culture dating from 12,500 B.P. The Jomon people were among the first in the world to produce pottery.

Kill site A place where prehistoric people killed and butchered animals.

KNM-ER 3733 The most modern looking fossil hominid form dating from the Pliocene-Pleistocene in East Africa. This form had a cranial capacity of 800 cm³, but is dated from 1.5–2 million years ago.

Knuckle walking Characteristic mode of terrestrial locomotion of orangutans, chimpanzees, and gorillas. These apes walk with a partially erect body posture, with the forward weight of the body supported by the arms and the hands touching the ground, fingers curled into the palm with the back of the fingers bearing the weight.

Language Characteristic mode of communication practiced by all human beings, consisting of sounds (phonemes) that are strung together into a virtually limitless number of meaningful sequences.

Late Horizon Final phase of Peruvian prehistory, dominated by the Inca empire and dated about 1438–1540, when Pizarro devastated the empire.

Late Preclassic (Formative) phase Final phase of the Formative period of Mesoamerican civilization, dated 300 B.C.–300 A.D. During this time political centralization appears to have increased, numerous ceremonial centers were built, and a calendar, writing, and mathematics invented.

Late Woodland period Period following the Hopewell in North America, dated from about 500–1100 A.D. The bow and arrow was invented during this period.

Laurasia The northern portion of Pangaea.

Laurel-leaf blade Cro-Magnon artifact associated with Solutrean tool kits. It is so finely worked, it is thought to have had a religious or ritualistic function.

Law of Independent Assortment Mendel's second principle. It refers to the fact that the particular assortment of alleles found in a given gamete is independently determined.

Law of Segregation Mendel's first principle. It states that in reproduction, a set of paired alleles separate (segregate) in a process called meiosis into different sex cells (gametes); thus, either allele can be passed on to offspring.

Lemur A nocturnal, arboreal prosimian having stereoscopic vision. Lemurs are found only on the island of Madagascar.

Levallois process A tool-making tradition characterized by flake tools and dating to the Riss-Würm interglacial in European and African Acheulian and Mousterian cultures.

Lexicostatistics See GLOTTOCHRONOLOGY.

Limbic system A group of structures in the brain important in expressing emotions and in regulating eating, drinking, sexual activity, and aggressive behavior. Relatively smaller in humans than in other primates.

Lineage The sequence of ancestral and descendant species.

Linguistics The systematic study of language.

Llano culture Upper Paleolithic culture in North America, famous for its fluted Clovis points. It was distributed all across the U.S., and most dates from kill sites range between 10,500–11,500 B.P.

Locus The position of a gene on a chromosome.

Lower Paleolithic Old Stone Age. Earliest stage in human culture, dated from about 2 million to 100,000 years ago.

Lower Perigordian culture The first Upper Paleolithic assemblage to appear in Europe. It was produced by big game hunters who dispersed across western Europe from 34,000 to 31,000 years ago.

Magdalenian culture The most advanced of the Upper Paleolithic cultures, dating from 17,000–10,000 B.P. Confined to France and northern Spain, the Magdalenian culture marks the climax of the Upper Paleolithic in Europe. The Magdalenians produced a highly diversified tool kit, but are most famous for their spectacular cave art.

Maintenance behavior Activities such as resting, moving, and self-grooming.

Marsupials Pouched mammals of the subclass *Metatheria*.

Maya civilization Best known Classic Mesoamerican civilization, located on the Yucatan peninsula, and dated around 300–900 A.D. Less intensely urban than Teotihuacán, it is marked by the building of huge ceremonial centers, such as Tikal in Guatemala.

Melanin The brown, granular substance found in the skin, hair, and some internal organs that gives a brownish tint or color to the areas in which it is found.

Mesolithic (Middle Stone Age) A term of convenience used by archaeologists to designate immediately preagricultural societies in the Old World; a frequently used diagnostic characteristic is the presence of microliths, small blades often set into bone or wood handles to make sickles for the harvesting of wild grains. In Europe it also featured the invention of the bow and arrow as a response to the emergence of forests with a shift from Pleistocene to Holocene climate.

Metallurgy The techniques of separating metals from their ores and working them into finished products.

Metatheria One of three subclasses of mammals. These are the pouched mammals, known as marsupials.

Microlith A small stone tool made from bladettes or fragments of blades, associated with the Mesolithic period, approximately 13,000–6,000 B.C.

Middle Kingdom Egyptian civilization dated from 2133 to 1786 B.C. Marked by centralized irrigation and mining projects.

Middle Paleolithic Part of the Old Stone Age, dated from 100,000–35,000 B.P. The age of *Homo sapiens neanderthalensis* and Mousteroid culture.

Milpa A technique of slash-and-burn horticulture as used by Maya Indians to make gardens in forested areas.

Miocene epoch Fourth of the six epochs that comprise the Cenezoic era. It dates from about 25–5 million years ago.

Mississippian culture North American culture, centered in the southeastern U.S., dated about 1000–1500 A.D., and characterized by the building of huge temple mounds.

Monkey Small or medium-sized quadrupedal primate. There are two groups of monkeys: Old World and New World. Only New World monkeys have prehensile tails. Most monkeys are arboreal, have long tails, and are vegetarians.

Monogenesis The theory that the human species had only one origin.

Monotremes Evolutionarily primitive, egg-laying mammals of the subclass *Prototheria*.

Morphological sex The physical appearance of a person's genitals and secondary sex characteristics.

Mousterian culture A group of European Middle Paleolithic assemblages characterized by prepared-core flake tools, dating from somewhat more than 80,000 to less than 40,000 years ago.

Multilinear evolution The study of cultural evolution recognizing regional variation and divergent evolutionary sequences.

Mutation A rapid and permanent change in genetic material.

Natufian culture Neolithic culture which emerged in Israel around 10,000 B.C. and lasted until 8000 B.C. It featured a successful broad spectrum life style.

Natural selection The process through which certain environmentally adaptive features are perpetuated at the expense of less adaptive features.

Neanderthal man (*Homo sapiens neanderthalensis*) A subspecies of *Homo sapiens* living from approximately 300,000 years ago to about 35,000 years ago and thought to have been descended from *Homo erectus*. See also HOMO SAPIENS NEANDERTHALENSIS.

Neolithic (New Stone Age) A stage in cultural evolution marked by the appearance of ground stone tools and frequently by the domestication of plants and animals, starting some 10,000 years ago.

Neontology A division of physical anthropology that deals with the comparative study of living primates, with special emphasis on the biological features of human beings.

New Archaeology Primarily an American development, the New Archaeology attempts to develop archaeological theory by using rigorous, statistical analysis of archaeological data within a deductive, logical framework.

New Kingdom Egyptian civilization dated from 1567–1085 B.C. It was characterized by the adoption of bronze tools and weapons, Middle Eastern techniques of warfare, and the building of cities.

Notched blade Upper Paleolithic stone tool with a depression chipped out of one side; it probably was drawn along the shafts of spears and arrows to smooth and straighten them.

Nucleotide The chemical unit comprising DNA and RNA.

Oasis hypothesis A theory of plant and animal domestication advanced by Childe, in which he suggests that in the arid Pleistocene environment, humans and animals congregated around water resources, where they developed patterns of mutual dependence.

Obsidian dating An absolute dating technique in which the standard of measurement is the rate at which freshly exposed obsidian absorbs moisture from the environment.

Oldowan culture Oldest recognized Lower Paleolithic assemblage, whose type site is Olduvai Gorge (Tanzania), dating from about 2.2 to 1 million years ago and comprising unifacial core (pebble) tools and crude flakes.

Oligocene epoch Third of the six epochs that comprise the Cenezoic era. It dates from about 35–25 million years ago.

Oligopithecus Oligocene ape form found in the Fayum area in Egypt.

Olmec culture The first civilization in Mesoamerica, and the base from which all subsequent Mesoamerican civilizations evolved. Located in the Yucatan peninsula, it is dated from 1500–400 B.C. Olmec art first appeared in 1250 B.C., and the civilization flourished at its height from 1150–900 B.C.

Order A taxonomic rank. *Homo sapiens* belongs to the order of Primates.

Orangutan *(Pongo pygmaeus)* A tree-dwelling great ape found only in Borneo and Sumatra. It has four prehensile limbs capable of seizing and grasping, and very long arms. The organgutan is almost completely arboreal.

Oranian culture Coastal Mediterranean Paleolithic culture with both Mousteroid and Gravettian features. It is the earliest culture (12,000–8,000 B.P.) with which modern human remains have been found.

Paleocene epoch Most ancient of the six epochs that comprise the Cenezoic era, it dates from about 70–60 million years ago.

Paleo-Indian tradition The four stages of early American prehistory, which lasted until about 11,000 B.P.

Paleolithic (Old Stone Age) A stage in cultural evolution, dated from about 2.5 million to 10,000 years ago, during which chipped stone tools, but not ground stone tools were made.

Paleontology, human A subdivision of physical anthropology that deals with the study of human and hominid fossil remains.

Palynology (pollen analysis) The study of fossil pollen; used in reconstructing ancient environments.

Pangaea The name given to the continental land masses when they formed one gigantic body some 300–225 million years ago.

Paradigm, scientific A concept introduced by Kuhn (1962): the orthodox doctrine of a science, its training exercises, and a set of beliefs with which new scientists are enculturated.

Parallel evolution The evolutionary pattern in which two organisms in the same taxonomic order evolve the same basic adaptive traits in response to a similar environment.

Participant observation A major anthropological field method originated by Malinowski, in which the ethnographer is immersed in the day-to-day activities of the community being studied.

Pebble tool The first manufactured stone tools consisting of somewhat larger than fist-sized pieces of flint that have had some six or seven flakes knocked off them; unifacial core tools; associated with *Australopithecus habilis* in Africa and also *Homo erectus* in East Asia.

Persistence hunting A unique hunting ability of humans in which prey is hunted over vast distances, often for days at a time.

Pharynx The throat, above the larynx.

Phenotype The visible expression of a gene or pair of genes.

Phoneme The basic unit of significant but meaningless sound in a language.

Phylogeny The tracing of the history of the evolutionary development of a life form.

Physical anthropology The study of human beings as biological organisms across space and time. Physical anthropology is divided into two areas: (1) paleontology, which is the study of the fossil evidence of primate evolution, and (2) neontology, which is the comparative biology of living primates.

Pigmentation Skin color.

Piltdown man A human skull and ape jaw "discovered" in England in 1911 and thought by some to be a "missing link" in human evolution. It was exposed as a fraud in 1953.

Plains Archaic culture Neolithic culture from the Great Plains of the U.S. and dated until 2000–3,000 B.P.; characterized by bison hunting and the gathering of a variety of plant foods.

Plano culture Upper Paleolithic North American culture that may have evolved out of the Llano.

Plastromancy The use of turtle shells to divine the future.

Plate tectonics Branch of tectonics that studies the movement of the continental plates over time; popularly known as "continental drift."

Platyrrhini One of two infraorders of the primate suborder *Anthropoidea,* consisting of all the New World monkeys; characterized by vertical nostrils and often prehensile tails.

Pleistocene epoch Most recent of the six epochs that comprise the Cenezoic era, it dates from about 2 million to about 10,000 years ago. Also, the earlier of the two epochs (Pleistocene, Holocene) which together comprise the Quaternary period.

Pliocene epoch Fifth of the six epochs that comprise the Cenezoic era, it dates from about 5–2 million years ago.

Polygenesis The theory that the human species had more than one origin.

Polymorphism A genetic characteristic that appears in more than one form in a population.

Polypeptide A chain of amino acids; a protein.

Polytypic species A species of wide-spread geographic location and an uneven distribution of its genetic variants among its local breeding populations.

Pongid A common term for the members of the *Pongidae* family, including the three great apes: the orangutan, gorilla, and chimpanzee.

Postclassic period Mesoamerican cultural period, dating from 900–1521 A.D., dominated first by the Toltecs and later the Aztecs.

Potassium-argon (KAr) dating Absolute dating technique that uses the rate of decay of radioactive potassium (K^{40}) into argon (Ar^{40}) as its basis. The half-life of $K^{40} = 1.3$ billion±40 million years.

Preceramic period Refers to regional variations of the Desert culture in the Southwest United States; so named because no evidence of pottery during this period has been uncovered.

Prehensile tail A gripping appendage found only in New World monkeys. It is characterized by tactile skin on its undersurface and is strong enough to support the body weight of the monkey.

Prehistoric archaeology The use of archaeology to reconstruct prehistoric times.

Primates The order of mammals that includes humans, the apes, Old and New World monkeys, and prosimians.

Primatologist One who studies primates.

Prosimian *(Prosimii)* The most primitive suborder of the order of primates, including lemurs, lorises, tarsiers, and similar creatures.

Protein synthesis The formation of polypeptide chains and the "packaging" of them into various functional combinations.

Prototheria The most primitive of the three subclasses of mammals. These are egg-laying mammals, known as monotremes.

Psychological sex The self-image a person holds about his or her own sex identity. Usually conforms to a person's (socially defined) morphological sex.

Quadrupedalism Locomotion by the use of four feet.

Quarry site A place where prehistoric people dug for flint, tin, copper, and other materials.

Quaternary period A geologic period comprised of two epochs—the Pleistocene and the Holocene—and dated from about 2 million years ago to the present.

Race A folk category of the English language that refers to discrete groups of human beings who are categorically separated from one another on the basis of arbitrarily selected phenotypic traits.

Radiocarbon (C^{14}) dating Absolute physical-chemical dating technique that uses the rate of decay of radioactive carbon (C^{14}) (present in all plants) to stable carbon (C^{12}) as its basis. The half-life of $C^{14} = 5568 \pm 30$ years. The technique is useful for dating remains from 5000 to 50,000 years old, although a new technique may extend its range to about 100,000 years while reducing the margin of error.

Ramapithecus A late Miocene hominoid, found in India, Kenya, and Europe, who lived in open woodland areas from 14 to 9 million years ago. *Ramapithecus* is accepted by many scholars as the first true hominid.

Random (genetic) drift Shift in gene and allele frequencies in a population due to sampling "error." When a small breeding population splits off from a larger one, its collection of genes may not adequately represent the frequencies of the larger population. These differences compound over succeeding generations, until the two populations are quite distinct. Along with mutation, gene circumstances.

Recessive allele Version of a gene that is not able to influence an organism's phenotype when it is homologous with another version of the gene. See also DOMINANT ALLELE.

Reformulation The modification of a cultural trait, or cluster of traits, by a group to fit its own traditions and circumstances.

Relative dating The determination of the sequence of events; a relative date specifies that one thing is older or younger than another.

Ribonucleic acid (RNA) Any of the nucleic acids containing ribose. One type—messenger RNA—carries the information encoded in the DNA to the site of protein synthesis located outside the nucleus.

RNA See RIBONUCLEIC ACID.

Robust australopithecines One of two lines of australopithecines, appearing some 3.5 million years ago and surviving until approximately 1 million years ago or even later; thought to have embodied two successive species, *Australopithecus robustus* and *Australopithecus boisei.*

Rosetta stone A tablet containing three parallel texts written in Egyptian hieroglyphics, demotic, and Greek. In 1822 Champollion used the stone to decode the hieroglyphics.

Salvage archaeology The attempt to preserve archaeological remains from destruction by large-scale projects of industrial society.

Sangoan tradition A tool-making tradition dated between 43,000–40,000 B.P. at Kalambo Falls in East Africa. The typical Sangoan tool is a stone pick, with one sharp and one blunt end.

Savanna Tropical or subtropical grasslands.

Scapulimancy The use of charred cracks in the burned scapula (shoulder bone) of an animal to divine the future.

Scientific racism Research strategies based on the assumption that groups' biological features underlie significant social and cultural differences. Not surprisingly, this kind of research always manages to find "significant" differences between "races."

Scraper Upper Paleolithic stone tool, made from blades, with a retouched end; used for carving wood, bone, and antlers to make spear points.

Seriation A technique of relative dating in which the relative dates of artifacts may be reconstructed by arranging them so that variations in form or style can be inferred to represent a developmental sequence, and hence chronological order.

Sexual dimorphism A difference between the males and females of a species that is not related directly to reproductive function.

Sexual identity The expectations about male and female behavior, established in children by the age of six, which affect the individual's learning ability, choice of work, and feelings about herself or himself.

Shang civilization The first fully developed Chinese civilization, dating from 1850–1100 B.C. The Shang were the first East Asians to write.

Sickle cell A red blood cell that has lost its normal circular shape and has collapsed into a half-moon shape.

Sickle cell anemia An often fatal disease caused by a chemical mutation which changes one of the amino acids in normal hemoglobin. The mutant sickle cell gene occurs in unusually high frequency in parts of Africa and the Arabian peninsula. Individuals heterozygotic for the sickle cell gene have a special resistance to malaria.

Site A concentration of the remains of [human] activities, that is, the presence of artifacts.

Slash-and-burn agriculture A shifting form of cultivation with recurrent clearing and burning of vegetation and planting in the burnt fields; also called swidden (or shifting) cultivation.

Social Darwinsim The doctrine that makes use, or misuse, of Darwin's biological evolutionary principles to explain or justify existing forms of social organization. The theory was actually formulated by Spencer.

Society A socially bounded, spacially contiguous aggregation of people who participate in a number of overarching institutions and share to some degree an identifiable culture, and that contains within its boundaries some means of production and units of consumption—with relative stability across generations.

Solutrean culture Localized European Upper Paleolithic assemblage that straddled the Pyrenees Mountains between 20,000–17,000 years ago. The Solutreans represent the summit of stone tool shaping.

Somatic cells The cells that make up all the bodily parts and that are constantly dying and being replaced; does not include central nervous system cells or sex cells.

Spacing mechanisms The behaviors between neighboring groups of animals that help to maintain them at some distance from each other.

Speciation The process of gradual separation of one interbreeding population into two or more separate, noninterbreeding populations.

Species The largest naturally occurring population that interbreeds (or is capable of interbreeding) and produces fully fertile offspring.

State A set of specialized, differentiated social institutions, in which the use of power is concentrated.

Stereoscopic vision Overlapping fields of vision resulting when the eyes are located toward the front of the skull, producing depth perception.

Stimulus diffusion The transfer of a basic idea from one culture to another, in which the idea is reinterpreted and modified to the extent that it becomes unique to the receiving group.

Strangled blade Upper Paleolithic stone tool with notches on both sides.

Strategic resources The category of resources vital to a group's survival.

Stratified society A society in which there is a structured inequality of access among groups not only to power and prestige, but also to the strategic resources that sustain life.

Stratigraphy The arrangement of archaeological deposits in superimposed layers or strata.

Structural linguistics The study of the internal structures of the world's languages.

Subsistence strategies Technological skills, tools, and behavior that a society uses to meet its subsistence needs.

Supraorbital ridge The torus or bony bar surmounting orbital cavities which is large and continuous in apes and quite small and divided in *Homo sapiens*.

Superposition The perception that, under normal circumstances, a stratum found lying under another stratum is relatively older than the stratum under which it is lying.

Swidden farming Shifting cultivation, with recurrent clearing and burning of vegetation and planting in the burnt fields. Fallow periods for each plot last many times longer than the periods of cultivation. See also SLASH-AND-BURN AGRICULTURE.

Synchronics The comparison of biological, linguistic, archaeological, and ethnographic data across a wide geographical area at one arbitrarily selected point in time.

Synthetic theory (of evolution) Modern theory of evolution based on the Darwinian theory, but emphasizing *differential fertility* (as opposed to differential mortality).

Systematics The study of the kinds and diversity of objects, and of the types of relationships existing among them.

Tabula rasa Concept proposed by Locke (1690) that people are born with blank minds, and that they learn everything they come to know through their life experiences, socialization, and enculturation into groups.

Tanged blade Upper Paleolithic stone tool made from blades, retouched so that a narrow stem extended down from a projectile point.

Tarsier Small East Asian arboreal, nocturnal prosimian.

Taxonomy The science of constructing classifications of organisms.

Technology A society's use of knowledge, skills, implements, and sources of power in order to exploit and partially control the natural environment, and to engage in production and reproduction of its goods and services.

Tell A stratified mound created entirely through long periods of successive occupation by a series of groups.

Territoriality Defense by an animal of a geographically delimited area.

Test pit A pit that is dug at carefully selected positions in a site to reveal information about buried artifacts and stratigraphy.

Thalassemia Like sickle cell anemia, a blood anemia carried by populations that are or have been in malaria-infested areas of the world—especially around the Mediterranean, Asia Minor, and southern Asia. Also represents an example of balanced polymorphism, like sickle cell anemia.

Therapsids Early reptile forms from which modern mammals are descended.

Thermoluminescent dating An absolute dating technique, used primarily on ceramics, that dates fired clay by measuring the amount of light emitted when it is heated to approximately 300°C.

Three-age system Concept delineated by Thomsen (1836) in which he identified three successive stages in cultural evolution: Stone Age, Bronze Age, Iron Age.

Toltec civilization Postclassic Mesoamerican civilization, dated from 900 to about 1300 A.D. The Toltecs perpetuated many of the themes of Classic culture. Their capital of Tula was sacked around 1160 and they were eventually replaced by the Aztecs.

Tradition (archaeological) The similarity in cultural elements and forms over a considerable span of time at a given site or group of sites in a geographically delimited area.

Tree-ring dating (dendrochronology) An absolute dating technique that uses as its basis the fact that trees add a ring to their cross sections each year.

Tribe A relatively small group of people (small society) that shares a culture, speaks a common language or dialect, and shares a perception of its common history and uniqueness. Often a term used to refer to unstratified social groups with a minimum of, or no centralized political authority at all.

Type site Site used to represent the characteristic features of a culture.

Typology A method of classifying objects according to hierarchically arranged sets of diagnostic criteria.

Ubaid culture Lowland Mesopotamian culture dating from about 5000 B.C. and reaching the height of its development by 4350 B.C.

Underwater archaeology The retrieval and study of ships, dwellings, and other human remains that have been covered over by waters in the course of time.

Uniformitarianism The theory, developed by Lyell, that the geological processes shaping the earth are uniform and continuous in character.

Unit of deposition All the contents of each stratum in an archaeological site, conceived to have been deposited at the same point in time (as measured by archaeologists).

Unit of excavation Subdivision of an archaeological site made by an archaeologist to record the context in which each remain is found.

Upper Paleolithic culture The culture produced by modern *Homo sapiens sapiens,* beginning about 35,000 years ago. It is characterized by pervasive blade tool production, an "explosion" of artistic endeavors (cave painting), highly organized large game hunting, and the efficient exploitation of previously uninhabited ecological niches—including the population of the New World, perhaps beginning as early as 40,000 years ago.

Uruk phase Cultural phase of the Sumerian civilization, located in lower Mesopotamia and dated around 3200 B.C. It marks the rise of civilization in Mesopotamia.

Valdivian culture Coastal Ecuadorian culture, dated from 3200 B.C., where the earliest pottery found in the Americas has been unearthed. Many archaeologists believe the pottery was introduced to the New World by Japanese visitors from the Jomon culture.

Varve dating An absolute dating technique that exploits the fact that in regions where glaciers once lay, their annual spring melt produced laminated layers of sediments called varves.

Venus figures Human female statues produced by the Gravettian culture. They have attenuated hands, feet and legs, stylized heads, and exaggerated buttocks, breasts, and vaginas. It is thought that they were used in fertility rituals.

Vertical excavation An approach to the excavation of a site that involves digging all the way down through the site at a few strategically located places.

Wattle-and-daub A type of construction technique in which stakes or rods are placed in the ground; twigs or branches are then interwoven with them, and finally they are plastered with mud.

Wernicke's area The brain site where verbal comprehension takes place, located in the temporal lobe of the dominant hemisphere.

Woodland culture Neolithic culture in the eastern U.S. woodlands, which followed the Archaic tradition beginning around 3500 B.C. The culture produced well-developed pottery, which along with its burial mounds and early agriculture distinguish the Woodland from the Archaic.

Workshop site A place where the remains left by prehistoric people engaged in specialized tasks, usually the processing of raw materials into artifacts, are found.

Würm glacial period The most recent glacial period, and the only one that has been accurately dated. It lasted from 75,000 to about 10,000–15,000 B.P.

Yang-shao culture The earliest farming culture discovered in East Asia, located around the Huangho Valley, and dated between 3950 and 3300 B.C.

Ziggurat A Mesopotamian terraced pyramid with outside stairways leading to a temple on the top, and dating from about 3200 B.C.

Zinjanthropus A 1.75 million year old australopithecine fossil found in Kenya by Mary Leakey and thought to be a form of *Australopithecus robustus*.

78 79 80 81 82 9 8 7 6 5 4 3 2 1